Capitalism at Work

To Charles G. Koch,
free-market capitalist

Capitalism at Work

Business, Government, and Energy

Robert L. Bradley Jr.

M & M Scrivener Press

Published by   M & M Scrivener Press
3 Winter Street, Salem, MA 01970

www.mmscrivenerpress.com

Conflicts and Trends® in Business Ethics
Series Editor: Nicholas Capaldi

Cover design by Hannus Design

Library of Congress Cataloging-in-Publication Data
Bradley, Robert L., 1955–
Capitalism at work: business, government, and energy /
Robert L. Bradley Jr.
p. cm.—(Political capitalism; 1)
Includes bibliographical references and index.

ISBN 978-0-9764041-7-0 (hbk.: alk. paper)

1. Corporations—Moral and ethical aspects.
2. Corporations—Political aspects.   3. Capitalism.
I. Title.

HF5387.B687   2008
330.12'2—dc22   2008024425

Printed in Canada on acid-free paper.

Contents

We may well turn to the "wisdom of the ages" in our
human quest to understand reality,
for that wisdom contains a truly inexhaustible contemporaneity.
—Josef Pieper, *The Four Cardinal Virtues* (1954)

Preface

DURING MY LAST TWO YEARS at Enron (2000–2001), I was asked to gather information for a history of the company—with particular emphasis on its chairman, Ken Lay. In this period, Enron declared victory on its mission to become the world's leading energy company and embarked on a new one: to become the world's leading company. Expectations were high for an eventual book with a title such as *The Making of the World's Leading Company*. Joining me as codirector of the Enron Oral History Project was a leading business historian and energy specialist, Joseph Pratt, Cullen Professor of History and Business at the University of Houston.

In the course of the project, we gathered the recollections of key employees and members of the board of directors, past and present. Reminiscences from Ken Lay's old economics professors and former bosses were recorded. One interview was with Lay protégé Jeff Skilling, who gave nary a hint of Enron's brewing troubles. His impressions were akin to a hall-of-fame acceptance speech—how the company came together, endured tough industry conditions, and finally triumphed—as if it were game, set, and match Enron. This mentality never wavered, at least in Skilling and Lay, despite Enron's bankruptcy and despite subsequent revelations of blatant wrongdoing. Enron was a *great* company, Skilling maintained. Enron had an *unassailable competitive advantage*, Lay insisted.

In retrospect, Skilling and Lay suffered from extreme overconfidence, hubris, even delusion. So long as everyone *believed*, and got others *to believe*, a healthy ENE stock price would make everyone a winner, they thought. Doubters were dumb and, within the walls of Enron, not considered good team players.

But Enron could not invent its own reality forever. Real value was not being created. Cash flow was inadequate. Enron's problems came from a combination of many bad bets and the poor execution of some good bets—and were magnified by a paucity of midcourse corrections. What is remarkable, in retrospect, is that the company did not implode sooner.

When the extent of the company's machinations came to light after the bankruptcy, the great majority of employees came to revise their thinking about the company they had once admired. Only then could they get beyond Enron and get on with their lives. But Lay and Skilling did not, partly because of their inviolable egos and partly because of their audacious legal strategy. But this was antireality, a continuation of their failings while steering Enron. Ken Lay died delusional and disillusioned; a defiant Skilling *still believes*, behind bars.

Needless to say, Enron collapsed before the work of the Enron Oral History Project could be fashioned into a book. I was part of the mass layoff of December 3, 2001, the day after Enron filed for bankruptcy in a Southern District of New York courtroom. But having published widely on energy history and policy, I decided to write my own version of events, combining what I had learned from my 16 years at the company (almost as long as Lay's own tenure) with what I came to know about Enron after my layoff, which was considerable and troubling.

I embarked upon this project despite being asked by Ken Lay to help him prepare an autobiography—something he undoubtedly saw as part of his come-back strategy. I declined, and no such book was evidently written. Aided by antidepressants, Lay, still chairman of the bankrupt Enron, saw himself as a victim of the debacle. But the real story was different. Ken Lay was the philo-sophic enabler of the whole sordid affair and was emotionally wed to the man who had done so much (however unintentionally) to ruin him: Jeff Skilling.

Sensing this, I chose instead to write a detailed retrospective from a more neutral vantage point, something I was able to do thanks to the generosity of a group of distinguished individuals and foundations, many Houston based, who wanted a lessons-learned chronology that would stand the test of time. Still, given the final result—a trilogy and publication years after most other Enron books—some explanation is in order.

Why didn't I pen a shorter, "timely" Enron book, tapping into the mass readership of, say, *The Smartest Guys in the Room* or *Conspiracy of Fools*?

First, I am a political economist and industry historian, not a commercial writer, although this book is geared for nonacademics as well as academics. From the beginning, my goal has been to identify cause and effect by telling the *whole story*, not only its poignant highlights. But the story had not run its course. The trial of 2006 was Part II of the Ken Lay/Jeff Skilling tragedy, and the final tallies of the company's debacle would not come before the last remnants of Enron were sold off and the final trial appeals were exhausted. Any comprehen-sive look at what is one of the most important stories in business history would have to wait until these events unfolded.

Second, my research into the prehistory of both Enron's businesses and Ken Lay's Enron career uncovered fascinating material concerning two of America's greatest and most regulated industries, electricity and natural gas. Because this history offered important context and striking similarities and contrasts to Enron and Ken Lay, and because little of it is known by today's historians and industry practitioners, I believed that it merited inclusion.

Third, and perhaps most important, *I did not know enough to write a definitive summary of the multifaceted Enron story.* Yes, I was a longtime employee and was Ken Lay's speechwriter for most of our last seven years together at Enron. I knew the history of the energy industry and was Enron's anointed historian. And I had unique documentation and records, including many speeches and notes by Lay himself, not to mention access to many colleagues who could fill in the gaps of a very complicated story. Still, I simply was not knowledgeable enough to rush out a book that would stand up to history. Time was needed to let the dust settle, survey the post-Enron world, and evaluate the many other Enron-related books and articles.

I have taken that time and prepared a trilogy on the theory and practice of political capitalism, with Enron as the touchstone. Book 1 presents a multidisciplinary worldview capable of analyzing Enron in its many dimensions. Book 2 examines a famous case similar to Enron (the rise and fall of the legendary Samuel Insull) and then describes Enron's prehistory, as well as Ken Lay's early career. Book 3 describes and interprets Enron, Ken Lay, Jeff Skilling, and the post-Enron world.

Such an effort required much more than my prior experience and expertise; it necessitated new investigations into the fundamental principles of the capitalist worldview. The good news was that those principles had already been set forth by a dozen or so major authors, ranging from philosophers to economists. The challenge was to integrate their contributions to illuminate both Enron and the related episodes covered in this trilogy. To the extent that this has been accomplished, I will have succeeded. But the true test of this reintegrated worldview is whether it can be more broadly applied to business practices and public policy, both to understand the past and offer insight for a better future. For the practical consequences of a wrong worldview are all too evident in the unhappy fates of Samuel Insull and Ken Lay.

·◌·

Books of this scope and detail are rarely started and seldom completed, and it took more than a lone author to pull it off. Thus, I have many individuals and institutions to acknowledge and thank.

My first thanks goes to my persevering family—three generations' worth— and particularly to my wife, Nancy. I also thank the board of directors of the Institute for Energy Research for their patience and support. Major funding came from the late Gordon Cain, a heroic capitalist whose autobiography, *Everyone Wins! A Life in Free Enterprise*, is testament to a life well lived. Jerry Finger's enthusiasm for the project helped get me over some early humps. George Peterkin Jr. got behind the project and got others interested on my behalf. Leo Linbeck Jr., capitalist intellectual, was one such distinguished supporter.

Other support is gratefully acknowledged from W. J. Bowen, Jeremy S. Davis, the late James A. Elkins Jr., Frank A. Liddell Jr., John H. Lindsey, W. R. Lloyd, Doris Fondren Lummis, W. R. Lummis, Robert C. McNair, Clive Runnells, L. E. Simmons, David M. Smith, R. Graham Whaling, and Wallace Wilson. I also benefited from the generosity of the George R. Brown Foundation, Earhart Foundation, Ray C. Fish Foundation, Liberty Fund, and Walter Looke Family Fund.

Roger Donway provided invaluable research help and edited the entire volume. When I reached my intellectual limit on a matter, Roger was always there for help and resolution. Richard Fulmer provided a keen editorial eye. And fellow Enron-ex Jean Spitzner, now with Bowne & Company (Houston), provided the expert graphics herein.

The following individuals critically reviewed one or more chapters in their area of expertise: M. A. Adelman, Joe Bast, Robert Bryce, Robert Campbell, Nicholas Capaldi, Douglas Den Uyl, Richard Gordon, Gil Guillory, Stephen Hicks, Jack High, John Jennrich, Dwight Lee, Leo Linbeck Jr., the late Stephen McDonald, Robert Michaels, Robert Murphy, William Niskanen, James Otteson, Valentin Petkantchin, Sheldon Richman, Colin Robinson, John Ryan, Chris Matthew Sciabarra, Elaine Sternberg, and Jonathan Wight. To these and others unnamed, I offer my profound thanks for their spirit of expertise sharing.

A particular thanks goes to Charles G. Koch, who has built Koch Industries into the world's largest privately owned company. My intellectual career has benefited from his philanthropy from the beginning, and it is his book, *The Science of Success* (2007), that offers the most compelling antidote to Enron-like behavior in print today. Koch's business philosophy of Market-Based Management® points the way to a sophisticated ethic of free-market capitalism in the post-Enron world. This is why I have dedicated this book to him.

One comment on documentation: I have kept footnotes to a minimum while instead providing full reference information in the Source Notes section and the Bibliography. I believe this format meets the highest standards for scholarly research, while rendering the book more accessible to nonacademics, who have an important role to play in the cause of advancing realism in the humanities and social sciences. For academics desiring more discussion or documentation on technical issues, I have posted 52 appendixes on the Internet at www.politicalcapitalism.org. Each is cited in a footnote of this book.

Finally, there was one publisher who stayed on the phone after I said the word *trilogy*. Martin Scrivener, founder and chairman of M & M Scrivener Press, has aided in numerous ways with the book project, from title suggestions to all the details behind the publication of a handsome book. I am very grateful to him and to Evelyn Pyle, whose intelligent final edits put the book over the top.

Any shortcomings, of course, are my responsibility alone.

September 23, 2008

Introduction

SUCCESS, ARROGANCE, PROBLEMS, DECEIT, more problems, more deceit . . . *spectacular failure*. That sequence describes the heady boom and decisive bust of Enron Corporation, the most chronicled and dissected business story in history.

But hubris, dishonesty, and obstinacy were not the exclusive franchise of Enron and its two principals, Ken Lay and Jeff Skilling. This destructive pattern was present in the record bankruptcy of Bernard Ebbers's WorldCom, which came just months after Enron's collapse in December 2001, not to mention other corporate scandals that greeted the new century. Looking back, the virus was also operative in the fall of Samuel Insull's titanic energy-utility empire during the Great Depression, a failure that was in some ways the Enron of its era.

The same failings characterized the 1904 bankruptcy of Houston Oil Company of Texas, which had been capitalized at a princely $30 million just three years earlier. Houston Oil, which emerged from receivership four years later, was a predecessor company to Enron.

History can meet itself coming and going.

The central figures in these three debacles were revered business titans. In the first third of the twentieth century, Insull was the Great Man of the electricity industry, as well as Mr. Chicago. Ken Lay was the Great Man of natural gas for much of the 1980s and 1990s—and Mr. Houston as well. Houston Oil centered on the bigger-than-life John Henry Kirby, the Mr. Houston of his day. Kirby would recover from Houston Oil's early stumbles, but his reign ended with his personal bankruptcy in 1933, a time when Samuel Insull was living abroad to avoid his legal woes. In the end, an extradited Insull was acquitted of his alleged business crimes, but such was not the case for Ken Lay, who in two trials was found guilty on all counts by jury and judge. Yet Lay escaped the prospect of life in prison, receiving what his sympathizers called a pardon from God—death from a heart attack just weeks before his sentencing.

"The bigger they come, the harder they fall," goes an old adage. And yet history mostly remembers the winners: Astor, Carnegie, Morgan, Rockefeller, Vanderbilt. By contrast, the lives of Kirby, Insull, and Lay are riches-to-rags stories, with Enron representing perhaps the *ideal type* of business failure—and thus a near-perfect specimen for lessons and learning.

What was the socioeconomic system within which Enron thrived—and then perished? Why did such a revered company collapse, and just who was responsible? What incentives, ideas, and habits led the perpetrators astray? How did deviations from common sense and standard business practices lead to unintended outcomes, slippery slopes, and such a disastrous finale? Most important, what are the lessons for business and government going forward? These questions are the inspiration for this trilogy. Book 1 examines the capitalist worldview; Book 2 focuses on Insull, Kirby, and Enron's prehistory (including the career of Ken Lay); and Book 3 chronicles Enron's rise, fall, and aftermath.

⌁

Bad habits acquired in boomtime, in addition to old-fashioned fraud, go a long way toward explaining dramatic business reversals. But Enron was something more. Ken Lay's company was not the largest bankruptcy in U.S. history (WorldCom's filing, listing $107 billion in assets, was double Enron's claimed amount) or the most overtly fraudulent. What set it apart was that Enron's sins seemed to involve every commandment and every pew. It was what journalist George Will called a "systemic failure," encompassing academics, accountants, boards of directors, consultants, credit-rating agencies, investment bankers, journalists, lawyers, politicians, regulators, securities analysts, and more. Thus, American business, even capitalism itself, was placed on trial, prompting Princeton economist Paul Krugman to declare in the *New York Times*: "I predict in the years ahead Enron, not September 11, will come to be seen as the greater turning point in U.S. society."

George Will was right. Enron shamed professions and institutions, not only individuals. Ken Lay's handiwork made Adam Smith's invisible hand tremble. Still, Krugman missed the boat, as did other pundits, including Robert Kuttner, who declared in *BusinessWeek* that Enron refuted free-market economics. These critics thought that the system that had made an Enron possible was capitalism and that free-market economists from Adam Smith to Milton Friedman had thus encountered their equivalent of stagflation (simultaneous high inflation and high unemployment), which had humbled Keynesian economics a quarter century before. Philosophically, these critics equated Enron Man to Capitalist Man, with one-and-the-same running footloose in an inadequately constrained system. The 2005 movie documentary *The Smartest Guys in the Room* linked Enron to Ronald Reagan, deregulation, and California's alleged electricity-deregulation experiment to make the same point.

Not surprisingly, these new-era populists championed more regulation in the attempt to plug the gaps in existing regulation. And more than that, a new ethos of corporate social responsibility was urged for business, complete with redoubled efforts to imbue students with business ethics through the academic curriculum, as if the problem at Enron was a lack of philosophical training. In a *Journal of Corporate Citizenship* essay, "Are Business Schools Silent Partners in Corporate Crime?" two university business ethicists asked why Washington policymakers had not investigated business schools in reference to the corporate scandals, given that many of the culpable MBAs were taught from an "approach to business education that elevates narrow self-interest above broader values of community and corporate citizenship."

So rather than rely on invisible hands and old-fashioned virtue, the call had come for New Capitalist Man and the Accountable Corporation. "The wisdom and resourcefulness of regulators, activists, and above all, corporate management itself," concluded a four-volume guidebook for corporate governance in the post-Enron era, "will shape a healthy future for the modern *accountable* corporation."

·◇·

How did an enterprise that sought to become the world's leading company become the very worst? How did Enron prosper for so long, seemingly achieving one ambitious vision after another? How did Ken Lay gain and command so much trust among vast constituencies? What created an aura of corporate invincibility that fooled virtually everyone—including Enron's own employees—as well as Lay himself?

Part of the answer is the *new economy* mantra (an economy-wide arrogance, in retrospect), which Jeff Skilling, in particular, exploited by positioning Enron as the world's premier dot-com energy company. In the knowledge economy, Enron had a corner on brilliance, he thought. But something more fundamental was at work, quite the opposite of the free-market whipping boy postulated by Krugman, Kuttner, prominent business ethicists, and others.

The socioeconomic framework that enabled Enron—and also contributed to its demise—was political capitalism. Unlike free-market capitalism, political capitalism is a variant of the mixed economy, in which business interests routinely seek, obtain, and use government intervention for their own advantage, at the expense of consumers, taxpayers, and/or competitors. Ken Lay, despite his claimed allegiance to a free-market economy ("I believe in God, and I believe in free markets," he would say), was at the epicenter of America's mixed economy. In fact, the scope and scale of Enron's politically dependent profit centers was unprecedented.

Who was Ken Lay, the architect and chairman of Enron from its formation in the mid-1980s until its bankruptcy? The once-celebrated visionary of the energy industry was not an engineer, as were many leaders in the energy sector. Lay did not possess an accounting or finance background, as did some senior executives. He never clawed his way up the corporate ladder in various operational divisions, much less built a company from scratch. No, Enron's leader was a Ph.D. economist, interested in the big picture and the ways of political power. His résumé was top-heavy with Washington experience, acquired at three federal jobs, the last two regulating the energy industry.

Ken Lay's interests and skill set dovetailed with the political-capitalist system he found when he became a Washington energy regulator in the early 1970s. Predictably, then, when Lay reentered the private sector after nearly six years of government service, his niche became running federally regulated interstate natural gas pipelines, assets that he knew well from his time at the Federal Power Commission (now the Federal Energy Regulatory Commission).

And when Lay got his own show as chairman and CEO of a Fortune 500 company, he lost little time in applying his academic training, considerable smarts, uncommon energy, keen ambition, and soulful persona to the government-opportunity/government-favor game. He was an extraordinary, mile-a-minute political capitalist (or *rent seeker* in the jargon of economics), eager to deploy the political means to propel Enron to the top of the energy industry—and then the whole business world.

As his career took off, Ken Lay's lofty ambition turned into overambition and then into blind ambition, complete with an almost messianic confidence. Increasingly, he focused externally, playing political cards for Enron's benefit. The Great Man of his industry and hometown, Houston, became a philanthropist and kingmaker, the modern equivalent of John Henry Kirby, who in his day had gathered almost too many awards, connections, and constituencies to list.

For a number of years, Enron did well by supplementing its consumer-driven profit centers with politically derived business opportunities. In particular, Enron scored big under a new regulatory regime, *mandatory open access*, whereby companies were required to open their natural gas pipelines and power transmission systems to outsiders needing interstate transportation services. Such "infrastructure socialism" enabled first-mover Enron to become the most profitable and largest wholesale marketer of gas and electricity in the United States. (Europe was being conquered too.) But other companies followed Enron's lead in the unregulated commodity business, and Enron's margins shrank despite the company's ongoing innovation. That required Ken Lay and marketing guru Jeff Skilling to find the next big thing—the next big *political* thing—to retain their first-mover advantage. The urgency was heightened by bad investments that threatened to take the bloom off Enron's rose, something Ken Lay could not accept professionally or personally.

But Enron's focus on the political means, rather than on the economic means of profitably anticipating and fulfilling consumer needs, proved challenging and problematic. Some government-created niches were more mirage than moneymaker from the get-go. And shifting political winds could reverse even the best of opportunities, as Enron discovered during the California electricity crisis of 2000–2001. Enron's supersized paper profits in the Golden State could not be monetized, and the company's power-trading opportunities shrank in the political melee that went national. Enron lost what it once thought was its ace in the hole, hastening its judgment day.

Book 3 in this trilogy details Ken Lay's tireless efforts to profit from government intervention. Government favor propelled Enron's profit centers in domestic power plants, natural gas and electricity marketing, wind and solar power, infrastructure in underdeveloped countries, and unconventional natural gas production. Enron was all about complex federal laws and administrative regulations, such as special provisions within the Natural Gas Policy Act of 1978, Public Utility Regulatory Policies Act of 1978, Omnibus Budget Reconciliation Act of 1990, and Energy Policy Act of 1992—or FERC rulings, such as Regulation of Natural Gas Pipelines after Partial Wellhead Decontrol (FERC Order No. 436: 1985), Pipeline Service Obligations and Revisions to Regulations Governing Self-Implementing Transportation Under Part 284 of the Commission's Regulations (FERC Order No. 636: 1992), and Promoting Wholesale Competition Through Open Access Non-discriminatory Transmission Services by Public Utilities; Recovery of Stranded Costs by Public Utilities and Transmitting Utilities (FERC Order 888: 1996). The arcane was pure gold to Enron.

And then there was the legislative reform that Enron could not land. In the 1980s, Lay's company failed to persuade lawmakers to enact a sizable oil tariff to reduce interfuel competition to the company's natural gas operations. Enron also fell short in its 13-year drive to persuade the federal government to regulate greenhouse-gas emissions, particularly carbon dioxide (CO_2), an intervention that promised profit opportunities in no less than seven company divisions. Still, as an ex-Greenpeace official observed, Enron was "the company most responsible for sparking off the greenhouse civil war in the hydrocarbon business."

And despite a desperate eleventh-hour attempt by company lobbyists, there would be no federal mandate for open access (to solve the so-called "last-mile" problem) to jump-start one of Enron's most languishing and fraudulently represented businesses, Enron Broadband Services.

Enron exploited the machinery of political capitalism in still another way. As the company's problems grew, Lay and Skilling's best and brightest manipulated the highly prescriptive—indeed *politicized*—tax and accounting systems to create the illusion of profitability. However clever, such an elevation of form over substance only postponed and worsened the inevitable. Creditors would end up getting only nickels on the dollar from the core assets of a company that was more broke than bankrupt.

Thus, the collapse of Enron was not a failure of capitalism proper. Enron played all sides of the political aisle to make itself an extraordinary company on the way up and on the way down. Public perception aside, Enron was not "a problem for anyone who believes in markets," as the *Wall Street Journal* editorialized soon after the collapse. It was a logical, albeit grotesque, outcome of the mixed economy writ large.

In retrospect, Enron could have been a sizable, sustainable company without special government favor. There were sound consumer-driven divisions that achieved scale economies through merger. But by the economic (versus political) means alone, it could never have become America's Most Innovative Company, as it was designated by *Fortune* magazine for six years running. Ken Lay himself would have needed to develop and deploy a different skill set to reach the top in a free-market order, where success is less about personality and political connections than it is about meeting shifting consumer demand expeditiously and cost-effectively.

<small>◇</small>

The impressive rise and stunning fall of Samuel Insull's energy utility empire offers a vivid comparison with the story many decades later of Ken Lay and Enron. To be sure, Insull was a far better businessman than Lay. Insull's deep intuition about energy technology, combined with his other business skills, made him a consummate doer and, indeed, the father of the modern electricity industry.

It was Insull who pioneered scale economies by replacing isolated generating plants with large, centrally located power plants that could electrify whole areas. It was Insull who broadened the market for electric appliances in a most exciting way and in so doing became, according to Forrest McDonald, his biographer, "the crucial link between Phineas T. Barnum and Madison Avenue." Insull matched the consumption profile of the city and farm to run his units more efficiently and to promote universal electricity service. And it was Insull who pioneered innovative financing techniques to meet the needs of his rapidly expanding businesses. He was one of the leading business pioneers of all time, doing nearly as much for his industry as Rockefeller and Ford did for theirs.

Yet Insull, like Lay, had a political side and had personality flaws that would transform him from an undisputed Great Man into a national villain. Insull sold his industry on the benefits of the *regulatory covenant*, whereby cost-based rate regulation was accepted in return for franchise protection against would-be entrants. (Such entrants had become a burden to established providers, and no end to their market raiding was in sight.) But public utility regulation proved not to be the safe harbor Insull imagined, and it contributed to a wide-ranging hubris that would bring down the nation's largest holding company, as well as the Babe Ruth of business himself.

Insull failed to overcome success, as it were, in a most dramatic way late in his career. Throwing caution to the wind, and working to create monuments rather than fundamental business value ("I think I'm going to establish a dynasty, and thereby render myself immortal," Insull confided to a friend), America's most revered businessman became a train off the tracks when the Roaring Twenties gave way to the Great Depression. Insull expanded his investments as the economy contracted, even venturing into areas well outside his core expertise. "He took on greater and greater burdens until it appeared as if he were attempting to carry the entire American economy on his shoulders," McDonald noted.

Insull's crash, trial of the century, and final years provide a climax of Book 2, after which case studies related to Ken Lay and Enron's prehistory are presented for their business and political lessons.

◇

How did the Enron-enabling mixed economy arise?

America's *political capitalism* took root in the nineteenth century and flourished in the twentieth. No sector became more politicized than energy, particularly during Ken Lay's career. Much of this was inherited, but Enron's chairman drove the mixed economy, too. Government intervention, existing and prospective, became core to Lay's business model. Indeed, it would take the new CEO less than a year to turn lightly regulated Houston Natural Gas Corporation into highly regulated HNG/InterNorth, which would soon be renamed Enron.

Unlike Marxism or Keynesianism, political capitalism was not the result of a master plan or ideology. A century and more ago, most business leaders praised free markets but were not principled capitalists. Few people were. Business leaders and others felt little constraint in seeking tariffs, subsidies, entry restrictions, and other species of corporate welfare. To win political support, there was always a high-sounding argument, such as aiding an infant business, promoting domestic security, or stabilizing a cyclical industry. Business lobbying often bore fruit, as a firm or an industry's concentrated effort outdistanced the countereffort (if any) of the less-organized, less-represented taxpayers or consuming public. (Business-versus-business spats were more complicated and less predictable in outcome.) Such intervention begat more intervention, sometimes to address the unintended consequences of the prior intervention and sometimes in the attempt to level a playing field for another party. In the process, the mixed economy became more imbued with interventionism.

Political capitalism hardly started with Ken Lay or even Samuel Insull. But both powerfully advanced the interaction between business and government during their reigns. And the dramatic failure of both men's companies put capitalism itself on trial, leading inflamed legislators to regulate corporate governance in ways far beyond the free society's common-law strictures against force and fraud.

What about America's Progressive Era, when the intellectual class helped to convince politicians to leash capitalism? Didn't this limit political capitalism—and by implication Enron's political machinery to come? Here, many textbooks got it wrong. Much so-called reformer legislation was actually, on close inspection, *by business* and *for business*. The fact that much so-called antibusiness intervention had organized support from business constituencies should have tipped off the reformers that their drive for a mixed economy would have unintended consequences—and undesirable outcomes for the public good.

Thus, the intellectual class that loudly proclaimed the imperfections and injustices of free-market capitalism was complicit in the growth of political capitalism, which, ironically, created an environment hospitable to the private-sector excesses they came to lament. However unintentionally, reformers created a framework that enabled further corporate manipulation.

Enron *had been* a favorite of the intelligentsia. The *New York Times* and just about every other media outlet sang its praises. Ken Lay's company was a champion of all things politically correct. Enron was *progressive*, practicing *social corporate responsibility* and *stakeholder theory*. Enron supported racial quotas internally and politically. Ken Lay courted Houston's minority community and cultivated Jesse Jackson—all part of Enron's political machine. Enron even formed a subsidiary to invest in inner-city, minority-owned firms (it was a bust).

On the environmental front, Enron practiced so-called sustainable development by sounding the alarm over man-made greenhouse-gas emissions beginning in 1988, supporting Clinton/Gore's 1993 proposal for a Btu tax, aggressively investing in solar power in 1994, jump-starting the ailing U.S. wind industry with the purchase of Zond Corporation in 1996, spearheading the effort behind what became the nation's strictest renewable-energy mandate (in Texas in 1999), and lobbying the Bush/Cheney administration (unsuccessfully) to regulate CO_2 emissions. Enron received a climate-protection award from the EPA and a corporate-conscience award from the Council on Economic Priorities. The company advanced the interventionist agenda of the President's Council on Sustainable Development, Aspen Institute, Business Council for Sustainable Energy, Pew Center on Global Climate Change, and Heinz Center for Science, Economics, and the Environment, as well as sponsored Earth Day events in Texas, California, and Oregon. Ken Lay's Enron was pointing the way to a sustainable-energy future—or so it was thought.[1]

With dollars and time, Enron was also a philanthropic leader—and made sure that everyone knew it. Ken Lay's private foundation gifted hundreds of organizations in hometown Houston. Such philanthropy (or do-goodism to critics) was part of making Enron the world's leading company, for that required Enron's becoming the world's *favorite* company. Where image was reality, such favor trading (and conflicts of interest) was a way up the stock-price ladder, Lay thought, with each step creating more wealth to redistribute to keep the music

---

1. Lay, as a director of Resources for the Future and the American Enterprise Institute, pushed the need for government to price CO_2. Lay was not formally associated with any libertarian groups, although he occasionally spoke at their conferences when Enron's agenda involved, to some degree, free markets.

playing. It was a charm offensive not seen since the heyday of Samuel Insull in Chicago, a subject of Book 2.

The many academics, environmentalists, journalists, politicians, and regulators who touted Enron in the boom cast a cold, embarrassed eye upon the company come bankruptcy. Ken Lay's goodwill vanished overnight when thousands of his employees found themselves stranded during the holiday season with a modicum of severance pay. It became a populist morality play with millionaire management on one side and rank-and-file victims on the other. This was thought to be cruel capitalism—despite the fact that Enron was hardly a capitalist-spirited company. This was the unhappy consequence of oil-and-gas Republicanism—never mind that the Texas Republican governor, George W. Bush, had gifted Enron Wind Corporation with his signature on a so-called electricity-deregulation bill, part of which mandated the nation's most aggressive renewable-energy quota.

In all, far too many failed to appreciate how a politicized economy created the conditions that allowed the worst in business to get on top. Along with the accountants, analysts, bankers, executives, and lawyers, the intellectual mainstream was part of that which George Will decried: systemic failure.

·◇·

The story of Enron is one of the most important benchmarks in the history of mixed-economy capitalism. Books, essays, and movies have told the company's riveting story in myriad ways. But such storytelling has only superficially probed into fundamental incentives and motivations: the *why* behind the why. Political pundits and academics have often jumped to conclusions that missed the underlying causes. So rather than revisiting the regulatory morass that invited Enron's legendary gaming in the first place, more regulation of corporate governance was prescribed, not to mention a new ethics in a quest to reform Capitalist Man.

Challenging the conventional view of Enron's rise, fall, and lessons requires an alternative worldview, which is the subject of Book 1. The sister disciplines of economics, history, philosophy, political economy, political science, and psychology all come into play..And it is here that the story within the story emerges. For the flawed mainstream thinking in the social sciences and the humanities, which resulted in political capitalism (replete with unintended consequences, including Enron), itself suffered from the aforementioned hubris/deceit/obstinacy virus. The smartest fell victim to their own smartest-guys-in-the-room problem when it came to understanding capitalist reality and the political economy of business and government.

What, then, is the neglected worldview that explains Enron's fate in hindsight and offers a best-practices framework for avoiding organizational failure in the future? What time-honored capitalist wisdom might have saved Samuel Insull, John Henry Kirby, and Ken Lay from themselves? And more broadly, how does the same framework define sustainable enterprise and thus heroic capitalism?

A reconstruction can begin with the works of three leading capitalist philosopher-moralists (Part I of this book). Adam Smith, Samuel Smiles, and Ayn Rand elucidated the character traits, mental models, and interpersonal conditions behind success and failure, while differentiating sharply between free-market entrepreneurship and political rent-seeking. Their concern was less the material outputs of capitalism, however substantial, than the moral inputs of capitalism.

In the eighteenth century (chapter 1), Adam Smith championed the "prudent man" and warned against "over-weening conceit" and "self-deceit" in the pursuit of gain. The Scottish philosopher stressed the need to have an *impartial observer*, a concretized, tell-it-like-it-is confidant capable of giving constructive criticism leading to appropriate change. (Kirby, Insull, and Lay had no such check when they needed it most.) Smith distrusted do-gooders and political capitalists and placed great stock in what he called "sacred rules," the very thing Enron eschewed.

Smith recognized a confluence of sentiments, a moral order, based on empathy ("mutual sympathy") among buyers and sellers in commerce. He understood how good business drove out bad, and yet he recognized that the worst case of bad business, financial bankruptcy, was the exception, not the rule, in a system of natural liberty. Smith would have been disappointed—but hardly surprised—by the systemic failure that characterized Enron, given the conceit and self-deceit of the company's leaders, as well as the mixed economy that invited political rent-seeking and gaming and allowed Ken Lay to reach the top.

In the nineteenth century (chapter 2), Samuel Smiles explained the timeless virtues behind productivity and identified the bad motivations and habits that led to failure. Perseverance trumped genius and luck in his book. Smiles chronicled how attention to detail, authenticity, common sense, and integrity won in the marketplace. He exposed deceit in its many varieties and warned against shortcuts and keeping appearances. "How many tricks are resorted to—in which honesty forms no part—for making money faster than others!" he complained in his early day. Smiles's capitalism with character reveals Enron's bad actors to be old vinegar in new bottles.

In the twentieth century (chapter 3), the philosophy of Objectivism, formulated by Ayn Rand, explains how Enron's financial bankruptcy was at root a philosophic one. Enron was the embodiment of subjectivism (or *postmodernism*, in academic parlance), given how the company came to believe that wanting, believing, and saying something to be true could make it so. (Objectivism posits that reality is independent of one's consciousness—and hence is *objective*.) Ken Lay was a second-hander, a *philosophic fraud*, trying to be all things to all people, acting on convenience rather than principle, living a corporate life from the outside in instead of the inside out. For him, the ends came to justify the means despite his many righteous sermons about Enron's values and public goodness. But business strategy based on pretense is a recipe for failure sooner or later.

Yet Rand, as powerful as her philosophy is for understanding the tragedy of Ken Lay and Enron, was party herself to a blow-up born of arrogance and self-deceit. Events in her personal life, chronicled in appendix A, created a crisis for the nascent Objectivist movement, bewildering and victimizing thousands of devotees.

An Enron can strike in any walk of life.

Smith, Smiles, and Rand did much to frame what can be called *heroic capitalism*, or what contemporary businessman/intellectual Charles Koch has codified as *Principled Entrepreneurship*™, defined as "maximizing long-term profitability for the business by creating real value in society while always acting lawfully and with integrity." In Koch's framework, political rent-seeking is rejected because it redistributes and destroys wealth rather than creates it. Koch's ideal is about the economic means, in the tradition of Adam Smith's *invisible hand*, Samuel Smiles's *great work*, and Ayn Rand's *virtue of productiveness*. It is this rich worldview that has been absent in so much of the post-Enron analysis and learning—and that should be part of the debate in the classroom and the boardroom.

Part II of this book turns from philosophy to economics. Its excursion into the history of business and capitalist thought details how a hearty band of academics advanced their reality-grounded theories only to find that the mainstream was not listening. Each of these academics formulated logical, real-world concepts and challenged their colleagues' entrenched thinking—but to little avail. For example, Ludwig von Mises defended economic realism over mathematical formalism, only to witness the triumph of false assumptions (chapter 4). The remaining chapters of Part II go on to explain precisely what economic realism reveals capitalism to be: a highly competitive environment that requires business to improve or deteriorate—or cheat by resorting to the political means. Real commerce is about entrepreneurship, dealing with risk and uncertainty, economic calculation (profit-and-loss accounting), and the nature of the firm. All four concepts have particular application to the business model of Ken Lay and Jeff Skilling at Enron, as well as to business strategy more generally.

Intellectual realism is also a major theme of chapter 5. In particular, Joseph Schumpeter took the economics profession to task for using a highly idealized theory of competition that misconstrued capitalist reality as monopolistic. That error would keep many historians from seeing how pressured and even desperate business executives embraced the political pursuit of success, both before and during the so-called Progressive Era.

This propensity of business leaders to seek special government favor can be understood in the simple terms of diffused costs (to the public) and concentrated benefits (to the firm or industry). The gains of a few come at the expense of the many, a bad bargain that grows worse as more play the rent-seeking, wealth-redistribution game. By such political capitalism, in theory and practice, America inadvertently set the table for a Ken Lay and Enron.

The mixed economy began with intermittent government favor, as well as reformer efforts in the name of rationalizing and civilizing capitalism. But because business support was crucial to many of these reform efforts, America's mixed economy soon became a creation of political capitalism first and outside reform second. Chapter 5 shows how two early American political economists, Simon Newcomb and William Graham Sumner, as well as the father of modern political science, Arthur Bentley, interpreted the legislative process as proceeding from specific lobbying pressure rather than from feel-good ideas (what Bentley dismissed as *idea ghosts*). Alfred Chandler undermined the muckraker narrative by interpreting business change as proceeding from market resources and entrepreneurial strategy rather than Marxist dialectic and capitalist greed (chapter 6).

Part III provides the foundation for understanding Enron's modus operandi in the 1980s and 1990s. Whereas chapters 4, 5, and 6 delineate the true nature of business enterprise under capitalism and the mixed economy, chapters 7 through 11 present a history of energy and sustainable-development thought against the backdrop of real-world political-economic developments. Capitalism and political capitalism, energy and fashionable notions of sustainable development: These are the stage upon which the drama of Enron played out.

Chapter 7 takes an in-depth look at the foundational, errant thinking of Thomas Malthus on population and W. S. Jevons on energy supply. Chapter 8 shows how Erich Zimmermann challenged the assumption of fixed, known, and depleting mineral resources in favor of a *functional* theory capable of explaining why mineral stocks grow even as record quantities are extracted. Chapters 9 and 10 relate the story of neo-Malthusianism—Malthusianism applied to natural resources—and its apotheosis in the 1970s. Finally, chapter 11 narrates the crusade of reformed Malthusian Julian Simon, who turned neo-Malthusianism on its head by demonstrating that human ingenuity can allow a rapidly expanding population to find and use ever more resources, without crises and without the need for government planning.

Mises, Schumpeter, Bentley, Chandler, Zimmermann, and Simon, in their different ways, are intellectual father figures of the business case studies examined in this trilogy.

The celebrated Enron whistleblower Sherron Watkins alerted Ken Lay to the accounting coverups that would soon bring down the company. Though less celebrated, the six social scientists named above were also whistleblowers in their disciplines. Each had, as Thomas McCraw wrote of Joseph Schumpeter, a "radical" message "indicting his own profession for what amounts to a capital crime": a neglect of observable, theory-driving reality. So did others in this book, such as M. A. Adelman, James Buchanan, Allan Nevins, Simon Newcomb, Colin Robinson, and William Graham Sumner.

Well known or obscure, each of the preceding realists challenged intellectual fashion with better theories about the social world. If their insights had been better understood and integrated into the core of the social sciences and humanities, free-market capitalism might have played a greater role than did political capitalism in twentieth-century America. And just maybe, a Ken Lay would not have ascended to the heights of the energy world, and Enron would have been unknown to history.

That is the major conclusion from Book 1. *But why did inferior thinking in the social sciences and humanities prevail?* Why was sounder, on-the-shelf theory neglected—even purposely ignored and deprecated? Why did the majority choose form over substance, opting for methodological and political fashion rather than a sober, truer understanding of the underlying social world? Why did these *intellectual Enrons* occur?

The answer is the by now familiar one: *arrogance.* Yet such academic failure did not lead to an unavoidable meltdown or judgment day. Immune from profit-and-loss accounting and lacking the verdicts of laboratory experimentation, errant social theory could survive and perpetuate itself as orthodoxy—even *consensus*—for two reasons. One was the perverse incentive structure under which the perpetrators were rewarded in academia, in the media, and in the halls of political power. A second was simply the bandwagon effect. Understanding and correcting such institutional failures must be part of the Enron postmortem—if the systemic failure identified by George Will is to be undone.

Capitalism proper—*free-market capitalism*, in both its moral and practical dimensions—deserves a new look in today's debates over corporate governance. Ken Lay's grand play in political correctness, corporate social responsibility, stakeholder theory, and second-hander strategies ended tragically. Sustainable wealth creation for a business and society requires a strict adherence to rational self-interest, sacred rules, like-it-or-not reality, and consumer-driven change, as well as allegiance to the economic rather than political means.

The fundamental lesson from Enron is this: Capitalism did not fail. The mixed economy failed. The capitalist worldview is stronger, not weaker, post-Enron. But there is another, deeper lesson that explains Enron and the mistakes of the intellectual mainstream before, during, and after Enron's active life: What in the Enron vernacular is called the *smartest-guys-in-the-room problem* can strike anytime and anywhere. Whether in business or academia—or any profession or association—conceit, deceit, and dogmatism are the bane of personal, intellectual, and organizational success.

Part I

Heroic Capitalism

Capitalism is too important and complex a subject to be left to economists.
—Jerry Muller, *The Mind and the Market* (2002)

Introduction

Enron and other corporate scandals put business ethics in the spotlight and capitalism on trial. As part of the national conversation, Alan Greenspan, then head of the U.S. Federal Reserve Board, testified in 2002 before a Senate committee that "infectious greed" had become commonplace in business, in part because "the avenues to express greed had grown so enormously." Greenspan endorsed greater regulation for the accounting industry, which the *New York Times* reported as a "remarkable turnaround for an economist who for many years was a close friend and colleague of Ayn Rand, the high priestess of unfettered capitalism."

Many books written on Enron and related corporate controversies have also concluded that more regulation and better policing are needed to save capitalism from itself. "Whether dealing with securities laws or energy regulation, with corporate governance or corporate audits," wrote Loren Fox, "the message is clear: Capitalism is a complicated enterprise, and the system won't work without referees." Kurt Eichenwald placed blame on "a government willing to abide absurdly lax rules." From a more academic perspective, Professor Frank Partnoy complained that Enron-era markets "are now like Swiss cheese, with the holes—the unregulated places—getting bigger each year, as parties transacting around legal rules eat away at the regulatory system from within."

A book written by Mimi Swartz in collaboration with Enron whistleblower Sherron Watkins concluded, "Enron represented the whole sorry devolution of American capitalism at the end of the twentieth century." Another newsstand book, noting that Enron's leadership "was morally, ethically, and financially corrupt," indicted the system that allowed the company to work its mischief for so long and in so many areas. Still another volume called the Enron saga "an American brand of individualism gone badly wrong." This dominant interpretation was neatly encapsulated in the title of a review of three of the aforementioned books by the chief financial correspondent of the *New York Times*, Floyd Norris: "Business Ethics and Other Oxymorons."

Writing five years after Enron's collapse, Gabriel Kolko, the New Left historian who in the 1960s documented how business lobbying corrupted many of the high-minded reforms of the Progressive Era, damned capitalism as follows:

> For decades the United States held itself as the example of what capitalism abroad should seek to become. But the Enron and all-too-many other promotional scandals revealed that American capitalism was a hypocritical chimera. Business people in the United States wished to become wealthy, in any way possible and necessary, fraudulent as well as technically legal, and that has remained the essence of the system since the nineteenth century.

Interventionists and socialists alike, it seemed, now had a trump card to play against laissez-faire in theory and practice.

But what is the socioeconomic system that these critics are attacking? Free-market capitalism, an economic system premised on private property and voluntary exchange, and one in which businesses compete without special treatment from government, has evolved into something quite different in practice. To properly interpret today's complex economic events, capitalism proper must be differentiated from its quasi- and even anticapitalist descendants, prominently including political capitalism, whereby businesses use the political means to succeed in the marketplace. To get from what *was* to what *should have been,* and from what *is* to what *ought to be,* real capitalism must be defined and carefully applied to the business case studies at hand.

Capitalist thought concerning personal, social, professional, and political ethics can be gleaned from the writings of two of capitalism's greatest philosophers—Adam Smith of the eighteenth century and Ayn Rand of the twentieth—as well as from the moralist Samuel Smiles of the century between. Their complementary views cast today's capitalism in a different light and offer unique insight into contemporary corporate controversies. At the same time, these philosopher-moralists point the way to *heroic capitalism*, an ethical, sustainable framework of behavior that is applicable to all participants in commerce, all businesses within an industry, and all industries within an economy.

Courses in business ethics would do well to consider the Smith/Smiles/Rand worldview as the foundation of modern capitalist thought—and as the foundation of ethical business itself. Individuals, after all, make up the business whole, and their combined moral outlook becomes the true corporate culture of an organization. Business participants should consider this triadic worldview as providing timeless insight into best practices—even the margin between success and failure. Public policy should recognize philosophically grounded capitalism as sustainable and avoid the imposition of complex corporate-governance rules in the ultimately vain attempt to reform Capitalist Man.

1

The Soul of Commerce: Adam Smith

A S WITH MANY THINGS BUSINESS and economic, contemporary corporate scandals cannot be understood without attending to the worldview of Adam Smith (1723–90). But the Smith of our interest is more the Professor of Moral Philosophy of the University of Glasgow than the economist of later fame.

Adam Smith explained and defended voluntary market relations against impositions from a central authority. In his day, government typically imposed high taxes, set wage rates, prescribed the so-called just price for articles in commerce, and protected merchants from imported goods. Government edicts even prohibited transporting bundles of goods deemed unsightly and other mundane practices. Yet through this thicket, there was enough unregulated commerce for the social science genius to recognize the benefits of voluntary exchange and to challenge the intellectual foundations of government-directed economic life.

Smith's masterwork, *An Inquiry into the Nature and Causes of the Wealth of Nations* (1776), set a new direction for Europe and promoted limited, constitutional government in the nascent United States. The book's "acute insight into the nature of the economic process" made its author the founder of *political economy*, a social science that would later become *economics*. "The first human was Adam, the first economist . . . Adam Smith," wrote Paul Samuelson in his preeminent economics textbook two centuries later. Yet Adam Smith did not invent capitalist theory or economics, although his was the first treatise in political economy. The "great architect" borrowed and synthesized the ideas of others to explain the interplay of motivations, markets, and government.[1]

---

1. Smith's place in the history of economic thought is considered in Internet appendix 1.1, "A Worldly View," at www.politicalcapitalism.org/book1/chapter1/appendix1.html.

Adam Smith's ideas are considered to be the foundation not only of economics but also of capitalist thought. And so his worldview came to be scrutinized in the post-Enron debate about capitalism. The editor of the journal *Business Ethics*, Marjorie Kelly, concluded from the Enron debacle: "The ideal of the unregulated free market is flawed, and it's time we said goodbye to Adam Smith's 'invisible hand.'" Attorney Ira Millstein, assessing the lessons learned from Enron, concluded: "The failure of Adam Smith's 'man' to 'do the right thing' resulted in the reform pendulum swinging from the private sector to the regulators."

In congressional hearings several months after the company's collapse, S. David Freeman of the California Power Authority stated, "We must recognize that the so-called invisible hand of Adam Smith was Enron and their fellow gougers picking the pockets of Californians to the tune of billions of dollars." Paul Ehrlich, whose dire warnings against economic growth made him a doyen of the environmental Left, chimed in: "Market failures occur when Adam Smith's 'invisible hand' doesn't function properly . . . as in the Enron fiasco [where] . . . criminal executives . . . knew the true state of corporate finances but denied the information to employees and investors." With Enron in mind, economist and *New York Times* columnist Paul Krugman blamed what he called "the current crisis of capitalism" on "deregulation," "loving free markets too much," and "rigid free-market prejudices." Crucial economic matters, he proclaimed, could not be "entrust[ed] . . . to the magic of the invisible hand."

But did Adam Smith's views about a natural economic order neglect the moral side of economic behavior? Do individuals engaged in commerce really have desirable character traits that can be relied upon to promote market order?

Can Smith's theories enlighten our understanding of political capitalism relative to free-market capitalism and help us understand and judge Samuel Insull and Ken Lay, the major fallen business titans of our story? Adam Smith, after all, was concerned not only with economic behavior but also with the motivations of Economic Man. Smith was a perceptive observer of business success and failure, including financial bankruptcy.

Sympathy: The *Moral* Invisible Hand

Adam Smith was impressed by the fact that the commoners of his day were materially better off in many respects than the nobility of ages past. Why did this progress occur, and what might create "universal opulence" in the future? This brought Smith face to face with self-interested practices in the marketplace, what he called "the obvious and simple system of natural liberty" (what later would be called capitalism). Smith asked: Does a broader good emerge from narrow, self-regarding commerce? Is there, perhaps, a natural order that tends toward national prosperity, thus obviating the need for government

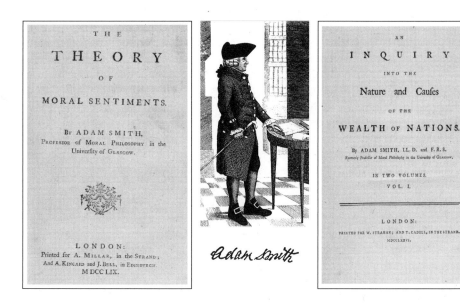

Figure 1.1 Adam Smith, who never married and was childless, described himself as a "beau in nothing but my books." His eighteenth-century insights are relevant to the post-Enron debate over capitalism and business ethics.

to direct economic life "as the hand arranges the different pieces upon a chess-board"?

Smith's celebrated answer was that self-interested behavior in commerce promoted the common good as if "led by an invisible hand." But why must this be true? If the products and services of others are needed, why would not some or many simply abscond with the goods or otherwise try to get something for nothing?

In fact, the invisible-hand simile of *Wealth of Nations* was undergirded by a moral philosophy in Smith's *Theory of Moral Sentiments* (1759).[2] It was the latter work that an authority of the day, Dugald Stewart, described as "a singular effort of invention, ingenuity, and subtilty" that "had the merit of directing the attention of philosophers to a view of human nature which had formerly in a great measure escaped their notice." If Smith became the Isaac Newton of social science by uncovering the principles behind social order, his achievement rested on his insight into both self-interested action and the nature of cooperation.

Smith opened his treatise on moral philosophy: "How selfish soever man may be supposed, there are evidently some principles in his nature, which interest

---

2. The last edition (1790) of *Theory of Moral Sentiments* was subtitled *An Essay Towards an Analysis of the Principles by which Men Naturally Judge Concerning the Conduct and Character, First of Their Neighbours, and Afterwards of Themselves.*

him in the fortunes of others, and render their happiness necessary to him, though he derives nothing from it except the pleasure of seeing it." Smith called this principle "mutual sympathy," described as the tendency of individuals to put themselves in the place of others, empathizing with their situation and emotional reactions. On the basis of such identification, a person feels either an accord or a discord with the other's emotions and wants. "Whatever is the passion which arises from any object in the person principally concerned," Smith observed, "an analogous emotion springs up, at the thought of his situation, in the breast of every attentive spectator." If the spectator feels a perfect concord with the emotion of the person observed, Smith explained, the observer judges the person's emotions to be right and just.

Among the most important emotions identified are *grief, joy, pity, compassion*, and *gratitude*. Another important emotion for Smith is *resentment*, "a disagreeable passion" that is nonetheless part of "justice and the security of innocence," which is needed to "beat off the mischief which is attempted to be done to us, and to retaliate that which is already done."

Thus, in one interpreter's words, Smith recognized "an unintended system of moral order," arising from identification with the situations of others and from feelings of accord or discord with their emotions. Such empathy, when it results in approval by others, creates a process of reciprocal self-improvement. The individual's desire for "self-love," Smith reasoned, leads him to seek approval. "The love and admiration which we naturally conceive for those whose character and conduct we approve of," Smith explained, "necessarily dispose us to desire to become ourselves the objects of the like agreeable sentiments, and to be as amiable and as admirable as those whom we love and admire the most." Although this feedback loop may encourage virtue, it does not guarantee it. What completes the transformation is one's desire to be *justly* approved of by an impartial observer—a final step that may or may not occur.

Smith's invisible hand in commerce explains how those who tend to serve themselves (and not others) end up serving others, thus creating a broad, unintended economic order. In parallel, Smith's theory of sympathy explains how those who tend to judge others (and not themselves) end up judging themselves, thus creating a broader moral order of mutually shared views toward virtue and vice. Empathy creates an interpersonal process whereby one judges many and many judge one, with virtually all desiring sympathetic approval. This gives rise to such "praise-worthy qualities" as "prudence, vigilance, circumspection, temperance, constancy, firmness," as well as "economy, industry, discretion, attention, and application of thought." All this promoted good behavior and, in the world of trade, good business—as if led by an invisible hand.[3]

---

3. Smith's invisible-hand view of economics is discussed in Internet appendix 1.2, "Adam Smith and Societal Order," at www.politicalcapitalism.org/book1/chapter1/appendix2.html.

Support for Smith's insights about voluntary social cooperation and norms—what James Otteson has called the "marketplace of morality"—has accumulated in the 250 years since the publication of *Theory of Moral Sentiments*. A review article in *Nature* (2003) pointed toward "experimental evidence indicating that repeated interactions, reputation-formation, and strong reciprocity are powerful determinates of human behaviour."[4] Indeed, the relatively new discipline of experimental economics has found that well-channeled self-interest—Smith's *moral* invisible hand of sympathy—is at work with *positive reciprocity* (trading favors) and *negative reciprocity* (not offering favors where none are offered by others). The Golden Rule, it seems, is not only a virtuous end but also a means to the end of winning just esteem.

In the field of cognitive neuroscience, scientists analyzing the magnetic imaging of brain activity have identified how trust in financial interactions results from tit-for-tat behavior and is eroded by betrayal. The bilateral trading that characterizes honest relationships in markets thus leads to trust and to predictable behavior in a variety of situations, smoothing economic life.

Labeling Adam Smith a behavioral economist, several researchers have declared that the "psychological perspective" of *Theory of Moral Sentiments* "suggests promising directions for economic research that have not yet been exploited." Smith's Economic Man, it was found, includes elements of benevolence and fairness, internalizing, as it were, some of the negative externalities of their market behavior. "In short," the authors conclude, "Adam Smith's world is not inhabited by dispassionate, rational, purely self-interested agents, but rather by multidimensional and realistic human beings." Smithian Man serves as a standard by which to judge Enronian Man, at least the amoral variant that became so prominent during the artificial boom that led to the company's dramatic bust.

Prudence

A cardinal virtue of Smithian morality is *prudence*, defined as "the care of the health, of the fortune, of the rank and reputation of the individual, the objects upon which his comfort and happiness in this life are supposed principally to depend." The reward for prudence, Smith concluded, is "success in every sort of business."

The prudent man is "perfectly genuine," "always sincere," "cautious in his actions," and "reserved in his speech." He is marked by "the steadiness of his industry and frugality." Insofar as he seeks praise from the ideal and impartial

---

4. Revisiting Adam Smith's 1759 book, another group of authors defined strong reciprocity as *"a predisposition to cooperate with others, and to punish (at personal cost, if necessary) those who violate the norms of cooperation, even when it is implausible to expect that these costs will be recovered at a later date."* However, such behavior may well be more self-interested and less altruistic than these authors imply.

observer, he "always studies seriously and earnestly to understand whatever he professes to understand, and not merely to persuade other people that he understands it." Although not always "brilliant" or "distinguished by the most exquisite sensibility," he is steadfast. He is internally focused and quite the opposite of the "imprudent pretender" and "artful imposter." Furthermore:

> The prudent man is not willing to subject himself to any responsibility which his duty does not impose upon him. He is not a bustler in business where he has no concern; is not a meddler in other people's affairs; is not a professed counsellor or adviser, who obtrudes his advice where nobody is asking it. He confines himself, as much as his duty will permit, to his own affairs, and has no taste for that foolish importance which many people wish to derive from appearing to have some influence in the management of those of other people.

The prudent man applies "steady perseverance . . . in the acquisition of fortune" and is forward looking. He avoids "vanity . . . profligacy" and "imprudence" and does not succumb to immediate gratification and the "love of ease, of pleasure, of applause." Knowing that "capitals are increased by parsimony, and diminished by prodigality and misconduct," Smith's prudent man would recognize the actions that destroy viable companies as the height of imprudence—a wholesale absence of the *self-command* attributes of "temperance, decency, modesty, and moderation."

Becoming intoxicated by one's good intentions, or thinking of oneself as a *great man*, was unsettling to Adam Smith. He noticed that "the great mob of mankind are the admirers and worshippers . . . of wealth and greatness" and acknowledged this impulse as a buttress to social order. But inordinate admiration and trust can contribute to social disorder—and did in the cases of Samuel Insull and Ken Lay.

Still, the "passion properly called ambition" was virtuous to Smith. Without it, the prudent man "commands a certain cold esteem, but seems not entitled to any very ardent love or admiration." We would not think much of "a private gentleman who did not exert himself to gain an estate, or even a considerable office, when he could acquire them without either meanness or injustice." By contrast, the "man of enterprise" was to be respected. Here, Smith was on the trail of *heroic capitalism*, whereby both the captains and the commoners of commerce possess ambition and sympathy alongside a "sacred regard to general rules." For any man, stated Smith,

> it is this which constitutes the most essential difference between a man of principle and honour and a worthless fellow. The one adheres, on all occasions, steadily and resolutely to his maxims, and preserves through the whole of his life one even tenour of conduct. The other, acts variously and accidentally, as humour, inclination, or interest chance to be uppermost.

A lack of Smithian prudence brought down Samuel Insull's empire after the Roaring Twenties abruptly ended, as Insull adopted a damn-the-consequences attitude: He *would* maintain control of his companies against any takeover; he *would* sustain his stocks' prices in the face of a bear raid; he *would* continue expanding despite the crash of 1929. Basking in his own power and conceit, and without an impartial observer to check his ambitions, Insull refused to rein in his gargantuan ambitions until it was too late.

Smithian prudence also stands in stark contrast to the actions of Enron executives and the many who failed in their roles as Enron's gatekeepers—accountants, boards of directors, credit-rating agencies, investment bankers, lawyers, regulators, securities analysts, and more. The opium of Enron's time—the *new economy*, revolutionary change over incremental improvement, government-directed energy transformation, and newfound personal riches and success—caused leaders of the company to change personally, and not for the better.

The 1999 waiver of the company code of conduct for Enron's chief financial officer—perhaps the single greatest mistake the company made—was certainly a violation of the "sacred regard to general rules." The ends would never justify the means for Smith's prudent man. This person, the rule abider and rule enforcer, was the check to the overly ambitious, those "candidates for fortune" who to Smith "too frequently abandon the paths of virtue."

Self-Deceit

The practice of virtue requires that we "become the impartial spectators of our own character and conduct." But there emerges a problem—"self-deceit"—because "there is not in the world such a smoother of wrinkles as is every man's imagination, with regard to the blemishes of his own character." This fog in the "moral looking glass" creates a situation whereby one's *conscience*—the inner impartial observer—is disabled. Thus, to be successful, a person must receive and take to heart the input of the outside impartial observer.

Self-deceit festers from a lack of critical feedback. "The propriety of our moral sentiments is never so apt to be corrupted," Smith explained, "as when the indulgent and partial spectator is at hand, while the indifferent and impartial one is at a great distance." When is this most likely to occur? Smith warned:

> Are you in prosperity? Do not confine the enjoyment of your good fortune to your own house, to the company of your own friends, perhaps of your flatterers, of those who build upon your fortune the hopes of mending their own; frequent those who are independent of you, who can value you only for your character and conduct, and not for your fortune.

This wisdom applies to the tragic figures of our trilogy—Ken Lay, Samuel Insull, and John Henry Kirby in particular—who reached the heights of success only to be brought down by that success. The seeds of business and personal destruction were planted and watered during the heady times of prosperity, when caution and respect for underlying reality gave way to an emphasis on *perception*, and perception gave way to ever greater *deceit*.

Smith identified two roads by which one may deserve, acquire, and enjoy the respect and admiration of mankind. One is the "study of wisdom and the practice of virtue"; the other is "the acquisition of wealth and greatness." Wisdom and virtue are the high road to such esteem, but Smith was candid enough to admit that wealth and greatness are more admired by the world, as much as he regretted others' inclination to "proud ambition and ostentatious avidity." Fortunately, in the middling condition of commercial and professional life, wisdom and virtue are generally the road to at least a modicum of wealth, whereas vice and folly are almost always paths to ruin. And what was true in Smith's day is equally true in ours.

Arrogance—what Smith called "over-weening conceit"—is a particularly destructive trait in the modern business world, where unprecedented success and prosperity can suddenly descend on an individual, firm, industry, and even a whole economy. Smith, although cognizant that "every individual, in his breast, naturally prefers himself to all mankind," asserted that a person "dares not look mankind in the face, and avow that he acts according to this principle." To the rest of mankind, after all, each person is an insignificant part of the whole. Thus, Smith warned, the individual must "humble the arrogance of his self-love," lest others, and certainly the impartial spectator, view such behavior as "excessive and extravagant." Consequently, Smith observed how interpersonal relationships teach the individual to "bring . . . down" his self-opinion to "something which other men can go along with."

Smith warned against the hubris of planning by a political or intellectual elite to perfect society. It was the "the highest degree of arrogance," Smith stated, for a lawmaker "to erect his own judgment into the supreme standard of right and wrong." Such an imposed "ideal plan of government" would result in the "highest degree of disorder" if the edicts went against the self-interest of the subjects. Indeed, though Smith ardently believed in the virtue of prudence, he was exceedingly skeptical of any attempt to impose it. He noted in *Wealth of Nations* that, given how poorly government behaves, "it is the highest impertinence and presumption, therefore, in kings and ministers, to pretend to watch over the œconomy of private people, and to restrain their expence either by sumptuary laws, or by prohibiting the importation of foreign luxuries."

Smith also cautioned against social elites, who "are themselves always, and without any exception, the greatest spendthrifts in the society." Smith advised them to tend to their own business and "trust private people with theirs."

Smith's "man of system," the utopian visionary, "apt to be very wise in his own conceit," was footloose at Enron during the company's artificial boom of the 1990s. These individuals were not part of government, but many were enabled by government favor and accounting deceits to pursue their illusions. Adam Smith would have appreciated the title of one of the more substantive accounts of the rise and fall of Enron, *The Smartest Guys in the Room*.

"The Laws of Justice"

Adam Smith is known to history as the father of capitalist thought. His view of public policy was neatly encapsulated in one of his most quoted statements (1755): "Little else is requisite to carry a state to the highest degree of opulence from the lowest barbarism but peace, easy taxes, and a tolerable administration of justice: all the rest being brought about by the natural course of things."

But Smith's case for liberty, which came from his recognition of mutual sympathy, the desire for right approbation, and the workings of natural economic order, did not blind him to human imperfections. The "unsocial . . . mean-spirited . . . poor-spirited" person who annoys our sensibilities or leaves good things undone "should have little respect." Beyond the reprobate was the criminal who could pervert the norm and, if unchecked, bring down the whole social order. Thus, as Smith wrote in *Lectures on Jurisprudence*, "the first and chief design of every system of government is to maintain justice; to prevent the members of a society from incroaching on one anothers property, or seizing what is not their own."

Smith's *laws of justice* delineated three categories of protection, covering "life and person . . . property and possession . . . [and] personal rights, or what is due to him from the promises of others." The crimes of "fraud, falsehood, brutality, and violence" prompt sympathy with the victims and "excite in every human breast . . . scorn and abhorrence," prompting others to strip the perpetrators of their ill-gotten gains by legal means.

The laws of justice applied to business rivalry. "In the race for wealth, and honours, and preferments, he may run as hard as he can, and strain every nerve and every muscle, in order to outstrip all his competitors," Smith said. "But if he should jostle, or throw down any of them . . . it is a violation of fair play."

Modern corporate malfeasance would no more surprise Smith than the deceit of tradesmen in his own day. But in the case of Enron, Smith would want to understand *why* a breakdown of the moral order and invisible-hand guidance occurred on such a grand scale and *why* it involved so many different institutions that constituted the checks and balances of the marketplace. Why the seemingly universal lack of *prudence*? As it turns out, Adam Smith's own insights come into play to help answer this highly important—and oft-debated—question.

Bankruptcy

Declarations of financial bankruptcy have long been the exception and not the rule. "The number of prudent and successful undertakings is every where much greater than that of injudicious and unsuccessful ones," Adam Smith observed in his day. "After all our complaint of the frequency of bankruptcies, the unhappy men who fall into this misfortune make but a very small part of the whole number engaged in trade, and all other sorts of business; not much more than one in a thousand." And in the post-Enron era, the bankruptcy rate has been just this—about 1.2 per thousand, according to the American Bankruptcy Institute, for the five years ending 2006.

There was good reason for such infrequency, as Smith explained:

> Bankruptcy is perhaps the greatest and most humiliating calamity which can befall an innocent man. The greater part of men, therefore, are sufficiently careful to avoid it. Some, indeed, do not avoid it; as some do not avoid the gallows.

Smith saw two common patterns behind bankruptcy. One was a "presumptuous hope of success [in] hazardous trades." Another was in the "trade of speculation" whereby "a bold adventurer may sometimes acquire a considerable fortune by two or three successful speculations; but is just as likely to lose one by two or three unsuccessful ones." This would prove to be true in an oil-trading scandal that rocked Ken Lay's Enron in 1987, a foretaste of what would reappear in grander form just over a decade later to decisively destroy the company.

Smith explained how under England's bankruptcy law, "the debtor, on giving up all his substance to the creditors, is freed from all farther distress." The moral philosopher/political economist sanctioned the safe harbor of bankruptcy as fair and as an impetus for risk taking. Smith's contemporary, the esteemed jurist William Blackstone, also defended the common law of debt forgiveness, reasoning:

> Trade cannot be carried on without mutual credit on both sides: the contracting of debts is therefore here not only justifiable, but necessary. And if by accidental calamities, as by the loss of a ship in a tempest, the failure of brother traders, or by the non-payment of persons out of trade, a merchant or tradesman becomes incapable of discharging his own debts, it is his misfortune and not his fault.

The laws of England, Blackstone added, "allow the benefit . . . of bankruptcy to none but actual *traders;* since that set of men are, generally speaking, the only persons liable to accidental losses, and to an inability of paying their debts, without any fault of their own."

Adam Smith did not wince at his homeland's draconian penalty toward those who violated the terms of bankruptcy. If the bankrupt person took above 20 pound sterling (about $2,500 today) beyond of the exemption of "his and his wifes wearing apparel," the punishment was death! Smith explained how the bankrupt person received a "great benefit" under the law's forgiveness of debt. "But besides this, there is no fraud which is more easily committed without being discovered" since "one may take 1000 ways to conceal his effects; and the loss of the creditors may by this means be very great."

The penalty fit the temptation in Smith's system of jurisprudence.

In the United States, legal forgiveness of debt was codified with the Bankruptcy Act of 1898, as amended in 1938 and 1978. Such laws, emanating from the British tradition, are not incompatible with capitalist philosophy, as evidenced by their support from Smith and Blackstone. In 1829, U.S. Supreme Court Justice Joseph Story, who had declared the rights of property to be sacred, elsewhere wrote:

> The general object of all bankrupt and insolvent laws is, on the one hand, to secure to creditors an appropriation of the property of their debtors *pro tanto* to the discharge of their debts, whenever the latter are unable to discharge the whole amount; and, on the other hand, to relieve unfortunate and honest debtors from perpetual bondage to their creditors, either in the shape of unlimited imprisonment to coerce payment of their debts, or of an absolute right to appropriate and monopolize all their future earnings. The latter course obviously destroys all encouragement to industry and enterprise.

However, in more recent times, leading capitalist philosophers have dissented, arguing that *debt nonpayment is a fraud per se*. Even the best of intentions and efforts of the debtor are not enough for the legal discharge of debt, in their view. Bankruptcy provisions would have to be negotiated in the original loan agreement or consented to by the creditor ex post. Bankruptcy law is thus seen as usurping voluntary negotiation and violating contract sanctity, or a government intervention into the free market.[5]

A financial bankruptcy may or may not involve fraud. But Enron's bankruptcy resulted from the fraud of all frauds, both prosecutable and philosophical (a distinction explored in chapter 3). Small deceits cascaded into bigger and then into giant ones. It was an extreme failing, one in which (in Smith's words) "the negligence is so great as that no man could have been guilty of the like in his own affairs." Insull's great empire went bankrupt also, although his acquittals in court suggest that the frauds involved were strictly or largely philosophical.

Owners versus Managers in Commerce

Smith had a keen eye for the activity in the bazaars and shops around him. The small capitalists of his day—the craftspeople and tradespeople, farmers and planters, merchants and storekeepers, printers and publishers—predated the rise of big business, which awaited the transportation and communication revolutions. Thus, Smith did not imagine a situation in which the checks and balances of commerce could be so thoroughly falsified and disguised by a façade of prosperity. Yet even if he had, Smith might well have suspected that more than free-market capitalism was at work in this extreme situation.

---

5. Divergent capitalistic views of bankruptcy law are further examined in Internet appendix 1.3, "On Bankruptcy Theory," at www.politicalcapitalism.org/book1/chapter1/appendix3.html.

Figure 1.2 Adam Smith integrated crucial insights on the nature of market interaction, gained from observing street merchandizing, with knowledge gained from voracious reading and discussion. This picture shows Edinburgh a generation after Smith lived there.

Smith's questioning of one aspect of commerce in his day has remained controversial within capitalist thought: the potential misalignment of incentives between managers and stockholders. In *Wealth of Nations*, Smith unfavorably compared the limited-liability, joint-stock company to the "private copartnery," since management of the former might not always keep the outside owners' best interests in mind. "The directors of such companies, however, being the managers rather of other people's money than of their own," Smith believed, would not "watch over it with the same anxious vigilance with which the partners in a private copartnery frequently watch over their own." He analogized:

> Like the stewards of a rich man, they are apt to consider attention to small matters as not for their master's honour, and very easily give themselves a dispensation from having it. Negligence and profusion, therefore, must always prevail, more or less, in the management of the affairs of such a company.

Here, Smith identified what in today's academic jargon is called the *principal/agent problem*. But unlike many modern corporate critics, he did not focus on management's lining its pockets at the expense of shareholders. Rather, he noted management's temptations to negligence (it is not the managers' money) and extravagance, or "profusion" (managers tend to believe that a grand company should act grandly, with their personal lifestyles not far behind).

Smith also noticed a difference between the nominal shareholder-owners of a limited-liability company and real owners:

> The greater part of those proprietors [of a limited-liability company] seldom pretend to understand any thing of the business of the company. . . . This total exemption from trouble and risk, beyond a limited sum, encourages many people to become adventurers in joint stock companies, who would, upon no account, hazard their fortunes in any private copartnery.

A third potential problem can be added to these two identified by Smith: the difference between long-term stockholders and short-term stock speculators.

The colossal failure of Enron's management was related to the principal/agent problem. Adam Smith would have been greatly troubled by the agency problem in that company and other large enterprises today. When everyone from the top down conceives of himself or herself as the agent of anonymous owners, personal morality and financial prudence can get lost in the subordinate's impulse to perform well at all costs. In a Smithian framework, James Q. Wilson described how pragmatism neutralizes conscience and the impartial observer, for both the management *order givers* ("'I don't care how you get it done, just get it done'") and the employee *order takers* ("'I can't help it, I'm just following orders'"). Smith himself stated that without a "sacred regard to general rules, there is no man whose conduct can be much depended upon."

Capitalist critic John Kenneth Galbraith posited that Smith today would shock corporate heads by telling them that "their enterprises should not exist." Yet Smith, an open-minded student of commerce, may well have changed his mind, recognizing the corporation as, in the words of a contemporary defender of capitalism, Michael Novak, "the most successful, transformative, and future-oriented institution in the modern world." The legal framework of limited liability has allowed the general public to effortlessly own and transfer stock in many thousands of companies, capitalizing capitalism. Wealth creation and wealth diffusion are still the rule; bankruptcies, the exception.

Adam Smith respected the ability of the free, open marketplace to settle questions of business form. Smith also limited his criticism of corporations in three ways. He recognized the superior ability of limited-liability companies to raise capital; he noted that concentrated ownership reduces the owner/manager divergence; and he conceded that routine business activities are not prone to divergence problems. Smith's chief concern with capitalism was *barriers to competition*, not the organizational form of its business.

Mercantilism: The Root of Political Capitalism

Smith challenged the notion, promoted by leading merchants in conjunction with political authorities, that protection against foreign goods increased national wealth. In Smith's day, the wealth of nations was equated with the accumulation of gold and silver bullion, an idea that fostered a policy of restrictions against imports in order to keep foreign goods out and bullion in. This fallacious economic doctrine, *mercantilism*, which held sway from about 1500 to 1800, sanctioned a business and political elite that worked together to restrict competition from abroad.

Modern mercantilism, better known today as *protectionism*, is rationalized as necessary to help so-called infant or temporarily distressed firms and industries gain a foothold for later success without government aid. Unlike other forms of government intervention, which were on the wane in Smith's day, protectionist laws were on the ascent. Protectionism was *the* major issue for political economy, for if wealth were really a zero-sum game, with losses canceling out gains, trade between nations was "a form of undeclared warfare."

The wealth of nations is not bullion from net exports, Smith explained, but "the plenty and cheapness of provisions" that comes from trade itself. Thus, Smith denounced "exclusive priviledges [that allowed] the butchers and bakers [to] raise the price of their goods as they please, because none but their own corporation is allowed to sell in the market." Such action "diminishes public opulence [by raising the] market price above the natural one."

"The mercantilist authors," as one historian observed, "were pamphleteering and proselytizing men of affairs, more characteristically advocates of self-promoting policies than dispassionate scholars, who shared certain perspectives and biases and concerns of economic purpose and practice." Adam Smith, sympathizing with the commoner, passionately disliked the mercantilists and their government cronies.

Smith knew that trade restrictions narrowed the division of labor and benefited the few at the expense of the many. It was free trade between sovereign territories, an international division of labor, that promoted wealth creation. Indeed, *Wealth of Nations* is most critically aimed against "the mean rapacity, the monopolizing spirit of merchants and manufacturers, who neither are, nor ought to be the rulers of mankind."

The history of England, which Smith knew well, was filled with examples of exclusive privilege in commerce. In the incipient energy field, Parliament in the seventeenth century granted a business consortium a 21-year monopoly on the sale of coal mined in Newcastle—an arrangement that included a coal tax for the king. London was forced to pay an "extravagant price [for coal from the] outrageous monopoly," one historian noted.

Smith criticized such political capitalism. "The proposal of any new law or regulation of commerce which comes from . . . any particular branch of trade or manufactures," he warned, "ought always to be listened to with great precaution, and ought never to be adopted till after having been long and carefully examined, not only with the most scrupulous, but with the most suspicious attention." Smith's love of commerce was moderated by his distrust of the leaders of commerce in a political venue.

Smith famously warned that a meeting of "people of the same trade" would invariably inspire a "conversation end[ing] in a conspiracy against the publick, or in some contrivance to raise prices." This statement has been invoked time and again by capitalism's critics to warn about monopoly practices in unregulated markets. But a close reading of Smith offers another interpretation. Such meetings were described as infrequent. Any laws against them would sacrifice "liberty and justice"—and might fail anyway. Smith went on to explain the real threat: "exclusive privilege," arising out of government-facilitated or government-sponsored business meetings. In a private letter, Smith expressed this concern regarding a live situation:

> I expect all the bad consequences from the chambers of Commerce and manufacturers establishing in different parts of this country, which your Grace seems to foresee. . . . The regulations of Commerce are commonly dictated by those who are most interested to deceive and impose upon the Public.

Thus Smith feared the disproportionate role of special interests on lawmaking and considered this a reason to separate politics from business: "The legislature, were it possible that its deliberations could be always directed, not by the clamorous importunity of partial interests, but by an extensive view of the general good ought . . . to be particularly careful neither to establish any new monopolies . . . nor to extend further those which are already established."

Adam Smith was no utopian or apologist for capitalism. He did not consider free and unfettered commerce as perfect, and he advocated a government role that went beyond being the arbiter of the laws of justice.[6] But he evaluated imperfect markets in light of more important considerations (liberty) and imperfect alternatives (government regulation). He also saw natural commerce as a process of improvement and a reason for optimism—or what in today's parlance is called sustainable business.

Crony Capitalism

Smith's inquiry into market morality and the political side of commerce led him to pass judgment upon what today would be called *crony capitalism*:

> In the courts of princes, in the drawing-rooms of the great, where success and preferment depend, not upon the esteem of intelligent and well-informed equals,

---

6. See Internet appendix 1.4, "Adam Smith and Public Policy," at www.politicalcapitalism. org/book1/chapter1/appendix4.html.

but upon the fanciful and foolish favour of ignorant, presumptuous, and proud superiors; flattery and falsehood too often prevail over merit and abilities. In such societies the abilities to please, are more regarded than the abilities to serve.

Divergence of station and abilities might have little consequence in "quiet and peaceable times," Smith continued. But there comes the time when "the solid and masculine virtues of a warrior, a statesman, a philosopher, or a legislator" are needed.

Smith associated phony talent and sycophantic praise in high places with political privilege. The "proud superiors" included the mercantilists and their sponsors. Cronyism was less in free and open commerce where, instead of "quiet and peaceful times," there is, to use the term that Joseph Schumpeter would popularize in the twentieth century, a "perennial gale of creative destruction."

Cronyism's deceit works in reverse when the (inflated) subjects return false praise and deference to their superiors. The "disposition to admire, and almost to worship, the rich and the powerful," Smith warned, is a "great and most universal cause of the corruption of our moral sentiments." "Inattentive observers are apt to mistake . . . wealth and greatness . . . for wisdom and virtue." He explained:

> It is from our disposition to admire, and consequently to imitate, the rich and the great, that they are enabled to set, or to lead what is called the fashion. . . . Even their vices and follies are fashionable; and the greater part of men are proud to imitate and resemble them in the very qualities which dishonour and degrade them.

Sycophantic followers can give a false sense of security to great and powerful deceivers, a theme that comes into play with our two examples of the Great Man of industry, Samuel Insull and Ken Lay. Both lowered their guard in a way that Smith warned against centuries before:

> The ambitious man flatters himself that, in the splendid situation to which he advances, he will have so many means of commanding the respect and admiration of mankind, and will be enabled to act with such superior propriety and grace, that the lustre of his future conduct will entirely cover, or efface, the foulness of the steps by which he arrived at that elevation.

Enron, perhaps more than any other major corporation in history, was about ends, not principled means. The modus operandi was to get things done; once done, few would care about the way in which it got done. But when the company collapsed, a wave of investigative journalism turned up the great "foulness of steps" that was, implicitly or explicitly, the Ken Lay way.

Natural Self-Interest

Smith recognized self-interest as natural, moral, and useful: "Every man is, no doubt, by nature, first and principally recommended to his own care; and as he is fitter to take care of himself than of any other person, it is fit and right that it should be so." Thus Smith was suspicious of those who by word or deed suspended self-interest in a quest to advance the public weal. "I have never known much good done by those who affected to trade for the publick good," he observed. "It is an affectation, indeed, not very common among merchants, and very few words need be employed in dissuading them from it."[7]

Smith's suspicion is relevant when interpreting the political economy of Enron and other energy firms that positioned themselves altruistically in the environmental debate over sustainable development in the 1990s. As Smith might have guessed, inconsistencies and hypocrisy were present among the righteous.

Criminal law discourages unjust behavior, rights wrongs, and punishes the guilty. Without justice, Smith explained, the social fabric would tear. But Smith saw competition's discipline on a merchant as the primary force that "restrains his frauds and corrects his negligence." Under open trade, he noted, any business can lose customers to better-performing rivals—unlike situations of "exclusive privilege," whereby a legal monopoly limits consumer choice and compromises the ability of customers to chasten inferior performance by patronizing elsewhere.

Smith's recognition of market sentiments and the laws of justice made him optimistic about commerce and society. One of the most famous passages in *Wealth of Nations* spoke to this point:

> The uniform, constant, and uninterrupted effort of every man to better his condition, the principle from which the public and national, as well as private opulence is originally derived, is frequently powerful enough to maintain the natural progress of things toward improvement, in spite both of the extravagance of government, and of the greatest errors of administration.

The "greatest errors," including "private prodigality and misconduct," were comparatively small compared to "the frugality and good conduct of others" in open competition, what today would be called free-market capitalism.

The Soul of Capitalism

In his introduction to the Modern Library edition of *Wealth of Nations* (1937), Max Lerner labeled Adam Smith "an unconscious mercenary [who] gave a new dignity to greed and a new sanctification to the predatory impulses." Lerner, if alive today, would likely point toward Enron-style corporate malfeasance as a refutation of Smith's invisible hand in theory and practice. But a truer understanding of Adam Smith—and growing evidence on the nature of human

---

7. Smith's view of altruism is considered further in Internet appendix 1.5, "Self-Interest and Self-Sacrifice," at www.politicalcapitalism.org/book1/chapter1/appendix5.html.

interaction—casts a decidedly different light on the father of capitalist thought and on recent corporate controversies.

Smith would have been disappointed at—but not mystified by—the scope of recent corporate malfeasance. If alive today, Smith would refer his critics—from Max Lerner to Paul Krugman—to *Theory of Moral Sentiments* passages that identified and counseled against the bad habits that presage spectacular failure. Indeed, Smith might have even commented that this was why he considered *Theory of Moral Sentiments* to be as or more important than *Wealth of Nations*.

Smith was no apologist for greed as the foundation of human progress or wealth as the foundation of happiness. "Surprising as it may seem to some, the real Adam Smith—in contrast to the caricature economists created of him in the 20th century—would have been appalled at both of these ideas," concluded one Smith scholar. In Smith's view, capitalism has a moral basis from which participants can be praised or criticized—and prosecuted in the event of coercion or fraud.

Smith determined that the "obvious and simple system of natural liberty," backed by the laws of justice, would cause mutual sympathy to predominate and goodness to prevail—with criminality and bankruptcy being the exceptions that proved the rule. But far from refuting Smith, Enron and other examples of corporate malfeasance offer support for the ageless profundity of the moralist-economist. Enron was not about free-market capitalism as much as it was about modern forms of mercantilism and old-fashioned deceit. Smith viewed political capitalists and do-gooders (such as Ken Lay) with great suspicion and prescribed limited government to curb their mischief. Smith also warned that nominally altruistic behavior (an Enron façade) be judged by its deeper motivations and results, not public declarations.

Seen through this lens, the fall of the House of Lay (and to an extent, the House of Insull) is less a crisis of invisible-hand capitalism than a cluster of errors that Smith warned against more than two centuries ago—imprudence, self-deceit, misplaced interest, cronyism, politics, and more. Still, additional insight is necessary to understand a complicated historical episode and to extract helpful lessons for corporate governance and public policy.

Capitalism has a soul. Success in a consumer-driven, free-market economy is about character—the subject of the next chapter, on the writings of moralist Samuel Smiles. Chapter 3, the final chapter of Part I, deals more specifically with the questions of self-interest, money making, and greed: issues that are central to the morality of capitalism and the values held by its prime movers.

2

Character and Success: Samuel Smiles

CORPORATE MALFEASANCE INVOLVES character flaws. Kurt Eichenwald, who formerly wrote about white-collar crime for the *New York Times*, blamed the Enron collapse on "shocking incompetence, unjustified arrogance, compromised ethics, and an utter contempt for the market's judgment." Such failings could be attributed also to Samuel Insull and John Henry Kirby of Book 2. Their debacles had similar causes: inattention to detail, overemphasis on the short run, overambition, overdelegation of core responsibilities, and a focus on maintaining appearances rather than on confronting problems. In the case of Insull's public utility empire and Ken Lay's Enron, there was also an overreliance on fickle government favor to succeed in a consumer-driven marketplace.

Capitalism depends on character and, in turn, molds it. A series of popular writings from more than a century ago by the Scottish moralist Samuel Smiles described the attributes for success in the workplace, where men and women spent half of most every day.[1] His books also isolated the bad habits, motivations, and scenarios that led to underperformance and even business ruin. The timeless wisdom contained in Smiles—whom some consider the father of the self-improvement movement that is today an industry of books and seminars—deserves a place in modern debates about capitalism, best-business practices, business ethics, and corporate culture. Smiles's uncommon common sense thus powerfully complements

---

1. A 12-hour day was normal for factory workers, shopkeepers, and women working in the home. A clergyman of the time commented, "One is heartily sorry that any man should be under the necessity of working twelve or more hours a day . . . but this is an age when all is going at railway speed. Every energy is valued forth in business, trade and profession."

Adam Smith's view of the moral side of capitalism and provides historians with a framework for understanding and judging commercial capitalism in action.

The Age of Improvement

"The greatest discovery of my generation," wrote American psychologist and philosopher William James in the late-nineteenth century, "is that a human being can alter his life by altering his attitudes." Attitude, however, had counted for little when reason and personal effort were suppressed by irrational doctrines and omnipotent government. Fortunately, this radically changed with the Enlightenment. Reason and the rule of law introduced economic order, capital accumulation, and rising productivity for the laboring masses. Common laborers and entrepreneurs alike had an incentive to *try harder* and *do better*. The Industrial Revolution, introducing mass production for mass consumption, lifted individuals from the vagaries of nature and a hand-to-mouth existence. Progress meant that one's hard-earned gain did not necessitate another's loss—the social Darwinism of the static precapitalist society. The best rose toward the top. A better future was envisioned—the phenomenon of *rising expectations*.

The urge for personal improvement and social advancement became a movement across Victorian England.[2] In Leeds, an industrial center halfway between Edinburgh and London, "there were societies for almost every form of human betterment—choral, floral, madrigal and motet, anti-monopoly, anti-slavery, temperance, a Society for Promoting Permanent Universal Peace, a Benevolent Strangers-Aid Society, a Guardian Society for Females Who Have Departed from the Paths of Virtue." Enter the editor of the *Leeds Times*, Samuel Smiles (1812–1904), a political reformer espousing free trade, woman's suffrage, and worker welfare.

In the mid-1840s, Smiles saw a higher calling in empowering each person to improve his or her character. Government policy was important, but the *individual* was the mainspring of social progress and good government. Smiles began lecturing and writing on these subjects. The grand result was *Self-Help, With Illustrations of Character, Conduct, and Perseverance*, first published in 1859 and revised for republication in 1866. Motivational self-help books were not new, but Smiles's 400-page opus was systematic, combining age-tested wisdom with knowledge of the industrial present, and profusely illustrated with stories of individuals-made-good in industry, engineering, the arts, and music.[3]

---

2. The Victorian era, though named after Queen Victoria, who ruled from 1837 to 1901, is defined by historian Asa Briggs as lasting only from 1851 until 1867, a period of uninterrupted prosperity, civility, high-mindedness, and national pride.

3. Also see Internet appendix 2.1, "*Self-Help* in the Self-Help/Motivational Literature," at www.political capitalism.org/book1/chapter2/appendix1.html. On the question of Smiles's advice applied to women, see Internet appendix 2.2, "Samuel Smiles and the Feminist Movement," at www.politicalcapitalism.org/book1/chapter2/appendix2.html.

Samuel Smiles, a medical doctor turned newspaper editor/political reformer turned businessman/moralist, would become the Adam Smith of applied commercial capitalism.

Smiles inspired thousands to take charge of their own lives, revisit their attitudes, refine their best efforts, and improve in the workplace. "*Self-Help* unambiguously celebrates individuality, autonomy, and civility," summarized one historian, "virtues central to the projects of other nineteenth-century institutions that actively encouraged cultivation of the intellectual and moral working-class self: the mechanics' institutes, public libraries, people's colleges, and lyceums." The self-help movement of Smiles's day predated England's Welfare State—but would eventually succumb to it.[4]

Smiles's writings inspired Samuel Insull, a Scottish lad who would go on to become the father of the modern electricity industry in the United States. On the occasion of his twenty-fifth anniversary as president of Commonwealth Edison Company in Chicago, Insull admonished his many employees to take greater advantage of the educational opportunities the company offered them. "Corporations today spend money to elevate their employees and cultivate their minds in a way that never existed when I was of your age," Insull said in a 1917 address. "The only inspiration that we used to get when I started work upwards of 43 years ago was from the books of such men as Samuel Smiles, who wrote *Self-Help* and *Lives of the Engineers* and books of that character, together with the inspiration of the literary and debating societies and the associations that one made in such company." Insull's message—"be ready when opportunity knocks"—was Smiles reincarnated. "It rests absolutely with you whether you ever get your chance" to excel and advance at Commonwealth Edison, he told the assemblage.

Many read and applied Smiles's message, but Insull, his biographer Forrest McDonald noted, "applied the formula and made it work"—at least for *most* of his storied career. Smiles's lessons were increasingly left behind when Insull reached the pinnacle of professional life. It was different with Ken Lay a half century later, if only because Smiles's *oeuvre* was not part of his rural Missouri upbringing. Perhaps it would have made a difference if the teachings of *Self-Help* had been in his soul, never to be unremembered, always to be applied. That wisdom could have saved Lay, like Insull, and their many associates, from a cruel business fate.[5]

---

4. England had *poor laws* in Smiles's era, but a universal system of social services—covering education, health care, pensions, and some housing—would come only in the twentieth century.

5. Samuel Insull Junior, born in 1900, was taught the Smilesian philosophy and "that most precious of human qualities, humility" by father Samuel and mother Gladys Wallis Insull. Junior would become a top executive in his father's utility empire and, as discussed in Book 2, rescue his embattled father.

A phenomenal 20,000 copies of *Self-Help* were sold in the first year, a number that would reach a quarter million in the next decades, easily outselling the literary classics of the day. Smiles's handbook for capitalism was translated into two dozen languages and dialects, becoming "a bible for western-inspired businessmen." One historian quipped, "Cholera itself could have traveled no faster."

The reception of *Self-Help* led Smiles to write three companion volumes: *Character* (1871), *Thrift* (1875), and *Duty* (1881). The author of more than 20 books, Smiles was also "the authorized and pious chronicler of the men who founded the industrial revolution." His biographies of great inventors and engineers—"strong-minded, resolute and ingenious men; impelled in their special pursuits by the force of their constructive instincts"—added heft to his moral teachings. Their stories, Smiles noted, served to "afford many valuable and important lessons of Self-Help, and to illustrate how the moral and industrial foundations of a country may be built up and established."

Figure 2.1 Throughout his life, Samuel Smiles had the physical appearance to complement the power of his message. (*Left:* © Mary Evans Picture Library/The Image Works.)

Smiles was a compelling reformer. The "cheery little soul," with his passionate delivery and "keen eye beaming benevolence," was a crowd favorite. Smiles's writings reflected meticulous research, and the few adages he did not know, he coined. He was a clear writer. Simplicity ruled; his stories spoke for themselves without unnecessary ornamentation. And Smiles lived as he preached, seeking perfection in all things, wishing to "retouch my life as the artist retouches his picture." His years in business (1845–72) helped him to understand the intricacies of the workplace. He was the working man's intellectual because he was a working man first and an intellectual second.

A Handbook for Capitalism

Self-Help was published on the centennial of Adam Smith's *Theory of Moral Sentiments*. Smith and a new generation of political economists had explained the moral and economic order of emerging capitalism. Now the Industrial Revolution was giving way to a new era of economic advancement. Personal opportunity abounded. Yet, as one historian noted, "pre-industrial experience, tradition, wisdom, and morality provided no adequate guide for the kind of behavior which a capitalist economy required." An on-the-ground perspective was needed—a guide to *applied capitalism* for artisans, merchants, inventors, and other ambitious souls. *Self-Help*, complemented by his other books, filled just that need.

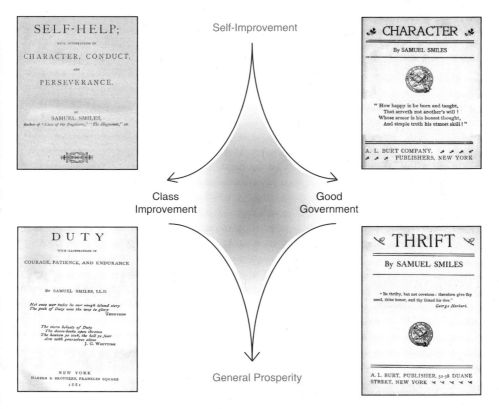

Figure 2.2 Samuel Smiles's message was that self-improvement would lead to class improvement and good government, beginning in homeland Britain.

Smiles sought to redress what he saw as the "deterioration of the standard of public men, of public morality, and of political principles." In the words of historian Asa Briggs, Smiles's "catalogue of social sins" included "scamped work, gambling, fraud, intemperance, dishonest advertisement, and sharp practices." Smiles also took aim at absenteeism and the foibles of lawmakers. In relation to Adam Smith's view of society, Samuel Smiles gave the *impartial observer* a tutorial in morality, advanced the process of *sympathy*, and fortified the *invisible hand*. He did so over many years, in many venues, beginning with candlelight talks to the Leeds Mutual Improvement Society and ending with a shelf of books for readers worldwide.

Smiles preached *self-respect, cleanliness, chastity, reverence, honesty, thrift, sobriety, politeness, courtesy, generosity, forethought,* and *economy*—not to mention what was perhaps his favorite virtue of all, *perseverance*. Happiness and prosperity would result from *truth* and *justice*. Vices that would foil the good life—and personal and business success—included *avarice, greed, miserliness, fraud, injustice, thoughtlessness, extravagance, selfishness,* and *improvidence*.

Smiles championed "energetic individualism" for all. Class, political party, and nationality mattered not. "Competence and comfort lie within the reach of most people, were they to take the adequate means to secure and enjoy them," he believed. Determinism was rejected. "The will is free," Smiles said. "Our habits, or our temptations, are not our masters, but we of them." In a later book, Smiles added, "Man is not the creature, so much as he is the creator, of circumstances." He quoted a brave and resolute man: "Nothing can work me damage but myself; the harm that I sustain I carry about with me; and I am never a real sufferer but by my own fault." To buttress these assertions, Smiles presented example after example of upward mobility and success emanating from "the ranks."

Projecting optimism and preaching opportunity for all, Smiles had the wind at his back. England's "golden age of high farming" put fears about the Malthusian doctrine to rest.[6] Coal to fuel the machines of the industrial age was being mined all around Leeds. Inventions and new industries were the norm. Smiles saw much more ahead, for "in an age of progress, one invention merely paves the way for another."

Economic Liberalism

Economic liberalism set the table for character development. Echoing Adam Smith, Smiles explained how the "free energy of individuals" had overcome "the effects of errors in our laws and imperfections in our constitution," creating the "vigorous growth of the nation." Thus, private-property rights were essential to character formation. The incentive and reward of physical possession

---

6. The views of Thomas Robert Malthus are discussed in chapter 7, pp. 190–94.

makes [men] steady, sober, and diligent. It weans them from revolutionary notions, and makes them conservative. When workmen, by their industry and frugality, have secured their own independence, they will cease to regard the sight of others' well-being as a wrong inflicted on themselves; and it will no longer be possible to make political capital out of their imaginary woes.

Smiles saw the connection between personal thrift (savings) and the funds for business expansion (investment). Capitalists were "among the most effective benefactors of the people." Machines *empowered* labor rather than, as Marx taught, alienated labor, although there were transition costs as labor moved from declining areas to expanding ones. Advancement was the story of machinery, "each stage of [man's] progress being marked by an improvement in his tools." The mother invention was James Watt's steam engine, fueled by England's coal, which gave labor the power to "drain their mines, blow their furnaces, roll and hammer their metals, thrash and grind their corn, saw their timber, drive their looms and spindles, print their books, impel ships across the ocean." Nature and resources, such as coal, were not sacrosanct but means to further human progress.

The intersection of capitalism and character produced many success stories for Smiles, none greater than those from the railroad industry. The transportation revolution represented all good things, from thrift-enabled capitalization to precision engineering. Railroad passage, once for the rich, was now producing a "notable" increase in third-class tickets. The "remarkable . . . degree of safety with which this great traffic has been conducted," he added, resulted in fewer deaths than from lightning bolts! This was more than luck; it was the result of "continuous inspection [by highly skilled] picked men."

Wealth creation and freedom from personal debt were the best weapons against *poverty*, "a great enemy to human happiness." Want of money, Smiles explained, "certainly destroys liberty, and it makes some virtues impracticable, and others extremely difficult." Savings was "husbanded power," the enabler of better tomorrows. Alcohol was a great barrier to savings, for every drink was a few pence lost for thrift. Drunkenness, a perennial temptation, magnified the problem. Smiles counted 17 drinking establishments in his community for every church— which inspired his career change from journalism to teaching personal reform.

Smiles rejected the socialist belief that "character is formed *for*, not *by*, the individual; and that society may so arrange 'circumstances' as to produce whatever character it pleases." He rejected as wholly impractical such notions as communal plenty and retirement by age 25. "The philosopher's stone was a child's toy compared to this arrangement," Smiles wrote in his memoirs.

Smiles rejected welfarism as well, for government redistribution was not an effective substitute for voluntary one-on-one charity. "The value of legislation as an agent in human advancement has usually been much over-estimated," Smiles wrote. "No laws, however stringent, can make the idle industrious, the thriftless provident, or the drunken sober." He drew upon experience and offered a theory:

We have tried to grapple with the evils of [misery] by legislation, but it seems to mock us. Those who sink into poverty are fed, but they remain paupers. Those who feed them feel no compassion; and those who are fed return no gratitude. There is no bond of sympathy between the givers and the receivers.

The path to minimize and manage poverty is "better habits [not] greater rights," Smiles wrote on the opening page of *Self-Help*. Better habits required improved character both for the Haves, so that they might *provide* charity, and for the Have-nots, so that they might *merit* it; charity, as Ayn Rand would argue a century later, should reward a person's virtues, not vices.

But there was much work to do, character being a work in progress. "The selfish part of [man's] behavior is over-developed; the sympathetic not at all," Smiles lamented early in his career. In the next decades, however, Smiles would become more optimistic and confident that heartfelt personal relationships were better than legislation to address the "enormous mass of poverty" that stood alongside unprecedented wealth.

Aristocratic Government (Political Capitalism)

"The function of government," Smiles stated on the opening page of *Self-Help*, "is negative and restrictive, rather than positive and active; being resolvable principally into protection of life, liberty, and property." Smiles's support for limited government reflected his distrust of coercion as a means for positive reform:

> Men are very slow to give up their faith in physical force, as necessary for the guidance, correction and discipline of others. Force . . . is the short way of settling matters, without any weighing of arguments. It is the summary logic of the barbarians. . . . Even civilized nations have been very slow to abandon their faith in force . . . [yet] the history of the world is, to a great extent, the history of the failure of physical force.

Smiles, like Adam Smith, stopped short of advocating strict laissez-faire. Among other things, Smiles championed universal (government) education and libraries to broadly distribute knowledge as part of the character crusade.[7] Still, he espoused public-policy reforms that went against mercantilist and feudalistic norms in England, not to mention the rest of the world. The dissenting radical did so as a member of the "uneasy" middle class, who more than once had to change professions to support his family. Smiles was never driven by envy toward the wealth and rank of others, but he cast a wary eye toward the aristocracy, which too often was peopled by landowners benefiting from import barriers on wheat and other agricultural products that unjustly inflated their wealth. It was the poor subsidizing the rich, for the commoners paid more for their food as the result of such protectionism. Would-be merchants of blocked

---

7. For Smiles's views on government, see Internet appendix 2.3, "Samuel Smiles and Laissez-Faire Capitalism," at www.politicalcapitalism.org/book1/chapter2/appendix3.html.

imports were also victims of the landed class, part of what a Smiles biographer called "the aristocratic-government complex."

Smiles worked to repeal the so-called Corn Laws, as well as a domestic bread tax that financed the political class. (*Corn* meant *grain*, and England's chief grain was wheat.) Repeal of the tariffs and tax was a bottom-up effort, aided by economists who saw the fallacies of protectionism. It was a triumph of honest work over privilege, moving England closer to a meritocracy and away from its feudalist past. "The spirit of commercial enterprise," Smiles rejoiced, "is destructive of feudal legislation" and "hostile to monopoly and to all exclusive rights and privileges."

The reversal of political capitalism in Victorian England was a hard-fought, come-from-behind crusade. Smiles, his emotions raw, "detested members of the House of Peers, who 'impoverished the people by their taxes and monopoly of agriculture, commerce, and legislation.'" The leisure and idleness of the politically endowed aristocracy violated Smiles's basic sense of fairness, for "if a man [does] not manage honestly to live within his own means, he must necessarily be living dishonestly upon the means of somebody else."

Good government required a character revolution across society, for "morals and manners, which give color to life, are of much greater importance than laws, which are but their manifestation." "Noble people will be nobly ruled," Smiles believed. Siding with his esteemed contemporary, John Stuart Mill, Smiles concluded: "The solid foundations of liberty must rest upon individual character; which is also the only sure guarantee for social security and national progress." Nations were as good as their citizens. Better societies came from better individuals. "National progress is the sum of individual industry, energy and uprightness as national decay is of individual idleness, selfishness, and vice."

Smiles held up his country's greatness for all to see. "It is this spirit [of industry], displayed by the commons of England, which has laid the foundations and built up the industrial greatness of the empire." England was a nondescript nation until she commercialized. "A number of ingenious and inventive men, without apparent relation to each other," Smiles explained, "succeeded in giving an immense impulse to all the branches of the national industry; the result of which has been a harvest of wealth and prosperity."

Self-Help is full of examples of England's creative, productive exploits, including those of Adam Smith, whose perseverance, Smiles noted, gave the world *The Wealth of Nations.* "Where would England have been now, but for the energy, enterprise, and public spirit of our manufacturers?" Smiles asked. It was time for the rest of the world to follow the same path to greatness.

The Discipline of Commerce

The rigors of business require candor, discipline, and good manners. "Trade tries character perhaps more severely than any other pursuit in life," Smiles noted.

"It puts to the severest tests honesty, self-denial, justice, and truthfulness; and men of business who pass through such trials unstained are, perhaps, worthy of as great honor as soldiers who prove their courage amidst the fire and perils of battle." Smiles invoked a magazine's lucid description of business as "high culture [involving] the perpetual call on a man's readiness, self-control, and vigor . . . the constant appeal to the intellect, the stress upon the will, the necessity for rapid and responsible exercise of judgment."

Smiles demurred from the argument that competition is "heartless . . . ruinous . . . [and a source of] poverty to the million." Rivalry puts the "lazy man . . . under the necessity of exerting himself," inspiring his best efforts in business, the arts, the clergy, and politics. Competition transforms problems into opportunities. "Put a stop to competition and you merely check the progress of individuals and of classes," Smiles found. Nations, too, advance under the discipline of competition.

"Integrity in word and deed is the backbone of character; and loyal adherence to veracity its most prominent characteristic," Smiles wrote in *Self-Help*. Smiles recalled the maxim *Always endeavour to be really what you would wish to appear* and warned: "Men whose acts are at direct variance with their words, command no respect, and what they say has but little weight; even truths, when uttered by them, seem to come blasted from their lips." In *Character*, Smiles identified some of the "many . . . forms [of] untruthfulness" that resonate today (bullet format added for emphasis):

- in reticency on the one hand, or exaggeration on the other;
- in disguise or concealment;
- in pretended concurrence in others' opinions;
- in assuming an attitude or conformity which is deceptive;
- in making promises, or allowing them to be implied, which are never intended to be performed; or
- even in refraining from speaking the truth when to do so is a duty.

Small things matter, for the whole is the sum of its parts. "'It will do!' has blighted many a character, blasted many a fortune, sunk many a ship, burned down many a house, and irretrievably ruined thousands of hopeful projects of human good," Smiles observed. He once defined character as "little things well and honorably transacted." "Where men or nations have broken down, it will almost invariably be found that neglect of little things was the rock on which they split," Smiles stated. He added a precept: "Trifles make perfection, and perfection is no trifle."

An ocean away from Smiles, John D. Rockefeller was hard at work on the little things. "As I began my business life as a bookkeeper," the great industrialist would write in his autobiography, "I learned to have great respect for figures and facts, no matter how small they were." Another American industrialist, Harvey Firestone, gave homage to the nitty-gritty of commerce:

> Success is the sum of detail. It might perhaps be pleasing to imagine one's self beyond detail and engaged only in great things. But . . . if one attends only to great things and lets the little things pass, the great things become little—that is, the business shrinks.

Neglecting the little things for grandeur is a major theme of the fall of business titans.

Smiles emphasized a number of attributes for success in commerce: focus ("one thing at a time"), accuracy, thoroughness, and promptitude—and a methodology for achieving all of them. There must be "quick perception and firmness in . . . execution." There must be action over words—"Philosophers discuss; decisive men act." The heart must be checked by the head. One "must drill his desires, and keep them under subjection, they must obey the word of command, otherwise he is the sport of passion and impulse." Leaders must set the example, for "immorality in high places never fails to exert a pernicious influence upon all classes of society."

There must be "elasticity to the spirit," Smiles said. "Spectres fly before it; difficulties cause no despair, for they are encountered with hope, and the mind acquires that happy disposition to improve opportunities which rarely fails of success." Interpersonal success ("peace with others") requires forbearance, given that "every man has peculiarities of manner and character . . . of form and feature."

Humility and temperance were also part of this elasticity. "The wise person gradually learns not to expect too much from life," Smiles said. "While he strives for success by worthy methods, he will be prepared for failures. He will keep his mind open to enjoyment, but submit patiently to suffering." Smiles saw consolation in disappointment, knowing that it was but a leg on a journey with many tomorrows. "Failure improves tempers and strengthens the nature," he noticed. "Even sorrow is in some mysterious way linked with joy and associated with tenderness."

Perseverance, Not Genius or Luck

Samuel Smiles was present at a mid-1840s Leeds improvement seminar at which railroad pioneer George Stephenson roared to the feverish crowd, "Young men, persevere, persevere, persevere; its been the making o' me." Smiles, in his early 30s, had found a hero. He went on to write a masterly biography of Stephenson, the father of the railways, and then *Self-Help*. "My object in writing out *Self-Help* . . . was principally to illustrate and enforce the power of George Stephenson's great word—PERSEVERANCE," Smiles recollected.

Smiles focused on the individual and presented numerous case studies from everyday life. He did not dwell on groups where causality could get lost, and he did not fictionalize greatness, as was done by Horatio Alger for his tens of millions of readers.[8] Yet Smiles's individualism avoided the extremes of *atomistic man* and *cellular man*. Man was a social being, not an island entire of itself, but neither was man a mere part of a superorganism called society.

Smiles's books chronicled failure as part of the process of betterment. "Failure, conquered by Perseverance, is always full of interest and instruction," he noted. He recited a proverb—"Crosses are the ladders that lead to heaven"—and a poem:

> Though losses and crosses
> Be lessons right severe,
> There's wit there, you'll get there,
> You'll find no other where.

Heroic man turned adversity into advantage. Setbacks and failure were part of the process of molding character for success. "He who never made a mistake," Smiles stated, "never made a discovery."

"The most important results in daily life are to be obtained, not through the exercise of extraordinary powers, such as genius and intellect," Smiles wrote in his autobiography, "but through the energetic use of simple means and ordinary qualities, with which nearly all human individuals have been more or less endowed." Business success is "usually the path of common sense," Smiles preached, not the result of brilliance, education, or nobility. "It is not the men of genius who move the world and take the lead in it so much as men of steadfastness, purpose, and indefatigable industry." Energy, not brilliance, "enables a man to force his way through irksome drudgery and dry details." Smiles placed more value on "diligent self-education" than on formal classroom study. Education to him started in the home and was well served by the study of biographies.

But lessons from the "school of experience" must be gained on the spot. Smiles explained:

> Precepts and instructions are useful so far as they go, but, without the discipline of real life, they remain of the nature of theory only. The hard facts of existence have to be faced, to give that touch of truth to character which can never be imparted by reading or tuition, but only by contact with the broad instincts of common men and women.

---

8. Horatio Alger Jr. (1832–99) authored more than 100 books of rags-to-riches ascents in which fictional heroes and heroines overcame the odds owing to their integrity, kindness, and perseverance. More than a hundred million copies of his works inspired a generation of Americans and led to the founding of the Horatio Alger Society in 1947, to which Ken Lay was elected in 1998. Ken and Linda Lay were scheduled to host the society's 2002 annual dinner and induction ceremony, but it was an appointment they would have to cancel.

Figure 2.3 Revered as the wise man of industrial England, Samuel Smiles offered those with ambition and drive a recipe for working success. *Left:* This painting depicts Smilesian hero George Stephenson lecturing the next generation on the value of hard work. *Right:* This cover image on a popular edition of *Self-Help* shows a typical Smiles theme. (*Right:* Reproduced with permission of Punch Ltd., www. punch.co.uk.)

Smiles would not have been taken with a business model predicated on hiring and unleashing *the smartest guys in the room*. An army of top MBAs, sprinkled with Ph.D. economists, would count for little unless they were degreed from the school of perseverance and possessed good character.

Perseverance is the stock of inventors who must laboriously advance by trial and error. Great inventions, Smiles found, were not the work of singular genius but of different individuals working over long periods of time—the genius of process. Discovery was more the story of incrementalism than of revolution, although the final product might be revolutionary. This finding was part of Smiles's suspicion of quick riches versus brick-by-brick progress.

Perseverance is the great equalizer. "Industry enables the poorest man to achieve honor, if not distinction," Smiles observed. He offered examples: "A working instrument-maker gave us the steam-engine; a barber, the spinning-machine; a weaver, the [spinning] mule; a pitman perfected the locomotive; the working-men of all grades have, one after another, added to the triumphs of mechanical skill."

Luck was no substitute for diligence in creating one's own good fortune. Luck, once a "popular belief," Smiles observed, was giving way to the realization that "diligence is the mother of good luck." "Sheer industry, application and hard work" came first and serendipity second in Smiles's chronologies of achievement. "Luck whines, Labor whistles," he concluded.

In his role as CEO of two Fortune 500 natural gas companies, Jack Bowen, a mentor to Ken Lay, took perseverance to heart. Bowen kept these anonymous, Smiles-like words of wisdom by his side in the workplace.

> *Press On*
> Nothing in the world can take the place of persistence.
> Talent will not;
> nothing is more common than unsuccessful men with talent.
> Genius will not;
> unrewarded genius is almost a proverb.
> Education will not;
> the world is full of educated derelicts.
> Persistence and determination alone
> are omnipotent.

Stopping the Buck

What should be known must be known. Excuses are no excuse. Smiles noted the failure of one investor who admitted that he "was ignorant of the multiplication-table" and had "contempt for arithmetic." Too often, Smiles noticed, the guilty are "apt to assume a tone of injured innocence, and conclude too hastily that everyone excepting themselves has had a hand in their personal misfortunes." The post-Enron blame game would involve the so-called gate-keepers of modern capitalism, those professionals (lawyers, accountants, financers, and so forth) who are trusted to serve as checks and balances to prevent, or at least discourage, catastrophic failure.

A related peril is passing the buck to others. "Important affairs must be attended to in person," Smiles intoned, citing the proverb "If you want your business done, go and do it; if you don't want it done, send some one else." In *Character*, Smiles shared the wisdom of an English lord who observed, "Those who shirk from facing trouble find that trouble comes to them." Smiles would smell failure in any business whose chieftain(s) delegated the key decisions of the company to others while focusing instead on external, big-picture company matters.

What today is called *groupthink* concerned Smiles. "The tendency of men is ever to go with the majority—to go with the huzzas." He was also suspicious of *culture*, in the new meaning that aesthetes gave to the term, fearing that it provided an excuse to abandon individual-centered principles. He warned:

> Many worship "culture." It is their only religion. It is intellectual cynicism and skepticism, with a varnish of refinement. The persons who profess it live in an atmosphere of exquisite superiority. . . . They sneer at the old-fashioned virtues of industry and self-denial, energy and self-help.

At Enron, *corporate culture* was a mantra: a supercharged vision of what the company was going to be; a description of values that was at once obvious and arrogant. It seemed harmless at the time—a road map, a way to outdistance the competition, an inspiration. In retrospect, the company's vision and values contributed to an environment that allowed the worst to get on top and brought out the worst in many others.

Stopping the buck includes blowing the whistle. Smiles quoted a well-known English merchant of the day who charged that since "all false appearances are lies . . . men act lies without speaking them." This wise man made a case for action:

> Hiding or screening the faults or errors of others is a system that has prevailed and caused much loss and injury—frequently to the offending party, always to the employer. . . . He . . . who seeing his employer injured, neglects to make it known, is equally guilty—with the addition that he is practicing a lie.

The absence or inability of whistleblowers to right the ship has allowed lies to live long enough to sink businesses—including ones described in this trilogy.

Anatomy of Failure

"Integrity of word and deed ought to be the very cornerstone of all business transactions," Smiles believed. He quoted a leading man who said, "We may succeed for a time by fraud, by surprise, by violence, but we can succeed permanently only by means directly opposite."

Smiles understood that "great work [was] the result of repeated efforts, and often of many failures." Perseverance was the bridge over failure. Still, Smiles could be disappointed with the sometimes spectacular business failures around him. "The spirit of the age," he complained in 1880, a time of bank failures and other business setbacks, "is not that of a trader, but of a gambler."

Smiles described greed and fraud in terms starkly applicable to recent corporate controversies. The "badness of trade" could be masked by fraudulent accounting. "In the arithmetic of the counting-house two and two do not always make four," he observed. "How many tricks are resorted to—in which honesty forms no part—for making money faster than others!" Smiles saw a pattern in which "young business men are often carried away" by the lucre of "the highest places in society."

> Young men are amazed at the splendor of the leaders of trade [who] . . . command the highest places in society. . . . [and] give balls, parties, and dinners. Their houses are full of pictures by the greatest artists. Their cellars are full of wine of the choicest vintage.

The enchanted juniors start fast, but their fortunes take a turn as complacency, arrogance, greed, or simply the law of averages sets in. Early mistakes are camouflaged, making the later reckoning sudden and complete. Smiles traced the scenario:

> The first speculation may be a gain. The gain may be followed by another, and they are carried off their feet by the lust of wealth. . . . Formerly every attempt was open; today everything is secret, until at length the last event comes, and everything is exposed. The man fails; the bills are worthless; the pictures are sold; and the recreant flies to avoid the curses of his creditors.

The collateral damage can reach widely, as when bank failures dissipate the savings of the commoners. "Men have been driven insane, and women have prayed to be delivered from their lives," Smiles related. He reproduced a poetic lament from a victimized group of elderly sisters:

> Pity us, God! There are five of us here . . .
> Five of us sitting in sorrow and fear . . .
> We could live on so little . . . cheerful and brave
> But to leave the old house, where old memories throng,
> For the Poorhouse! Oh, rather the peace of the grave!

The final cry comes from the perpetrator, also reproduced by Smiles:

> To what infamy I have come step by step, heaping crime upon crime. I am the cause of ruin, and misery, and disgrace to thousands. Oh, how I feel for those on whom this ruin must fall! I could bear all punishment, but I could not bear to witness their sufferings. It must be better than I should not live. Oh, that I had . . . resisted the first attempts to launch me into speculation! I might then have remained what I was—honest and truthful. I weep and weep now, but what can that avail?

All this was because "men already rich, but having to be richer, throw themselves into wild speculations with the view of making money more rapidly than before." Such a consequence did not begin with Enron's Andy Fastow.

Smiles knew the ultimate fate of the "unscrupulous, the over-speculative, and the intensely selfish, in their haste to be rich."

> The bubbles blown by unscrupulous rogues, when full-blown, usually glitter only to burst. [They], for the most part, come to a sad end even in this world; and though the successful swindles of others may not be "found out," and the gains of their roguery may remain with them, it will be as a curse, and not as a blessing.

Overambition and "keep[ing] up appearances . . . at the expense of honesty" are poison to sustainable success from which many can be victimized. The ruin of insolvency affects the many associated with those on top. Smiles observed:

> There is a constant struggle and pressure for front-seats in the social amphitheater; in the midst of which all noble, self-denying resolve is trodden down, and many fine natures are inevitably crushed to death. What waste, what misery, what bankruptcy come from all this ambition, to dazzle others with the glare of

apparent worldly success, we need not describe. The mischievous results show themselves in a thousand ways—in the rank frauds committed by men who dare to be dishonest, but do not dare to seem poor; and in the desperate dashes at fortune, in which the pity is not so much for those who fail as for the hundreds of innocent families who are so often involved in their ruin.

The fraud of kept appearances is related to a failure to deal with setbacks in a timely, resolute, corrective manner. Smiles could have guessed the fate of those who—again and again, with their bets rising—maintained appearances rather than confronted adversity. And so it was, spanning the twentieth century, with John Henry Kirby, Samuel Insull, and Ken Lay. "Though the ordeal of adversity is one from which we naturally shrink, yet, when it comes, we must bravely and manfully encounter it." It is good, if bitter, medicine. "Trials," explained Smiles, "train the character, and teach self-help; thus, hardship itself may often prove the wholesomest discipline for us, though we recognize it not."

Humanism, Not Darwinism

"Man is much more than a competing being," Smiles noted. "He has sensibilities, sympathies, and aspirations, which should induce him to unite and co-operate for the common good." Such considerations can and should be part of "unfettered individualism" to promote "the general happiness." Smiles spoke to this in *Self-Help* ("the duty of helping one's self in the highest sense involves the helping of one's neighbors") and began *Duty* with the paragraph:

> Man does not live for himself alone. He lives for the good of others as well as of himself. Every one has his duties to perform—the richest as well as the poorest. To some life is pleasure, to others suffering. But the best do not live for self-enjoyment, or even for fame. Their strongest motive power is hopeful, useful work in every good cause.

The gains from social cooperation made this imperative:

> The middle classes have accomplished more by the principle of co-operation than the classes who have so much greater need of it. All the joint-stock companies are the result of association. The railways, the telegraphs, the banks, the mines, the manufactories, have, for the most part, been established and are carried on by means of the savings of the middle classes.

Thrift is man enabling man, one's savings being another's investment capital. "The object of [thrift]," Smiles stated, "is to induce men to employ their means for worthy purposes, and not to waste them upon selfish indulgences."

Sympathy was an important character trait for Smiles—whether in the workplace or at home. "A consideration for the feelings of others, for his inferiors and dependants as well as his equals, and respect for their self-respect, will pervade the true gentleman's whole conduct." Workers need help and welcome empathy, not only a paycheck. "The political economists say that the relationship of master and servant is simply a money bargain—so much service, so much wage," Smiles observed. "But the moralist, the philosopher, the statesman, the man, should acknowledge, in the positions of master and servant, a social tie, imposing upon the parties certain duties and affections growing out of their common sympathies as human beings, and the positions they respectively fill." Sympathy must come from all sides. Smiles believed that happier homes and more prosperous workplaces would be the just reward of sympathy.

Smiles censured bullying. "Mind without heart, intelligence without conduct, cleverness without goodness," he said, "are powers in their way, but they may be powers only for mischief." He quoted Shakespeare: "It is excellent to have a giant's strength; but it is tyrannous to use it like a giant." The culture fostered at Enron by Jeff Skilling between 1997 and 2001—implicitly sanctioned by Ken Lay—is a case in point.

"Gentleness is indeed the best test of gentlemanliness," Smiles posited. Edging toward Adam Smith's concept of sympathy, Smiles explained how the gentleman

> values his character,—not so much of it only as can be seen of others, but as he sees it himself; having regard for the approval of his inward monitor. And, as he respects himself, so, by the same law, does he respect others. Humanity is sacred in his eyes: and thence proceed politeness and forbearance, kindness and charity.

Despite his passionate defense of charity between ranks of individuals, from the first edition of *Self-Help* to his last writings, Smiles continually had to dispel the notion that his manly individualism was license for selfishness and materialism. Smiles's preface of the second edition of *Self-Help* (1866) should have put the issue to rest:

> The title of the book . . . has led some . . . to suppose that it consists of a eulogy of selfishness: the very opposite of what it really is. . . . Although [the book's] chief object unquestionably is to stimulate youths to apply themselves diligently to right pursuits . . . it will also be found . . . that the duty of helping one's self in the highest sense involves the helping of one's neighbors.

Virtue and the Good Life

In an 1845 lecture to the Leeds Mutual Improvement Society, Samuel Smiles spoke of the "grand idea" of the age: "that every human being has a great mission to perform—has noble faculties to cultivate, great rights to assert, a vast destiny to accomplish." Smiles then described the utilitarian promise of labor-saving machinery to free people from constant toil. This was a very good thing, for Smiles's message of thrift, perseverance, and virtue did not mean all work, no play.[9] "Man, I insist, has a right to leisure—for the improvement of his mind as well as the preservation of his health;—leisure to think, leisure to read, leisure to enjoy." Neither was material success the end-all. Labor brings pleasure through cooperative endeavor and the self-love of accomplishment. Smiles saw in capitalist labor room for *heart*, *mind*, and *soul*, not just the means for subsistence.

The final section of *Thrift*, "The Art of Living," finds Smiles at his cosmopolitan best. "It is not wealth that gives the true zest to life, but reflection, appreciation, taste, culture." "Relax and exercise frequently" for good health. "Be happy!" Enjoy music and the arts. "Have a flower in every room, by all means." "Make the best of everything." "A benevolent Creator has . . . set [man] in a fair and lovely world, surrounded him with things good and beautiful, and given him the disposition to love, to sympathize, to help, to produce, to enjoy; and thus to become an honorable and a happy being."

Smiles warned against negativism. "Doom [a man] to dismal thoughts and miserable circumstances, and you will make him gloomy, discontented, morose, and probably vicious." Each person has a "strong natural appetite for relaxation and amusement"; take away "wholesome" pleasure and the opposite will be substituted. Smiles concluded the chapter and book, "And thus we link time to eternity, where the true art of living has its final consummation."

Eclipse and Resurrection

Smiles's fertilization of capitalism's roots drew scorn from various quarters. Help for the masses needed to come from without, not within, argued the socialists and welfare-state paternalists. Business was the opiate of the masses, argued Matthew Arnold, a leading social critic of the day. The "philistinism" of commerce, Arnold wrote in 1864, must give way to a cultural and intellectual renaissance. Intellectuals and government must educate and reorient the laboring class. Only then would the masses be "liberalized by an ampler culture, admitted to a wider sphere of thought, living by larger ideas, with its provincialism dissipated, its intolerance cured, its pettinesses purged away." Little surprise, then, that the Art and Culture Movement "sneer[ed] at the old fashioned virtues of industry and self-denial, energy, and self-help."

Back-to-nature philosophers and leisure utopians criticized Smiles as enabling industrialism. Unionists chided self-help as a diversion from the battle against the real enemy, factory owners. "Verily working men would be fools to dream of a better future, or seek its realization" through self-help, one labor leader opined.

---

9. Smiles, a workaholic ("I could not be idle"), left industry to write full time only after a stroke at age 59. Smiles worked days and nights while taking on his dual jobs; for everyone else, he recommended finding time after work for intellectual pursuit within a realm of leisure.

To critics all, self-improvement's "teachy-preachy fever" was a mix of propaganda, a new religion of secularism, utopianism, and apologia.[10] Still, for several decades at least, Smiles's message won out. "In many Victorian homes," noted one historian, *Self-Help* "had a status second only to the Bible."

The close of the century was a far cry from the 1860s when a national figure such as William Gladstone proclaimed in reference to Smiles, "It is SELF-HELP that makes the man." The political winds had been going the other way since at least the late 1880s when so prominent a figure in the United Kingdom as Sir William Harcourt declared, "We are all socialists now." Trade unionism, socialism, and government paternalism made the Smilesian philosophy appear trite and anachronistic.

Self-Help was no longer selling well. Smiles's final installment in his self-help series, *Conduct*, completed around 1898, was deemed noncommercial and after his death was destroyed by his publisher, Thomas Murray. A new genre of self-help was in vogue, represented by such books as *Money! Money! Money!* (1890) and *How to Get Rich Quick* (1907). Smiles's dogged incrementalism, PERSEVERANCE, became passé. "The success of tomorrow," read Ernest Bryant's *A New Self-Help* (1908), "lies with those who can devise new methods." The same philosophy of revolution-always over incrementalism would emerge a century later during Enron's new-economy run.

Smiles's message remained out of intellectual favor as the new century's decades came and went. The *new psychology* of Sigmund Freud saw behavior as the unconscious at work. The *new economics* of John Maynard Keynes preached the benefits of consumption over thrift. The *welfare state* supported the idle, as well as protected the unable. Collectivism was in; individualism, out.

Books by Smiles went in and out of print. Outside of one direct descendant, no biographer came forth to revive his work and institutionalize his memory until the 1980s. The once-storied philosopher of self-help became a dimly remembered figure—"a sort of British Horatio Alger." When Smiles was remembered at all, only *Self-Help* seemed to get mentioned from his bookshelf of work. Nevertheless, Samuel Smiles stands prominently between Adam Smith of the eighteenth century and Ayn Rand of the twentieth. In their different ways, all three recognized, warned against, and anticipated the vices that befall individuals and nations—and leaders of storied corporations.

Still, rumblings of rediscovery have been heard, particularly in Smiles's home country. Edward Heath, the leader of the British Conservative Party, warned in Smilesian terms in the 1960s that "we must change our whole attitude to work and its rewards" with an economic policy "directed at encouraging

---

10. Critics have had particular difficulty understanding Smiles's view of social class. See Internet appendix 2.4, "Some Misinterpretations of Smiles," www.politicalcapitalism.org/book1/chapter2/appendix4.html.

and rewarding industrial skill, hard work and initiative." Two decades later, Prime Minister Margaret Thatcher upheld the Victorian work ethic as part of a transformation away from nanny-statism and toward an enterprise culture. "Thatcherism shifted the emphasis from state responsibility to individual responsibility, and sought to give first priority to initiative, incentives, and wealth generation rather than redistribution and equality," Daniel Yergin and Joseph Stanislaw wrote. Nigel Lawson, a key figure in the Iron Lady's revolution, defined Thatcherism as "a mixture of free markets, financial discipline, firm control over public expenditure, tax cuts, nationalism, 'Victorian values' (of the Samuel Smiles self-help variety), privatization and a dash of populism." More recently, the Institute of Economic Affairs, a London-based think tank that germinated some of the ideas behind Thatcherism, published a new edition of *Self-Help* (1996) with endorsements from a new generation of intellectuals.

Business understanding and best-business practices can learn much from Smiles. Smilesian capitalism, or *capitalism with character*, is the self-help opportunity of the day coupled with political-economy reform to remove regulatory opportunism. *Self-Help*, in particular, "deserves to rise again."

3

Supply-Side Ethics: Ayn Rand

IN *THE WEALTH OF NATIONS*, Adam Smith demonstrated that the "obvious and simple system of natural liberty" was conducive to moral order, economic coordination, and wealth creation. Yet, Smith explained, it was not benevolence but "self-love"—as if "led by an invisible hand"—that was the driving force behind these happy outcomes. Nearly two centuries later, novelist-philosopher Ayn Rand (1905–82) defended and celebrated self-interest and capitalism in a deeper philosophic way. The virtues of capitalism are not an ironic product of selfishness, she concluded, but a logical expression of the fact that rational self-interest is the key to virtue. "When I met Ayn Rand I was a free enterpriser in the Adam Smith sense—impressed with the theoretical structure and efficiency of markets," remarked Alan Greenspan. "What she did was demonstrate to my satisfaction that capitalism is not only efficient and practical, but also moral."

Yet Greenspan, who in 1963 had described capitalism as a "superlatively moral system," in 1996 warned investors about "irrational exuberance" and, after the Enron collapse, testified to Congress that "an infectious greed seemed to grip much of our business community." Had he changed his mind about the positive role of self-interest under capitalism? Or did Greenspan now believe that the scandals of the early twenty-first century were something other than achieving success within capitalism?

It so happened that Greenspan spoke to that question upon receiving the last Enron Prize for Distinguished Public Service, awarded to him personally by Ken Lay on November 13, 2001, at Rice University's Baker Institute for Public Policy just weeks before Enron declared bankruptcy. Greenspan's remarks included a pointed comment on the importance of ethics in the marketplace.

> I do not deny that there are innumerable people who succeed in business by being less than wholly ethical. But I will say to you that those are the rare

examples; the best chance you have of making a big success in this world is to decide from square one that you're going to do it ethically.

Greenspan, gracious enough to honor his commitment as the storms thundered around Ken Lay's company, would leave his Enron-inscribed crystal award, as well as a stipend check, with the event organizers.

Soon, other commentators were debating whether what happened at Enron was licensed by Ayn Rand's worldview—or by its antithesis. For the first time since her death in 1982, Rand became newsworthy. The *New York Times* and *USA Today* reported that her ideas from a half century before were back in play. *Atlas Shrugged*, Rand's 1957 epic novel about capitalism and its enemies, was selling particularly well. The Objectivist Center, a Rand-inspired think tank, published analyses of how Enron's financial bankruptcy was at root a *philosophic* one. The Ayn Rand Institute busily differentiated Rand's thought from the motivations behind corporate malfeasance. No other philosopher or philosophic system was as prominent in the post-Enron debate over business ethics, although virtually all intellectuals had pronounced views on the issue.

What is Objectivism, the philosophy that provides Ayn Rand's moral defense of capitalism? Why is her integrated philosophy—tying together the personal, professional, and political—important for unraveling Enron's predicament and understanding the total, sudden demise of Ken Lay, the hitherto Great Man of the modern energy industry? How does Objectivism fit in with the actions of Jeff Skilling, the paragon of arrogance and greed in the Enron story? Was he a Randian capitalist or something quite different? Why is Objectivism important for interpreting some of the blind spots of other fallen notables, such as Samuel Insull and John Henry Kirby (discussed in Book 2)?

Why was Rand herself so personally controversial, not only attracting critics of the Left and the Right but also disowning seeming allies and engaging in personal behavior that detracted from the power of her philosophy? Did her personal failings reflect a blind spot in her philosophy, whereby the world is seen in such sharp shades of black and white that debate is not even possible? Even today, a quarter century after Rand's death, Objectivism as a living message must confront and overcome the dark side of its messenger.[1]

A New Capitalist Philosopher

Ayn Rand, born Alissa Rosenbaum, graduated at age 19 from Petrograd University with a degree in history and philosophy. Two years later, she escaped the growing terror of Bolshevik Russia, first by making her way through Western Europe and then by finding her home in the United States.

---

1. This dark side, which climaxed in an Enron-like scandal for Objectivism, is the subject of appendix A, "The Ayn Rand Problem," pp. 320–31.

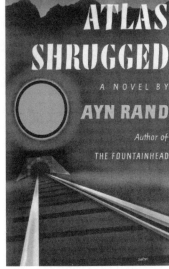

Figure 3.1 Ayn Rand's two most famous books—*The Fountainhead* (1943) and *Atlas Shrugged* (1957)—sold millions of copies and made her one of the most praised and criticized intellectuals in American history. Rand's public recognition led to a commemorative stamp from the United States Postal Service in 1999.

Precocious, self-taught in many ways, cerebral, and goal directed, she had been sketching screenplays and plotting novels since age 10. From the beginning, she was captivated by the struggle between good and evil, an epic theme that would remain with her always. One of the émigré's few possessions upon her arrival in New York City in 1926 was a typewriter, her tool for creating philosophically themed, romantic fiction and, later, philosophy and social commentary—writings that would make her one of the most important and controversial intellectuals of twentieth-century America.

Rand's novels conveyed a world of human relationships "as they might be and ought to be." Her stories took complex personal and economic relationships and turned them into triumph and tragedy based on her philosophical precepts. The nature of a just political system was never far from her focus. Rand's passion for political justice stemmed from the totalitarianism she escaped and the personal and economic freedom she relished. The naturalized citizen was a true American patriot,[2] yet she would always be an outsider to America's improvisational spirit and always be hypercritical of perceived imperfections.

---

2. Rand's love of her adopted country was apparent when, in the intellectual climate of post-Vietnam 1974, she told the graduating class of the United States Military Academy at West Point: "I can say—not as a patriotic bromide, but with full knowledge of the necessary

As a philosopher, Rand addressed three questions: *What is reality? How do we know reality? How should we act, given reality?* Her journey from *is* to *ought* resulted in an integrated philosophical system, which she christened Objectivism shortly after the release of *Atlas Shrugged* in 1957. When asked by a Random House salesman to summarize the book's philosophy "while standing on one foot," she obliged by answering:

1. *Metaphysics*: Objective Reality

2. *Epistemology*: Reason

3. *Ethics*: Self-interest

4. *Politics*: Capitalism

Rand translated her response into simple language in her inaugural column for the *Los Angeles Times* in 1962:

1. Nature, to be commanded, must be obeyed, or Wishing won't make it so

2. You can't eat your cake and have it too

3. Man is an end in himself

4. Give me liberty or give me death

These four areas can be tailored for our business story with the questions: *What is business reality? How is this reality being approached? What is the motivation behind business action? What is the nature of the economic system in which business operates?* Before judgment can be passed on John Henry Kirby or Samuel Insull or Ken Lay, the principal figures of our book, a philosophic framework is necessary for distinguishing *virtue* from *vice*.

Objectivism in Business

A is A—existence exists. Nothing could be simpler or more acknowledged— except by academic philosophers, who invoke traditions of thought denying that one's mind can separate the real from the unreal. The philosophy of Objectivism takes its name from *objective reality*, which gives rise to the law of causality—the necessary and identifiable connections that are always at work between entities and their effects, in nature and in human interaction. Individuals must discover, interpret, and account for reality to be successful in science, business, and personal life. Failure to identify and respect the objective world with the most diligent reasoning courts disaster. In the no-nonsense world of "Mrs. Logic," "good premises" always trumped "good luck."[3]

---

metaphysical, epistemological, ethical, political and esthetic roots—that the United States of America is the greatest, the noblest and, in its original founding principles, the *only* moral country in the history of the world."

3. The tenacity of Rand was reflected in an entry in her private journal in 1945, two years after the publication of *The Fountainhead* and at the beginning of what would be the 13-year

Yet entrepreneurship is an art and not a science, given the uncertainty of the future. Even the best-laid plans of revenue and cost can go wrong with the unfolding of events. Business professors cannot derive, much less teach, an algorithm for profitability. Neither can business executives do so for their staff.[4] Still, an underlying order of causality in the business sphere makes objectivity the North Star. The founder of the Ayn Rand Institute, Leonard Peikoff, stated:

> If you are to succeed in business, you must make decisions using logic. You must deal with objective realities—like them or not. Your life is filled with numbers, balance sheets, cold efficiency and rational organization. You have to make sense—to your employees, to your customers, and to yourself. You cannot run a business as a gambler plays the horses. . . . You have to *think*.

Two Objectivist professors added:

> To run a successful business . . . requires the most ruthlessly objective perception of reality, and constant, effective thinking to process and evaluate reams of information, which is only possible by separating the essential from the non-essential. The businessman must constantly ask himself and answer questions such as: What is the nature of my market? Who are my customers? What do they want? Am I giving it to them? What are my opportunities? What are my financial, technological, managerial and employee resources? Do I have enough? Am I using them effectively? What business am I actually in? What business should I be in? What should my business strategy be? How will circumstances change in the future? Any attempt to fake reality with respect to any of these issues is a recipe for disaster.

Economist Joseph Schumpeter restated A=A when he observed, "Both business success and business failure are ideally precise. Neither can be talked away."

Subjectivism (Postmodernism)

The philosophical morass that Objectivism sought to escape was *Subjectivism*, defined by Rand as

> the belief that reality is not a firm absolute but a fluid, plastic, indeterminate realm which can be altered, in whole or in part, by the consciousness of the perceiver—i.e., by his feelings, wishes or whims. It is the doctrine which holds that man—an entity of a specific nature, dealing with a universe of a specific nature—can, somehow, live, act, and achieve his goals apart from and/or in contradiction

---

Atlas Shrugged project: "My greatest personal mistake is ever to allow a word or a moment that 'doesn't count,' i.e., that I do not refer to my own basic principles. *Every word, every action, every moment counts.*"

4. Formulas also cannot be used to measure *resource depletion* or *competition*, two areas explored later in this book, where misplaced objectivism, or *formalism*, has led to analytical and public-policy error.

to the facts of reality, i.e., apart from and/or in contradiction to his own nature and the nature of the universe.[5]

The escape from reality sanctified by Subjectivism—a philosophy whose modern incarnation can be traced back to Immanuel Kant (1724–1804) and whose contemporary manifestation is broadly known as *postmodernism*—can be played out on a grand scale by government tyrants, on a large scale by business tycoons, or in the microcosm of personal relationships.[6] Postmodernism is a multidisciplinary movement whose "primary goal has been to challenge convictions about the objectivity of knowledge and the stability of language." Facts, truth, reality, communication, and open inquiry are more than questioned, as they are in the time-honored practice of *prove it*; they are *trivialized* as subjective and unknowable.

Postmodernism is a reaction to the outlook of *modernism*, "the notion of the freely acting, freely knowing individual whose experiments can penetrate the secrets of nature and whose work with other individuals can make a new and better world." To modernists, reality and truth are knowable and discoverable, language is understandable, and improvement is achievable by comprehending, communicating, and implementing the wisdom of social and natural science. *Human progress* is the goal and vindication of modernism.

What is the argument of postmodernism, variously described as *complete skepticism, contemporary relativism, cynicism, deconstructionism, nihilism, obscurantism, perspectivism, romanticism,* and *mysticism?* Postmodernists maintain that the biases of society, and particularly the predilections of those who wield power, make the disinterested search for truth a charade. "Objectivity," it is held, is "a disguise for power or authority in the academy." Perception *is* reality, since reality is nothing more than "suspect dichotomies on the flux of events." Reality is dismissed as a fleeting, impermanent subjective state. Natural science is viewed with suspicion; social science, wholly rejected. Predictably, postmodernists are especially opposed to "the modern, industrial, and urban way of life," because they sense what underlies it—reason, science, and freedom. Capitalism is despised as an arbitrary political economy with a class-based politics of truth.

Tensions and contradictions abound within postmodernism. It is a profoundly *anti-intellectual* intellectual movement. Postmodernists discredit themselves as seekers, communicators, and knowers of truth by questioning reality, language, and veracity. Somehow, they *know* that knowledge is unknowable.

---

5. Epistemological subjectivism is different from *economic subjectivism*, or subjective value theory applied to human action in the marketplace. See Internet appendix 3.1, "Epistemological Objectivism versus Economic Subjectivism," at www.politicalcapitalism.org/book1/chapter3/appendix1.html.

6. Also see Internet appendix 3.2, "The Roots of Philosophical Subjectivism," at www.politicalcapitalism.org/book1/chapter3/appendix2.html.

Postmodernists are "deeply disillusioned intellectuals" who want to change the world but cannot accept any end-states from capitalism to communism to anarchy. What began in literature and the arts as "a playful acceptance of surfaces and superficial style, self-conscious quotation and parody . . . and a celebration of the ironic, the transient, and the glitzy" turned into a nonsensical creed against human thought and progress.

Postmodernism creates a large void in place of what might otherwise be described as *workable reality*—a realm that is generally, albeit imperfectly, recognizable by seekers of truth. Not surprisingly, postmodernism is irrelevant outside the ivory tower. There are no postmodern how-to business books, for example, because any such effort would comically demonstrate the difference between consumer-grounded realism and whim. Any postmodern business would crash and burn.

Postmodernism, denying "the individual as knower and doer," becomes an ethos of *anything goes* and "never having to say you're sorry." Postmodernism allows Enron apologists to say that the company was "in great shape" and that outsiders "killed a great company." Far from being a hypothetical possibility, such statements were made by disgraced former Enron CEO Jeff Skilling during a nationally televised congressional hearing in February 2002. On the eve of his trial, Enron founder and chairman Ken Lay called on his former employees to step forward to "prove that Enron was a great company," presumably by joining Skilling and himself in declaring it to be a fact. For both Enron leaders, these declarations were not—at least, were not only—an attempt to tell the same story and protect each other at trial; they reflected a postmodern belief that a thoroughly shared narrative *is* reality. Enron was—and should always be remembered as—a *postmodern company*.

Postmodernists meet themselves coming and going in the Enron debacle. Enron created, in postmodern jargon, its own *language* and *truth* under the "hubris of power." Postmodernists must shine a critical light on themselves to ask, *Is the reality of Enron unreal? Was the Enron debacle—marked by executives fighting reality with perception— postmodernism in action?*

Subjectivism in Business

Enron's ill-fated leaders were not guided by Kantianism, Romanticism, or other subjectivist/postmodernist schools of thought. Still, those leaders became artisans of their own home-made variant of these schools. Appearances went from packaging the business message to being the message in the company's last years. The scale and scope of Enron imaging can be best described by a new *ism, perceptionism.*

Appearance as corporate strategy started small and snowballed at Enron. Executives and lieutenants were encouraged by past success and intoxicated by big plans. They were "smoking their own dope" and "drinking their own whisky," as a top Enron executive warned his colleagues prior to the ruinous

Skilling era.[7] Enron founder and head Ken Lay became "doped by his own publicity," to use a phrase Rand penned for *Atlas Shrugged*. A follow-the-leader and
group-think mentality was supercharged by peer-review and compensation
systems under which all judged all, and deviants were punished. Atlas—the
men and women of ability at Enron—shrugged.

Perceptionism was encouraged by the heady boom outside the window.
Were not the 1990s the most prosperous decade in world history—and nowhere
more so than in the United States? Accommodative monetary policy by the Fed;
the dot-com boom; the New Economy; discount brokers, day traders, and 24/7
markets; a surfeit of *buy* recommendations by stock analysts; self-fulfilling
prophecies: Was not a company's value what a buyer perceived at the moment?
Decades earlier, the *new economics* of John Maynard Keynes had brushed aside
the warnings of classical economics against quick fixes with the words "in the
long run we are all dead." Underlying company fundamentals for long-term
success: Wasn't that old-fashioned too? As it turned out, perceptionism was a
game of musical chairs with many chairs and winners in the beginning but few
chairs and many losers at the end.

Philosophic rot was at work. Perceptionism in the Enron story included a
financial-accounting approach that was geared less to understanding the true
state of business than to creating a mirage of profitability.[8] Necessarily, therefore, it included those Enron's gatekeepers who gave Enron what it coveted by
satisfying legal technicalities (gaming the rules) in return for lucrative fees. But
the philosophic rot of perceptionism at Enron also included extraordinarily
enabled departments of public relations and government affairs, dealmakers
"who couldn't take no for an answer [and] couldn't even take no from reality,"
as well as many ordinary people who cast their lot with "opinions about profit
over facts about cash." It included the governor of California, who sanctioned
price controls on electricity while lambasting the industry for the problems created by such regulation. But most of all, the philosophic rot included a chief
financial officer who thought he could turn stones into bread and never come to
judgment day and a Great Man of industry who spent more time cultivating an
image than understanding the inner workings of his own company. These individuals and institutions, in their different ways, counted on *perception to triumph
over reality*, forgetting or denying that, in the final analysis, as Rand stated in
1962, decades before Enron was born, "facts are facts, independent of man's
feelings, wishes, hopes, or fears."

---

7. Richard Kinder was Enron's president, and his departure in late 1996 presaged the company's demise. Kinder would go on to found Kinder Morgan, an anti-Enron energy company
in terms of business philosophy and results.

8. The language of deceit, many terms of which can be applied to Enron, are summarized
in Internet appendix 3.3, "Reality, Deceit, and Philosophical Fraud," at www.politicalcapitalism.
org/book1/chapter3/appendix3html.

Honesty versus Philosophic Fraud

The opposite of pretense, or unreality, is *honesty*. Honesty is more than a forthright relationship between two individuals; it is every individual's proper relationship to objective reality. To Rand, honesty is "the refusal to fake reality, i.e., to pretend that facts are other than they are."

Honesty is "developing an active mind . . . 'knowing what one does know, constantly expanding one's knowledge, and *never* evading or failing to correct a contradiction.'" Honesty is "more profound an issue than not telling lies to one's neighbors," noted Leonard Peikoff. "It means becoming a priest of truth in every aspect of one's mind, life, and soul." The dishonest person "fakes an interest in ideas as a form of role-playing, usually for the purpose of impressing others."

Dishonesty often turns from an *act* to a *process* because "reality is a unity; to depart from it at a single point . . . is to depart from it in principle." One falsehood can lead to another and another. Behavior can become more desperate and bizarre, because the evader is at war not only with the facts but also with everyone who knows the facts. Peikoff noted: "The con man . . . counts on his ability to manipulate others. People become to him more real than the fragments of reality he still recognizes. People become his means of survival, but in a form worse than that of the typical second-hander." Thus:

> The liar thinks he has turned others into his puppets, but his course makes him their pawn. It makes him a dependent of the lowest kind; a dependent not merely on the consciousness of others, which is bad enough, but on their unconsciousness. Such a man, in Ayn Rand's words, is a fool—"a fool whose source of values is the fools he succeeds in fooling."

Objectivism defines the attempt to escape reality as *philosophic fraud*. Rand explained:

> The law of identity does not permit you to have your cake and eat it, too. The law of causality does not permit you to eat your cake *before* you have it. . . . Whenever you rebel against causality, your motive is the fraudulent desire, not to escape it, but worse: to reverse it.

Philosophic fraud is distinct from the *prosecutable fraud* associated with violating commercial agreements. Still, the latter always involves the former, although the former does not always lead to the latter.

Inverting causality was a strategy of Enron executives during the company's artificial boom and especially when their seemingly unsinkable ship began to slow, list, and go down. Using a prescient example for what would be Enron's ultimate undoing, a lack of cash flow, Edwin Locke and Jaana Woiceshyn wrote:

> The businessman who refuses to acknowledge, despite clear evidence, that his facilities are outdated, his products uncompetitive and his cash flow inadequate, is dishonest just as the one who makes fraudulent claims to customers is dishonest. Both are trying, at the deepest level, to fake reality.

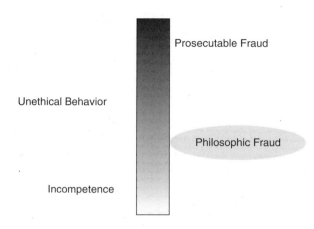

Figure 3.2 This illustration compares philosophical fraud with other categories of business error and deceit.

These two Objectivists warned that the flight from reality could emerge from small beginnings—another telling insight for understanding the Enron saga:

> If you breach the principle of honesty, you undermine the tie between your mind and reality by changing the focus from adhering to facts to deceiving other people. Once this is done, it is not easy to arrest the process, because you have switched from a principled approach to honesty to a pragmatic approach, viz., "I'll be honest most of the time, except when really tempted."

They described how "the dishonest businessman is at war with reality," because "he has placed his wishes and desires above the truth and above objective moral principles." They concluded, "Such a policy cannot work; evading reality will only destroy the evader." It did—in the cases of Ken Lay, Jeff Skilling, and particularly Andy Fastow, as well as others inside and outside Enron who played the perception game.

Authentic Leaders versus Second-Handers

The personal philosophy of a business leader drives company strategy and the mentality of the workforce. An entrepreneur must correctly judge the future state of the market to make a profit. Success in a free market percolates toward reality-grounded individuals who can resist the fads and whims of the day. This person is Adam Smith's "man of principle," possessing "one even tenour of conduct"—quite unlike the "worthless fellow" who "acts variously and accidentally." This is also Samuel Smiles's "man of character," "guided and inspired by principle, integrity, and practical wisdom."

Rand's "worthless fellow" is the *second-hander*, a person whose self-worth and aspirations are based on what he or she believes to be the values and preferences of others. In Rand's major novels, the day of reckoning comes when the second-hander finds that he or she has no inner core, just an illusory outer one. Rand described this tragic persona through the words of Howard Roark, the fictional hero of *The Fountainhead*:

> Second-handers . . . don't ask, "is this true?" They ask: "Is this what others think is true?" Not to judge, but to repeat. Not to do, but to give the impression of doing. Not creation, but show. Not ability, but friendship. Not merit, but pull. . . . Second-handers have no sense of reality. Their reality is not within them, but somewhere in that space which divides one human body from another. Not an entity, but a relation—anchored to nothing.

"The worst second-hander," Roark (Rand) adds, is "the man who goes after power."

Enron became a *second-hander company*. Blinding ambition made Ken Lay contort Enron into being all good things to all people—a company for Republicans, Democrats, deregulation proponents, environmentalists, minorities, charities, high society, generation X, the religious, nonconformists, sports fans, and more. Liberties with the truth, or simply not telling the whole story, became the means to a greater end—to a more exalted Enron that would benefit employees and stockholders. What was good for Ken Lay was good for Enron, and what was good for Enron was good for society. This would open the door to, among other things, special government subsidies for Enron, or political capitalism.

"The code of competence," Ayn Rand stated in *Atlas Shrugged*, "is the only system of morality that's on a gold standard." She saw through perception plays, whether they were in business, politics, or personal relationships. She advocated what in today's vernacular would be called *tough love* and advised all to "judge and be prepared to be judged." Excuses based on shiftless ignorance were not accepted. A character in *Atlas Shrugged* made Rand's point when he declared, "I'm heartless enough to say that when you'll scream, 'But I didn't know it!'—you will not be forgiven." In the business world, one must know what can reasonably be known—or suffer the consequences.

Ironically, Enron and some of its controversial principals (but not Ken Lay, a notorious second-hander) have been analogized to Objectivism in action. "Enron was, almost from the beginning, a company of carnivores," stated Mimi Swartz in her final look back at the company she chronicled for years. "It was every man for himself; these were people who took as gospel the work of Ayn Rand." Jeff Skilling was described by Bethany McLean and Peter Elkind as a cold capitalist in manner (arrogant, ruthless) and politics (Darwinian libertarianism). A rival to Skilling at Enron, Rebecca Mark, the executive who presided over some of the company's most costly failures, was described by McLean and Elkind as "'fierce and fearless' . . . a character in an Ayn Rand novel."

But the Randian hero or heroine is reality focused, laser honest, and *successful*. Skilling was a capitalist antihero under a Smith-Smiles-Rand standard. He evolved into a master corner-cutter, perceptionist, and political capitalist (rent seeker). Skilling was an amoral pragmatist—an ends-justify-the-means operator—who was far closer to the brutish Great Man of Friedrich Nietzsche (1844–1900) than to Randian Man.[9] Mark was more sizzle than steak, a woman of great persuasion and action but not, as it turned out, positive results. Like her hero Ken Lay (they had a mentor relationship), Mark was wildly optimistic, believing that her smarts and will could trump a mediocre world. When it came to her domain, "pigs *do* fly," she once said.

Firm, fair, realistic, and *consistent*: These Objectivist superlatives make *cronyism* and *nepotism* philosophic crimes. In Rand's formulation:

> Justice is the recognition of the fact that you cannot fake the character of men as you cannot fake the character of nature, that you must judge all men as conscientiously as you judge inanimate objects, with the same respect for truth, with the same incorruptible vision, by as pure and as *rational* a process of identification—that every man must be judged for what he *is* and treated accordingly.

Two Objectivist business consultants brought Rand's point home. "Cronyism and nepotism, as well as other forms of subjective and collective judgment, are commonly encountered in business," they wrote. "When they occur, the virtue of justice is subverted." Cronyism and nepotism, sanctioned by Ken Lay, were important parts of the rampant philosophical fraud present at Enron.

Capitalism

The primacy of objective reality and reason led Rand to endorse *capitalism*, "a system where no man may obtain any values from others by resorting to physical force, and *no man may initiate the use of physical force against others*." Rand was impressed by the efficiency and social beneficence of the free market, but her case "was not Adam Smith, F. A. Hayek or Milton Friedman's [utilitarian] defense of capitalism," as two libertarian philosophers noted. Her argument rested on the moral legitimacy of self-interest pursued through voluntary relations and the moral illegitimacy of any value seeking pursued by initiating coercion.[10]

Rand's case for the morality of capitalism had three steps. Life for humans requires the use of *reason*, not instinct as for the lower animals. Force is the antithesis of reason. Ergo, human relationships should be voluntary. Force can be used only *in response* to the criminal act of initiating force or fraud, a dictum akin to Adam Smith's laws of justice. The sovereign state is to have a monopoly on the use of force—to be used for retaliation only.

---

9. See also Internet appendix 3.4, "Jeff Skilling as a Nietzschean Great Man," at www.politicalcapitalism.org/book1/chapter3/appendix4.html.

10. Libertarian philosopher Robert Nozick used the phrase "capitalist acts between consenting adults" to convey this concept.

Rand's capitalism was logically dependent upon her first principles. As she explained in 1971:

> I am not *primarily* an advocate of capitalism, but of egoism; and I am not *primarily* an advocate of egoism, but of reason. If one recognizes the supremacy of reason and applies it consistently, all the rest follows. This—the supremacy of reason— was, is and will be the primary concern of my work, and the essence of Objectivism.

Rand saw her philosophical defense of capitalism as unique and essential. "Capitalism is the only system based implicitly on an objective theory of values— and the historic tragedy is that this has never been made explicit."

Rand's capitalism, like that of Adam Smith and Samuel Smiles, has a soul. Alan Greenspan, circa 1963, defended capitalism in an Objectivist framework: "Capitalism is based on self-interest and self-esteem; it holds integrity and trustworthiness as cardinal virtues and makes them pay off in the market place, thus demanding that men survive by means of virtues, not of vices." Of course, the objective virtues of capitalists can be used to satisfy many subjective preferences, such as aesthetic ones. Two Rand interpreters noted that her moral formulation "allows for a society that values primarily art and literature to be just as capitalistic as one that values automobiles and boats—so long as both respect individual rights."

Rand remarked: "The magnificent progress achieved by capitalism in a brief period of time—the spectacular improvement in the conditions of man's existence on earth—is a matter of historical record." She recited the statistics of increasing life expectancy in the United States from the turn of the century through 1968, in contrast to the significantly lower average in noncapitalistic countries. If Rand had been alive at century's end, she would have celebrated the stunning increase in life expectancy, wages, and leisure time recorded in the United States in the relatively capitalistic twentieth century (see Figure 3.3).

Moral action, by liberating human potential, was the fountainhead of this material progress. Rand praised the prime movers of business for raising living standards, but ultimately, it was the moral behavior of capitalists and not the wealth capitalism produced that led Rand to endorse the capitalist system and to reject all forms of economic collectivism.

Business on Trial

Reason, productive work, and political and economic freedom stand together in Objectivism's morality as values objectively based on human life. "Productive work is the central *purpose* of a rational man's life, the central value that integrates and determines the hierarchy of all his other values," Rand wrote, because it is productive work that undergirds human survival. "Reason is the source, the precondition of his productive work." The free market, in turn, "represents the *social* application of an objective theory of values."

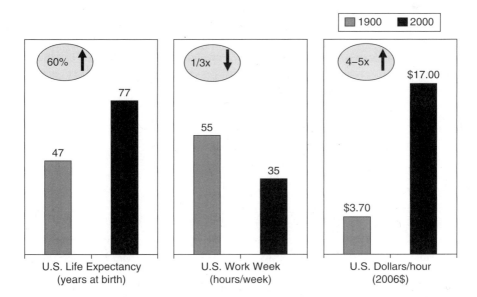

Figure 3.3 The twentieth century, the first measured one, put capitalism's stamp of progress on the human condition. The life expectancy of an American born in 2000 was 60 percent longer than that of someone born in 1900; leisure time grew by one-third; and wages, more than fourfold.

Of course, rational people do not personally create all the values that they need to live. In a complex society, people survive by creating economic value, ordinarily by taking jobs created by entrepreneurs. It is thus market entrepreneurship, profitably fulfilling consumer needs in open competition, that is the key to creating economic value.

The essence of market entrepreneurship is quite unlike the effort of political capitalists (the mercantilists of Adam Smith's day), whose success depends on governmental restrictions of competition or on other special favors. Rand made the distinction in no uncertain terms in a personal 1949 letter she penned while writing *Atlas Shrugged*:

> In my new book, I glorify the real kind of productive, free-enterprise businessman in a way he has never been glorified before. I present him as the most heroic type of human being. . . . *But* I make mincemeat out of the kind of businessman who calls himself a "middle-of-the-roader" and talks about a "mixed economy"—the kind that runs to government for assistance, subsidies, legislation and regulation.

In her nonfiction essays, Rand sharply distinguished between these two types of power, although she complained that the "chaotic mixture of free enterprise and government controls [was blurring] the dividing line between the earned and the unearned." In her words:

> Economic power is exercised by means of a *positive,* by offering men a reward, an incentive, a payment, a value; political power is exercised by means of a *negative,* by the threat of punishment, injury, imprisonment, destruction. The business-man's tool is *values*; the bureaucrat's tool is *fear.*

Rand warned political capitalists: "He who lives by a legalized sword will perish by a legalized sword." Insull and Lay were, in part, taken down by a bastardized regulatory system they helped create—and that had in part created them.

Capitalist Abundance

The Industrial Revolution introduced mass production for mass consump-tion. Friend and foe alike agreed on that fact, although interpretations and prog-nostications varied. "The bourgeoisie, during its rule of scarce one hundred years," wrote Karl Marx and Frederick Engels in *The Communist Manifesto* (1848), "has created more massive and more colossal productive forces than have all preced-ing generations together." Amid their accusations against capitalism, Marx and Engels acknowledged "the rapid improvement of all instruments of production . . . immensely facilitated means of communication . . . cheap prices of its com-modities," as well as "gigantic means of production and of exchange." They also spoke of the "exclusive political sway" of capitalists whereby "the modern state is but a committee for managing the common affairs of the whole bourgeoisie."

Nearly a century later, in 1945, John Maynard Keynes wrote, "We are enter-ing into the age of abundance." In the next decade, Harvard economist John Kenneth Galbraith attacked capitalism-cum-materialism in *The Affluent Society* (1958). His original version, entitled *Why People are Poor*, would have blamed poverty on Americans' refusal to provide the government with enough money for redistribution. In *The Affluent Society*, however, Galbraith turned the argu-ment around and second-guessed how Americans actually did spend their own money. The new rap on capitalism was rampant materialism, which led the productive forces of society to produce the wrong things. "To furnish a barren room is one thing," he declared in the tradition of Thorstein Veblen. "To continue to crowd in furniture until the foundation buckles is quite another."

Making "all wants urgent," Galbraith reasoned, was bringing "economic soci-ety to the brink of . . . make-work and boondoggling." Galbraith blamed "obsoles-cent thought" for what he saw as a "tense and humorless pursuit of goods." "Wealth is not without its advantages," the populist economist allowed, "but beyond doubt, wealth is the relentless enemy of understanding." "The rich man . . . will have a well-observed tendency to put it to the wrong purposes or otherwise to make him-self foolish." Galbraith concludes: "As with individuals, so with nations."

Galbraith called for revising the Puritan ethic (part of "the conventional wis-dom") of working to live and living to work, fearing "consumer demand creation, recurrent inflation, [and] social imbalances." He sought escape from "the thralldom of productive efficiency" and longingly looked toward public investments, such as the Soviet Union's "breath-taking series of scientific and technical advances." Communist Russia hardly had a track record of social good, but Galbraith and other Western intellectuals remained enamored with the possibilities of a centrally directed economy.

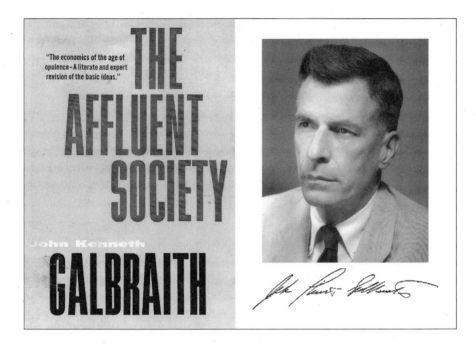

Figure 3.4 John Kenneth Galbraith's 1958 polemic *The Affluent Society*, as influential among intellectuals as Rand's *Atlas Shrugged* was with the public, censured capitalism for promoting inequality and rampant materialism.

The Affluent Society became an anticapitalist manifesto in the post-Keynesian era. Fellow Harvard professor Arthur Schlesinger Jr., the most esteemed historian of the day, pronounced the manuscript profound. Prominent reviews in the *New York Times* and *Washington Post* put the book on the best-seller list, as did glowing assessments in virtually every other intellectual organ. A few voices dissented. F. A. Hayek in the *Southern Economic Journal* took issue with the "non sequitur" that new consumer wants were not important, because they came after more basic needs were satiated. George Stigler, a Chicago school free-market economist and future Nobel laureate, professed shock that more Americans were learning about capitalism from Galbraith's new book than from Adam Smith's *Wealth of Nations*. The intellectual class—too modern for Adam Smith, too sophisticated for Samuel Smiles, and certainly not attracted to Ayn Rand—closed ranks around *The Affluent Society*.

Moneymaking and Virtue

The very things Galbraith found so deplorable were the things that Ayn Rand's *Atlas Shrugged* glorified: rational self-interest (which she called "a new concept of egoism") and the fruits of capitalist production. Rand ended her 1,168-page novel describing John Galt's triumphant return to society following his strike: "He raised his hand and over the desolate earth he traced in space the sign of the dollar." Rand's favorite symbol was the dollar sign, which represented free trade and free minds. She regarded money itself as "a frozen form of productive energy." At Rand's funeral, an admirer placed a six-foot-high dollar-sign floral arrangement beside the coffin.

Yet Rand criticized conspicuous consumption. Money was not glorified for its own sake. Entrepreneurs in her ideal world value money not only for its purchasing power but also as a *just reward for a job well done*. Money made is value provided, a reward system increasing value over time. Wealth is nothing to apologize for—or flaunt. The true capitalist, molded by incessant competition, is "committed to his work with the passion of a lover, the fire of a crusader, the dedication of a saint and the endurance of a martyr," with "his creased forehead and his balance sheets . . . the only evidence of it he can allow the world to see." The true entrepreneur, Rand continues, "learns everything he can about the business, much more than the job requires"—the opposite of the second-hander, who substitutes cronyism or other fakery for talent, execution, and toil. The capitalist is a doer, not a talker, in the spirit of John D. Rockefeller, who once said, "We do not talk much—we saw wood." He is a George Stephenson, the British railway entrepreneur, described by Samuel Smiles as "diligent and observant while at work, and sober and studious when the day's work was over."

In distinction to the capitalist "money-maker," there is the "money appropriator," who "may become a politician—or a businessman who 'cuts corners'—or that destructive product of a 'mixed economy:' the businessman who grows rich by means of government favors, such as special privileges, subsidies, franchises; that is, grows rich by means of *legalized force*." Rand further delineates the politicized businessman as an "essentially noncreative [person who] seeks to get rich, not by conquering nature, but by manipulating men, not by intellectual effort, but by social maneuvering."

On a more personal level, she sniped at the businessman who "hires personal press agents and postures in the public spotlight" and "flaunts his money in vulgar displays of ostentation, who craves 'prestige' and notice and hangs eagerly on the fringes of 'café society.'" To Rand, overacquisitiveness (what most would call *greed*) was not the malady of the reality-grounded capitalist but of the second-hander, political capitalist, and crony. As chapters 5 and 6 will show, it is also the result of a politicized system in which business has come to operate.

Rand wondered how such a pejorative as *greed* came to be associated with "the system that raised the standard of living of its poorest citizens to heights no collectivist system has ever begun to equal." "America's abundance," she explained, "was not created by public sacrifices to 'the common good' but by the productive genius of free men who pursued their own personal interests and the making of their own private fortune."

Many intellectuals in the tradition of Marx and Galbraith have continued to deride the psychology and morality of wealth-generating capitalism. Liah Greenfeld has deprecated the "addiction [of moneymaking as] a sport in which one tested oneself and found *certitudo salutis*, the surest way to and method of secular salvation." Historian Gabriel Kolko found it peculiar that the Boston Brahmins of the Progressive Era "worked frightfully hard" and quoted their confessions from letters and diaries. "I must be busy. I don't know how to stop. . . . I can't help seeing openings for profit, neither can I help availing of them," read one. And another, "I believe in toiling terribly, and the only thing that I ask of my body is to give me the power to work and work until I drop."

Such critics of the passion for work neglect several things. First, overdoing it is hardly unique to capitalists. Intellectuals, too, believing their work to be supremely important, and in some cases escaping personal demons, have worked themselves into premature decrepitude or death.[11] Indeed, every profession has its workaholics, and they include politicians and bureaucrats craving power. Hard-working and overworking businesspeople at least create wealth for consumers.

Second, on a purely monetary plane, entrepreneurs (like virtually all people) desire a more comfortable life and wish to leave an estate. Or, they may wish to use their wealth to pay for life-giving research, support needy talent, advance inspiring art movements, commercialize promising inventions, or back revolutionary start-ups. Thomas Edison and George Westinghouse, two founders of the electricity industry, valued the "stored energy" of money for enabling future research, production, and progress. Westinghouse defined his ambition as giving "as many persons as possible an opportunity to earn money by their own efforts." Then, too, business is in itself a creative activity, offering the same intrinsic pleasures of achievement as composing, painting, or sculpting.

It is simplistic to view moneymaking as drudgery necessary to acquire basic consumer goods, after which point it must be looked upon as a psychological obsession. Moneymaking is a multifaceted activity with many motives. Economist Joseph Schumpeter saw in entrepreneurship

> the joy of creating, of getting things done, or simply of exercising one's energy and ingenuity . . . the will to conquer: the impulse to fight, to prove oneself superior to

---

11. An example is William Stanley Jevons, a leading nineteenth-century social scientist whose views on mineral-resource depletion are highlighted in chapter 7, pp. 194–202.

others, to succeed for the sake, not of the fruits of success, but of success itself . . . the dream and the will to found a private kingdom . . . the sensation of power and independence.

Thus did historian Allan Nevins dismiss the muckrakers' robber-baron interpretation of industrial leadership as "grievously misconstrued." The greed of business leaders, he found, was for "competitive achievement, self-expression, and the imposition of their wills on a given environment," not very different from "Shakespeare [who] was greedy for fame, Lincoln greedy for political power, and [Eleonora] Duse greedy for applause." Money, like these other rewards, was a *byproduct* of something greater and grander. Clint Murchison, arguably America's leading venture capitalist of the mid-twentieth century and an important figure in Book 2, stated: "The real satisfaction in life is the knowledge of accomplishment, and in business making money is the result of successful accomplishment."

The will to succeed and the reward for success are not to be taken for granted. The optimism that progress can be made and life substantively changed began only in the seventeenth century, before which "economic stagnation seemed to be the natural order of things all over the world," and "people at every social level . . . arranged their lives accordingly."

Rand's views of moneymaking, wealth, and greed apply to the post-Enron debate over capitalism. The many authors linking Enron to capitalism are short on definition, explanation, qualification, and distinction. They have put the grandest *ism* on trial and rendered a verdict based on loose perceptions and half-reasoning. Rand questioned such guilt by association: "If [critics] do not choose to identify the nature and the actual working of capitalism, but reject it, offering no argument or theory except 'greed'—isn't that an illustration of the fact that the morality of altruism has made it impossible for philosophers to evaluate capitalism?"[12] Three questions for these critics are: *What system is being attacked as capitalism? What system should be implemented in its place? Would the new system be impervious to character flaws?*

The Moral Obligations of Capitalists

As the public face of capitalism, business leaders have a vital moral responsibility to explain the logic of free markets from a moral and economic viewpoint—and to demonstrate by example the noncoercive nature of trade by eschewing the political exploitation of consumers, taxpayers, and rivals. The actual words and deeds of corporate executives are quite different, however, and Rand was very disappointed in what she saw of business leaders. She would be more disappointed today.

---

12. Rand's crucial definition of altruism is explained in Internet appendix 3.5, "Selfishness versus Altruism Revisited," at www.politicalcapitalism.org/book1/chapter3/appendix5.html.

On the one hand, she pitied "businessmen as the greatest victims of the present philosophical trend (particularly of the altruist morality)." Muckrakers from different generations criticized and demeaned the great wealth creators, even those who benefited the masses without resorting to political means, such as John D. Rockefeller and Cornelius Vanderbilt.[13] On the other hand, Rand reviled the common business strategy of appeasing enemies, which was pronounced in Rand's time and has only grown worse since. She complained:

> As a group, businessmen have been withdrawing for decades from the ideological battlefield, disarmed by the deadly combination of altruism and Pragmatism. Their public policy has consisted in appeasing, compromising and apologizing: appeasing their crudest, loudest antagonists; compromising with any attack, any lie, any insult; apologizing for their own existence. Abandoning the field of ideas to their enemies, they have been relying on lobbying, i.e., on private manipulations, on pull, on seeking momentary favors from government officials. Today, the last group one can expect to fight for capitalism is the capitalists.

This was not an original lament, however. Adam Smith fretted about capitalists versus capitalism, and the Adam Smith of our era, Milton Friedman, observed: "The two greatest enemies of free enterprise in the United States . . . have been, on the one hand, my fellow intellectuals and, on the other hand, the business corporations of this country."

To Rand, appeasement of capitalism's opponents was philosophical surrender:

> Appeasement is a betrayal not only of one's own values, but of all those who share one's values. . . . It would be better if they kept silent rather than spread the horrible advertisements that make us cringe with embarrassment. By "us" I mean advocates of capitalism. Mobil Oil ran ads in the *New York Times* which stated the following (I quote from memory): "Of the expression free, private, responsible enterprise, we strike out 'free' and 'private' as 'nonessential.'"

The Mobil Oil of her day would be the BP, Cinergy/Duke Energy, DuPont, Enron, Exelon, and Shell of more recent times, all of which succumbed to ideologically motivated critics of carbon-based energy and timorously implicated their own emissions in causing potentially deleterious climate change from an enhanced greenhouse effect. In some cases, however, the motive has not been appeasement but rent-seeking—calculated profit seeking through the political process. The energy-sustainability debate is not only backpedaling by business leaders (as Rand saw) but *front-pedaling* for pecuniary gain at the expense of competitors—and consumers and/or taxpayers.

Rand set her sights high. She aspired for "the real businessmen—the first raters [to] give one hour of their eighteen hour work-day [to] check their philosophical premises—and their Public Relations Departments." Rand's intellectual

---

13. Market versus political entrepreneurship in late nineteenth- and early twentieth-century America is discussed in chapter 6, pp. 158–72.

businessman was akin to Adam Smith's "prudent man, [who] always studies seriously and earnestly to understand whatever he professes to understand, and not merely to persuade other people that he understands it." Rand's businessman would use his daily intellectual hour to read and contemplate the cultural and political forces necessary for wealth creation or wealth destruction—and seize opportunities to foster the first and fight the second.

Rand's thinker-doers would then "stop apologizing for their ability and their success" and use their speeches and resources to defend free-market capitalism. Her plea in the *Atlantic Economic Review* in 1958 was scarcely heeded during her era of American political capitalism, but it remains an ideal for a post-Enron, post-corporate-welfare era.

The 18-hour workday Rand posited for her executives reflected her own capacity for work. But long hours also reflected the growing rigors of a job for which ever more distractions and responsibilities were on the shoulders of business Atlases. Writing in 1946, one business historian noted how the entrepreneur had to "synthesize more appraisals of experts and advisers . . . be cognizant of more services from more service institutions . . . relate his decisions to a longer time space of past and future . . . [and be aware] of the data that he does not possess." The leader had to also appreciate the impact of actions and strategies not only for different parts of the company but also on competitors, customers, the general public, and *government*.

Pragmatism in the mixed economy naturally encouraged political entrepreneurship and second-hander strategies. The firm's decision making shifted, in part, from the home office to Washington, D.C., and other seats of political power. Management attention was diverted from employees, customers, and owners to pressure groups, regulators, and legislators. *Atlas Shrugged* is the fictional account of growing political capitalism and economic chaos. The interventionist dynamic that Rand described in the book has also been present in real life, particularly for energy companies in the highly regulated 1970s. And within corporations, the philosophic virus of perceptionism described in her novels was also playing out—foreshadowing the death spiral that engulfed Enron.

The Apex: *Atlas Shrugged*

Ayn Rand's first major novel, *The Fountainhead*, is the story of a lone professional struggling against the altruistic, collectivist norms of his profession, architecture. Her epic novel, *Atlas Shrugged*, describes what happens when men and women of accomplishment and honor withdraw their talent to defeat a parasitic, collectivist society. In her book plan, Rand described this plot as an anti–Industrial Revolution and instructed herself:

> Reverse the process of expansion that goes on in a society of producers: Henry Ford's automobile opened the way for industries: oil, roads, glass, rubber, plastics, etc. Now, in a society of parasites, the opposite takes place: a shrinking of industries and productive activities.

Originally titled *The Strike* because of this withdrawal of talent, the novel revolves around a theorist and inventor in the field of energy, John Galt, who leads the exodus, refuses under torture to save the bankrupt society, and then returns with the strikers to rebuild America on a rational, individualistic basis. *Who is John Galt?* has become a literary phrase that, like *Atlas shrugged*, is still in use today.

Atlas Shrugged contains a variety of business and business/government situations that impart Rand's views of positive and negative attributes of firms and their leaders. Although the work is fictional, a number of its insights anticipated the real-life blind spots of the major figures and events of Book 2 and Book 3. For example, the book's discussion of asset nationalization in the "People's State" anticipated Enron's problems in Peru in the 1980s and India in the 1990s.

The ideal in *Atlas* begins with the foundation of meaningful, inspired work and wealth creation. The rational, indeed heroic, business leader practices frugality, attends to detail, and strives for continual improvement, even perfection. The firm is reality centered, forward looking, and authentic. Government favors are not sought—market solutions are.

On the other hand, there are warnings about emotions in the workplace, conflicts of interest whereby businesspeople are put under obligation, cronyism and nepotism, extravagance, and a failure to take responsibility. The flash-in-the-pan company is focused on public relations and politics. It seeks and welcomes government subsidies. It appeases, rather than confronts, enemies of business.

Style-over-substance leaders have "a gift" for making their businesses popular and receiving "good press." They are detached from the nitty-gritty of the home office, working on what is considered bigger things in a marquee city. They have "Washington ability" whereby skillful actions result in legislative favor. There are "glossy" annual reports and many speeches to make. Great importance is given to the company's slogan, symbol, and "noble plan." Decision making is very hierarchical. Formalities are relished and public relation events emphasized. Diversity and "fairness" are considered alongside merit.

The flawed leader takes comfort in hiring "very promising young men, all of them guaranteed by diplomas from the very best universities." The CEO is a Great Man creating a legacy with an autobiography in mind. He is extremely confident, believing that reality will be what he wants it to be. When things go sour, this leader is full of excuses.

The preceding insights about substance versus façade foster an understanding of the fate of Enron and Ken Lay—and the ongoing success of the anti-Enron companies. Samuel Insull and John Henry Kirby, as well as other examples of business failure described in Book 2, also got off track in ways anticipated by the narrative of *Atlas Shrugged*.

The themes of *Atlas Shrugged* can be applied on any scale and in many situations. In the case of a failed business, the question arises: *Was Atlas shrugging?* Were the men and women with the solutions absent? Did they formally resign their employment, or did they choose not to work for the company in the first place? Were they physically present but mentally on strike, choosing not to engage in a rigged game?

In any case, why—and how? Was a race to the bottom created by a compensation system that rewarded those who destroyed wealth rather than those who created it? Speaking through Francisco d'Anconia, one of her characters in *Atlas Shrugged*, Rand explained the logical result of such a perversion:

> Money will not buy intelligence for the fool, or admiration for the coward, or respect for the incompetent. The man who attempts to purchase the brains of his superiors to serve him, with his money replacing his judgment, ends up by becoming the victim of his inferiors. The men of intelligence desert him, but the cheats and the frauds come flocking to him, drawn by a law which he has not discovered: that no man may be smaller than his [the briber's] money.

Or: Was Atlas *shoved*? Were the agents of constructive change—inside or outside a failed company—bullied into submission? Was their very ability feared and neutralized by the purveyors of deceit and philosophical fraud? In the case of Enron, the answers are a resounding *yes*.

Self-Interest and the Perils of Altruism

Objectivism posits *rational self-interest* as the proper guide to action—personally, professionally, and socially. Such egoism is not conceit or megalomania. It is not the amoral brute of philosopher Friedrich Nietzsche, claiming license to do anything imagined to be of personal benefit. Rand makes that distinction clear in the introduction to her provocatively titled book *The Virtue of Selfishness* (1964), which is subtitled *A New Concept of Egoism*—"new," in the sense of non-Nietzschean. "Rational self-interest," also described as "rational selfishness," flows from a personal morality based on life, reason, productive action, and moral striving—and the values that thereby accrue to the person.

As discussed in chapter 1, Adam Smith recognized self-interest as the norm and distrusted its opposite. *Altruism*, as defined by Rand, is the antithesis of rational self-interest. Considering and respecting the position of others, the "analogous emotion" of Adam Smith's *direct sympathy*, is often thought of as altruistic. Yet the empathy that Smith saw in interpersonal relations is based on the shared values of self-regarding people. Altruism-as-selflessness places others' values *before* one's own, sacrificing one's own judgment and well-being for a mechanistic call to duty. It is a flight from reality (Rand) and a form of self-deceit (Smith).

Altruistic ethics, putting the needs of the recipient ahead of the values of the giver, is short-sighted and corrosive. Benevolence is rooted in the ethics of creation, not distribution, for wealth must be produced before it is dispensed. As Rand noted:

> Men have been taught that the highest virtue is not to achieve, but to give. Yet one cannot give that which has not been created. Creation comes before

distribution—or there will be nothing to distribute. . . . We praise an act of charity. We shrug at an act of achievement.

This insight applies to any business that compromises its productive core in favor of image building—high-profile charity included. Milton Friedman warned of the "fundamentally subversive doctrine" of corporate social responsibility whereby firms work for ends other than maximizing shareholder wealth. He stated: "There is one and only one social responsibility of business—to use its resources and engage in activities designed to increase its profits so long as it stays within the rules of the game, which is to say, engages in open and free competition, without deception or fraud." Serving other masters begs the questions: Which masters, and why those rather than others?

Charity should not infest the productive processes responsible for wealth creation. Enron, practicing high-profile philanthropy and blurring the line between its profit and nonprofit activity, as documented in Book 3, destroyed shareholder value in the name of altruism.

The dismal history of sacrificial calls to duty, particularly in times of government-created crisis, is a powerful warning against misplaced altruism. When government price-and-allocation controls on oil and natural gas created debilitating energy shortages in the 1970s, national leaders scapegoated industry, jawboned consumers, and imposed new intervention. President Nixon, in the first peacetime energy address ever given to the nation (scripted in part by Ken Lay, then deputy undersecretary of energy at the U.S. Department of the Interior), called for voluntary conservation as an alternative to forced rationing. "We as a nation must develop a national energy conservation ethic," Nixon stated in April 1973. "I call upon every American to do his or her part." The message concluded, "Whenever we have been confronted with great national challenges in the past, the American people have done their duty. I am confident that we shall do so now."

Nixon's price-control program triggered an oil crisis even before the Arab embargo, joining a natural gas crisis that came from a longer-standing regime of price controls. (Ken Lay is part of that story, too, again from the government side.) The nadir of energy policy came in 1977 when President Jimmy Carter and his energy czar, James Schlesinger, blamed the limits of nature for the crisis and called for self-denial. "We have a classic Malthusian case of exponential growth against a finite source," complained Schlesinger. "Everyone will have to make some kind of sacrifice." In a nationally televised address from a chilly Oval Office with firewood ablaze, Carter, wearing a cardigan sweater, called for "sacrifices and changes in every life" to avert "a national catastrophe." The reality was that price controls had caused the shortages, and price *decontrol* could have ended them. More government intervention to address the distortions of prior intervention was chosen instead.[14]

---

14. The policy of *gapism* over deregulation is described in chapter 10, pp. 266–68.

Atlas Shrugged included energy-crisis scenarios caused by price controls. Authorities and their many followers in the fictional account called for mandatory conservation (including rationing) and personal self-sacrifice, not deregulation, to remove the root of the problem. Ayn Rand had seen this with energy and other goods during World War II, and now, two decades later, there was a peacetime equivalent of the crisis foreshadowed in her book.

"Pentagon commandeers oil supplies"; "New York sues 7 oil firms"; "New England faces voltage cuts"; "Truckers protest fuel crisis . : . launch strike"; "Allocation plans proposed"; "'Windfall' profits tax proposed"; "Rationing program unveiled"; "Speed limit lowered"; "Sunday gasoline sale ban urged"; "States act to save fuel"; "Emergency fuel plan adopted"; "[Europe] agrees on unity in oil crisis." These 1970s headlines were akin to the *Atlas Shrugged* narrative describing fuel shortages and power blackouts. This *right-out-of-an-Ayn-Rand-novel* scenario would be joined by another fiction-to-fact carryover 20 years later: the rise and spectacular fall of a powerful perception-based corporation.

Implicit Objectivism

The tenets of Objectivism are intuitively appealing and commonsensical. Not surprisingly, a variety of thinkers outside Objectivism have arrived at similar conclusions about the primacy of reason, reality-grounded business strategy, and capitalism.

Social Science Realism

Science is based on reality, not the whims or emotions of the scientist. The chapters of Book 1 present the worldview of methodological realists, beginning with Adam Smith, Samuel Smiles, and Ayn Rand and continuing with a group of political scientists, economists, and historians who challenged and corrected the leading lights of their profession on the nature of political capitalism. The revisionists' "victory for realism," noted one historian, was identifying "self-interest rather than high-minded regard for the 'public welfare' as the genesis of federal regulation." But this self-interest was Nietzschean, a regard for self outside a moral context and not consonant with Smith-Smiles-Rand heroic capitalism.

Ludwig von Mises (chapter 4) defended realism over mathematical formalism as the sine qua non of economics. Joseph Schumpeter (chapters 4 and 5) took the economics profession to task for using a highly idealized theory of competition to judge capitalist reality. Arthur Bentley (chapter 5) pleaded with political scientists to "find the only reality . . . in the proper functioning of the felt facts and the thought facts," not in imputed feelings and "idea ghosts." Alfred Chandler (chapter 6) substituted economic understanding for muckraker emotionalism in the interpretation of business history. Erich Zimmermann (chapter 8) challenged the hypertheoretical construct of fixed, known, and depleting mineral-resource supply. Julian Simon countered neo-Malthusian passion with facts,

facts, facts (chapters 10 and 11). Realism in social science theory is indispensable for understanding the business world and framing appropriate public policy. By contrast, *un*realism inaccurately portrays the business landscape and invites inappropriate public policy.

Best-Business Practices

"Awareness of reality," the business historian Alfred Chandler concluded, "is more important than indoctrination in generality." This has been borne out by business thinker Jim Collins (b. 1957), whose case studies in his 2001 best-seller, *Good to Great: Why Some Companies Make the Leap . . . and Others Don't,* identified realism as a chief characteristic of business success.

Having a good idea or a bold vision for greatness is just a start. "The good-to-great companies continually refined the *path* to greatness with the brutal facts of reality," Collins found. He quoted Winston Churchill, who stated, "There is no worse mistake in public leadership than to hold out false hopes soon to be swept away." Collins identified the winning firms as being led by those who exclaim "'Look! You'd better pay attention to this' [rather than] 'Aren't we great.'"

Failed entrepreneurs always had an excuse ("We lost some battles, but we were winning the war"). The losers "turned a blind eye to any reality inconsistent with [their] own vision of the world." Leadership, contrarily, proved to be all about vision *and* "creating a climate where the truth is heard, and the brutal facts confronted." Collins offered four steps to get business firms to move from instructing employees to "have your say" to giving them "the opportunity to be *heard.*"

1. *Lead with questions, not answers.*

2. *Engage in dialogue and debate, not coercion.*

3. *Conduct autopsies, without blame.*

4. *Build "red flag" mechanisms.*

Collins warned about the charismatic leader who "allows himself to become the primary reality people worry about, rather than reality being the primary reality." He told the charismatic leader to tone it down, in much the way that Adam Smith warned about self-deceit. Collins profiled Winston Churchill, who said that in wartime, *"Facts are better than dreams."* Such attention to objective reality helped Churchill achieve a very difficult victory—and avoid being a misguided visionary, believing that his mighty self could trump underlying realities to achieve the desired outcome.

Collins, who earlier in life was an honored professor at Stanford University's graduate business school, has now become the most-read and most-revered business thinker in the world. Collins eclipsed another business guru, Gary Hamel, who captured Ken Lay's imagination by proclaiming a theme of *revolution-always* rather than *incrementalism* as the key to excelling in the new economy. Collins's book and message went unread and unheeded, and by 2001, it was too late for Ken Lay and Enron.

Arthur E. Andersen (1885–1947), described as "a man of ideas and ideals," was the founding force of the accounting firm bearing his name. His motto, and that of his firm, was "*think straight—talk straight*," an adage given to him by his mother. "Never has it failed me," Andersen explained. "It has been as a firm rock to which I could anchor in a storm."

Andersen died at age 61, with his firm in its thirty-fourth year. At the memorial service, his pastor remembered him as

> a representative of principles as opposed to expediency. His principles got him into much trouble but that was trouble he liked, for to him there could never be any real trouble as a result of following principles. . . .
>
> Mr. Andersen could not be bought. He could not be bought with money, but what is more important, he could not be bought with power, influence, prestige or social position. And few, if any, were the people who could mislead him. . . .
>
> It was Mr. Andersen's belief that principles would go on working for you even when you were asleep. He believed that to be true of the short sleep of the night or the long sleep of death. He believed in honesty. By this he did not mean mere financial honesty, for that he took for granted. He believed in honesty of purpose and motive. He believed, of course, in truth; for him there was no alternative.

The eulogy added, "I am sure he would rather the doors [to his firm] be closed than that it should continue to exist on principles other than those which he established." The House of Andersen, with 85,000 employees worldwide, already moribund because of its transgressions, climaxing with Enron, ceased to be an ongoing concern in mid-2002 when it lost in trial against the Department of Justice over an Enron-related charge of obstruction of justice. Perhaps Andersen would have assented to his firm's fate, coming as it did on top of other transgressions.

The demise of one of the world's big-five accounting firms goes beyond the moral failings of some or many of its principals. It also had to do with a different rulebook and set of incentives in the 1990s than in the firm's early decades. Politicized accounting made financial gaming—a perverted form of financial engineering whereby the perpetrators devised the numbers from the story rather than the story from the numbers—a core competency and profit center at the company. The lost alternative was principles-based accounting standards whereby substance is elevated over form in depicting the state of a business at any particular time.

A contemporary example of a principled business with an implicit Objectivist framework is Koch Industries, now the largest privately held company in the United States. Long-time chairman Charles Koch (b. 1935) has stated: "My motivation has been an internal compulsion to understand reality and to develop a unified philosophy of life." Applying what is called Market Process Analysis,™

Koch Industries emphasizes a three-step framework to understand its entrepreneurial opportunities:

1. *Determine what facts are significant.*
2. *Simplify, see patterns, and understand causality.*
3. *Identify the problem and root causes.*

The reality-grounded nature of Koch Industries' business model is captured in one of Charles Koch's favorite quotations, which comes from the nineteenth-century philosopher and logician Richard Whately: "It is one thing to *wish to have truth on our side*, and another to wish sincerely to be *on the side of truth*."

Figure 3.5 Thinkers and doers outside the Objectivist tradition have captured the interrelationship between reason, reality, and business success under capitalism. Four notables (clockwise, from upper left) are business thinker Jim Collins (rayng.com), accounting firm founder Arthur Andersen, entrepreneur Charles Koch, and theologian Michael Novak.

The company's Web site explains the company's philosophy as follows:

At Koch Industries, we are firmly focused on long-term success. We believe in creating real value, rather than the illusion of value. To do so, we strive to live by core values and principles that include integrity, humility, respect and what we call principled entrepreneurship™. . . . We strive to make tough decisions, respond quickly to market opportunities and are willing to absorb volatility. We evaluate our financial performance in a way that fully represents economic reality.

Koch Industries is part of the Enron story. The philosophic approach and principles of Charles Koch were diametrically opposed to those of Ken Lay, political capitalist and perceptionist extraordinaire. Like Kinder Morgan, the company founded by Richard Kinder after he left Enron in 1996, Koch Industries is an anti-Enron. Enron and Koch Industries competed vigorously in some markets, and Enron executive Cliff Baxter, a tragic name from the Enron story, left Enron to work for Koch before returning to his old company, one that was more in line with his ambition—or overambition.

Religion and Reason

Rand's total devotion to reason and strictures against faith made her an enemy of the religious establishment. Still, a reconciliation of religion and reason has been pursued within the capitalist ethos. Capitalist theologian Michael Novak (b. 1933) has argued:

> Reason is central to capitalism. Capitalism is very much (as the word suggests) a system of the head. Practical intelligence orders it in every detail. It promotes invention and fresh ideas. It strives constantly for better forms of organization, more efficient production, and greater satisfaction. It plans for the long run as well as the short. . . . It organizes means and ends. It constantly studies itself for improvement. It is ordered toward continuous enterprise longer than the life of any individual.

Theologian Jacques Maritain (1882–1973) made a case for carefully separating, or removing, faith from reason's expanse:

> Faith in its own domain—in the things which are *of faith*—unites minds absolutely and upon certainties absolutely essential to human life; it alone can create such a unity of minds. But faith only creates unity of minds at the top; it does not create unity of doctrine or of behavior in any of the categories of our activities which touch only human affairs, which are not of *faith*. . . . Faith itself wants reason to be free in human affairs.

In the same vein, Maritain warned against "intellectual opportunism [and] trickery" that mixes faith with reason in the "pursuit of truth." Such a lack of differentiation applies to Ken Lay, who dotted his business persona with religion and cloaked himself in the deity as he made controversial after controversial decision.

German Catholic philosopher Josef Pieper (1904–97) grounded goodness in an understanding of and respect for reality. In his book on the four cardinal virtues, the first of which is prudence, he wrote:

> The pre-eminence of prudence means that realization of the good presupposes knowledge of reality. He alone can do good who knows what things are like and

what their situation is. . . . So-called "good intention" and "meaning well" by no means suffice. Realization of the good presupposes that our actions are appropriate to the real situation . . . and that we therefore take this concrete reality seriously, with clear-eyed objectivity.

Pieper continues, "The prudent decisions, which, when realized, shape our free action, are fed from . . . 'the universal principles of reason and the singulars with which ethical action is concerned.'"

New Relevance—and Old Baggage

There are few neutral opinions about Ayn Rand among those who have read her novels or studied her worldview. Millions have reacted positively to her general precepts of reason, rational egoism, and voluntary social and economic relations. The results have been more mixed, however, among those who graduated from Rand's idealistic fiction into formal study of her philosophy—particularly in her lifetime. A rigid interpretation of Objectivism, fostered by Rand herself, resulted in a cultish movement in the 1950s and 1960s. Rand's inner circle interpreted the world in black and white, even extending right-and-wrong to the arts. Deviancy in matters small and large was denounced and disparaged within her group, which facetiously but tellingly called itself "the Collective."

Figure 3.6 During the 1950s, Ayn Rand's inner circle, known as "the Collective," included (from left to right) Leonard Peikoff, Nathaniel Branden, and Alan Greenspan. Of this group, Peikoff would remain resolute and found the Ayn Rand Institute in 1985, following Rand's death.

The dreary existence of virtually all of Rand's inner circle at the time has been chronicled in gripping biographies of Ayn Rand by two of her closest associates. One was by Nathaniel Branden, with whom Rand had a decade-long affair and bitter break, which ended a thriving period for Objectivism as an

organized movement in 1968.[15] The other was written by Nathaniel's wife during his affair with Rand, Barbara Branden, who (unlike Nathaniel) would eventually reconcile with Rand. But time would heal wounds, and in his 2007
autobiography, Alan Greenspan fondly remembered his mentor as "a wholly original thinker, sharply analytical, strong-willed, highly principled, and very insistent on rationality as the highest value."

Critics of Objectivism have often cited her moral authoritarianism in personal relationships as a reason to dismiss her philosophy. But although there is
much to regret—and learn from—regarding the arrogant personal side of the
early Objectivist movement, Rand's books and essays were relatively consistent
and carefully reasoned. It is her writings, not persona, that scholars and laypersons alike must evaluate in the post-Rand era.

Criticism of Rand's novels and ideas from the secular Left and religious
Right, summarized in an appendix,[16] made her one of the most controversial
intellectuals of her time. Thus, it was not wholly surprising when editorialists
at some of the nation's leading papers cited Enron, WorldCom, and Adelphia as
a prima facie refutation of Rand's philosophic defense of capitalism. Alan
Greenspan was also tainted by his early association with Rand's inner circle.

A *New York Times* article in mid-2002 reported, "Forty-five years after the
publication of [*Atlas Shrugged*] . . . greed apparently represents a greater danger
to capitalism than government bureaucrats." The article noted how former Randian Greenspan admitted that he was wrong for not having previously endorsed
government regulation of the accounting industry. A response in the *Times* several
days later from David Kelley, head of The Objectivist Center, reminded the
reader that Rand considered fraud a crime. Furthermore, "she was no advocate
of greed, at least not in the sense that Mr. Greenspan seems to have meant in
speaking of 'infectious greed': the pursuit of wealth as an end in itself, without
regard for achievement. Indeed, she wrote with scathing insight about such
unprincipled, dishonest, manipulative behavior." Once again, the press had
revealed its superficial view of morality and capitalism as developed by Adam
Smith, Samuel Smiles, Ayn Rand, and other leading capitalist philosophers.

The Ayn Rand Institute distributed an opinion-page editorial, which the
Houston Chronicle titled "There Isn't Too Much Greed, It's Just Wrong Kind":

> Far from being too "greedy," too many of America's chief executive officers are
> not greedy enough. They are pragmatic corner-cutters who fail to recognize
> that there is far more wealth to be achieved by a consistent, long-range policy

---

15. "The Rand/Branden split also splintered the Objectivist movement [because they]
were perceived as radiant, rational, heroic mother/father figures to Objectivists, the living
example, as Rand would often tout them, of the fact that real heroes of the sort she wrote
about could and did exist."

16. See Internet appendix 3.6, "Critics of Objectivism," at www.politicalcapitalism.org/
book1/chapter3/appendix6.html.

of honesty—by creating a quality product and maintaining the company's reputation over many years—than by squeezing out some momentary advantage.

Still, Rand's unconventional use of the terms *greed, selfishness*, and *altruism* has made it easy for critics to caricature her views.[17] Applied Objectivism is still marred by this choice of terms—and by the inability or refusal of critics to understand and communicate Rand's definitions.

The Enron debacle did not refute Rand's views, or Objectivism broadly considered. Enron was a case of entrepreneurial error and fraudulent cover-up. In terms of public policy, it was a classic case of *government failure* and the unintended social consequences of *political capitalism*, not free-market failure. The energy trading, accounting, and tax systems at the center of many Enron controversies were so imbued with regulation that they invited gaming and abuse. But more to the point regarding Rand and Objectivism, such entrepreneurial error and government failure were abetted by *philosophic failure* on the part of key Enron executives, the very thing that Ayn Rand explained and warned against decades before. That is why it was an Objectivist thinker, Roger Donway, who first explicated the philosophic bankruptcy that resulted in the financial one.[18] Political capitalism and form-over-substance postmodernism come together in the full autopsy of Enron.

Objectivism was encapsulated by Ayn Rand as "the concept of man as a heroic being, with his own happiness as the moral purpose of his life, with productive achievement as his noblest activity, and reason as his only absolute." "Man" is the men and women of enterprise, contributing to companies and an economic system that is much greater than the sum of its parts.

Objectivism offers numerous insights into the *why* of sustainable business success and even spectacular business failure. These lessons include the importance of identifying and acting upon underlying realities, as well as being loyal to ideas and principles—and not to a Great Man or groupthink. Objectivism also warns about the dangers of giving Atlas a shove or a reason to shrug.

Objectivism points the way toward *heroic capitalism*. The philosophy developed by the Russian émigré provides a *moral* defense for an economic system typically judged by its materialistic fruits. Among them, Adam Smith, Samuel Smiles, and Ayn Rand have placed self-interest and voluntary exchange on a high pedestal for serious debate. The three also provide a framework for understanding complex historical business events, including the rise and fall of seemingly unsinkable companies and their iconic leaders.

---

17. This and other reasons for Rand's unpopularity among many intellectuals and academics are discussed in Internet appendix 3.7, "Objectivism in the History of Philosophy," at www.politicalcapitalism.org/book1/chapter3/appendix7.html.

18. See "The Collapse of a Postmodern Corporation," at www.objectivistcenter.org.

Part II

Business Opportunity, Political Opportunism

I see no force in modern society which can cope with the power of
capital handled by talent, and I cannot doubt that
the greatest force will control the other forces.
—William Graham Sumner, "Economics and Politics" (1905)

Introduction

The business entrepreneur has two avenues to success. The first is the *economic means*, whereby goods and services are voluntarily produced and sold to consumers in open competition. Where profits are won, private and public wealth is created, and very few except the less-efficient competitors are made worse off.

Free-market capitalism is the institutionalization of the economic means. As explained in chapter 4, entrepreneurs formulate their business plans based on economic calculation, but consumers ultimately determine the number, size, and functions of firms. Profits reward the successful participants, shifting the resources of land, labor, and capital to the more able from the less able.

A growing economy allows more firms to succeed than fail, but no enterprise is forever. The invisible hand of the market includes the process of creative destruction. Even bankruptcies are manifestations of progress amid change in a free economy, as good replaces bad and better replaces good.

But there is a second avenue to business gain. The *political means* are used when entrepreneurs turn to government to supplement, and even override, consumer choice. Consumers, business rivals, and/or taxpayers lose whenever these political capitalists win. Examples of political entrepreneurship include an industry establishing certification requirements to block new entry or a domestic seller acquiring tariffs to hamper foreign rivals.

Political capitalism is the intersection of business opportunity and political opportunism. Samuel Insull and Ken Lay were political capitalists extraordinaire. John Henry Kirby, Clint Murchison, Jack Bowen, and Robert Herring, important figures of Book 2, also had a political side. But their machinations were hardly the exception in an era rife with business/government relations, often instigated by business, for business.

It is not surprising that entrepreneurs have leveraged their power for political gain. The consumer is a tough taskmaster, and businesses have not been prohibited from seeking or receiving special government favor (aka *corporate welfare*). Within civil society, there has not been a common belief strong enough to ostracize those who use the political means. Indeed, beginning in the late nineteenth century, the intellectual class sanctioned an active, open-ended role for government in business.

The economics of politics in theory and practice, the subject of chapters 5 and 6, respectively, provide context for understanding how the two central entrepreneurs of our trilogy were brought up in a mixed economy, advanced it, and were partially brought down by it. Ironically, the very intellectuals who vehemently criticized Samuel Insull and Ken Lay had a worldview that helped create the mixed economy that both men masterfully exploited.

·◌·

Capitalism is of comparatively recent origin. Seventeenth-century England was its cradle, but America became its bastion. The United States embodied a voluntary political and economic order for the world to observe and emulate. America was conceived in liberty by statesmen who tried to institutionalize economic and political freedom. Economist Milton Friedman was near the mark when he observed that America started "with a clean slate: fewer vestiges of class and status; few government constraints; a more fertile field for energy, drive and innovation; and an empty continent to conquer."

But after some decades of relative separation between economy and state, business and government interests increasingly came together to move the economy away from its quasi-laissez-faire orientation. The process began at the local and state levels and was eventually federalized through the regulation of interstate commerce. Most of this government intervention was business sponsored, but some sprang from the pressures of organized labor, as well as from intellectuals and reformers who championed ideas different from those of most of America's Founding Fathers.

In the name of accelerating economic development, pure business opportunity was supplemented by taxpayer subsidies in the eighteenth and nineteenth centuries. The transportation industries—beginning with turnpikes and canals and continuing with railroads—were the main beneficiaries of these government handouts. Expertise-driven regulation—a "peculiarly American institution" according to two regulatory historians, although its genesis can be traced to Bismarck's Germany—emerged in the 1880s. A new class of well-educated civil servants used sophisticated rationales to justify regulating gas and electricity as public utilities, two industries that are of particular importance for this trilogy. Regulated capitalism was much more sophisticated than earlier mercantilism and was quite distinct from the socialism embraced by England in the mid-twentieth century.

For much of the twentieth century, public policies toward business were more the workings of political capitalism than of reformer capitalism. The majority of government intervention in the economy was prompted—or crucially shaped—by business interests rather than by academics and pundits critical of free-market reliance. But as interventionism matured, other lobbying groups with specific agendas entered the fray. These later reformers—representing not only labor but also the aged, consumers, the environment, minorities, religious groups, and other constituencies—helped shape America's middle way between free-market capitalism and a government-managed economy. More than ever before, business interests found themselves on the defensive, either trying to avoid unwanted government intervention or striving to retain the desired level of intervention. Business was still very much involved in the legislative process, but now social reformers could set the agenda. The raw political capitalism of decades past broadened into special-interest capitalism.[1]

How did America move from an ideology-based, liberty-dominated economy to a mixed economy? Why did government intervention become so commonplace and varied? How much intervention was the result of companies seeking competitive gain at others' expense, and how much was the work of intellectual reformers or nonbusiness special interests? Was the growth of interventionism sequential, with each stanza building on the one before, or was it haphazard? And what was the role of *ideas* in this transformation?

Deciphering the past helps us understand the *is* of the present and the *ought* for the future. If "American capitalism is ripe for reinvention," as one Enron-inspired muckraker claimed, American capitalism itself must first be understood. The next three chapters describe the socioeconomic system that accelerated the rise of two of the most important figures in the history of U.S. political capitalism: Samuel Insull in the first third and Ken Lay in the last third of the twentieth century.

---

1. The growth of government intervention in the private sector was also propelled by welfare programs and military expenditures, the latter prominently involving business as suppliers. The federal government's share of the gross domestic product (GDP) rose from 3 percent in 1900 to a peak of 40 percent during World War II, before falling to around 20 percent in 2000.

4

Business Opportunity

A THEORY OF ENTREPRENEURSHIP and business strategy is necessary to decipher complex business events, such as the rise and fall of Samuel Insull's energy empire and Ken Lay's Enron. Such high theory was developed in the first half of the twentieth century by a handful of economists who were methodological realists. They rejected their colleagues' overly theoretical approach, in which perfect knowledge was assumed and decision making under conditions of uncertainty postulated away.

These realists asked: What is the role of the *entrepreneur* in business and the general economy? What determines an entrepreneur's *business model*? How is a firm to be properly sized and tasked in order to be successful? How are strategies chosen that fit the firm's opportunity? Where, when, and how do firms make baby-step improvements versus grand leaps of advancement? How is uncertainty managed and, at times, reduced to insurable risk?

Answering these questions helps us to understand how a reversal of business fortune can occur. The central entrepreneurs of our story had business models that worked well and then spectacularly failed. Why did this occur?

Basic economics explains how profit and loss allocates resources between firms and promotes economy-wide coordination. But such economic calculation is also at work within firms, shifting resources between and within departments. Financial accounting describes the state of a business—and more. Measured profit and loss, cash flow, and assets versus liabilities indicate trends and signal the need for business adjustments. Properly interpreted, future profitability and economic efficiency are enhanced. Accounting information that is manipulated, falsified, or disregarded, on the other hand, can mislead a firm (and outside parties) and misallocate resources. The results can even be tragic, as in the case of Enron.

The market is a process, not a static state of equilibrium. Business adjustments are necessary to anticipate and react to shifts in technology, consumer demand, and other economic conditions. Step-by-step change can be part of a process of continuous improvement—or part of a slippery slope to ruin. Thus, business participants must unfailingly comprehend and respect underlying realities in the open-ended, trial-and-error business world.

The Four Horsemen of enterprise economics—Joseph Schumpeter, Frank Knight, Ludwig von Mises, and Ronald Coase—rank among the great economists of all time. In the first half of the twentieth century, an era memorialized in the discipline as the years of hard times and high theory, each made seminal contributions to decipher the nature of business reality. All four conceptualized the "economics of disorder" around the concept of entrepreneurship and the market process, whereas their rivals—economists as technicians—were working out the equilibrium-limited "economics of tranquility." Harold Hotelling, a central figure of chapter 8, was a tranquility theorist, mathematically solving for the allocation of fixed resources over time. Yet analyzing highly conditional states of equilibrium, to the exclusion of real-world processes, is shadowboxing with reality.[1] Asked one student of tumult: "What sense did it make to assume perfect knowledge in a world where every morning's newspaper was opened in fear and scanned with foreboding?"

The challenge of business is to advance from profit *seeking* to profit *making*. But the opportunity for profits also means the potential of losses, even business failure. There are two sides to the capitalist coin, because fickle consumer demand and shifting supply-side conditions (not government guarantees) determine business outcomes.

Entrepreneurship: Joseph Schumpeter

Joseph Schumpeter (1883–1950) was the conscience of his profession, questioning the relevancy of an equilibrium-only approach for understanding business competition and economic growth. Schumpeter was a methodological realist interested in the actual workings of capitalism, what he called *capitalist reality*.[2] He also had a contrarian streak. He claimed allegiance to no school of thought and even feared becoming the orthodoxy himself. "When I see those

---

1. Economic equilibrium can be mathematically and diagrammatically described by assuming *perfect knowledge* for all market participants and *perfect divisibility* for economic goods (to create continuous curves for differential calculus). For the limits of such theory, see Internet appendix 4.1, "Equilibrium versus Market Process," at www.politicalcapitalism.org/book1/chapter4/appendix1.html.

2. Schumpeter's views on capitalist reality and business competition are explored in chapter 5, pp. 126–30.

who espouse my cause," he averred, "I begin to wonder about the validity of my position."

Schumpeter's theory of capitalist development centered upon the entrepreneur, a "swashbuckling . . . quasi-heroic" figure who disrupted routines and forged a new menu for consumers. Innovation was less about economizing within a known framework than about creating wholly new vistas. The Schumpeterian entrepreneur did not say *If it ain't broke don't fix it* but rather *Break it and make it better!* Incremental improvement was about routines and managers; by contrast, "the function of entrepreneurs," Schumpeter stated, "is to reform or revolutionize the pattern of production by exploiting an invention or, more generally, an untried technological possibility for producing a new commodity or producing an old one in a new way, by opening up a new source of supply of materials or a new outlet for products, by reorganizing an industry and so on." In this vein, Schumpeter spoke elsewhere of the "New Firm," "New Plant," and "New Men."

This perspective led to a profound conclusion from the Austrian-born-and-trained economist: "The problem that is usually being visualized is how capitalism administers existing structures, whereas the relevant problem is how it creates and destroys them." Schumpeter analogized firms to the cycle of human life itself:

> Like human beings, firms are constantly being born that cannot live. Others may meet what is akin, in the case of men, to death from accident or illness. Still others die a "natural" death, as men die of old age. And the "natural" cause, in the case of firms, is precisely their inability to keep up the pace in innovating which they themselves had been instrumental in setting in the time of their vigor.

He continued:

> No firm which is merely run on established lines, however conscientious the management of its routine business may be, remains in capitalist society a source of profit . . . . Everyone who looks around knows the type of firm we are thinking of—living on the name, connections, quasi-rent, and reserves acquired in their youth, decorously dropping into the background, lingering in the fatally deepening dusk of respectable decay.

No equilibrium box could hold the Schumpeterian entrepreneur. Automatons populate equilibrium; human innovators preclude it. Many economists abandoned the study of entrepreneurship because it was not amenable to mathematical and diagrammatic portrayal. They were right, but the wrong thing was discarded. The open-ended world of disequilibrium was the reality that had to be comprehended, even if mathematical economics had to be demoted. Much empirical study was required to formulate the relevant concepts and to identify patterns. Theoretical economists had to team with business historians to understand in-the-flesh entrepreneurship. As discussed in chapter 6, Schumpeter found his home at Harvard University less and less in the economics department and more and more in the graduate business school, where he could pursue entrepreneurial studies.[3]

"Every piece of business strategy," Schumpeter famously wrote in 1942, "must be seen in its role in the perennial gale of creative destruction; it cannot be understood irrespective of it or, in fact, on the hypothesis that there is a perennial lull."[4] During the Great Depression and World War II, when stability and uniformity were sought, Schumpeter's conception of capitalist progress found little interest. But that changed in the postwar period. "The Age of Keynes" became "The Age of Schumpeter" as managerial capitalism gave way to entrepreneurial capitalism. Schumpeter's 1942 book, *Capitalism, Socialism, and Democracy*, would be translated into 15 languages and go through many reprintings. Business consulting became a thriving new field, helping firms deal with unprecedented change, complexity, and growth. A leading strategist was Peter Drucker, whose 1968 book *The Age of Discontinuity* described the new reality of the equilibrium-shattering, value-creating entrepreneur.

Drucker (1909–2005) was no trained economist, but he knew that economics had fallen down on the job when it came to emphasizing capitalism's prime movers. "We need a theory of economic dynamics in addition to the theory of equilibrium, which is all we have now," he lamented. The "new economics" was dismissed as "static, rather lifeless, and mechanistic." Drucker longed for a theory of organizations that took into account what equilibrium analysis assumed away: "scattered" knowledge, new knowledge, expectations, uncertainty, ignorance, technological change, advertising, price adjustments, growth, and product differentiation. "We will have to understand the reality of the market in terms of what it is rather than what it is not," he told his many readers. The spirit of Schumpeter (who died in 1950) lived on in Drucker's *Age of Discontinuity*, although he was hardly mentioned. Drucker would pay tribute elsewhere, however, calling Schumpeter in 1983 the figure "who will shape the thinking . . . on economic theory and economic policy for the rest of this century, if not for the next thirty or fifty years."

Schumpeter himself was a revolutionary, writing definitive books and presenting new theories, some wrong, from his twenties until his death at age 67. And the *wunderkind* had a personality to match his professional bona fides. His many exploits and imbroglios made him one of the most colorful of all economists, certainly the polar opposite of the sedate Adam Smith. Schumpeter enjoyed taking different sides in a debate and found something to like in just about everything. "Given the choice between being right and being memorable," remembered colleague John Kenneth Galbraith, "Schumpeter never hesitated."

---

3. See pp. 154–55 and Internet appendix 4.2, "Entrepreneurship in Economics: From Unknown to Missing," at www.politicalcapitalism.org/book1/chapter4/appendix2.html.

4. *Creative destruction* has become the second-most-famous phrase in economics next to Adam Smith's *invisible hand*. Schumpeter's term *business strategy* in the same sentence, which was new, became seminal too.

Capitalism, Socialism, and Democracy

By

JOSEPH A. SCHUMPETER

CHAPTER VII

THE PROCESS OF CREATIVE DESTRUCTION

Figure 4.1 Joseph Schumpeter's personality was as big as his economics. Brilliant, blithe, eclectic, and obsessive, the immaculately attired aristocratic scholar captured the essence of entrepreneurial capitalism with his terms *creative destruction* and *business strategy.*

Among his students, "Schumpy" was a hit because of his grand presence, masterful scholarship, and personal reminiscences. "I set out to become the greatest lover in Vienna, the greatest horseman in Austria, and the greatest economist in the world," Schumpeter would fondly recall. "Alas, for the illusions of youth," he then deadpanned, "as a horseman, I was never really first rate." It was as much jest as braggadocio, remembered one student, M. A. Adelman, who was destined to become the dean of energy economists in his time. But if Schumpeter wasn't the world's greatest economist in the first half of the century, he certainly came close.[5]

---

5. The darkly romantic side of Schumpeter was illustrated by an experience early in his career when he headed a bank in Vienna. Living extravagantly, Schumpeter was asked by his board of directors to be more discreet in his personal affairs. "In response," a friend recalled, "he rented a pair-drawn open [carriage] and rode up and down Kärtnerstrasse—a main boulevard in the inner city—at midday with an attractive blonde prostitute on one knee and a brunette on the other."

᭪

There was no jest a half century later when Ph.D. economist Ken Lay proclaimed a goal for Enron to *become the world's leading company*. His Schumpeterian
view of business strategy drew upon Drucker's *Age of Discontinuity*, which Professor Lay had taught to his graduate economics students at George Washington
University in the early 1970s. A quarter century later, as head of Enron, Lay
discovered Gary Hamel, the leading business guru of the high-flying 1990s.
Also a Drucker disciple, Hamel brought the discontinuity/revolution theme to
new heights, as discussed in Book 3. Hamel's coauthored *Competing for the
Future* (1994) and his *Leading the Revolution* (2000) fueled Enron's vision, values,
and corporate culture. The admiration was mutual. "As much as any company
in the world," Hamel reported in 2000, "Enron has institutionalized a capacity
for perpetual innovation." "Gray-haired revolutionary" Ken Lay, Hamel continued, had "helped create an organization where thousands of people see
themselves as potential revolutionaries." Hamel was a member of the Enron
Advisory Council when the eight-member outside strategy group dissolved
with the company's bankruptcy in December 2001.[6]

The charge at Enron was *Ask Why?* An Enron logo read, *Will you change the
world today?* Ken Lay's business model was to employ and empower the best and
brightest in order to capture the pools of profit that went unnoticed or unexploited
by the stodgy competition. Failures were blessed at Enron, because revolutionary
firms have more misses, not only more hits. Like others in the Schumpeter-Drucker-
Hamel tradition, Ken Lay might have substituted the words *enterprise* for *knowledge*, and *profit* for *learn* in philosopher Karl Popper's declaration:

> To avoid error is a poor ideal; if we do not dare to tackle problems which are so
> difficult that error is almost unavoidable, then there will be no growth of knowl-
> edge [enterprise]. In fact, it is from our boldest theories, including those which
> are erroneous, that we learn [profit] most.

Only it would not be that easy. Shooting for the very top landed Enron at the
very bottom. Ken Lay's company did not have the business model, discipline, or
supermen and -women to match its grandiose vision. Schumpeter, Drucker, and
Hamel could not be blamed. No company should have forgotten self-discipline
in the pretense that genius trumps execution. Path-breaking entrepreneurship
must be accompanied by good management—what Schumpeter called the
"adaptive response" after the *"creative response."* No company, battered by the
competitive gales, should abandon its compass by disregarding and abusing its
accounting systems. But Enron did. Gary Hamel, embarrassed, rushed out a
second edition of *Leading the Revolution*, removing Enron from its pedestal. He had
been fooled, as just about everyone else had, including virtually all Enron's own

---

6. Also see Internet appendix 4.3, "Schumpeter, Drucker, and Hamel," at www.political
capitalism.org/book1/chapter4/appendix3.html.

Figure 4.2 The call for nonlinear business change over incrementalism, enunciated by Peter Drucker and later Gary Hamel, fueled the mighty ambition of Ken Lay and Enron. A slogan for Enron employees stressed the importance of revolutionary change.

employees. The revolution-over-incrementalism model of business strategy was not as robust as had been thought before its exemplar exploded. Revolutionary ambition at Enron yielded revolutionary failure.

Schumpeter recognized a *tendency* toward equilibrium between revolutionary changes. The equilibrating process meant a convergence of costs and selling prices, eliminating profits and losses. Schumpeter's "law of cost" was no more than resources leaving unprofitable areas for profitable ones, which in the absence of further entrepreneurial disruption would leave returns at the rate of interest (zero profits and zero losses). Outside of equilibrium, however, uncertainty prevails: Profits and losses are everywhere and changing and, from the viewpoint of equilibrium, nonordinary.

The "progressive diminution" of entrepreneurial profits and losses means that the first mover must *continually move first* in the quest for extraordinary returns. Enron was caught on both ends of the law of cost. The company's first-mover profits from its premier cash generator, wholesale energy trading, were narrowing, a fact that the company artfully hid with a black-box (non)explanation of how it made its money. With these core earnings under pressure, Enron raced to become the first mover in numerous new ways, many highly experimental and away from its core, in order to keep aloft. Because of institutional breakdowns, however, the company, flying blind, inevitably crashed, disintegrating suddenly and completely once the full nature of its operations became known.

Enron's failed attempt at grand revolutionary change took almost everyone by surprise. There had been little warning, because the company's financial accounting had been falsified so thoroughly and for so long. But a *change-always* business model is very demanding on any firm, even the best. There must be a system of controls to flag and eliminate loss ventures in a timely manner. There must also be respect for broad rules that are intended to check quick-fix decisions and to avoid slippery slopes. As one student of business change wrote: "the more radical the change—the more radical the deviation from the customary path—the more abstract will be the institutions necessary to change, create, or otherwise redirect concrete capabilities in an effective direction." Enron infamously ditched its checks and balances, even time-honored rules of corporate America, in a pell-mell pursuit of first-mover profits.

There are good revolutions and bad ones. There must be continual improvement, or incrementalism, between sea changes. Often, if not quite always, revolution comes by steps, not bounds. Business thinker Jim Collins enriched the Schumpeter-Drucker-Hamel view by noting how good-to-great companies were *disciplined* change makers whose entrepreneurship was less about revolutionary *moments* than revolutionary *process*. In his words:

> Good-to-great transformations never happened in one fell swoop. There was no single defining action, no grand program, no one killer innovation, no solitary lucky break, no wrenching revolution. Good to great comes about by a cumulative process—step by step, action by action, decision by decision, turn by turn of the flywheel—that adds up to sustained and spectacular results.

Success was "an organic evolutionary process . . . a pattern of buildup leading to breakthrough." The "doom loop," noted Collins from his case studies, was "big programs, radical change efforts, dramatic revolutions, chronic restructuring—always looking for a miracle moment or new savior." Collins saw greatness in disciplined thought and action; failure, in "fads and . . . management hoopla." There was no silver bullet, no magic, that could substitute for sustained, well-directed effort.

Gary Hamel touted Enron as a model of successful revolutionary change. Collins, although not mentioning Enron (he had not formally studied it), offered a general theory that was capable of detecting cancerous malignancy at the very time the company was booming. Enron was an *ideal type* for failure in Collins's good-to-great paradigm.

Risk versus Uncertainty: Frank Knight

Frank Knight (1885–1972), much like his contemporary Joseph Schumpeter, questioned professional convention in the area of competition and entrepreneurship. Knight's central interest was business realism, not perfect knowledge and equilibrium. A student of Knight who would go on to win the Nobel Prize in economics, James Buchanan, remembered how "Knight gave those of us who bothered to listen the abiding notion that all is up for intellectual grabs, that much of what paraded as truth was questionable, and that the hallmark of a scholar was his courage in cutting through the intellectual haze."[7] The wholesale substitution of perfect information for business reality had left a vacuum aching to be filled. And it was Frank Knight, noted Schumpeter, who advanced economics by formulating "a profit theory that linked . . . non-insurable uncertainty . . . to rapid economic change."

Knight's doctoral dissertation, published in 1921 as *Risk, Uncertainty and Profit*, challenged the bedrock assumption of "practical omniscience on the part of every member of the competitive system." It was profound and pathbreaking—"the first work of any importance, and in any field of study, that [dealt] explicitly with decision-making under conditions of uncertainty," Peter Bernstein wrote 75 years later in *Against the Gods: The Remarkable Story of Risk*.

Business and the economy were about profits and losses, both reflecting *true uncertainty* borne by entrepreneurs. Knight elucidated capitalist reality by differentiating between measurable *risk* and unmeasurable *uncertainty*. "Uncertainty must be taken in a sense radically distinct from the familiar notion of Risk, from which it has never been properly separated," he explained in one of the most famous dissertation books in the history of economics. "It will appear that a measurable uncertainty, or risk proper . . . is so far different from an unmeasurable one that it is not in effect an uncertainty at all."

Knight gave the example of "throwing a perfect die [versus] the chance that a building will burn." The difference was *qualitative*, not only quantitative. "The first, mathematical or a priori, type of probability is practically never met with in business, while the second is extremely common." Indeed, "it is difficult to think of a business 'hazard' with regard to which it is in any degree possible to calculate in advance the proportion of distribution among the different possible outcomes. This must be dealt with, if at all, by tabulating the results of experience."

Grading uncertainties—and knowing which ones to remove through insurance and hedges—is the stuff of entrepreneurship. "The collection, digestion, and dissemination in usable forms of economic information is one of the staggering

---

7. Knight championed "integrity, competence, and humility" as the paths to truth and objectivity in science, views that were seconded by his fellow economist and methodological soul mate, Ronald Coase.

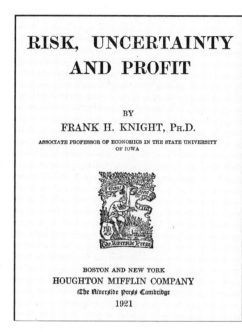

Figure 4.3 Frank Knight's 1921 book advanced economics by differentiating between risk and uncertainty and describing how the former was the exception, given that entrepreneurs incurred costs in the present and received revenues in the future.

problems connected with our modern large-scale social organization," Knight explained. *Intuitive judgment* was the best and only substitute for equilibrium-like information. Error was therefore unavoidable. "The best men would fail in a certain proportion of cases and the worst perhaps succeed in a certain proportion," Knight noted. But the element of bad or good luck would even out over time as more ventures were undertaken. The best entrepreneurs would rise to the top in a market economy.

Knight followed Schumpeter in spelling out the law of equilibration (Schumpeter's law of cost). "The primary attribute of competition, universally recognized and evident at a glance," Knight explained, "is the 'tendency' to eliminate profit or loss, and bring the value of economic goods to equality with their cost." Market learning brings new entrepreneurship through the door opened by prior entrepreneurship. Enron was a first mover in natural gas and electricity trading, a major new area of competitive space created by changes in long-standing government regulation of the industry. Aquila, Duke, Dynegy, El Paso, Williams, and other Fortune 250 companies offered products similar to Enron's and even hired Enron's traders as part of the emulation process. Houston's Smith Street became known as *energy alley,* with several major rivals housed near one another.

Enron's Jeff Skilling, perhaps more than anyone else, saw his company's trading margins shrink through market maturity and sought the Next Big Thing. Meanwhile, Skilling, Lay, and Enron *talked up* the Next Big Thing in order to buy time to find it. There could be no stumbles. The momentum-driven stock was richly priced, and the upward trajectory had to be steep to become (per Lay) the *world's leading energy company* and then the *world's leading company*. Book 3 will describe the harrowing details of a company stuck on a quickening treadmill to trouble.

Knight's distinction between risk and uncertainty elucidates an important façade at Enron. In its last years, the company paraded as a logistics company, a risk manager, arbitraging within and across markets, telling investors that its daily trading positions were hedged. Many trades were offset, but Enron was also taking speculative (nonhedged) positions where price movements of the underlying commodity created net gains and losses. Enron was immersed in uncertainty, not taking the actions necessary to make their trading book price neutral going forward. The company's vaunted "house advantage" as the leading market maker in natural gas and electricity did generate profits, particularly in times of extreme volatility, as during California's electricity crisis of 2000/2001. But Wall Street discounts speculative profits as an indicator of future earnings relative to less risky returns. Enron's ruse, hidden in its big black box, allowed the company's stock to be valued higher—to have a higher price-earnings ratio— than it otherwise would have had. It was a fable of Knightian proportions.

Economic Calculation: Ludwig von Mises

If Joseph Schumpeter was not the world's greatest economist in the first half of the twentieth century, fellow Austrian Ludwig von Mises (1881–1973) could claim the prize. Mises did what no other economist could or would: ground economics on the methodology of purposeful human action and erect a unified, integrated theory upon that edifice. Sober-minded, judicious, uncompromising, and a master logician, Mises took the best from his fellow economic theorists (including Schumpeter and Knight) and unmasked the fallacies that had long plagued the science. His *Human Action: A Treatise on Economics* (1949) is a classic of twentieth-century economics and remains definitive today.

Misesian economics is about mind-centered causal relations, not measurement as in the natural sciences. Equilibrium is not the focus but the foil to reality. Mathematics is demoted as a dangerous distraction because Economic Man does not act mathematically. Markets are not in equilibrium but in flux. A favorite maxim of Mises—"The market is a process"—spoke volumes about his view of business competition and capitalism. Mises was a Schumpeterian and Schumpeter a Misesian on this point, as much as the two diverged in other areas of economic theory.

The firm is a process. These five words also speak volumes but were rarely on the economists' lips, including Mises's. Firms incrementally evolve just as markets and whole economies do, and markets are nothing without firms. Great companies emerge through long sequences of sound decisions, and companies become troubled from the cumulative effect of many unsound choices. Even white-collar crime has a prehistory, a build-up phase, often reflecting a corporate culture amenable to shortsightedness and an ends-justify-the-means mentality.

Intrafirm processes revolve around *economic calculation*, a core concept developed by Mises to contrast capitalism (where such calculation was possible) and socialism (where it was not). Calculation applies to each firm and, indeed, to each and every economic transaction within a firm. The sum of the parts is economic calculation under capitalism.

Informational Chaos under Socialism

In a seminal 1920 essay, Ludwig von Mises refuted the theoretical notion that socialism was economically superior to capitalism. "Where there is no free market, there is no pricing mechanism; without a pricing mechanism, there is no economic calculation," Mises demonstrated. Yet central planning by government had far too much momentum in the 1920s and 1930s to be stopped by a lone essay written in German, a language that many English speakers, including the influential John Maynard Keynes, could not read well. But more important, few intellectuals were *seeking* the verdict that Mises presented in his essay and in the wide-ranging book that followed, *Socialism: An Economic and Sociological Analysis* (1922). There could be no revolution, because so few believed—or even wanted to believe—in the cause.

It would take the economics profession more than a half century to realize the power of Mises's economic-calculation argument. Political victory came for capitalism with the fall of the Berlin Wall in 1989 and the collapse of the Soviet empire shortly thereafter. Intellectual victory was recognized for Mises with an about-face by a popular economist in the socialist camp, Robert Heilbroner, who had previously concluded that Mises's argument had been "effectively demolished."[8] The challenge for socialism, Heilbroner had argued, was less about economics than politics—avoiding bureaucratization at the central planning boards. Heilbroner was the author of 20 books, including *The Worldly Philosophers*, a volume that sold nearly 4 million copies, second only to Paul Samuelson's *Economics* among economics texts. Thus, Heilbroner's revised verdict was heard 'round the intellectual world.

"Less than seventy-five years after it officially began, the contest between capitalism and socialism is over: capitalism has won," Heilbroner wrote in *The New Yorker* in 1989. In "After Communism," a follow-up essay, he recalled how "socialism seemed within easy grasp" back in his student days at Harvard, a

---

8. Mises's student F. A. Hayek was also an intellectual victor in this debate. The views of Hayek, who shared the 1974 Nobel Prize in economics with socialist Gunnar Myrdal, are presented in Internet appendix 4.4, "Economic Calculation Revisited," at www.politicalcapitalism. org/book1/chapter4/appendix4.html.

half century before. The economic-calculation argument of Mises (caricatured as "an Austrian with extremely conservative views") had been glossed over because capitalism itself seemed full of problems. Now, with decades of actual experience with central planning boards, and in light of capitalism's superior output, Mises's argument was revisited. "It turns out, of course, that Mises was right," Heilbroner now concluded.

What was Mises's calculation argument, long ignored but now seen as a prescient explanation of what few had predicted: the collapse of central planning in its strongest of strongholds, Soviet Russia and Eastern Europe? And why was Mises's demonstration, in the opinion of two economists, Peter Boettke and Christopher Coyne, "the most significant contribution to political economy made in the twentieth century"?

"We cannot act economically if we are not in a position to understand economizing," Mises wrote in 1920. Yet no person, not even a genius, can "master all the possibilities of production" in order to rationally decide among them. There are different ends and different means to a chosen end (such as what material to use to build a house). What is needed in all but the most primitive economies is a computational system to register relative scarcities of supply to demand. The common denominator of money is the starting point. But money prices for goods and services cannot be determined willy-nilly. They must reflect *marketplace realities* as determined by consumer decisions to buy and entrepreneurial decisions to produce and sell. The free market accomplishes this as if led by an invisible hand, to use Adam Smith's metaphor.[9]

Economic calculation is absent under socialism because the factors of production are not privately owned. The factors are owned by one giant legal monopoly— the state—which buys and sells to itself in most stages of the structure of production (except at retail). Scarcity prices cannot emerge, because separate firms do not compete. There is no entrepreneurship when entrepreneurs do not own resources and cannot enter, exit, and otherwise compete with new products and terms of purchase. There cannot be consumerism where the bureaucracy, not rival firms, determines the economy's who, what, when, where, and how. Paradoxically, economic planning cannot rationally plan an economy.

Economic calculation is premised upon private-property rights. Private property connotes *ownership*, or "full control of the services that can be derived from a good." Legal rights and institutions establish who owns what at any one time and in what ways property can be used. Owners can sell or trade what they own, lease their property for income, or borrow against their property for

---

9. For questions about prices not capturing the full social costs and benefits, see Internet appendix 4.5, "Externalities and Economic Calculation," at www.politicalcapitalism.org/book1/chapter4/appendix5.html.

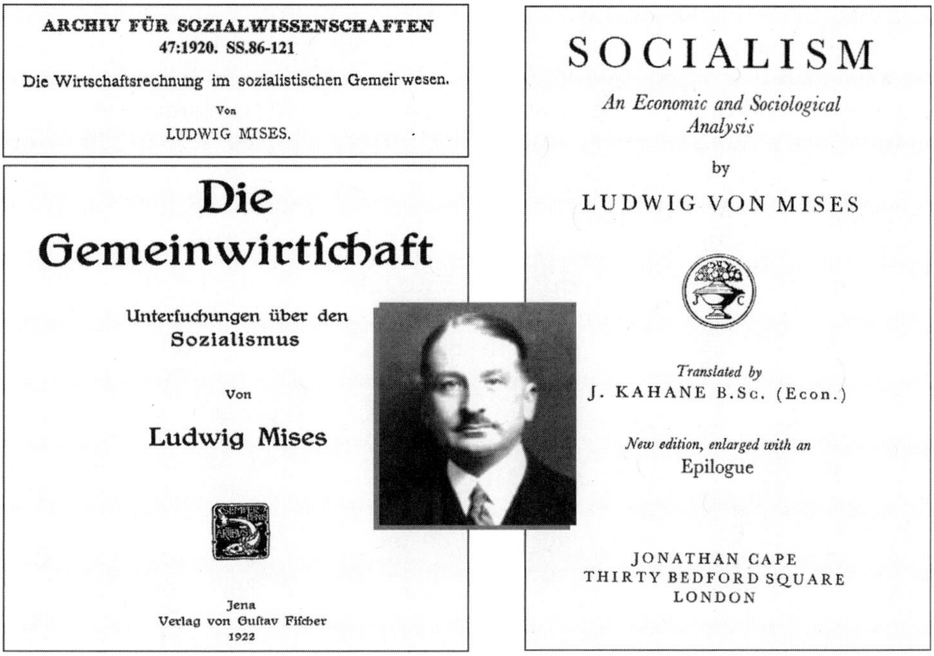

ARCHIV FÜR SOZIALWISSENSCHAFTEN
47:1920. SS.86-121
Die Wirtschaftsrechnung im sozialistischen Gemeirwesen.
Von
LUDWIG MISES.

Die
Gemeinwirtſchaft
Unterſuchungen über den
Sozialismus
Von
Ludwig Mises
Jena
Verlag von Guſtav Fiſcher
1922

SOCIALISM
An Economic and Sociological Analysis
by
LUDWIG VON MISES
Translated by
J. KAHANE B.Sc. (Econ.)
New edition, enlarged with an
Epilogue
JONATHAN CAPE
THIRTY BEDFORD SQUARE
LONDON

Figure 4.4 Ludwig von Mises's concept of economic calculation showed how profit-and-loss capitalism is rational and why socialism works in the dark. Mises's theory, formulated in 1920 and elaborated in book form two years later, entered the professional mainstream of thought after his death in 1973.

capital. And property owners have legal recourse against any person or entity (including the state) that steals or damages their assets.

Unowned assets, however, are not property but *dead capital*, stuck in an extralegal sector governed by political whim and/or the vagaries of an underground economy. Economic incentive is dulled, transaction costs magnified, and capital formation stymied without the wealth-creating advantages of *real* property. Economic calculation—efficiently choosing among competing alternatives—is hampered or entirely removed.[10]

"Capitalism is in crisis outside of the West," noted Peruvian economist Hernando de Soto, "not because international globalization is failing but because developing and former communist nations have been unable to 'globalize' capital

10. For further discussion of this point, see Internet appendix 4.6, "The Institutional Framework of Economic Calculation," at www.politicalcapitalism.org/book1/chapter4/appendix6.html.

within their own countries." Without the institutions to turn assets into property—to turn dead capital into self-help capital—reform efforts have fallen short and even been reversed. Investment climates have worsened. U.S. companies, prominently including Enron, that aggressively invested in countries with insecure property rights and unpredictable regulatory regimes have paid a heavy price.

Accounting and Capitalism

Private property and voluntary exchange through a monetary medium create an array of scarcity prices from which meaningful profit/loss accounting is possible. Indeed, "the fundamental purpose of accounting," stated Arthur Dewing, "is to determine whether or not the business is making a profit." The *income statement* conveys profit or loss during a period; the *balance sheet* and subsidiary information indicate the net worth of a business, or the profit or loss that might be expected for the owner if sold. Such evaluation is part and parcel of economic calculation as explicated by Mises.

In his 1944 book *Bureaucracy*, Mises paid tribute to "the elaborate methods of modern bookkeeping, accountancy, and business statistics" that gave entrepreneurs their bearings. Accounting was both the "compass" and "conscience" of business. He added:

> The devices of bookkeeping and accountancy are so familiar to the businessman that he fails to observe what a marvelous instrument they are. It needed a great poet and writer to appreciate them at their true value. Goethe called bookkeeping by double-entry "one of the finest inventions of the human mind." By means of this, he observed, the businessman can at any time survey the general whole, without needing to perplex himself with the details.

The "sober" work of the financial accountant gives each business scheme, from the simplest to the most elaborate, a verdict. "The cool-headed reckoner is the stern chastiser of the ecstatic visionary," Mises warned, not knowing how prescient his words would be for accounting-related corporate controversies a half century later.

But financial accounting, noted Mises, is not a precise, cut-and-dried exercise. Overhead costs must be assigned to revenues in a nonprecise way. Asset valuation based on historic cost can be very different from market value—and more so in times of inflation.[11] Cost accounting is backward looking; economic calculation, forward looking. Accountancy, as valuable as it is, must always be a step behind in a world of change. Explained Mises:

---

11. Fair-value accounting in place of historic-cost accounting, whereby the firm and auditors estimate the market value of assets, has invited manipulation by firms to help achieve short-term objectives.

> Commercial usages and customs and commercial laws have established definite rules for accountancy and auditing. There is accuracy in keeping of books. But they are accurate only with regard to these rules. The book values do not reflect precisely the real state of affairs. . . . Cost accounting is therefore not an arithmetical process which can be established and examined by an indifferent umpire. It does not operate with uniquely determined magnitudes which can be found out in an objective way. . . . Attempts to establish cost accounts on an "impartial" basis are doomed to failure.

Entrepreneurship, the art of interpreting and profitably acting on imperfect information, includes understanding imperfect financial statements. *Judgment* is necessary, states Mises, making intention and honesty an important component in sustainable business success.

Economic profit (loss) is defined as the excess (deficit) of revenue relative to cost in a particular accounting period. Mises placed great faith in "the incorruptible judgment of an unbribable tribunal: the account of profit and loss." Traditionally, income accounting has matched revenue to associated costs not only when money changes hands (the cash basis) but also when a transaction is finalized and cash is either paid or owed (the accrual method). In either case, the purpose is to portray the true financial state of a business. But accounting method is not intended to help a company be other than what it really is—such as creating a result that helps a business meet an earnings expectation. Reality-based (not cosmetic or otherwise misused) accounting is what Mises associated with market entrepreneurship and capitalism.[12] Mises, after all, did not say that financial accounting *causes* economic calculation; he stated that accounting *enables* economic calculation if market participants gather and interpret the information correctly. "Financial statements must reflect economic reality," as one Misesian-influenced business entrepreneur has emphasized, adding: "Remember, anywhere profit and loss is measured, analysis is also needed to understand what drives those results."

But political influences have distorted the U.S.-codified Generally Accepted Accounting Principles (GAAP).[13] Taking a highly prescriptive, rule-based approach, in large part owing to federal regulation,[14] GAAP has invited firms

---

12. Mises would argue that good accounting would drive out bad given the positive nature of truth and transparency for viable entrepreneurship in a market economy. Or restated, the market would learn to guard against, discount, and ultimately discourage perception-inspired accounting methods and results.

13. Charles Koch adds that where GAAP accounting does not achieve its purpose of describing economic reality, Koch Industries prepares a set of internal statements in addition to its GAAP-conforming external statements.

14. Beginning in the mid-1960s, and particularly from the 1970s onward, the Securities and Exchange Commission, Department of the Treasury, and Congress increasingly came to

(publicly traded firms in particular) and compliant auditors to engage in "earnings management" to achieve a predetermined, desired result. Instead of the *end* of representing reality, accounting became a *means* to make the numbers in order to placate investors. Instead of working from the numbers to the story, a firm could work from the story to the numbers.

Such manipulation has dulled the mighty signals of profit and loss, weakening economic calculation and capitalism itself. A 2005 essay in the *Journal of Economic Perspectives* documented "the deteriorating quality and reliability of corporate profit reports" in the United States, specifically, the routine restatement of earnings to true-up prior accounting opportunism and/or to undo instances of accounting fraud. GAAP opportunism has included accelerating income to the current period, deferring costs to a later period, or manipulating balance-sheet items to dress up the income statement. Enron notoriously played these games, particularly after 1996, when Jeff Skilling replaced Richard Kinder as president of the company. Tax-minimization strategies, such as those used at Enron, have also contributed to the deviation of reported profit and loss from underlying economic reality.

Politicized accounting and taxation in the business sector have contributed to a crisis in corporate accounting. This would not have surprised Mises, who was a critic of government intervention and cognizant of how one intervention leads to another. Gaming regulatory systems is predictable and common, as evidenced by oil trading in the United States under price controls in the 1970s, electricity trading under retail-price ceilings in California in 2000/2001, and accounting and tax-minimization strategies at many times and places.

Market participants learn from mistakes and work to become more successful going forward in free-market capitalism. Accounting abuses of recent years have sharpened the incentive and ability of investors to see through the gloss to find the substance. Still, even imperfect accounting, Mises concluded, "gives to the system of free enterprise that versatility and adaptability which result in an unswerving tendency toward improvement."

Accounting information is a major determinant of resource allocation in a market economy. But *trust* is also a determinant when decisions are made on the basis of interpersonal evaluations rather than numbers. Great trust was placed in Samuel Insull and Ken Lay during their respective heydays. Employees worshiped them. Stockholders *believed*, including laypersons who bought

---

determine, or at least influence, accounting standards otherwise set by private-sector bodies. Predictably, then, corporate lobbying in the standards-setting process accelerated. "On four occasions [from 1985 and 1996], as the flexibility to produce favorable earnings grows in importance to CEOs, industry places pressure on [the Financial Accounting Standards Board] to be more responsive to its objections," one accounting historian found.

stock based on heroic images. Lenders and others believed in the top-of-the-world, indeed *celebrity*, executives. *Great Man* hyperbole inflated the values of Samuel Insull's public-utility empire and Lay's Enron well beyond what was justified in retrospect. Trust can powerfully expedite market decision making, but in the cases of Insull and Lay, trust was placed on an engine that left the tracks.

The Theory of the Firm: Ronald Coase

Economics has long studied the behavior of firms. But the firm itself was assumed rather than explained—a "rhetorical device" depicted by a few cost and revenue curves on a page or blackboard. The firm was defined as a collection of resources under a common management that transformed inputs into outputs. Firms grew with profits and contracted with losses; firms had become bigger and less localized with falling transportation costs; and firms had become more specialized in response to a growing division of labor. Economists also recognized how entrepreneurs and managers sought to uncover—department by department, product by product, person by person—the moneymakers and money losers in order to initiate change.

But why does a firm exist in the first place? Why do people band together in one enterprise rather than work separately, each selling his or her services to the other in the arm's-length marketplace? Relatedly, what determines the boundaries of a firm? Why are some firms big and others small, some firms integrated and others not? An inquiring young mind would formulate the right questions and find the answer.

Ronald Coase (b. 1910) entered the London School of Economics in 1929 to pursue a business degree. In his second year, he attended a seminar taught by Arnold Plant, a "commonsense" economist who specialized in business. There, Coase was introduced to Adam Smith's notion of the invisible hand. "[Plant] explained that the economic system was coordinated by the pricing system," remembered Coase. "I was a socialist at the time, and all this was news to me." The seminar on industrial organization discussed why firms expanded horizontally (buying a competitor) or vertically (buying a supplier for, or purchaser of, its own products).

Coase was puzzled. Markets worked and socialism did not, because of the prerequisite of competitive pricing to perform economic calculation. Yet the firm ("that little planned society") was outside the price system (open market) as defined by arm's-length transactions. Corporations seemed to be getting bigger and bigger, and Lenin had talked about Russia as One Big Factory. How did all this square?

To find out, Coase traveled to the United States in 1931/32 on fellowship. It was an active, productive venture, although his destination was in the throes of the Great Depression. Coase visited many leading companies—Allis Chalmers,

Ford Motor, General Motors, Montgomery Ward, Sears Roebuck, and Union Carbide, among others. He quizzed leading economists and even happened upon classes taught by Frank Knight at the University of Chicago. Coase sought out Norman Thomas, the Socialist Party candidate for president of the United States, and read books on business organization, including studies by the Federal Trade Commission. Coase studied the business directory in the cities he visited, fascinated by the division of companies within each industry. All this effort was much better than reading the "absolute bilge" in the economics journals, Coase remembered.[15]

It took innumerable queries and worn-out shoes, but Coase found his answer. "I was then twenty-one years of age and the sun never ceased to shine," Coase would tell a gathering in Stockholm, Sweden, in December 1991. "I could never have imagined that these ideas would become some 60 years later a major justification for the award of a Nobel Prize."

Coase's theory, which he had formulated to his satisfaction in 1934, was published as "The Nature of the Firm" in *Economica* three years later. "The main reason why it is profitable to establish a firm would seem to be that there is a cost of using the price mechanism," Coase famously stated. But what did this mean, exactly?

A firm exists, he explained, because it is cheaper to work collectively under a few broad rules and open-ended contracts than it would be for the employees to split apart, rely on arm's-length agreements, and get the same business done ("using the price mechanism"). Compared to the *you're hired* handshake and working alongside one another, pursuant to a general understanding regarding salary, budget, and office norms, individuals as firms would have to spend more time negotiating and renegotiating arm's-length contracts, inspecting performance, and resolving disputes. Knocking on the door of an officemate is easier than more formal communications to get expectations realigned or a contract amended. "The operation of a market costs something, and by forming an organization and allowing some authority (an 'entrepreneur') to direct the resources, certain marketing costs are saved," Coase noticed. "It is true that contracts are not eliminated when there is a firm but they are greatly reduced." Coase's marketing costs—the costs of arranging economic activity—would come to be called *transaction*, *information*, or *friction* costs, terms that every business and economics student learns today. Organizational theory, building on

---

15. "When economists find that they are unable to analyze what is happening in the real world," Coase explained, "they invent an imaginary world which they are capable of handling. It was not a procedure I wanted to follow in the 1930s. It explains why I tried to find the reason for the existence of the firm in factories and offices rather than in the writings of economists, which I irreverently labeled as 'bilge.'"

ECONOMICA   [NOVEMBER 1937]

The Nature of the Firm
By R. H. COASE

Figure 4.5 A youthful Ronald Coase solved a problem that economists had hardly bothered to ask: Why do workers bundle together in a firm rather than operate autonomously in a market? His Nobel Prize–winning insights from 1937 would influence Enron's business model under CEO Jeff Skilling.

Coase, recognizes the role of *nonprice planning* in a firm and the competitive advantage gained from, in Edith Penrose's words, "the cumulative growth of knowledge, in the context of a purposive firm."

Coase's breakthrough allowed him to understand the boundaries of the firm. The entrepreneur uses economic calculation (money prices) to assess the costs and benefits of adding or subtracting a function (or resource, given a function). The question is always, *Should the function be done inside the firm or purchased on the market?* The more often the economic calculation is made to perform the activity internally, the larger the firm (and vice versa), other things being equal.[16]

---

16. Also see Internet appendix 4.7, "Markets within a Firm," at www.politicalcapitalism. org/book1/chapter4/appendix7.html.

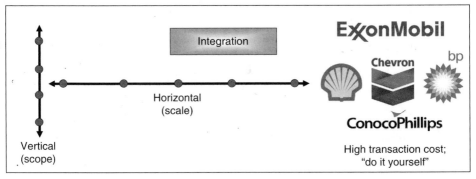

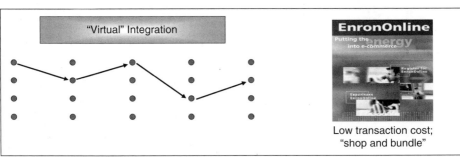

Figure 4.6   EnronOnline was touted by CEO Jeff Skilling as an effective substitute for vertical integration in the new world of low transaction costs. Companies could *virtually* integrate by buying and assembling the parts via the Internet.

"I have made no innovations in high theory," Coase humbly began his Nobel acceptance speech. But with his concept of marketing costs, Coase *was* immersed in high theory, which unlocked the nature of the firm and led to whole new ways of thinking. Yet Coase distanced himself from mainstream economics, since microeconomics was mired in the equilibrium-always, perfect-knowledge world, where information costs were zero and firms were frozen. Not being formally trained in economics was a blessing. "I started . . . with an education in commerce," recalled Coase, so "when I began to study economics it was with a view to using it to understand what happened in the real world." Still, in time, Coase's contribution would become core to economics, complementing the work of Schumpeter, Knight, and Mises in understanding the nature of capitalist enterprise.

Ronald Coase's theory of the firm was a driver at Enron. Whereas Ken Lay's business model was broadly Schumpeterian, Jeff Skilling's model was specifically Coasian. Enron's wholesale marketing operation, encompassing hundreds of products, mostly in gas and electricity but also pulp and paper, steel, water, and broadband, went online in late 1999. EnronOnline soon became the leading business-to-business offering on the Internet, just as Amazon.com became the leading business-to-consumer retailer. Skilling pronounced the coming end of the integrated oil company, given the radical reduction of transaction costs provided by the new medium. "You will see the collapse and demise of the integrated energy companies around the world," he said. "They are going to break up into thousands and thousands of pieces." At a minimum, for example, such a firm would pick its most preferred activity—say, refining—and sell its assets in exploration and production, transportation, and wholesaling to other parties and then turn to the Internet to deliver the whole product to its name-brand dealers (see Figure 4.6).

Enron would declare bankruptcy about one year after then-CEO Skilling gave this new-economy speech at Arthur Andersen's Energy Symposium 2000. Ken Lay would be back as CEO of Enron, reassuming the title he had awarded to Skilling six months before. Skilling, meanwhile, holed up in his River Oaks mansion just a few miles from his old company, watched Enron implode, terrified. It had been just three months since he had quit his once dream job, citing exhaustion and frustration with the company's sagging stock price. Obviously, there was a great disconnect between Coase's unassailable theory and the business model Skilling based on it. Disequilibrium economics explained, but certainly did not financially insulate, uncertainty-bearing entrepreneurship. What was responsible for this divergence of theory and practice will be covered in Book 3.

Conclusion

Economics is about business in the real world. Real-world business is about entrepreneurship. Entrepreneurship is about risk versus uncertainty, economic calculation (profit/loss accounting), and the theory of the firm. Yet these central concepts can hardly be found in many contemporary textbooks in microeconomics or managerial economics.

Apologetic professors like to say *We know all that* when it comes to the contributions of the Big Four of enterprise economics. But by failing to make the economics of uncertainty and change explicit, even in introductory material, a good bit of the common sense behind business activity is left unappreciated by students and businesspeople. Complained Mark Blaug, a leading historian of economic thought:

> It is a scandal that nowadays students of economics can spend years in the study of the subject before hearing the term "entrepreneur," that courses in economic development provide exhaustive lists of all the factors impeding or accelerating economic growth without mentioning the conditions under which entrepreneurship languishes or flourishes, and that learned comparisons

between "socialism" and "capitalism" are virtually silent about the role of entrepreneurship under regimes of collective rather than private ownership.

Business reality is core economics, bringing theory and experience together in a compelling way. Such high theory helps one to unravel complexity and understand the rise and fall of business titans and their companies.

5

The Business of Politics

NEWSPAPER EDITORIALISTS, AUTHORS, and academics have closely linked Enron to capitalism. In so doing, they have used different terms to describe the economic system in which Enron thrived and then perished: *American capitalism, modern capitalism, cowboy capitalism,* and *crony capitalism.* Each modified *ism* was intended to portray how greed, opportunism, and boom/bust cycles overwhelmed an inadequately regulated system.

Holders of the Enron-as-capitalism view had the scent but failed to bag the prey. Enron was more a creature of political capitalism than of free-market, consumer-driven capitalism. Ken Lay was an adroit political entrepreneur—exploiting and creating private/public opportunities in his grand and ultimately tragic quest to create the world's leading company. The magnitude and range of Enron's political dealings—in natural gas production, transmission, and marketing; electricity generation and marketing; air-emissions trading; and international infrastructure development—were unique. The high-flying company mined the politicized tax and accounting codes to advantage—even fathering a few provisions along the way. Enron was the best at what it did, but the company's business boom and political largesse, and at times machinations, could not have occurred outside the vibrant framework of largely symbiotic business/government relations built up through the course of U.S. history.

Ken Lay and Enron were the political heirs of Samuel Insull, whose industry leadership and lobbying are the subject of Book 2. Insull's energy-utility empire formed the nation's largest holding company by the early 1930s, a culmination of his half century in electricity. Enron rose to the top of the natural gas industry and then challenged electricity providers by changing the rules and entering their markets. In important ways, political capitalism in twentieth-century America began with the rise of Samuel Insull and climaxed with the fall of Ken Lay.

◇·

Historical interpretation is only as sound as the theory behind it. The theory of political capitalism draws on three premises. The first is the *primacy of economic motivation*—which posits that pecuniary ends, rather than any nonmonetary values, drive business decision making. Dollar-driven executives have pragmatically sought government help in an environment in which it was considered permissible not only by their peers but by intellectuals, the media, and consumers as well.

The second tenet is *capitalist reality*, the incessant pressure on firms to make profits and avoid losses under open competition, even after resorting to mergers and informal alliances in the attempt to tame rivalry. There has never been a free-market era in which bigness insulated a firm from the gales of competitive destruction.

The third premise of political capitalism is the *economics of politics*, which holds that government officials are open to, and benefit from, aiding business. The intersection of business and government is the meeting of demand and supply. Business demands or buys intervention to enhance profitability; government supplies or sells intervention for favors received. Self-interest propels the deal from both sides, which also means that business may not seek or want government involvement if it is not to its benefit, and politicians and regulators may not want to grant special favors to businesses (aka corporate welfare) if doing so would be unpopular with voters. Or, politicians might side with reformers or other special interests against business groups for particular reasons. Still, for most of American history, government intervention in the economy often has been business driven.

Political Capitalism

Political capitalism (as opposed to free-market capitalism) is a socioeconomic system in which legislation and ensuing regulation are inspired and influenced primarily by organized business interests. Historian Gabriel Kolko defined political capitalism as "the utilization of political outlets to . . . allow corporations to function in a predictable and secure environment permitting reasonable profits over the long run." Although alternatives exist in theory, such as *laissez-faire capitalism* on one end and *social-welfare capitalism* on the other,[1] Kolko's research led him to conclude that "political capitalism has been inherent in capitalism at every stage."

But contra Kolko, capitalism did not *have* to be political. Kolko's Marxist framework viewed entrepreneurial capitalism as inherently unstable, thus

---

1. Social-welfare capitalism is not as easily specified as is laissez-faire capitalism (the separation of government and economy), but it can be described (in ideal terms, at least) as capitalism modified by pluralistic, public-interested, and enlightened government intervention. See appendix B, pp. 332–35.

inevitably leading business executives to the government trough in search of acceptable profits.[2] Libertarian theorist Murray Rothbard, while embracing Kolko's historical findings, came to different conclusions. To Rothbard, free-market capitalism was a rational, price-coordinated system driven by entrepreneurial profits and losses. The free market did not have to be political, but it could be (and was) political, because interventionism was embraced by intellectuals, voters, government, and business leaders.

Political entrepreneurship, called *rent-seeking* in the academic literature,[3] drives political capitalism. Deal making typically starts on the private side when a business or a trade association seeks a subsidy or a regulation for competitive advantage. The losers—taxpayers, consumers, and/or targeted competitors—typically have been less politically organized.

Business interests are not monolithic. "There are as many objections as there are differing economic interests," a federal court arbitrating a regulatory dispute once noted. Often, a firm or a business group opposes another firm or business group on a legislative or regulatory issue. Any combination of special interests or reformers can join a business interest against another business interest. The crucial question is: *Would the intervention have taken place without active business support?* In a regime of political capitalism, the answer is typically no.

Business can include a variety of parties on either side of a transaction (e.g., shippers or railroads). Political capitalism occurs when any particular business or business class, big or small, shifts the balance toward or against passage of legislation. It may be the case that reformer-driven politics causes business interests to participate in a defensive role. Nevertheless, to the extent that the final legislation is amended because of business participation, political capitalism slips in through the back door.

Political capitalism can morph into *special-interest capitalism* under which a variety of constituencies, not only business, win special favors outside a consumer-driven, free-market process. Their particular cause may or may not be in the public interest. Good intentions are not enough where there are many losers from intervention. In recent decades, a plethora of public-interest groups have imparted greater pluralism than ever before, but business interests may also lurk within these groups (which critics see as being front groups for business).

Political capitalism was alive and well during the eras of Samuel Insull and Ken Lay. Business in some organized form has been the single most important driver of legislation and administrative regulation in twentieth-century America. It was, truly, a century of political capitalism, as chapter 6 documents.

---

2. See Internet appendix 5.1, "Kolko and Schumpeter on Capitalist Stagnation and Instability," at www.politicalcapitalism.org/book1/chapter5/appendix1.html.

3. James Buchanan has defined rent-seeking as "allocatively unnecessary payment [made] in institutional settings where individual efforts to maximize value generate social waste rather than social surplus."

Capitalists versus Capitalism

To a merchant, positive competition is that which drives down costs by reducing the price of what is bought, whereas negative competition is what drives down the merchant's income by reducing the price of what is sold. Thus, from time immemorial, pragmatic merchants have insisted that *good* competition be free of government interference, while demanding that government address *unfair* competition. Adam Smith warned against those tradesmen who "in order to confine the competition to as small a number of persons as possible, endeavoured to subject the trade to many burdensome regulations." The wealth of nations did not come from protecting merchants from their rivals, domestic or foreign, Smith explained. Wealth came from the cheapness of goods created by an international division of labor. The protected firm was a drag on the system. "To be merely useless, indeed, is perhaps the highest eulogy which can ever justly be bestowed upon a regulated company," the father of economics declared.

Adam Smith's concern about the "monopolizing spirit" of capitalists made him an early foe of political entrepreneurship—and political capitalism as a system. Two centuries later, Ayn Rand expressed contempt for what she called the "money appropriator," the phony capitalist who mined the system for political spoils. Following earlier libertarian theorists, Rand sharply distinguished between the economic and political means to business success. The former concerns voluntary patronage in an open marketplace; the latter coercively seeks to limit competition or gain special subsidies. The former produces wealth; the latter merely redistributes it. The political is a "parasitic relationship," she added, because wealth must be *created* before it can be *redistributed*. Adam Smith and Ayn Rand, two centuries apart, recognized the difference between capitalism and political capitalism and fought a common foe.

To their credit, many leading advocates of an open, free, competitive economy were sincere and consistent reformers, opposed to class gain through government favor and special favor to business such as subsidies or tariffs.[4] They were not apologists for the status quo; nor did they try to redefine laissez-faire to include probusiness intervention, as did some intellectuals.

But a very different view of capitalists versus capitalism entered the textbooks. "FDR's historic function was to rescue capitalism from the capitalists," observed historian Arthur Schlesinger Jr. Was President Roosevelt chastising business executives for undermining capitalism by rent-seeking? Hardly! Schlesinger's Keynesian worldview portrayed FDR as galloping in on a white horse, with swords held high, to save the system from itself. One saber was his alphabet soup of social-welfare programs designed to comfort the victimized masses;

---

4. Such promarket intellectuals in the annals of libertarian thought included Herbert Spencer, William Graham Sumner, Edward Atkinson, and Benjamin Tucker in the United States and Vilfredo Pareto, Gustave de Molinari, Frederic Bastiat, and J. B. Say in Europe.

the other was macroeconomic planning to lead America out of the Great Depression and prevent its recurrence. But did capitalism really cause the economic collapse that began in 1929 during the presidency of Herbert Hoover? And did FDR's New Deal, which began after his election in 1932, end it?[5]

Chapter 6 challenges Schlesinger's interpretation. The New Deal predated FDR in many respects from the public side (Herbert Hoover) and the private side (rent-seeking capitalists). Seen in this light, FDR rescued *political* capitalism for the political capitalists, not capitalism from the capitalists.

The debate continues. *Saving Capitalism from the Capitalists* (2003) by Raghuram Rajan and Luigi Zingales disputes the conventional view that the Enron collapse occurred because "markets have become too free." Enron's markets were regulated typically because the involved (political) capitalists wanted them that way. "Under the continuous pressure of vested interests, markets are always too restricted, never too free," the authors posited.

Business is institutionalized opportunism. Its leaders are pragmatic and seize political as well as market opportunities to capture profits. The mercantilist era (1500–1800) cemented business/government activism. Thus it was not surprising to find that merchants and builders in America's first few decades were alert to the possibilities afforded by government favor. The doctrine of laissez-faire had general appeal as a founding principle of the nation, and the platitudes of freedom of association were trumpeted by business leaders in labor disputes. But this line of argument was quickly forgotten when subsidies and protective regulation were in reach.

The vestiges of doctrinal laissez-faire weakened as government intervention grew. Business leaders, remarked Gabriel Kolko, increasingly came to "regard politics . . . as an important part of their larger position in society." Business pleas for government rules to promote reasonable profits became commonplace. Small and large businesses sang from the same hymnal, although song and verse could be different.

Business executives preferred to avoid peripheral issues, reflecting, in the estimation of Robert Heilbroner, "a profound unwillingness to get embroiled in anything that might take them away from their jobs, or that might not look good in the newspapers, or that might displease their main customers or their boards." But it was an entirely different matter when their profitability was on the line.

Political entrepreneurship has been primarily *reactive*, responding to emerging threats to established product lines. *Proactive* rent-seeking to create new profit centers has been rarer. Through it all, a "striking absence of real world

---

5. The Keynesian underconsumption/overproduction theory of the Great Depression is critically examined in Internet appendix 6.1, "'Overproduction' and the Business Cycle," at www.politicalcapitalism.org/book1/chapter6/appendix1.html.

political commitment," as Heilbroner put it, allowed leaders to straddle different issues differently—and sometimes inconsistently.

Enron's Ken Lay, a Ph.D. economist and former regulator with a gift for all things interpersonal, was a master political capitalist. His political forays could be reactive—addressing downturns in Enron's mature business lines from unwanted market shifts—or proactive—creating wholly new opportunities outside the free market. This story, as well as that of another gifted political rent seeker, Samuel Insull, comes later in this trilogy.

The Primacy of the Economic

Moneymaking was alive and well in the petty-capitalist era. "A passion for bourgeois comfort spread everywhere in the seventeenth century," wrote historians Charles and Mary Beard. "A frenzy for traffic animated all classes in England; the love of money and the trading spirit 'permeated all departments of life and influenced almost every sentiment.'" This was the world of commerce that fascinated Adam Smith and other Scottish Enlightenment thinkers studied.

The "fundamental proposition" of *The Communist Manifesto*, published by Karl Marx and Friedrich Engels in 1848, was that "the prevailing mode of economic production and exchange, and the social organization necessarily following from it, form . . . the political and intellectual history of that epoch." At the turn of the century, social critic Thorstein Veblen recognized that "modern politics is business politics." Not only domestic but also foreign policy, he added, "has much of a pecuniary color."

These disparate thinkers—capitalist critics all—recognized the fundamentality of economic motivation in human action and thus the pecuniary demand side of the business/government exchange. Religious and philosophical motivations were present in some or many issues, but the chief concern of American householders was securing the economic necessities of life and, perhaps, even leaving a residual for their descendants. Business legislation reflected the interests of many hungry breadwinners.

Thus, it was natural for business interests to seek and win pecuniary favor from government. It did not go unnoticed. "I see no force in modern society which can cope with the power of capital handled by talent, and I cannot doubt that the greatest force will control the other forces," wrote American economist William Graham Sumner in 1905.

A decidedly *economic* interpretation of American history sprang forth from prominent American intellectuals after 1900. Instead of understanding America's past as the manifestation of a particular philosophical theme—such as freedom, tolerance, democracy, or equality—or tracing the intellectual history of a few great men, the *progressive historians* saw economic interests as primary to social and political change. New interpretations of the origins of the Constitution (Charles Beard, 1874–1948), the frontier (Frederick Jackson Turner, 1861–1932), and reform (V. L. Parrington, 1874–1948) made America's past, according to Richard Hofstadter, "relevant to the political intellectual issues of the moment."[6] A political scientist, Arthur Bentley, was also part of this development, discussed later in this chapter.

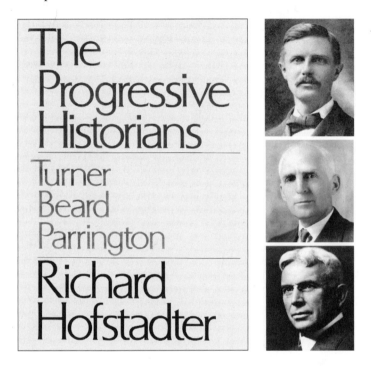

Figure 5.1 After the turn of the century, a new school of historians saw U.S. history as an economic and political conflict among various interests. The three most important were (top to bottom) Frederick Jackson Turner of the University of Wisconsin, Charles Beard of Columbia University, and V. L. Parrington of the University of Oklahoma.

Interest-group politics—"rough and sordid, hidden and neglected"—was now the historians' Rosetta stone. Business life and political economy came to the fore. The operative question became, "Who has control, and what do they want?"

The study of history took on higher meaning. What was once simply a pastime for the contented and well-to-do became intellectual grist for "new

---

6. This did not mean that their analyses were correct. Beard's thesis, in particular, would come under withering criticism from later historians who determined that the founding fathers were ideologically driven by the good of social and political freedom and not financially driven by their nation-building work.

types of Americans who were beginning to constitute a productive, insurgent intelligentsia."[7] Much work remained to turn the new, economically conscious, reform-minded history into a sound understanding of rapid industrialization and capitalistic progress. That would prove to be a major challenge for the next generation of historians—and political scientists as well.

Capitalist Reality

Understanding free-market competition, or what economist Joseph Schumpeter captured in the notion of "capitalist reality," is crucial for the Insull and Enron stories. Schumpeter's conception of incessant change and *creative destruction* has entered the mainstream of thought today, but he fought and lost an important debate within the economics profession in his day on the nature of competition in the real world.

By the 1940s, when Schumpeter presented his theory, mainstream economics embraced the benchmark of *perfect-competition*, an idealized theory predicated on the assumption of numerous, identical firms selling an identical product, thus driving prices down to the cost of production.[8] The maximum quantity was produced with the minimum of resources and sold at the lowest sustainable price—hence *perfect-competition*. Although a few agricultural products and the stock market might approximate some of these conditions, little else did.

Despite its overly theoretical nature, and one at odds with the real world's entrepreneurial adjustment process, perfect-competition became the yardstick by which the market was measured—and found wanting.[9] Big business, with its monopolistic practices, including seller influence over price, left capitalism with a black eye—or what economists called *imperfect* and, later, *monopolistic* competition.

Schumpeter dismissed the theory of perfect-competition as "imaginary," a "textbook picture" that failed to comprehend either capitalism or progress. Neither was it an ideal. "A perfectly competitive industry was apt to be routed

---

7. Richard Hofstadter described American historians in the nineteenth century as "working in the tradition of the great amateurs," "a conservative class of men writing for a conservative public."

8. The technical conditions assumed by the perfect-competition model include a very large number of identical rivals, costless (free) entry and exit by each individual firm, perfect information, perfect product divisibility and homogeneity, no unpaid-for costs or benefits (no externalities), and no increasing/decreasing returns to scale. Such unrealistic assumptions defined Harold Hotelling's 1931 derivation of the rate of depletion of a fixed resource (chapter 8), which misled a generation of energy economists.

9. The attraction of perfect-competition in the economics profession is described in Internet appendix 5.2, "The 'Remarkable' Influence of Perfect-Competition Theory," at www.political capitalism.org/book1/chapter5/appendix2.html.

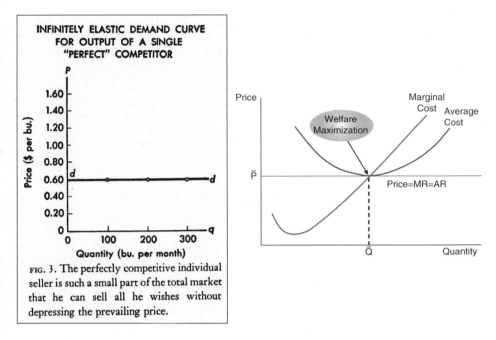

FIG. 3. The perfectly competitive individual seller is such a small part of the total market that he can sell all he wishes without depressing the prevailing price.

Figure 5.2 Despite its limiting assumptions, perfect-competition theory became a benchmark for judging business performance. Over the objections of some leading economists, the theory would dominate the classroom and journals, beginning from at least Paul Samuelson's first edition of *Economics* in 1948 (left).

under the impact of progress or of external disturbance that is big business," he argued.

Translated: Capitalism's spectacular success in raising living standards had very little to do with perfect-competition. Capitalism was a "perennial gale of creative destruction" by which entrepreneurship introduced *change*—what Schumpeter identified as "the new consumers' goods, the new methods of production or transportation, the new markets, the new forms of industrial organization." Schumpeter's world of leap-frog innovation added value in large denominations, whereas perfect-competition hypothetically wrung pocket change from preexisting goods and services.

Schumpeter's entrepreneurship, indeed, is not about perfecting routines in a sea of givens—the closest perfect-competition can get to reality. Capitalism is all about firms continually innovating to, in Schumpeter's words, "keep on their feet, on ground that is slipping away from under them." Progress comes from creation and obsolescence under conditions of constant change—what metaphorically can be called "disequilibriating" movement.

"Creative destruction," Schumpeter explained, is "what capitalism consists in and what every capitalist concern has got to live in." Free-market competition is "an ever-present threat" that "disciplines before it attacks." Not even the sole provider of a particular good or service was immune from competition so long as new entry was *possible* (that is, not illegal). This explains why leaders of incumbent utilities sought the regulatory covenant of franchise protection in return for rate regulation, a battle that Samuel Insull fought and won for the electricity industry. The so-called *natural monopolists* were not so natural after all.[10]

Joseph Schumpeter was not on the professional fringe with his contrary view of competition. Schumpeter stood as "the most interesting economist of his time." A combination *enfant terrible* and *wunderkind*, he began his career in the 1910s with a flurry of publications reexamining the foundations of economics. He died in 1950 at age 67 as Harvard University's most distinguished professor of economics.[11]

How could one of the most respected economists of the twentieth century, common sense in hand, fail to dislodge the benchmark of perfect-competition? Like Erich Zimmermann's functional theory of mineral resources, the subject of chapter 8, Schumpeter's creative-destruction theory flew in the face of methodological fashion. The "invariant conditions" of perfect-competition may not have been geared for capitalist reality, but the construct's continuous curves of cost, revenue, price, and quantity gave so-called neoclassical economists a model for mathematical derivations and equilibrium diagrams. *Let's assume* would launch many an economist joke, but *let's assume* also launched innumerable research programs and journal articles for the ranks.[12]

Entrepreneurial competition—the real world of capitalism that interested Schumpeter—cannot be mathematically captured. Economic magnitudes are lumpy, not continuous functions amenable to differential equations. The passage of time introduces intractable unknowns and, indeed, the very profit or loss that a world of perfect certainty cannot generate. So-called literary economists can describe the capitalistic process, and economic historians (applied economists) can mine real-world examples for insight and wisdom. But only a gifted few can advance the theoretical edifice. Schumpeter, one of those few, was unable to persuade the majority of his colleagues to forego their mathematical

---

10. Book 2 details Insull's lobbying effort, as well as an example of firm-to-firm competition in natural gas distribution in Houston, Texas, involving Houston Natural Gas, a predecessor company to Enron.

11. Schumpeter's résumé included the presidencies of the American Economic Association, Econometric Society, and International Economic Association.

12. Many academic economists chose their profession precisely because they enjoyed and were skilled at mathematics, diagrammatic exposition, and model building. With a different methodology in economics, many of these individuals would have chosen another profession, perhaps in the natural sciences or engineering, where reality was amenable to their method.

THE BUSINESS OF POLITICS

fun. The triumphant majority, intoxicated with technique and basking in originality, was engaged in obscurantism and irrelevancy, portraying something
other than what was really at work. Schumpeter could only fret about the traffic
of professional essays and government reports that judged business strategy
and events statically. Perfect-competition against the backdrop of the real world,
he complained, was like *"Hamlet* without the Danish prince."

·◇·

"Schumpeter's preoccupation with the dynamics of economic life broke the
spell of the static approach to economic problems," reported an entry in a leading encyclopedia of economic thought. If only that were true! Schumpeter
scarcely turned the ship. Paul Samuelson, with an economics textbook translated into more than two dozen languages schooling tens of millions, judged
the imperfect world from a perfect-competition standard. Said his inaugural
edition, dated 1948:

> An even more serious deviation from perfect-competition [than entrepreneurial
> error] results from *monopoly elements.* These result in wrong pricing, distorted
> profit uses, incorrect and wasteful resource allocation. A monopolist is not a fat,
> greedy man with a big moustache and cigar who goes around violating the law.
> If he were, we could put him in jail. *He is anyone important enough to affect the prices
> of the things he sells and buys.* To some degree that means almost every businessman,
> except possibly the millions of farmers who individually produce a negligible
> fraction of the total crop.

A textbook on business regulation published a decade later also used perfect-
competition as its normative ideal:

> One of the basic requisites of a private enterprise economy . . . is competition.
> Competition refers to the market situation among buyers and sellers of goods
> and services in which no one person, or group of persons acting in concert, is able
> to exercise any control over the conditions of sale. . . . Actual markets, however,
> manifest many imperfections.

From this prima facie foundation of the-more-the-better, markets with large
firms were judged *oligopolistic* or *monopolistic.* As one economist described it, the
"workhorse statistic" of concentration ratios—measuring the market share of the
top four or eight firms in an industry—became shorthand for describing competition or the lack of it and thus the basis for the Federal Trade Commission to
approve or block a merger. Competition as a measurable state rather than a
ceaseless process of entrepreneurial adjustment was a far cry from the Schumpeterian view of capitalist action in which success changed from day to day, and
a firm's market share was the fleeting residue of the competitive process.

The lost paradigm of real-world rivalry would be kept alive by a small but
talented band of economists in the next decades, each exploring such disequilibrium concepts as *discovery, alertness, experience, knowledge, error, revision,* and

feedback. Institutions, the legal and social framework governing exchange, were important to understanding competition. Other disequilibrium touchstones, *discontinuity* and *revolution*, would be key terms in the Enron lexicon.

But these Schumpeter-inspired concepts could not be portrayed by diagrams or mathematics—the language of choice for academic economists. Technique defeated everyday business understanding in competition theory—and defeated a whole school of logic-based, qualitative economics: Austrian School, or market-process, economics.[13]

Decades after Schumpeter's death, entrepreneurship reentered the discussion of theoretical economics, and perfect-competition came to be forthrightly characterized for what it was all along—a highly conditional theory. But the demotion was through the back door and only as an afterthought. Meanwhile, two generations of capitalist critics and mainstream historians followed perfect-competition theory down a blind alley. These lost souls saw the American economy as monopolistic rather than as a hotbed of competition, and they failed to grasp how capitalism evolved into political capitalism: how *market entrepreneurship* routinely turned into *political entrepreneurship* in times of business need. Mainstream economists' "wishful thinking," as Schumpeter put it, blinded government officials and other social scientists into thinking that competitive stress under capitalism was "all make-believe."

Competition theory is important to the Enron story in yet another way. In the 1990s, Enron affiliate Transwestern Pipeline Company used a Schumpeterian/capitalist-reality framework in an attempt to persuade the Federal Energy Regulatory Commission (FERC) to find its interstate gas market sufficiently competitive for rate deregulation. FERC, wed to perfect-competition theory and rigid formulas for determining workable competition, disagreed. Not only that, FERC instructed Transwestern to withdraw its testimony because it uncomfortably challenged the neoclassical theory on which the agency judged competition.

The Self-Interest Theory of Government

Politics has always had a manipulative side. James Madison (1751–1836) wrestled with the problem of how constitutional government could check "the violence of faction," whereby "men of factious tempers, of local prejudices, or of sinister design, may, by intrigue, by corruption, or by other means, first obtain the suffrages, and then betray the interests, of the people." To Madison, the challenge of a "well constructed Union" was to defuse conflicts of interest "by giving

---

13. Austrian economics was founded by Carl Menger (a contemporary of chapter 7's W. S. Jevons) and was developed in the twentieth century primarily by Ludwig von Mises (1881–1973) and F. A. Hayek (1899–1992). Schumpeter grew up in Austria, trained in Austrian School economics, and held an Austrian School view of competition, but his other views were too eclectic to label him a mainstream Austrian School economist.

to every citizen the same opinions, the same passions, and the same interests." The father of the Constitution and future president of the United States was no idle thinker; his wisdom was distilled from years of legislative wrestling in the Virginia Assembly and then the U.S. Congress.

Madison's beginning would be complemented by a tradition of thought that only recently has entered into the mainstream of social science. It began with some early political economists whose work was marginalized by intellectual fashion. It was advanced by Arthur Bentley, the man who would become the father of modern political science. Only with the emergence of the Public Choice School of economics in the 1970s, adding empirical heft to the rediscovered insights of Bentley, would the economic theory of government enter the textbooks.

Early Political Economists

Economics was once all about the real world. A group of early American economists, political economists all, recognized how and why special interests violated the general interest. Tariffs were the great educator, as they were for Adam Smith. Arthur Perry, the holder of an endowed chair in history and political economy at Williams College, wrote in *Elements of Political Economy* (1878) that "our present tariff and all such tariffs . . . are always laid at the instance, and under the pressure, of the special interests protected." The opposite was scarcely imaginable. "No legislator, on general principles, and without solicitation from individuals, ever framed, or would ever have thought of framing, such a tariff as ours."

America's leading astronomer in the late nineteenth century was also a distinguished political economist. Simon Newcomb (1835–1909) was a mathematician and professor who adopted economics as his avocation while working on the *Nautical Almanac*. In 1885, he published *Principles of Political Economy*, a treatise that Joseph Schumpeter praised as "the outstanding performance of American general economics in [its] . . . epoch." John Maynard Keynes described the book as "one of those original works which a fresh scientific mind, not perverted by having read too much of the orthodox stuff," could generate for "a half-formed subject like economics."

Newcomb's book addressed "the burning question [of] whether any economic advantage can be gained by government interference with the liberty of the individual." His answer presented what today would be called *the interest-group theory of regulation*.

Newcomb favored separating the economy from the government (the "let-alone principle") because of "the custom for Congress to attend almost exclusively to special 'interests' in shaping its policy, thus losing sight of the general public welfare." The problem occurs because the government does not independently, or neutrally, study legislative issues. Instead, the party requesting the intervention predominates in the subsequent hearings. Newcomb illustrated his point with a hypothetical. Assume that a proposed law would confer benefits of $500,000 to a business firm and cost each American a penny. Individuals "could not send a letter, or print a handbill, or call a meeting of his neighbors without spending more time than the question was worth." But the business could underwrite books, editorials, lectures, and public meetings to generate petitions for the cause, as well as "provide a body of able lawyers to plead with individual members of Congress." Thus, the special interest wins over the underrepresented general interest.

To Newcomb, the case for remedial legislation had to show more than "individuals use their liberty to their own injury." Any law had to effectively address the specific shortcoming *and* not produce "other evils equally great." This comparison was a forerunner of today's debate between *market failure* (an economic failure creating a social problem) and *government failure* (a problem resulting from trying to politically correct a market failure).

A contemporary of Newcomb, William Graham Sumner (1840–1910), the first holder of the chair of political and social science at Yale University and a renowned sociologist and social critic of his day, similarly exposed what he called "the fallacy in the philosophy of state interference." State interaction with business was not the democratic ideal, as many of his fellow intellectuals wrote and taught. It was *plutocracy*, government by "clique or faction," whereby the politically active "serve[d] their own interests at the expense of everybody else." Government open to regulatory bidding could not be expected to "repel all the special interests and keep uppermost the one general interest of the welfare of all." Sumner cautioned:

> The opinion of the people is almost always informal and indefinite. A small group, therefore, who know what they want and how they propose to accomplish it, are able by energetic action to lead the whole body. Hence the danger which arises for us, in this country, from incorporated or combined interests.

Regulation to "control . . . interests" did not level the playing field but resulted in "more crafty and secret modes of action" by the interests. The "lamentable contest" between government officials and business lawyers to shape regulation and operate under it was one reason that the *effects* of regulation could be "far other than those which were expected and intended."

Sumner warned political capitalists about their strategy. Invoking the experience of the Interstate Commerce Act of 1887, the first major federal law regulating trade between states, Sumner warned business leaders to stick to business, for "when once the fatal step is taken of invoking legislation, the contest is changed in its character and in its arena." Sumner explained to the would-be political capitalist:

> Although you may be in possession of the power of the state to-day, and it might suit you very well . . . to triumph over your business rivals and competitors . . . you would far better consent to forego your satisfaction, lest presently your rivals . . . should beat you in a political struggle; and then you must suffer wrong and in the end be forced to . . . devote your whole energy to the political struggle, as that on which all the rest depends.

Figure 5.3 Simon Newcomb and William Graham Sumner were first-generation American political economists who grasped the nature and perils of political capitalism for business and society. (*Left:* © Mary Evans Picture Library/The Image Works.)

Sumner feared that "the power of capital handled by talent" would strain and corrupt political institutions by forcing them "to act as governor, patron, and receiver for the rest of America." The political game brings out "politicians, editors, economists, *littérateurs*, lawyers, labor agitators, and countless others who, in one way or another, have something to make out of it." Sumner cautioned against what today would be called the politicization of economic relations, whereby "every industrial interest is forced more or less to employ plutocratic methods." His answer was to "minimize to the utmost the relations of the state to industry."

Sumner, "the late nineteenth-century thinker American history textbooks most like to hate," was caricatured as a social Darwinist and business apologist. Yet, as a leading proponent of laissez-faire, Sumner was critical of the all-too-common business strategy of controlling government for narrow benefit. On a personal level, he championed "hard work and self-denial over material luxury, and public good over individual gratification." Sumner's philosophy was one of constrained, not unbridled, self-interest, not unlike that of Adam Smith or Samuel Smiles.

Despite the sophistication of their analyses, Newcomb and Sumner, as well as other first-generation political economists, were labeled "old school" and overrun by a new breed of economists, many of them younger scholars newly degreed from German universities, which at the time were the intellectual center of the universe. The so-called German historical school of economics embraced an activist role for government to solve social problems, rejecting the worldview of Adam Smith and other classical liberal scholars.

Richard Ely was one of many students who studied in Germany and returned to the United States passionate about social change. In 1885, he founded the American Economic Association (AEA) on a platform that "laissez-faire is unsafe in politics and unsound in morals." In a private communication, Ely provided a more pointed reason: to "combat the influence of the Sumner and Newcomb crowd." Some of the old school were not invited to join the economics fraternity; others were invited but refused to join.

Traditional political economy was weakened but not extinguished by the groundswell toward activist economics. A decade after the AEA was formed, Harvard professor S. M. Macvane warned his colleagues to resist the "denunciations of benevolent enthusiasts whose schemes for the improvement of the world [the science of political economy] has had to oppose." He explained:

> Well-intending visionaries take it amiss to be reminded of the hard realities of life. The offense of political economy is that it insists on getting at the true causes of the poverty and misery that are so sadly prevalent in the world. It rejects all remedies that do not address themselves to the seat and source of the disease. For this, eloquent enthusiasts have denounced it as "the gloomy science," and an enemy of human progress. They have no doubt turned many against it. Yet political economy is but reason and common sense applied to practical affairs.

But such caution would be overrun by political fashion.

Arthur Bentley

Political science, the study of political behavior and public policy, was professionalized with the founding of the American Political Science Association in 1903. One of the discipline's most significant books came just five years later. *The Process of Government* by Arthur Bentley substituted realism for idealism, offering a firm foundation for the young science of government. Alas, the book was ahead of its time.[14]

Bentley (1870–1957) began his professional life as an academic, but his book would be equally shaped by his years as a writer and editorialist in the Chicago

---

14. Also see Internet appendix 5.3, "The Realism of Arthur Bentley," at www.political capitalism.org/book1/chapter5/appendix3.html.

newspaper world, where "all the politics of the country, so to speak, was drifting across my desk." Part of this bailiwick was the public utility regulation and municipalization that involved Samuel Insull and the Chicago Edison Company.

With the newspaper requiring only "two hours a day . . . to earn my pay," Bentley burrowed into Chicago's Crerar Library to pen what in time would be "hailed by many scholars as a work of genius." It was like shooting fish in a barrel, for the ivory tower's political science was remarkably unsophisticated. "It was still possible to write reputable descriptions of politics without even mentioning political parties or pressure groups," a political scientist would later write of that era.

Figure 5.4 In *The Process of Government* (1908), Arthur Bentley reoriented political science to give the subject a firm, realistic ground. It would take decades, but Bentley's *group politics* approach to governmental decision making penetrated the mainstream to make him America's "greatest political theorist."

Policymaking, Bentley explained in *The Process of Government*, is less about individual characteristics (feelings, faculties, ideas, ideals) and abstract principles (truth, ideals, freedom, equality, welfare) than the actionable desires of "powerful group pressures." *Felt* and *thought* facts, not generalities (called "soul-stuff" or "idea ghosts"), inspire individuals to come together to impact government decision making. Within groups, particular individuals at certain times and places—*activity at the margin*—is decisive.

The group needs the *interest* as much as the interest needs the *group*. "If we try to take the group without the interest, we have simply nothing at all," he concluded. Thus, Bentley criticized a leading theoretician of the day who attributed legislative change to a "society [that] selects ideas and individuals."

Unlike Gabriel Kolko and others working in the Marxian tradition, Bentley did not believe that economic interests were the sole driver of the process of government. Bentley recognized the role of inertia, crosscurrents, and public opinion in driving legislative change. But public opinion had to be separated from such holistic concepts as "'objective utility,'" "'social whole,'" or "'established condition.'" The causality of "the opinion, the theory, the creed" had to be established by also looking at "differentiated activity" (group activity) to see public opinion at work, whether it be manifested in newspaper editorials, church sermons, or just social conservations. "Freedom, liberty, independence, and other similar rallying cries in the governmental process all need the same kind of interpretation," Bentley argued.

At the same time, Bentley did not naïvely believe that a well-organized, funded, active special interest could automatically prevail over the sensibilities of the majority. The opposition had to be not only unorganized but also relatively indifferent to the action at the margin. Legislators must have the expectation that their water carrying will not incite a backlash. And in "distorted" cases in which "the concentrated pressures of smaller group interests" prevailed over majority opinion, "we see the formation of a group interest directly aroused in opposition to the interests which have gained objectionable power."

Bentley defined government as "the organization of forces, of pressures." The "raw material" of politics was the organized interest group, whether operating at the legislative or the administrative level. To Bentley, political change could not be gleaned from "the lawbooks . . . [but from] the 'law' behind the lawbooks . . . the proceedings of constitutional conventions . . . essays, addresses, appeals, and diatribes on tyranny and democracy . . . the 'character of the people,' in their specific 'feelings' or 'thoughts,' in their 'hearts' or 'minds.'" The "very flesh and blood of all that is happening" came from *pressure groups*, "freely combining, dissolving, and recombining in accordance with their interest lines." A perennial conflict is between larger, weaker interests and smaller, stronger interests, he explained.

Evidence for Bentley's thesis abounded—if intellectuals would have allowed themselves to step back from *ought* to recognize *is*. The U.S. House of Representatives began requiring lobbyists to register with the clerk in 1876. Massachusetts, home to a "body of professional lobbyists," imposed a similar requirement in 1890, as did many other states in the next decades. And some top political economists of the day had the explanation if anyone wanted to know.

Bentley frontally attacked what he called "dead political science." He disparaged "your political scientist" who "thinks he is going a long way afield and . . . meritoriously portraying 'actual' government when he inserts in his work some remarks on the machine, the boss, and the practical virtues and vices of men practicing politics." These players could be as vital as "the president or governor," Bentley explained, and from there one must "go behind to find . . . the real interests that are playing on each other through his agency."

Bentley in some ways was his own enemy. His 500-page tome was hard reading—"long, crabbed, difficult" in the estimation of one esteemed historian. Bentley's book made enemies by stridently debunking the big names in political science. In a book review in *Political Science Quarterly*, Charles Beard, the leading historian of the day, described Bentley's work as "unnecessarily rude," although a "thought-provoking book that will help to put politics on a basis of realism, where it belongs." Another reviewer, among the flogged, pleaded innocent and called the book "worthy of rank as an event in the history of social science." Still, the work failed to gain traction among political scientists or sociologists.

A second release of *The Process of Government* in 1935 went without notice. Political scientists did not see Bentley as one of them. His Ph.D. was in social science, not political science.[15] The iconoclast did not attend professional meetings, write for the journals, or teach. Fighting physical problems and mental depression, Bentley for many years had tended to his fruit orchard in a small Indiana town, not much more. But he would return to research and writing, and by his death in 1957, his *oeuvre* had expanded to where he was championed as "one of America's distinguished pioneers in political science, sociology, psychology, and the logic of scientific inquiry."

The awakening toward Bentley began with the third release of *The Process of Government* in 1951. Accolades flowed to the scholar who four decades before had reoriented political causality from *words* to *deeds*, as one reviewer put it. Bentley was "the founder of the 'group theory' of modern political science," reported Mancur Olson in his influential book *The Logic of Collective Action* (1965). The rediscovery of Bentley as the father of interest-group theory was part of a larger development whereby a strong core of sociologists (who held that "the structure of society is associational"), historians, political scientists, and economists, separately and together, comprehended the true nature of government—finally.

Public Choice School

The self-interest view of political behavior was relegated to the backwater until a group of economists interested in public-sector decision making coalesced in the 1960s and 1970s. The *Public Choice school*, studying "choices by political

---

15. Bentley remembered how, at Johns Hopkins University, where he received his Ph.D., "political economy hung from the ankles of political science, and political science hung from the ankles of history. In other words I was on the loose."

people with power over the lives of other people," brought supply-and-demand analysis from markets to politics (the political market). The so-called *new political economy*, or *interest-group theory of government*—also called "politics without romance," or "who wins and who loses" theory—created a new urgency for realism and reshaped political science. It was also a rediscovery, or reconfirmation, of what a few hearty political economists had grasped nearly a century before.

The modern economic theory of government can be traced to a 1962 book by James Buchanan and Gordon Tullock, *The Calculus of Consent.* Their study on constitutional democracy independently rediscovered the central idea of Arthur Bentley by focusing on the organized pressure group as the manifestation of economic interest. *Public interest* and *public welfare* as public-policy drivers were demoted as ambiguous and scarcely definable outside of individual perception and action.

The politics-as-exchange paradigm looked at the profitability of group activity in terms of the size of the public sector and government budget. Among the book's insights was that "differential advantages" caused more and more pressure groups to organize. The authors also recognized a "spiral effect"—with intervention breeding more intervention—in "federal income-tax structure, federal tariff legislation, federal resource-development projects, and many other important areas of economic legislation." Enron would have its hand in many of these money pots.

Public Choice economics begins with the recognition that there is a demand for and supply of government favor—both motivated by identifiable self-interest. The demand for intervention emanates from organized interests, whether led by business leaders or outside reformers. Generally speaking, the organized triumph over the unorganized, the more organized over the less organized, and the more influential over the less influential. Decisions to participate in legislative or regulatory matters have become more sophisticated (or in economics jargon, *rational*) whereby, as a general rule, "political markets are characterized by the interaction of rationally ignorant voters and rationally less ignorant special interest groups."

In the tradition of Arthur Bentley and Public Choice theory, Gary Becker, a Nobel laureate from the Chicago school of economics, defined the political equation in the vernacular of neoclassical economics: "Political equilibrium has the property that all groups maximize their incomes by spending their optimal amount on political pressure, given the productivity of their expenditures, and the behavior of other groups." A popular business school textbook, *Managerial Economics and Organizational Architecture*, restated Becker's point:

> The economic theory of regulation is based on those who demand regulation (special interests) and those who supply it (politicians). Special interest groups who are made better off by the regulation will lobby in its favor, whereas those harmed will lobby against it. Politicians are made better off by brokering these transactions.

That book goes on to tell students (presumably tomorrow's business leaders):

> To develop strategies that both create value and capture value—it is not enough to build a better mousetrap—you must limit entry by competitors. The most direct way to limit competition is a government regulation limiting entry. . . . A less direct method . . . is a government regulation that imposes a cost on certain competitors and potential entrants.

Political entrepreneurship and rent-seeking were mainstreamed.

Public Choice dispensed with the romantic view of politics and identified government officials as self-interested. "Benevolent despots do not exist," James Buchanan stated; "government policy emerges from a highly complex and intricate institutional structure peopled by ordinary men and women, very little different from the rest of us." Abraham Lincoln's notion of government of, by, and for the people is recast in Public Choice terms as *government of, by, and for some people.* "It is government 'of the Busy (political activists), by the Bossy (government managers), for the Bully (lobbying activists),'" as one Public Choice economist put it.

Figure 5.5 James Buchanan (top left and bottom) and Gordon Tullock (top right) launched a new intellectual subdiscipline with *The Calculus of Consent* (1962). Public Choice entered the mainstream of economics, whereas political science continued to hang on to much of its public-sector idealism despite the growing influence of Arthur Bentley.

The Calculus of Consent built a small but dedicated movement. A year after its publication, the authors founded the Public Choice Society and launched a journal, *Public Choice*, to put a backlog of stranded articles into print. It would be slow sledding, but the efforts of a growing cadre of Public Choice economists would bear fruit when Buchanan received the 1986 Nobel Prize in economics for "transfer[ing] the concept of gain derived from mutual exchange between individuals to the realm of political decision-making." His "realistic view," the Royal Swedish Academy of Sciences continued, overthrew the notion that "public authorities could apply relatively mechanical methods to correct different types of so-called market failures." The announcement concluded, "Individuals who behave selfishly in markets can hardly behave wholly altruistically in political life."

Still, the model of a benevolent, impartial regulator, popular for most of American history, the pet idea of so many prointervention intellectuals, would prove hard to dislodge. Political scientists in particular continued to characterize government employment as *public service*, seeing truth and justice as consonant with officialdom. The wise, far-seeing bureaucrat who set aside the political pressures of the moment—the *exception*—was made the rule.

Public servants themselves from time immemorial have been prone to polish their own pedestal—if a professional historian did not do it for them (as Arthur Schlesinger Jr. did for the Kennedys). George Otis Smith, the former head of both the Department of the Interior and the Federal Power Commission, for example, wrote in *Public Utilities Fortnightly* in the 1930s how his faith in the "regulation principle" sustained him in the "thankless task of serving a public so critical in this particular field of service." He and his brethren would "hang their heads in sorrow" when someone had "too close a contact with big business." Almost with embarrassment, Smith noted "a type of profit motive even in public office, the true nature of which the political profiteer may not like to admit even to himself."

If penned today, such an article would invite not only skepticism but also ridicule. Suppositions of a monolithic, definable public weal; selfless public servants; and neutral experts are no longer taken at face value. Bureaucrats and politicians often, though not always, act in distinctly self-interested ways and bear the burden of proof to show otherwise. Rule upon rule has been enacted to distance public-sector decision making from private interests, but the interplay has continued. Even setting aside the temptations posed from private special interests, bureaucrats often find themselves vying for more employees, larger budgets, and other signs of prestige in the public sector, whether or not it is in the public's best interest. In William Niskanen's words, the bureaucrat "is a 'chooser' and a 'Maximizer' and . . . not just a 'role player' in some larger social drama."

Conclusion

"Analysts of American politics have generally been much impressed by the power of narrow interests," wrote the president of the left-leaning Brookings

Institution in a 1985 review describing a decade of deregulation. A retrospective on the same subject by a free-market institute similarly concluded, "There is hardly a regulatory program anywhere that does not benefit some industry or subset, most often at the expense of rivals or consumers." Moreover, "almost no area of regulation is free from strategic planning by firms to disadvantage rivals for higher profits." Thus had awareness dawned, on scholars of the Left and the Right, a full century after Simon Newcomb defended his let-alone principle on grounds of a probable takeover of public policy by special interests and three-quarters of a century after Arthur Bentley developed the special-interest theory of government.

Government goes to those who show up. The political side of business has grown substantially as all branches of government have intervened in the economy under the general-welfare and commerce clauses of the U.S. Constitution. Government intervention has spawned further intervention—often to correct collateral problems created by the prior intervention. Pragmatic business strategies seeking government favor have inspired more such efforts by competitors—another dynamic of intervention. Eschewing a government-affairs effort in such an environment would be to put employees and stockholders at risk relative to the politically active and able companies. This was the world that Samuel Insull worked to create. It was also the world that Ken Lay inherited—and powerfully advanced—after he became head of Houston Natural Gas Corporation in 1984, the company destined to become Enron.

6

U.S. Political Capitalism

AT-CAT CAPITALISM and the Republican ascendancy were surely on the ropes after the Enron debacle. "I predict in the years ahead Enron, not September 11, will come to be seen as the greater turning point in U.S. society," wrote Paul Krugman in the *New York Times*. "Enron is to George W. Bush what Teapot Dome was to Warren G. Harding," opined Robert Kuttner in the *American Prospect*, invoking the memory of a scandal in the early 1920s that involved oil leasing on public land and that tainted a presidency and an industry.

Octogenarian Arthur Schlesinger Jr. also went on the attack. "The business scandals exposed in the first years of the twenty-first century—Enron, Arthur Andersen, Tyco, WorldCom, Adelphia, et al.—would have fitted perfectly into the excesses of the 1920s," he stated. The 1920s *New Era* and 1990s *New Economy* had the same stench: "the dynamics of speculation, of euphoric self-delusion, of market fundamentalism, of the deceptions wrought by greed." Yet the Enron et al. bubble did not lead to a general collapse, Schlesinger continued, "for one simple reason: the Great Crash brought on the New Deal." He listed the New Deal programs still in place that saved twenty-first century America from the excesses of the new "'economic royalists'": macroeconomic stabilizers, unemployment insurance, minimum-wage law, Social Security, bank-deposit insurance, farm price supports, and securities regulation.

Corporate malfeasance, led by Enron, had given New Deal liberalism a second wind.

The Enron story has deep meaning for American history. Yet the preceding interpretation, based on a particular view of twentieth-century business/government relations, fathered by Schlesinger and other leading academics of his generation, should be critically reconsidered.

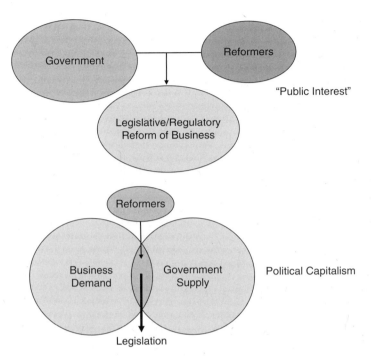

Figure 6.1 The standard interpretation of American political history, the public-interest model (top), has posited government and reformers as distinct from business in policy-making. A truer interpretation of twentieth-century interventionism is the political-capitalism model (bottom), which sees a symbiotic relationship between government and business.

"Liberalism in America," according to Schlesinger, was a "movement on the part of the other sections of society to restrain the power of the business community." Yet the government-reformer, business-resister view of American history—in which laissez-faire was gradually weakened and then replaced by the mixed economy to civilize capitalism, or save capitalism from itself—has been challenged from both ends of the ideological spectrum. The *public-interest* interpretation of the Progressive Era and New Deal was taken to task by New Left historians in the 1960s and 1970s. Economists joined in by examining the data in greater detail, jettisoning faulty Keynesian/Marxist precepts, and forwarding a stronger case for a separation of business and state.[1] The resulting

---

1. The charge of inherent macroeconomic instability under capitalism is criticized in Internet appendix 6.1, "'Overproduction' and the Business Cycle," at www.politicalcapitalism. org/book1/chapter6/appendix1.html.

history—the *real history*—must be understood in order to put in context the rise and fall of Samuel Insull's energy empire and Ken Lay's Enron.

Intellectuals as Reformers

At the beginning of the twentieth century, investigative journalists and academics formed America's first critical intelligentsia. These thought leaders distrusted the natural order of laissez-faire and saw great potential for government-led reform.

The first generation of investigative journalists, the *muckrakers*, wrote in popular magazines about "the bribe, the rebate, the bought franchise, the sale of adulterated food, the desperate pursuit of life in the slums." An estimated two thousand articles between 1903 and 1912 documented a variety of ills, including corruption and undue influence in business/government relations. A fascinated public saw industrialization and big business in a negative way and could not help but wonder whether a variety of social problems could be addressed by the stroke of a government pen.

As discussed in chapter 5, a group of reformist scholars and clergymen founded the American Economic Association (AEA) in 1885.[2] "While we recognize the necessity of individual initiative in industrial life," its platform read, "we hold that the doctrine of laissez-faire is unsafe in politics and unsound in morals." "A vast number of social problems," the document continued, require "the united efforts of Church, state and science." Richard Ely, the principal founder of the AEA, was eager to demote the "old school" of economics that "had nothing to say when industrial progress and new economic formation brought to the front fresh problems for solution."

The AEA's interventionist/reformist agenda was not homespun. At a time when "English universities were concerned with turning out gentlemen, not scholars," American intellectuals, including Ely, were receiving advanced degrees in Germany, the academic center of the world. Their professors taught that government-sponsored cooperation was superior to market competition and that government welfare programs were necessary for the citizenry. These were the policies championed by the chancellor of Germany from 1871 to 1890, Otto von Bismarck, who rewarded the professors with the status and pay

---

2. Prior to 1870, economics was taught in the philosophy department as a branch of moral philosophy. Laissez-faire was a quasi-religious doctrine, often taught as being of providential design. Harvard economist Francis Bowen wrote in his 1877 textbook: "Laissez-faire; 'these things regulate themselves,' in common phrase; which means of course, that God regulated them by his general laws, which always, in the long run, work to good." Stand-alone economics departments first emerged at Harvard (1871), Yale (1872), Johns Hopkins (1876), and Columbia (1879). The growth of economics departments, associations, and professional journals accelerated rapidly from there.

accorded to very top bureaucrats. "The German 'socialists of the chair' certainly fulfilled the ideal of progressive politicians and laymen—the ideal of the professor who preaches reform and denounces obstructing interests," Joseph Schumpeter remarked.

Other associations were formed in America by historians, sociologists, and political scientists to lend expertise to the cause of bigger and better government. Graduate study at Brown, Chicago, Columbia, Harvard, Johns Hopkins, Michigan, Stanford, Wisconsin, and Yale excited the radical scholars' students about open vistas of benevolent government in place of the invisible hand.

The new professionalism had its rewards. New careers were created in government and industry as public utility regulation expanded from the railroad industry to manufactured/natural gas, electricity, water, streetcars, and telecommunications. Economic planning during World War I "exhilarated . . . professors, social workers, and other university-trained men and women" who cherished "public ends rather than private profit." New Deal planning repeated the experience in peacetime. Members of FDR's so-called brain trust were college-degreed, except for a few who "had come up through the university of hard knocks." Deciding the right fiscal policies to combat the redepression of 1937/38 created a "battle of the Ph.D.s." Ken Lay, brandishing an economics Ph.D., would engage in his own public-policy battles two generations later.

The American Bar Association was established in 1878 and the American Association of Public Accountants in 1887. Through such organizations, jurisprudence and accountancy became licensed occupations and graduated certified professionals to deal with a host of new regulations, prominently including the federal taxation of business income (begun in 1909) and personal income (begun in 1913), as well as the Uniform System of Accounts governing public utilities.

Public-Interest History: Inadvertent Misdirection

The so-called *Progressive Era*, which stretched from the 1880s until World War I, has been intensely studied to understand how politics grew with urbanization and industrialization. Interpreting these decades was not easy, given "shifting coalitions around different issues, with the specific nature of these coalitions varying on federal, state and local levels, from region to region, and from the first to the second decades of the century." Still, although the legacy of Progressivism is "steeped in ambiguity," as Thomas McCraw concluded, general themes were there for the finding, and in some important respects, the mainstream historians fell short.

The failure of historical perspective and analysis went beyond the Progressive Era. It also covered the most important stanza in U.S. economic history, the

1920s boom and ensuing Great Depression. The misinterpretation came in part from not appreciating how effectively business leaders embraced interventionism. There was never a golden era of laissez-faire. There was incipient political capitalism, mostly at the local and state levels, that later would expand and become federalized.[3]

What was the mythology that leading lights of the American Historical Society advanced? The consensus view, beginning with Charles Beard (1874–1948) and continuing with Richard Hofstadter (1916–70) and Arthur Schlesinger Jr. (1917–2007), was the *triumph of Progressivism over conservative, laissez-faire economics*. In their view, government intervention in the economy was a manifestation of middle-class pluralism over business elitism, making America an economic democracy, not just a political one. Harvard University's Schlesinger wrote how President Woodrow Wilson, campaigning for a second term in 1916, "stood clearly for strong government, for administrative regulation, for some intervention on behalf of the farmer and the worker—in short, for affirmative federal action aimed to produce equality of opportunity." Wilson's "people's government . . . had to be stronger than business if popular rule were to be effective." Wilson himself had announced some years before that "no one now advocates the old *laissez faire*."

The New Deal's response to America's Great Depression, in Schlesinger's view, was a noble attempt to "save the system rather than to change it": to continue private ownership rather than have the federal government take over the economy as was done with railroads after World War I. Franklin Roosevelt, this view continues, elected in 1932 to reverse Herbert Hoover's do-little response to the crisis, was a hero in word and deed. FDR's National Recovery Administration "helped preserve American unity" in the face of what could have been a "permanent depression," Schlesinger found.

The most revered historian of his generation had interdisciplinary help with his worldview. Schlesinger expressed gratitude in his books for the economics tutelage received from two Harvard Keynesians: John Kenneth Galbraith and Seymour Harris. Thus, student, like teachers, blamed capitalism for the Great Depression and credited government intervention for recovery.

Schlesinger's interpretation was seconded by another icon of the history profession, Richard Hofstadter. Hofstadter had been writing on Progressivism since the 1940s, and in 1963 the Pulitzer Prize winner summarized his interpretation in a mass paperback published by Prentice Hall for classroom use.

Progressivism, "a major episode in the history of the American conscience," was in response to economic advances that "had been achieved at a terrible cost

---

3. For a brief discussion of social legislation in this period, see Internet appendix 6.2, "Progressivism and Statism," at www.politicalcapitalism.org/book1/chapter6/appendix2.html.

in human values and in the waste of natural resources," Hofstadter wrote. "The land and the people had both been plundered," which necessitated "orderly social change [to] remedy the accumulated evils and negligences of a period of industrial growth."

Figure 6.2 Arthur Schlesinger Jr. espoused the *consensus view* of regulatory reform, an interpretation that saw society join together to overcome the vested interest of business in laissez-faire capitalism. Richard Hofstadter, "the historian's historian," similarly interpreted the Progressive Era as an enlightened transformation to a welfare state, although his later views became more nuanced.

A political solution required "civic alertness and the combative mood of a great part of the public." It succeeded, thanks to the "heroic efforts" of different constituencies: rural citizens, an urban middle class, and a new generation of well-to-do professionals with "high civic ideals." There were younger politicians who "never acquiesced in the crass and ruthless materialism" of post–Civil War industrialization. A new crop of intellectuals across the humanities—economics, jurisprudence, history, political science, philosophy, education, and sociology—gave academic weight to reform. Muckraking journalists and the clergy joined academics in the noble quest of putting government and economic life back in the people's hands, Hofstadter continued.

It was a great challenge and achievement to enact local, state, and federal legislation that restrained business practices. "In their struggles against railroads, utilities, insurance companies, and other business organizations, reformers were driven to do constant battle with the political machines fed by contributions from businessmen." The result was all the more impressive because it occurred during a time of national prosperity, Hofstadter explained.

Leading textbooks on the origins and practice of government intervention in the U.S. economy provided a like interpretation. Political economist Clair Wilcox, for example, described regulation as reformer driven and a necessary evil:

> Government does not willfully interfere with business. It intervenes only when it is forced to intervene. It acts reluctantly, deliberately, and tardily, in response to overwhelming pressures. Criticism of public intervention is criticism, not of dictatorship, but of the results of the democratic process.

Wilcox closed his 900-page tome *Public Policies toward Business*: "In their total effect, in the perspective of history, the policies of government toward business in the United States appear to have been sound."

Subsequent editions of this classroom staple and other business/government books would remain on point. *Business: An Introductory Analysis* (1962) by Bayard Wheeler, for example, a new genre of textbook examining American enterprise "as a dominant institution in our culture," described regulation as public-spirited. "Negative restraints, in the public interest, are found in the regulatory laws administered by government agencies, such as the Justice Department and the Federal Trade Commission," he wrote. In this version of American history, regulatory history, and business practice, government wore a white hat.

From Muckraking to Business History

The apogee of muckraking historiography came with Matthew Josephson's *The Robber Barons*, published during the Great Depression. Leading industrialists were portrayed as antiheroes whose enormous wealth came at the expense of workers, natural resources, and competitors. The final page of his book spoke of the "fearful sabotage practiced by capital upon the energy and intelligence of human society," whereby workers and patriots were reduced to "idle and hungry louts" and "rebels and lawbreakers." Josephson identified Samuel Insull as one of the barons of "Frenzied Finance," part of an era whose "mismanagement and stupidity" revealed capitalism's "inherent contradictions."

Josephson was a social reformer whose worldview came from a range of anticapitalist writings, including Karl Marx's *Das Kapital*. Josephson promised his publisher that he would expose "the whole character of [the robber barons'] construction, rotten at the core by virtue of the profit-making motive that fixed its character, and the inevitable maldistribution that brings successive waves of disaster." The book hit the bestseller lists and became required reading for New Deal bureaucrats. The public was drawn to a writer "with the verve of a pamphleteer and the style of the romantic novelist" who offered a whipping boy—greedy industrialists—for the great economic ills of the day, including 20 percent unemployment.

Josephson, meanwhile, one of a number of Western intellectuals who thought that capitalism was on its last legs, was studying state collectivism in the Soviet

Union and would wait to hear about his book's success. He was pleased with what he found in the USSR, although he noticed a paucity of conveniences that were enjoyed back home. "I like their life and their spirit," he wrote his editor during the trip. "They are completely sold . . . on the present political program. The intellectual class in any case is remarkably well off in Russia. It has work up to the neck, but gets everything it wants."

What he did not see, or what was kept from him, was the ongoing extermination of millions of Russians by Joseph Stalin in a quest to create a new Marxist Man. It was not a social garden but a grotesque gulag.

The muckrakers often had personal circumstances and motives for their antibusiness crusades. Henry Demarest Lloyd, author of *Wealth against Commonwealth* (1894), was an independently wealthy social reformer who supported the Socialist Party. Ida Tarbell, author of *The History of the Standard Oil Company* (1904), was the daughter and sister of bitter competitors of John D. Rockefeller. Josephson ardently supported the Communist Party platform, while doubling as a *bourgeois bohemian*. All were spinning errant history, no matter how factually researched their final product was, how exciting and moralistic their prose, and however well intentioned they thought themselves to be.

What explains the muckrakers' preconceived notion that business titans were predatory promoters injuring the natural competitive order and public weal? Why did these writers—at least prior to 1929—give so little weight to the *results* of industrial change—improved affordability, better products, and mass production for mass consumption? As Harvard business historian Thomas McCraw would later explain, these writers did not have an adequate theoretical foundation to understand the whys and wherefores of commerce:

> Without the benefit of a vocabulary that distinguished conceptually between center and peripheral firms, productive and allocative efficiency, vertical and horizontal integration, economies of scale and transaction cost, these observers had only their personal sensibilities and political ideologies to guide them. And both their personal and political values concerning the nature of liberty, the meaning of opportunity, and the promise of America were directly threatened by the trusts.[4]

The despair of boom gone bust made for an angry decade, one in which intellectuals rushed forth with ideas and proposals that precluded key free-market reforms. The intelligentsia, in fact, had much to do with Hoover/FDR interventionism.

It did not have to be this way. Eighteenth century's Adam Smith and a long line of capitalist thinkers after him would have asked and determined *why* some products and firms were so successful. They would have differentiated between

---

4. See also Internet appendix 6.3, "The 'New Vocabulary,'" at www.politicalcapitalism. org/book1/chapter6/appendix3.html.

the market and political means to success and praised or criticized accordingly. Smith would have seen John D. Rockefeller, Andrew Carnegie, and Cornelius Vanderbilt as classic market entrepreneurs—capitalists practicing capitalism. Smith would have applauded Vanderbilt's victories against Robert Fulton and Edward Collins, two business rivals wed to political means. The Scottish professor would have been disappointed in, but hardly surprised by, the likes of railroad titans Henry Villard, Leland Stanford, and Jay Gould, who feasted off government subsidies and/or legislatively blocked new entrants.

Allan Nevins and Historical Revisionism

The bar of business history was raised in 1940 with the publication of the two-volume *John D. Rockefeller and the Age of Heroic Enterprise* by Allan Nevins, a historian at Columbia University. Declaring his preference for a "free competitive economy," Nevins painted a different picture than did the muckrakers.

"Our industrial history since the Civil War can hardly be understood without a clear grasp of the principal facts of Rockefeller's work," Nevins stated in the preface. His 1,400 pages described an "inextricably mingled [mix of] exceptional constructive ability and astute destructive strategy," making extreme praise or vilification of Rockefeller unwarranted. Nevins applauded Rockefeller's prominent role in the "Great Game" of the late nineteenth century, one that rationalized resources and expanded the economic pie for many Americans. Rockefeller, added Nevins, possessed an intellectual purity that his critics did not.

> Rockefeller was a realist; one of those realists who . . . have a better grasp of realities than the intellectuals who operate with theories and ideals. Partly by intuition, partly by hard thought, he divined the real nature of economic forces, and the real motives operative in American industry. He and the other leaders of the "heroic age" in American business development thus constituted the guiding elite, in a modern sense, of our industrial society.

Muckraking was more propaganda than explication, Nevins's revisionism concluded.

Nevins saw little that was heroic in "journalists who had learned that [muckraking] boosted circulation and politicians who knew there were votes in it." Journalists, not only businesspeople, were self-interested, fallible, and even susceptible to greed. Intellectuals and academics were too, a point made in an essay published in *Business History Review* by a young graduate student at Harvard. "All historians have values," wrote Gabriel Kolko, and "the denial of their influence in written history serves no useful purpose." The key was to have objective values consonant with a sound theoretical framework.

Nevins's zeal for a new, better history transcended the ivory tower. Two years after his Rockefeller reinterpretation was published, Nevins wrote in the *New York Times Magazine* that historical research was now "broader, deeper and more mature" than the traditional military and political fare. History needed social, economic, and psychological analyses. "A thorough, accurate and intelligent knowledge of our national past—in so many ways the brightest national record in all world history—is the best ground for faith in the present and hope for the future."

In a speech before the Institute of American History in 1951, Nevins decried the older view of American capitalism as simplistic and wrongheaded.

> In the past our historians . . . were apologetic about our dollars, our race to wealth, our materialism; they mentioned deprecatingly our worship of size and deplored our boastfulness about steel tonnage and wheat production. They spoke scornfully of the robber barons, who were not robber barons at all.

Nevins declared that the new history would be "more intent on proving that our way of life, called decadent by our enemies, has proved historically to be freer, more flexible, and more humane than any other in history."

Nevins's outcry found praise. *The New York Times* seconded his hope for better history. *Fortune*, the nation's premier business magazine, called his address a potential "turning point" to improve the reputation of business. Still, there was much resistance in the academic ranks to Nevins's new view.

In 1954, Nevins butted heads with Matthew Josephson in the *Saturday Review of Literature* on the question, *Should American history be rewritten?* Nevins argued for the affirmative: "Not one historian in fifty knows as much as he should of the tool called statistics, or of psychology, or of economic geography, or of ecology." The "superior penetrative power" of a multidisciplinary approach made for much richer history than before. And based upon the analysis, it could be shown that America rode on the shoulders of its great firms and industrial might to win world wars and become the most productive economy in the world. That was worth a lot.

Josephson shot back that a McCarthy-like campaign against established history was using the ends of economic growth to justify the means. Nevins's own words—"Great business aggregations . . . frustrating, crushing, or absorbing multitudinous small enterprises"—were cited against him. But this argument begged the question of *what* was legally or morally permissible and what was economical given consumer preference, something neither historian came to grips with.

Josephson, despite support from many historians, was on the defensive. The remarkable postwar economic boom made the business of America once again business. The alternatives to capitalism had lost much luster as well. Josephson's 1962 introduction to a new printing of *The Robber Barons* explained how his original (1934) edition was written amid economic gloom and upheaval when the "paradise of freebooting capitalists, untrammeled and untaxed" seemed over. Some industrialists were adventurous and "of heroic stature," he allowed, but they were envied and disliked by many if not most Americans.

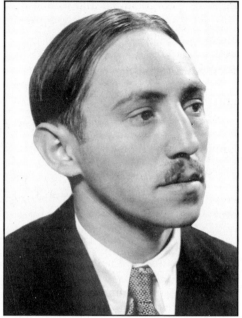

Figure 6.3 Allan Nevins (left) wrote revisionist history and attacked muckraking, including that of Matthew Josephson (right), as simplistic and misleading. Nevins's probusiness worldview failed to differentiate between free-market and political capitalism, a shortcoming also present in his opponents' anticapitalist view.

And it was not he but "embattled" Kansas farmers who coined the term *robber barons* in reference to their railroad masters.

Josephson's retrospective again threw the baby out with the bathwater, damning capitalism without distinguishing between consumer-driven entrepreneurship and political entrepreneurship, the latter seeking profitability at the expense of consumers, competitors, and taxpayers. Still, the long-overdue reconsideration of industrial history was bigger than Nevins knew, for a new school of historiography was about to emerge.

Nevins's scholarship only began to bury the entrenched robber-baron interpretation of the U.S.-led Second Industrial Revolution.[5] What was missing was a real-world conception of competition and efficiency that mainstream economics had failed to teach. Their framework of perfect-/imperfect-competition left the market process, enterprise economics, and Joseph Schumpeter's notion of creative destruction unexplained and unappreciated. A static view of competition, which assumed all variables as known and given, espoused by such leading

---

5. The First Industrial Revolution (1760s–1840s) was led by Great Britain; the Second Industrial Revolution, by the United States.

lights as George Stigler and Kenneth Boulding, crowded out the entrepreneurial theories of some of the old lions of the profession, including Frank Knight
and Joseph Schumpeter. This state of affairs would be partially rectified by business professors whose offices were often right down the hall from those of
economists.

Harvard Business School

Harvard Business School (HBS) opened its doors in 1908 with 15 faculty
members and 80 students. The nation's second graduate business school (the
University of Pennsylvania's Wharton School of Finance had begun in 1881),
HBS offered courses in accounting, commercial law (contracts), banking and
finance, economic resources, industrial organization, and transportation (railroads), insurance, and public business (municipalities).

HBS's founding dean, Edwin Gay, was also interested in something that was
not in the curriculum: business history, or *entrepreneurial strategy in action*. Following his colleague Joseph Schumpeter, Gay recognized "the self-centered,
active individual" as "a disruptive force." Gay saw a "rhythm of history" in
commerce: short-run change whereby "the cake of custom must be broken,"
and longer-run strategies that contributed to "social stability." Business historians keyed on the former; political economists and political scientists were concerned with the latter.

In 1925, Dean Gay founded the Business Historical Society within HBS to
study the dynamics of business change. The society's findings were dissemi-
nated in a mimeographed, hand-stapled *Bulletin* each month. Two years later,
the nation's first chair in business history was filled at Harvard with the appointment of Norman Gras. Recalled his former student, business historian Henrietta Larson, "Gras saw in the market the central factor in economic life and the
most important of the dynamic factors in economic change and development."

Gay and Gras were prime movers of a new discipline straddling business
and economics. Gay became the first president of the Economic History Association in 1940 as part of a career that would title him the "first real American
economic historian." Professor Gras founded the Business History Foundation in 1947, from which academics wrote business histories under contract
with companies and trade associations. The first major grant, from the Standard Oil Company of New Jersey, resulted in an acclaimed multivolume history of the company that is today ExxonMobil. Professors from Harvard, New
York University, Northwestern University, and elsewhere wrote histories,
many on the petroleum industry, with full autonomy and open access to company records and employees. Such studies gave readers, including business
managers, a hitherto unavailable perspective of the dynamics of their firm
and industry.

A third Harvard figure who shaped the new field of business history was
Arthur Cole, who was appointed president of the Economic History Association in 1946, the year of Gay's death. Cole became the historian of business

historians, outlining a research agenda for the new discipline and chronicling his colleagues' contributions.

Cole lamented the economics profession's neglect of short-run change in its rush to work out the mathematics of long-run equilibrium. What mattered were *multifactor processes*, "the integrated sequence of actions, taken by individuals or by groups operating for individual business units, in a world characterized by a large measure of uncertainty, such actions being modified in greater or less degree by contemporary economic and social forces." Citing Schumpeter, Cole identified the entrepreneur as "the central figure" in economic theory and economic history.

Anticipating the work of the greatest business historian of them all, Alfred Chandler Jr. (who would come to call himself "a Schumpeterian"), Cole identified "the real purpose of business strategy" as effectively managing uncertainty. Documenting how this was done across companies and industries was new territory. "The area of entrepreneurial history stands open to the present generation of research workers, almost as unworked as the 'significance of the frontier' when Frederick Turner first voiced his hypothesis."[6] Economists had bypassed this core activity; business scholars, some trained in economics and others not, were needed to fill the void.

Arthur Cole, like Edwin Gay, was a man of action at Harvard Business School. Under Cole's direction, the Baker Library became the world's leading depository of business documents, and he cofounded the Research Center in Entrepreneurial History in 1948 with a grant from the Rockefeller Foundation. The intellectual inspiration of the Center was none other than Joseph Schumpeter, the grand old man of the economics department. "Without his zeal and support," Cole remembered, "the Center might readily have 'died aborning.'"

Schumpeter knew that economics was all about the business world—the everyday grappling with uncertainty. Schumpeter spoke volumes when he said, "Every economist knows—if he did not, he could not help learning it from conversation with businessmen." Or every economist *should know* by talking to the doers rather than retiring to the ivory tower to theorize unrealistically.

Schumpeter was laboring on a treatise on the history of economic thought in his last years when he circled back to his first love, entrepreneurship. With mainstream economics embracing arcane theory, the "entrepreneur of entrepreneurial history" found a "new reference group" in business historians and sought to bridge the gap. "Economic historians and economic theorists can make an interesting and socially valuable journey together, if they will," Schumpeter wrote. Investigating "the sadly neglected area of economic change" promised "new hypotheses and the marshalling of factual data, old and new."

---

6. Frederick Turner's *frontier thesis*, introduced in his 1893 paper "The Significance of the Frontier in American History," identified the frontier as the wellspring of America's exceptionalism and vitality.

Figure 6.4 Edwin Gay, Norman Gras, Arthur Cole, and Joseph Schumpeter (clockwise from upper left) shaped the new discipline of entrepreneurial case studies at the Harvard Business School, setting the stage for a new generation of business historians.

The new business historians set out to understand the rise of large-scale enterprise in terms of underlying economics and business principles. The *Business History Review*, which replaced the homespun *Bulletin* in 1954, was a venue for a growing number of scholars whose essays did not quite fit into the traditional history or economics journals. Good work now had an outlet, but much remained to be done. A new star and new generation were needed.

Alfred Chandler and the New Business History

That star emerged in a Harvard-trained business professor at the Massachusetts Institute of Technology, Alfred Chandler Jr. (1918–2007). The man destined to become the father of business strategy splashed onto the scene with his paradigm-building book *Strategy and Structure: Chapters in the History of American Industrial Enterprise* (1962), described as "one of the classic works of American historical scholarship." Chandler set a new standard for understanding the economics of enterprise by determining how America's 70 largest corporations dealt with complexity and growth.

Chandler's breakthrough was understanding profit maximization via business principles. His introduction read: "My goal from the start was to study the complex interconnections in a modern industrial enterprise between structure and strategy and an ever-changing external environment." Business strategy drove structure, and crisis (underperformance) drove strategy, in a never-ending cycle of "resources accumulated, resources rationalized, resources expanded, and then once again, resources rationalized." This was capitalism at work. "The market, the nature of their resources, and their entrepreneurial talents have, with relatively few exceptions, had far more effect on the history of large industrial firms in the United States than have antitrust laws, taxation, labor and welfare legislation, and comparable evidences of public policy," he observed. Chandler ended his 400-page treatise with characteristic humility: "If it does nothing else, this exploratory study should provide the student of business history and business administration as well as other scholars with some suggestions for significant areas of investigation."

Never before had a historian analyzed industrial giants "without turning an ideological hair." Chandler's focus on dynamic performance was so *clinical* that the traditional question of good (*industrial statesman*) or bad (*robber baron*) was bypassed. Business change could now be comprehended in familiar terms of the modern business vernacular: *technology, economies of scale and scope*, and *logistics*. Interestingly, and perhaps crucially, Chandler never took a course in economic theory in graduate school. His training in economic history, unencumbered by sterile theory, left him to grapple with real-world causality.

Chandler was a student of change—of *process*. He elevated Schumpeter's entrepreneur to "a collective entity, institutionalized among teams of managers operating within structures they themselves designed." "Dynamic forces" were central. As Chandler explained in the opening paragraph of one of his earliest essays, appropriately published in the *Business History Review*:

> The historian . . . must be concerned with change. What made for change? Why did it come when it did, and in the way it did? . . . What in the American past has given businessmen the opportunity or created the need for them to change what they were doing or the way they were doing it? In other words, what stimulated them to develop new products, new markets, new sources of raw materials, new ways of producing, processing, or marketing the goods they handled? What encouraged them to find new methods of financing, new ways of managing or organizing their businesses? What turned them to altering their relations with their working force, their customers and competitors, and with the larger American public?

Chandler's long-overdue research program caught two disciplines AWOL—history and economics. Adam Smith would have been proud of the new development but puzzled about why it arrived so late.

Formal economics had little to say about entrepreneurship. Applied economics was not directed toward real-world decision making under uncertainty.

Figure 6.5 Alfred Chandler Jr.'s new approach to business history went beyond political presuppositions, understanding business change as driven by forces designed to maximize efficiency and thus profits.

Economics, once known as political economy, was under a spell of false and simplifying assumptions that allowed hypertechnical theorizing by practitioners who could claim originality. Entrepreneurial history had much to offer compared to this fare. But Chandler knew that such research was not a business leader's nirvana, a road map to profitability. In his words:

> History can teach businessmen little about specific techniques. They change too fast in the modern world. The lesson to be learned from history is rather that awareness of reality is more important than indoctrination in generality.

Chandler's realism and humility toward the use of business history was quite unlike that of many social scientists whose flights from reality came with few caveats for either students or policymakers.

Chandler provided a wake-up call to the history profession, which had an ideological problem (as opposed to the methodological problem plaguing economics). "Many historians had an a priori distaste for business," Thomas McCraw explained, "and particularly for the big companies that so fascinated Chandler." This bias, resulting in superficial analysis, left business economics unexplored.

The result was emotive history, misleading rather than informing.[7] But a reconsideration of America's industrial past was under way, with Chandler in front.

Strategy and Structure became the most widely read business book of the day. "'Strategy precedes structure' became a byword of corporate management during the 1960s and 1970s," thanks to Chandler, "not only in the United States but all over the world, perhaps most notably in Japan." His approach opened up the field of business consultancy that was embraced by one firm in particular, McKinsey & Company, the pre-Enron employer of Jeff Skilling.

Jeffrey K. Skilling (b. 1953) entered Harvard Business School in the fall of 1977. A National Merit Scholar, Skilling attended Southern Methodist University on scholarship, where he received a degree in business. He then worked two years in corporate planning at the (now-defunct) First City National Bank, Houston's second largest after Texas Commerce Bank (now part of JPMorgan Chase). After becoming the youngest officer of the bank, Skilling decided to leave to attend graduate school. A formidable interview won him a scholarship to pursue the most prestigious MBA in the world at Harvard University.

Skilling graduated from Harvard two years later as a Baker Scholar, an honor reserved for the top 5 percent of his class. "Jeff may have been the single best student I ever had," remembered Harvard professor Irwin Bupp, "and he did not suffer fools."

In the course of his studies, Skilling discovered business history. The student of capitalism devoured such books as Allan Nevins's Rockefeller reassessment, which gave him a perspective on energy and integration, an area that would shape his future career.

Upon graduation, Skilling joined McKinsey & Company, the most respected and cerebral business consultancy. The McKinsey worldview—"which reduced a chaotic world to a series of coolly clinical logical observations"—was Chandlerian. Skilling, whose client list included InterNorth, a large Midwestern natural gas company that would purchase Houston Natural Gas (Ken Lay's company) in 1985, became one of the youngest partners in the firm. He rose to senior partner, overseeing McKinsey's worldwide energy and North American chemical consulting practice. Skilling would go on to extensively consult with Enron on natural gas product development before joining a division of the company in 1990. Skilling's 11-year Enron career is described in Book 3.

The Diminishing of Laissez-Faire

In a 1955 issue of *Business History Review*, Robert Lively of the University of Wisconsin surveyed 25 books and articles describing the role of government

---

7. McCraw added elsewhere: "Most histories of business remained atheoretical and immature until . . . Chandler. Fus[ing] economics and sociology with history, Chandler firmly established the subdiscipline of business history, worldwide."

before and after the Civil War. He was surprised at what he unearthed. The literature documented at the local and state levels what a new breed of historian would soon uncover at the national level—proactive business/government teamwork moving public policy away from laissez-faire.[8]

Government tax and spend policies shaped American capitalism in the nineteenth century. What activist states, such as Massachusetts, Pennsylvania, and Georgia, did not do, localities did. "Public-spirited undertakings [became] neomercantilism" as towns, cities, regions, provinces, and states competed with one another to construct internal improvements.[9] One study counted 2,200 laws in 36 states as part of the "local aid movement." "From Missouri to Maine, from the beginning to the end of the nineteenth century, governments were deeply involved in lending, borrowing, building, and regulating." Nothing was more popular for the public dollar than railroads. "Enterprise demanded and received vital support from public treasuries so long as there was a mile of American railroad track to be laid," Lively found.

The politics of business was there to see. Scholars had only to document where business interests actively sought and received favors beyond the simple right to compete. There was anticorporate sentiment, especially when times got hard and public investments turned sour, but the record of largesse spoke for itself. There was a pound of business favor for every ounce of denial.

"King Laissez Faire," Lively concluded, "was ... not only dead; the hallowed report of his reign had all been a mistake." What was there in its place? No term was provided, but a new descriptor, *political capitalism*, would soon be on its way—and from one of Lively's students no less.

The business/government nexus did not go unnoticed and uncriticized. *The Nation* editorialized in 1873 for what was by then a fading ideal of the separation of business and state:

> The Government must get out of the "protective" business and the "subsidy" business and the "improvement" and the "development" business. It must let trade, and commerce, and manufactures, and steamboats, and railroads, and telegraphs alone. It cannot touch them without breeding corruption.

As it turned out, too many historians were focused on national issues and missed the capitalist-led anticapitalism at the local and state levels. "The error was one of monumental proportions, a mixture of overlooked data, interested distortion, and persistent preconception," Lively surmised. The misinterpretation

---

8. Government was much smaller in the nineteenth century than in the twentieth; still, there was neither a period of laissez-faire nor sea change to political capitalism. See Internet appendix 6.4, "Early Political Capitalism," at www.politicalcapitalism.org/book1/chapter6/appendix4.html.

9. Regional neomercantilism is part of the Insull (Chicago) and Lay (Houston) stories in Book 2 and Book 3, respectively.

would flow over to a misunderstanding of Progressivism; the good news was that there was a golden opportunity for correction.

Gabriel Kolko: "Political Capitalism"

As Richard Hofstadter's primer on Progressivism came off the press by the thousands, a newly minted Ph.D. in history, Gabriel Kolko, reworked his doctoral dissertation into two books: *The Triumph of Conservatism: A Reinterpretation of American History, 1900–1916* (1963) and *Railroads and Regulation, 1877–1916* (1965). These works, along with budding research from other historians, mostly from the New Left, singed the consensus view of Progressivism and gave exalted meaning to the term *revisionist history*.

Kolko's central thesis in *The Triumph of Conservatism* was a cannon shot across the bow of his elders: "The dominant fact of American political life at the beginning of this century was that big business led the struggle for the federal regulation of the economy." The Progressive Era, he documented, was more about business control of government than government control of business. Kolko, who "combined exhaustive archival research with an intellectual ruthlessness in seizing on crucial questions," could not be ignored. With a new set of questions and a curiosity to challenge the conventional wisdom, he found the proverbial rest of the story in the dusty bins of university libraries, corporate archives, and government depositories.

The reality Kolko uncovered was less reformer-driven Progressivism than probusiness conservatism—or what he called *political capitalism*. Business leaders feared instability, and capitalism was "a perennial gale of creative destruction," as Joseph Schumpeter had taught. Many firms merged or cooperated in newly formed trade associations, but the gales continued. "If economic rationalization could not be attained by mergers and voluntary economic methods, a growing number of important businessmen reasoned, perhaps political means might succeed," Kolko explained. Business leaders traveled a political path in each of six industries he studied: iron and steel, automobiles, agricultural machinery, telephones, copper, and meat packing. The railroad industry, Kolko's most detailed (and controversial) example, merited a book of its own.

Business leaders favored competition when it kept their costs down. Let employees compete rather than be part of a monopolistic labor union! Do not enact tariffs on my inputs! But when it came to sales, unrestricted competition was decried as "cut-throat," even "ruinous," Kolko found. "Laissez faire provided the businessman with an ideological rationale on an intellectual plane, but it also created instability and insecurity in the economy." "Ironically," Kolko continued, "contrary to the consensus of historians, it was not the existence of monopoly that caused the federal government to intervene in the economy, but the lack of it." Competition was not declining in the first decades of the new century; it was "intense" and "growing."

Figure 6.6 Gabriel Kolko's novel interpretation of the Progressive Era provided a new framework for historical analysis. Instead of Progressivism, he documented a continuation of probusiness government intervention into the economy, what he called *political capitalism.*

Outside reformers often helped business effectuate political capitalism. "Many well-intentioned writers and academicians worked for the same legislative goals as businessmen," Kolko noted, "but their innocence did not alter the fact that such measures were frequently designed by businessmen to serve business ends, and that business ultimately reaped the harvest of positive results." This alliance with intellectuals, he added, "was possible because of a naïve, axiomatic view that government economic regulation, per se, was desirable." It was also due to something not mentioned by Kolko—business funding of proregulation academic research. Such was part of a strategy used by Samuel Insull and other leaders in the electric utility industry to secure public utility regulation, a subject of Book 2.

It takes two to tango, and government leaders were typically in step with their business counterparts. Kolko explained why: "The business and political elites knew each other, went to the same schools, belonged to the same clubs, married into the same families, shared the same values—in reality, formed that phenomenon which has lately been dubbed The Establishment."

The capture of politics by business was not conspiratorial. "It is . . . a fact that people and agencies acted out of public sight, and that official statements frequently had little to do with operational realities," Kolko found. Yet "there was a basic consensus among political and business leaders as to what was the public good, and no one had to be cajoled in a sinister manner." Progressivism was a continuation of, not sharp break from, the past—a "triumph of conservatism" whereby a business and political elite stayed on top. So-called Progressivism, really political capitalism, "did not die in the 1920's, but became a part of the basic fabric of American society."

Political capitalism before and after the Civil War matured into a far more sophisticated form, going from old-fashioned tariffs and subsidies to rate-and-entry regulation in many states. The process was also federalized, Kolko noted, business interests preferring one standard to "random state economic regulation." In fact, as some historians and economists noticed, nationalized reform was part of a cumulative process whereby regulation was broadened to address the problems of prior regulation.

Political Railroading

Kolko's companion book, *Railroads and Regulation*, focused on the origins and first decades of federal railroad regulation. His revisionist—and still controversial—thesis: "The railroads, not the farmers and shippers, were the most important single advocates of federal regulation from 1877 to 1916."

Kolko's reconstruction went as follows. Local and state authorities found themselves in the middle of a business fight between shippers desiring lower fares and railroads seeking higher fares. Open entry, price wars, and low margins—"the railroad problem"—made industry leaders sympathetic to formalized, comprehensive regulation where an impartial body set rates. The rates were nominally maximum rates, but by eliminating secret rate discounts off the published fares, the legal rates acted as rate floors. Entry would also be regulated—the other part of the so-called regulatory covenant. Statewide regulation, however, could not apply to interstate routes.

The first draft of a federal railroad bill, Kolko discovered, was authored by an attorney of the Philadelphia and Reading Railroad in 1876. Eleven years later, the Act to Regulate Interstate Commerce, better known as the Interstate Commerce Act of 1887, was enacted, which introduced elements of public utility regulation for much of the industry. Rates were to be "published" and "just and reasonable" to encourage uniformity and to discourage discrimination—as well as price wars, of great interest to the regulated industry. Different groups with different motives brokered the deal, but proregulation railroads were central, in Kolko's view. Without their support, the resulting law and responsibilities of the Interstate Commerce Commission would not have been the most important single regulatory foray of nineteenth-century America.

With rebates, free passes, and other forms of secret discounts prohibited, profitability improved as the supportive industry wanted the new law to do, Kolko noted. Yet industry overcapacity guaranteed tension between carriers and shippers—and between the regulators and the regulated. Political constraints on market signals guaranteed roil, inefficiency, and shifting fates among the private contestants. (The political sector had few losers.) Resulting regulation would be a two-edged sword, hurting as well as helping industry parties, as later studies would document. Nonetheless, railroad and other business support introduced the weapon.

Part of Kolko's railroad story concerned the paragon of high-brow, public-interest regulators in the nineteenth century, Charles Francis Adams Jr., the architect behind the first powerful state regulatory body, the Massachusetts Board of Railroad Commissioners (formed 1869). After leaving the commission to head the Union Pacific Railroad, Adams reiterated his support for federal regulation: "We would welcome the rigid and literal enforcement of every provision of the interstate commerce act."

Union Pacific would become a footnote to history when it successfully challenged a state law denying it a compensatory rate schedule as traditionally accorded under public utility regulation. The U.S. Supreme Court in *Smyth v. Ames* (1898) ruled that legislators and regulators had to allow subject firms a "fair return upon the value of that [property] which it employs for the public convenience." The *fair-value doctrine* would be a centerpiece of state and federal regulation across different industries, including natural gas and electricity. It also cemented a safe haven for many a political capitalist.

Kolko's interpretation of the enactment of the Interstate Commerce Act relied heavily on a report by the Senate Committee on Interstate Commerce, which noted in January 1886, the year before the federal law's enactment:

> The committee has found among the leading representations of the railroad interests an increasing readiness to accept the aid of Congress in working out the solution of the railway problem which has obstinately baffled all their efforts, and not a few of the ablest railroad men of the country seem disposed to look to the intervention of Congress as promising to afford the best means of ultimately securing a more equitable and satisfactory adjustment of the relations of the transportation interests to the community than they themselves have been able to bring about.

Still, historians have put Kolko's thesis under the microscope to find that although many railroad leaders pragmatically supported federal help to maintain rates and profitability, the final law was more the work of large merchant-shippers and not to the railroad industry's liking. Even so, *combined* shipper and railroad interest in regulation—state and then federal—was political capitalism in action.[10]

State regulation, less scrutinized by Kolko, also exhibited examples of leading railroad operators and shippers finding common ground to set uniform rates and eliminate secret discounting for business stability. California, for example, enacted public utility regulation in 1911 with support from the Southern Pacific Railroad Company and the California Fruit Growers Association. In

---

10. Kolko's analysis of federal railroad policy between 1877 and 1916 is critically reviewed in appendix C, pp. 336–42.

words that Kolko could not have scripted better, the head of Southern Pacific, William Sproul, reminisced four years later:

> It is well that those practices [rebating] have been abolished. Neither the railroads nor the shippers could themselves abolish them. Both the railroads and the shippers were dealing with competitive conditions as they found them; they could not control the conditions, and regulation in this regard had undoubtedly been in the public interest.

Kolko's Worldview

Gabriel Kolko, in one historian's words, "reached down the Progressive lion's throat, grabbed its tail, and pulled the creature inside out." How did a historian at the beginning of his career upstage his superiors, including an esteemed member of his Harvard dissertation committee, Arthur Schlesinger Jr.? Voracious reading and research by a gifted chronicler explains only part of it. Kolko's real advantage was a different worldview, one that made fresh facts important and old facts worth another look. Kolko went past (in his words) the "ideological intonations in election speeches, much exaggerated by historians," to uncover the real thing: a "movement to establish stability and control within the railroad industry so that railroads could prosper without the fearful consequences of cutthroat competition."

Robert Wiebe, who lit the revisionist fires along with Kolko, documented how social reformers strategically downplayed the support they received from business interests. "A crusade belonged to the pure," Wiebe explained, and "during the progressive era one either stood with the people or with the interests." Thus "descriptions of reform acquired a classic form," whereby "the simplified version provided convenient shorthand for proving authenticity, convincing doubters, and communicating with other reformers." Wiebe, like Kolko, was not misdirected by the "war cry" of the chambers of commerce to "'get the government out of business.'"

From the get-go, Kolko was suspicious of the public-interest interpretation of regulation. He knew that a golden age of laissez-faire was "mythology." He also recognized how business and political leaders were socially intertwined. It would take a sea change to reverse this symbiotic relationship, which otherwise could be expected to continue to expand along with bigger business and bigger government, Kolko and other New Left historians believed. They could not imagine capitalism without the political given the inherent contradictions of capitalism that Karl Marx had divined.

Kolko seized on another fact that mainstream historians failed to comprehend: Despite consolidation and mergers that increased concentration, at least for a while, and despite informal agreements between rivals to soften competition, competition remained intense. The merger movement was overrated. "The heyday of the merger movement was restricted to a few years [1897–1901]," observed Kolko, "and ended almost as abruptly as it began." A growing economy and high rate of inventions and innovations meant entrants galore and red-hot rivalry among the old guard. Historians fooled themselves into believing that major industries, from railroads to banking, were "sufficiently concentrated and internally cohesive not to need the assistance of political agencies." Why? Although underappreciated by Kolko, *mainstream historians bought into perfect-competition theory, which made American capitalism look monopolistic and big business appear not in need of political relief from competition.* Kolko, having bailed out of his only economics class at Harvard after two weeks because "it had nothing to do with reality," saw only real-world competition—Schumpeter's *capitalist reality*—in the statistics and actions of business leaders.

A fourth reason for Kolko's breakthrough was that he avoided the "idealization of the state." Many intellectuals saw in government the image of society, a pluralism that left little room for business dominance. Yet capture, or at least disproportional influence, is exactly what happened when the organized and powerful few advanced their interest at the expense of the less-organized and weaker many, even during the so-called Progressive Era.

Political capitalism was not an ideology. It had no champions. It did not have a clear beginning or end. It naturally evolved from many strands. "Because there were precious few business advocates of political capitalism preaching over time, and never a general theorist in the true sense of that term," Kolko explained, "reform became an incremental process intended to compensate for the failure of traditional means to cope with new problems." Holistic thinking about *society*, *state versus business*, and *laissez-faire versus socialism* masked what was happening in bits and pieces, in fits and starts, beneath the surface. Political scientist Arthur Bentley was right; political change was happening *at the margin*, where organized groups drove the outcomes affecting the many.

New Left History

Kolko and other New Left intellectuals longed for an alternative to capitalism. They rejected laissez-faire as inherently unstable as a whole, as in its parts, and exploitative of the working·class (proletariat). The Keynesian/Marxian notion of a mismatch between aggregate supply and demand—capitalism's "underconsumptionist dilemma of productive capacity exceeding consumer demand"—was their core economics, however fallacious. Ipso facto, business downturns at home necessitated imperialism abroad as businesses sought to find new markets capable of buying their surplus. In Kolko's estimation, "intrinsically mercurial ... regulated capitalism" necessitated "America's constant, increasingly violent effort to control and redirect a world moving ever further beyond any nation's mastery."

Capitalism's benefits, this interpretation continued, came with weighty political baggage. "The main tendency within American capitalism since the Civil War," Kolko explained, "has been to require ever more comprehensive political, economic, and social solutions to the challenges it has confronted, even as the political and intellectual conditions both for articulating precisely and implementing these answers have become increasingly elusive and transcended the system's capacities." The system he preferred to capitalism (really political capitalism) was some form of democratic socialism requiring a "new politics."[11]

Kolko's research inspired other New Left historians. In *The Corporate Ideal in the Liberal State* (1968), socialist James Weinstein documented how "businessmen were able to harness to their own ends the desire of intellectuals and middle class reformers [for] . . . stabilization, rationalization, and continued expansion of existing political economy." Weinstein's historiography exposed the fiction that so-called rugged individualists embraced Darwinian competition and laissez-faire. "In the current century, particularly on the federal level, few reforms were enacted without the tacit approval, if not the guidance, of the large corporate interests," he concluded. Like Kolko, Weinstein was not a conspiracy theorist. The fact that "businessmen were able to harness to their own ends the desire of intellectuals and middle class reformers" was the result of influential corporate heads acting independently to promote their own interests.

Weinstein had little stomach for the standard interpretation of Progressivism by Arthur Schlesinger Jr., whom he deprecated as the "intellectual in residence of the Kennedys." The barb had substance. When Schlesinger was not writing flattering prose about a Kennedy, he was often on the phone with one of them. Gabriel Kolko recalls how his dissertation adviser was, for this reason, seldom available.

Weinstein was impressed by the sophistication of key business leaders in the business/government alliance, including the energy titan Samuel Insull. Weinstein's book focused on the National Association of Manufacturers (formed 1895) and the National Civic Federation (formed 1900), which represented the most powerful of the powerful. Insull, a founder of the latter, was a leader of this elite.

Kolko and Weinstein helped resurrect the career of the father of New Left history, William Appleman Williams, whose work had once been disparaged as "farcical [and] argument rather than history" in the *Journal of American History*. Williams's renaissance included his election as president of the Organization of American Historians for 1980/81. As empty (and tragically wrong) as Marxian/socialist economics would turn out to be, the New Left provided an important contribution to historical scholarship.

---

11. Although stopping short of endorsing socialism, Kolko has spoken about "new options" and "radical humanist change" requiring societal transformation. He more recently (1994) stated: "While the term 'socialism' itself would warrant a replacement if a better definition could be devised, the much larger rationalist, internationalist, humanitarian, and radical tradition from which it evolved, and which long preceded Marxism and was ultimately irrevocably committed to the goals of equality and social cooperation both between nations and within them, remains more imperative than ever."

Political Energy

America's energy industries have been a bastion of political capitalism for much of their history. Leading gas and electricity firms sponsored state and then federal public utility regulation during the Progressive Era and New Deal, as discussed in Book 2 and Book 3. They, like other so-called public utilities, welcomed the prospect of making commission-approved reasonable profits in an entry-restricted environment, rather than taking their chances in open-entry markets.

The U.S. coal industry longed for federal aid as well. "The bituminous coal industry has been one of the most chaotic industries in the United States in recent years," an Ohio University economist wrote in 1940. "Because of this lack of order it has recommended itself to the Nation as an industry urgently in need of social control and, as a result, it has come to serve as a significant laboratory for experiments in certain types of government regulation." The industry was *too competitive*, he posited, necessitating "minimum price regulation . . . to prevent excessive exploitation of the industry by its consumers in other industries which are in a better position to exercise a sabotage of production." Coal producers could not be happier with what at least one Ph.D. professor was saying.

Integrated and independent oil companies were against public utility regulation, on the other hand. Cost-based rate ceilings were not considered compensatory for the risk of exploration and production. And gasoline service stations could hardly be cost-and-entry regulated without regulating refiners and, in turn, producers. Still, political capitalism roared in with the oil gushers in the 1920s. What Norman Nordhauser described as the *quest for stability* involved state efforts to limit oil production to market demand—a regulatory regime called market-demand proration—to achieve a price of $1 per barrel (about $12 per barrel today). "Dollar oil," a rallying cry among producers, also necessitated federal measures to limit imports. Preferential, industry-secured tax breaks for exploration and production was the third leg of what Alfred Kahn in the *American Economic Review* identified as a domestic oil-industry cartel.

Energy companies were a political force. Noting that "big business is powerfully organized and integrated," John Ise, in his 1946 textbook *Economics*, ranked the most powerful lobbying associations of the nearly 400 in Washington. The Edison Electrical Institute was first, the American Petroleum Institute fifth, and the National Coal Association eighth. Ise warned that "under pressure from special interests, the government itself has done much to foster monopoly and so to weaken our capitalist economy."

Pro-oil-industry regulation, which continued through the 1960s, required ever more government intervention, which led Alfred Kahn to observe: "One interference with competition necessitates another and yet another, and an industry of 'rugged individualists' becomes more and more tightly enmeshed with the government to which they originally turned in hope of protecting themselves from competition." In 1971, fellow economist George Stigler, a future Nobel laureate, identified the petroleum industry as a "political jugger-naut [and] immense consumer of political benefits."

But political capitalism came to haunt the oil industry a short time later when growing demand, flat world supply, and the unintended consequences of government intervention sent oil prices to record levels. The age-old domes-tic programs to support prices—state-level wellhead proration and import restrictions—were no longer necessary in the new environment. Oil politics reversed as populist politicians turned against the industry with price controls and tax increases. The first head of the U.S. Department of Energy, James Schle-singer, rationalized federal price ceilings by noting how the oil industry had politically raised prices for so long. An energy study by the Ford Foundation made the same point: The oil industry won with government policy during periods of low prices; consumers should now win relief from high prices. This price-control era (1971–81) would turn out to be worse for consumers than it was for domestic producers, but that is another story.

Business in Political Action

Overcapacity and price wars were not unique to energy. They were emblem-atic of other businesses competing in open markets as economic growth gave entrepreneurs more capital and consumers more options. Tariffs became "more protective and more inclusive" from the 1860s to the 1930s, giving a variety of domestic industries breathing room from foreign competition. The Sherman Antitrust Act of 1890, an aid to smaller competitors and supported by them, became a quid pro quo for the McKinley Tariff Act, enacted in the same year. Tariffs bred domestic trusts, but lawmakers felt that federal antitrust law could undo the excesses of the trusts. This sinister logic caused the *New York Times* to reverse its support for the Sherman Act soon after it was enacted. But it was too late; the act and the tariff were law.

The muckrakers' and politicians' "bogey of monopoly" did not incite con-sumer unrest, because big business was delivering more goods at lower prices. Bigness would be prosecuted from time to time, and new areas of antitrust law made just about any pricing strategy legally questionable. Charging higher prices could be called monopolistic; charging the same price, collusive; lower prices, predatory. The Federal Trade Commission, ostensibly created to promote competition, was the machinery used by smaller firms to attack "unfair" com-petition from larger firms. Not surprisingly, businesses found plenty of room to use antitrust to attack competitors and soften competition. Private antitrust suits would outnumber federal suits by 6 to 1 in the 1940s and 1950s and by 20 to 1 in the next decades.

The throttling of competition by the selective application of the very regula-tions that were intended to promote competition led two economists to dust off and rephrase the opening of *The Communist Manifesto*:

> There is a specter that haunts our antitrust institutions. Its threat is that, far from serving as the bulwark of competition, these institutions will become the most powerful instrument in the hands of those who wish to subvert it. More than that, it threatens to draw great quantities of resources into the struggle to prevent effective competition, thereby more than offsetting the contributions to economic efficiency promised by antitrust activities.

Antitrust, far from promoting the reformer's reform, was a sharp tool of political capitalists.

Some more salient examples of political capitalism will cement the main point of this chapter: Business input into the legislative and regulatory process was narrowly conceived, sophisticated, and persuasive before, during, and after the so-called Progressive Era.

Long-standing tariffs protecting agricultural markets were joined by the Agricultural Marketing Act of 1929, a Hoover-era law authorizing the use of taxpayer dollars to support farm-product prices. Federal subsidies for agricul-tural products accelerated during the Great Depression and are entrenched today. From the beginning, the politically powerful farm bloc has dictated public policy at the expense of less-powerful consumers, an example of thoroughgoing political capitalism.

The Shipping Act of 1916 extended public utility regulation to vessels engaged in interstate or coastal commerce at the request of the to-be-regulated as well as railroad interests desiring less intermodal competition. By 1940, water-borne carriers were regulated as a public utility, joining railroads, oil pipelines, and motor trucks at the Interstate Commerce Commission. The "nationalistic and protectionist" Merchant Marine Act of 1936 began the long-standing practice of granting cash subsidies to ships built in domestic shipyards at higher costs owing to U.S. labor laws. Needless to say, the program had as much support from shipbuilders as from labor.

Food standards codified in the Pure Food and Drug Act of 1906 resulted from "the cumulative interaction of commercial and bureaucratic competition." Conflicts before and after the law's passage "were not contests between good and evil, or purity and adulteration, or honesty and fraud," two scholars found. "They were contests over who would benefit and lose from regulatory activity." The saga also featured a quite self-interested bureaucrat, Harvey Washington Wiley, who "captured the pure food movement and used it as the basis for expanding his bureau." Gabriel Kolko himself had noted the episode but did not look deeply enough to find further support for his own thesis.

Federal child-labor law reflected the interests of the northern textile industry seeking to erase the labor-cost advantage of its southern rivals. "The banking community in general, and large bankers specifically" won passage of the Federal Reserve Act of 1913, which provided centralization, stability, and an "elastic currency" to promote cheap credit for business expansion.

The American Petroleum Institute successfully lobbied the Oregon legislature to enact the first gasoline tax in 1919 to fund road building, a public-finance breakthrough that would lead to all 48 states following suit in the next decade. Big oil envisioned more roads for more gasoline sales, a strategy that dovetailed nicely with that of the paving contractors, another influential lobbyist group then—as now.

·◇·

Two particular examples of common-good, Progressive Era legislation can be better understood in light of their business origins. One concerns public-land management around the turn of the last century; the other, coal-mining safety regulation.

The *conservation movement* is considered one of the most public-spirited initiatives of a period that witnessed ever-increasing mineral and timber harvesting from public (as from private) lands and the so-called closing of the frontier. President Theodore Roosevelt in 1907 urged the nation to "look ahead and to substitute a planned and orderly development of our resources in place of a haphazard striving for immediate profit." With experts claiming to see a coming exhaustion of timber and coal, among other resources, Roosevelt withdrew more than 200 million acres of federal land from private development. Development henceforth would be for *all* the people, he declared, not "monopolized by a few men."

Historians followed the Roosevelt line to interpret public-domain conservation as the victory of science and husbandry over the short-term excesses of the oil, coal, copper, timber, water, and cattle industries. Gifford Pinchot, a leader of the conservation movement,[12] described his work as replacing "the law of Business [with the] law of self-preservation." The "morally imperative" action required politics to rid itself of the special interests. Pinchot declared:

> In a day when the vast increase in wealth tends to reduce all things, moral, intellectual and material, to the measure of the dollar; in a day when we have with us always the man who is working for his own pocket all the time; when the monopolist of land, of opportunity, or power or privilege in any form, is ever in the public eye—it is good to remember that the real leaders are the men who value the right to give themselves more highly than any gain whatsoever.

---

12. The personally wealthy Pinchot, "America's first forester," was described as "a perfect example of the type of patrician reformer who cast his lot with the Progressives, not because of economic deprivation, but out of a desire for greater status, service, and power."

But Pinchot spoke differently when he told a gathering of the Society of American Foresters: "The object of our forest policy is not to preserve the forests because they are beautiful . . . or because they are refuges for the wild creatures of the wilderness . . . but . . . [for] the making of prosperous homes."

The people-versus-interests interpretation of the conservation movement has been challenged as gloss over substance. Reformers and business groups worked together for legislation that was pro-elite and probusiness. Much favor trading—so-called logrolling—was needed to satisfy different industry groups, such as the American National Livestock Association, National Rivers and Harbors Congress, and the National Water Users Association. Business and the new efficiency experts designed federal legislation to "place a premium on large-scale capital organization, technology, and industry-wide cooperation and planning to abolish the uncertainties and waste of competitive resource use." Timber titans, such as Northern Pacific Railroad, Kirby Lumber, and Weyerhaeuser Lumber, welcomed taxpayer-funded research and management by the Bureau of Forestry, a new division within the Department of Agriculture. Using the rationale of conservation, railroads pushed for measures that increased tourism or increased the value of their land grants on each side of the track. The "barbed-wire people, who got huge orders whenever forest sections were withdrawn from entry," were also active. Political capitalism was sophisticated and thorough.

Safety standards for mining coal and other metals "was, above all, a business reform." Mining companies were behind the establishment of the Bureau of Mines in 1910, a pet measure of Pennsylvania congressman George Huff, who was first and foremost a coal operator. The bureau offered the mining industry an entrée to what the many other regulated industries had politically sought: "stability, predictability, and security." A single federal mining standard was preferable to different state standards, and resource studies, safety inspections, and other bureau work would be funded by taxpayers, not the industry. Mining companies set the agenda once the Bureau of Mines was created. "In short," historian William Graebner concluded, "the emphasis of Gabriel Kolko and James Weinstein on the primacy of business in the reform process seems appropriate to the Progressive coal-mining safety movement."

·◇·

Amid the business community's boiler-plate pronouncements for less government came moments of truth. Theodore Vail, head of American Telephone & Telegraph, hailed his company's work in securing regulation in telephony. "We believe in and were the first to advocate state or government control of public utilities," he wrote in 1914, "in order that waste and duplication of effort may be avoided and uniformity of purpose and common control be enforced." J. P. Morgan operative Henry Davison told Congress in 1912, "I would rather have regulation and control than free competition." His view, Kolko noticed, was "a truism that was widely appreciated at the time but overlooked by scholars over the next half-century." Even some in the milk industry tried to qualify as a public utility to qualify for government relief from open entry and price wars.

Political capitalism became an open fount of excess during the Great Depression. "The average trade convention is a perfect hothouse of proposals for government regulation," one journalist wrote in *Harper's*, with hundreds of trade associations "begging Mr. Hoover's bureaus to look them over and . . . tell them how to improve the management of their affairs." The intellectuals seconded the notion of business/government cooperation as a recovery tool. "By 1931–32 interest in so-called economic planning had become almost a popular craze," one historian found. "Socialists, liberals, and business men joined in the movement, though the methods they proposed were not the same." The *Quarterly Journal of Economics* published a survey on the burgeoning literature of government planning. The dean of the Harvard Business School, W. B. Donham, among others, called on business leaders to embrace government planning with a social purpose.

FDR's New Deal continued the largely probusiness policies of his predecessors, including Herbert Hoover,[13] with a new rationale: government-aided cooperation for business profitability and, in turn, general recovery. The National Recovery Administration (NRA), established in 1933, set 847 industry codes of fair competition, regulating 150 types of rivalrous practices to minimize competition and improve profitability. This experiment in by-business-for-business regulation, blessed by the intellectual class, crashed when the Supreme Court ruled the NRA unconstitutional in May 1935.

The Business of Business—and Politics Too

"The business of America is business," President Calvin Coolidge famously remarked during the Roaring Twenties. He could have added that the business of government is also business. The Great Depression and World War II quieted such confident talk of commerce, but in the postwar period, America's business was again booming business.

A collection of speeches given in 1966/67 by the president of the U.S. Chamber of Commerce was published by McGraw-Hill as *The Business of Business: Private Enterprise and Public Affairs*. M. A. "Mike" Wright, chairman of Humble Oil & Refining Company (now part of ExxonMobil), urged his fellow executives to be more proactive in public and government affairs to improve the business environment and better society. "Virtually every business decision today is affected by public laws, regulations, and policies," he stated, yet industry leaders were often "indifferent" or "negative" rather than "creative" and "positive"

---

13. For an interpretation of President Hoover as the first New Dealer, see Internet appendix 6.5, "The Hoover Mythology," at www.politicalcapitalism.org/book1/chapter6/appendix5.html.

toward lawmaking. A new emphasis on statesmanship and the common weal was necessary for the business community to meet the unprecedented challenges posed by "urbanization, industrialization, and internationalism." The "new ... executive" of the "'new capitalism'" had to understand and participate in "government-business relations, public affairs, investment analysis, international trade, union relations, public relations, social welfare, diversification, [and] cultural development." The CEO's "daily education" needed to be as much about "legislative trends and developments in Washington as on the latest production or marketing techniques."

The speeches, and now published essays, offered little historical context. The issues of the day—inflation, price controls, welfare transfers, tax policy, pollution, public education, antitrust suits, labor relations—were simply taken as the starting point. Business was portrayed as an innocent bystander rather than, historically speaking, the *shaper* of much government activism. The real message from the book was that political capitalism was getting more difficult to manage for its progenitors as new interests organized and pluralism increased.

The book's fare was not unlike what journalist John T. Flynn criticized in the 1920s as sloganeering, including "that which burns upon the banners of the United States Chamber of Commerce: *More Business in Government and Less Government in Business.*" Flynn scoffed because the new laws were coming far less from the imaginations of legislators than from "the legislative program committees of trade associations or from the special counsel of trade groups . . . backed often by resolutions from trade conventions and chambers of commerce." Yet the chamber, complained Flynn, was selling a picture of business "as a huge giant, gagged and shackled like a moving-picture galley slave to his oar." Flynn forwarded his own ideal for the chamber: *"Less business interference in government and more statesmanship in business."*

That was the 1920s; this was the 1960s. The policymaking environment was more competitive and pluralistic, even if *The Business of Business* provided no inkling about how then-current politics evolved from a century of mostly business-driven politics. Joining the traditional government/business/labor triad were new players that could frustrate the legislative agenda of any business, including that of the oil industry. Business-versus-business tiffs alone could leave any company or trade association defeated, as Humble Oil knew firsthand from its skirmishes with independent oil firms on policies regulating domestic production and imports. On the natural gas side, Humble Oil and other producers were losing a fight to deregulate wellhead prices as legislators, regulators, and presidents sided with prointervention gas-distribution companies and municipalities instead. The depletion allowance and other cherished wellhead tax breaks for oil and gas producers were under fire. Environmental issues were complicating the political equation for the first time. Political capitalism was a win-some/lose-some game more than ever before for big companies, as it could also be for small firms.

The game had changed for business in general. "Corporate plans for advertising campaigns, for mergers and acquisitions, for changes in employment practices, for new stock issues, for changes in the manner of computing and reporting earnings, for pricing to different groups of customers—all can raise questions that the management must put to its legal staff," noted one historian in the late 1960s. In the same period, Alfred Chandler declared the day over when business leaders devoted all their time to internal matters. As a result of the affluence they helped to create, "non-economic challenges are now becoming more critical than the economic ones." Special interests were proliferating, some or many with an antibusiness and anticapitalist agenda.

The sweep of contemporary economic issues in *The Business of Business* was beyond the reach of a lifelong engineer and busy company head. Mike Wright had a speechwriter and ghostwriter, an up-and-coming corporate economist by day and Ph.D. economics candidate at the University of Houston by night. Kenneth Lee Lay, age 25, was smart and well educated. He had a large capacity for work and got to the essence of things quickly. He possessed sound organizational instincts and strong people skills. He wrote clearly and imaginatively. Dr. Lay, as he would soon be titled, had a big future.

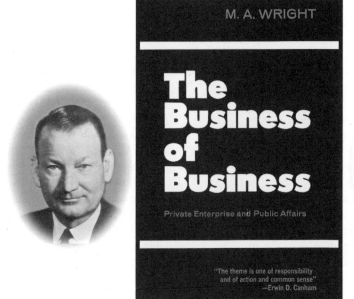

Figure 6.7 *The Business of Business* (1967), a guidebook by Humble Oil & Refining head Mike Wright (left) for business leaders in the mixed economy, was ghostwritten by Ken Lay (right), a corporate economist who had joined the company two years earlier after receiving his master's degree in economics from the University of Missouri.

·◇·

In the older days of political capitalism, legislative affairs could be handled by companies through Washington contacts and occasional trips to the District by company executives. Few firms had their own Washington office. By the late 1960s, however, companies were regularly opening a Washington branch, in addition to participating in their D.C.-based trade associations, all dealing with some 50 new federal regulatory programs in such areas as consumer and environmental protection. "The corporate executive may be most concerned about the award of public contracts or about actions taken by the Internal Revenue Service, the Antitrust Division of the Department of Justice, the Federal Trade Commission, the S.E.C., the N.L.R.B., and the other regulatory agencies," one study found. This study noted something else new—"the top echelons of the modern corporation are filled with men who have come to know Washington."

The new CEO might attend meetings with the president, testify before a congressional subcommittee, serve on a special committee, or even have once taken a "tour of duty" in Washington. Such experiences made business chiefs empathetic toward the party in power and partial toward compromise and cooperation in public policy. Ken Lay would go on to become a prototype Washington insider.

Between 1970 and 1980, an estimated 130 major new federal laws "brought the Fortune 500 to Washington, along with tens of thousands of lawyers." Walter Heller, President Johnson's chief economic adviser, reported that most business groups were on board with the "new economics" of fine-tuning the economy. President Nixon would soon declare, "I am now a Keynesian." In 1972, the Business Roundtable was created in Washington, the first organization "to be based on the principle of the personal participation of the corporate CEO." Three years later, Atlantic Richfield Company became the first major public corporation to mobilize its employees, retirees, and stockholders—a group numbering in the tens of thousands—to back its political issues. Other firms, many in the highly regulated energy industry, mobilized their constituencies to make the company's voice heard in an increasingly noisy political environment. Some firms started political action committees (PACs) in response to the Political Reform Act of 1974, which limited individual donations to $1,000 per candidate per election but allowed companies to contribute up to $5,000 to political causes from employee contributions.

The mobilization was in line with the message of Mike Wright/Ken Lay: Ratchet up or be left behind. But even with this greater effort, the business of politics was less a sure thing than it typically was in the past. Business took much of the blame for the 1970s stagflation and energy shortages, which presented an unprecedented public relations problem. "Why is it that in the United States government and business have so often appeared as adversaries?" Alfred Chandler Jr. asked at the close of the troubled decade. "The question is particularly intriguing since such a relationship between government and business did not always exist in the United States." The deans of Harvard's Graduate School of Business Administration and School of Government also lamented the "present

adversarial relationship between business and government" that was not resulting in good public policy.

Government affairs departments, once the province of defense contractors and companies regulated as public utilities, became the norm for many
other companies by century's end. "Government relations has been described
as '*the* principal new responsibility added to top corporate management's
traditional functional concerns' in the past two decades," one textbook
reported. The process that was once so simple—a top business leader con-
tacting a top government official in times of need—came to require a fully
staffed public and government affairs office, rich in "analytic and technical
responsibility."

It would be none other than Ken Lay's Enron that brought this analytic capability to new heights with a computer program named *the matrix*, which quantified legislative and regulatory risk/reward to drive the company's lobbying
efforts. "The matrix illustrates the brash, calculating methods that Enron managers used to play Washington politics," the *Washington Post* reported soon after
the company's collapse. "The company that made headlines by erasing rules
and ignoring convention in the business world applied the same principles in
Congress, state capitals and the Administration, bragging that its shrewd political tactics blew past customary constraints."

Enron's economist behind the matrix lamented about how his company had
no weighting for the public good: "They only cared if this was good for Enron."
But such an ambitious, amoral corporate culture hardly began with Ken Lay's
political entrepreneurship. A template had been created at Ford Motor Company in the decade prior to Enron's formation, as chronicled by a principled
free-marketeer who worked in its government affairs department in the late
1970s.

In *The Suicidal Corporation* (1988), Paul Weaver described Ford Motor's
"*corporatism*—broadly, the management of a nation's markets and politics by
companies, unions, and/or other producer groups in their own interest, backed
up where necessary by the power of government." The mentality among his
peers was "less a set of ideas than an attitude" that

> whatever would benefit the company was all right for them to seek. They believed
> that any method that would secure those benefits was all right for them to use.
> They believed that pursuing corporate advantage through the public-policy pro-
> cess was their duty and right. Whatever my colleagues felt like doing, they did.

Political promiscuity was joined by public- and investor-relations promiscuity. Ford's press releases were "Good News Only and No Bad News," even as
billions of dollars in losses were recorded. "We lied," Weaver remembered.

"Boundless ambition" created a "good for Ford, good for society" mindset.
Conscience-free political capitalism and perception-over-reality public relations
went together.

Ford's rent-seeking reached a peak in 1980 when senior management decided to lobby for federal import restrictions against Japanese automobiles, ironic for a company that in the era of Henry Ford and Henry Ford II had been a force for open trade and internationalism. Ford's chief economist, William Niskanen, who left a tenured position at the University of California at Berkeley in 1975 to join the company, was nonplussed. In meetings and memos, he bluntly admonished Ford's top brass to either meet the competition or get out of the car business. One memo came with a philosophical flourish: "A common commitment to refrain from seeking special [political] favors serves the same economic function as a common commitment to refrain from stealing."

Ford went hard for automobile protectionism, and Niskanen was dismissed for his intransigence. "In this company, Bill, the people who do well wait until they hear their superiors express their views," his boss explained. "Then they add something in support of those views."

Ford's political and personnel actions were hardly surprising. Corporate rent-seeking was old hat, as economists from Adam Smith to Milton Friedman documented. A corporation is not a free-market think tank. Niskanen went to war and lost. An in-the-ranks uprising at Enron over the company's renewable-energy and global-warming strategy replayed the tape a decade later, although Ken Lay found a compromise to prevent a high-profile firing, as discussed in Book 3.

William Niskanen went on to bigger and better things. He was appointed to President Reagan's Council of Economic Advisers soon after leaving Ford and in 1985 became chairman of the libertarian Cato Institute in Washington, D.C. One of Niskanen's most important projects at Cato would be corporate accountability and regulatory standards in the wake of the Enron debacle, resulting in two learned books: *Corporate Aftershock* (2003) and *After Enron: Lessons for Public Policy* (2005).

Revisionism for Deregulation: Kolko's Legacy

Gabriel Kolko's revisionist books and articles "became staples of graduate seminars and professional convention sessions," yet there would be no Pulitzer Prizes for him as there were for Schlesinger and Hofstadter. Kolko carried the baggage of the New Left, and his treatment of the elites hit too close to home for some prominent academics. Still, Kolko's new history would triumph as a part of a reform movement. It began when free-market capitalists seized upon Kolko's findings to bolster the case for *pure capitalism*, a bittersweet development for him.[14] It culminated with the removal of some of the regulations whose unholy origins Kolko had exposed.

---

14. Kolko complained: "With the unimportant exception of a few conservatives who ignored everything which undermined their case, no one paid much attention to my economic exposition, preferring to focus on my political narrative—which generated considerable attention and dispute—rather than its integral economic context."

An "intellectual weakness of libertarianism," economist-philosopher Robert Heilbroner charged in 1970, was "its failure to trace the part played by business-men themselves in the erection of the state apparatus that presumably curtailed their freedom." New Left historians may have beaten the free-marketeers to the punch, but capitalism's leading lights were not soft on political capitalism, despite their failure to document the extent of the virus. Capitalist theoreticians quickly embraced the New Left's revisionism, substituted a different economic interpre-tation, and forwarded a new urgency for the separation of business and state.

Libertarian scholar Murray Rothbard reviewed Kolko's "brilliant" *Triumph of Conservatism*, arguing that "monopoly privilege can only be created by the State and not as a result of free-market operations." George Stigler, a leader of the free-market Chicago school of economics, concluded in an influential 1971 essay: "Regulation is acquired by the industry and is designed and operated for its benefit." His statistical approach elevated the capture theory of regulation to expose the Progressive thesis of public-interest regulation as sophomoric. The synthesis of New Left history and free-market economics to censure the practice of political capitalism inspired a new term, the *Kolko/Stigler thesis*.

Intellectual change was also propelled by a group of disillusioned Leftists, some former Marxists, and other "liberals mugged by reality." The so-called neoconservatives rebelled against many of the outcomes of modern liberalism, including regulation plagued by the "law of unintended consequences" and a perceived moral decay resulting from welfare dependency. "The neocons were intellectuals," Daniel Yergin and Joseph Stanislaw wrote, "engaged in an ideo-logical struggle against a set of dominant ideas that had held the commanding heights in American thinking for several decades." Neoconservatives, writing in such magazines as *Public Interest* and *Commentary* and on the editorial page of the *Wall Street Journal*, became as much a part of the new thinking "as the Hayeks and Friedmans," Yergin and Stanislaw added.

Democrats greeted the Ford administration's regulatory reform effort in 1975 with the words: "While 'regulatory reform' is a cliché whose time has come, one person's regulatory reform is another's environmental, consumer rip-off, unconscionable cancer risk, or return to the robber baronies of yester-year." Yet just a few years later, "regulatory reform embraced the entire political spectrum." It was "the 'economist's hour,'" stated regulatory historian Thomas McCraw of Harvard Business School. Politically correct *de*regulation came in those areas where regulation was prima facie protectionism. Gabriel Kolko's revisionism was vindicated in the halls of power, although it came with an irony. Kolko's thesis of business-dominated politics led to the very reform that weakened his case for the inevitability of political capitalism.

Ideas matter too.

Kolko also won in the intellectual arena, even though his own writings had disparaged the power of ideas as a causal factor. Harvard Law School's Stephen Breyer (a future U.S. Supreme Court justice) published a tome discrediting the

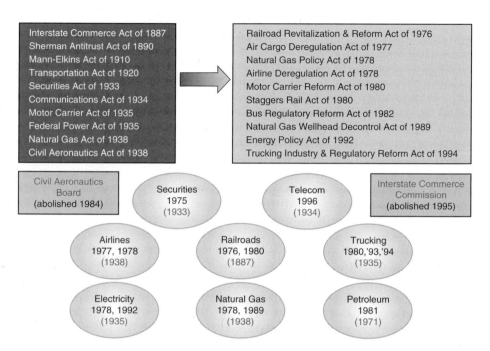

Figure 6.8 A number of American industries lost their Progressivism/New Deal protection in whole or in part in the 1970s and 1980s. Two long-standing agencies were abolished: the Interstate Commerce Commission and the Civil Aeronautics Board.

public-interest theory of regulation. Studies from the Chicago school of economics were influential in the drive to get from *capture* to *competition*: Major transportation industries, among other parts of the U.S. economy, were partially or substantially deregulated for the first time in decades. The Interstate Commerce Commission (1887–1995) was abolished soon after its centennial.

Natural gas and electricity, the two energy industries still under federal public utility control, were *partially* deregulated. The Natural Gas Policy Act of 1978 (NGPA) mixed deregulation and regulation in one weighty, complicated law. One provision (Section 311) opened up the wholesale gas market, allowing spot-gas transactions and transportation fees for the interstate pipeline industry for the first time in the history of the Natural Gas Act of 1938. This beginning, supplemented by administrative orders by the Federal Energy Regulatory Commission (FERC) in the 1980s, created a spot market in natural gas and a major new business—*natural gas marketing*. Enron, more than any other company, drove FERC gas policy and profited from so-called mandatory open access.

A provision tucked inside the 373-page Energy Policy Act of 1992 (EPAct) deregulated commodity transactions in the *wholesale* (interstate) electricity market.

For the first time since the enactment of the Federal Power Act of 1935, utilities and independent power producers could buy and sell electricity at unregulated prices so long as the power was resold by a utility or municipality to a final user. (Commodity transactions in retail—distribution—markets remained entry and price regulated at the state level.) This EPAct provision, authored by Enron lobbyists, was the proverbial camel's nose under the tent for restructuring the huge U.S. electric power industry. Enron would become the nation's largest power trader in addition to being the largest natural gas marketer—all from regulatory change.

Yet partial deregulation—some mix of deregulation, reregulation, and continued regulation—was not deregulation. A study by Stephen Vogel across industries and nations concluded:

> In most cases of "deregulation," governments have combined liberalization with reregulation, the reformulation of old rules and the creation of new ones. Hence we have wound up with freer markets and more rules. In fact, there is often a logical link: liberalization requires reregulation.

But liberalization does not *require* reregulation. It simply turned out that way in some key industries (gas, electricity) owing to a particular confluence of lobbying pressure and, to an extent, the ideas held by key decision makers. And under partial regulation, decisions by administrative agencies became crucial, inspiring much behind-the-scenes activity by business (and environmental) interests. Enron would be a deft player in this process to shape important new business lines.

How did decades-old, entrenched regulation and bureaucracy fall victim to major reform? The short answer is that intellectuals and politicians of different stripes rebelled against a system of Robin Hood in reverse—taking from consumers to give to corporations. Ralph Nader, Consumers Federation of America, Common Cause, and Consumers Union found a type of regulation that they did not like—probusiness. Senator Edward Kennedy (D-MA) joined in, and in 1977, President Jimmy Carter declared his intent "to free the American people from the burden of over-regulation." Enough Republicans were promarket rather than probusiness to make the effort bipartisan. The reformist-led retreat was an all-too-rare moment in the history of twentieth-century political capitalism.

Carter's greatest victory came after he appointed Alfred Kahn head of the Civil Aeronautics Board (CAB) in 1977. The CAB had long regulated the airlines as the ICC regulated railroads and motor carriers. Its clients did not want change, despite (or because of) the rampant inefficiency with which the controls allowed them to operate. Kahn, with the help of "an odd coalition of academic economists, Naderite consumerists, liberal Democrats, and conservative Republicans," won the day with the Airline Deregulation Act of 1978, which deregulated entry and rates for commercial air travel for the first time since 1938. The same dynamic resulted in deregulation in other transportation industries and elsewhere.

"As in physical nature the flash of lightning always precedes the roll of thunder," historians Charles and Mary Beard once wrote, "so in human affairs the flame of thought has always gone before a transformation in the social arrangements of mankind." Intellectuals acquiesced to business stabilization during the Progressive Era and New Deal; their passion now worked for deregulation of the protected industries. Experience has been called the great teacher, but it took the right *interpretation* of experience to effectuate change. The joined interpretation of the "left-liberal theory of political participation [and] conservative free market economic theory" began with Gabriel Kolko in the 1960s. All of which shows: *Ideas can have consequences.*

Free-market reform in the 1970s and 1980s added a pluralistic element to the politics of business. Political capitalism could be torn down, not only constructed. Still, the historical record of most of the twentieth century remains invariant: *the triumph of political capitalism over capitalism,* led by business interests in many cases and abetted by academics, the media, and other intellectuals.

Conclusion

The Economist, founded in London in 1843 as a brief for free trade, published a somber commemorative issue 18 months after the Enron collapse. "Our happy 160th anniversary is an unhappy time for capitalism," it reported. Intellectuals were angry at capitalism because corporate interests were dominating the state. Not only was corruption by business and individuals a problem in democracies, the essay lamented, but also "governments remain far too keen to do businessmen's bidding even when no money is offered."

Foremost among the magazine's "radical birthday thoughts" was to advocate a "pro-market, not pro-business" line. Governments were urged to "keep their distance from businesses and their bosses." The "household name" Enron stood atop the essay's "scandal sheet" of recent corporate malfeasance. Enron was hardly the epitome of capitalism, the essay noted, but the fall of the once-revered company threatened capitalism as a perceived ideal nonetheless.

"The problem with socialism is socialism; the problem with capitalism is capitalists." So it has been said. Moral and economic perfection is beyond any social system—that is one defense of the capitalists. But a different hypothesis can be forwarded: *The problem with socialism is socialism; the problem with capitalism is political capitalists.* The case studies of Samuel Insull and Ken Lay in particular offer support for this view.

Part III

Energy and Sustainability

Is there any more single-minded, simple pleasure than viewing with alarm?
—Kenneth Boulding, "Fun and Games with the Gross National Product" (1970)

Introduction

"Here is a planet, whirling in sunlit space," reads the opening of Rose Wilder Lane's *The Discovery of Freedom: Man's Struggle against Authority*, penned during the dark days of World War II. "The planet is energy," she continues. "Every apparent substance composing it is energy. The envelope of gases surrounding it is energy. Energy pours forth from the sun upon this air and earth."

Energy is pervasive and liberating. It moves people, makes things, and provides incalculable services. It vanquishes darkness, literally and figuratively. "Since early men ignited the first fires in caves," it has been noted, "the unleashing of energy for light, heat, cooking, and every human need has been the essence and symbol of what it is to be human."

In economic terms, energy is the resource of resources, the *master resource*. Energy transforms mineral and natural resources from their raw form into consumable goods. Energy must be expended to create more energy and to refine energy into more usable forms. Thus, energy can be considered the *fourth* factor of production, in addition to the textbook triad of land, labor, and capital.

In business terms, energy has been, and will likely always be, the world's biggest enterprise. The energy sector has spawned some of history's great entrepreneurs. John D. Rockefeller shaped the American and world oil industry more than a century ago. Mr. Petroleum was one of the greatest, if not *the* greatest, business doers in U.S. and world history.

Second to Rockefeller in the history of the U.S. energy industry is Mr. Electricity: Samuel Insull. An émigré who teamed with Thomas Edison to build the company that emerged as General Electric, Insull ventured on his own and built America's largest gas and electricity empire. But his fortunes spectacularly reversed in the early 1930s. The dramatic rise and fall of the father of the modern electricity industry, "the Babe Ruth, the Jack Dempsey, the Red Grange of the business world," is still the subject of contemporary books and articles.

In the 1980s and 1990s, another figure cut a unique path in the energy sector: Mr. Natural Gas, Kenneth L. Lay. He made a case for methane as the economic and environmental answer to America's energy challenges and positioned Enron as the world's first natural gas major. Lay's star power put him in a league with the biggest names of the industry at the time, such as John Browne of BP and Lee Raymond of ExxonMobil. In early 2001, Paul Portney, president of Resources for the Future, declared, "In his role as chairman of Enron Corp., Ken Lay has almost singlehandedly made the world rethink what it means to be a modern energy company."

But Ken Lay was a shooting star. He was no Samuel Insull, much less a John D. Rockefeller. Still, he was an industry driver and energy changer, as evidenced by Enron's role in restructuring the natural gas and electricity markets in the United States and Europe. History should also note that Enron helped resuscitate the ailing domestic wind-power industry, however unproductive this may turn out to be in the sweep of history. The energy world is different today because of Ken Lay.

For Rockefeller, Insull, and (for the most part) Lay, energy was a far different commodity from that utilized during all of mankind's previous history. The energy of old was *renewable*—falling water, burning wood and plants, harnessed wind and sunlight. The new energy, which powered the machines of the Industrial Revolution and which today has an 85 percent share of the global energy market, is *fossil fuel*, which in all its varieties is vastly more concentrated, powerful, reliable, and transportable than what it replaced.

The carbon-based energy era began with coal and its derivatives, coal gas and coal oil. Petroleum and natural gas joined in. These energies came from the sun's ageless work, creating a mineral *stock* far superior to the irregular, dilute energy of the sun's *flow*. Little wonder that the new energy overwhelmed what came before, powering industrialization and accelerating the capitalist-led transformation to modern society.

Free minds and free markets created an energy boom that is now in its third century. That boom began in England in the eighteenth century and continues today worldwide with ever-greater quantities of carbon-based energy produced and consumed. But therein lies a peculiarity. In a physical sense, oil, gas, and coal are nonrenewable, with each extraction from a known supply leaving less for the future. As nature's hydrocarbon glass is emptied, the thinking goes, extraction costs and selling prices must increase.

History tells a different story. As more oil, gas, and coal have been produced, more has been found. New substitutes within the carbon-based fuel family have emerged. So-called depleting resources have been replenished—and more. This paradox of plenty is a fact that few people, even economists, have been able to understand, much less explain.

In fact, the experts have told us time and again that energy demand will outrace supply, pushing prices up and stalling progress. More often than not, such alarmism has been the conventional wisdom. Times of energy adequacy are only temporary, it is warned. Optimists are like the person who jumps off a tall building and gives a good report on the way down.

The coal panic of the 1860s is the peak-oil debate of today—nearly a century and a half later. Samuel Insull feared coal depletion during his reign as "The Chief" of the U.S. electricity industry in the first third of the twentieth century. Coming out of the 1970s energy crisis, Robert Herring, chairman of Houston Natural Gas Corporation—a predecessor company to Enron—sought a "versatile substitute" for natural gas. At Transco Energy Company, Jack Bowen and his protégé, Ken Lay, looked to coal gas as the future for methane.

But when natural gas shortages turned to surpluses in the 1980s (the so-called gas bubble), the outlook shifted. Brandishing his Ph.D. in economics, Lay, now CEO of Enron, became a national voice for resource optimism. Countering skepticism about the gas supply was a key part of Enron's natural gas strategy.

⌒

The following five chapters revisit the perennial issue of energy pessimism versus energy optimism. The fixity-depletion view of fossil fuels was popularized by William Stanley Jevons in the 1860s, mathematically explicated by Harold Hotelling in 1931, and geologically quantified by M. King Hubbert in the 1950s and 1960s. The budding environmental movement gladly seized upon Hubbert's analysis to warn of an impending crisis and urge a government-restructured ecological society. "What will we do when the [gasoline] pumps run dry?" asked Paul and Anne Ehrlich in 1971.

But some hearty souls championed a quite different view. To them, energy was a growing, not depleting, resource. The concept of resource expansionism was conceived by Erich Zimmermann in the 1930s, documented by resource economists beginning in the 1950s and 1960s, and codified into a general view by Julian Simon thereafter. Simon, originally a Malthusian, changed his mind after being contradicted by the statistical record. Simon put a theory to the data, concluding that human creativity had kept and would keep the cupboard full, given free minds and free markets. Human ingenuity—what he called the *ultimate resource*—was not a depletable resource but an expanding one, with each invention setting the stage for new breakthroughs. "I'm not an optimist, I'm a realist," he would plead to the neo-Malthusian holdouts. But the apocalyptists would have none of it, deprecating Simon as wrong and incompetent.

Resource adequacy is part of the wider environmental issue of *sustainable development*, defined as "development that meets the needs of the present without compromising the ability of future generations to meet their own needs." A sustainable energy market is one in which the quantity, quality, and utility of energy improve over time. Sustainable energy becomes more available, more affordable, more usable and reliable, and cleaner. Energy consumers do not borrow from the future; they subsidize the future by continually improving today's energy economy, which the future inherits.

The energy-sustainability debate relates to Enron in several important ways. The depletionist mindset that became a political force during the 1970s energy crisis created a movement to husband fossil fuels, over and above the behavior engendered by the price signals of the marketplace. *Conservationism*, or conservation for its own sake, became a mantra of environmentalists, and it continued unabated despite energy surpluses in the 1980s and 1990s. Government at all levels enacted mandates and subsidies to reduce energy usage. Nowhere was this done more than in California, a pivotal energy market in Enron's history.

Riding the conservationism wave, Enron became the nation's largest provider of energy-efficiency services—to great applause. This was part of a new genre of capitalism—*natural capitalism*—environmentalists thought. But energy outsourcing, whereby large commercial and industrial businesses turned over their energy operations to Enron Energy Services (EES), turned out to be a billion-dollar bust. EES's advertised energy savings of 10 percent (or more)—making firms "Kyoto compliant" under one proposed EES marketing scheme—was fiction. Driven by the profit motive, its corporate customers had already achieved most of the potential energy savings themselves. Most of EES's contracts were unprofitable, as were those of other so-called energy service companies, or ESCOs. This case study in entrepreneurial error and public relations overreaching in the name of environmental correctness was a cost of the creed of conservationism, which in turn came from the mindset of depletionism.

Enron was an energy company at heart. Ken Lay declared victory on three successive visions, which were to become

- *The leading integrated natural gas company in North America*
- *The world's first natural gas major*[1]
- *The world's leading energy company*

Enron focused on natural gas throughout, touting the fuel's environmental and economic advantages over coal, in particular. But under its third mission, Enron set a vision within a vision—*to become the world's leading renewable energy company*. Enron's positioning as a so-called green energy company, however, was at odds with other company priorities and would result in financial losses and even criminality.

Enron was at the pinnacle of the energy-sustainability debate, with its Ph.D. economists and MBAs preparing energy outlooks, organizing conferences, and writing articles and books on resource availability, climate change, and national energy policy. *Dr.* Kenneth L. Lay actively participated in energy debates as a board member of Resources for the Future and the American Enterprise Institute; as a keynote speaker at major conferences worldwide; as a member of the Clinton administration's President's Council on Sustainable Development (1993–99); and as a popular panelist at the World Economic Forum in Davos, Switzerland. Enron representatives set the agenda within various industry trade associations and pushed legislation at all levels of government in the United States and Europe. Thus, the big picture of energy thought and policy is fundamental to the Enron story (Book 3) in many and varied ways, as well as other industry case studies (Book 2).

---

1. *Natural gas major* was an analog to the *oil major*, or the global integrated oil company.

7

Malthusianism

PESSIMISM AND MELANCHOLY have a long history. The Book of Genesis tells of mankind losing an idyllic mode of existence at the dawn of human life. The Greek poet Hesiod, writing about 800 BC, believed that the world had degenerated into its fifth, last, and worst stage. During the third century, Saint Cyprian, an early Christian writer, described mankind's "wasteland" in stark, complete terms:

> The world has grown old, and does not remain in its former vigour. It bears witness to its own decline. The rainfall and the sun's warmth are both diminishing; the metals are nearly exhausted; the husbandman is failing in the fields, the sailor on the seas, the soldier in the camp, honesty in the market, justice in the courts, concord in friendships, skill in the arts, discipline in morals. This is the sentence passed upon the world, that everything which has a beginning should perish, that things which have reached a maturity should grow old, the strong weak, the great small, and that after weakness and shrinkage should come dissolution.

Subsistence living would be the human lot for many more centuries. Philosophical obstacles hampered the development of scientific theories and their technological application. Confiscatory taxation and economic controls perpetuated destitution. Famine, disease, and war depressed population. The outlook was for more of the same.

But the climate for scientific advances and political liberties improved gradually. Historians note a great improvement during the *Age of Reason* in the seventeenth century. The offshoots of reason—science and capitalism—blossomed in the next century's *Age of Enlightenment*. Private property, voluntary exchange, and profit/loss incentive and signals coordinated markets, however rudimentary. Worker productivity rose with savings and investment. International trade gave consumers new and cheaper goods and created cross-border friendship. Wealth surged, and the "populationist attitude" emerged, a belief that "a numerous and increasing population was the most important *symptom* of wealth; it was the chief *cause* of wealth; it *was* wealth itself—the greatest asset for any nation to have." Rising expectations were in stark contrast to "the ancients [who] had no conception of progress; they did not so much reject the idea; they did not even entertain the idea."

The Industrial Revolution, which began in Great Britain in the mid-eighteenth century and quickly spread to continental Europe and to the United States, was the coming together of reason, science, property rights, voluntary exchange, capital accumulation, and internationalism. Newtonian mechanics and fossil energy merged in a dramatically positive way. Mechanical laws and in-place resources had always been there for the taking, but only now did the conditions bring them into play. Machines made a world of new things possible—but only with concentrated, storable, transferable, plentiful, *cheap* energy to run them. The Industrial Revolution was also the *machine age* and the *coal age*.

Representative, limited government grew up alongside reason, science, and progress. Two masterworks by Adam Smith explaining the moral and economic order of voluntary commerce supported political liberalization. So did the genius and farsightedness of the Founding Fathers, who created the Declaration of Independence and the Bill of Rights for the United States.

Looking back, it is hard to believe that humans lived in a wasteland for so long before the conditions emerged for sustainable progress. A graphical look at the "great breakthrough" (Figure 7.1) shows how recent and unprecedented it was in human history.

Trepidation came with progress. There was little precedent for believing that future gains were ensured, much less probable—quite the opposite. The writings of the optimists, even the great Adam Smith, were just theories. Alarmism would soon appear.

From "Misery or Vice" to "Moral Restraint"

The happy economics of Adam Smith was jolted on a summer day in 1798 when an unsigned pamphlet appeared in London bookstores. The author of *An Essay on the Principle of Population* was 32-year-old Thomas Robert Malthus (1766–1834), but he remained anonymous to avoid embarrassing his father, whose entrenched view was "every day in every way, the human race is getting better and better."

Malthus's "incontrovertible truths" reached a gloomy conclusion. Although "the passion between the sexes" would increase population geometrically (2, 4, 8, 16, 32, 64 . . .), the agricultural means to sustain them would grow only arithmetically (1, 2, 3, 4, 5, 6 . . .). Growing families would overwhelm the ability to feed them, given the fixity of land and impossibility of "mak[ing] every acre of

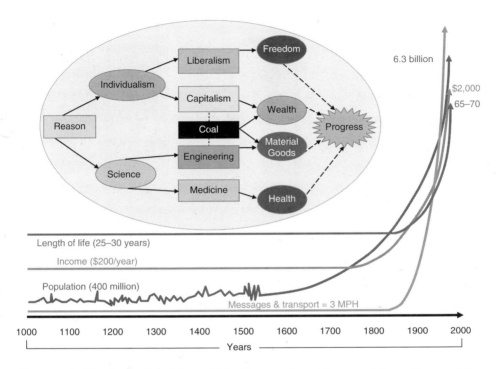

Figure 7.1 The "great breakthrough" in life expectancy, income, information, and the general quality of life hit full stride in the mid-eighteenth century with the intersection of reason, science, and capitalism. These developments were abetted by carbon-based energies, beginning with coal.

land in the Island like a garden." To Malthus, this incompatibility left "misery or vice"—some combination of disease, famine, and foregone marriage, or barbarianism and war—to bring population down to a sustainable level of subsistence. "The argument is conclusive against the perfectibility of the mass of mankind," he declared, and "decisive against the possible existence of a society, all the members of which should live in ease, happiness, and comparative leisure."

Malthus understood that population did not have to increase geometrically. It did in the United States, where a doubled population in 25 years escaped misery or vice because of a "rapidity of [agricultural] increase, probably without parallel in history."[1] Population growth was slower in Europe, yet there was "frequent distress of the common people." Poverty was common, and government

---

1. The United States, Malthus explained, was blessed with large quantities of rich, open land and low taxation, which resulted in aggressive tilling and production.

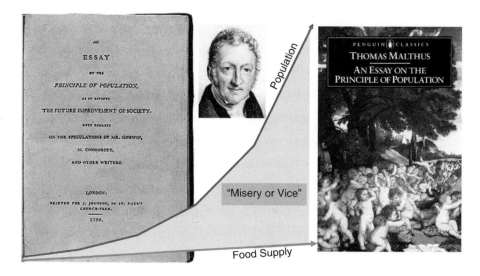

Figure 7.2 T. R. Malthus put economics in a dark light by concluding that increases in food supply could not keep pace with population growth. His pessimistic theory would be applied two generations later to coal and later still to petroleum and natural gas.

poor relief was burdensome and growing. Europe's only lifeline was postponed or forgone marriage owing to "the foresight of the [economic] difficulties attending the rearing of a family." This abstinence from marriage was *misery*, but sex out of wedlock was *vice*, which to Malthus was the greater evil.[2]

The "preventative check" of fewer children from foregone marriage was much milder than the "positive check" of death to reduce overpopulation, leading Malthus to observe: "Necessity has been with great truth called the mother of invention," and "the first great awakeners of the mind seem to be the wants of the body." Malthus ended his tract with a pious plea for "constant exertion to avoid evil and to pursue good [to] smooth many of the difficulties that occur," including that "from the principle of population."

∽

Although the argument that food would be inadequate for a growing population was not original with Malthus,[3] his sophisticated essay on population provoked a firestorm and "warfare of pamphlets," spurring Malthus to revisit his thesis. He studied, discussed, and traveled far in search of facts. Five years later,

---

2. "It is difficult to conceive any check to population which does not come under the description of some species of misery or vice," Malthus believed.

3. See Internet appendix 7.1, "Pre-Malthus Malthusianism," at www.politicalcapitalism.org/book1/chapter7/appendix1.html.

a much-enlarged second edition appeared under his name. His introduction began defensively. The original effort had been done on "impulse" and "from the few materials which were then within my reach." He was now presenting "a new work," and it introduced a new remedy. Beyond misery or vice was "moral restraint." This involved postponing marriage and procreation (a "preventative check," as in the first edition), but it would not be vice if one avoided "promiscuous intercourse, unnatural passions, violations of the marriage bed, and improper arts to conceal the consequences of irregular connections." So, the "superior power of population" could now be overcome by some combination of *moral restraint, misery,* or *vice.* Malthus had gone from Malthusian in 1798 to Malthusian-lite by 1803.[4]

What about agriculture? In his final edition of *An Essay,* Malthus compared the potential "unexhausted vigor" of population with the fixity of cultivatable land. "Man is necessarily confined in room," he said, cementing his argument about the arithmetic increase as an upper bound of food production. Yet some asides in Malthus's other major book, *Principles of Political Economy* (1820, revised 1836), offered rays of optimism. "There can be no doubt of the improvements in agriculture," he noted. "No instance has occurred, in modern times, of a large and very fertile country having made full use of its natural resources." Labor-saving, productivity-enhancing materials were "the result of the ingenuity of man." Capital growth "facilitate[d] supply." In a broader vein, he warned: "How very dangerous it is, in political economy, to draw conclusions from the physical quality of the materials which are acted upon, without reference to the moral as well as physical qualities of the agents." Still, the "fertility of soil" was seen as a given, with little idea about how *elastic* capital and ingenuity could make it. It would remain for twentieth-century thinkers, drawing upon a far richer empirical record of resources and population, to expand the idea of human ingenuity into a full-blown theory of resource expansionism.

In Malthus's time, population was growing—but the supply of foodstuffs was expanding faster! The great die-offs came from disease, not resource limitations. Studies in the 1820s began to suggest an inverse relation between wealth and population change: The greater the wealth, the lower the rate of population growth. Population concerns faded by 1850, and the Industrial Revolution, however miserable as judged by today's standards, was improving living conditions.[5] Yet the "dismal science" of Malthusian economics would take a new turn. The new concern was whether coal could continue to affordably fuel English industry and ensure the country's global prominence. England occupied a

---

4. See Internet appendix 7.2, "Did Malthus Change His Mind," at www.political capitalism.org/book1/chapter7/appendix2.html.

5. The role of coal in England's Industrial Revolution and its net benefits are discussed in Internet appendix 7.3, "Coal: The Great Liberator," at www.politicalcapitalism.org/book1/chapter7/appendix3.html.

tiny 0.04 percent of the world's land mass and was home to 2.5 percent of global population. Yet England produced more than half of the world's annual output of coal to power domestic industry and to sell abroad.

"The Coal Panic"

The year after Malthus's death, William Stanley (W. S.) Jevons (1835–82) was born in Liverpool. By his late twenties, Jevons had become a gifted thinker and a struggling academic in search of a breakthrough. A tract on the value of gold, although intellectually respected, did not afford him public prestige. But his next effort, a book-length examination of the future of coal in the United Kingdom, published in 1865, succeeded in a way not seen since Malthus's *Essay* more than a half century before. *The Coal Question: An Inquiry Concerning the Progress of the Nation, and the Probable Exhaustion of Our Coal Mines* reached a stark, troubling conclusion: England's coal abundance was coming to an end, and the nation's industrial and competitive might was living on borrowed time.

Jevons resurrected a dormant Malthusianism by creating "the coal panic." The book's factual detail, straightforward logic, and startling conclusion sparked a debate in British government about policy reforms to soften the coming decline. W. E. Gladstone, the Chancellor of the Exchequer (minister of finance), cited Jevons's "grave and . . . urgent facts" to argue that England should retire its national debt. The distinguished political economist John Stuart Mill seconded the argument in the House of Commons, citing Jevons's "almost exhaustive" research. Parliament established a Royal Commission on Coal Supplies in 1866 to update Jevons's findings.

Now with reputation, Jevons would assume distinguished academic positions, including Professor of Political Economy at University College in London. The versatile academic launched into new fields of studies that would make him one of the foremost social scientists of his age.

The Coal Question transcended its time. Adam Smith and the classical school of economics dealt only with goods that human labor could reproduce without limit; Jevons dealt with a perceived *depletable* resource, whereby each unit of production and consumption left less for the future. A new discipline was founded, mineral-resource economics, from which would emerge *energy economics* and the study of worldwide oil, natural gas, and coal issues.[6] All this was launched by Jevons in 1865.

Jevons's argument began simply enough. Coal was king—the "all-powerful" enabler of the age of steam and iron and "mainspring of modern material civilization." "With coal almost any feat is possible or easy; without it we are thrown

---

6. *Mineral resources* are different from *natural resources* like plants and water because minerals cannot be produced by nature or man in human time frames. Thus, terms associated with mineral resources include *fixed, depletable, nonrenewable, nonreproducible,* and *exhaustible* supply.

THE

COAL QUESTION;

AN INQUIRY
CONCERNING THE PROGRESS OF THE NATION,
AND THE
PROBABLE EXHAUSTION OF OUR COAL-MINES.

BY

W. STANLEY JEVONS, M.A.
FELLOW OF UNIVERSITY COLLEGE, LONDON, AND OF THE STATISTICAL SOCIETY.

London and Cambridge:
MACMILLAN AND CO.
1865.

Figure 7.3 Jevons's "powerful face" (as J. M. Keynes called it) was worn at age 42 (lower) in contrast to his carefree visage of 20 years before (upper). The "pioneer of modern economics" founded mineral-resource economics and became the energy heir of the gloomy worldview of Malthus.

back into the laborious poverty of earlier times," Jevons wrote. Such material decay would bring "moral and intellectual retrogression." Hence the epigraph of *The Coal Question,* which quoted Adam Smith: "The progressive state is in reality the cheerful and the hearty state to all the different orders of the society; the stationary state is dull; the declining melancholy."

Jevons considered "the necessary results of our present rapid multiplication [of demand] when brought into comparison with a fixed amount of material resources." "For the present," he found, "our cheap supplies of coal, and our skill in its employment, and the freedom of our commerce with other wide lands, render us . . . out of the scope of Malthus's doctrine." But the "painful fact" was that "in the increasing depth and difficulty of coal mining we shall meet that vague, but inevitable boundary that will stop our progress."

Fixed supply was controlling in Jevons's system, which meant that coal would become more expensive as reserves diminished. Recognizing that "everything is a question of cost," Jevons calculated the relative expense of mining different seams of coal, to construct what economists would later call a marginal-cost curve (the cost of producing additional supplies). Projected demand growth of 3.5 percent per year was assumed, given recently experienced growth and trends in population, industry, and international trade. Comparing demand to supply, he projected that "more than a century of our present progress would exhaust our mines to the depth of 4,000 feet, or 1,500 feet deeper than our present deepest mine." A "threatening" rise in fuel costs, "perhaps within a lifetime" and certainly within a century, was inevitable, Jevons concluded.

The problem was absolute for England but relative for the rest of the world. Other areas would gain what the homeland would lose. "The exhaustion of our mines will be marked *pari passu* by a rising cost or value of coal," Jevons wrote, "and when the price has risen to a certain amount comparatively to the price in other countries, our main branches of trade will be doomed." Imported coal could not save the day, because of its higher cost in England compared to its costs to new industries in new coal lands. The United States was deemed heir to England's energy greatness because of the vast prospects of coal-laden states, such as Pennsylvania.

With "all events tending to an indefinite increase of the consumption of coal," staying a course that had seen demand increase tenfold during Malthus's life, England's fate was sealed. "Our anxiety must be indefinitely increased in reflecting that *while other countries mostly subsist upon the annual and ceaseless income of the harvest, we are drawing more and more upon a capital which yields no annual interest, but once turned to light and heat and force, is gone for ever into space.*"

In Malthusian prose, Jevons concluded that "after a time we must either sink down into poverty, adopting wholly new habits, or else witness a constant annual exodus of the youth of the country." He closed *The Coal Question* with an ultimatum for his fellow citizens and lawmakers:

> If we lavishly and boldly push forward in the creation and distribution of our riches, it is hard to over-estimate the pitch of beneficial influence to which we may attain in the present. *But the maintenance of such a position is physically impossible. We have to make the momentous choice between brief greatness and longer continued mediocrity.*

"To allow commerce to proceed until the course of civilization is weakened and overturned," Jevons warned, "is like killing the goose to get the golden egg." To arrest this future, Jevons recommended "a more or less heavy" export tax to keep domestic coal at home, as well as retire the national debt "towards [the goal of] compensating posterity for our present lavish use of cheap coal."

Energy Sustainability: First Views

The Coal Question, which Jevons revised a year later with a new introduction rebutting his critics, was praised in its time and is still revered today for its "thorough, scientific" analysis. Jevons conscientiously examined the best available evidence and logically deduced its implications. His focus on changing scarcity over time led him to reject the notion that coal would run out in a physical sense; the cost of producing it would simply rise over the medium to long term in the United Kingdom until there was a cessation of mining activity. Yet unfortunately, by continuing to use the term *exhaustion*, which literally means *to consume entirely*, Jevons created confusion where he least meant to do so. To his credit, he avoided speculating about *global* depletion, about which little was known. Extrapolating from the part to the whole would be the bane of future depletionists.

Jevons's treatise dealt with resource depletion, efficiency and conservation, and renewable energy, each part of the contemporary energy-sustainability debate. Ken Lay's entrepreneurial vision at Enron dealt with these same issues. As the leading voice of the natural gas industry from the mid-1980s until Enron's demise in 2001, Lay challenged the argument from coal interests that North American gas reserves were inadequate to meet increasing demand. Enron Energy Services purveyed energy-efficiency services to large commercial and industrial customers with much fanfare about promoting energy sustainability. Also in the name of energy sustainability, Enron Renewable Energy Company became one of the world's major solar and wind providers.

Jevons viewed U.K. coal as a "fixed amount of material resources." Production would rise, peak, and then fall as finding costs inexorably climbed. This view would be mathematically formalized by an American economist in the 1930s and presented as a bell curve of production by an American geologist in the 1950s, the subject of the next two chapters.

Jevons linked rising coal consumption to "the very economy of its use." Increasing efficiency lowers energy usage in existing uses, he reasoned, but such cheapness broadens usage and leads to new applications, increasing energy demand overall. In his words:

> It is wholly a confusion of ideas to suppose that the economical use of fuel is equivalent to a diminished consumption. The very contrary is the truth. As a rule, new modes of economy will lead to an increase in consumption, according to a principle recognized in many parallel instances.

Jevons observed how "the reduction of consumption of coal, per ton of iron, to less than one-third of its former amount" in Scotland's iron works was followed by a "ten-fold total consumption, not to speak of the indirect effects of cheap iron in accelerating other coal-consuming branches of industry." The efficiency of the steam engine increased "ten or fifteen-fold" in less than a century, yet coal demand surged due to "the cheapness of the power it affords." Future improvements, he added, "will only accelerate anew the consumption of coal."

Jevons considered the renewable energies of the day—wind, falling water, heat from the earth's interior, and burning wood and plants—as inadequate to take the place of domestic coal. Wind was "irregular," too dilute to "supply the force required in large factories or iron works," and limited to "open and elevated situations." Hydropower was too dependent "upon local circumstances." Wood production required much more land than was available for planting and cultivation. Geothermal sources tappable near the surface were rare. These problems led the United States, like the United Kingdom, to shift to coal and then other concentrated, reliable fossil energies, beginning in the nineteenth century.

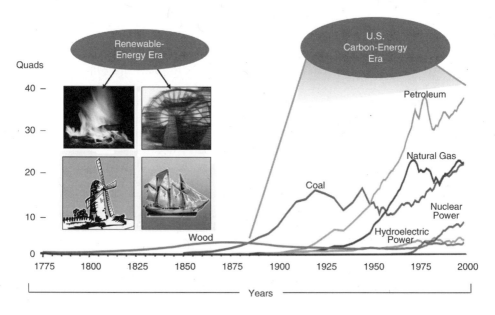

Figure 7.4 U.S. energy usage was not unlike the energy transformation in the United Kingdom and other industrialized nations. The first energy era (not shown here) was composed of human and animal muscle power—the *animate-energy era*. The *renewable-energy age* then dominated until the nineteenth-century transformation to the *carbon-energy*, or *fossil-fuel*, *era*—coal, natural gas, and oil.

Jevons was the first intellectual to question the ability of renewables to serve as primary energies for industrial society. The carbon-based energy era superseded renewables because coal—and crude oil and natural gas to come—were more concentrated, portable, dependable, flexible, and economical energies to capture, convert, and consume. Jevons's long-forgotten insight explains why Enron's foray into renewables, particularly wind power, was financially problematic even upon a bed of government subsidies.

Anatomy of a False Alarm

W. S. Jevons worked in the tradition of Malthus,[7] whose theory of population had not been intellectually refuted, simply demoted amid the real problems of everyday life. As it would turn out, the findings of Jevons were misleading both as a guide to England's situation and as a theory of mineral-resource development. His prediction that "the voracious iron-furnaces will exhaust our seams as they exhausted our woods" would prove false, and his "threatening" rise in coal costs would prove illusory. The production history of U.K. coal during and in the decades after Jevons's life is shown in Figure 7.5.

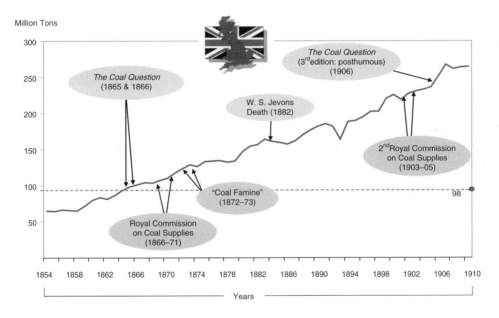

Figure 7.5 Continuing a long trend, coal production in the United Kingdom rose in the 40-year period between the first edition and the third (posthumous) edition of Jevons's *The Coal Question.* The feared coal problem was always in a future that would recede as it was approached.

Where did Jevons go astray? Jevons's assumption of annual coal consumption growth of 3.5 percent per year—based on recent experience that coincided with a peak in railway construction—proved to be high of the mark. Actual annual growth averaged 3 percent in 1865–80, 2 percent in 1881–1900, and less than 1 percent in 1901–65 (see Figure 7.6). Part of this weakening demand in the

---

7. See Internet appendix 7.4, "Jevons as a Malthusian," at www.politicalcapitalism.org/book1/chapter7/appendix4.html.

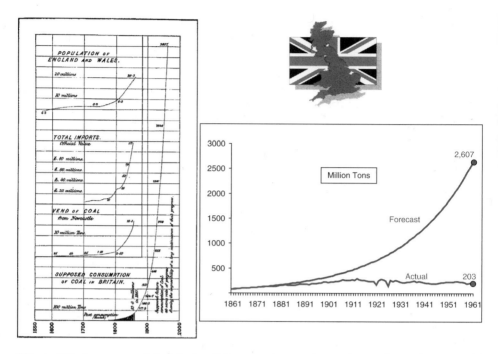

Figure 7.6 Jevons predicted that a 3.5 percent annual growth rate in coal use would overwhelm low-cost supplies and raise prices. But because of increasing efficiency, fuel substitution, and economic stagnation (the so-called British disease), the actual growth rate for his forecast period (to 1961) averaged less than 1 percent per year.

twentieth century, however, was the preventable result of an ailing, government-constrained economy.

On the supply side, Jevons severely underestimated the ability of advancing knowledge to counter the economic law of diminishing returns.[8] (Globally, the same was true, with new coal reserves outracing consumption.) To him, "ingenuity" was no match for coal extraction's "fair fight with difficulties." Jevons recognized how coal and steam power "cheapen[ed] extraction," yet he failed to appreciate the cost-reducing effect of improving technology, whether in locating reserves or inventing new extraction devices. He also neglected to consider how capitalism's investment capital growth could expand and improve mining operations. All these things had a history of progress during the Industrial Revolution, yet the meticulous Jevons missed them.

---

8. The concept of diminishing returns is discussed in Internet appendix 7.5, "Precedents for Jevons," at www.politicalcapitalism.org/book1/chapter7/appendix5.html.

Jevons dismissed the prospects of interfuel substitution. "There is no probability that when coal is used up any more powerful substitute will be forthcoming," he concluded. Global crude oil supply was seen as "far more limited and uncertain than that of coal," despite annual oil imports into the United Kingdom of millions of gallons. (There was no domestic oil production.) Natural gas was given nary a thought. Oil and gas manufactured from coal only brought the question back to coal—Jevons was at least right on that.

᳁·

Jevons became the first in a long line of intellectuals to proclaim a crisis in depletable-resource supply was coming. "I naturally pass to consider whether there are yet in the cost of coal any present signs of exhaustion," Jevons wrote in *The Coal Question*. Yet a decade later in a public lecture, he boldly interpreted England's 1872/73 "coal famine [as] the first twinge of the scarcity which must come."

Could he be sure? As Jevons himself stated in his seminal book, there could be *"a retardation of the price after a considerable rise has already taken place."* The historical record suggested that coal was becoming more plentiful, not less. England's centuries-old coal industry had increased production to meet home demand and to export *without* higher production costs or retail prices. Total coal output went from 3 million tons per year in 1700 to 30 million tons annually by 1830 and continued to grow through Jevons's lifetime. Coal prices, adjusted for inflation, were stable from 1600 to almost the time of Jevons's book. Meanwhile, coal experts were *increasing* their estimates of remaining supply as more data was accumulated. Jevons would have been just as wrong in 1700, 1750, 1800, or 1850 as he was in 1865—as was his own son a half century later.

Coal output in the United Kingdom finally took a downward turn around World War I, but this hardly vindicated Jevons's depletionist warnings of a half century before. Yes, international competition had grown stronger. But it was growing regulation and labor union obstructionism that stopped and reversed progress in the domestic coal industry. It began with union mandates and spiraling regulation that culminated with a governmental takeover of the coal mines between 1917 and 1921. Problems continued with the General Strike of 1926, the Great Depression, and government-decreed restrictions on output intertwined with price supports. Nationalization of the U.K. coal industry in 1947 did not end until 1994. In the late 1960s, natural gas from the North Sea offered power plants and industrial users a home-grown substitute for coal for the first time, a development that was accelerated by a coal strike in 1984/85. Yet a Jevonian depletion signal never appeared in the United Kingdom or Western European coal market in these decades.

The British disease—low productivity from economic collectivism and labor obstructionism—resulted in an inefficient coal industry that struggled to cover its bloated costs even with government price supports. Subsidies, featherbedding, strikes, and a mix of heavy regulation and outright socialism, not depletion, destabilized output in the industry. Coal operators in Germany and Belgium had fully mechanized their industries by the 1930s, whereas operations in the United Kingdom were less than 40 percent mechanized. "British [coal] entrepreneurs did not keep up with progress in other countries," one historian documented.

Jevons, focused almost exclusively on supply and demand, missed the role of *public policy* and *institutions* in resource development. Painting the full picture to explain resource scarcity would be the contribution of a future generation of resource economists.

⌒

Jevons was an ultraproductive scholar who worked furiously in subjects as diverse as meteorology, logic, scientific principles, empirical economics, and political economy. His work pace was his medicine to fight personal depression, but by his early forties, Jevons was sickly. The end came just shy of his forty-seventh birthday when he chanced swimming against doctor's orders on the last day of a vacation in Sussex. As the *Manchester Examiner and Times* mournfully reported, "Almost within sight of his wife and children, at a spot known to be dangerous except for good swimmers, the waves closed over him, and he was seen no more alive."

Jevons never altered his depletionist view toward coal, despite contrary evidence. He went out an unrepentant Malthusian, and his pessimism carried over to the personal side. After his death, the family found a hoard of paper, whose purchase, noted John Maynard Keynes in a biographical sketch of Jevons, had been "more in the nature of speculation than for his personal use, since his own notes were mostly written on the backs of paper, of which the proper place was the waste-paper basket." This, continued Keynes, was "a psychological trait, unusually strong in him, which many other people share, a certain hoarding instinct, a readiness to be alarmed and excited by the idea of the exhaustion of resources."[9]

The issue of coal depletion, like the population issue some decades before, receded from popular concern by the 1870s. But Parliament remained very interested in the future of the industry because of the powerful coal union. A second Royal Commission on Coal Supplies (1903–05) updated the statistics and reiterated Jevons's conclusion. A third and final edition of Jevons's *The Coal Question*, published posthumously in 1906, was little changed and lacked critical comment by its editor, A. W. Flux. Opportunity after opportunity passed without any explanation of why the bleak future was not happening.

Second-Generation Alarm

Herbert Stanley (H. S.) Jevons (1875–1955), son of William Stanley, published *The British Coal Trade* in 1915. The weighty volume reported how the output

---

9. See Internet appendix 7.6, "Unnecessary Alarmism," www.politicalcapitalism.org/book1/chapter7/appendix6.html.

of coal and other fuels had increased more than anticipated, efficiency gains did not moderate demand, and better business organization kept costs down. Still, although these unforeseen developments "may tend somewhat to postpone a serious rise in price which would deal a heavy blow to English industry and shipping," the younger Jevons concluded, "the danger is nevertheless still with us."

"Englishmen must take heed," he warned.

Petroleum was becoming a competitive force against U.K. coal, yet H. S. Jevons dismissed the "scare writings of people with vivid imagination who saw in recent engineering progress 'the dawn of the oil age.'" His conclusion that "the supply of oil is strictly limited" was based on declining oil production in Colorado. Yet petroleum output was rapidly increasing most everywhere else in the country, and total U.S. output tripled between 1900 and the publication of his book. Crude oil production was also increasing in Latin America, Russia, and elsewhere—with global supply tripling. These available facts did not suggest scholarship of the first rank. Surely, had the elder Jevons written *The Coal Question* in 1915 rather than in 1865, he would have recognized and explained what he did not 50 years before—robust interfuel competition and substitution.

The younger Jevons's predictions turned out badly. He foresaw a peak for crude supply at around 120 billion barrels per annum come 50 to 60 years. World production in 1970, however, would be five times greater. "Practically

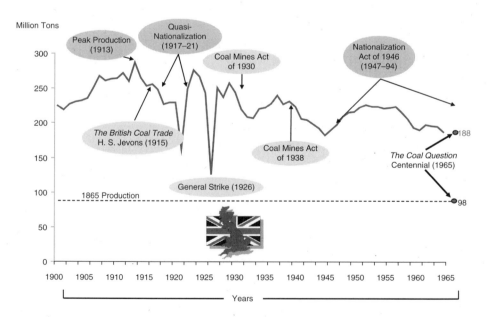

Figure 7.7 Declining twentieth-century coal production in the United Kingdom was caused by rival fuels and government intervention rather than resource depletion. U.K. coal output in 1965 (the centennial of *The Coal Question*) was almost double that in 1865.

complete exhaustion of the world's petroleum reserves may be looked for within 100 years," he said. Proved reserves today are at an all-time high of 1.25 trillion barrels, and much more remains to be found and so classified. Jevons *fils* also anticipated that coal supply, coming from "much deeper or thinner seams," would lag behind demand and cause prices to "gradually increase" for 40 to 50 years and accelerate more rapidly thereafter. Coal prices would gradually increase in the United Kingdom—ending a 250-year period of relative price stability—but labor obstructionism, nationalization, and high taxes were the primary culprits.

What was the cost of production, as reflected in the selling price of coal in London? In the century following publication of *The Coal Question*, the per-ton price was in a range of approximately 30 to 60 pounds sterling, adjusted for inflation.

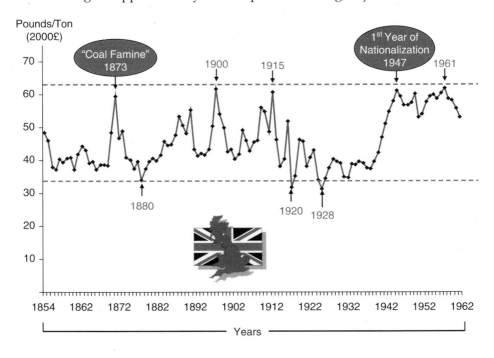

Figure 7.8 W. S. Jevons's predicted rise in coal prices failed to occur. Inflation-adjusted U.K. coal prices show little change compared to the period that Jevons intensely studied for writing his book. Higher prices after World War II reflected government price supports.

The elder Jevons predicted in 1865 that U.K. coal seams down to 4,000 feet would be exhausted in a century. In fact, coal-mining depths in 1965 were just more than 3,000 feet, although the quantity of mined coal was much less than he projected.

What about natural gas, a substitute that Jevons *père* failed to mention? Jevons *fils* asserted that "the life of the supplies of natural gas found in Western

Canada and the Western States of North America is still more fleeting" than petroleum—and let it go at that. That left coal—"our only great ultimate source of power"—and its future wasn't considered promising.

The interfuel reality that the younger Jevons could not or would not envision began with increasing amounts of imported petroleum and continued with domestic oil and natural gas production from the North Sea later in the century (see Figure 7.9). Coal for heating and generating electricity was displaced by oil and particularly natural gas. The "dash for gas" included the construction of the world's largest electricity-generating plant fueled by natural gas combined-cycle technology, built by Enron in 1993 at Teesside in the United Kingdom.

False energy alarms: like father, like son.

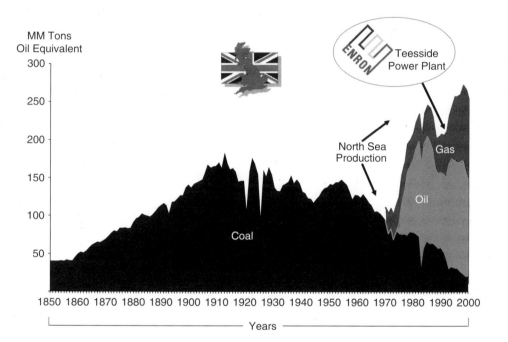

Figure 7.9 Energy production in the United Kingdom was radically transformed with the discovery of gas and oil in the North Sea in 1968. Enron was at the center of the "dash for gas" in the United Kingdom.

U.S. Coal: From Plenty to Problems

President Theodore Roosevelt created the National Conservation Commission (NCC) in 1908 to undertake the first inventory of domestic natural resources. Its findings, which Roosevelt called "an imperative call to action," were disconcerting, particularly concerning energy. The nation's known natural gas fields were expected to run out within 25 years and its oil fields by midcentury. Coal, the nation's most plentiful mineral resource, appeared to be adequate until the middle of the twenty-first century.[10]

Coal was the least of the nation's worries, for good reason. The United States was the global leader in coal production, coal exports, and reserves—just as the elder Jevons envisioned. Nonetheless, in 1922, just 14 years after the NCC disbanded, President Warren Harding created the United States Coal Commission (USCC) to study the increasing challenges faced by the coal industry. The "exhaustive" study surveyed "our coal problem" and concluded, *"There is no easy panacea for this troubled industry!"*

The 11-month, 500-person, 3,000-page study was as alarmist for the United States as *The Coal Question* had been for the United Kingdom more than a half century before. "Already the output of [natural] gas has begun to wane," the report found. "Production of oil cannot long maintain its present rate." Coal faced the difficult task of keeping up with a geometric growth in demand. The commission opined:

> In the hundred years from the end of the Napoleonic Wars to the outbreak of the World War, the world increased its consumption of mineral fuels a hundredfold. This increase cannot continue, and the task of developing a service of heat and power that will make the most of our remaining resources deserves the most earnest attention.

The study stopped short of offering public-policy ideas, reflecting political sensitivities. "Guided by facts rather than rumors, by information rather than prejudice," it stated, "the people will be able to exercise wisely the powers of the Government over this type of private business." But facts do not speak for themselves; there was a reason why such a resource-mighty industry was so badly underperforming.

What happened in the decade after 1909 that turned the U.S. coal industry upside down? The roots of the problem came during the period of coal surpluses and price wars, when the industry, after failing to cartelize itself to improve profitability, went hat in hand to the government to tame competition. Spiraling government involvement, coming on top of labor union problems, turned resource plenty into want and decline. World War I's Food and Fuel Control Act of 1917 (Lever Act) made coal, along with banking, one of the most regulated industries in the American economy. Federal action setting prices, allocating supply, licensing operators, and forcibly taking from (requisitioning) firms not acting in the "public interest" created the nation's first bona fide energy

---

10. The alarmist findings of the 1909 report led to a provision in the Revenue Act of 1913 to allow producers of oil, gas, and coal to subtract part of their income from their federal tax liability. The depletion allowance would be a controversial part of the federal tax code, attracting criticism from many economists, including free-marketeer Milton Friedman.

crisis—"lightless nights," "heatless Mondays," shutdowns of "non-essential" industry, fuel riots, even death. Fuel czar Harry Garfield, head of the U.S. Fuel Administration, called coal operators "robber barons of the Rhine" and threatened the industry with nationalization. His small army of energy planners threw new regulations at bad and even made arrests on grounds that "the law of humanity took precedence over property rights."

The domestic oil and natural gas industries also ailed from wartime price and allocation edicts, which increased the burden on coal. In one historian's estimation, railroads operating under the Interstate Commerce Commission's "completely uncoordinated government priority system," added to coal's problems. Nationalization of the railroad industry followed.

The first U.S. energy crisis did not arise from physical depletion. Manmade, or *institutional*, factors were responsible for turning resource plenty into resource want. A theory was badly needed to explain *why* depletable resources were not depleting in an economic or business sense and *why* resource crises came not from nature but from man-qua-government. That theory would soon appear.

8

A Joined Debate

THE RESOURCE VIEWS OF T. R. Malthus and W. S. Jevons impressed intellectuals and excited the public in their day. As time passed, however, the predicted problems failed to materialize, and attention drifted away. Although agricultural specialists saw the error in Malthus's thinking about replenishable food products, Jevons's mineral depletionism remained in high esteem. Growth statistics aside, everyone *knew* the bell would toll for coal because depletable resources, by definition, deplete. There was no countertheory to suggest why what was always just around the corner might be a mirage. This would finally change with the publication of the first treatise on mineral resources since Jevons's *The Coal Question* seven decades before. Erich Zimmermann's breakthrough in the 1930s would be joined in the 1950s and 1960s by major empirical studies that documented how mineral resources were growing more abundant, not scarcer, thanks to the ultimate resource of human ingenuity. A new think tank, Resources for the Future, established in 1952 by the Ford Foundation, was at the forefront of the fact finding. In theory and practice, this was a happy time for mineral resources and mineral-resource economics.

"Resources *Are Not, They Become*": Erich Zimmermann

His name is not found in economics textbooks or histories of economic thought. Where it does appear, his Germanic surname is often misspelled. His contribution is virtually unknown in the world's vast mineral-resource industries today. Government policies owe little or nothing to him. Yet Erich Zimmermann (1888–1961) developed a new theory to explain why fixity and depletion were the wrong way to view minerals in an economic and business sense. Thus, his is one of the great contributions in the history of resource thought.

Zimmermann's 1933 *World Resources and Industries* began a line of analysis that would explain a paradox of economic life—the growth of supposedly depletable supply, whether measured as current production or known reserves. Although incomplete, Zimmermann's theory provided a novel and compelling way of comprehending the economics of so-called exhaustible resources.

What was Erich Zimmermann's breakthrough? And why would the economics profession, in its moment of need, turn away from the breakthrough to a mathematical exposition of depletionism based on unrealistic assumptions? More puzzling still: Why did Zimmermann himself fear depletion despite the optimistic *gestalt* that his theory pointed toward? These questions surround the most important and studied mineral resource of all: carbon-based energy.

Economists from Jevons forward focused on a conception of *known* resource quantities that, by definition, depleted as they were mined and consumed. Future production costs would rise as mining progressed from superior to inferior deposits. Resource prices were destined to increase in the face of continuing demand and, certainly, demand growth. The increasing scarcity of mineral resources might be gradual or rapid, but the direction was not in doubt, even allowing for improved exploration and extraction technology.

Zimmermann rejected this outside-in view that saw resources as a knowable, fixed quantity. Such a perspective was for the natural sciences, not economics. Instead, he started from the inside out: "the appraising mind of the economic decision-maker." Resources, defined as "the environment in the service of man," exist only as a result of "human wants and abilities." Resources without humans are not resources. The interaction between people and environment is central.

To Zimmermann, resources are not fixed, permanent things but what technology creates for want satisfaction at any moment in time. Coal and copper were not resources once and may not be resources at some future time. Resources come in and out of existence, part of what economist Joseph Schumpeter would call *creative destruction*. "Creating the better," Zimmermann stated, "we must often destroy the good." Different resources, Zimmermann continued, are more than *variety*; they are potential substitutes. Substitution grows from the cumulative nature of scientific discovery whereby "each invention gives rise to numerous others." This insight would be seized by later thinkers to bring Zimmermann's functional theory of resources to a grand conclusion: recognition of the vast human potential to overcome, even overwhelm, diminishing returns and the perceived fixity of resources.

⟨·◦·⟩

The second edition of *World Resources and Industries* (1951) added precision and elegance to Zimmermann's original exposition. "Resources are highly dynamic functional concepts; they *are not, they become*, they evolve out of the triune interaction of nature, man, and culture, in which nature sets outer limits, but man and culture are largely responsible for the portion of physical totality that is made available for human use." His poignant, pregnant conclusion: "Knowledge is truly the mother of all other resources."

Physical to functional; objective to subjective; absolute to relative; static to dynamic: Zimmermann presented a *real-world* theory to help intellectuals, industrialists, and policymakers solve the paradox of nondepleting depletable resources. The University of North Carolina named him a distinguished professor soon after *World Resources and Industries* was published, and by the second edition, Zimmermann was ensconced at the flagship school of the nation's leading oil and gas state, the University of Texas at Austin, with a dual professorship in economics and natural resources. All seemed in order for the titan of resource thought.

1933   1951

Figure 8.1 Erich Zimmermann's functional theory of resources was not accepted into mainstream economics, despite its real-world qualities. Nonetheless, his is one of the greatest contributions in the history of mineral-resource thought.

However, by the time of his second edition, Zimmermann knew that something was wrong—not with his theory but with the *influence* of the theory. The academic reviews were positive. Leading industry economists, such as Richard Gonzalez of Humble Oil and Refining Company, were moved, and the American Petroleum Institute distributed his book to its members. Yet academic economics was going in another direction. Instead of realism, professors were resorting to enabling assumptions that objectified economic life to allow mathematical description, diagrammatic exposition, and statistical testability. One of the new breed, Paul Samuelson, who would go on to receive one of the first Nobel prizes in economics, wrote in the *American Economic Review* in 1952 that "mathematical economics is flying high," eclipsing the work of the "literary economist." Zimmermann was certainly the latter.[1]

Quantified economic data promised a new domain for the discipline. Ivory-tower economists longed for their science to become as rigorous as the natural sciences—and provide precise information for policymaking. Calculus was useful for mathematically describing natural phenomena, including energy. Could technical analysis be equally useful in prescribing the optimal rate of production of a depletable resource?

Zimmermann warned his peers in the first edition, "To those who are used to viewing resources as material fixtures of human nature, this functional interpretation of resources must seem disconcerting." But the gulf had not been bridged, and in the second edition, Zimmermann challenged his colleagues in no uncertain terms:

> Nothing is more fatal to a realistic and usable understanding of resources than the failure to differentiate between the constants of natural science and the relatives of social science, between the totality of the universe or of the planet earth . . . and . . . the ever-changing resources of a given group of people at a given time and place. . . . One has but to recall some of the most precious resources of our age—electricity, oil, nuclear energy—to see who is right, the exponent of the static school who insists that "resources are," or the defender of the dynamic, functional, operational school who insists that "resources become."

Erich Zimmermann's functional theory brought in *institutional* factors, such as technology, politics, war, science, and culture, to explain the availability and changing nature of resources. This was a powerful supplement to the rigid, one-dimensional interpretation that spawned depletionist thinking. "A functional interpretation of resources," Zimmermann explained, "makes any static interpretation of a region's resources appear futile; for resources change not only with every change of social objectives, respond to every revision of the standard of living, change with each new alignment of classes and individuals, but also with every change in the state of the arts—institutional as well as technological."[2]

This was economic realism at its highest, although Zimmermann missed a grand opportunity to place his contribution in a broader context, namely, within Austrian economics, a whole school of economics that adopted mind-centered analysis as the common denominator of a reality-based science of human action.[3]

---

1. See also Internet appendix 8.1, "Zimmermann—A Forgotten Economist," at www.political capitalism.org/book1/chapter8/appendix1.html.

2. See also Internet appendix 8.2, "Zimmermann and Institutionalism," at www. politicalcapitalism.org/book1/chapter8/appendix2.html.

3. See also Internet appendix 8.3, "Zimmermann's Methodological Isolation," at www. politicalcapitalism.org/book1/chapter8/appendix3.html.

The Calculus of Depletion: Harold Hotelling

Zimmermann aside, economists became wedded to the fixity notion of mineral resources. In a 1913 essay that set the agenda for the rest of the century, L. C. Gray wrote:

> Minerals afford a tolerably clear-cut type of resources which are absolutely limited in supply and non-restorable. It is necessary to make a definite choice between present and future. Normally, when once used, the supply is exhausted practically for all time. . . . This is absolutely true in the case of coal, petroleum, and natural gas.

The issue of how to produce (consume) declining supply, *the problem of conservation*, Gray added, "is the determination of the proper rate of discount on the future with respect to the utilization of our natural resources."

Taking Gray as his starting point, Harold Hotelling (1895–1973), a mathematician and statistician who was attracted to technical economic issues, published a seminal essay in 1931 applying the calculus of variations to derive the optimal allocation of a fixed (depleting) resource over time. His constrained-maximization problem, originally rejected for publication because of its abstruse mathematics, became a classic once the economics profession deciphered his technique and envisioned its possibilities.

Hotelling began by noting that the standard economic analysis was "plainly inadequate for an industry in which the indefinite maintenance of a steady rate of production is a physical impossibility, and which is therefore bound to decline." Hotelling proved that *if* the total resource base was known, fixed, and of identical quality; *if* capital investment was fixed; *if* minerals were mined in order of (objectively known) least cost; *if* resource prices were known in each time period; and *if* the entire market had perfect knowledge, the entire quantity would be mined and sold at a net price (marginal revenue minus marginal cost) that rose at the rate of interest (Hotelling's Rule).[4] This price premium, or *depletion value*, also known in the literature as *user cost*, was a revenue stream that only a fixed (exhaustible) supply could command through time.

Hotelling achieved his purpose of finding a rational production profile, a "golden mean," between the "wholesale devastation of irreplaceable natural resources" and the conservationist dilemma where "exploitation . . . can never be too slow for the public good." The dormant depletionism of Jevons was given new life—at least theoretically.

Hotelling's formalistic approach to mineral-resource issues was in the vanguard of emerging economic theory. Students flocked to Hotelling's courses in mathematical and statistical economics at Columbia University and, later, just four years after Zimmermann departed, at the University of North Carolina.

---

4. The interest rate represents the premium on money available today versus the future. A 4 percent interest rate means, for example, that $100 today exchanges on the market for $104 that is available after a year of waiting.

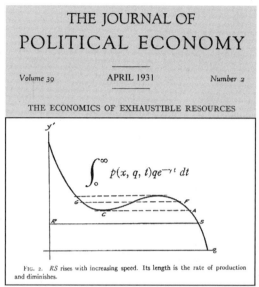

Figure 8.2 Harold Hotelling's mathematical demonstration of the optimal allocation of a fixed resource over time was technically correct but unsuited for the real world. Hotelling's Rule would eclipse Zimmermann's functional theory by giving theoretical rigor to the doctrine of depletionism.

"The Mecca," as Paul Samuelson described him, had created his own momentum, although his theory of mineral pricing would attract little development for decades. The reason for the lack of attention was subtle but profound: Resources believed to be depletable were not depleting but greatly expanding by any economic or business measure.

Harold Hotelling's derivation was elegant and intuitive. It rigorously proved an insight that was recognized from at least the time of Adam Smith: Expectations about future availability affect present prices. But the assumption giving rise to depletionism—*fixed supply*—was exactly wrong for the real world that Hotelling aimed to inform. So too was his assumption of perfect knowledge that banished entrepreneurship toward resources, or *resourceship*. The institutional framework was ignored or simply assumed away. Once Hotelling's "ideal state" was relaxed to allow for improving technology, capital reinvestment, interfirm rivalry, resource substitution, institutions, and business strategy and entrepreneurial change, Zimmermann's functional theory was the better one. But economists did not see Zimmermann as a framework for analysis, leaving Hotelling as the heir to Jevons's theory of mineral resources. This would come to haunt the profession when leading economists turned to Hotelling's Rule to explain the oil-price explosion in the 1970s, the subject of chapter 10.

Zimmermann Stalls Out

Zimmermann belittled Hotelling's contribution as "a jumble of numbers." There is no evidence that Hotelling referenced, much less knew about, Zimmermann's functional theory. The protagonists were both right but working in different paradigms—a hypothetical one of fixed, known resources and a real-world, open-ended one of business opportunity.

Zimmermann, however, fell short of presenting a systemic countertheory to Jevons-Gray-Hotelling depletionism. *Despite* teeing up a theory with rich implications for expanding supply and interresource substitution; *despite* presenting an array of price and quantity statistics showing how oil, gas, and coal were expanding resources; and *despite* declaring the vision of Malthus "obsolete," Zimmermann was a depletionist at heart. His particular concern was rapid production of oil and gas in the United States under the rule of capture, a particular property rights assignment for migrant minerals. But his angst extended to hard minerals as well.

Zimmermann recognized a conservation (efficiency) ethic at work toward reproducible goods under capitalism. But profit maximization toward exhaustible resources was another matter. "To the average individual the oil resources of the year 2000 may be of little concern; their size and accessibility do not interest him, for his imagination cannot follow his children and his children's children far enough into the future," he wrote in 1933. To Zimmermann, the statistics of plenty were not the triumph of human ingenuity and evidence of an open-ended resource future; it was a sign of *overproduction*, of "warped appraisal" in favor of present output. This "tempo problem" for Zimmermann was a *market failure* and a concern of government, which "as the political embodiment of the group . . . takes in the conservation of the limited non-renewable resources."[5]

On an aggregate level, Zimmermann differentiated between a "transient" civilization based on exhaustible resources and a permanent one based on renewables. The Jevons-Gray-Hotelling view of mineral resources, banished by Zimmermann from the front door, reentered though the back. Ironically, Zimmermann feared the very thing that his functional theory demoted—fixity.

Zimmermann was one of a number of economists concerned over the rapid pace of resource extraction in the United States. Most, if not all, advocated a role for government to slow down exploitation, whether it was with timber on the public domain or with oil and gas on private land. State and federal wellhead conservation regulation of oil and natural gas, enacted at the request of the industry for the most part, is part of the U.S. political-capitalism story of chapter 6.

---

5. See also Internet appendix 8.4, "Zimmermann and Petroleum Conservation," at www.politicalcapitalism.org/book1/chapter8/appendix4.html. The concept of market failure is more generally considered in Internet appendix 9.3, "Welfare Economics," at www.political capitalism.org/book1/chapter9/appendix3.html.

Hayek on Conservation

The conservation debate attracted the attention of one of the century's leading critics of government planning, F. A. Hayek (1899–1992). In *The Constitution of Liberty* (1960), Hayek evaluated "the necessity of central direction of the conservation of natural resources," a view that was "particularly strong in the United States, where the 'conservation movement' has to a great extent been the source of the agitation for economic planning and has contributed much to the indigenous ideology of the radical economic reformers."[6] Although not denying that economic error could produce real waste in the "consumption of irreplaceable resources," Hayek cautioned that government was unlikely to have the knowledge of future conditions of price and scarcity that would enable it to impose an efficient solution.

Although speaking of fixity, Hayek's dynamic analysis complemented that of Zimmermann by urging consideration of the *resources totality*, not its parts. "Any natural resource represents just one item of our total endowment of exhaustible resources, and our problem is not to preserve this stock in any particular form, but always to maintain it in a form that will make the most desirable contribution to total income," Hayek wrote. "The existence of a particular natural resource merely means that, while it lasts, its temporary contribution to our income will help us to create new ones which will similarly assist us in the future."

This *more-creates-more* view was a missing piece of a thoroughgoing alternative to depletionism. Hayek was onto something bigger than he realized—at least until he discovered the work of Julian Simon, a story told in the next two chapters.

Hayek's assessment of conservation planning noted a circularity problem: Postponed consumption was *still* supply lost for the future. Quoting a fellow economist (Anthony Scott), Hayek noted the irony that "the conservationist who urges us 'to make greater provision for the future' is in fact urging a lesser provision for posterity." In other words, consumption had to be avoided indefinitely, not merely postponed, or it was not conservation. Yet this would create perpetual nonusage in the present—an impossibility.

A decade prior to Paul Samuelson's dig at the literary economist, Hayek argued oppositely: "It is probably no exaggeration to say that every important advance in economic theory during the last hundred years was a further step in the consistent application of subjectivism." Objectivist formalism, whereby the statistical residue of human action is divorced from human plans and purpose, is the methodology of mathematical economics; subjectivism, the creed of literary economists and the methodological framework that Zimmermann

---

6. Hayek, like other economists of the time, defined conservation as *preservation* rather than more efficient or so-called *sustainable* utilization, the latter being the common usage today. The changing meaning of conservation is discussed in Internet appendix 8.5, "The Rise of Conservation Economics," at www.politicalcapitalism.org/book1/chapter8/appendix5.html.

needed to codify his argument. Zimmermann needed Hayek, and Hayek needed Zimmermann. But they never joined, leaving different parts of the theory for others to discover independently and expand into a full-fledged alternative theory to depletionism.

Paley Commission

The United States undertook its first comprehensive mineral stocktaking nearly a century after England grappled with the coal question and a quarter century after President Harding investigated the U.S. coal situation. It was long in coming. There had been the so-called closing of the frontier, which involved the conservation movement of President Theodore Roosevelt. Resource concerns had been paramount during World War I, World War II, and the Korean conflict. The United States had turned from a net exporter to a net importer of oil in 1947. New books painted a gloomy resource future. At the call of many in the federal government, President Harry Truman appointed a presidential commission in 1951 to study "the broader and longer range aspects of the nation's materials problem as distinct from the immediate defense needs."

The President's Materials Policy Commission, also known as the Paley Commission for its chair, William Paley, the head of Columbia Broadcasting System (CBS), mobilized more intellectual firepower than had ever been dedicated before to an economic study. A full-time staff of 50 worked with top academicians, industry leaders, and government agency officials over 18 months to produce a five-volume report, *Resources for Freedom* (1952).

Figure 8.3 The Paley Commission, named after its chair, William Paley of CBS, resulted in the five-volume *Resources for Freedom* (1952). Directing the study was Edward Mason of Harvard University, one of five members of the commission.

The study documented an unprecedented increase in material requirements in the first half of the century, including a 26-fold increase in natural gas usage and 30-fold rise in crude oil consumption. The nation's annual usage of materials was running at 2.5 billion tons, or 18 tons per person per year, a quantity that few had ever contemplated. The study asked, *Could the U.S. meet its resource needs out to 1975—and beyond?*

The obligatory nod to depletion—"the time will come . . . when civilization's energy needs will outrun nature's declining store of fossil fuels"—was noted. Yet the core of the report was not alarmist—at least not for the forecast period out to 1975. The moderating voice that kept Malthus, Gray, and Hotelling at bay was Harvard economist Edward Mason (1899–1992), the academic joining Paley, two other businessmen, and a journalist on the five-person steering committee.[7]

Mason was a *what-do-I-really-need-to-know* scholar who depended on his juniors to keep him apprised of the increasing technical literature of economics. A simple-mannered man with a gift for simplification, Mason was a great teacher whose students fondly called themselves members of the "Masonic Lodge." Mason was also a leader. "Where Ed Mason sat, there was the head of the table," remembered his Harvard colleague John Kenneth Galbraith. But most important for the Paley Commission, Mason was a *realist* whose interest was less on highly conditional theories than on the actual workings of the economy.

Mason viewed the quantity of each resource as *inventory that could be replaced at a cost*. Jevons had sagely focused upon the mining cost for coal but underestimated technological change and interfuel substitution. Hotelling left the real world behind without realizing it. Zimmermann stopped short of where his theory and evidence pointed. Mason assembled the factual record, added a dollop of commonsense economics, and showed how well human ingenuity was stacking up against what would otherwise be diminishing returns of minerals extraction.

The Paley report presented mineral-resource theory in a new and optimistic light. A "popular fallacy" was challenged: "our resource base" being "a fixed inventory which, when used, up, will leave society with no means of survival." A "related fallacy [was that] physical waste equals economic waste." The study explained: "Hoarding resources in the expectation of more important uses later involves a sacrifice that may never be recouped; technological changes and new resource discoveries may alter a situation completely." Besides, "using resources today is an essential part of making our economy grow; materials which become embodied in today's capital goods, for example, are put to work and help make tomorrow's production higher."

The comprehensive statistics spoke loudly for human resourcefulness. Volume III on energy resources reported an increase in U.S. oil reserves from less than 4 billion barrels at the turn of the century to more than 27 billion barrels—despite interim consumption of almost 8 billion barrels. Prices of petroleum products had fallen 16 percent in the last quarter century, adjusted for inflation. Although left unmentioned, such a result was the opposite of that suggested

---

7. One of the businessmen was George R. Brown, whose investment group purchased (and converted to natural gas) the Big Inch and Little Inch oil pipelines from the government after World War II to form Texas Eastern Gas Transmission, a transaction described in Book 2.

by Hotelling's Rule, which calculated price increases for fixed resources. But then Hotelling's assumptions were not operative. In the Paley Commission framework, supply was not fixed, investment was not static, and entrepreneurs had resourcing to do.

Turning to public policy, recognition was given to "the free price system" as "the great 'allocator' of resources and materials." The report supported a global division of labor—the internationalism of Adam Smith and other free traders. "The United States must reject self-sufficiency as a policy and instead adopt the policy of the lowest cost acquisition of materials wherever secure supplies may be found." The staunch free-trade position of the report would be later recognized as "a courageous act in the face . . . of vociferous calls for protection of domestic industries" operating in a buyers' market.

Some conclusions and recommendations of the Paley study foreshadowed the muddled energy-sustainability debate of nearly a half century later, one in which Enron actively engaged. A vaguely defined energy problem required "prudence in the face of uncertainty," a position that decades later came to be formalized as the *precautionary principle*. The study urged a "comprehensive energy policy" as follows:

> The Nation's energy problem must be viewed in its entirely and not as a loose collection of independent pieces involving different sources and forms of energy. So numerous and vital are the interrelations among all sectors of the energy field, that problems in any one sector must be dealt with always in full consideration of the side effects on all other sectors. The aim must be to achieve a constant pattern of policies and programs throughout the entire energy field.

What was the nation's energy problem? Setting up the Jevonian logic of increasing scarcity, annual world energy demand growth since 1860 was found to be 2.2 percent—with the United States at a higher compounded rate of 3 percent. "If we are to avoid the risk of seriously increased real unit costs of energy in the United States," the study warned, "then new low-cost sources should be made ready to pick up some of the load by 1975." Atomic energy was calculated to provide no more than one-fifth of the growth, which left the energy flow from the almighty sun, since "the United States supply of solar energy is about 1,500 times the present requirement." A policy directive followed: "It is time for aggressive research in the whole field of solar energy—an effort in which the United States could make an immense contribution to the welfare of the free world." Coal and coal-based synthetics, not oil or gas, were expected to bridge this open-ended solar future. This view of the energy future would become a mantra in the 1970s.

The study was supply-side oriented. The first premise of the report was: "We share the belief of the American people in the principle of Growth." The economist-dominated study assumed that the price system registered scarcities and guided usage rationally. There was little mention of market failure or appeal for energy conservation for its own sake—conservationism. Environmental issues were not discussed. The Organization of Petroleum Exporting Countries

(OPEC) was not yet in existence, and the Persian Gulf was just another body of water. Wind power, unmentioned, was something down on the farm. Such was the energy world in the early 1950s.

Commission member Eric Hodgins, a longtime writer for *Fortune*, oversaw the final drafting of the Paley Commission report. Knowing that the opening pages would be the most read, Hodgins could not resist language that was more alarmist than that suggested by a literal reading of the study itself. Provocative terms, such as "threat" and "many causes for concern," turned what the core of the report characterized as a *conceivable* long-term problem into an urgent one.

Not surprisingly, the popular press seized upon Hodgins's wording to warn of problems ahead. "A Crisis in Raw Materials Found Imperiling Security," announced the *New York Times* on page 1. "Developing shortages and mounting costs of raw materials had raised grave questions for the nation's security and living standards," the story read. But this was misdirection. Indeed, President Truman had congratulated the commission for its "heartening" finding that neither living standards nor national security was imperiled and for its conclusion that solutions to the nation's resource challenges could be found.

The country's premier business magazine did worse in an article titled "The Crisis in Raw Materials"—again the work of Hodgins. The piece reworded the report to add spin to spin. This incident, hardly noticed at the time, underscored the proclivity of the media to sensationalize the news. This incident would be repeated in greatly magnified form in a tiff over the executive summary of a major international global-warming study released in 1996, part of Enron's political-capitalism, sustainable-development story, described in Book 3.

The Paley Commission report, a compromise among many voices, warned against the extremes of pessimism and optimism. The economic logic that underlay the report was a good foundation, however, and few could dispute that the resource future looked bright for at least the next decades. Only *after* the forecast period did concern creep in. This hardly created a stir akin to the coal panic of Jevons's day; the public was too busy basking in resource abundance and economic prosperity to be swayed by pundits.

Resources for the Future

William Paley was determined to continue the commission's work. His initial idea was to move his activity to the National Security Resource Board, a civil defense agency established in 1947 as part of the cold war's National Security Council. An overture to that effect was rejected by President Eisenhower as a step toward economic planning.

Paley and leaders from academia, government, and conservation groups then interested the Ford Foundation in funding an organization that could provide "substantial groundwork" on "a problem of increasing importance to the

IN 1950 the Trustees named five general areas to which Ford Foundation activities would be directed for the public welfare:

1. The support of activities that promise significant contributions to world peace and the establishment of a world order of law and justice.

2. The support of activities designed to secure greater allegiance to the basic principles of freedom and democracy in the solution of the insistent problems of an ever-changing society.

3. The support of activities designed to advance the economic well-being of people everywhere and to improve economic institutions for the better realization of democratic goals.

4. The support of activities to strengthen, expand, and improve educational facilities and methods to enable individuals more fully to realize their intellectual, civic, and spiritual potentialities; to promote greater equality of educational opportunity; and to conserve and increase knowledge and enrich our culture.

5. The support of scientific activities designed to increase knowledge of factors which influence or determine human conduct, and to extend such knowledge for the maximum benefit of individuals and of society.

Figure 8.4 The Ford Foundation, endowed with Ford Motor Company stock from the estates of company founder Henry Ford (top left) and his son Edsel (top right), would dive into energy and public policy, beginning with the creation of Resources for the Future in 1952. Henry Ford II (lower left), instrumental in turning around the fortunes of Ford Motor, guided his namesake foundation and its first mission statement.

American people"—a "wiser use of resources."[8] The result was a new Washington, D.C.–based think tank, Resources for the Future (RFF),[9] which opened its doors in 1952 and hosted a major conference on resource issues, reminiscent of the White House Conference of Governors in 1908, led by Teddy Roosevelt and Gifford Pinchot. The Mid-Century Conference on Resources for the Future, backed by the Conservation Foundation and Izaak Walton League of America, both active in the incipient environmental movement, produced *The Nation Looks at Its Resources*, beginning the "era of the big books" at RFF. The stocktaking provided many opinions from different perspectives, including President-elect Eisenhower's kick-off admonition: "We have got to be intelligent all over the United States, and not let pressure groups or any extremists lead us into erroneous directions."

---

8. The Ford Foundation was just spreading its wings. In 1952, it also founded the Population Council, and millions of dollars were spent on other public-policy projects. Still, half of the Foundation's early funding went to RFF.

9. Other names considered by the RFF founders included the Natural Resources Association and, lightheartedly, Dynamic Prosperity, Inc.

Through the 1960s, RFF would publish a stream of studies on resources, particularly energy, that presented virtually all available statistics of cost, supply, and price.[10] The data showed that resources were becoming more plentiful even as more was being consumed—contradicting, implicitly at least, the tenets of depletionism. RFF's newsletter, *Resources*, had on its masthead: "Every discovery that has extended the circle of the known has enlarged the perimeter of the unknown." The static view of the world embedded in Malthusianism was challenged at the pinnacle of resource thought.

  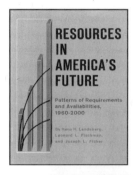

  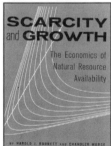

Figure 8.5 Studies sponsored by Resources for the Future documented how, in economic terms, nonreproducible resources were expanding, not depleting, despite their record production and use. Four of the books shown here were published in the early 1960s; *Energy in the World Economy* was released in 1971.

In 1962, RFF's positive findings were joined by a U.S. Senate study. *Report of the National Fuels and Energy Study Group,* authored by representatives of the oil, gas, and coal sectors, pronounced the domestic energy resource base adequate until the end of its forecast period—1980. Resources were deemed abundant across the board—and none more so than petroleum. Indeed, state and federal regulators were managing a surplus by limiting domestic oil production and restricting oil imports. Natural gas, with more supply than demand, was

---

10. These volumes are listed on pp. 344–45 in appendix D.

increasingly going into pipelines and reaching new markets instead of being discharged and flared at the well site.

Although many RFF studies were heavy on documentation, *Scarcity and Growth* (1963) by Harold Barnett and Chandler Morse painted the big picture in such a way as to inspire a new generation of resource economists, including M. A. Adelman of the Massachusetts Institute of Technology (MIT) and Julian Simon of the University of Illinois. Between the Paley report and *Scarcity and Growth*, not to mention the ongoing abundance of a variety of natural and mineral resources, expansionism gained the upper hand in academia and government.

Scarcity and Growth reviewed the history of resource economics, politics, and modeling to conclude that although "no society can escape the general limits of its resources . . . no innovative society need accept Malthusian diminishing returns." With a nod to what social critic John Kenneth Galbraith labeled *the affluent society*, the authors framed the "modern natural resource problem [as] not diminishing returns, but social adjustment to a variety of adverse indirect effects of technological change and economic growth." The energy problem was becoming more nuanced in a world of resource plenty.

The book paid passing tribute to the "gestaltist" Erich Zimmermann and his "monumental *World Resources and Industries.*" But the praise was marred. Not only was Zimmermann's functional theory not explained, but also the last name of the pioneer of mineral-resource economics, just two years deceased, his theory in the shadows, was misspelled.

An Eye Trained on Scarcity: M. A. Adelman

M. A. Adelman (b. 1917) was a particularly able student whose award-winning dissertation on antitrust, under Edward Mason, was published in the Harvard Economics Series in 1959. Adelman began to specialize in oil and gas issues in the 1960s and became a leading exponent of resource expansionism. Like Mason, Adelman was also a great teacher, with such energy scholars as Paul Bradley, Les Cookenboo, Richard Gordon, Michael Lynch, Zenon Zannatos, and Martin Zimmerman to his credit during a long career as professor of economics at MIT.

For Adelman, as for his mentor Mason, "the basic idea was that resources were inventories; what we needed to know was the cost of renewal," which meant discerning "what is in the mind" of mineral prospectors. Adelman's contribution would include many learned books, articles, and lectures. But a particularly significant moment occurred at a talk before a geophysics association in 1970 when he almost unknowingly completed the expansionist line of thought. Adelman mused: "Perhaps the very concept of exhaustible reserves ought to be discarded as wrong or irrelevant. Not much of the resources we know today will ever be used because better ones will be found. Or the need itself may disappear before the resource." This insight was a logical progression

Harvard University   Massachusetts Institute of Technology

Figure 8.6 Harvard University economics professor Edward Mason (left) produced a top student in M. A. Adelman (right), who would specialize in the most enigmatic mineral resource of all, petroleum, and mentor a generation of leading energy economists at MIT.

from his idea that "resources, like other assets, are not found but made," an echo of Erich Zimmermann's "resources *are not, they become.*"

Undiminished growth of mineral-resource stocks in the United States and around the world made the depletion question seemingly one for some distant future. The statistics of plenty were published for all to see. The functional theory of Erich Zimmermann stood ready, with some improvements, to add theoretical heft to the data and further challenge the Jevons-Gray-Hotelling orthodoxy. Instead of arguing about how much water was in the glass, the question was turning against the concept of a glass (fixity) itself. Still, just about everyone *knew* that depletable resources depleted. That gut premise would inspire a neo-Malthusian movement in the 1960s and carry the day when energy markets went from surplus to shortage in the 1970s, the subject of the next two chapters.

9

Neo-Malthusianism

IN THE 1950s AND 1960s, notable voices challenged the resource optimism emanating from Resources for the Future (RFF). The oil industry's best-known geologist, M. King Hubbert, forecast declining U.S. oil and gas production by the early 1970s and falling world oil output by century's end. E. F. Schumacher, economic adviser to the U.K. National Coal Board, warned that demand would overtake supply for each of the fossil fuels. Paul Ehrlich, a population biologist at Stanford University, wrote a best-seller declaring that hundreds of millions of deaths were inevitable from imminent shortfalls of fossil fuels and foodstuffs, among other goods. These currents came together on Earth Day, 1970, when thousands of events at high schools, colleges, and universities elevated environmentalism to a national movement and political force. A neo-Malthusian doomsday book, *Limits to Growth* (1972), sponsored by the Club of Rome, an international group of intellectuals and business leaders, sold millions of copies worldwide.

When energy markets began to encounter problems in the late 1960s and early 1970s, the intellectual mainstream jumped toward the fixity-depletion theory of mineral resources. Some former leading resource optimists would retreat or simply not be heard from. Others were ignored. Despite the odds, a notable contrarian emerged. Julian Simon, a statistics expert and data hound, reversed his Malthusian mindset after finding stubbornly positive correlations between population and improvement that others did not see—or want to see, much less believe. It would be Simon, not the economists at RFF, who would expound optimism in the face of record population growth and ever-growing mineral consumption.

Dismal Geology: M. King Hubbert

The American Association for the Advancement of Science (AAAS) celebrated its 100th anniversary in 1949 in Washington, D.C. "Energy from Fossil

Fuels," a paper presented at the centennial symposium, was T. R. Malthus and W. S. Jevons reincarnated. M. King Hubbert (1903–89), associate director of the Exploration and Production Research Division at Shell Oil Company, declared: "One of the most disturbing ecological influences of recent millennia is the human species' proclivity for the capture of energy, resulting in a progressive increase of the human population." Estimating increasing rates of coal and oil production, he asked: "Where is it taking us? How long can we keep it up?" Although not offering specifics, Hubbert warned that, without major changes, "overpopulation, exhaustion of resources and eventual decline" lay ahead.

Hubbert became the talk of the industry seven years later, in March 1956, when he specifically predicted coming peaks in U.S. oil and gas production and in world oil production at a meeting of the American Petroleum Institute. His superiors at Shell tried to dissuade him from giving his message, but Hubbert, an honored scientist with a stubborn streak, went ahead.[1] Geology was now the dismal science.

Hubbert presented life-cycle estimates for each of the carbon-based fuels that coupled recorded production with estimated remaining supply. The result was a simple set of curves that showed expanding, peaking, and then declining production over time. *Hubbert's peak* was easier to grasp than Hotelling's Rule and attracted a following in the earth sciences. Hubbert "became something of a folk hero for conservationists" as well.

Hubbert concluded that the earth's fixed carbon-energy endowment—the result of "500 million years of geological history"—faced "progressive exhaustion" from "industrial exploitation." As a template, he plotted the ascent of Ohio's oil production from the 1860s to its peak in the 1890s and steady decline thereafter. Then came Hubbert's grand leap: *extrapolated* production rates and geological exhaustion for the United States and the world. He predicted that domestic oil and natural gas output would peak by 1970 and that global oil output would peak about 2000. (He did not model global natural gas supply, which was not an international commodity.) Plentiful coal would not peak in the United States or the world until the twenty-second century, in his estimation—little worry or potential falsification there.

In 1969, Hubbert added new forecasts for global production/consumption of fossil fuels. He predicted that oil and gas production/usage (crude oil, natural gas, coal, gas liquids, tar sands, and shale oil), would "exhaust the middle 80 percent of the ultimate resources . . . [in] only about a century." World coal

---

1. For the published version of his talk, Shell Oil persuaded Hubbert to rephrase his original statement that "there is a vast difference between the running of an industry whose annual production can be depended upon to increase on the average 5 to 10 per cent per year and one whose output can be depended upon to decline at that rate." It now said that "the culmination for petroleum and natural gas in both the United States and the State of Texas should occur within the next few decades."

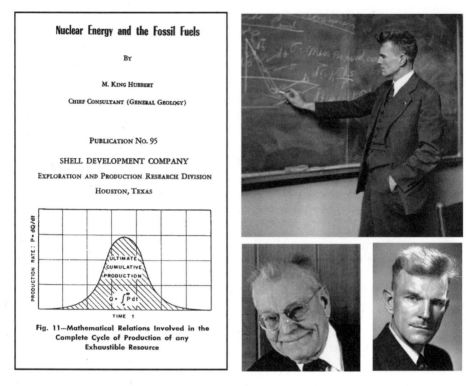

Figure 9.1 M. King Hubbert's bell-curve heuristic, which he described as the "mathematical relations involved in the complete cycle of production of any exhaustible resource," provided a seemingly simple empirical basis to depletionism.

would exhaust the same 80 percent in "about 300 to 400 years (but only 100 to 200 years if coal is used as the main energy source)."

A known, fixed (albeit estimated) resource base was the key for Hubbert as it was for Hotelling—although the two exercises were different and never cross-referenced. Hubbert's prediction of a coming peak in U.S. oil production would prove to be on the mark, but his prediction for domestic gas was wrong, as would be his global forecast for oil. Actual production has exceeded Hubbert's theoretically predicted quantities, the slope of the decline curves notwithstanding. The Zimmermann framework explained why. Hubbert's preoccupation with objective quantities blinded him to the crucial role of economics (scarcity pricing, etc.) and institutions (property rights, etc.) in enhancing the resource base and directing interregional production. Hubbert's self-styled "powerful means of estimating the time scale for the complete production cycle of any exhaustible resource in any given region" was a simplified, misleading look at the real world, where ingenuity and politics mattered too.

Kenneth Deffeyes, a later-day proponent of Hubbert's geological model, admitted that his teacher's "inspired guess . . . was just barely within the envelope of acceptable scientific methods." Yet Hubbert's lone correct prediction of peak U.S. oil production became legend, and his overall approach became a staple of the neo-Malthusian popular literature. His geology curves of a half century ago are still the basis of predicted imminent declines in global production today.[2]

Small as Beautiful: E. F. Schumacher

A second voice of resource pessimism during the period belonged to the economics adviser to Britain's National Coal Board, an agency that assumed the functions of the industry under the Coal Industry [Nationalization] Act of 1946. As early as 1952, E. F. Schumacher (1911–77) warned that depleting oil and gas was destined to increase the burden on coal. Two years later, Schumacher sounded the energy alarm in a way that his homeland had not heard since Jevons's *The Coal Question* nearly a century before:

> We are living off capital in the most fundamental meaning of the word. . . . Only in the last hundred years has man forcibly broken into nature's larder and is now emptying it out at a breathtaking speed. . . . Adaptation and invention [to forestall shortage] continually demands the expansion of one product, namely energy. The whole problem of nature's larder, that is the exhaustion of non-renewable resources, can probably be reduced to this one point—Energy. If one asks about the future of the economy, ultimately one is asking about the future of an energy economy.

In 1958, Schumacher warned the Federation of British Industry that "the first signs of a world oil famine [were] visible"—reminiscent of Jevons's 1875 public lecture claiming to see "the first twinge" of coal depletion. But few were listening to Schumacher. There was a resource problem, but it concerned too much and industry demoralization, not too little and consumer pain. Energy regulators on both sides of the Atlantic were grappling with producer angst over high production and low prices, not depletion and rising prices.

Schumacher's Malthusianism became spiritual when he left atheism for Zen Buddhism. "A Buddhist economy," he wrote, "would make 'the distinction between "renewable" and "non-renewable" resources.'" A socialist, Schumacher was "concerned more about people than efficiency." Like John Kenneth Galbraith an ocean away, Schumacher attacked affluence and materialism. "Modern man has built a system of production that ravishes nature and a type of society that mutilates man," he wrote. The solution was a "magnanimous kind of

---

2. See appendix 11.4, "Contemporary Hubbert Analysis," at www.politicalcapitalism.org/book1/chapter11/appendix4.html.

Figure 9.2 E. F. Schumacher, as economic adviser to the U.K. National Coal Board, popularized the notion of coal, gas, and oil as *capital fuels* rather than *income fuels*, portending a supply crisis to come. His ideas became popular with President Carter when energy problems hit in the 1970s.

prudence" leading to "justice, fortitude, and *temperantia*, which means knowing when enough is enough."

The "voice in the wilderness" would emerge triumphant when the global energy surplus disappeared in the 1970s. The British establishment, from Queen Elizabeth to Royal Dutch Shell, sought his company and advice. California Governor Jerry Brown, President Jimmy Carter, and thousands of newly minted neo-Malthusians embraced the new guru of less-is-more. Schumacher's 1973 book, *Small Is Beautiful*, sold hundreds of thousands of copies before and after his death in 1977.

Doomsday! Paul Ehrlich and John Holdren

Around the turn of the century, the first environmental movement coalesced around the *wise use* of public lands and their resources. The *preservation movement* had Malthusian roots, but it was also an offshoot of an increasingly affluent society in which some citizens of means embraced countervalues to industrialization and materialism. Groups such as the National Audubon Society (established 1866), Sierra Club (1892), Wilderness Society (1935), and National Wildlife Federation (1936) were dedicated to the great outdoors in their different ways, but each would become much more than simply a private group using private resources to achieve its ends. All would become highly political and participate in the energy debates of Enron's era—and sometimes debates involving Enron itself.

The 1960s brought together a number of natural scientists, soon to be labeled *ecologists* and *environmentalists*, concerned about population growth, pollution, and resource depletion. A catalyst for the new movement was biologist Rachel Carson's *Silent Spring* (1962), a critique of chemical use in agriculture, which found an unexpectedly large and passionate audience. Pollution, once tolerated as a byproduct of a growing economy, became part of the dark side of business-dominated society. Whereas John Kenneth Galbraith questioned *affluence*, the new consciousness targeted *effluence*. To many critics of U.S. capitalism, the two were flip sides of the same coin.

In 1968, just in time for the presidential election, Paul Ehrlich, head of the graduate biology program at Stanford University, published a sensational bestseller, *The Population Bomb*. The opening chapter, "The Problem," contained three subtitles: "Too Many People," "Too Little Food," and "A Dying Planet." "The battle to feed all of humanity is over," the book began. "In the 1970's the world will undergo famines—hundreds of millions of people are going to starve to death in spite of any crash programs embarked upon now." Malthus's *misery* was Ehrlich's "death-rate solution." The United States, Ehrlich emphasized, would not be spared.

Ehrlich's neo-Malthusian tract was followed by other writings that focused on resource problems, particularly with oil. In one book, Ehrlich paid homage to M. King Hubbert and asked, "What will we do when the pumps run dry?" Ehrlich brought his doom-and-gloom message to millions on popular television in the 1970s, including appearances on *The Tonight Show Starring Johnny Carson*. New groups, such as Zero Population Growth, cofounded by Ehrlich, began an international campaign to slow birth rates. It was a late start from Ehrlich's point of view, given that "hundreds of millions of people are going to starve to death in spite of any crash programs embarked upon now."

◇

A pessimistic echo came from a physicist at the Lawrence Radiation Laboratory, University of California, Livermore, Ehrlich collaborator John Holdren, who took a particular interest in energy issues. In 1971, Ehrlich and Holdren formulated the first version of what became the I=P•A•T equation, or Impact *equals* Population *times* Affluence *times* Technology. The greater the impact, the worse the ecological consequences (and vice versa), which made population, affluence, and technology bad in themselves.

Figure 9.3 Paul Ehrlich's *The Population Bomb* (1968) sold more than 3 million copies. Ehrlich's message of strict population control and sharp cuts in energy use brought hardcore Malthusianism into the modern age.

Figure 9.4 Paul Ehrlich (left) and energy specialist John Holdren (later picture, right) coauthored books and essays in the 1970s and 1980s warning about the perils of society's business-as-usual energy path. Both mentor and protégé equated a negative environmental impact (I) to increasing population (P), affluence (A), and technology (T).

In their 1977 textbook, *Ecoscience*, Holdren and Paul and Anne Ehrlich, declaring themselves "firmly in the neo-Malthusian camp," described the "vexing . . . predicament" of people's interaction with nature. This "gloomy prognosis," they added, was shared by "a growing number of scholars and other observers" calling for "organized evasive action: population control, limitation of material consumption, redistribution of wealth, transitions to technologies that are environmentally and socially less disruptive than today's, and movement toward some kind of world government."

The energy alarmism of Holdren and Ehrlich would extend to air pollution, water runoff from power plants, global cooling, and global warming.[3] Holdren would become a leading intellectual voice for energy alarmism and policy activism as Professor of Energy and Resources at the University of California, Berkeley, and then as Teresa and John Heinz Professor of Environmental Policy at Harvard University's John F. Kennedy School of Government. His views on the coming problem of global climate change from fossil fuel combustion would influence the thinking and strategy of Enron under Ken Lay.

Earth Day, 1970

Modern environmentalism came of age on Earth Day, April 22, 1970. Oil pollution was a catalyst. Smog and other air pollution problems were impacting major U.S. cities, particularly Los Angeles. An offshore oil platform blowout near Santa Barbara, California, spilled 100,000 barrels over several hundred square miles of ocean. Environmentalists led by Rachel Carson, neo-Malthusians led by Paul Ehrlich, and politicians led by President Nixon headlined events at some 12,000 schools and colleges around the country.

Denis Hayes, the event's chief organizer, flew to six events around the United States on Earth Day to tell the throngs that this movement was about revolution, not incremental change. "I suspect that politicians and businessmen who are jumping on the environmental bandwagon don't have the slightest idea what they are getting into," he said. Business leaders "are talking about filters on smokestacks while we are challenging corporate irresponsibility." Politicians are "bursting with pride about plans for totally inadequate municipal sewage treatment plants." In contrast, "we are challenging the ethics of a society that, with only six percent of the world's population, accounts for more than half of the world's annual consumption of raw materials."

At one of many events on Earth Day 1970, two professors at the University of Illinois in Urbana-Champaign squared off before an audience of 2,000 at the campus auditorium. Economist Julian Simon (1932–98), having jettisoned his initial Malthusian beliefs, argued that the statistical record demonstrated a *positive* relationship between population and progress over time. Simon boldly predicted

---

3. See Internet appendix 9.1, "Thoroughgoing Alarmism: Paul Ehrlich and John Holdren," at www.politicalcapitalism.org/book1/chapter9/appendix1.html.

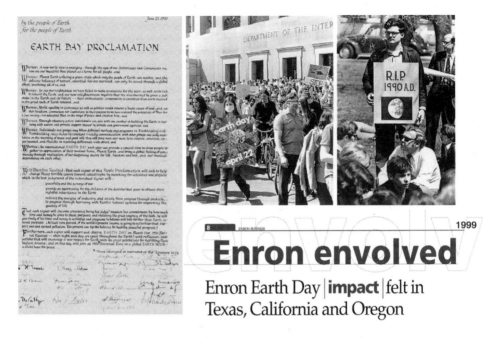

Figure 9.5 Millions participated in marches, teach-ins, debates, and other activities on the first Earth Day, April 22, 1970. The "new agenda" targeted "solid waste, pesticides, chemicals, population growth, [and] industrial development." Enron would sponsor Earth Day events in Houston, San Francisco, and Portland three decades later to buttress its image as a green energy company.

that the earth's carrying capacity could be a *multiple* of the current population— and at a higher level of prosperity—before sitting down to tepid applause.

Zoologist Paul Silverman, citing a number of official studies, tied a range of problems to the 3 billion current world inhabitants and predicted far worse in a more populated future. "We are in the process of destroying and polluting our environment at a rate which may soon put its redemption beyond human intervention," he warned. Energy was of particular concern. With a nod toward M. King Hubbert, he cited a National Research Council study that reported that 80 percent of potential oil reserves would be produced within 20 to 30 years. Silverman then questioned Simon's credentials and values in presenting a view so opposite from mainstream scientists, before sitting down to ringing applause.

The confrontation resumed a few days later at a campus cocktail party at which Simon launched three gin-and-tonics at Silverman. The outburst was part of Simon's professional frustration and clinical depression, but he found solace in dogged research and writing. Simon would soon gain full confidence in his coun-tertheory, which posed a new challenge for him: *How could he break through the*

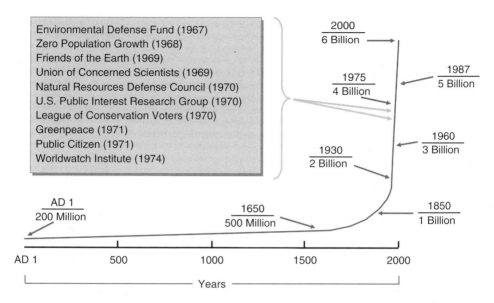

Figure 9.6 Surging population growth gave rise to a strong, emotional neo-Malthusian movement. Some of the new interest groups formed between 1967 and 1974 to challenge population trends, affluence, and high energy usage would praise Ken Lay and Enron in the 1980s and 1990s.

Malthusian fog, the anticapitalistic establishment, to reach the public with the good news about population growth? The challenge was now marketing.

His breakthrough would come.

⟡

"Ecology," noted political economist Robert Heilbroner in 1970, was now "the thing." He continued:

> There are ecological politics, ecological jokes, ecological bookstores, advertisements, seminars, teach-ins, buttons. The automobile, symbol of ecological abuse, has been tried, sentenced to death, and formally executed in at least two universities (complete with burial of one victim). Publishing companies are fattening on books on the sonic boom, poisons in the things we eat, perils loose in the garden, the dangers of breathing. . . . In short, the ecological issue has assumed the dimensions of a vast popular fad.

But the new environmentalism was more than a fad. Some of its roots were in *deep ecology*, a quasi-religious movement that put nature and animals on a par with humans.[4] The new environmentalists were also helping society play catch-up against various forms of pollution that had lagged behind the will

---

4. See Internet appendix 9.2, "Deep Ecology," at www.politicalcapitalism.org/book1/chapter9/appendix2.html.

and means to address them. "Aside from property damage, visibility reduction, and general destruction of the amenities," Allan Kneese of RFF wrote back in 1962, "there is strong circumstantial evidence indicating the adverse health effects of continued exposure to the array of contaminants found in the air of numerous urban areas." But this problem was not due to capitalism or affluence per se; it was rooted in a *tragedy of the commons* whereby air and water assets were not privately owned, managed, and protected through nonregulatory means.[5] As it would turn out, pragmatic business interests were positioning themselves alongside politicians for what would be a long regulatory journey in which incrementalism—and steady ecological improvement—would win out, whether or not it was achieved at least cost.

The number of prominent environmental groups that were founded around 1970 at home and abroad was testament to the power of the new conservationism that tapped into the youthful discontent toward the Vietnam War. Local and state regulation of air and water was powerfully supplemented by tough federal statutes, led by the Clean Air Act Amendments of 1970 and the Water Pollution Control Act Amendments of 1972. Energy production, transportation, and consumption were in the middle of the development of new standards.

The Limits to Growth: Club of Rome

Paul Ehrlich's *The Population Bomb* was just a warm-up for an international best-seller by a group of authors who claimed the prestige of the Massachusetts Institute of Technology and the novelty of a computer model of world production and consumption. *The Limits to Growth: A Report for THE CLUB OF ROME'S Project on the Predicament of Mankind* (1972), destined to sell 9 million copies in 29 languages, calculated the exhaustion of a variety of natural resources, including oil and gas, by century's end. The collision between "exponential growth" in resource demand and "a finite world" led to a confident, dark conclusion:

> Although we have many reservations about the approximations and simplifications in the present world model, it has led us to one conclusion that appears to be justified under all the assumptions we have tested so far. *The basic behavior mode of the world system is exponential growth of population and capital, followed by collapse.*

The prescribed policy to avoid catastrophe was *global equilibrium*, a state of nongrowth. The book longed for "a totally new form of human society—one that would be built to last for generations." What was needed was "a realistic, long-term goal [to] . . . guide mankind to the equilibrium society"—and the powers of government and personal transformation to get there.

The Limits to Growth, critics noted, was "Malthus with a computer." The sponsoring group, an "invisible college" of "intellectual technologists," reflected the predilections of its founder, Italian industrialist Aurelio Peccei, who saw a

---

5. The externality problem created by commonly owned resources (versus privately owned assets) is discussed in Internet appendix 9.3, "Welfare Economics," at www.politicalcapitalism.org/book1/chapter9/appendix3.html.

"fundamental imperative" to "transform society" via renewable energy and energy conservation. The "astonishingly young (the oldest was 30), touchingly idealistic, very eager, naive, and bright" authors were true believers. After completing the book, Dennis and Donella Meadows retreated to a New Hampshire farm "to learn about homesteading and wait for the coming collapse." "We definitely felt like Cassandras," Donella Meadows added, "especially as we watched the world react to our work."

Figure 9.7 *The Limits to Growth* (1972) had academic veneer, international backing, and corporate sponsorship. The five authors pictured here are (left to right) Jorgen Randers, Jay Forrester, Donella Meadows, Dennis Meadows, and William W. Behrens III. Economist Robert Solow (upper right) proved a trenchant critic of the study associated with his university, as did a group of scholars in *Models of Doom* (1973).

The study was unveiled to 250 opinion makers, government officials, and environmentalists at the Smithsonian Institution in downtown Washington in March 1972. "We dearly hope that the debate which starts here today will have wide repercussions, opening a new phase of awareness, inquiry, and finally, political action," stated Peccei. Dennis Meadows, "the soft-spoken 29-year-old director of the project," as the *New York Times* described him, pointed to computer-generated graphs hanging from the walls and claimed that even the *most optimistic* projections about future energy supply could not avert collapse.

One of the chief exhibits was a table showing the remaining years for the "known global reserves" of 19 minerals. Three estimates in consumption years were provided: reserves divided by current demand (static years), reserves divided by exponentially growing demand (exponential years), and reserves multiplied by 5 divided by exponential demand (exponential index).

Mineral	Static Years	Exponential Years	Exponential Index Years
Aluminum	100	31	55
Chromium	420	95	154
Coal	2,300	111	150
Cobalt	110	60	148
Copper	36	21	48
Gold	11	9	29
Iron	240	93	173
Lead	26	21	64
Manganese	97	46	94
Mercury	13	13	41
Molybdenum	79	34	65
Natural Gas	38	22	49
Nickel	150	53	96
Petroleum	31	20	50
Platinum Group	130	47	85
Silver	16	13	42
Tin	17	15	61
Tungsten	40	28	72
Zinc	23	18	50

Source: Donella Meadows et al., *The Limits to Growth* (New York: Universe Books, 1972), 56–60.

The Limits to Growth was not derailed by problems that would have discredited less fashionable efforts. *Science* magazine dissected the unusual Xerox-financed public relations strategy behind the project. The project did not seek or receive any input from the top MIT social scientists who could have sharpened the analysis—and likely reversed the findings. One of the excluded, Robert Solow, an economist who would go on to win a Nobel Prize for his work in growth theory, ridiculed the computer model created by Jay Forrester, an MIT business school engineer who scarcely understood economics. "'Doomsday Models' are worthless as science and as guides to public policy," Solow argued.

Garbage-in, garbage-out—rephrased as "Malthus in, Malthus out" by one critic—plagued the computer runs behind the dire prognosis of *The Limits to Growth*. Indeed, tweaked model algorithms generated contrary results. A *Washington Post* book review by two scholars at Resources for the Future expressed "serious doubts" about an effort jerry-built on questionable assumptions and repeatedly referencing unpublished papers "housed somewhere at MIT."

A follow-up study by the Club of Rome two years later, funded by Volkswagen, allowed for a modicum of economic growth—a "startling shift" that Peccei explained as an "evolving strategy." Still, *Mankind at the Turning Point* (1974), alarmist and shrill,[6] could not duplicate the splash of *Limits to Growth*. Malthusian studies had become old hat, and the Club's message had become obscure. A 1976 Club of Rome event, for example, warned that unsustainable global trends would necessitate "a technocratic version of oriental despotism, of which Stalinism and Nazism have already given us an anticipated view."

A retrospective on the limits-to-growth debate by Resources for the Future called for a clean break from the Club of Rome's "fictitious data and dubious methodology," harsh words indeed. Still, RFF, ever mindful of the middle ground, warned against the "didactic arrogance of the would-be prophets—whether of doom or utopia," the latter characterized as having an "almost undiluted technological optimism."

The authors of the original Club of Rome study would be heard from once more in full alarmist cry. The story of the Carter administration's swan song, *Global 2000*, is told in the next chapter.

Back-to-Malthus Economists

Neo-Malthusianism would gain a toehold in the economics profession in the 1960s and early 1970s, building upon earlier work done by A. C. Pigou (1877–1959) and John Kenneth Galbraith (1908–2006). Pigou, the father of welfare economics, posited market failure—an excess of social costs over social benefits from private activity—with an eye toward corrective government intervention. Mineral depletion was of particular concern. Writing in 1920, Pigou declared it "the clear duty of Government to watch over, and, if need be, by legislative enactment, to defend, the exhaustible natural resources of this country."[7]

Galbraith, a professor of economics at Harvard University, had questioned capitalist affluence as a social ideal in the influential *The Affluent Society* (1958). "The problems of an affluent world, which does not understand itself, may be serious, and they can needlessly threaten the affluence itself," he wrote. In the book's final chapter, "Security and Survival," Galbraith spoke of "the problem . . . of a burgeoning population and of space in which to live with peace and grace, or . . . the depletion of the materials which nature has stocked in the earth's crust and which have been drawn upon more heavily in this century than in all previous time together."

---

6. The book, the prologue of which began with the quotation "The World Has Cancer and the Cancer is Man," called for "the creation of a new mankind" to avoid "traumatic experiences if not . . . catastrophes."

7. Also see Internet appendix 9.3, "Welfare Economics," at www.politicalcapitalism.org/book1/chapter9/appendix3.html.

E. J. Mishan

Pigou and Galbraith opened the door, but it would be economists E. J. Mishan (b. 1917) and Kenneth Boulding (1910–93) who would shed their technical economic skin to emote about the evils of materialism and a loss of people's spiritual side. Mishan's *Technology and Growth: The Price We Pay* (1970), a popularized version of his technical *The Cost of Economic Growth* (1967), attacked "growthmania" as "unimaginative and unworthy" and causing negative "spillover effects." "One may concede the importance of economic growth in an indigent society," he allowed, but not for advanced countries, including his Great Britain. Mishan listed some disagreeable features of modern society:

> post-war "development" blight, the erosion of the countryside, the "uglification" of coastal towns, the pollution of the air and of rivers with chemical wastes, the accumulation of thick oils on our coastal waters, the sewage poisoning our beaches, the destruction of wild life by the indiscriminate use of pesticides, the change-over from animal farming to animal factories and a rich heritage of natural beauty being wantonly destroyed.

Some of Mishan's sharpest criticism was reserved for modern forms of energy. "We do not need the oil companies' advertisements to inspire us to become 'get-away people,'" he said, wondering where people needed to go. Mishan called the invention of the automobile "one of the greatest disasters to have befallen the human race." He saw benefit in the then-greatest electricity blackout in world history (New York, 1965), which "broke the spell of monotony for millions of New Yorkers [who] enjoyed the shock of being thrown back on their innate resources and into sudden dependence upon one another." He added, "as the darkness brought them stumbling into each other's arms, so the hard light scattered them again."

Kenneth Boulding

Kenneth Boulding, a much-honored economist who spent his academic career at the University of Michigan and then University of Colorado, described himself as

> something of an ecologist at heart, mainly because I am really a preacher, and we know that all ecologists are really preachers under the skin. They are great viewers with alarm. Is there any more single-minded, simple pleasure than viewing with alarm? At times it is even better than sex.

In a 1966 lecture at Resources for the Future, Boulding argued that mineral depletion required the earth to recycle its inputs to survive. "The Economics of the Coming Spaceship Earth" deprecated the status quo as a *cowboy economy*, associated "with reckless, exploitative, romantic, and violent behavior, which is characteristic of open societies." With exhaustible inputs shrinking, the earth would transition to the "spaceman economy" whereby inputs and outputs were

part of a "cyclical ecological system [in which] lessened throughput is a gain."
Boulding added, "This idea that both production and consumption are bad
things rather than good things is very strange to economists, who have been
obsessed with the income-flow concepts to the exclusion, almost, of capital-
stock concepts."

Boulding grew alienated from his profession's premise of wealth maximization and economic growth. "Economic development is the process by which the
evil day is brought closer when everything will be gone," he wrote. "It will
result in final catastrophe unless we treat this interval in the history of man as
an opportunity to make the transition to the spaceship earth." John Holdren
and Paul Ehrlich seized upon Boulding's "evil day," welcoming the eminent
economist into the ecological camp.

Boulding ridiculed what at that time was the intellectual center of resource
optimism:

> Resources for the Future says, "We're all right, Jack. We've got a hundred years."
> Its report points to our fossil fuels and our ores, and reassures us that they will be
> adequate for a century. After that, the deluge.

Boulding confidently urged economists, governments, and the public to
reconsider economic growth. "Bigger is not necessarily better," he wrote. "For
the poor, growth in income is entirely desirable; for the rich, it may simply mean
corruption and luxury." Boulding urged "a fundamental change in human consciousness," one that admittedly would require "an adjustment of our ethical,
religious, and national systems which may be quite traumatic."

Mishan and Boulding were the exceptions in their profession, as other ecological economists, such as Herman Daly and Robert Constanza, would be a
generation later. On the other hand, environmental economics, led by Nobel
laureate Robert Solow, among others, would swim closer to the mainstream,
applying standard microeconomic theory to issues of market failure, negative
externalities, public goods, and social versus private discount rates.

Cloudy Days

The era of energy tranquility was on its last legs by 1970. An RFF energy
review for 1969 spoke about the emerging "collision" between growing electricity demand and environmental constraints:

> At issue are principally air pollution from fossil fuel combustion; water pollu-
> tion from discharges of cooling water at temperatures sufficiently above those
> of the recipient water body to affect the aquatic environment; and, in the case of
> nuclear facilities, discharge of radioactive material into the water and air and
> the hazards associated with the remote possibility of accidental escape in plant
> and in transit.

Still, there was enough supply to meet demand across the energy board.

RFF's summary for 1970 was more ominous. "Behind the Energy Crisis" spoke of electricity brownouts and blackouts, a doubling of fuel-oil prices, and threatened shortages of natural gas. The promise of nuclear power as the savior of electricity was fading. Middle East politics was looming larger over oil imports. Government regulation of oil imports and of interstate natural gas prices was problematic. Environmental concerns over fossil-fuel emissions were accelerating. Electricity generation seemed unable to keep up with roaring demand. But bad times for energy were good times for alarmism. Neo-Malthusianism, an emotionally powerful worldview for critics of capitalism, was finally getting here-and-now empirical support—at least so it seemed.

Empirically, professionally, and politically, a sea change away from resource optimism toward resource pessimism was at hand. But a few voices rang out in dissent against the popular, well-funded, trans-Atlantic, neo-Malthusian movement. In addition to Julian Simon in the United States, John Maddox, a U.K. scientist and editor of *Nature* magazine, wrote a book entitled *The Doomsday Syndrome* (1972). The opening paragraph read:

> *Prophets of doom* have multiplied remarkably in the past few years. It used to be commonplace for men to parade city streets with sandwich boards proclaiming "The End of the World Is at Hand!" They have been replaced by a throng of sober people, scientists, philosophers, and politicians, proclaiming that there are more subtle calamities just around the corner.

Little did the optimists know just how much energy markets were about to be rocked by a combination of international developments and domestic politics, which would make their world very small.

10

The Dark Decade

THE STATISTICS OF ENERGY PLENTY changed dramatically in the 1970s. Oil prices hit record highs time and again. Periodic shortages of natural gas and petroleum products made people's problems much worse than simply a pinch in the budget. A new term, *energy crisis*, became as ubiquitous as *inflation* and *recession* during the troubled presidencies of Nixon, Ford, and Carter.

The energy crises had well-defined causes outside the limits of nature. Federal price ceilings artificially discouraged supply and encouraged consumption, causing shortages in the near term and higher prices over time. Energy shortages that occurred during World War I and World War II under price controls now happened in peacetime—*for the same reason*. California, with a peculiar regulatory regime of fixed retail prices and floating wholesale prices, would painfully learn this lesson with electricity at century's end.

Political control of vast oil regions outside of North America also contributed to what turned out to be *the great resource false alarm*. The 1973/74 oil embargo against the United States by Saudi Arabia was facilitated by the nationalization of the Arabian-American Oil Company (Aramco) in the same period, which shifted production decisions from (former) asset owners Exxon, Gulf, Texaco, and Chevron to the Kingdom. The absence of market-driven resource extraction in the Middle East and other parts of the world was bad news for consumers—as it was for would-be resource owners and entrepreneurs in the private sector.

Yet many experts faulted geology rather than politics for the energy problem. Their root error was a fixity view of minerals, a view that neglected the primacy of entrepreneurship and the market process. Erich Zimmermann's functional theory of resources had not been incorporated into the social-scientific mainstream, much less energy policymaking.

The politics of depletionism created *conservationism*, an *ism* predicated on the belief that less energy consumption was good per se. W. S. Jevons a century earlier had rejected conservation as a means of "neutralizing the evils of scarce and costly fuel." To him, freezing energy usage meant that "Britain should be stationary and lasting as she was, rather than of growing and world-wide influence as she is." In contrast, the 1970s' neo-Malthusians, at odds with affluence, saw salvation on the demand side. They welcomed constraining economic activity to the perceived limits to nature. James Schlesinger, the first head of the U.S. Department of Energy, premised Carter-era conservationism on "a classic Malthusian case of exponential growth against a finite resource." The creed of non-use would not recede when energy abundance resumed in the 1980s.

Among intellectuals, the crosscurrent that formed against resource optimism in the 1960s became a raging river in the 1970s. Economists excitedly applied Hotelling's Rule to new data indicating increased energy scarcity. M. King Hubbert confidently updated his geology-based case for impending production declines. Across the Atlantic, E. F. Schumacher raised the specter of inadequate fossil-fuel supplies. A spreading neo-Malthusian movement, which found voice in Paul Ehrlich and a manifesto in *The Limits to Growth*, gained a library of books and legions of intellectuals. Sparks of crises created a wildfire of worry.

Ken Lay was busy at ground zero during this tumult. Regulator Lay began at the Federal Power Commission (the predecessor of the Federal Energy Regulatory Commission) dealing with natural gas shortages. When oil problems emerged during the Nixon price-control program, he joined the Department of the Interior to help allocate short supply. It was thankless work, and after several years, Lay repositioned himself in industry to deal with natural gas issues. The great mineral-resource debate would never be far from his mind later in his career when he was head of Enron.[1]

Fathering a Crisis: Richard Nixon

Richard Nixon (1913–94) got on the wrong side of economic law three years before he resigned the presidency for his role in the Watergate scandal. In August 1971, in a surprise decision intended to quell inflationary expectations, Nixon imposed the first peacetime wage-and-price controls in U.S. history. Businesspeople reined in their surprise to pragmatically offer support. John Kenneth Galbraith and Paul Samuelson offered quick congratulations. But free-market economist Milton Friedman, knowing that shortages lay ahead, lambasted the move.

Nixon's edict disabled the market process responsible for coordinating supply with demand and allocating resources to their most profitable use.

---

1. References to Ken Lay and Enron in this chapter foreshadow discussions of greater depth in Book 2 and Book 3.

Predictably, oil shortages developed, which resurrected long-dormant deple-tionist thinking and pointed policymakers toward conservationism. After all, if price controls did not allow prices to rise and regulate demand to available sup-ply, government had to—at least according to the majority of policymakers and neo-Malthusians, whose worldview dovetailed nicely with public sentiment against the energy industry.

The oil crisis, contrary to popular remembrance, *did not begin with the Arab embargo of October 1973*. It began with petroleum-product shortages that arose in late 1972 when price controls became constraining. In February 1973, Senate hearings on fuel shortages demonstrated, in the opinion of committee chair Henry Jackson (D-Wash.):

> One, there has been an unprecedented breakdown in our energy supply and dis-tribution system; two, the fuel shortages now being experienced are far more extensive than anticipated; three, more severe shortages of fuels, particularly gasoline, are in the offing.

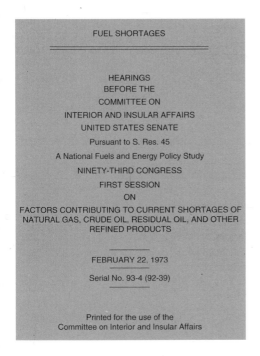
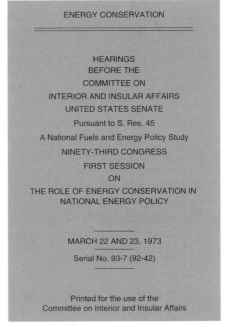

Figure 10.1 Senate hearings in first-quarter 1973 indicated how the nation's oil prob-lems were under way before the imposition of a production cutback and oil embargo against the United States later that year by Arab members of OPEC. President Nixon's wage- and price-control program created oil shortages, which directly led to government mandates for energy conservation.

Expert testimony was heard about how 18 months of price controls were at the root of the supply shortfall, as were the lingering constraints of an earlier federal program designed to help the domestic industry in a time of oil surplus, the Mandatory Oil Import Program.

The U.S. Senate convened a meeting on energy conservation, identified as "the first congressional hearings to be devoted to this subject." Demand was now decoupled from supply, creating an industry of thought, opinion, and passion as to what demand *should be* and what role government should play to correct oil-market problems.[2] The game was rigged thanks to Richard Nixon, whose original 90-day freeze would be the first of five price-control phases, as well as the starting point for more than seven years of price-and-allocation regulation under the Emergency Petroleum Allocation Act of 1973.

The March 1973 hearings attracted the first wave of energy conservationists and environmentalists from such organizations as the Environmental Defense Fund, the Friends of the Earth, and the Sierra Club. Testimony was also heard that day from Irwin Stelzer, founder of National Economic Research Associates, a prominent consultancy. Stelzer, a Ph.D. economist, would befriend Ken Lay in the 1970s and become one of Lay's go-to consultants in the Enron years.

Ford Foundation's Energy Policy Project

The Ford Foundation, which had launched Resources for the Future (RFF) two decades before, was ready to make its own splash in energy research and policy. RFF had become a bastion of fact-based resource optimism, whereas Ford was moving sharply left under "liberal domestic reformer" McGeorge Bundy. In late 1971, the world's wealthiest private foundation launched a three-year, $4 million ($20 million today) effort headed by S. David Freeman. An engineer and lawyer by training, Freeman had worked in various capacities for government, most recently as head of Nixon's energy policy staff. Bundy defended Freeman as "a man of stature and integrity," but Freeman was other things as well—arrogant, an interventionist ideologue, and an implacable foe of the energy industry.

The final product of the Ford Foundation's initiative was *A Time to Choose: America's Energy Future*, released in 1974, a time of energy upheaval. The 500-page study came to three major conclusions:

- The energy crisis is real and long-lived.
- "Conservation is as important as supply."
- The United States needs an integrated national energy policy.

Fossil-fuel *production* was the orphan of the study. Apart from a weak endorsement for increasing output from the lower 48 states, the report was devoid of a

---

2. Terms in the field of welfare economics, such as *market failure*, would be used to justify government activism in energy markets. See chapter 9, pp. 237–39.

supply-enhancement strategy. Energy development in frontier areas, along with downstream infrastructure to turn resources into usable energy, was rejected in favor of conservationism and, over the longer term, unconventional (nonhydro-electric) renewables. A federal yardstick enterprise was proposed for oil and gas development, akin to electricity's Tennessee Valley Authority (TVA), where Free-man had once worked. Public utility regulation of exploration and production was suggested—an idea once floated during the New Deal but rejected by the industry and government. Nationalization was raised "if historical growth is the nation's choice, and the energy industry repeatedly fails to satisfy the public's energy appetite within reasonable profit limits." A tariff on oil imports was prof-fered to finance a domestic oil stockpile equal to 90 days' consumption—an intertemporal distribution, not production, policy. The report also recommended eliminating wellhead tax breaks in favor of a revamped tax system tied to a "high enough" price set by government.

These ostensibly supply-side policies were more than anti-industry. They were *intentionally* supply limiting, with an aim to raise prices in order to check economic expansion and promote energy conservationism. "The net effect of a highly favorable economic climate for energy supply could amount to a 'self-fulfilling prophecy' for energy growth," the report warned. Energy usage was bad, and less energy was less bad. Never had this argument been made in such a forthright, high-profile way.

Energy conservation in the Ford/Freeman report went well beyond self-interested *economic* conservation—economizing in the face of higher prices. The report proposed ending energy-demand growth by creating a federal-level Energy Policy Council. Assisted by a Citizens' Advisory Board, the council would set conservation goals for the nation, each region, and each industry sec-tor. A first step was to set "a uniform system of accounting for energy" for indus-try to follow.

Social concerns were raised in the report's recommendation that a contin-gency program allocate energy stamps to low-income users in the event of an energy emergency. Campaign finance reform was advocated to counter the oil industry's "unique combination of political advantages." This agenda was to the left of anything that was emanating from the big think tanks, certainly Resources for the Future, and even the Brookings Institution with its leanings toward the Democratic Party.

Freeman's large staff and sizable budget created a strong base of support. The Ford Foundation enhanced his power by setting up a largely friendly advi-sory board with limited powers of oversight. There were no principled free-marketeers despite a claim that the 20-member board was "selected to reflect a broad range of individual outlooks." Freeman's polar position was also facili-tated by a Republican president whose regulation-driven energy policy included Project Independence, a quixotic plan to eliminate energy imports by 1980. Such intervention made the Ford/Freeman study seem as much visionary as radical.

A Time to Choose, however, did not get a free ride. Upon release, the report was "blasted . . . thoroughly by everyone from the editor of *Harper's* to market-oriented economists to the president of the Mobil Corporation." A rejoinder, *No Time to Confuse*, gave pen to free-market proponents, the very group whose views Freeman had ignored. UCLA economist Armen Alchian complained that *A Time to Choose* "regrettably confuses energy and environmental issues, enters the Guinness books of records for most errors of economic analysis and fact in one book, is arrogant in assertions of waste and inefficiency, is paternalist in its conception of energy consumption management, is politically naïve, and uses demagoguery." Herman Kahn criticized "a belief that the federal government is willing and able to create a coherent plan on a subject as complex as energy policy; a belief that they have deduced the public interest . . . and . . . can achieve the objectives of the plan." M. A. Adelman complained, "Everything said about oil and gas in this book was said about coal by W. S. Jevons in 1865." The study, he added, "completely ignores the interaction of supply and demand [and] . . . market processes." Adelman could only note the political irony: "The book's viewpoint is 'liberal' . . . yet it coincides perfectly with the outlook and policy of a conservative Administration."

The head of Mobil Oil, William Tavoulareas, was incensed at Freeman's extreme anti-industry positions and baiting tone. He felt duped because he had been promised a major say as the lone adviser from the oil and gas industry. Tavoulareas was given room to comment in the back of the report, and his comment was by far the most critical. But he demanded more. The Ford Foundation was persuaded to publish his full critique, complete with a comment/rebuttal by fellow adviser and MIT professor Carl Kaysen. *A Debate on A TIME TO CHOOSE* (1977) was notable for three things: an introduction by a Ford Foundation official tying the original report to Freeman and not the foundation, Tavoulareas's animated criticism of the antisupply and progovernment nature of the original report, and Kaysen's lukewarm defense of the original report. While applauding *A Time to Choose* for "helping to make energy conservation a respectable subject for analysis and policy," Kaysen criticized Ford/Freeman as "unhelpful for choosing among supply options; too willing to replace the market with the administrator; one-sided in both its praise for conservation and its attacks on the oil industry."

Kaysen was right about the study's direction. Government-led energy conservation made its way into core policy at all levels of government. Another first in *A Time to Choose* was its trinity of energy, environmental, and social objectives, which foreshadowed the definition of sustainability formulated a quarter century later by the President's Council on Sustainable Development (PCSD). A project of Vice President Al Gore Jr., the PCSD would also wall out free-market intellectuals. But what was radical in the 1970s was, by the mid-1990s, respectable and even visionary; the PCSD's two leading members from the energy industry—Chevron's Kenneth Derr and Enron's Ken Lay—supported both the process and the final report.

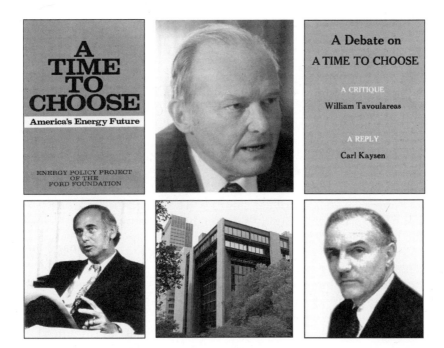

Figure 10.2 *A Time to Choose* (1974) injected an anti-industry, statist agenda into the energy policy debate. The controversial report by S. David Freeman (bottom left) was rebutted by Mobil head William Tavoulareas (bottom right) in *A Debate on A TIME TO CHOOSE*. Freeman's enabler was McGeorge Bundy (top), the controversial head of the Ford Foundation.

Freeman's report was a black eye for the Ford Foundation not only because of the end product but also because of the heavy-handed process and arrogance involved. Among other things, Freeman announced the conclusions of the study before receiving input from the project's advisers and consultants. Freeman also testified before Congress several months before the report's release that he was "troubled" about a free-market energy policy, since "in a very real way the marketplace has failed us in the last decade." The Ford Foundation study was the antithesis of the Paley Commission's report (1952) in approach, not only substance.

As it would turn out, some top consultants to Ford/Freeman were not averse to applying free-market solutions to existing energy problems. A 1975 book published as part of the Ford project concluded: "Almost everyone now concedes that the field prices for natural gas set by the Federal Power Commission have been kept too low, creating shortages and the consequent need for rationing." Another publication warned that "although there may be significant market imperfections, there are no readily available instruments to correct the problems they create." By this time, however, the Ford Energy Policy Project had made its splash, and David Freeman had moved back to energy policymaking in government.

⌒·

The enabler and alter ego of Freeman was the president of the Ford Foundation, McGeorge Bundy (1919–96), "a scion of wealthy Boston Brahmins," former dean of Harvard University, and prointerventionist national-security adviser to Presidents Kennedy and then Johnson.[3] Not only was Bundy running a "highly conceptualized, interventionist, sometimes confrontational, and accident-prone foundation program," one critic noted, his controversial investment philosophy and aggressive spending were producing "shocking losses" at a foundation whose wealth was equal to one-sixth of the entire combined endowment of America's 25,000 private charities. The foundation's worth fell from $3.7 billion to $1.7 billion in Bundy's first eight years, and more problems before and after his exit in 1979 magnified the total loss. The largest dissipation of philanthropic wealth in history required the foundation's 1,500 staffers, heavily represented by "academics and intellectuals," to be pared significantly.

With Bundy's hiring, the Ford Foundation had set out to replace its "whisper" with a "roar." It got that and much more. Two Enron-like projects early in his presidency set the tone for his 13-year tenure. At Bundy's insistence, the foundation constructed an architecturally controversial, lavish office building in the heart of New York City that "resulted in a sixfold increase in office costs at one stroke." Bundy also implemented a "quasi-investment, quasi-philanthropic" practice under which the foundation invested in "social criteria" projects, such as low-income housing. "A policy breakthrough had been made," one study concluded, "but great difficulties were later encountered in identifying and in carrying out such . . . projects." Thirty years later, Enron would find out much the same with its ill-fated Enron Investment Partners, a venture-capital fund that invested in minority, inner-city projects, and the lavish Enron Center, partially occupied before the company's bankruptcy in late 2001.

Ford's Energy Policy Project "reconfirmed the impression that Bundy as a philanthropic gardener personally had rather a brown thumb." This and other Bundy actions led the last family trustee of the foundation, Henry Ford II, to step down in 1977 after 34 years of service. Bad philosophy and bad management were just too much, although Ford tried to be as diplomatic as possible. "I am not playing the role of the hard-headed tycoon who thinks all philanthropoids are socialists and all university professors are communists," his resignation letter read. "I'm just suggesting to the trustees and the staff that the [capitalist] system that makes the foundation possible very probably is worth preserving."

---

3. One study of McGeorge Bundy revealed: "Many in Congress and elsewhere had come to believe that Bundy had played a key role in the Bay of Pigs and the Dominican Republic interventions and in the escalation of the Vietnam War."

Bundy responded curtly: "He has a right to expect people to read the letter carefully, but I don't think one letter from anyone is going to change the foundation's course." So exited the man who rescued Ford Motor Company from the mismanagement of his ailing grandfather, who with his mother activated the Ford Foundation, and who served as chairman of the trustees in the foundation's formative years.

The next time around, in 1979, the Ford Foundation chose Resources for the Future to administer its energy study. There would be no more David Freeman, who had had his fun and more. Just months after the release of *A Time to Choose*, Freeman published his own book, *Energy: The New Era*, which added arguments even too strong for his Ford study. He declared, per M. King Hubbert, that low-priced energy was a thing of the past. He likened producer complaints about inadequate incentives to a "sit-down strike." On the demand side, Freeman advocated a "new ethic, ... which regards waste as a form of theft." He questioned "the whole structure of our material-oriented, energy-intensive ... basis of our civilization." His worldview was about ends, not only means.

Freeman joined the Carter presidential campaign and authored the candidate's energy statements espousing conservationism first, productionism second, and free markets last. Freeman would go on to become deputy to Carter's neo-Malthusian energy czar, James Schlesinger, and then leave Washington to manage a succession of federal and state power agencies, including the Los Angeles Department of Water & Power (LADWP) during California's electricity crisis in 2000/2001. Freeman, long a critic of energy-company profiteering, found himself in the middle of his own price-gouging controversy at LADWP as seller, not buyer. Governor Gray Davis then hired Freeman to oversee California's multibillion dollar long-term electricity purchases, which turned out to be a very expensive mistake.

Soft Energy Paths: Amory Lovins

Another tract for the times, one that would have nine political lives, was a 1976 essay in *Foreign Affairs* by Amory Lovins, the 29-year-old energy representative of the U.K. environmental group Friends of the Earth. In "Energy Strategy: The Road Not Taken?" Lovins coined the term *soft energy paths* to differentiate energy conservation and decentralized renewable technology from the *hard* path of central-station power plants fueled by oil, gas, coal, or uranium. Neo-Malthusians, such as Paul Ehrlich and John Holdren, sang his praises, and the article became the most-reprinted piece in the history of *Foreign Affairs*. Lovins was soon testifying before the U.S. Congress and advising President Carter on the proposition that the least-cost energy option was not to produce energy but to *save* it.

Unlike David Freeman, Lovins, an Oxford don, specialized in the technical minutiae of energy and wrote, footnoted, and argued his opponents into despair, never mind how much his analyses and recommendations contradicted demonstrated market preferences. Lovins became *the* most-talked-about energy guru in the world during the crisis period, with a deceptively simple message that *less was more*. To critics, however, Lovins was "selling a dream without presenting the bill."

Lovins held a deep-rooted suspicion—even phobia—about the energy market. "It is hard to think of any current energy technology in extensive use that does not hold the potential for serious long-term environmental risks—risks which may today be wholly unsuspected," he warned. From this premise came his worldview, later dubbed *whole-systems thinking*, that saw current energy usage—thus production—as a massive market failure. "We must devise a science and a technology of energy impact analysis so that we can make energy *a critical variable in all policy decisions*, rather than leaving it to emerge *de facto* from decisions taken on other grounds," he wrote in 1975. "Boundary conditions on the energy inputs are now needed." This message was new to the U.S. energy debate, although the "small is beautiful" theme of E. F. Schumacher was already popular in Europe.

Lovins's first order of business was to push for a short-term phaseout of nuclear power—a signature issue for Friends of the Earth. Lovins feared that the rapid depletion of oil and gas would segue to superabundant coal and nuclear—a bad transition and worse long-run lock-in to him. Lovins wanted "transitional technologies that use fossil fuels briefly and sparingly to build a bridge to the energy-income [i.e., energy-renewable] economy of 2025." However wrong this would turn out to be, Lovins would fare better with his second aim: full-scale deployment of conservation technologies to reach a "realistic long-term goal" of "modest, zero, or negative [energy] growth" per unit of output.

Figure 10.3 The technical minutiae of Amory Lovins gave energy conservationism great allure. Lovins's holistic view that "conservation is far cheaper than increasing supply" made him popular with not only Congress but also President Carter.

Lovins's technical optimism toward soft energies was missing when it came to conventional technologies. Admitting that the then-higher energy prices were still too low to effectuate his desired transition, he argued that his alternative was *theoretically* cheaper when social factors and depletionism were factored in. The hard path, Lovins charged, was littered with "subsidized $100-billion bailouts, oligopolies, regulations, nationalization, eminent domain, corporate statism." But most of these complaints were about political capitalism, not capitalism proper. To get beyond such political capitalism would have required a completely different framework for energy—free-market capitalism to determine market share for hard and soft energy alike. But that was hardly the soft-energy agenda, which required government mandates. And not even this was enough, as shown two decades later by Enron's failed investments in energy efficiency and renewables.

Lovins was an eloquent conservationist. At a time when pervasive regulation left markets in turmoil, it was Lovins who with diagrams, sound bites, and bushels of footnotes explained why market participants got it wrong, but his blueprints and government intervention could get it right. Part of his approach was to calculate the energy savings if today's embedded assets could be instantaneously transformed to the most energy-efficient technology—an engineering-over-economics approach.[4] Another part was making Malthusian-/Hotelling-like assumptions, such as imputing a higher long-run replacement cost for fossil energies, to compute a social cost high enough to make his alternative affordable. The soft-energy path was not cheap, Lovins admitted, "only cheaper than not doing it."

Lovins presented his views in romantic, something-for-everyone packaging. As he told a congressional subcommittee in 1977:

> A final feature of the soft energy path that I wish to commend to this committee as politicians is that it helps to avoid conflict between constituencies by offering advantages to all of them; jobs for the unemployed, capital for businesspeople, environmental protection for conservationists, increased national security for the military, opportunities for small business to innovate and for big business to recycle itself, savings for consumers, world order and equity for globalists, energy independence for isolationists, exciting technologies for the secular, a rebirth of spiritual values for the religious, radical reforms for the young, traditional virtues for the old, civil rights for liberals and states' rights for conservatives.

Many of Amory Lovins's positions ("we could advantageously be running this country with no central power stations at all," "we could eliminate oil imports if we would stop living in sieves and stop driving petrol pigs") put him at odds with virtually every energy economist. His characterization of the hard-energy

---

4. Given purchase and installation costs, continued reliance on older assets can be less expensive (more economical) than installing new equipment even if the energy savings from new assets lower operating costs.

path—"Strength Through Exhaustion"—was recycled Malthusianism. Yet for an era when market forces were disabled and distortions abounded, Lovins had an alluring message. The wider academic, media, and political class welcomed a new approach to energy to correct alleged market failure. A special report in *Business Week* (1977) captured the spirit of the day:

> The idea is rapidly gaining support that conservation may be a cheaper and better—if unfamiliar—way to solve the nation's energy problem than developing new supplies. And there is a deep-rooted feeling in Washington that if energy conservation is to be effective on the scale that federal planners now believe is essential, it will require demand management on an unprecedented scale.

Energy consumption would flatten out in the next decade as Lovins predicted, but it was hardly natural. It resulted from a wrenching adjustment to government-induced distortions—physical shortages of natural gas and petroleum products, energy price spikes, and, relatedly, economic stagnation for much of 1980–82. Compounded energy growth would rebound toward 2 percent per annum between 1986 and 2000, with hard energy as the workhorse—not the scenario predicted by Lovins and by Daniel Yergin.[5] Lovins's upperbound prediction of 95 quadrillion British thermal units (quads) of primary energy usage by 2000, however, was only 4 percent short because of a lost decade of demand growth. His same forecast estimating a continuing drop to 75 quads by 2025 promises to be wildly off the mark—barring massive government intervention and distortion as occurred in the 1970s.[6]

Lovins's "urgent" hard-to-soft transition had a champion in physicist John Holdren. A figure from chapter 9, Holdren in 1973 founded a multidisciplinary studies program at the University of California, Berkeley, to train "the next generation of scientists and professionals who will need to cope with the even more complex environmental and international-relations issues of the future." Berkeley's Energy and Resources Group, which Holdren would codirect for the next two decades, was praised by Lovins for launching "a soft path study for California in cooperation with many other people and groups," including the left-moving Resources for the Future. California would become the soft-energy laboratory of the United States (and world) with a plethora of special subsidies for wind power, solar farms, and utility-demand reduction programs. The result would be the highest power rates in the country, legislative reform to address the problem, and the electricity crisis that Enron would inherit and infamously drive in 2000–2001.

John Holdren was at the beginning of a long career as a pronounced critic of the carbon-based energy economy. By the 1990s, he would emerge as a leading

---

5. Daniel Yergin's evolving energy views are discussed later in this chapter, pp. 258–60.

6. In 2007, the U.S. Department of Energy forecast U.S. energy consumption in 2025 at 124 quads, which would be 65 percent above Lovins's estimate.

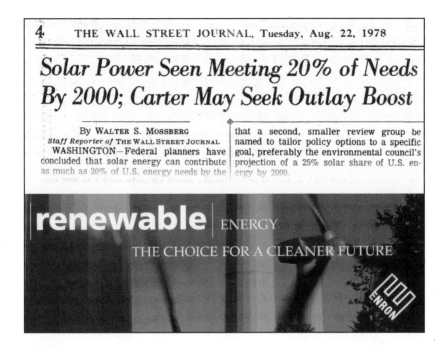

Figure 10.4 The push for renewables (called solar) in the energy-troubled 1970s would be resurrected two decades later by Enron, which invested in solar and wind facilities in a quest to become the world's leading renewable-energy company.

voice of energy alarmism and a revered figure of the left-of-center private foundations and the Clinton/Gore administration. Ken Lay and Enron would heed his energy views as well.

Presidential Alarmism

Alarmism rang forth from official quarters. Nixon's "temporary" price controls continued for petroleum after the rest of the economy was decontrolled in 1973. Nixon's Project Independence Report, "the most comprehensive energy analysis ever undertaken," was fatalistic about domestic energy and the international petroleum market. Its look at energy alternatives offered virtually nothing to replace petroleum in the transportation market—and thus virtually no progress toward its stated end of energy independence. Gerald Ford's mini-term started with free-market aspirations but ended in continued energy statism from, in part, a post-Watergate Democratic takeover of Congress. Vice President Nelson Rockefeller's proposed $100 billion taxpayer-subsidized program for high-cost/high-risk energy projects (about $400 billion today), launched with Ford's blessing, was scarcely a free-market alternative to the

Democrats' energy program. Such a government-engineered supply enhancement created its own *ism, productionism,* joining conservationism—all in the name of addressing the problems created by price controls.

Ford's successor, Jimmy Carter, an engineer by training, would bring government energy management to its apogee. Carter's 1977 *National Energy Plan* opened as ominously as Jevons's 1865 *Coal Question* closed:

> The diagnosis of the U.S. energy crisis is quite simple: demand for energy is increasing, while supplies of oil and natural gas are diminishing. Unless the U.S. makes a timely adjustment before world oil becomes very scarce and very expensive in the 1980's, the nation's economic security and the American way of life will be gravely endangered.

The 100-page blueprint of energy alternatives and conservation was a dream for anti-industrial environmental groups that had already seized upon radical energy change as a core activity. Nine national environmental organizations

Figure 10.5 Energy problems plagued the ignoble pragmatist Richard Nixon (1969–74), caretaker Gerald Ford (1974–77), and "preacher and engineer" Jimmy Carter (1977–81). Nixon is shown announcing price controls in August 1971; Ford, outlining his energy program in his 1975 State of the Union Address; and Carter, in his cardigan sweater, during his energy address of February 1977. *Inset:* Carter's energy czar and the first secretary of the Department of Energy, James Schlesinger.

jointly praised the plan as "fundamentally fair and farsighted." The Sierra Club added, "The energy message sounded like we wrote it ourselves."

Carter's *National Energy Plan II,* issued two years later, warned that "over the next decade, the energy security problems facing the U.S. could worsen." Its 367 pages outlined government strategies to balance supply and demand. Reliance on the freely functioning price system to achieve the same ends was politically verboten.

Carter's energy czar was Harvard-trained economist James Schlesinger, who counted among his teachers the late Joseph Schumpeter. But Schlesinger, who became the first secretary of the newly established Department of Energy—a 20,000-person, $10 billion agency—was no resource optimist (as Schumpeter was) or free-market advocate. His economic views, as a Brookings Institution study put it, "were closer to French indicative planning than to the invisible hand of Adam Smith, Alfred Marshall, or Milton Friedman."

"Shar[ing] a deep belief in the impending exhaustion of fossil fuels," Carter and Schlesinger applied "righteous pragmatism" to energy policy. Schlesinger

Figure 10.6 Major government energy studies during the 1970s included the Nixon administration's *Project Independence Report* (1974), the Ford administration's *National Energy Outlook* (1976), and the Carter administration's *National Energy Plan* (1977) and *National Energy Plan II* (1979).

became point man for federal price and allocation controls, a policy endorsed by few economists other than John Kenneth Galbraith, whose early career included a stint as a dogmatic price controller during World War II. Perception and interventionist ideology ruled under the populist Carter. This political scenario would recur two decades later in the energy regime of California Governor Gray Davis.

Jimmy Carter stated in his memoirs, "The comprehensive program put into effect during my term has now reversed the movement toward [energy] disaster." Yet what he had called "the moral equivalent of war" in April 1977 was won only because his national energy policy—after years of distortion and abject failures—incorporated enough energy liberalization to *finally* put market processes over the top. Still, there was much to regret. Phased oil decontrol came only after disruptive gasoline lines in many cities during the summer of 1979, as well as a pernicious wealth transfer from oil producers to oil resellers, explained later in this chapter. Very complicated natural gas legislation left the industry half-slave, half-free. Carter's cabinet-level Department of Energy would be a focal point for politicizing energy over the next decades, although the work of DOE's Energy Information Administration would provide a reality check to starry-eyed energy planners.

The Great Turn: Hotelling's Hour

The pessimism of the day reached an unexpected quarter: Resources for the Future. Before the energy crisis, RFF books chronicled the growing availability of resources and stayed clear of the fixity/depletion view. For example, a 1968 study, *U.S. Energy Policies: An Agenda for Research*, reported a "widespread belief that energy requirements for the next twenty years or more can be met without serious upward pressure on real costs."

RFF launched the National Energy Strategies Project in 1976 with a major grant from the Mellon Foundation. The final 550-page report, *Energy in America's Future: The Choices before Us* (1979), paid little homage to the past, much less to the worldview of Erich Zimmermann or the ongoing analysis of M. A. Adelman, examined later in this chapter. The message of the book was not dissimilar to Carter's national energy plan:

> While the petroleum and natural gas era is not over, the contribution of these fossil fuels to world energy requirements will probably pass its peak within the lifetime of most persons now living. Real energy prices will almost certainly rise before that peak is reached. These changes will demand many adjustments.

In the section "Energy Costs and the Shrinking Pie," Jevons-Hotelling-Hubbert depletionism was resurrected as theory and fact with added emphasis on institutional change:

> The increase in energy's cost to U.S. consumers has come from the higher costs of producing it, from an increase in the cost of using energy now rather than the

future, from monopoly exactions by oil exporting countries, and from additional costs now paid by U.S. consumers to overcome environmental, health, and safety costs of energy acquisition and use.

RFF's new flagship book had a different tone from the think tank's past work. "Fairness," "environmental insults," "market failure," "social costs," and technology "decentralization" were the new stock in trade. Energy modeling and demand-side planning (conservationism) were accepted at face value as grist for the policy mill. Intellectuals such as Amory Lovins were prominently cited, whereas promarket voices advocating fundamental deregulation went unheard. Near the end of the book, a call for deregulation was tinged by a conclusion that even a deregulated "private" price of oil would be below its "true marginal cost"—even adding a modest tariff on oil imports and whatever "'profit margin' oil exporting countries choose to add to their production costs." Free-market principles, Economics 101 principles, were lost amid the book's heady activism.

The self-described "balanced perspective" on a complex, far-ranging, and ideological issue had an introduction by RFF president Charles Hitch. He urged Americans to accept as fact the "increasingly limited availability" of fossil fuels and opt for an energy policy premised on "'satisficing'" (a new term coined by Nobel laureate Herbert Simon blending *satisfying* and *sacrificing*) instead of "'optimizing.'" The give-a-little to gain-a-little was neo-Malthusianism lite.

The lead author of the study, Sam Schurr, spoke gravely about America's energy future in his presidential address to the newly formed International Association of Energy Economists. After reviewing the book's findings, he expressed his "personal view [that] we are running out of time for devising and implementing policies to meet long-term energy needs." What was needed was a "consensus" in mainstream America for goals that "would provide an essential starting point for launching the necessary technical and policy initiatives." Means and ends, it was implied, could not be left to market forces alone in the United States.

RFF had taken not only an economic but also a political turn during the most troubled decade in U.S. energy history. It would recur in Enron's day with global-warming alarmism—a focus pushed in part by RFF board member Ken Lay.

A second effort published in the same year by RFF, under the sponsorship of the Ford Foundation, reached similar conclusions. Among the authors of *Energy: The Next Twenty Years* were Harvard professors Robert Stobaugh and William Hogan[7] with their pet recommendations. In the introduction, McGeorge Bundy, in one his final acts as president of the Ford Foundation, praised the RFF-led

---

7. Hogan would be a thorn in Enron's side when electricity restructuring came of age in the 1990s, advocating a *Poolco*, or centralized approach, over Enron's more decentralized, bilateral model for the power grid.

effort for giving "heavy emphasis to the role of market forces," while admitting that the Ford Foundation–sponsored *A Time to Choose* "did not sufficiently consider those forces." Principled free-market arguments were scarce in the volume, but anticipated higher prices from oil and natural gas decontrol were part of the conservationist agenda. The push to "vigorously pursue conservation as an energy source" and promote solar energies were other reasons for Bundy's strong endorsement. The Ford Foundation and RFF had moved rightward and leftward, respectively, to common ground.

·◌·

A key explanation of higher energy prices in RFF's 1979 manifesto, *Energy in America's Future*—"an increase in the cost of using energy now rather than in the future"—harked back to Harold Hotelling. RFF's economists were hardly alone. The economics profession's "explosive revival of interest" in Hotelling's 1931 "The Economics of Exhaustible Resources" had created a new field, *natural resource economics*, based on the theory that depletable resources were *different*; that is, their prices were destined to rise over time as demand increased.

Just days after Hotelling's death, Robert Solow paid tribute in a keynote address at the 1973 annual meeting of the American Economic Association. The story-telling MIT economist explained how "having, like everyone else, been suckered into reading *The Limits to Growth*," he decided to study the economics of exhaustible resources. He worked up a paper based on Hotelling's classic only to encounter in each day's mail a paper from some top economist on the very same subject! But the esteemed MIT economist, like just about everyone else, concluded that the rediscovered Hotelling was right.

Indeed, Hotelling was to the energy crisis what John Maynard Keynes was to the Great Depression: the economist of choice in a time of acute need. The American Economic Association had named Hotelling a *distinguished fellow* in 1965, the first year of the honor. Now, amid the energy crisis, he was an icon. But Hotelling's fame as a sage of depleting resources would prove to be short-lived, as described in chapter 11.[8]

Daniel Yergin

Other voices found popularity in heralding a new energy era of depletionism and conservationism. One was Daniel Yergin, (b. 1947), a lecturer at the Kennedy School at Harvard. Yergin would later win a Pulitzer Prize for a book on the history of the global oil industry, *The Prize: The Epic Quest for Oil, Money & Power* (1991), and establish the leading consultancy to the energy industry, Cambridge Energy Research Associates (CERA). But he first hit stride with a coedited book, *Energy Future: Report of the Energy Project at the Harvard Business*

---

8. Also see Internet appendix 10.1, "Hotelling's Sophism," at www.politicalcapitalism. org/book1/chapter10/appendix1.html.

School (1979). Although favoring "greater reliance on the free market," *Energy Future* painted a "bleak outlook" for U.S. energy and longed for a government-directed "transition to a more balanced energy system."

Pessimism toward conventional energies was evident from such chapter titles as "The End of Easy Oil" and "Natural Gas: How to Slice a Shrinking Pie." Two chapters offered optimism for a reconstructed energy future: "Solar America" and "Conservation: The Key Energy Source." Indeed, Yergin and coeditor Robert Stobaugh concluded that "the government must be the champion of conservation and solar." Two goals were outlined: a 20 percent market share for renewables (aka solar) "within two decades" and a reduction in energy usage of 30–40 percent with only "modest adjustments in the way people live." This was not a free-market program or outcome.

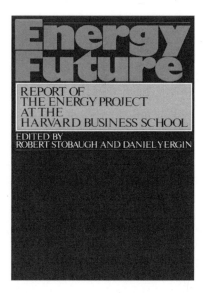

Figure 10.7 Government intervention made energy matters less for the market and more for the intellectuals. The new research / policy paradigm mixed three doctrines: depletionism, conservationism, and gapism. Two prominent studies published in 1979 by scholars at Resources for the Future (left) and Harvard University (right) are shown here.

Stobaugh and Yergin sought the middle ground between the "romantics opposed to economic growth" and the "even more powerful romanticists . . . who believe that it is possible to return to an era of unlimited production." They concluded: "Now is the time for the United States to come to terms with the realities of the energy problem, not with romanticisms, but with pragmatism and reason. And not out of altruism, but for pressing reasons of self-interest."

Energy Future, perfectly timed with America's summer gasoline shortages, became the most popular energy book of its day. The *New York Times* called it "the best single examination of America's energy problem in print." Back-cover endorsements came from Paul Samuelson (the world's foremost Keynesian economist and a Nobel laureate), Shell and ARCO executives, Amory Lovins, and Jim Harding, Lovins's successor at Friends of the Earth. The book's chapters, particularly Yergin's on conservation, codified the new approach to energy policy evident in the scattered writings of David Freeman, Lovins, and economists at Resources for the Future, among others. The orthodoxy was set.

Daisy Chaining: The Great Oil-Trading Boom

The nation suffered through periodic petroleum shortages during the 1970s. Yet for the most part—from 1975 through 1978, for example—supply and demand meshed despite federal price controls. Seen another way, U.S. consumers paid record prices for petroleum products *despite* maximum-price regulations, at all stages of the domestic industry, designed to insulate consumers from the government cartel, the Organization of Petroleum Exporting Countries (OPEC). How did this happen?

Part of the answer was well recognized by analysts and regulators. U.S. refiners were free to pay the world price to import much-needed crude oil—or the United States would, in effect, embargo itself as international cargoes would go elsewhere to receive market prices. Unregulated imports put refiners in a position to *bid up* the price of foreign crude that was mixed with regulated (underpriced) domestic oil—so long as the refiner's total cost was not more than the downstream market would bear. Such regulatory-induced averaging, which by one estimate increased the cost of imported oil between 10 percent and 20 percent, negated some of the benefit of regulated oil for consumers.

Yet another process was at work, which few outside the industry and the Department of Energy grasped. The oil-reseller boom (1973–81) was one of the most bizarre cases of unintended consequences in U.S. regulatory history. Such regulatory gaming (called *superfluous entrepreneurship* in the economics literature) would recur during the California power crisis of 2000–2001, a saga prominently involving Enron and David Freeman.

Regulation can create profit opportunities, not only remove them. In the case of oil, effective price controls, by definition, create prices that are below market levels. If party A cannot legally receive a market price from party B, party C has an incentive to step in, buying from A and selling to B, to capture some or all of the unrealized gain. Regulators tried to prevent such opportunism by price controlling each downstream transaction so that the savings from price controls at the crude-oil producer level (the wellhead) could flow downstream to end users.

But because of a *regulatory gap*, this plan did not work. Although oil could be produced, transported, refined, transported (wholesaled), and retailed only once—the physical, value-added traditional industry functions—*intermediaries* could buy and resell the oil without limit. Many oil trader/reseller firms sprang up with little other purpose than to buy and resell price-regulated oil until it reached its market-clearing price level. Many of these middlemen had little more than a telephone, fax machine or telex, and bank letters of credit to do their work. They were unlike the pre- and postregulation oil gatherers that used hard assets to physically collect and move bought-and-sold oil. The opportunists had a regulatory setup.

To be sure, each reseller was subject to a maximum price based on its cost and allowed margin. The trick was to buy and sell the same oil back and forth—labeled *daisy chaining*—so that the regulated margins stacked up: smaller margins over many transactions rather than killings on the whole differential—at least if it was done legally.[9]

In the 1970s, hundreds of resellers consummated hundreds of thousands of transactions with crude oil between the wellhead and the refinery, and with oil products between the refinery and retail outlets. The good news is that such price arbitrage (increasing the price of regulated oil to its market-clearing level) typically kept motorists out of the gasoline lines. The bad news is that domestic oil producers were prevented from producing an estimated million more barrels per day than if they had received their (higher) free-market price.[10] The revenue that should have gone to those finding and producing oil instead went to foreign oil producers and fly-by-night resellers, some of whom became "regulatory millionaires."

The extravagance of oil resellers who were allowed to pass through their full costs before receiving their allowed margin—and thus were motivated to maximize their costs—is a story in itself. Another story was the rulemakings and litigation by regulators under the Emergency Petroleum Allocation Act (1973–81) trying to arrest opportunism by defining what was or was not a legitimate industry practice.

---

9. For illustration, assume that the free-market price of crude oil would be $20 per barrel but that federal law limits the first sale of crude oil to $15 per barrel, creating underpricing of $5 per barrel. Also assume that resellers are limited to a margin of $0.20 per barrel and that the refiner is under a regulated margin constraint. This regulatory schema invites 25 *legal trades* to get the price up to its free-market level ($20 per barrel), because the refiner cannot make more money under regulation from buying underpriced (regulated) crude oil. A similar example could be constructed for petroleum products between the refiner and retailer under stage-by-stage price controls.

10. The irony of price controls subsidizing imports at the expense of domestic producers was noted by two Harvard economists: "The publicly stated U.S. policy objective ... has been energy independence. In fact, the effects of petroleum price regulations have been exactly the opposite of the professed goal."

This arcane episode offered a precedent for opportunistic trading by Enron in California after the state restructured (not deregulated) its electricity industry in 1998. It is also important to understand the high risk of speculative trading when the oil industry returned to free-market conditions in early 1981. Taking *nonhedged* (naked) positions in a free market (versus *arbitraging* in regulated markets) could be big-money makers—or big-money losers, as Enron found out in a near-death oil-trading scandal in 1987.[11]

Media Alarmism

The media had its own energy problem. Few journalists were conversant with energy when the crisis hit. Most newspaper and magazine stories suffered from a combination of technical error, superficiality, omission, sensationalism, demagoguery, and scapegoating. Writers thrust onto the energy beat did not grasp the fundamental linkage between price controls and shortages and the uphill battle—even impossibility—of reestablishing order outside the market process. Time constraints or (less charitably) laziness encouraged what one critic called the "Initial Simplistic Explanation," which combined some mix of the aforementioned shortcomings.

To an extent, the energy industry had itself to blame for the media problem. The sector's long history of giving and receiving political favors did not sit well with journalists or politicians from the energy-importing Northeast and Northwest.[12] The views of Senator Edward Kennedy (D-Mass.), Henry Jackson (D-Wash.), corporate critic Ralph Nader, industry gadfly Edwin Rothschild, and government energy experts drowned out free-market views, which were lumped together with those of Big Oil. Statements from oil-company heads came across as industry greed, whereas neo-Malthusian opinions from energy czar James Schlesinger were reported as self-evident. Michael Jensen, the energy scribe of the *New York Times*, was particularly at fault.

Swimming against the tide was the editorial page of the *Wall Street Journal*, a reliable home to free-market analyses. Milton Friedman in his *Newsweek* column also addressed energy issues—often pleading with the government to stop regulating and with the industry to stop asking for it. In his PBS series and bestseller, *Free to Choose* (1979), the Nobel laureate explained the energy crisis with spoonfuls of Economics 101, asking:

> Why has this simple and foolproof solution [of price decontrol] not been adopted? . . . To the despair of every economist, it seems almost impossible for most people other than trained economists to comprehend how a price system works. Reporters

---

11. Enron's Valhalla oil-trading scandal, detailed in Book 3, revealed the personal and managerial weaknesses of Ken Lay and foreshadowed the demise of Enron less than 15 years later.

12. Political capitalism in the history of the U.S. energy market is outlined in chapter 6, pp. 167–68.

and TV commentators seem especially resistant to the elementary principles they supposedly imbibed in freshman economics. Second, removing price controls would reveal that the emperor is naked—it would show how useless, indeed harmful, are the activities of the 20,000 employees of the Department of Energy.

Media focus on price and allocation controls as the root problem would have unmasked the crisis for what it really was—government engineered—and put federal energy planning under the microscope. The market could have adjusted much sooner than it did, compressing the price cycle and thus the boom and bust experienced by the industry. Industry publications that made this point (such as those from the American Petroleum Institute) could not be expected to carry the day. And if any think tank had the media's ear on energy, it was Resources for the Future, not the American Enterprise Institute.

International Alarmism

Depletionist assumptions and government activism were prevalent in Europe as well. The environmental movement took off in the United Kingdom with the formation of Friends of the Earth in 1969 and Greenpeace two years later. European countries responded to higher oil prices in the 1970s by raising retail taxes, not imposing price ceilings. These countries not only raised revenue in the name of promoting energy conservation but also avoided what America did not—lines (queues) at the service station. Tax-inflated motor-fuel pricing remains a staple of European energy policy today.

But the international response to price hikes by OPEC had an American flavor. Secretary of State Henry Kissinger sought to create a consumer-nation cartel to counter OPEC. Europe took the lead, and in 1974, the International Energy Agency (IEA) was created within the 24-nation Organization for Economic Co-operation and Development (OECD, established in 1961). A multivolume OECD study concluded that "market distortions [from] excessive" demand for low-cost oil supplies (primarily in the Middle East) threatened the "economic and social wellbeing of OECD countries." The report warned against "a false sense of security as to the extent to which economic policy can rely on the automatic adjustment through the market mechanism."

The IEA set policies among its 16 members—which included the United States, Canada, Britain, and Japan—to cope with oil-supply disruptions on "reasonable and equitable terms," as well as undertake "long-term co-operative efforts on conservation of energy, on accelerated development of alternative sources of energy, on research and development." But Kissinger wanted more—an international floor oil price adhered to by IEA to promote conservation and to provide security for synthetic fuel projects should prices break. (President Ford had set a goal of producing 1 million daily barrels of synthetic fuel by 1985.) This extraordinary proposal was not adopted, but member nations did move ahead by establishing modest strategic petroleum reserves in case of future cutoffs.

Whereas Kissinger wanted a consumer OPEC, or OPCC (Organization of Petroleum Consuming Countries), others wanted an international energy agency within the United Nations to make planning truly global. Much of this sentiment was predicated on depletionism.

Jimmy Carter's complaint that the United States was "the only developed nation without an energy policy"—intended to rally public support behind the National Energy Plan and the new Department of Energy—was true to the extent that national energy planning was in vogue. Short of international coordination, virtually all foreign countries had government-dominated energy sectors, which could raise prices in the name of conservationism. By wanting the United States to join this club, Carter was rejecting the coordinating and demand-regulating role of impersonal market forces.

As it turned out, the International Energy Agency was long on form and short on action. A 20-year retrospective published by IEA in 1994 dedicated 412 pages to its rules and regulations and a scant 8 pages to its major achievements. "IEA was shaped to deliberate rather than act," one energy historian concluded.

Industry Alarmism

Resource pessimism afflicted the leaders of the oil and gas industry itself—thanks in no small part to the influence of Hotelling-school economists and M. King Hubbert's bell curve. In 1977, keynote articles in the 75th anniversary issue of the *Oil & Gas Journal* revealed a gloomy, defensive mentality. Maurice Granville, head of Texaco and chairman of the American Petroleum Institute, began his piece, "Although we in the oil industry have known it for a long time, most Americans only recently became aware that petroleum is a limited resource and that the era of 'cheap energy' has ended." Mobil head Rawleigh Warner predicted that future historians would see the petroleum age as but a "brief interlude between the wood-burning era that lasted well into the 19th Century and the era of nuclear, solar, and other energy sources that will characterize the 21st Century and beyond." Still, he added, Mobil was "committed to remaining an energy company" despite its diversification program away from energy and chemicals.

On the natural gas side, George Lawrence, head of the American Gas Association (AGA), foresaw a coming era when methane would no longer fuel "low-priority" industrial boilers and power generation but high-priority residential and commercial users—the very customers of AGA utilities. Gasified coal and other supplemental methane sources, Lawrence assured his readers, would increasingly join the supply mix to ensure enough gas for the residential market at century's end.

Exxon was not immune from the depletionist virus and made nonenergy investments to prove it. Chairman C. C. Garvin Jr. told a group of environmentalists in 1981 that oil use in the United States had peaked and was on the way down, implying the same for world oil consumption and the production to meet it.

Government fix-it was not far behind such industry defeatism. In particular, the Powerplant and Industrial Fuel Use Act of 1978 restricted gas burning, targeting coal and fuel oil for powerplant and industrial boilers. It was a decision that the gas industry, regulators, and environmentalists would regret when clean-burning gas went from shortage to surplus soon thereafter.

Industry prognostications of the beginning of the end for fossil fuels were squashed by the 1980s. Fossil fuels were again crowned king—at least until 1997 when Royal Dutch/Shell, in a public relations mode, forecast that half of global energy could be produced from renewable sources by 2050 (versus the then current 8 percent). Neo-Malthusians would hail Shell as a visionary energy company, as did business guru Gary Hamel, who preached revolution over incrementalism. Yet caution was in order. As W. S. Jevons noted in the 1860s, renewables were unsuited as primary energies for the industrial age, and his reasons had not gone away. (Shell has since repudiated its forecast.)

Depletionist thinking turned out to be costly for industry investors, employees, and consumers, as well as taxpayers. Some of the world's largest energy companies diversified into uranium, synthetic fuels, renewables, fuel cells, and nonenergy lines, such as copper mining, office products, and department stores, only to lose most or all of their investment. The federal government's Synthetic Fuels Corporation, hailed upon its founding in 1980 as "the cornerstone of U.S. energy policy," was shut down after five controversial years. The Strategic Petroleum Reserve, hatched as part of comprehensive energy legislation signed into law by President Ford in 1975, was fiscally under water by the early 1980s, with its expensive crude waiting for a crisis that was not in sight. Federal energy policy discouraging gas-fired electricity-generation capacity in favor of coal-fired capacity soon found gas in surplus and coal at the center of air pollution concerns. President Carter's temperature regulation in commercial buildings—no lower than 78 degrees in the summer and no higher than 65 degrees in the winter—brought the energy police to the door.

Federal price regulation created a crisis that depletionists thought verified their theory. Yet nature's cupboard was hardly bare. The 1970s would have been a very different energy decade if two American presidents had made different decisions. Natural gas shortages could have been avoided had President Dwight Eisenhower not unexpectedly vetoed a wellhead price-decontrol bill in 1956. Oil-supply interruptions from the Middle East could have been weathered had President Nixon addressed inflation in 1971 by restricting the growth of monetary supply rather than by regulating prices, a classic case of attacking symptoms rather than causes. Depletionist thinking—and its handmaiden, conservationism—could have been arrested as well. The 1970s energy experience underscored a major lesson of political economy: *the propensity of government intervention to expand from its own shortcomings*, with one intervention leading to another.

Voice of the Market

In the wake of the first oil crisis and with natural gas problems several years old, the American Enterprise Institute (AEI, established 1943) launched its National Energy Project. For AEI, a promarket, Republican-oriented think tank, it was back to basics—if *Republican* still had free-market connotations after the Nixon and Ford administrations.

Edward Mitchell (b. 1937), professor of business economics at the University of Michigan, directed the project and authored its first study, *U.S. Energy Policy: A Primer* (1974). Mitchell began his tract by quoting free-market economist Milton Friedman on the cause of systemic microeconomic dislocation, such as the United States was experiencing with energy:

> Economists may not know much. But we do know one thing very well: how to produce shortages and surpluses. So you want to produce a shortage of any product? Simply have government fix and enforce a legal *maximum* price on the product which is less than the price that would otherwise prevail. . . . Do you want to produce a surplus of any product? Simply have government fix and enforce a legal *minimum* price above the price that would otherwise prevail.

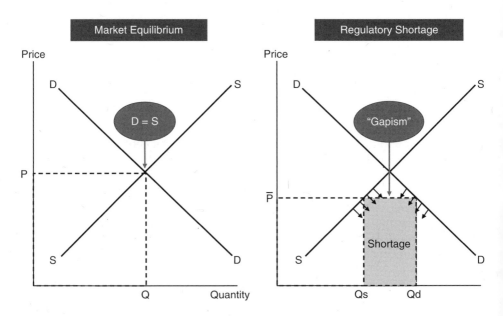

Figure 10.8 Equilibrium (left) is graphically represented as the point at which a market price coordinates supply with demand. Disequilibrium (right) results when price regulation causes demand to exceed supply (Qd > Qs). *Gapism* attempts to undo the physical shortage by shifting the supply curve down and to the right, and the demand curve down and to the left, given the maximum regulated price (P̄).

Figure 10.9 The American Enterprise Institute's National Energy Project (1974–76) and Studies in Energy Policy (1976–85), directed by Edward Mitchell, shown here, was a home for free-market energy analysis. Five of AEI's 25 studies are pictured here, including Mitchell's notable primer (upper left).

The federal government, explained Mitchell, was explicitly following a shortage policy by legislating oil and gas ceiling prices. Underlying resources had not suddenly grown scarce. Production costs had not suddenly soared. Price controls, coupled with other interventionism, were giving consumers, producers, and society the worst of all worlds. But rather than allow higher prices to reduce demand and increase supply, government was following an expensive, haphazard policy of "gap-reducing"—using taxpayer-funded programs and edicts to engineer a supply-demand balance given the mandated price. The "gapologist" (Mitchell's term) was the lobbyist seeking a particular subsidy or planner effectuating supply-side or demand-side fixes, such as efficiency mandates, tax-code provisions, public land directives, and research and development grants. Gapism was conservationism and productionism.

Five printings later, in 1980, Mitchell's message was unchanged—testament to its underlying logic. Few other books or essays from that decade would hold up as well to critical scrutiny as Mitchell's monograph still does today.

The message of the primer (and more specialized studies in the series by such economists as Kenneth Arrow and Joseph Kalt of Harvard University, Paul MacAvoy of Yale University, and Walter Mead of the University of California,

Santa Barbara) was that *markets work* and *government interventions distort*—
sometimes surprisingly so. This was a tonic at a time when private foundations
were often funding their favorite interventionist notions and the analyses of the
American Petroleum Institute, however sound, carried the stigma of Big Oil.
Only later would two newly formed think tanks—the Cato Institute (established
1977) and the Heritage Foundation (established 1980)—join AEI in carrying the
free-market energy flag in the nation's capital. This would be more necessary
than ever with the mixed message coming from Resources for the Future.[13]

Trinity of Dissent: Adelman, Simon, Robinson

M. A. Adelman (b. 1917), his eye trained on oil-production costs, was a hold-
out from the Hotelling-inspired groupthink of the economics profession. His
1975 essay in the *Quarterly Journal of Economics* noted that "an altogether new
chapter in economic history, that of a cartel or shared monopoly of a group of
sovereign states," had begun. This sellers' market "has nothing to do with real
scarcity, and is explained simply by the change from a slowly retreating monopoly into a rapidly advancing one."

Adelman's point was that the 13-member OPEC had become an effective
cartel with Saudi Arabia's nationalization decision in 1973–74. With the country's production taken from Exxon, Gulf, Texaco, and Chevron, Arab OPEC in
October 1973 began reducing output by 5 percent per month to protest U.S.
foreign policy. The United States, meanwhile, was locked into federal price and
allocation controls, a political fix that worked against the very supply and
demand adjustments that were needed to avert an energy crisis. Nixon, however unintentionally, put the oil industry on a treacherous course with his economy-wide wage-and-price control order, and the political majority kept it in
place during the Ford and Carter years. Only after belated market adjustments
and full decontrol in 1981 would the consumer crisis turn into a producer predicament of falling commodity prices and financial losses, a development totally
unpredicted by Harold Hotelling's economic paradigm for mineral resources
and by neo-Malthusian thinking more generally.

By 1973, Julian Simon, whose entrance into the sustainability debate was
described in chapter 9, was confident that population and progress were positively correlated, just the opposite of what the neo-Malthusians believed and
what he once believed.[14] Simon became a man on a mission, laboring mightily on
a fact-laden treatise to prove his case. It would not be easy. The magazine *Science*
rejected Simon's powerful warm-up, an essay challenging the "population

---

13. See appendix D, pp. 343–50.

14. See Internet appendix 10.2, "The Conversion of Julian Simon," at www.politicalcapital
ism.org/book1/chapter10/appendix2.html.

controllers." Long delays were encountered with his manuscript. But finally, *The Economics of Population Growth* (1977) was published by Princeton University Press. His book surveyed the population literature and offered statistical support for his contra-Malthus finding: "If population has a tendency to increase geometrically, output has a tendency to increase geometrically and at least as fast—without apparent limit."

Despite its depth of documentation and Princeton imprimatur, the book drew little academic attention and found no champions within the population establishment. Invoking David Hume, Simon could only remark how his book "fell deadborn from the press." Malthusianism was entrenched, particularly among natural scientists armed with a social agenda. The antipopulation movement had turned into a financial juggernaut, complicating scholarly debate. The economic ills of the day, from inflation to recession to energy shortages, did not engender optimistic opinion. Simon's consolation was a fan letter from F. A. Hayek, who told him how the book "provided the empirical evidence" for what had been "a life-time of theoretical speculation." To Simon, it was "the most valuable letter of my life."

Simon's book presented a new way of viewing natural resource and population issues. In retrospect, it was Simon's most significant work, full of well-documented novel findings presented in a forceful manner at a most inhospitable time. *Energy is the master resource. Oil is not becoming scarcer, because finding costs were well below its record-high selling price. The future supply of energy is limited only by "the human imagination." Human ingenuity is "the key resource!" Faster population growth is positively correlated with per worker income and other economic indicators in the long run* (defined as between 30 and 80 years).

Sustainable-development theory would never be the same, at least to those scholars who examined both sides of the issues.

·◇·

A lone European think tank questioned the consensus of depletionism and government as energy manager. The Institute of Economic Affairs in London, founded in 1957 to promote free-market thinking, published several studies in the 1970s by Colin Robinson (b. 1932), a professor of economics at the University of Surrey. Robinson advocated ending the ban on coal imports and repealing the fuel-oil tax to subject the domestic coal industry to market forces. He noticed that government regulation spawned more regulation—a "kind of ratchet effect which seems to lead to accumulating intervention over time." Perhaps liberalization could create its own dynamic, he thought.

After the world oil market turned in 1973, Robinson had depletionism to counter as well. The available evidence "throws much doubt on the extreme views about energy 'famine,'" he dissented. "The energy doom prophets either confuse oil with energy in general, or confuse the global resource problem with . . . pollution and monopoly issues."

Meanwhile, E. F. Schumacher, lionized as the prophet of energy scarcity for his warnings in the 1950s and 1960s, was riding high. His 1973 book, *Small Is Beautiful*,[15] a best-seller on both sides of the Atlantic, castigated society for "treating [fossil fuels] ... as income items although they are undeniably capital items." Mankind's "gigantic" task in the "foreseeable future" was to increase the market share of the "income fuels" from their current 4 percent to as much as 90 percent. Energy was Exhibit A for Schumacher's wider angst that "modern man has built a system of production that ravishes nature and a type of society that mutilates man." Crossing the ideas of Galbraith, Ehrlich, and Lovins, Schumacher sought to replace "the philosophy of materialism" with a "magnanimous kind of prudence."

Colin Robinson, not Schumacher, was now the voice in the energy-policy wilderness. But whose voice was false and whose true would not be decided until the world oil market resumed its pre-1970s course in the 1980s and beyond.

---

15. The irony of a socialist advocating smallness should not be overlooked. Socialism by definition is one giant monopoly—a bureaucracy providing every good and service without competition from autonomous firms.

11

New Light

THE 1970s WITNESSED "a flood of books, articles, speeches, and conferences on the subject of energy, produced by politicians, economists, physicists, ecologists, and even mystery writers." Instant energy experts, many with pet proposals, were everywhere. Energy economics became a subdiscipline of economics with its own professional association, trade journals, and textbooks. Energy modeling became "one of the fastest growing [fields] in the industrialized world." If impersonal market forces could not address the economic questions of *what, where, when,* and *for whom,* economists as the *smartest guys in the room* would.

The Department of Energy (DOE) stood as the newest of 12 Cabinet-level departments. A small army of physicists and technocrats at DOE worked on what was described in chapter 10 as *gapism* (aka "gapology"). Conservationism was a livelihood for many and a religion for more. Richard Nixon's 1974 call for energy independence—"Let us set our national goal, in the spirit of Apollo, with the determination of the Manhattan Project"—had not lost fervor in the Ford and Carter administrations.

Darkness for energy lifted in 1981. Ronald Reagan's total decontrol of oil ended Carter's phased deregulation program, although a crude-oil windfall-profit tax was capturing some of the higher prices for government. Higher natural gas prices permitted under the Natural Gas Policy Act were having their intended effect of increasing supply and decreasing demand. As market forces strengthened, the energy problem shifted from *consumers* to *producers.* Too many domestic producers, particularly independents, were under a spell that depletable resource prices were destined to rise over time. They believed Hotelling-school economists predicting $100 per barrel oil (about $225 in 2007 dollars). Sorely disappointed, vulnerable firms would practice political capitalism.

Things were happening on the intellectual front too. MIT's M. A. Adelman emerged triumphant over the iconic Harold Hotelling. A scholar's scholar, Adelman's focus on production costs as the best measure of resource scarcity proved to be on the mark.[1] The fixity/depletion prism came under assault. Although no technical errors were uncovered in Hotelling's seminal 1931 essay, his premise of an ever-scarcer stock simply did not comport with the real world. And, as the capstone of the new era, Julian Simon popularized a full-fledged theory of expansionism to challenge—at long last—the neo-Malthusians in theory and in fact. These complementary developments set the stage for the business and intellectual environment that Houston Natural Gas (soon to become Enron) inherited in the mid-1980s under its new chairman, Ken Lay.

Doomslayer: Julian Simon's Expansionism

Science magazine in mid-1980 published an essay by Julian Simon that "raised the blood pressure of the scientific community a good twenty points," one Malthusian environmentalist recalled. "Resources, Population, Environment: An Oversupply of False Bad News" presented official statistics to refute high-profile media scare stories. In so doing, Simon challenged the interrelated notions of a fixed supply of land, fixed and depleting resources, a growing inadequacy of food supply, an inverse relationship between population and progress, and a worsening environment. Simon's cherry-on-top was answering, "Why do we hear phony bad news?" Part of his explanation was that "bad news sells books, newspapers, and magazines: good news is not half so interesting." He asked, "Is it a wonder that there are lots of bad-news best-sellers warning about pollution, population growth, and natural-resource depletion but none telling us the facts about improvement?"

The provocative essay, published on the home turf of the neo-Malthusians, put Simon's ideas in play. Princeton University Press rushed ahead to publish what became Simon's signature book, *The Ultimate Resource*. The sustainability debate was finally joined.

In response to Simon's cannon shot, a flood of dissent filled the offices of *Science*'s publisher, the American Association for the Advancement of Science (AAAS). Paul Ehrlich asked: "Could the editors have found someone to review Simon's manuscript who had to take off his shoes to count to 20?" Paul and Anne Ehrlich, John Holdren, and John Harte in a reply challenged Simon's contention that oil was not becoming permanently scarcer. "The fact is that OPEC's price hikes and the 'improved market power' of coal and uranium *both* reflected

---

1. A *festschrift* for Adelman, published in 1987 by his students and colleagues—a who's who of energy economists—began: "Morry Adelman is the complete scholar. He has made major contributions to our understanding of industrial organization and antitrust policy, the economics of natural resource discovery, and (most recently) the world petroleum market."

a new reality based on emerging scarcity of oil and natural gas." Record oil prices gave at least superficial credence to their depletionism, but Simon, like M. A. Adelman, would soon have the upper hand.

A New Paradigm

The Ultimate Resource (1981) was designed to irresistibly engage Simon's opponents. Using as his model John Kenneth Galbraith's *The Affluent Society*, Simon sought to write a popular book that would influence academia via the general public. Thus, Simon turned over his trump cards in the introduction.

> Hold your hat—our supplies of natural resources are not finite in any economic sense. . . . If the past is any guide, natural resources will progressively become less scarce, and less costly, and will constitute a smaller proportion of our expenses in future years. And population growth is likely to have a long-run *beneficial* impact on the natural-resource environment.
>
> Energy. Grab your hat again—the long-run future of our energy supply is at least as bright as that of other natural resources, though political maneuvering can temporarily boost prices from time to time. Finiteness is no problem here either. And the long-run impact of additional people is likely to speed the development of a cheap energy supply that is almost inexhaustible.

Twenty-three chapters and thousands of data points later, his book ended: "The ultimate resource is people—skilled, spirited, and hopeful people who will exert their wills and imaginations for their own benefit, and so, inevitably, for the benefit of us all." This was Erich Zimmermann resurrected—but backed by a much richer empirical record within a wider framework. It was Zimmermann who had written decades earlier, "Freedom and wisdom, the fruits of knowledge, are the fountainhead of resources."

A science of expansionism and the integration of depletable resources in the corpus of general economics were at hand.

The Ultimate Resource, condensing and building upon Simon's 1977 book, *The Economics of Population Growth*, offered a new way to view the world. Two decades before, science historian Thomas Kuhn had explained the whirlwind that Simon now found himself in. In Kuhnian terms, Simon's time-series data revealed a gaping "anomaly" in an entrenched neo-Malthusian "paradigm." The process of "normal science" had now to give way to "extraordinary science," a "scientific revolution" whereby a new "gestalt" came forth. Not surprisingly, the establishment, viewing the world in a "preformed and relatively inflexible box," was "intolerant" of the new theory.

"Paradigm shifts," Kuhn explained, overturn the established order. Emotions run high. The process begins with "scientists . . . behav[ing] differently" and continues with "pronounced professional insecurity" whereby years and perhaps lifetimes of work and writing are put at risk. If the paradigm is powerful and useful, with open questions answered, it prevails until only "a few elderly hold-outs remain."

Figure 11.1 Julian Simon's *The Economics of Population Growth* (1977), challenging deeply ingrained Malthusian notions, was largely ignored. Simon's *The Ultimate Resource* (1981) reached a wider, though limited, audience. Together, Simon's books represented a new paradigm of thought as defined by Thomas Kuhn in *The Structure of Scientific Revolutions*.

Simon's "shift of vision" was not verifiable as in the laboratory sciences, where experimentation under controlled conditions can objectively settle matters. While taking into account physical laws, social science issues, such as the costs and benefits of population growth, offered plenty of wiggle room for scientists to interpret the data differently or to hold out for new data. Julian Simon would practically have to go it alone until economists—a few, more, then many—joined him against an entrenched core of largely environmental scientists wed to Malthusian notions.

The implications of Simon's worldview were profound for science, public policy, philanthropy, the media, and the public psyche. If history supported increasing resource availability and improving human welfare, all while population surged, people were not the problem but the solution. What John Holdren, Paul and Anne Ehrlich, and John Harte called the "mass of human protoplasm" were not only mouths to feed but also limbs that converted calories into productive work and minds that multiplied means and ends. Malthusians from Malthus to Ehrlich were errant, as were depletionists from Jevons to Hotelling to Hubbert. What Adelman saw with petroleum, what Zimmermann outlined with resources, what Adam Smith and F. A. Hayek sensed across the economy, and what Ayn Rand envisioned in her Objectivist world, Julian Simon saw in all human activity within a regime of "truth and liberty."[2]

Simon's *The Ultimate Resource* was as well timed for the energy-surplus era as Stobaugh and Yergin's *Energy Future* was for the energy crisis, yet book sales for Simon were far less. A popular audience was much harder to find for good news than for bad, and few in the intellectual class were seeking to overturn the orthodox view of sustainable development. Still, Simon's "gestalt switch" (in Kuhnian terms) was fact based and theoretically robust. It would, over time, overcome trenchant resistance. F. A. Hayek predicted as much in a missive to Simon upon reading *The Ultimate Resource*:

> Though you will be at first much abused, I believe the more intelligent will soon recognize the soundness of your case. And the malicious pleasure of being able to tell most of their fellows what fools they are, should get you the support of the more lively minds about the media. If your publishers want to quote me they are welcome to say that I described it as a first class book of great importance which ought to have great influence on policy.

This was no small praise from the 1974 Nobel laureate in economics, a thinker whose own renaissance after decades in the intellectual wilderness was at hand. By the time Hayek died in 1992, at age 91, he was regarded as one of the top social scientists of the century and a theoretical victor over John Maynard Keynes and others who had argued that central planning, in part or in whole, could outdistance markets. Although few in the 1970s realized it, the intellectual underpinnings of *gapism* had been refuted by the worldview of F. A. Hayek.

A second notable free-market economist, Israel Kirzner, was struck by the "parallels" between the insights in Simon's new book and his own theory about open-ended entrepreneurial discovery. Simon's empirically based prediction of long-term plenty was a modern version of Joseph Schumpeter's "spirited debunking forty years ago of the stagnation thesis," noted Kirzner. But Simon went further, identifying each person with his "'unlimited . . . thoughts'" as "'the ultimate resource.'"

But Simon, Kirzner cautioned, paid precious little attention to the *institutional* conditions enabling the prime movers, the entrepreneurs, to continually move and improve. (Simon, in fact, did not focus on entrepreneurship per se.) "My own grounds for challenging the premise of long-run finiteness of resources has been more cautious and depends heavily on the scope permitted by the institutional environment for the free exercise of entrepreneurship," Kirzner wrote in 1983. "Horizon-expanding discoveries" require free-market capitalism, he argued.

---

2. Also see Internet appendix 11.1, "Julian Simon as Paradigm Builder," at www.political capitalism.org/book1/chapter11/appendix1.html.

And so it would come to be. Kirzner's caveat would not seem to apply to the energy-rich 1980s and 1990s. But in Enron's final years (2000–2001) and the post-Enron era, energy-price increases can be understood as a lack of incentive and means for entrepreneurial discovery in a world whose resource capabilities became dulled by virulent statism and nationalism. Simon, if alive today (he died in 1998), would surely agree with Kirzner that institutions not only matter but indeed can make all the difference.

Simon's 1981 book gained a foothold but not the mass appeal of neo-Malthusian tracts. Harold Barnett, coauthor of *Scarcity and Growth*, called *The Ultimate Resource* "ideal" to counter the popular alarmism of the 1970s. Sympathetic if not positive reviews followed in a variety of publications, including the three leading business magazines: *Forbes*, *Fortune*, and *Business Week*. A *New York Times* book review simply titled "Antineomalthusian," concluded:

> The 1970's have not demonstrated the physical limits to growth, rather the social limits to non-growth. We have exhausted our tolerance for stagnation. In the short run at least, the prospects are dismal for the doom-mongers. "The Ultimate Resource" is perfectly timed.

Paul Ehrlich was nonplussed—again. He had scolded *Science* for publishing Simon's breakthrough essay, and he now equated Simon's view on population with "physicists arguing for a flat Earth." What Thomas Kuhn identified as "pronounced professional insecurity" was breeding sophomoric intolerance toward Simon. Meanwhile, Paul and Anne Ehrlichs' own book of 1981, *Extinction*, ceding almost nothing to "the economists," was as grim as ever. The husband-and-wife team wrote:

> The enemy is not only "us" but virtually all human activities. The crisis is terribly mundane, but terribly serious. Unless appropriate steps are taken soon to preserve Earth's plants, animals, and microorganisms, humanity faces a catastrophe fully as serious as an all-out thermonuclear war.

Modern energy, the Ehrlichs explained, was central to the problem.

A Famous Wager

The sudden turn to energy surplus by the early 1980s gave Julian Simon a new opening. Still, he knew that more was needed to win popularity for his good-news message. His entrepreneurial side, cultivated by his background in marketing and advertising, went to work. Inspired by one of Paul Ehrlich's wild predictions—"If I were a gambler, I would take even money that England will not exist in the year 2000"—Simon got an idea. *What if he publicly challenged his archrival to a wager?* So, in the front of *The Ultimate Resource*, he challenged "the doomsdayers to put their money where their mouths are" by betting on the future scarcity of minerals—whichever ones his opponents chose. Ehrlich was mentioned by name and goaded with his prediction about England. But there was nothing flip about Simon's proposal. If the future price of the minerals rose after adjusting for inflation, Simon would pay; if the price dropped, the depletionists would pay.

In an exchange with Simon in *Social Science Quarterly*, Ehrlich and associates John Holdren and John Harte announced that they would "accept Simon's astonishing offer before other greedy people jump in." After conducting research, five metals were chosen by the Ehrlich consortium: chrome, copper, nickel, tin, and tungsten. The settlement date was September 1990, a term of 10 years. At Ehrlich's insistence ("the lure of easy money can be irresistible"), the stakes were raised and the contract finalized.

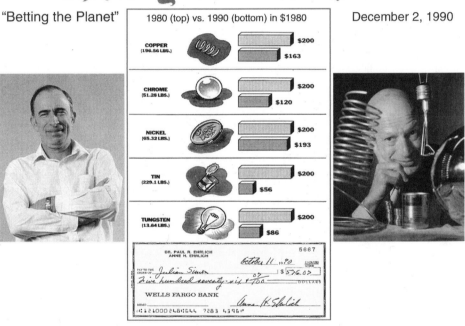

Figure 11.2 The most famous wager in the history of economics was won by Julian Simon (right) against his neo-Malthusian critics, led by Paul Ehrlich (left). His victory demonstrated the viability of a seemingly illogical proposition: the growing supply of so-called depletable resources. John Tierney's 1990 *New York Times Magazine* article told the story to a national audience.

The outcome of the most famous wager in the history of economics was a resounding victory for Simon. Most of the picked minerals had fallen in nominal terms between 1980 and 1990, and each fell in inflation-adjusted terms—despite 822 million more earthlings consuming so-called depletable resources. The Ehrlichs paid up, and Simon's public call to renew the bet at double the stakes was rejected.

The Ehrlich group would have lost more money had it chosen oil, gas, or coal. More than anyone knew, resource nationalization and price controls had created an artificial scarcity of oil, driving prices to record levels. The belated market response to such distortion was lost demand, which made the price collapse (supply glut) even greater than if the price spike had been less—as it would have been in a more free-market environment. As with all artificially generated business cycles, the boom exacerbated the bust.

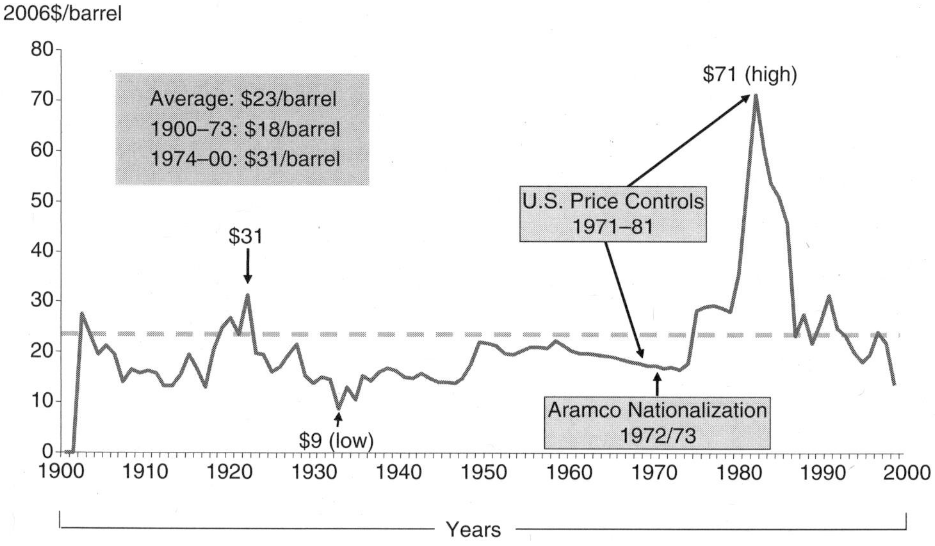

Figure 11.3 The surge in oil prices in the 1970s was unprecedented. Falling prices in the next decade indicated how government activism (nationalization, regulation) can create artificial scarcity outside the natural-resource base.

Ehrlich would have to alter his position on resource scarcity. Although "prices of more raw materials are indeed dropping than rising," Paul and Anne Ehrlich wrote in 1996, "market prices don't capture the full social costs of resource harvesting and consumption." The perceived energy problem was becoming more nuanced, a sign of a Kuhnian clash between *normal* and *extraordinary* science.

Challenging Global 2000

Simon produced study after data-packed study to back his working hypothesis of "more people, greater wealth, expanded resources, cleaner environment."[3]

---

3. This was the subtitle to Simon's last public lecture, on December 4, 1997, given in the Kenneth L. Lay Lecture Series in Global Economic Issues, cosponsored by the University of Houston and the Houston Forum.

Figure 11.4 Julian Simon's prolific research and passion led to a school of expansionist thought as evidenced in *The Resourceful Earth* (1984). This multiauthor effort rebutted the Carter administration's *Global 2000*, a million-copy best-seller that was translated into five languages.

In 1984, Simon coedited a book with Herman Kahn, *The Resourceful Earth*, directly responding to a study by the exiting Carter administration that predicted what a business-as-usual world would look like in 20 years. *Global 2000 Report to the President*, a best-selling neo-Malthusian tract that the incoming Reagan administration ignored, concluded:

> If present trends continue, the world in 2000 will be more crowded, more polluted, less stable ecologically, and more vulnerable to disruption than the world we live in now. Serious stresses involving population, resources, and environment are clearly visible ahead. Despite greater material output, the world's people will be poorer in many ways than they are today. . . [unless] the nations of the world act decisively to alter current trends.[4]

---

4. *Global 2000* shied away from making a bold prediction on the future price of oil, but President Carter foresaw oil at $100 per barrel (in 1980 dollars) by 2000. The actual price in 1980 dollars was below $15 per barrel in 2000.

Simon and Kahn stood this conclusion on its head with their own prognostication:

> If present trends continue, the world in 2000 will be *less crowded* (though more populated), *less polluted, more stable ecologically,* and *less vulnerable to resource-supply disruption* than the world we live in now. Stresses involving population, resources, and environment *will be less in the future than now. . . .* The world's people will be *richer* in most ways than they are today.

The authors' chapter on the future of oil supplies reviewed the failed history of alarmism and cautioned that although a transition away from oil in the next hundred years "seems likely . . . there is still much uncertainty as to if, when, and how this transition will occur."

The 25 contributors to the Simon/Kahn rejoinder included Harold Barnett, a past voice of expansionism at Resources for the Future. This was noteworthy. RFF had once been a bastion of natural-resource analysis and optimism. Now it was Simon, with funding support from the newborn Heritage Foundation, who was carrying RFF's old banner—and attracting interest from the Reagan administration. RFF's board and donors were pointing the organization in a different energy direction—environmentalism and conservationism. RFF hereafter would periodically weigh in on resource availability but almost as an aside to its burgeoning work product in other areas.[5]

A Slow Retreat: RFF and Daniel Yergin Hold Out

The depletionist outlook at Resources for the Future lingered despite a reversal of the national and world energy picture. In *Energy Today and Tomorrow: Living with Uncertainty* (1983), authors Joel Darmstadter, Hans Landsberg, and Herbert Morton stated that "the world will not run out of oil, but it will have to pay more for it." Hotelling-like, they continued: "As oil becomes more costly to find, extract, and transport from remote places, its use will decline." Environmental issues associated with carbon-based energy were also emphasized, including man-made global warming from the enhanced greenhouse effect, an issue that was not yet in the public mind.

This was a far cry from what the RFF economists could have proclaimed during and after the troubled 1970s: Energy shortages were the result of government policy, not free markets or even OPEC's monopolistic actions. Longer term, "the ultimate quantity of oil under the ground is (as Professor M. A. Adelman tells us) unknown, unknowable, and, most important, uninteresting." Edward Mitchell and his adjunct scholars were saying these things under the auspices of the American Enterprise Institute instead.

∽

Daniel Yergin, evolving from a Cambridge-trained, Harvard-based intellectual to an energy consulting entrepreneur, was also slow to break away from

---

5. See appendix D, pp. 343–50.

depletionism. "Low-cost reliable supplies of energy, and especially of oil, do not appear available," he wrote in a 1982 book. Increasing demand in such circumstances "may pose a threat to sustained economic growth." Yergin warned against the new "glut psychology," in that "by 1982, many people wanted to pretend that the events of 1979–80 had occurred in the distant past, as though they had no relevance to the present and the future." Yergin faulted the Reagan administration for "virtually dismantl[ing] . . . the infrastructure—programs, institutions, financing, people—needed to accelerate alternatives and conservation."

Figure 11.5 Daniel Yergin went from conservationist critic of Reagan energy policy to cofounder of Cambridge Energy Research Associates (CERA), a consulting firm. After authoring *The Prize* (1991), he coauthored *The Commanding Heights* (1998), a chronicle of the ascent of free markets. A PBS miniseries of the latter book was sponsored by Enron, eager to portray itself as a free-market company (it was not).

Yergin's policy activism reached the international market. The Ph.D. in international studies sought "an energy security system for the developed nations [from] the International Energy Agency, the economic summits, and the European Community." He wondered, "Can adjustment outrun crisis?"

In 1983, Yergin cofounded Cambridge Energy Research Associates (CERA), a "research and consulting firm that specializes in the analysis of current energy issues and basic energy trends." CERA aimed to bridge the gap between academic research and the real world for its clients. Thus, Yergin dispensed with his depletionist thinking as energy markets turned to surplus. But he found solace in his conservationist past. Comparing 1982 to 1973, Yergin noted that the U.S. economy had grown (by 18 percent), and yet energy usage had declined (by 5 percent). Thus, his prediction in *Energy Future* that such contrary trends were about to occur, considered "heresy" at the time, had been vindicated. David Freeman pointed to these same statistics to identify conservationism as "our outstanding achievement" in a 10-year retrospective on *A Time to Choose*, published in the inaugural issue of the *Energy Journal*. Yet such conservation was a bitter legacy of interventionism—price spikes, shortages, inconvenience, and mandates—and not of free markets. Energy growth would resume in the less-distorted period to follow, even as government conservation programs grew because of falling energy prices and a stronger economy.

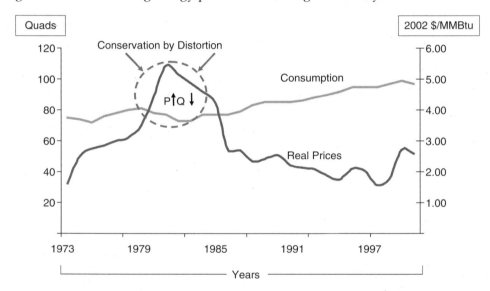

Figure 11.6 Declining U.S. energy usage during parts of the period 1973–83 was the result of government distortion, not natural consumer behavior. A free-market policy in the 1970s would have prevented shortages and flattened out the price curve, resulting in greater energy consumption.

Depletionism was not the only doctrine challenged by the new energy reality. Government programs instituted in the name of energy security were also put on the spot. Like the U.S. Strategic Petroleum Reserve, the International Energy Agency's efforts to store oil for a rainy day would have little to show to offset the costs. Stockpiling in response to resource pessimism—a practice that was not unlike W. S. Jevons's paper hoarding a century before—had long been uneconomic. Julian Simon identified it as a real cost of incorrect thinking. But not all was lost for the believers of energy-market failure. A new rationale, and one not so easily falsified, was on the way: the allegedly deleterious climate change that resulted from carbon dioxide emissions from power plants and motor vehicles. Conservationism, as well as a new policy promoting (non-hydroelectric) renewable energy to replace carbon-energy dependence, would accelerate even as depletionism and oil-security concerns moderated.

The Creed of Conservationism: Amory Lovins

The conservationism of Amory Lovins did not wither in the surplus era. In 1982, Lovins and his wife, Hunter, founded the Rocky Mountain Institute, a "think and do tank" promoting energy efficiency from a superinsulated, solar-powered, earth-sheltered structure near Aspen, Colorado. Funding came in, and staff positions were filled. Public and private parties were intrigued with the energy-saving ideas and gizmos that were being pushed by the evangelical technician.

Lovins was opposed to free-market materialism but from a different angle than were John Kenneth Galbraith and Paul Ehrlich. Lovins argued less about new social priorities and lifestyle changes than about implementing the very latest in technology to pare energy usage. Lovins saw the solution on the shelf—or as hundred-dollar bills on the ground, waiting to be picked up. He did not play the depletionist card and, in fact, chided the Ehrlich team for making their natural-resource bet against Julian Simon.

As in the 1970s, Lovins remained a fierce critic of centralized electricity generation. He boldly predicted that increasing energy efficiency could cost-effectively cancel out demand growth. "The long-term prospects for selling more electricity are dismal," he told *Newsweek* in 1984. Claiming that he could not find any instances "where it is cheaper to generate power than to save it," Lovins declared the national fleet of power plants obsolete and the era of building new plants "over." The future was not megawatts but "negawatts"—avoided electricity through ratepayer-funded conservation programs.

Lovins's urgings, pronouncements, and predictions from the 1980s would not hold up well. Between 1984 and 2000, electricity capacity and production increased by 19 percent and 22 percent, respectively, *despite* a multibillion-dollar effort by utilities, municipalities, localities, and government to reduce electricity usage at the expense of ratepayers and/or taxpayers. Energy efficiency improved for just about all applications and the economy as a whole, but more people and a plethora of new uses for electricity ensured overall demand growth. Something else was also happening. What W. S. Jevons recognized in the 1860s—increasing energy usage *from* increasing efficiency—was at work more than a century later.

Lovins's advice to stop building new power plants and focus on demand-reduction policies and (uneconomic, intermittent) renewables was taken very seriously in California, the soft-energy capital of the world. The result—the state's electricity rate crisis in the 1990s and electricity shortage thereafter—was hardly nirvana.

Amory Lovins would be a big fan of Enron Energy Services, which managed the energy function for large companies under long-term outsourcing contracts. But the cheerleading stopped when it came to light that Enron's much-celebrated energy and cost savings were illusory. A pillar of what Lovins (et al.) thought was a "new era of natural capitalism" was not so distinct. The value proposition of unexploited energy-conservation opportunities was much less than advertised. *Economical* conservation opportunities had been mined by self-interested businesses for the most part, and decades of government-mandated and taxpayer/ratepayer conservationism had done its work. There was not that much unexploited savings left. The (contrived) accounting profitability of Enron's outsourcing contracts was not matched by underlying economic profitability. Cash flow, *negative* cash flow, would tell the real story.

The conservation of natural capitalism was hardly born in the 1980s and 1990s, however. "Today the conservation movement is led by sober business men and is based on the cold calculations of the engineers," Erich Zimmermann declared back in the 1930s. "Conservation, no longer viewed as a political issue, has become a business proposition."

A Cul-de-Sac: Harold Hotelling Rejected

The influence of Harold Hotelling's "The Economics of Exhaustible Resources," which had fathered the boom in mineral-resource analysis in the 1970s, was now petering out. Hotelling-inspired articles continued, but the results were not robust. Simply put, economists could not find a depletion signal in the data to support Hotelling's Rule. A eulogy of sorts was given by the president of the International Association for Energy Economics in 1992:

> The [Hotelling] Principle sees net prices of "exhaustible" resources as following a rising trajectory dictated by the rate of interest. . . . [Yet] the petroleum industry seems to have been unimpressed by this philosopher's stone, supposedly the key to the pricing behavior of the very resource it produces. . . . Empirical evidence for the Principle is largely absent.

An essay published six years later in a journal of the American Economic Association, surveying some 125 articles and books in the 65-year Hotelling-related literature, was little kinder. Hotelling's theory was elegant but misplaced. Real-world phenomena could be explained only by relaxing the assumptions, the review article concluded.

Many of Hotelling's critics still saw value in his mathematical exercise, despite its limited operational value. But Julian Simon thought otherwise:

> Hotelling's analysis has no descriptive or prescriptive power due to its being founded on a contrary-to-fact assumption. . . . To the extent that it affects decision-makers, Hotelling's Rule is perverse, and imposes a cost because it is misleading; it focuses economists upon an analysis which leads to wrong conclusions

for all known situations. And it wastes the time of economists who could be devoting themselves to more profitable activities.

Somewhere in the sky, Erich Zimmermann could claim victory over a foe whose one article had captured the imagination of the economics mainstream—and led it astray.

Two Revolutions: Reagan and Thatcher

The tag line *dismal science* was reapplied to economics during the dark decade of the 1970s, but the 1980s would be different. It began during the 1980 presidential election when candidate Ronald Reagan dismissed Carter's call to address energy shortages with "sacrifices and changes in every life." Reagan retorted: "People who talk about an age of limits are really talking about their own limitations, not America's." But Carter was a true Malthusian. Undeterred by the easing of the energy crisis, his farewell address spoke of danger ahead:

> There are real and growing dangers to our simple and our most precious posses-sions: the air we breathe, the water we drink, and the land which sustains us. The rapid depletion of irreplaceable minerals, the erosion of topsoil, the destruction of beauty, the blight of pollution, the demands of increasing billions of people, all combine to create problems which are easy to observe and predict, but difficult to resolve. If we do not act, the world of the year 2000 will be much less able to sustain life than it is now.

Reagan cast an altogether different light toward the nation's problems in his inaugural address of January 1981:

> We're too great a nation to limit ourselves to small dreams. We're not, as some would have us believe, doomed to an inevitable decline. I do not believe in a fate that will fall on us no matter what we do. I do believe in a fate that will fall on us if we do nothing. So, with all the creative energy at our command, let us begin an era of national renewal. Let us renew our determination, our courage, and our strength. And let us renew our faith and our hope. We have every right to dream heroic dreams.

Reagan also rejected the central-planning mentality that had grown alongside energy problems:

> In this present [energy] crisis, government is not the solution to our problem; government is the problem. From time to time we've been tempted to believe that society has become too complex to be managed by self-rule, that govern-ment by an elite group is superior to government for, by, and of the people. Well, if no one among us is capable of governing himself, then who among us has the capacity to govern someone else?

Reagan walked the talk by deregulating petroleum a week later. "Ending price controls is a positive first step towards a balanced energy program," he announced, "a program free of arbitrary and counter-productive constraints, one designed to promote prudent conservation and vigorous domestic production."

Reagan's address was a sea change from pessimism, despair, and governmentism. Noted one historian at the time:

> The contrast with both traditional conservatism and post-Humphrey liberalism could not be more striking. Gone are the dour conservative prescriptions of austerity and self-sacrifice and returning to the past. Gone is the Carter-era pall of limited resources, complexity, and a world in which "more is not better." Reaganism is kinetic, expansive, and endlessly (critics would say mindlessly) optimistic about the future.

·◌·

The leadership of Prime Minister Margaret Thatcher in the United Kingdom from 1979 until 1990 also "recast attitudes toward state and market, withdrew government from business, and dimmed the confidence in government knowledge." Thatcher praised the free and open economy as a worthy ideal in stark contrast to Britain's tradition of democratic socialism. One of her greatest tests was the British coal strike of 1984–85, which was broken after a year. Electricity generation and distribution were privatized in 1990, and the coal industry, which had been nationalized in 1946, soon followed.

Upon privatization, Enron boldly constructed the world's largest gas-fired cogeneration plant at Teesside, United Kingdom. As part of the lobbying/permitting process, Ken Lay befriended the U.K. Secretary of State for Energy, John Wakeham, who would later join Enron's board of directors. Teesside was at once a great success and harrowing experience for Enron—the sign of a risk-taker extraordinaire.

A lacuna in Thatcher's reign concerned her alarmist beliefs about the human influence on global climate. Perhaps she wanted to sport her undergraduate degree in chemistry. Maybe it was because of her fight against the CO_2-intensive coal-mining industry or because she came under the sway of several U.K. environment-oriented scientists. In any event, Thatcher spoke ominously on climate change to the Royal Society in September 1988, just several months after James Hansen's U.S. Senate testimony on the same subject. "It is possible . . . we have unwittingly begun a massive experiment with the system of this climate itself," she said. This would require more, not less, government "for energy production, for fuel efficiency, for reforestation," she concluded. Thatcher's government went on to found the Hadley Center for Climate Prediction and Research and gave early direction to the Intergovernmental Panel on Climate Change (IPCC) to elevate the issue at home and abroad.

In her retrospective, *The Downing Street Years* (1993), Thatcher, although wary of "green socialism," described how her environmental concern expanded from stratospheric ozone to "another atmospheric threat," man-made global warming. Yet her next book, *Statecraft: Strategies for a Changing World* (2002), declared war on "the doomsters' favorite subject . . . climate change."

Figure 11.7 New U.S. and U.K. political leadership elevated free-market thinking, including resource optimism in place of Malthusianism. Ronald Reagan and Margaret Thatcher looked to such intellectuals as Milton Friedman and F. A. Hayek, respectively. Reagan's decontrol order of January 28, 1981, ended the oil-crisis era that Nixon had begun nearly a decade before with his program of wage and price controls. (*Bottom right:* © Manchester Daily Express/SSPL/The Image Works.)

What had changed for Thatcher in less than a decade? First, she found the findings of climate science less alarming than before. Second, an "ugly . . . anti-growth, anti-capitalistic, anti-American" political agenda had emerged around the issue. Harking back to her free-market roots, Thatcher forwarded her own version of the precautionary principle: "Government interventions are problematic, so intervene only when the case is fully proven."

Thatcher's about-face can be chalked up to experience and regret about helping to create what became the anticapitalist Kyoto Protocol (1997).[6] Another explanation is that Thatcher's bitter battle against the nationalized, unionized coal-mining industry, which to her "symbolize[d] everything that was wrong

---

6. This 1997 agreement among developed nations to curb greenhouse gas emissions by an average 5.2 percent was praised by an Enron lobbyist as "good for Enron stock!!" He explained: "The potential to add incremental gas sales, and additional demand for renewable technology is enormous. . . . The endorsement for emissions trading was another victory for us."

with Britain," was over. A new rationale to demote coal was needed in the 1980s, but the economics-driven *dash for gas* cut the coal lobby to size in the 1990s.[7]

◆

A sea change had taken place on both sides of the Atlantic. Capitalism was in and socialism out. F. A. Hayek and Milton Friedman were appreciated; John Maynard Keynes and John Kenneth Galbraith were passé. Government studies began to give voice to optimism. The World Bank lowered its concern about the effect of population growth on natural resources for the first time in its 1984 *World Development Report*. Two years later, the National Research Council of the National Academy of Sciences reached a similar conclusion, reversing its 1971 findings. These official studies drew upon the work of population and growth economists who now saw distinct benefits as well as costs in higher population growth. These economists were catching up to the trailblazer, Julian Simon.

Prior energy problems became a distant memory as the 1980s progressed. Falling oil prices in 1981/82 caused a contraction of wellhead activities, and a sudden, severe oil-price collapse in 1986 raised a hue and cry from U.S. independent producers and refiners for petroleum tariffs to protect U.S. "national security" from the whims of OPEC. Enron too joined the protectionist bandwagon as power plants were leaving natural gas for cheaper residual fuel oil at the expense of Enron and other natural gas suppliers. This push for an oil tariff by Ph.D. economist Ken Lay would not have pleased—or surprised—Adam Smith.

Daniel Yergin's resource pessimism faded with the facts, but John Holdren remained convinced that the decade of the 1970s was a revolution that would not be undone. The MacArthur genius-grant recipient wrote in a 1990 *Scientific American* article that "expensive energy is a permanent condition, even without allowing for its environmental costs" because "the trends that once held cost at bay against cumulative depletion . . . have played themselves out." The fact that fossil-fuel prices had fallen by more than one-half between 1981 and the time of his article did not give him pause. Prestigious awards would keep coming Holdren's way—but not Simon's. When asked about his chances of receiving a genius award, Julian Simon mused: "MacArthur! I can't even win a McDonald's!"

Milton Friedman, now the world's most revered economist, believed that Julian Simon deserved a Nobel Prize in economics. But Nobel prizes can be awarded only to the living, and Simon lost whatever small chance he might have had in 1998 when he died of a heart attack after his daily exercise routine at his home in Chevy Chase, Maryland. Paul Ehrlich, also 65, lost his chief adversary, a man whom he refused to debate or even meet face to face.

Official estimates of remaining oil and gas reserves, found and probable, grew higher in the 1980s, adding to the paradigm problem for neo-Malthusians.

---

7. See Internet appendix 11.2, "Margaret Thatcher and Global Warming," at www.political capitalism.org/book1/chapter11/appendix2.html.

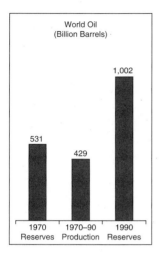
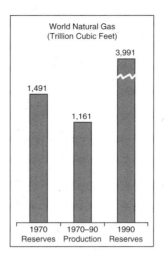
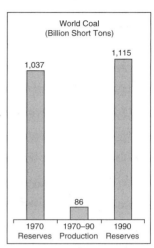

Figure 11.8 The data anomaly for neo-Malthusians is evident from these statistics showing an increase in estimated proved reserves for fossil fuels despite 20 years of increasing, record consumption. Longer time-series data would make the same point more dramatically.

The news was also favorable on the pollution front, where emissions were falling even as energy combustion was increasing, thanks to technological improvements and regulatory incrementalism. U.S. air-pollution emissions fell 18 percent during the 1980s even as total energy usage rose 8 percent. The earlier fear of Paul Ehrlich and John Holdren—"our limited knowledge of the details of air pollution permits little hope for early relief"—proved far off the mark. Also exaggerated was Ehrlich's view that Los Angeles was unlikely to control smog as long as "we have an automobile industry centered on the internal combustion engine and a social system which values large overpowered cars as status symbols."

An additional alarm concerning petroleum—insecure imports—was also proving exaggerated. National and international preparation for oil embargoes and other supply disruptions was akin to waiting for Godot. A greater role for free-market forces in the United States, the world's pivotal consumer and second-leading producer (behind Russia and ahead of Saudi Arabia)—was proving a match for the Organization of Petroleum Exporting Countries. Non-OPEC production, which stood under 50 percent of world supply in the early 1970s, rose to 62 percent by 1990. Between 1970 and 1990, energy usage, while unchanged per capita, fell by one-third per unit of gross domestic product. Julian Simon's improvement process was at work. Human ingenuity really was the ultimate resource in the free world.

Still, there was the question of what might have been. *What if free-market pricing had allowed U.S. markets to adjust to world markets in the 1970s, removing the false alarms and the turn to gapism?* Record high prices surely would have eased sooner, and much energy politicization could have been avoided. Perhaps political energy's *smartest guys in the room* could have lived prosaically in the private sector or in academia, with, say, Amory Lovins as an engineer, Daniel Yergin as a political scientist, and John Holdren as a physicist.

A Nuanced Energy Problem

The Malthusian energy problem had to be reframed—or *rearticulated* in the Kuhnian vocabulary—in the face of growing anomalies. The discovery of a potential human role in global climate change from emissions of greenhouse gases, and in particular carbon dioxide (CO_2) emissions from fossil-fuel combustion, fit the bill perfectly.

Measurements in 1957–58 first documented the increasing concentration of CO_2 in the atmosphere, portending a warming of the earth's surface by an *enhanced* greenhouse effect. This was a theoretical concern only. The worry of the 1970s was anthropogenic global cooling, a phenomenon linked to increasing sulfur dioxide (SO_2) emissions from coal and oil combustion. Mankind's energy emissions were culpable in either direction.

The global-cooling trend that had begun in the 1940s changed into a warming trend by the late 1970s. As early as 1979, the Carter administration debated whether its proposed synthetic-fuels program would increase global warming. Synfuel production and combustion were estimated to emit 40 percent more CO_2 than directly burning coal to generate the same energy. Gus Speth, acting chairman of the President's Council on Environmental Quality, and soon-to-be cofounder of the Natural Resources Defense Council (NRDC), warned Carter personally about this "very important and perhaps historic" scientific development.

When surface-temperature records continued to show warming in the 1980s, the culprit from fossil-fuel emissions shifted from SO_2 (the cooling gas) to CO_2 (the warming gas). Resources for the Future began targeting global warming as a potentially major issue in the early 1980s. By the end of the decade, the meteorological debate was ensconced in the public mind, thanks to highly publicized Senate hearings, featuring NASA scientist James Hansen, held by Al Gore (D-Tenn.) during the heat wave and drought of the summer of 1988.

In 1992, John Holdren reoriented the energy problem, a sign of a paradigm under strain.[8] Holdren's claim of rising energy costs in the face of contrary evidence now had a new component: a social cost that should be added to the paid price. "'Cost' must be understood to include not only monetary but also environmental and sociopolitical components," he stated. Holdren's original position— "the most accessible and cheaply producible oil and gas hav[e] already been

---

8. See Internet appendix 11.3, "Broader Energy Alarmism," at www.politicalcapitalism. org/book1/chapter11/appendix3.html.

depleted"—now had reinforcement with the alleged social costs of import dependence and "higher environmental costs of harvesting and using the more distributed fossil fuels." Then came a third social cost—the costs of substitute nuclear and renewable energies "that avoid the environmental and political liabilities of fossil fuels but create others."

Holdren's nuanced energy problem was not home free. His social costs were shrinking. Air and water pollution were diminishing, and 1970s-style oil interruptions and shortages were nowhere. His ace in the hole, however, at least hypothetically, was anthropogenic climate change. This issue would bring the alarmists out in full force, just as other energy problems receded.

Depletionism, however, was hardly slain. M. King Hubbert died in 1989 at age 86, but the baton was in the hand of geologist Colin Campbell, who wrote in the same year: "Shortages [of crude oil] seem to be inevitable by the late 1990s, but knowledge of an impending supply shortfall may trigger an earlier price response." Campbell, like Hubbert, would reset his global crude-oil peak as his prior prediction dates came and went.[9]

The redefined energy problem of the neo-Malthusians was a major retreat with negative implications for their credibility. "Having rightfully failed to convince people of the threat of exhaustion," one leading energy economist concluded, "the resource pessimists may be seeking new rationales that appear more plausible." To the pessimists, however, the *real* death knell of the modern energy economy had finally surfaced—anthropogenic climate change from the emissions from the carbon-based energy economy. The human influence on climate could only be bad, not neutral or positive. To the true believers in a potential global-warming apocalypse, the optimists, although right on some issues, now had a paradigm problem of their own.

For Enron, the climate-change issue was an opening that Ken Lay would seize upon to differentiate his self-described clean-energy company from the pack. Natural gas (for coal), wind and solar generation, energy-conservation services, emissions trading for greenhouse gases: It worked—to a point. Enron was building foreign power plants that were fired by oil, not natural gas. Solar, wind, and energy services were not profitable—but a quietly formed coal subsidiary was. It was a battle between perception and reality. Adam Smith would have shook his head, Samuel Smiles would have frowned, and Ayn Rand would have chuckled. Energy was no different from anything else. The political means of political capitalism offers transient opportunities, not assured profitability. Underlying consumer demand is primary. The creative destruction of the marketplace would have the last say for Ken Lay, Jeff Skilling, and Enron.

---

9. Also see Internet appendix 11.4, "Contemporary Hubbert Analysis," at www.political capitalism.org/book1/chapter11/appendix4.html.

Epilogue
Surreal Enron, Real Capitalism

T HE ANALYSES OF THE PREVIOUS CHAPTERS point toward three major conclusions.

1. True capitalism is not only uniquely wealth creating but also *moral*. Simple-rules capitalism is an ethically superior socioeconomic system because it maximizes voluntary relations among consenting adults and minimizes the initiation of force (coercion). It requires persuasion and thus inspires reason. Good behavior is encouraged and rewarded, with one judging all and all judging one via impersonal market forces. What Samuel Smiles wrote in 1871 remains true today: The "high culture" of trade "tries character perhaps more severely than any other pursuit of life."

2. Pervasive government intervention disrupts and corrupts the market's natural moral and economic order by encouraging gaming and corner–cutting, while creating economic problems that give rise to further inter-vention. The corrosive process feeds on itself and gradually changes a culture of consumer-driven entrepreneurship to one of politicking, in which the worst can gain advantage and get on top.

3. A long history of industry-sponsored government intervention in energy markets, combined in the 1970s with pernicious price regulation and Malthusian thinking, thoroughly politicized U.S. energy markets. This set the stage for an aggressive, gifted young Ph.D. economist to reach the top of the energy field and, later, for a time, the whole business world. As a company builder and visionary, Ken Lay is arguably the third notable figure in the energy industry to date, after John D. Rockefeller and Samuel Insull. But because of his bad choices at Enron and after, Lay will be remembered as one of the most nefarious businessmen of modern times.

The full story of Ken Lay and Enron—replete with surprises, ironies, and implications—is developed later in this trilogy. But *Capitalism at Work* has illuminated the core flaws of Enron in order to develop some wider lessons for business and society. In particular, the mainstream interpretation that Enron represented a failure of capitalism is erroneous, as is the corollary thesis that Enron proves that market-driven self-interest must be modified to achieve what is called *corporate social responsibility* (CSR).

Enron's many critics have underestimated the codependence between Ken Lay's company and politically manipulated markets (the interventionist state). Enron should be remembered as the *antithesis* of a true capitalist enterprise. In terms of public policy, greater government intervention in search of effective corporate governance is a hair-of-the-dog, tar-baby exercise. Academically, the fundamental tenets of CSR should be revisited. Too many corporate decision makers, policymakers, and business ethicists have scarcely considered capitalism's anti-Enron philosophy, which begins (at least) with Adam Smith's *The Theory of Moral Sentiments* (1759), and continues through the writings of Samuel Smiles in the nineteenth century, the political philosophy of Ayn Rand in the twentieth, and most recently Charles Koch's *The Science of Success* (2007).

Misinterpreting Enron: Capitalism as Whipping Boy

Enron in its heyday was considered a prototype New Economy company and a socially responsible corporation. Then, after its financial collapse in December 2001, the company was vilified. At first, there were a few defenders, on the Left and on the Right.[1] But as the truth seeped out about the inner workings of the company, there were virtually no apologists, apart from ex-Enron defendants who sought to exonerate the company as part of their trial strategy.

In particular, the Left pounced on Enron as a failure of capitalism, a failure of self-interested, profit-maximizing Capitalist Man in an inadequately regulated system. Free-market advocates—such as the *Wall Street Journal* editorial page and the Cato Institute, interpreting Enron as a problem for the free market's ethos—sprang into damage control, which prompted *BusinessWeek* editorialist Robert Kuttner to comment: "Defenders of deregulation are mounting a heroic effort to insist that the debacle was merely a business model gone bad, not an impeachment of freer markets." Kuttner opined elsewhere: "Enron should signal a whole new era of re-regulation—of everything from electricity to pensions to accounting standards."

Alice Rivlin of the Brookings Institution, a venerable think tank associated with left-of-center public policy, added: "The problem of Enron and too many

---

1. Neoconservative Irwin Stelzer complimented Enron "for leading the fight for [natural gas and electricity] competition." Liberal Bill White stated: "Enron . . . called on industry to address the issue of global warming even as some companies feared the impact of pollution control on their bottom lines." The full motivations—and inconsistencies—of Enron's positions in these areas are detailed in Book 3.

other corporations ... demonstrates that we do not yet have the rules of the game right." Specifically, "the accounting rules have not caught up with the rapidly increasing complexity of business transactions."

Thus, a common view was seemingly reconfirmed: Adam Smith's *invisible hand*, while holding true in some ways and for some eras, was now a bygone relic. Thomas McCraw, writing in the post-Enron era, likened Smith's metaphor to the eighteenth-century waterwheel in relation to modern energy infrastructure. The Straus Professor of Business History Emeritus at Harvard Business School added:

> *Modern* capitalism must be actively nurtured and controlled, with sophistication and resolve. Without constant promotion by entrepreneurs and careful monitoring by regulators (a necessity much underestimated by many advocates of the free market, including [Joseph] Schumpeter himself), it cannot achieve or maintain its full potential. Like the actual engines that loom so large in creative destruction—steam, electric, diesel, gasoline, jet—the capitalist engine can slow down, sputter, overheat, explode, or die.

This mindset, attributing Enron's sins to self-interested free-market activity, damned the wrong socioeconomic system. Enron's modus operandi was to escape or manipulate market forces via government forces, not to operate under free-market consumer verdicts. Government intervention was sought to create and shape so-called markets where there were none before. Special government subsidies were demanded and accepted. Only in certain areas—such as rate-and-entry policy for interstate natural gas pipelines—did Enron work to *lighten* the regulatory hand. But those were pragmatic positions, not the result of a philosophy that championed the economic means for business success. Pushing truly free markets was more the exception than the rule at Ken Lay's company.

The false conflation of Enron and capitalism resulted from not only a superficial understanding of Enron's business model in light of ethical, best-practices capitalism but also an incomplete, even naïve, view of business/government relations. For example, a four-volume post-Enron study, *The Accountable Corporation*, made these unchallenged points in regard to America's political capitalism.

- "Since the early years of the nation the government has regulated commerce and business practices to serve the public interest."
- "Many managers believe the best regulation of business consists of no regulation."
- "A serious lesson has been learned—again. Scandal begets regulation."[2]

---

2. Another Enron-inspired tome on corporate governance speaks of "many" corporate lawyers acting as "libertarian antinomian(s)," reflecting "an express contempt for, and disapproval of, law and regulation."

These misconceptions are not new. The discipline of business ethics grew up around just such a flawed belief that business was antipathetic toward regulation. For example, Howard Bowen's pioneering *Social Responsibilities of the Businessman* (1953) concluded: "Businessmen ... are opposed—in principle at least—to restrictions on competition."[3]

But as shown in chapters 5 and 6, the public interest has been compromised, time and again, by the private interest acting in concert with those in political power. A powerful driver of government intervention in America's mixed economy has been prointervention business lobbying, whether for a tariff or quota against imports, an entry restriction on a would-be competitor, forced price transparency, access requirements placed on a service provider, financial subsidies, or special tax provisions. Free-market economists from Adam Smith to Milton Friedman criticized the use of the political means to business ends, as did capitalist moralist Ayn Rand, for whom "the aristocracy of pull" was abhorrent.

In addition to scandal begetting regulation, regulation has also begotten scandal, which, in turn, has led to more intervention. The government-exacerbated and -prolonged Great Depression (or "Great Duration," as one historian called it) set the stage. The fall of the House of Insull, despite the protective umbrella of public utility regulation, resulted in two signature pieces of New Deal legislation: the Securities Act of 1933 and the Public Utility Holding Company Act of 1935. And nearly seven decades later, the collapse of politically driven Enron was a catalyst for passage of both the Public Company Accounting Reform and Investor Protection Act of 2002 (Sarbanes-Oxley Act) and the Bipartisan Campaign Reform Act of 2002. The Financial Derivatives Act of 2002, very much Enron inspired, almost became law. Provisions of the Energy Policy Act of 2005 were designed to prevent a future Enron. However, all these political reactions, furthering intervention rather than removing it, were chasing the symptoms of the problem rather than removing root causes.

Reinterpreting Enron: The Perils of the Mixed Economy

"We definitely have a problem with bad apples," concluded Kim Clark, then dean of the Harvard Business School, in the aftermath of Enron. Yet the Enron-era problem went deeper, he added: "Too many people crossed too many lines. But if you dig into it, we also have a problem with the barrel. We have systemic problems where good people are put into a position where their values are compromised."

Bad apples and business bankruptcies will never be eliminated entirely. But when incentives are market driven, they can be "not much more than one in a thousand," as Adam Smith noted in 1776 with regard to business failures. What

---

3. A second suspect notion permeating business-ethics thought is that capitalism is an *amoral* business system. Bowen states here: "Ethical man was permitted to abdicate to a hypothetical economic man."

Clark's barrel problem reflected were the deep *malincentives* of the mixed economy: the perverse, unintended consequences of the New Deal–launched, half-century-plus effort at rulemaking and oversight undertaken in the elusive quest to govern corporations in the public interest. Prescriptive rulebooks, representing direct or indirect regulation for the most part, have invited opportunistic business behavior—strategies that satisfy the letter rather than the intent of the law and allow form to trump substance.

"Ultimately," concluded author Kurt Eichenwald, "it was Enron's tragedy to be filled with people smart enough to know how to maneuver around the rules, but not wise enough to understand why the rules had been written in the first place." Well said, but what Eichenwald failed to grasp was that the apple of temptation lay in the overprescribed rules themselves. For the opportunists— and there will always be those—weighty rulebooks are not as much an obstacle as a safe harbor, a way to use legal technicalities to camouflage informational misdirection. Contrary to Alice Rivlin, complex rules for a complex world have proved less a cure than an enabler for corporate malfeasance. This is yet another case of unintended consequences from government intervention, a major theme of political economy.

A different approach would be to stop throwing new regulation after bad. Instead of prescribing the *means* of compliance (which can be a frustrating, prolonged process), the focus would turn to *intent-via-result*: a good-faith description of the true state of the business. General principles, not legal minutiae, would govern corporate governance. Common sense and purpose would rise to the fore. The fact of deceit and/or intent to mislead would be the issue posed to judge and jury under a common-law standard that asked whether harm had occurred and redress was needed.

"The proper response to more complex societies should be an ever greater reliance on simple legal rules," concluded Richard Epstein, a professor of law at the University of Chicago, "including older rules too often and too easily dismissed as curious relics of some bygone horse-and-buggy age." This perspective favors general rules and the application of tort law to corporate malfeasance, for, as Epstein states, "government works best when it establishes the rules of the road, not when it seeks to determine the composition of traffic."

A simple, predictable legal framework harks back to Adam Smith's "sacred regard to general rules" and "laws of justice." It is akin to Milton Friedman's dictum that business practices should "confor[m] to the basic rules of the society, both those embodied in law and those embodied in ethical custom." And it is a precondition for entrepreneur/intellectual Charles Koch's admonition that businesses follow "the general rules of just conduct."

Surveying the ruins of Enron, Richard Epstein warned:

> The greatest tragedy of the Enron debacle is not likely to be the consequences of
> its bankruptcy, but from the erroneous institutional reforms that will take hold if

its causes are not well understood. . . . [We must] walk a fine line between complacency in the face of failure and overreaction through excessive regulation.

Yet the feared overreaction occurred. Intellectuals and politicians sold their belief that new regulation and better enforcement could and should corral the elusive Capitalist Man. But to the extent that such prescriptions are at odds with self-interested activity, an iterative process of business-side circumvention and government-side dike plugging will only continue. Thus, it should not be a surprise that the post-Enron rules have produced unintended consequences. "One lesson of Enron was that the idea that companies could make profits without taking any risk proved to be as ridiculous as it sounds," the *Wall Street Journal* reported nearly six years after the company's collapse:

> Regulators made a great show of slamming closed that loophole [in financial reporting]. But as the current situation . . . [of] burying risks in off-balance-sheet vehicles . . . makes clear, they not only didn't close it all the way, but the new rules in some ways made it even harder for investors to figure out what was going on.

The debate over corporate-governance reform in the wake of Sarbanes-Oxley is examined in more detail in Book 3 of this trilogy.

<small>◇·</small>

Political economists have long recognized the challenge of getting regulation right in a mixed economy. "A scheme of state interference for the attainment of some social or economic benefit," stated Hubert Smith in 1887, "will in general succeed or fail according as it is able or unable to cause a change in the nature, habits, and disposition of those whom it affects." A century later, regulatory economist Sanford Ikeda reached a like conclusion: "Interventionism is really a process of entrepreneurial adjustments in both the private and public sectors, where these adjustments tend to be both unanticipated and undesirable (from the viewpoint of the interveners) owing to radical ignorance, complexity, and dispersed information." Some historians have noted the same. The Progressive Era's "stunningly rapid bureaucratic triumph," Richard McCormick wrote in the *American Historical Review*, resulted in "open-ended and unpredictable" state and federal regulation. "Consequences are often unexpected, outcomes surprising when matched against origins."

Even business ethicists dismissive of simple-rules capitalism have acknowledged the limits of government fiat. For example, Duane Windsor states: "It is infeasible fully to regulate a complex economy." The alternative, in this view, is that *Social* Capitalist Man must be classroom coached before entering the thicket of the mixed economy, where an estimated 300,000 potential federal offenses lie in waiting.

However, rule inflation does more than create criminals out of ordinary people, even among those who could be acting ethically. It creates disrespect for the law and breeds opportunistic circumvention, as well as cost-inflating full employment for accountants, lawyers, and other specialists whose only purpose is making sense out of the imposed labyrinth. The danger is that in trying to neuter the bad actors with ever more rules, the good actors are trapped or constrained, and wealth-creating activity is compromised. It might be higher expenses here or greater uncertainty there, all of which serves to undermine the entrepreneurial opportunity of those who work within the environs of fair field, no special favor.

Students and practitioners of regulation have recognized the gulf between passionate intent and hallowed ends on the one side and results on the other. During the 1970s regulatory avalanche, parts of which would be undone by Democrats and Republicans, John Dunlop, the head of the U.S. Department of Labor, critically dissected "the more intensive approach of governmental promulgation of mandatory regulations." Drawing upon the experience at his own agency, whose regulatory programs grew from 18 in 1940 to 40 by 1960 and stood at 134 in 1975, Dunlop identified 11 problem areas, which he described in part as follows:

- "Regulation . . . encourages simplistic thinking about complicated issues" and sets expectations too high in regard to what can be accomplished.

- "Designing and administering a regulatory program is an incredibly complicated task."

- "Oftentimes policies that appear straightforward will have unintended consequences which can create problems as severe as those with which the regulations were intended to deal."

- "The rule-making and adjudicatory procedures of regulatory agencies tend to be very slow, creating conflicts between the different groups involved, and leading to weak and ineffective remedies for the people the programs aim to help."

- "The rule-making and adjudicatory procedures do not include a mechanism for the development of mutual accommodation among the conflicting interests."

- "Regulatory efforts are rarely abandoned even after their purpose has been served."

- "Legal gameplaying between the regulatees and the regulators" results from the fact that "no set of men is smart enough to write words around which others cannot find holes when the stakes are high."

- There are difficulties "encountered by small and medium size firms in complying with the regulations of the various agencies," as well as "problems the government has in trying to enforce compliance."

- "Over time as the rule-making and compliance activities of regulatory agencies become routine, it grows increasingly difficult . . . to attract highly qualified and effective administrators into leadership positions."

- "Uniform national regulations are inherently unworkable in many situations because the society is not uniform."

- "[There is] 'regulatory overlap,' where a number of different regulatory agencies share some of the same responsibilities."

"The central issue," stated Dunlop, is that "the country needs to acquire a more realistic understanding of the limits to the degree to which social change can be brought about through legal compulsion." Although not espousing wholesale deregulation, he longed for "new attitudes" and "new relationships and procedures" so that command-and-control could give way to self-help's "persuasion, mutual accommodation and problem-solving."

Reorienting Business Ethics

"We live in a post-Enron world" begins an essay by legal scholar and business ethicist John Hasnas. "The corporate scandals that rocked American business over the last four years have brought renewed attention to the importance of ingraining the principles of business ethics into the corporate environment."

This obligatory cliché, a "vacuous bromide" Hasnas playfully confesses, indicates the extent to which Enron has become a defining event in corporate governance and a call to arms for teaching ethics to business students. But fundamental questions relating to the cause and cure of systemic corporate malfeasance are unsettled in the still-young post-Enron era. And that is good news, for much of what has been concluded to date is incomplete at best and misleading at worst.

Enron's fall is explicable in terms of questionable business plans, poor execution, and a lack of midcourse correction. The company's Icarus-like ambitions did it in. Many norms and rules were violated in the desperate attempt to placate investors, including thousands of Enron employees whose stock ownership in ENE (Enron's ticker symbol) was vital to their wealth. It was a hothouse for that "badness of trade" codified by Samuel Smiles more than a century before.

The scale, scope, and surprise of the debacle—the "systemic failure" identified by journalist George Will—requires getting to the *why* behind the why. The case study of Ken Lay and his company, it turns out, illuminates the capitalistic worldview of ethical, successful, sustainable business practice in a unique, powerful way—with important implications for the study and teaching of business ethics, that uneasy hybrid of philosophy and commerce.

Competing Views

Business ethics has been defined as "the study of what constitutes right and wrong, or good and bad, human conduct in a business context." As an academic discipline, business ethics is relatively new. It reached critical mass in the 1970s, leading to the formation of the Society of Business Ethics in 1980. But the movement has a longer history, as evidenced by Milton Friedman's 1962 attack on the "social responsibility" of business and labor as a "fundamentally subversive doctrine." Friedman's stark verdict was spelled out in the *New York Times Magazine* in a 1970 essay that remains a touchstone in the debate today.

Business, Friedman argued, can effectively serve only one master—its owners—by winning profits in accord with investor expectations, while respecting legal and ethical norms. Friedman warned about serving multiple masters: "If businessmen do have a social responsibility other than making maximum profits for stockholders," he asked, "how are they to know what it is?"

Working in the Friedman tradition, Elaine Sternberg has identified maximizing long-term owner value as the *very essence* of being a business. In her conception, a firm that purports to be a business but seeks to be a charity or a surrogate for government does more than simply lose its comparative advantage. For Sternberg, such activity contradicts what *being a business* is all about. In a corporate context, deviations from wealth creation also run afoul of the principal/agent relationship, which raises a separate host of ethical issues. Thus, the CSR notion that "refraining from business [is] the condition of being ethical in business" represents a "central contradiction." Nevertheless, she acknowledges that "even when the purpose of a business is conceived narrowly, as nothing but the maximization of long-term owner value, business must still take into account everything that affects achievement of that limited goal."

Sternberg identifies two constraints that value-maximizing businesses must respect to be ethical: classical distributive justice (proportionally rewarding contributions to the organizational objective) and "'ordinary decency': honesty, fairness, avoiding physical violence and coercion, and a presumption in favour of legality." She warns that pandering to a nonbusiness objective or other unethical conduct "can lead to very substantial charges, both legal and financial . . . [and] can cost a business its very life."

CSR theory speaks of the need for business to meet a *triple bottom line* whereby profit making is joined by environmental and social metrics. But agreeing on, much less applying, noneconomic metrics makes any "sustainable capitalism transition," as advocated by John Elkington, tenuous at best. Elkington himself warns that the exercise is "one of the most complex our species has ever had to negotiate."

In theory and practice, CSR introduces ambiguities and complexities that are not present for self-interested activity under simple-rules capitalism. Social values and objectives are in the eye of the beholder and can be diametrically opposed, depending on one's economic analysis or emotional predilections. "The discussions of 'social responsibility' are notable for their analytical looseness and lack of rigor," complained Milton Friedman in 1970. Nearly 35 years later, Duane Windsor admits that "it is very difficult to offer a logically compelling definition of discretionary corporate social responsibility, as distinct from a prudential altruism to forestall greater government regulation."

What Friedman saw in corporate social responsibility decades ago many see today: a hidden agenda, a *driving assumption*, that business is underregulated, that market failures abound, and that self-interested profit taking is suspect. In other words, government is either not doing enough or simply cannot do enough, requiring a subdiscipline to apply ethics to business in order to check the default impulse of capitalist self-interest toward profit making.

Business philosopher Tibor Machan has complained that the usual fare of business ethics is "thinly veiled business bashing" predicated on the belief that "what we need to do is tame business by government intervention, regulation or litigation." He adds: "Instead of seeing business as the institutional expression of . . . virtue—the good deeds people engage in carrying out economically prudent endeavors—business itself, as a profession, is something that is mostly distrusted and denigrated."

Not surprisingly, business ethics as a discipline was developed by critics of capitalism, necessitating defensive responses from capitalism's advocates, such as Friedman and Machan. Defenders of simple-rules capitalism, on the other hand, see good and bad business as fairly self-evident, assuming private-property rights and the rule of law are in good order, complete with market-oriented approaches that better internalize the negative externalities of so-called commons problems.[4] A good business is one that plays by the rules of just conduct and creates wealth by the economic means; a bad business is one that breaks the rules and/or lives by political favor. Good businesses prove themselves by registering profits over time; bad businesses fail the market test and contract or disappear. Good and bad in business *can* be fathomed from common sense and standards of ordinary decency, despite a view from one business ethicist that it is "dangerous" to believe "that ethics is what we learn at our parents' knees." For business success, stated Samuel Smiles more than a century ago, is "usually the path of common sense."

Misplaced Activism

The disconcerting revelations that emerged after Enron's bankruptcy inspired a group of Houston business and law professors to study what went wrong at the once iconic hometown company, as well as to draw lessons for the classroom and for public policy.[5] One of those professors was Duane Windsor, a business ethicist at Rice University, who wrote an open letter to the Association to Advance Collegiate Schools of Business (AACSB)—supported by 200 of his academic colleagues and two business-ethics associations—asking that the

---

4. Commons areas include public land, many water areas, and the air. The challenge for market-oriented reform is to "create the right incentives for productive behavior at low administrative cost." Privatization, for example, can allow the new owner to apply stewardship to increase capital values, while using the rule of law to challenge and redress invasion and harms.

5. *Enron: Corporate Fiascos and Their Implications* (2004), edited by the dean of the University of Houston Law School and a chair business professor at Rice University, had 32 contributors, 8 of whom were from these two Houston universities alone.

accreditation agency require a stand-alone ethics course in every MBA curriculum. One-third of the nation's business schools had such an offering, but Windsor saw the "crisis" of corporate governance as requiring "a universal and essential mandate in the public interest."

Business ethicist Diane Swanson of Kansas State University also fronted the effort, expressing alarm that "most MBAs will graduate without an anchor in social and environmental management," leaving them with "an amoral, even brutish theory of management [that] has long been taught in business schools." She stoked the controversy by asking whether business schools were complicit in the recent spate of corporate malfeasance by not requiring or properly teaching business ethics—and even asked for a federal inquiry to this end.

To Windsor, the problem got back to "the Enron value set" of "an extreme laissez-faire ideology of absolutely 'free' (i.e., absolutely unregulated) markets." Amoral Enroners in amoral markets created the immorality and crisis that Windsor, Swanson, and others sought to redress, one student and one executive at a time.

But this misdiagnosis raises questions about the proffered educational remedies. The conclusion-turned-assumption that Enron represented capitalism par excellence suggests that reform is needed less in the business of capitalism than in the business of business ethics.

To repeat: Enron lived, thrived, and perished in and through the mixed economy. Enron's artificial boom and decisive bust was an extreme outcome of interventionism and its philosophical antecedents that, ironically, had to do with academic and political correctness. Ken Lay's meteoric rise and stunning fall was not the saga of a capitalist wildcatter; it was a tragedy of political rent-seeking, second-hander strategies, and postmodernist thinking. Unfortunately, interventionism in America's mixed economy was pervasive enough to allow Enron to get on top. Fortunately, the free market was robust enough to render a swift verdict once the philosophic and prosecutable frauds of Enron became known.

Enroners themselves were extremely well educated—even overeducated relative to on-the-job experience. The hundreds of newly minted MBAs rolling into Enron yearly were drilled in corporate social responsibility by *Dr.* Kenneth L. Lay. Enron brandished a detailed code of ethics (50+ pages), and Lay repeatedly emphasized his handpicked values for the company: *respect, integrity, communication*, and *excellence*. Enron dedicated employees and formed a $2 million task force to advance CSR. But Enron found it hard being green in an environmental, not only financial, sense. Like BP (the old British Petroleum, which now styled itself Beyond Petroleum), Enron became distracted by trying to be too many things to too many people. Its triple-bottom-line aspiration destroyed wealth and was, according to the Sternberg view, most unbusiness-like.

In retrospect, Enron's many and far-flung operatives, working within a mother-may-I mixed economy, threw niceties overboard in the exigencies of the often troubled moment. There were too many deals to execute, projects to complete, numbers to meet. There was always more fire than water. With a safe harbor of meeting legal technicalities, there was room to be amoral (or worse) to dodge those 300,000 tripwires.

Business schools cannot be expected to educate away opportunistic behavior in the heavily mixed economy, where overregulation begets rule breaking and even scandal. There will always be an underclass of opportunists. Simple-rules capitalism, not proscription, creates an environment in which the good actors can dominate the quick-buck artists.

An Honorable Profession

Profit making in an open, competitive economy requires foresight and discipline. Milton Friedman noticed how "the difficulty of exercising 'social responsibility'" was a backdoor confirmation of "the great virtue of private competitive enterprise—it forces people to be responsible for their own actions and makes it difficult for them to 'exploit' other people for either selfish or unselfish purposes." Antisocial behavior, in other words, can be addressed by the market process.

True capitalism's prime movers—by virtue of their success in an economic system marked by voluntary relations—tend to be principled and ethical. The so-called doer in open commerce—as spelled out by Adam Smith, Samuel Smiles, and Ayn Rand in their different eras—is self-interested, authentic, realistic, and honest. Each has an intellectual side and guards against conceit and self-deceit. Rules are respected, even inviolate. Successful businesspeople persevere and accept accountability. Prudence and self-reliance check cronyism, extravagance, groupthink, nepotism, overambition, and political plays.

Free-market corporations are about heroic vision and goodwill for successful tomorrows, not only daily dollar grubbing. The entrepreneurial prophets behind entrepreneurial profits have humane vistas too. Perhaps even a smidgen of CSR practice predated the advocacy of wholesale CSR. "We cannot interpret the motives of businessmen solely in terms of profit maximization," wrote Howard Bowen in 1953. "He recognizes increasingly that his own long-run self-interest calls for the adjustment of his policies and actions with a regard to their social effects."

But the perennial danger is that the social avocation of the entrepreneur will become the primary vocation, leading to second-hander strategies, foregone wealth creation, even business ruin. All this is unnecessary, for business leaders are generally checked and balanced by civil society. And in less political settings, with no regulatory technicalities to provide the safe harbor of amoral compliance, civil society's discipline on business activity can be expected to strengthen, not diminish.

A reorientation of business ethics should consider the moral issues present in noncapitalistic institutions. Regimes of political power around the world are plagued by cronyism, nepotism, and power plays. The ethics of consumer-driven profit-and-loss enterprise is different from the ethics of bureaucracies (not only government agencies but also nonprofits, including educational institutions such as business schools). Such an inclusive view of ethics in action could rescue the study of business ethics from itself, for as Elaine Sternberg has warned: "If 'business ethics' is taken to denote a separate business ethic, a set of ethical rules that apply exclusively in business and nowhere else, then there is indeed no such thing."[6] In such a reconstruction, courses in "Corporate Citizenship," "Corporate Social Responsibility" and "Business Ethics" could be recast as "Organizational Ethics," or even "Organizational Success."[7]

Enron Lives! Political Energy Today

In one important respect, Enron lives and thrives today. The issue concerns the energy-sustainability debate, a pillar of the modern CSR movement. Coal, oil, and natural gas emissions have been linked to global climate change through an enhanced greenhouse effect. Alarm over anthropogenic (man-made) global warming has created a political movement to mandate reductions of fossil-fuel emissions through supply-side substitution of low-carbon (natural gas) or no-carbon (wind, solar) energies and through demand-side reductions in energy usage.

Enron championed climate alarmism/energy transformation between 1988 and 2001 (most of its solvent life) and built important profit centers around climate-related government policies. The "green MBAs" lauded by Diane Swanson had a home at Enron as at few other corporations of the 1990s. And what CSR champions today regarding energy policy is little different from Ken Lay's vision for Enron.

As chronicled in Part III, energy alarmism has a cautionary past. It began with the "coal panic" of W. S. Jevons, whose 1865 book, *The Coal Question: An Inquiry Concerning the Progress of the Nation, and the Probable Exhaustion of our Coal-mines*, was smartly reasoned but ultimately errant in some of its important conclusions, as explained in chapter 7. Coal demand in England grew far less than Jevons projected, and there was much more economically recoverable coal on the island than he thought, because of what today is recognized as the *ultimate* resource—human ingenuity. Coal costs and prices would not surge, and depletion would not leave the island with a shell of its most valuable resource industry.

---

6. Applying ethics to the teaching of business ethics would remind instructors that it is "a professor's duty . . . not to indoctrinate [his students] but to clarify, familiarize, explain, and provide a just treatment of a subject by considering major viewpoints on it." The Statement on Professional Ethics of the American Association of University Professors also speaks to "intellectual honesty" and "critical self-discipline and judgement" and the "professor's . . . deep conviction of the worth and dignity of the advancement of knowledge."

7. Business ethics as a discipline would also benefit from a greater appreciation of methodological individualism, discussed in Internet appendix E.1, "Ethical Individualism," at www.politicalcapitalism.org/book1/Epilogue/appendix1.html.

England's coal industry would encounter severe challenges in the twentieth century, but it was not because of a shortage of resources. Rather, it resulted from a surplus of government, whereby interventionist public policies stymied the market's entrepreneurial process.

America became the center of alarmism soon after its energy industry became the world leader. Running-out-of-oil predictions were periodically heard, but it was not until the 1960s (population-bomb scare: Paul Ehrlich) and the 1970s (mineral-resource scare: The Club of Rome) that neo-Malthusianism took hold, as told in chapter 9. However, this scientific consensus—after all, everyone *knew* that minerals must deplete—was challenged by the data and one indefatigable researcher in particular. Julian Simon broke through the emotional, virtually unified opposition of the natural-science community and brought many in the economics profession to his viewpoint. Neo-Malthusianism was in open debate, despite Ehrlich's and others' protestations.

Embracing Climate Alarmism

Another scare, mentioned in chapter 11, concerned man-made global cooling, which was blamed on rising sulfur dioxide (SO_2) emissions from coal plants. SO_2 was considered a cooling agent, and the world was in a cooling trend between the 1940s and 1970s. Then, as now, coal caught the heat from its impact on climate.

But by the 1980s, a global warming trend was evident, something that had been theoretically predicted beforehand. Now, with measurements confirming an increasing concentration of greenhouse gases (GHG) in the atmosphere, a new alarm was sounded: Human activity was making the climate warmer and wetter and raising the sea level. For "a planet [that] has been delivered in perfect working condition and cannot be exchanged for a new one," stated Paul Hawken, Amory Lovins, and L. Hunter Lovins, this was a scary thought.

The alleged climate crisis is at the center of a powerful contemporary neo-Malthusian movement that has judged self-interested economic activity to be incompatible with a healthy environment. A variety of ills are linked to the existing and anticipated (man-made) greenhouse signal. The new neo-Malthusianism rejects a nonpolitical solution that relies on free-market wealth creation and adaptation. Just such a strategy, however, is the one that society will increasingly employ, for two reasons. First, long-lived GHGs in the atmosphere have predetermined future climate change. Second, consumers favor affordable, plentiful energy over its government-engineered opposite.

Still, there is a political push to *mitigate* business-as-usual GHG emissions to prevent some portion of the future human influence on climate, however small and however costly the effort. To one degree or another, the carbon-reduction crusade will raise energy prices, increase the up-front price of energy-using equipment, and otherwise ration energy usage. These negatives apply to the developed world where piecemeal government intervention is taking hold (as predicted by Ken Lay and Enron). But these costs lie in waiting for the more than 1 billion people who are eager to receive modern energies for the first time to replace primitive biomass and dung as their primary fuel sources. The immediate opportunity for fossil fuels to alleviate energy poverty in the developing world is a practical and moral challenge to neo-Malthusianism energy policy today.

Carbon dioxide (CO_2) is the predominant man-made greenhouse gas. Yet it is essential to life and not a pollutant in the ordinary sense of the term (humans exhale it; plants breathe it). Societal progress has gone hand-in-hand with increasing fossil-fuel consumption and concordant GHG emissions. A climate-policy expert at the U.S. Department of the Interior, Indur Goklany, summarized the key statistics:

> In the last two centuries, global population has increased more than seven-fold from about 900 million to about 6.5 billion today; manufacturing industry by more than 75-fold; carbon dioxide emissions from fossil fuel combustion by 600-fold; and global economic product has increased more than 60-fold.

"The data indicate that human well-being has improved and continues to improve for the vast majority of the world's population," Goklany concludes. Part of this improvement, he adds, has been the work of CO_2, which has boosted agricultural productivity from fertilization, longer growing seasons, and increased water-use efficiency.

Thus, to the critics of climate neo-Malthusianism, the distinct advantages of carbon-based energies over renewables (as explained by Jevons nearly 150 years ago) make coal, natural gas, and oil part of the *solution* to future challenges with climate and weather. Energy—abundant, affordable energy—is humankind's "master resource" to prepare for and adapt to an uncertain, changing future.

Energy consumerism limits government mitigation strategies. Two decades of ferocious debate and political posturing have produced little apparent change in either consumer energy patterns or GHG emissions. The current market share of carbon-based fuels, in the United States and globally, exceeds 80 percent, an amount that is expected to continue for the next decades. And given growing energy demand, particularly in the developing countries, global GHG emissions are forecast to rise by more than one-half by 2030. Neo-Malthusians face a tears-in-the-ocean problem in terms of the solution to their defined problem.

·◇·

Beginning in the late 1980s, global warming became a bread-and-butter issue for Ken Lay, Enron's leader and up-and-coming industry visionary. Enron in the 1990s became a full-fledged *green* company, practicing so-called energy sustainability with its investments in energy-efficiency services, environmental services, solar power, and wind power.

No U.S.-based company sounded the tocsin over climate change more than Enron. What John Browne did as head of the international energy major BP, Ken Lay did in the United States, working with interest groups and political leaders to push the energy industry and public toward CO_2 regulation. Lay had his reasons—seven in terms of company profit centers, all of which stood to gain from government restrictions on carbon emissions. The profit centers involved

- Natural gas production (relative to oil and coal)
- Natural gas transmission (relative to oil and coal)
- Natural gas–fired electricity generation (relative to oil and coal)
- Energy outsourcing (aka energy efficiency) services
- Renewable energy generation (wind and solar)
- CO_2 emissions trading (joining company trading in sulfur dioxide and nitrogen oxide)
- Environmental outsourcing (aka environmental services)

Of these, Enron's natural gas activities were core, profitable activities (and win-win economically and environmentally, in their important applications). But the last four areas were problematic from the start and never profitable, even with special government favor. In retrospect, almost no amount of government subsidy would have been enough for these nascent businesses.

But there was always hope. In late 1997, an elated Enron lobbyist reported that a climate-change accord was reached in Kyoto, Japan, among 38 Annex 1 countries (the developed world) to reduce their collective greenhouse-gas emissions by 5.2 percent by 2008–2012 compared to base 1990 levels. The United States, itself committed to a 7 percent decrease, at least in principle, would need new waves of government intervention to reduce its emissions, which meant more subsidies and new mandates for politically correct renewable energies (wind and solar, not hydropower) and energy-conservation programs. Thus, Enron's John Palmisano wrote from Kyoto:

> If implemented [the Kyoto Protocol] will do more to promote Enron's business than will almost any other regulatory initiative outside of restructuring of the [electricity] and natural gas industries in Europe and the United States. . . . The endorsement of emissions trading was another victory for us. . . . This agreement will be good for Enron stock!!

It was time to turn deeds into dollars, he added. "Enron now has excellent credentials with many 'green' interests including Greenpeace, WWF [World Wildlife Fund], NRDC [Natural Resources Defense Council], GermanWatch, the US Climate Action Network, the European Climate Action Network, Ozone Action, WRI [World Resources Institute], and Worldwatch [Institute]," reported Palmisano. "This position should be increasingly cultivated and capitalized on (monetized)."

Enron was popular at Kyoto. Palmisano spoke on panels and received an award from the Climate Institute on behalf of Ken Lay and Enron. And the praise continued. Worldwatch Institute's *State of the World 1998* identified Lay's company as a key player in a coming "energy revolution," explaining that

"Enron, originally a large Texas-based natural gas company, has made a strong move in the renewables field with its acquisition of Zond, the largest wind power company in the United States, and its investment in Solarex, the second largest U. S. manufacturer of photovoltaic cells."

Although closely associated with both Bush administrations, Lay was ideologically closer to another political figure on the issue of climate change. As Enron's chairman once declared: "In *Earth in the Balance*, Senator Al Gore stated: 'Higher taxes on fossil fuels . . . is one of the logical first steps in changing our policies in a manner consistent with a more responsible approach to the environment.' I agree."

Enron and Lay have come and gone. Today, Al Gore has declared a "planetary emergency" from rising concentrations of CO_2 and other man-made greenhouse gases in the atmosphere. For him, this emergency is all about 5 billion people using carbon-based fuels. (But another emergency is that 1.5 billion are living in energy poverty without access to oil, gas, and coal.) The EU has adopted the cap-and-trade program that Enron sought. The United States is considering the same. Wind and solar are seen as staples of a new energy future. Energy efficiency well beyond what has been achieved so far (about a one-third improvement since the 1970s) is seen as a necessary but not sufficient condition to achieve so-called energy sustainability. These post-Enron trends have everything to do with Ken Lay's business model, yet that model failed Enron in its parts and as a whole strategy.[8]

But was Enron right when it adopted the CSR view of sustainable energy? Should new light be cast on a company that banked on the right issue but simply failed to turn it into profits? Should Ken Lay, an empathetic, well-meaning man to many who really knew him, be considered as a prophet, a Paul Revere, for getting corporate America to confront the issue of the human influence on climate? Or was Enron's energy-sustainability play merely opportunism, simply another example of a promiscuous modus operandi based on political rent-seeking?

Certainly, guilt by association is not argument enough to conclude that the current mantra for government-driven energy sustainability is off track. But Enron certainly did not know the answers to the very complicated, multifaceted climate debate. The company was not a science institute or a think tank; it was playing what it perceived to be a political high card in the United States and Europe, one that gave it a significant rent-seeking advantage, to help outdistance the oil majors and become, at least in Lay's mind, *the world's leading energy company*.

Ken Lay was, foremost, a pragmatist—and hence an opportunist. While president of Transco Energy, a natural gas company with coal interests, he blessed a primary role for coal, the most carbon-intensive fossil fuel of all. "Over time we as a nation, and the world for that matter," he said in 1982, "will have

---

8. In each year and for each division (energy outsourcing, environmental outsourcing, solar, wind), Enron incurred losses under realistic, full-cost accounting.

to increasingly rely on coal as one of our basic energy fuels, along with oil and gas." But that was before climate concerns hit full stride. Enron expected and hoped that the human influence on climate was just enough of a problem to drive government energy policy, and to this end Enron worked diligently to help the green lobby outdistance both the oil lobby and the coal lobby.

Corporate Social Responsibility

In the fall of 2001, Ken Lay's words set the tone for what would be Enron's last Environmental, Health, and Safety Management Conference:

> We believe that incorporating environmental and social considerations into the way we manage risk, govern our projects, and develop products and services will help us maintain our competitive advantage. As we move forward, we will leverage our intellectual capital and innovative capabilities to promote sustainable business practices around the world.

At this meeting, Enron's CSR task force listed its accomplishments as follows:

- Secured board oversight of social/environmental performance
- Expressed support for Universal Declaration of Human Rights
- Completed corporate responsibility task force
- Developed and pilot-tested human rights audit
- Developed security and human rights guidelines
- Established formal partnerships with WBCSD [World Business Council on Sustainable Development], IBLF [International Business Leaders Forum], and CI [Conservation International]
- Identified language to strengthen code of ethics
- Providing project support—Calypso, Transredes, Dabhol and Cuiabá
- Responding to stakeholder concerns on an ongoing basis

The task force recommendations and goals included the following:

- Formally adopt CERES Principles . . .
- Complete indigenous people's [sic] policy . . .
- Specify social/environmental expectations in formal relationships with vendors and contractors . . .
- Review results of stakeholder survey and develop strategy to address outcome
- Create awareness of social/environmental trends among [Enron's] origination and investment groups . . .
- Add corporate responsibility performance attribute to PRC [Performance Review Committee] process . . .
- Present task force recommendations to Dr. Lay and senior management

Make no mistake: Enron was *trying* to practice CSR in order to monetize its so-called green energy model. This had been Lay's strategy for a decade with natural gas, as well as internationally, as with Enron Global Affairs's 1999 launch of the Social and Environmental Responsibility Program.

Enron's CSR initiatives came to a screeching halt in December 2001, along with all the company's other discretionary activities. The company was out of money and out of time. But the ship went down with its green lights on.

"I have never known much good done by those who affected to trade for the publick good," Adam Smith cautioned in 1776. "It is an affectation, indeed, not very common among merchants, and very few words need be employed in dissuading them from it." Milton Friedman said the same in his 1970 essay on the social responsibility of business.

Politically Correct Investments

On close inspection, Enron was trying to have its cake and eat it too. The company was building oil-fired power plants internationally and erecting (sans press releases) a profitable coal subsidiary. This created internal tensions, but Enron president Jeff Skilling assuaged the concerns of one of his coal executives with the words: "Mike, we are a green energy company, but the green stands for money." Still, with $300 million (and counting) invested in coal properties and the imminent prospect of becoming the world's leading coal trader, coming on top of a decision to sell the solar division, Enron's head of European government affairs warned in 1999, "Our position as a 'green' company is getting thin."

It was not easy being green. Environmentalists lambasted Enron for building energy projects in pristine areas, even wind turbines in southern California. Wind (when blowing) was mostly backing out natural gas, the cleanest of the fossil fuels, which created a financial downside for natural gas giant Enron.

Enron stayed silent on the patent disadvantages of wind relative to natural gas in terms of cost and reliability. Wind is a free energy input, but turning wind into electricity is much more capital intensive than generating electricity with relatively BTU-intensive fossil fuels. Wind power has been propped up by disproportionate tax subsidies, as well as by state-level mandates requiring that utilities buy renewable energy whether or not they need it. In particular, the wind-power boom in Texas has not been about economics. It originated in a successful lobbying effort by Enron Wind Corporation in 1999 to include the nation's strictest renewable quota mandate in an electricity restructuring bill. Texas Governor George W. Bush aided Ken Lay on that one.

Solar power was (and still is) several times more expensive than wind power—and hopelessly uneconomic compared to gas-fired generation. Yet Enron hoodwinked the public in 1994, claiming that its proposed $150 million project could produce solar power "at rates competitive with those of energy generated from oil, gas and coal."

A business-section feature in the *New York Times*, "Solar Power, for Earthly Prices: Enron Plans to Make the Sun Affordable," reported Enron's pledge to deliver power to the federal government for $0.055 per kilowatt hour from a 100-megawatt solar farm within two years, comparable to the average cost of delivered electricity across the nation. Enron's rate was unheard of, exceeding even the most optimistic estimates from environmental pressure groups. But it was highly contrived, depending on a raft of government subsidies (some in the law; others, requested), as well as questionable assumptions about delivery schedules, financing, and technology. The rate was also back-loaded, with compounded annual cost escalations for 30 years.

Still, the quoted rate was taken at face value, as if a new era of solar affordability had suddenly dawned. Two officials from the Clinton administration's Department of Energy were quoted in the *New York Times*. "This establishes the benchmark we want and restarts a stalled solar industry," said the head of DOE's photovoltaic section. Deputy Secretary William White (aka Bill White, later mayor of Houston, and one of Enron's last defenders) stated his intention to try to help make the economics of the project work. But the smoke-and-mirrors project was too much even for the Clinton administration. The project languished and quietly died. Nevertheless, it provided a heady PR moment for a politically correct company.

Turning from the supply side to the demand side, Enron excited environmentalists (as well as stock analysts) with Enron Energy Services (EES), known in the trade as an energy service company (ESCO). EES offered energy outsourcing services for large commercial and industrial customers under long-term contracts. Under these contracts, the company and Enron would split the energy-cost savings, at least theoretically. Who could complain about private-sector strategies that saved money and reduced energy usage and emissions at the same time?

EES cochairman Thomas E. (Tom) White estimated the customer cost savings around 20 percent. Ken Lay put the energy-use savings near 10 percent, which inspired some within the company to advocate certifying customers as "Kyoto compliant." (The idea was ultimately rejected.)

But such reductions were only the beginning, according to energy conservationists Amory Lovins and Joseph Romm. They argued in articles, books, and talks that so much more energy savings and greenhouse-gas emission reductions were profitable that compliance with the Kyoto Protocol was possible, if not easy.

"ESCO's are DEFINITELY the future," Joe Romm e-mailed Enron. In his book *Cool Companies* (1999), Romm wrote: "Cool buildings that cut energy use—and hence greenhouse gas emissions—*in half* are increasingly commonplace." He saw massive opportunities for easy savings. *"The entire notion that low-hanging fruit is easily exhausted turns out to be a myth,"* Romm wrote in italics.

EES bought 200 copies of *Cool Companies* to give to existing and potential customers. The respect was mutual. Enron is "a company I greatly respect," Romm e-mailed.

And then there was Amory Lovins, whose conservationist vision went beyond even that of Romm. "Something like 80% or 90% of the electricity now sold is uncompetitive with electricity-saving technologies," Lovins told *BusinessWeek* in

1984. Consequently, he predicted that the demand for electricity would fall and that new power plants would not be needed.

Eighteen years later, with EES smoldering in ruins, Lovins estimated that the nation's electricity bill could be cut in half, with energy efficiency leading the way. "That's not a free lunch," Lovins proclaimed. "It's a lunch you're paid to eat."

But EES's (much smaller) energy savings consisted mainly of speculation and accounting tricks. EES's contracts were liabilities parading as assets. The division was closed as an operating concern upon the parent's bankruptcy filing and proved to be unsalable. Moreover, the entire ESCO business was in disarray, with market leaders, such as PG&E Energy Services and DukeSolutions, calling it quits. Saving energy profitably, above and beyond what companies had been doing prior to outsourcing, was skinny on profits relative to risk. The Romm/Lovins idea of free lunches was highly exaggerated. Free or low-cost compliance with the Kyoto Protocol was little more than a postmodernist dream on both the demand side and the supply side—at least as far as what buyers naturally choose.

Enron's PR pitch from beginning to end was loud and clear: that renewables and step-change efficiency improvements were tomorrow's energy. "We've bet on the future, while others have bet on the past," John Palmisano proclaimed to the trade press in December 1997 from Kyoto, Japan. But W. S. Jevons circa 1865 offered better insight about energy's past and future. He explained how increasing energy efficiency—then in stark evidence—was accompanied by *increasing* overall energy usage and, in fact, was a cause of it. Jevons also explained why renewable energies were unsuitable for the industrial age. Falling water, wind, and burning wood did not have the economy and/or reliability to power the machine age, a statement that still holds true today. The concentrated energy embedded in coal, natural gas, and oil—the sun's work over the ages—was a quantum leap over the dilute, irregular energy flow from the sun. Coal, gas, and oil are also easily stored and transported compared to most forms of renewables.

As smart and educated as he was, Ken Lay—the industry visionary—was not a true intellectual. Unlike Jevons, he did not fathom the place of fossil fuels relative to renewables in the energy equation. Unlike Samuel Insull, Ken Lay did not really understand energy technology. He read as many executive summaries as anyone, but in the final analysis, he was not a truth seeker, one who challenges his own beliefs and makes necessary, even humbling, midcourse changes. He was a how-can-it-help-me now, what-politically-do-I-need-to-do opportunist. As it turned out, Lay failed to comprehend true energy sustainability (as judged by technical realities and consumer choice) and overplayed his political hand beyond his company's natural gas core.

A New Consensus?

Potentially catastrophic climate change, it is said, necessitates a government-led transformation of the U.S. and world energy market to so-called clean fuels and energy efficiency. The debate is over, and neo-Malthusianism—finally—has grounding in reality. Ken Lay was just ahead of his time. Or so it may appear.

In reality, this is an old song, new verse. Chapters 10 and 11 chronicled how a like consensus, long on emotion and dismissive of contrary data, was falsified by reality. And so it has been in other great policy debates of our time. Ludwig von Mises and F. A. Hayek fought against the central-planning consensus—and won. Economist Milton Friedman did likewise against the Keynesian consensus. "The Doomslayer" of our story, Julian Simon, has good company.

The physical science behind climate change is not settled in favor of alarmism—much less an imperative that governments worldwide mandate a new energy future. Climate models predicting distant pessimistic climate scenarios are problematic. Actual warming has lagged behind predicted warming, suggesting that climate sensitivity to GHG forcing is less severe than thought. Skeptics of climate alarmism/policy activism argue that the human influence on climate has positive economic and environment effects too, and policy action against consumer-driven business-as-usual energy markets has significant costs that must be compared to, and discounted against, the alleged future benefits.

Climate alarmism is very much a two-sided debate in its physical, economic, and policy dimensions. The scientific method does not work by agendas, emotion, or even consensus. The fact that virtually everyone *thought* that Enron was a great company did not make it one. The fact that scientists *thought* that the world was running short of resources did not mean that it was true. And just because the United Nations' Intergovernmental Panel on Climate Change has declared that the climate is or will be in crisis and that major government action is necessary does not make it true. There is an independent reality beyond consciousness, and no amount of posturing in the debate will change either the underlying physical reality of climate science or the technological choices dictating economic tradeoffs with energy alternatives and the environment.

Political capitalism has brought out the worst in American business. Government funding may have done the same with the current generation of atmospheric scientists and those of other disciplines who are locked into a neo-Malthusian mindset. To these true believers, there is little pause in the face of great uncertainties, such as the gulf between modeled and real climate, and the public-policy tradeoffs of government energy activism. For them, the science is settled, and political decision making should trump the welfare of energy consumers.

Only the future will tell for sure, but the climate debate shows signs of yet another classic case of an arrogance, form-over-substance, and obstinacy problem, which can be traced back to heart-over-head emotionalism, groupthink, and personal conceit and deceit. As the middle ground of this debate slowly emerges, more troubling analogies to Enron may well come to light.

Toward Heroic Capitalism

"Corporate social responsibility," one critic noted, "remains more a set of complaints and criticisms than it is a real managerial alternative to traditional views of corporate organization and purpose." Indeed, stakeholder theory has proved troublesome in practice, reflecting its conceptual ambiguities. Defining specifically what a business should do outside of its self-determined profit-and-loss calculus is debatable, difficult to measure, and, ultimately, subjective. After all, a business is not a government agency or a nonprofit charity. Neither is a business a club, family, or hobbyist league.

A profit-and-loss enterprise must be sustainably wealth creating over time, satisfying owner expectations. The firm cannot use coercion or commit fraud. The firm should uphold the sanctity of private property and the rule of law upon which its wealth-creating ability and legitimacy depend. As a practical matter, a firm in a free society must also honor contracts and engender goodwill among its customers, suppliers, and workers. All these characteristics define *the heroic enterprise* as described by John Hood in his book *The Heroic Enterprise: Business and the Common Good.*

The wider good, even "responsibility" of heroic business, explains Hood, can be assessed by "examining in detail how actual companies, in their day-to-day operation, confer broad and measurable benefits to the society in which they operate." These benefits, he emphasizes, do not come from practicing CSR but by *avoiding* it to the extent that a contrived "guardian activity" hinders market wealth creation.

A New Business Standard

A similar but more precise and market-tested view of the heroic enterprise has been put forward by Charles Koch, an MIT-trained engineer and free-market intellectual. As the architect of Koch Industries, now the world's largest private company, he has articulated a think-and-do strategy for organizational success. His model, explicated in *The Science of Success* (2007), covers the private *and* social aspects of a profit-and-loss business, thus offering an alternative to the CSR model that is espoused by many business ethicists today.

In the capitalist tradition, Koch stresses the timeless personal attributes required for success. He pays homage to *a culture of virtue*—"the sense of urgency, discipline, accountability, judgment, initiative, economic and critical thinking skills, and risk-taking mentality necessary to generate the greatest contribution to the company." Koch contrasts this with bad behaviors and habits: "cynicism, form over substance, bureaucracy, command-and-control, or destructive, self-serving behavior," "emotion and gut feeling," "impulsive action," "mindless application," "gimmicks or false advertising," "entitlement and unaccountability," and "inaction, abdication or finger-pointing."

But for Koch, this personal morality is only the beginning. Individuals must have an organizational framework to incite good personal behavior *and* contribute to sustainable business success. The goal is *Principled Entrepreneurship*™ (PE), defined as "maximizing long-term profitability for the business by creating real value in society while always acting lawfully and with integrity." Principled behavior, integral to which is reliance on the economic means to success (as opposed to the political means), places Koch's philosophy squarely in the tradition of Adam Smith's "man of enterprise," Samuel Smiles's "great work," and Ayn Rand's "virtue of *Productiveness.*"

Koch's roadmap to get from virtuous employee behavior to PE is called Market-Based Management® (MBM), defined as "a philosophy that enables organizations to succeed long-term by applying the principles that allow free societies to prosper." After decades of profit-and-loss testing, Koch has found that businesses, as "miniature societies," perform best when "property rights are clearly and properly defined and protected, people are free to speak, exchange and contract, and prices are free to guide beneficial action." Thus, as in whole capitalistic societies, a business's ethical, wealth-creating rules, grounded in reason and persuasion, can result not only in owner and employee success but also in broader societal success.

MBM has five dimensions. It begins with the entrepreneurial *vision* (how and where to create value) and continues with identifying *virtue and talents* (how to get the right people in the right roles), *knowledge processes* (how to communicate to win profits), and *decision rights* (how to empower the right people). The process culminates with individual *incentives* (employee rewards for wealth creation), which Koch summarizes by modifying Karl Marx's dictum to "'From each according to his ability, to each according to his contribution.'"[9]

Koch's framework eschews specific commands in the corporation's internal markets. "Over-specifying and enforcing particulars undermines prosperity by encouraging inaction," he warns. General rules should govern particulars. What he has in mind are the universal and commonsensical attributes of "honesty, respect for others and their property, making a contribution, being responsible and taking initiative."

MBM centers on the means and ends of profit making and thus is congruent with the social business model classically advanced by Milton Friedman. But there are important conditions and amplifications. Profit maximization is defined by Koch as "creating real, long-term value," which transcends preoccupation with short-term returns, such as quarterly or even annual earnings, as with public companies. (Being privately held is seen as part of Koch Industries' competitive advantage.) Also, for Koch, profit making is legitimate if and only if the gains are won "in harmony with sound principles," including the use of the economic means rather than the political means. Employees not only are

---

9. Koch recognizes the challenge of avoiding "perverse incentives" that set employee actions at odds with what the owners want done (the so-called principal/agent, or agency, problem).

prohibited from directly engaging in coercion but also are discouraged from relying on indirect coercion via special political favor. Thus, MBM is a *moral* system because it marries reason and persuasion with wealth creation. Such ethical wealth creation via free-market entrepreneurship advances the social good as if, in Adam Smith parlance, led by an invisible hand.

Anti-Enron Business

MBM represents the antithesis of the business model and practices at Ken Lay's Enron.[10] Yet MBM has been shaped by what Charles Koch himself describes as expensive failures and humbling setbacks. Recognizing and learning from failure—and a spirit of humility going forward—is a core aspect of MBM.

Humility is the opposite of arrogance, closed-mindedness, intimidation—all parts of Enron's *smartest-guys-in-the-room* problem. And as *Capitalism at Work* has demonstrated, these same attitudes have been a barrier to academic scholarship in important areas of social theory and political economy.

MBM is about open-ended learning in a world buffeted by change, where profit opportunities come and go but must be noticed and properly seized upon to create wealth. And even when handsome profits are won, the market's creative destruction steps in to normalize and even reverse returns over time.

Given an open-ended world, core competency via MBM transcends individuals, industries, or products. Such concretes come and go. MBM is about engendering a "set of capabilities" that applies across the business landscape. MBM itself is thus a living embodiment of a modernist philosophy, emphasizing a rigorous attention to reality regardless of the subject involved. Koch Industries is offered as the proof of the pudding: a conglomerate with an extensive history of entering and exiting very different businesses, yet a company that has been consistently and extraordinarily profitable to date.

By contrast, postmodernist mental models characterized Enron's principals. For Ken Lay and Jeff Skilling, fanciful thinking continued even after the company's bankruptcy, compounding the tragedy. Against such a mindset, Koch warns: "We must constantly remind ourselves that just because we believe or want a thing to be true does not make it so." Instead, "decisions should be made using economic and critical thinking, logic and evidence, rather than emotion or gut feeling," and "style should never take precedence over substance."

The underlying assumption of MBM is that there is an objective means for identifying success and for becoming successful (thus the *science* of success). The terms *reality* and *truth* are taken as self-evident, although there is a warning that correctly interpreting reality takes hard work and proper values. For example, profit-and-loss measurement should not be profit maximizing for its own sake (to impress others or increase bonuses) but for the sake of value creation

---

10. In Kuhnian terms, if Enron represents an *anomaly* in the entrenched CSR *paradigm*, Koch's MBM represents a *shift of vision*, even *extraordinary science*.

(by realistically matching period costs and revenues, in order to learn). Koch explains:

> A business can best determine where and how to create value when it is organized into profit centers . . . [But profit-and-loss] financial statements must reflect economic reality. Remember, anywhere profit and loss is measured, analysis is also needed to understand what drives those results.

Enron's postmodernism, in contrast, gamed the accounting rules. The resulting unreal profitability was philosophic fraud, whether or not it was prosecutable.

For Koch, the prescriptive Generally Accepted Accounting Principles (GAAP) are not an end in themselves. To be sure, GAAP should not be abused in determining financial outcomes of the reporting period for tax purposes or for other reasons. But where GAAP is judged inadequate for internal learning and decision making, Koch creates separate accounts to better gauge financial realities and assist internal decision making.

Avoiding hyperbole and half-truths is a necessary strategy for long-term results, for trust and goodwill are essential to a free economy. "A company's reputation is critical to how it will be treated by others and to its long-term success," states Koch. "We must build a positive reputation based on reality, or others will create one for us based on speculation or animus."

Rejecting Political Capitalism

How does a company ethically and profitably perform within an environment of political capitalism and the mixed economy where regulation can be not only unproductive but also punitive? Here, too, Koch Industries has learned expensive lessons and made changes, resulting in a retooled approach to government relations, or what is called Public Sector Capability.

First, MBM starts from a position of full compliance with the law, even though individuals or the company may oppose a regulation or law for business and/or intellectual reasons. Second, MBM eschews gains for itself through political means (and seeks no disadvantage for others). Third, from a position of good-faith compliance, the company can seek reform. Koch explains:

> Striving to comply with every law does not mean agreeing with every law. But, even when faced with laws we think are counter-productive, we must first comply. Only then, from a credible position, can we enter into a dialogue with regulatory agencies to demonstrate alternatives that are more beneficial. If these efforts fail, we can then join with others in using education and/or political efforts to change the law.

Koch also believes that a company should not be exempt from regulation (even bad regulation) "because it is small or favored politically." In "a free and prosperous society," he argues, "people must be treated according to their individual merits, not by group association." This is part of the principle of "equality before the law." Implicit in this view is that bad regulation should be repealed wholesale and that beneficial results, reason, and trust should set the standard for regulated and regulators alike—in place of emotions and agendas that hurt the private and public interest.

"Practicing MBM in a political world" is a challenging area for a free-market-oriented company. But as a long-term strategy, it is arguably a means to both maximize profits and improve public policy in an open, democratic way.

The methodology outlined in Koch's *Science of Success* is ethical; that is, it employs free exchange to produce wealth-creating companies And precisely because it is ethical, MBM is practical. Consumers, employees, and others must gain in an open, free economy in order for owners to win. Regulation is respected but always challenged (like every part of the business) in an atmosphere of mutual trust and according to a standard of actual results.

·〜·

Applauding the social benefits of a prosperous business is hardly controversial. One hears the refrain in many retrospectives by respected businesspeople, such as Jack Welch, the successful longtime head of GE, the company that Samuel Insull helped father a century before.

Friedman-like, Welch states that "a CEO's primary social responsibility is to assure the financial success of the company." He continues:

> Only a healthy enterprise can improve and enrich the lives of people and their communities. When a company is strong, it not only pays taxes that provide for important services. It also builds world-class facilities that meet or exceed safety and environmental standards. Strong companies reinvest in their people and their facilities. Healthy companies provide good and secure jobs that give their employees the time, spirit, and the resources to give back to their communities a thousand-fold.

Although much of the preceding is undoubtedly true, Welch's altruistic model differs from MBM's ethical individualism.[11] A good-for-GE, good-for-society position does not preclude—and might even encourage—achieving profitability via the political means of wealth redistribution rather than by a principled reliance on the economic means of wealth creation. After all, if communities and governments benefit from GE's profitability, why should they not help make it happen with special favors? That is an argument for political capitalism by political capitalists. And, indeed, by buying Enron Wind from the parent's estate, GE assumed part of Enron's political capitalism model.

Heroic capitalism involves heroic firms, and heroic firms are created by heroic entrepreneurs—as well as by every worker who is trained to be ethical

---

11. The congruence of self-interest and moral good is further examined in Internet appendix E.2, "Self-Interest and Ethics," at www.politicalcapitalism.org/book1/Epilogue/appendix2.html.

and entrepreneurial within that miniature society. Systemic, egregious business failure, as at Enron, can be linked to a flawed morality that substitutes second-hander mentalities for virtuous behavior and rampant mixed-economy strategies for free-market processes.

Amid the mixed-up mixed economy, the good news is that capitalist philosophers have developed a framework for ethical business practices and sustainable wealth creation. This worldview comes into greater focus in Book 2 and Book 3.

Finale

Enron's bankruptcy profoundly challenged business-as-usual in the corporate world. Many companies took a second look at their practices to make sure that substance matched form. The flawed *interpretation* of Enron described herein should also be a challenge to business-as-usual in the academic, media, and policy realms. The regulation-intensive approach to corporate governance, as well as the stakeholder-driven philosophy of CSR, is less the solution than the problem. For Ken Lay's company brought to life many behaviors that capitalist philosophers have long recognized as incongruent with best-business practices and limited government. A new model of heroic capitalism based on principle-driven, free-market entrepreneurship deserves a central place in business-ethics thought and action.

Capitalism at Work has described how Malthusian and neo-Malthusian thinking has repeatedly led to false alarms and promiscuous calls for government energy planning. This book has advanced the thesis that complex regulation in place of simple-rules capitalism disrupts market processes and corrupts business incentives. What is perhaps more important, *Capitalism at Work* has argued that free enterprise is a system that is not only superbly wealth creating but also morally superior to coercion-based alternatives. It is ethical because it is based on the *self-love* of Adam Smith, the *self-help* of Samuel Smiles, and the *rational self-interest* of Ayn Rand. Yet far from being atomistic or amoral, capitalism driven by self-interest is an intensely *sociable* system; its supply-side ethics rewards society's wealth creators, person by person, thus creating goodwill and empowering philanthropy. From the innumerable parts comes a robust civil society, its individuals dually directed, as it were, by the economic invisible hand of markets and the moral invisible hand of human benevolence. In the post-Enron world, capitalism deserves a second look by even its most trenchant and intransigent critics.

Appendix A
The Ayn Rand Problem

This appendix is intended to understand Ayn Rand's personal shortcomings in order to better appreciate Objectivism, the importance of humility and open communication (versus arrogance), and the importance of respecting general rules (setting boundaries) in personal relationships. It is not meant to disparage Objectivism by criticizing the personal choices of its founder.

OBJECTIVIST PHILOSOPHY HOLDS that individuals can understand the world and live best through the pursuit of reason-based, peaceful activities. Objectivism is also an intellectual tool for historians (such as the present writer) to elucidate causality and understand success and failure in the social world. The demise of seemingly invulnerable business titans can be comprehended in terms of second-hander strategies and philosophic fraud (reality falsification), not only politics-over-market strategies. The same framework can be used to interpret individual and organizational failure within the Objectivist movement itself, in which successes led to arrogance, and arrogance led to failure, deceit, and disaster.

Objectivism as a thriving, popular intellectual and practical framework has been held back by its founder in various ways. As mentioned in chapter 3, Ayn Rand sometimes couched her views in counterproductive rhetoric that her critics could exploit in sound-bite denunciations. Her unusual definitions and usage of the words *selfishness* and *altruism* were problematic, allowing critics to portray Objectivism as cold and heartless rather than as a philosophy for rational, productive living. Rand also defined and used the terms *faith* and *mysticism*, *egoism* and *sacrifice*, *pride* and *humility*, and *mercy* and *pity* unconventionally. But this was more of a strategic problem for Rand than an intellectual one, for her critics are under an obligation to understand and explain terms as they are defined and meant by their author.

Far more important, Rand made personal choices that caused a crisis in her life, the lives of some of her closest associates, and the entire Objectivist movement. This outcome could have been avoided by rational thinking, something that Rand's philosophy championed in so many other ways. Walking the talk in this case would have avoided much personal anguish, for as Scott Peck has written, "Mental health is an ongoing process of dedication to reality at all costs."

Rand's writings and philosophy point toward a strong inward-out self: the self-sufficient person. Yet she herself suffered from personal insecurities and a high need for approbation, however much she might have tried to deny or hide it. She attracted an inner circle of admirers and students who were psychologically whipped into a cult of obedience to her. But this was part of something else that came to engulf Rand: a relationship addiction, called *codependency* in the mental health literature, with her protégé-turned-lover Nathaniel Branden. Rand placed her happiness, her self-esteem, in the hands of another person. Like a narcotic, Rand's arrangement worked for a while. But the situation became less and less sustainable over time, leading Rand and Branden to dodge realities in their own ways to avoid a great crash. Predictably, such evasion would make the final result worse, not better.

Such a disaster is hardly unique. Mental falsification from emotional dependency is also the story of Ken Lay, who clung to a preferred reality that stemmed from his own personal insecurities. His Enron was different from the real Enron, just as Rand's dreamt relationship with Branden became different from the real one. In these cases (and many others, from other walks of life), the dichotomy brings turmoil—or worse. For as Rand said in *Atlas Shrugged* (speaking through her hero, John Galt): "Reality is not to be wiped out, it will merely wipe out the wiper." It did wipe out Ken Lay—reputationally, emotionally, and physically. And it brought the "goddess of reason," Ayn Rand, to her knees.

Like the missteps that brought down Enron, the codependency (or love addiction) that engulfed Rand started small and spun out of control. It was a slippery slope that began by violating what Adam Smith called "a sacred regard to general rules." It was heart over head, forgetting Samuel Smiles's admonition that a person "must drill his desires, and keep them under subjection" to avoid becoming "the sport of passion and impulse."

Also, as in the case of Enron, Branden and Rand made no midcourse corrections but engaged in vivid imagining, role playing, and mutual deceit in an attempt to get to a fanciful *other side*. The two embarked on an unsustainable path, enjoyed an Enronish boom, prolonged an artificial situation, and suffered a painful crash. The real tragedy was not that their peculiar Objectivist (or anti-Objectivist) experiment ended badly but that it started wonderfully. In other words, the affair should not have begun, and once begun, it should have ended quickly, with contrition.

Because Rand created and largely controlled the spread of Objectivism, her persona became almost as important as the philosophy itself—a dangerous development for any movement in which ideas must trump personalities. (Ken Lay's image as the buoyant Mr. Enron would have a similar, insidious effect.) Her death in 1982 left Objectivism to stand on its own, although a wing of her supporters has continued to equate not only Rand's ideas but also her *actions* with Objectivism. Such idolatry aside, fully evaluating Rand's philosophy requires understanding and abstracting from Ayn Rand's personal shortcomings—then applying that understanding and those abstractions to the core subject of our trilogy.

The Affair/Addiction

Objectivism as an organized intellectual movement was ruptured in 1968 by the acrimonious split between Ayn Rand and her heir apparent, Nathanial Branden. At the time, he headed the 10-year-old Nathaniel Branden Institute (NBI), which with Rand's consent and participation offered courses in Objectivism in 80 cities around the United States. Her sudden, shocking repudiation of Branden ended the enterprise, to the bewilderment of thousands of serious students of Objectivism. (The NBI mailing list at the time had grown to 80,000 names— "all people who had attended lectures, subscribed to the magazines, etc.")

The complete, acrimonious break resulted from a conflict between reason and emotion in a real-world, intimate relationship, one that turned out quite differently from Rand's fictionalized ideal. Rand, married to Frank O'Connor, and Nathaniel, married to Barbara Branden (neé Weidman), began having an affair in 1954, which was during the writing of *Atlas Shrugged*. At this time, Nathaniel was an impetuous 24 and Rand a mature (but needy) 49.

The affair began with emotional intimacy between the two in front of their spouses. Then, with a full explanation to their (reluctant) spouses, Ayn and Nathaniel began a platonic affair, scheduling time together when husband Frank would leave Rand's apartment so that she and the visiting Nathaniel could be alone. Five months later, in January 1955—again, with an announcement to the spouses—a physical affair started. So began, in Barbara Branden's words, "the nightmare that was to last for fourteen years, and was finally to smash many hundreds of lives."

Ayn and Nathaniel rationalized their intimacy as reason- and reality-based, corresponding to the highest moral values of love between a man and a woman. Both emphasized to Frank and Barbara that they loved their marriage partners just as before. Rand also stated that because of their 25-year age difference, the physical part would last only a year or so. But the affair engendered, in whole or in part, anxiety attacks for Barbara, a marginalization of and possible alcohol abuse by Frank, codependency and self-described "torture" for Rand, and a lifestyle of deceit and agony for Nathaniel.

All four, sworn to secrecy about the affair, engaged in a widening web of lies to keep the situation from others. Recalled Nathaniel:

> Earlier, there had been the lie to Barbara and Frank that 'nothing will change,' and now we were lying to everyone in our circle. But, of course, *lie* was a word we never used. We didn't have to. We had a philosophical explanation for everything.

Rand reputedly said, "Well, I don't like it either, but reality is reality," as though her desires were supreme and deceit simply an unfortunate byproduct. After all, wasn't such secrecy keeping up appearances in violation of a tenet of Objectivism?

The affair's honeymoon period lasted through the completion of *Atlas Shrugged* in 1957. The affair proved distracting to the book's completion, however, as Rand habitually spent hour after intoxicating hour with her young lover in deep emotional conversations and physical intimacy. (The 60-page speech of John Galt climaxing the book took two years to complete.) Rand was attempting to live a love scene from one of her novels, Barbara would later realize.

The affair cooled when Rand grew despondent at the negative critical reaction that greeted the publication of *Atlas Shrugged*. Collectivists of all stripes panned the book, as might be expected. But Rand's secular case for reason, individualism, and capitalism made enemies among conservatives as well. The worst conservative attack came in William F. Buckley's fortnightly magazine, *National Review*, when reviewer Whittaker Chambers slammed Rand's "mountain of words" as "remarkably silly" and "preposterous." Behind the book's free-enterprise message was a totalitarian psychology, Chambers claimed. Randian man was likened to Marxian Man, a Big Brother through the back door. "From almost any page of *Atlas Shrugged*, a voice can be heard, from painful necessity, commanding: 'To a gas chamber—go!'"

Rand viewed life grimly in this period. "The bitterness that had always been part of her makeup was becoming more pronounced," Nathaniel noticed. "She was impatient, irritable, angry, and quick to condemn—Frank, me, Barbara, Leonard [Peikoff], anyone in the Collective who said or did anything even slightly ambiguous or questionable." The physical part of the affair became less intense and stopped altogether, whereas the emotional side became erratic. Nathaniel, age 29, found himself in a situation in which he had ceased to be either "a lover to Ayn or a husband to Barbara." Rand, Ms. Objectivism, meanwhile, had emotionally slipped to the point that her self-esteem was based on another person.

The Break

Nathaniel was willing and able to continue the emotional side of his affair with the person who remained "the rock of my life." He also admitted to having, at least in his relaxed moments, "a kind of love for Ayn, at times very intense, and I showed this plainly." And given the big business that NBI had become, Branden was also in an employee relationship with Rand, because her endorsement propelled the enterprise.

A major disconnect emerged in 1963 when Rand, feeling more like her old self, asked Nathaniel to resume the sexual side of their relationship—and really to resume the emotional/physical oneness of before. But the 58-year-old was going in just the opposite direction from her 33-year-old intimate. Aging and isolated, Rand looked to Nathaniel as her primary joy and bedrock for the future, her Galt-like Atlas. She feared anything less than a full return to the affair's former glory—despite the fact that much had changed in the relationship in the past six years. And both still had their own spouses, who, by definition, were supposed to preclude such otherness.

Nathaniel, in fact, was no longer attracted to his mentor as a lover. Part of this was because of their ever-more-pronounced physical divergence and the years of enduring Rand's moodiness. But the other part was the inevitable that now happened: 34-year-old Nathaniel found a true love. The object of his affection, and soon his lover, was one of his Objectivist students, a fashion model 10 years his junior.

Patrecia Gullison, who herself had recently gotten married, was more than simply beautiful. According to Barbara Branden, she possessed "an unusual emotional spontaneity and openness and, at times, a startling acute sensitivity." Patrecia loved Nathaniel immensely—and did not place endless demands on him as did Rand. Before long, the love-starved, conflicted Nathaniel was in a new passionate affair. For her part, Barbara began having an affair with Nathaniel's understanding but not his formal consent.

Thus, any desire by Nathaniel for a physical relationship with Rand was out of the question. Furthermore, Patrecia meant that the emotional oneness with Rand was over too.

But rather than own up to his feelings and set boundaries on the relationship, even at this late date, Nathaniel made excuses to try to placate Rand. This was not deceit for its own sake. It was ends-justifies-the-means pragmatism to try to give Rand enough of what she needed and preserve what he did like about and need from their relationship. The truth, he feared, would devastate their personal and business relationship (as in fact it did).

Rand by this time was classically codependent. To her, it was all or nothing—and had to be all. Her husband, Frank, hardly existed in her Nathaniel-centric world, and her relationship with him predictably suffered. Insecurities abounding, Rand increasingly came to view her world through Nathaniel rather than, as a mentally healthy person would, through herself.

With Nathaniel inventing a reality in an increasingly desperate attempt to allow Rand to have hers, the two were engaging in endless "psycho-epistemological" sessions by late 1967.[1] Rand—not getting logical explanations

---

1. Rand's role as psychotherapist to Branden multiply violated the rules by which clinical psychologists now practice. The therapist should not have any intimate relationship with the client, yet Nathaniel was her lover and employee. A therapist must be in a position to be able to recommend ending the affair—something that Rand was determined not to do. Professional guidelines set by the American Psychological Code of Ethics (available at www.apa.org/ethics/code2002.pdf) caution against "harm" (Section 3.04), "multiple relationships" (3.05), "conflict of interest" (3.06), "exploitative relationships" (3.08), and "sexual intimacies with current therapy clients/patients" (10.05).

and fearing what she was not hearing—reached out to Barbara to cope—or to control Nathaniel. Frank O'Connor, passive by nature, and now in a dysfunctional husband/wife relationship, was powerless and a target of Rand's unhappiness.

Sensing Nathaniel's withdrawal, Rand became more and more desperate and controlling toward her intellectual heir, so-called. As she became more manipulative, Nathaniel became more evasive, knowing what would happen if Rand found out that she had been replaced by an intellectual inferior and physical superior. Nathaniel was trapped, for he knew that the truth would "result in the total collapse of the life I had built . . . the end of everything." This included any chance for NBI, which was taking the next step of getting a new address: the Empire State Building, Rand's beloved skyscraper and a grand statement of how far he and Objectivism had come.

The Brandens' marriage was irrevocably broken by Nathaniel's new love. When Nathaniel told Rand that he and Barbara were separated, she responded with the words he did not want to hear: "Now, darling, perhaps there will be a chance for us to be in love again." Nathaniel at this point wanted to be "the best and closest of friends."

◇

In emotional turmoil, Rand wrote pained, furious entries in her personal diary. "I am *dead* in his mind already," she agonized. "I can't help this feeling. He makes me *feel dead*." She complained elsewhere about the relationship's "*total* chaos," and her personal "horror" at where things were going. "Why don't I break with him now?" she pleaded with herself. (She could not—addicts cannot, short of recovery.) For his part, Nathaniel admitted: "I knew that I was putting her through hell." But he did not mean to do it—he *hated* doing it. He was simply trying to engineer—somehow, someway—a soft landing rather than a crash.

Rand feared reality! She knew that anything short of total love meant that Nathaniel would find, sooner or later, a true love, and that she, Rand, would be trapped in her own triangle. Indeed, for a time, a hypothetical "Miss X" became a major focus of their psychoepistemological sessions.

In summer 1968, three bomb blasts would demolish the relationship. The first was when a fearing, exhausted Nathaniel handed Rand a letter he wrote explaining why age was a barrier to a romantic relationship. Rand's diaries had been filled with suspicions that the physical was driving the emotional, and here was the dreaded confirmation. But the letter did not mention another reason: "her rage, her grandiosity . . . had long ago extinguished any romantic feelings I had for her." Also, his relationship with Patrecia was left unmentioned, though she was the very person who Rand finally now suspected of being Miss X.

Rand reacted harshly, realizing that the 14-year affair had to come to an end in abject failure. Emotionally sick from trying to control Nathaniel and to construct her desired reality, Rand screamed at Nathaniel, summoned Barbara, and went through a litany of what-to-do-nows. Nathaniel, his worst fears confirmed, was now "passionately sorry" that he had not confessed to Rand years earlier. "But it was also the first step toward a return to reality and the rebuilding of my self-esteem."

To cope, Rand returned to her diary. This time she wrote out a careful outline before proceeding with a 12,000-word entry—no doubt for posterity. (Indeed, she would not destroy her diary or stipulate that it not become public—which it finally did, in part, with James Valliant's book, discussed later.)

Rand tried to contain her rage at "the worst traitor and the most immoral person I have ever met." But she did rage at "the total hell (for me) and the terrible torture of the last five months of 'psycho-epistemological therapy.'" Remarkably, there was no mention of Frank O'Connor as she reviewed and parsed the history of the affair and the rabbit-trail truth sessions. Rand described her "stunned awe at the magnitude of the horror involved in such a phenomenon—at such an ignominious end for what had been, potentially, such rare and authentic greatness," as if the affair could and should have been a lifelong joy to all parties. She ended her entry with a soft touch—a last hope, really—that Branden could see the light, recover, to make at least part of her reality become real. "Well," Rand wrote, "I wish him the best premises—in the name of the best within him."

Rand decided to let Nathaniel continue at NBI. The two visited strictly on business matters and actually shared their feelings about the pain that both were going through from the relationship pullback. But Rand was still codependent. As she told her new best friend, Barbara Branden, in this period: "There is nothing for me to look forward to, nothing to hope for in reality. My life is over. He has forced me into a permanent ivory tower. He took away this earth."

The second blast came when Nathaniel confessed that he was in love with Patrecia to an intermediary Rand had chosen to help them cope with the new reality. When Rand received this news, she broke into rage and announced that she would never speak to Nathaniel again. Rand sent him a set of demands for being able to continue at NBI. When he agreed to those, new demands followed.

Then the third and final blast came. Barbara, finding out that she was to replace Nathaniel as heir to Rand's estate should Ayn outlive Frank O'Connor, could no longer continue to keep a deceit: the affair between Nathaniel and Patrecia. With Nathaniel's permission, Barbara confessed this fact to Rand, whereupon—hell hath no fury. It suddenly became clear: Nathaniel had been lying systemically. It was all his fault, Rand now knew.

But Nathaniel had concocted an alternative reality to avoid devastating his mentor-turned-lover-turned-codependent—and to save the nonromantic side of their relationship, not to mention his business life. He certainly was not out to hurt Rand; he simply wanted the romantic switch turned off. Yet Rand was addicted—to him. She was *allowing* Nathaniel Branden to torture her rather than realistically concluding: *This is not romantic love, this can't be romantic love, this should have never been romantic love, so let's reground the relationship.* Branden's deceit was about not bursting Rand's bubble, for he wanted Rand as mentor and dearest friend—and needed her endorsement for professional reasons and for the continued growth of the Objectivist movement itself.

Upon receiving the full story from Barbara, Rand immediately summoned Nathaniel, whereupon she verbally, emotionally, and physically attacked him in a final meeting that ended with her hiss:

> If you have an ounce of morality left in you, an ounce of psychological health, you'll be impotent for the next twenty years! And if you achieve any potency sooner, you'll know it's a sign of still worse moral degradation!

Nathaniel may have been a pitiful liar and hypocrite, but Rand was a sick codependent who had put her happiness in another's hands and got crushed.

∽

NBI was dissolved, and Nathaniel moved from New York City to California to begin life anew with Patrecia, who became his second wife in 1969. Rand, with all her influence and through her remaining intimates, conducted a scorched-earth policy in an attempt to discredit and otherwise ruin Nathaniel. Rand even would expunge references to Branden's work when her original articles were reprinted—as if his intellectual contributions to Objectivism were now null and void.

Nathaniel had Patrecia and little else; Ayn had Frank and a lot. It was time for both to lick codependency, for such "recovery is when fun becomes fun, love becomes love, and life becomes worth living."

Rand may never have recovered, however, for recovery requires coming to grips with the reasons for the addiction—owning up to one's insecurities and recognizing the inadequacies in one's other relationships—and accepting responsibility. But Rand, viewing herself as the exemplar of what people should be, could not admit that the affair had been wrong *in principle*. And so to her last breath, she saw herself as a victim of the other party in the codependency and thus was unable to understand, forgive, and forget—or really recover.

Rand explained the sudden, stunning break—as stunning as the Enron collapse was in a different context—by resorting to half-truths, a method she philosophically condemned elsewhere as a "very vicious form of lying." Rand would never own up to the circumstances leading to the split, personally or publicly, placing all blame on others. She was *in denial*, in the vernacular of addiction science, as much as Nathaniel Branden himself can be blamed for his bad choices and tar-baby deceit.

The split between the Brandens and Rand was part of a pattern. Many in Rand's inner circle suffered from "paralyzing alienation." Barbara recollected how during that time, "a philosophy that exalted individualism and joy was becoming, in practice, a set of dreary duties and a source of agonized emotional repression. A philosophy that was a mighty hymn to the possibilities of human life was becoming, in practice, a dirge."

Some left Rand's inner circle, but others could not, owing to "a deadly mixture of idealism and a vulnerability to guilt." One of the few survivors was

Leonard Peikoff, who became heir to Rand's estate and founded the Ayn Rand Institute (ARI) in 1985. ARI not only is dedicated to the veracity of Rand's writings in toto but also defends Rand's personal life as consonant with Objectivism. It is as if the moral perfection of Rand is necessary for Objectivism, something which it is clearly not.

Relationship Addiction (Codependency)

Codependency, or relationship addiction, is defined by the National Mental Health Association (NMHA) as a "learned behavior . . . that affects an individual's ability to have a healthy, mutually satisfying relationship." The codependent cannot emotionally disentangle from a "one-sided, emotionally destructive and/or abusive" relationship. Misplaced caretaking for the partner leaves the codependent "feeling choiceless and helpless in the relationship," yet the codependent is "unable to break away from the cycle of behavior that causes it."

Codependency is "a disease of lost selfhood," a "dysfunction . . . from focusing on the needs and behavior of others." It also has been called "the addiction to looking elsewhere." The values and practices characteristic of codependency run contrary to the self-reliance that is taught by Objectivism. Melody Beattie begins her book *Codependent No More: How to Stop Controlling Others and Start Caring for Yourself* with an Objectivist-like, commonsense quotation (from Agnes Repplier): "It is not easy to find happiness in ourselves, and it is not possible to find it elsewhere."

Why couldn't Ayn Rand find happiness in herself or at least in her own husband, Frank O'Connor? Did Rand's depression and deep-rooted insecurities have a physiological basis? Was it due to her prior drug usage (Dexamyl, a combined amphetamine and barbiturate)? Could today's antidepressants have allowed her to be more satisfied with her accomplishments and more optimistic about her future—and thus have a sustainable relationship with Nathaniel Branden and her own husband? These questions can only be raised, not answered.

Scarcely understood in Rand's time, codependency has become a well-studied emotional disorder. Rand (and Nathaniel) exhibited its classic behavioral characteristics, described in part by NMHA as:

- An exaggerated sense of responsibility for the actions of others . . .
- A compelling need to control others . . .
- Fear of being abandoned or alone . . .
- Rigidity/difficulty adjusting to change
- Problems with intimacy/boundaries
- Chronic anger
- Lying/dishonesty

- Poor communications
- Difficulty making decisions

Another descriptive can be added to these: *chronic depression*. And indeed, Rand was in such a state, and Nathaniel was not far behind.

There were many telltale signs of codependency in their relationship. Rand heaped increasing praise upon Nathaniel, even telling him that she could not survive without him. She dedicated *Atlas Shrugged* to him in addition to her husband—then used the inscription against Nathaniel as if it were a marriage bond. Interminable discussions between the two included statements from her that ranged from inordinate praise to devilish threats (Rand's own form of deceit, or a deceit fighting Nathaniel's deceit):

- "If anything goes permanently wrong between us, I'm finished. Every-thing is finished. You're my lifeline to the world and to any chance at happiness I'm ever going to have."
- "The man to whom I dedicated *Atlas Shrugged* would never want anything less than me! I don't care if I'm ninety years old and in a wheelchair."
- "You [want] a personal life away from me? . . . You have no right to casual friendships, no right to vacations, no right to sex with some inferior woman!"

Rand was unable to see the reality she did not like. "Ayn's blindness on some issues is incredible," Barbara remarked to Nathaniel in the period right before the breakup, continuing: "You've got to find a way to help her see the truth. A way that won't devastate her. Not that Ayn would ever admit to being devas-tated. Poor Ayn. Poor Nathan."

Codependency brings out the worst in the afflicted. Nathaniel remembers Rand's "near paranoia, violent temper, and general blindness to any context but her own." He was engulfed in his own hell, lacking any perceived way of escape without dramatic consequences. "The only thing worse than feeling trapped in a nightmare," he summarized, "is forbidding oneself to know that one feels trapped in a nightmare."

Despite her own teachings on the primacy of self-reliance and personal responsibility for one's own happiness, Rand put herself into an untenable situ-ation with the affair. She placed her emotional state and happiness in the hands of another person—and not her husband at that. Nathaniel himself remarked "how disastrous it was to allow my self-esteem to become involved with my relationship with Ayn."

~·

The psychological explanation of codependency is not mentioned once in James Valliant's 400-page attempted exoneration of Rand, *The Passion of Ayn Rand's Critics*, based in part on newly released entries from Ayn Rand's personal diary. (A full release of Rand's diaries has not been made, which will be necessary to further understand the dysfunctional relationship under review.) Valliant casts blame almost entirely on Nathaniel—with some reserved for Barbara Branden. In Valliant's interpretation, Rand was "a romantic soul [who was] cruelly manipulated by a man to whom she had given her highest trust and affection." The author goes so far as to conclude at the end of the book that "[Nathaniel] Branden's psychology shows a striking similarity to the *psychology of a rapist.*"

Valliant's black-and-white reinterpretation is problematic. Although it is possible that Nathaniel and even Barbara have misconstrued parts of the story with their recollections, Valliant throws the baby out with the bathwater to suggest that their memoirs each are "monuments of dishonesty on a scale so profound as to literally render them valueless as historical documents."

But given the facts (marital circumstances, age difference, etc.) and Rand's mental makeup, was an emotional and physical affair between Nathaniel and Ayn really sustainable? Valliant admits: "Certainly, the average contemporary husband would find such a situation [as between Ayn and Nathaniel] intolerable." He also shares Rand's answer to the question once posed to her in public about whether a person can be romantically in love with two people at the same time. Rand answered (before the blowup when, *presumably,* she was in love with Frank O'Connor): "It's a project that only giants can handle." Thus, she viewed herself as a *giant,* one who could live life by a set of rules different from everyone else's, different from the nongiants' rules. Still, Rand shuddered at the prospect that Nathaniel would find his own love, one that could require a triangle where she was not at the apex.

If Rand had not drifted into codependence but was emotionally strong enough to end the physical side of the relationship—and thus the emotional intimacy that went with it—Nathaniel's own behavior would have been far less evasive and dishonest than it turned out to be. A much healthier relationship, and certainly greater productivity and happiness, could have resulted from setting emotional and physical boundaries. Sadly, Frank O'Connor was not what Ayn could accept, at least after she entered into an emotional/physical oneness with her protégé.

Lessons

Nathaniel Branden possessed personality flaws and has regretted his authoritarian, insensitive years at the feet of Ayn Rand. Nathaniel could have and should have ended the affair much sooner, as Rand should have. Without the affair, Rand surely would have been more productive and less controlling, although the latter was apparently a deep-seated trait that might have still manifested itself.

As it turned out, the affair brought out the very worst in Ayn Rand—as it did in Nathaniel Branden. "The luckiest beneficiaries of her work are the people who read her and never see her, never meet her, never have any reason to deal with her in person," Nathaniel concluded from the ordeal. "Then they get the best of what she really was."

Nathaniel interpreted Rand's blind spot as follows: "If you have created a new intellectual system—or new in important respects—which rightly or wrongly you perceive as a highly integrated structure, the desire to preserve it in its totally undiluted form is as understandable as it is unrealistic." But Rand had deep-seated insecurities that contributed to her absolutist, controlling nature.

Another of Rand's closest and best students also saw the situation more clearly after leaving Rand's inner circle. The linkage between the bad and the good in Rand's character led Barbara Branden to conclude:

> One must wonder if the dogmatic absolutism of her certainty, the blinding conviction of her own rectitude and her special place in the world, the callousness of her intolerance for opinions that were not hers, the unwavering assurances that she was alone to know the truth and that others must seek it from her—the eyes that looked neither to the left nor to the right, but only at the path ahead—the savage innocence of her personality was not the fuel for the height of achievement she attained.

She goes on to ask:

> Would a lesser conviction have made it possible? The unyielding intransigence distorts the life and corrupts the personality of the innovator. But is it a tragic flaw—or is it, in the end, when one pushes past the rubble and the pain, neither tragic nor a flaw?

But, again, it did not have to be this way. A mentor/business relationship would have brought out the best (instead of the worst) in the principals, their loved ones, and their friends. This would have been a godsend to the whole Objectivist movement compared to what actually transpired.

Adam Smith once contrasted the brilliant ideas of Voltaire with his erratic personal behavior. Voltaire was one of a genre of great thinkers who, said Smith, "distinguished themselves by the most improper and even insolent contempt of all the ordinary decorums of life and conversation." Smith added, "They have thereby set the most pernicious example for those who wish to resemble them, and who too often content themselves with imitating their follies, without even attempting to attain their perfections."

The Ayn Rand problem retarded the intellectual development of Objectivism in her lifetime. Today, the split reverberates between the orthodox Ayn Rand Institute, founded three years after Rand's death, and a breakaway organization, the Objectivist Center (now the Atlas Society), which was founded as a "more open, tolerant, and independent alternative to orthodoxy."

The existence of different Rand-influenced organizations—small tent and big tent, closed philosophy and open philosophy—indicates that Objectivism is outgrowing its founder's persona. The Ayn Rand problem will continue to recede as the personalities of Objectivism's past give way to the ideas of Objectivism itself, although the lessons of the whole affair and the crisis of 1968 should never be forgotten.

Appendix B

A Taxonomy of Political Capitalism

T HE SEPARATION OF GOVERNMENT and economy has been called *laissez-faire (laissez-passer) capitalism, laissez-faire liberalism,* "unhampered capitalism," and "Manchesterism." A free-market business system—or free-market capitalism or free economy—has also been labeled *commercial capitalism, industrial capitalism,* and "financial capitalism." Economists also liken capitalism to "a system of decentralized decision-making."

Terms closely associated with capitalism include the *industrial revolution* and "consumer economy," or simply *classical capitalism.* Capitalism revolves around the *economic means* of voluntary trading, which is the opposite of the *political means,* or "forcible appropriation."

Interventionism

An economic system between the poles of laissez-faire capitalism and comprehensive socialism has been termed *interventionism,* the *mixed* or *middle-way* economy, the *regulatory state,* and "regulatory capitalism." Other terms are the "positive state," "third way," "third road," "third system," "third solution," "hampered market economy," and *"Keynesianism."*

The mixed economy has been often described as the *public-interest state* and "interest-group pluralism." *Public-interest theory* was the original mainstream view of business/government relations, one that "lies behind both the 'official' view of legislative intent and the many scholarly analyses which look at the history of regulatory origin." This view "abounds with faith in the administrative process not only to protect powerless consumers, but also to affect rationality and fairness in the economy generally." Nonpartisan, impersonal agencies staffed by experts and continuously in session are the manifestation of public-interest regulation.

"Capture theory," also called "self-interest theory," is a more recent paradigm of business/government relations that identifies business as the key constituency behind the state's regulatory functions. A term in the capture-theory literature, *the strategic use of regulation*, is also used to describe "any attempt by a firm or collection of firms or others with similar interests to alter the political or legal structure of the economy to their advantage." Other terms used in chapter 5 are *rent-seeking* and *political profit making*. Piecemeal, probusiness intervention has been called *corporate welfare*.

A vast vocabulary has described the close relationship between business interests and government—what this book, following Gabriel Kolko, calls *"political capitalism."* Kolko describes political capitalism as "the merger of the economic and political structures on behalf of the greater interests of capitalism." Under political capitalism, "the welfare of government and business, is, in the largest sense, identical."

The following terms connote *political capitalism* (my preferred term, following Kolko): "administrative state," "American capitalism," "American monopoly statism," "American oligarchy," "American state corporatism," "American statism," "American syndicalism," "aristocratic-government complex," "associative state," "broker state," "[c]aptive [s]tate," "corporate-administered stage of capitalism," "corporate capitalism," "corporate capitalist order," "corporate commonwealth," "corporate liberal state," "corporate liberalism," "corporate state," "corporate statism," "corporate syndicalism," "corporate welfare state," "corporation capitalism," "corporation political economy," "corporative state," "corporativism," "government capitalism," "industrial corporate capitalism," "interest group liberalism," "liberal corporate capitalism," "liberal corporatism," "liberal state," "lobbying-industrial complex," "modern corporate state," "monopoly capitalism," "national capitalism," "neo-fascism," "neomercantilism," "New Deal capital[ism]," "positive state," "plutocracy," "private government," "progressivism," "regulated capitalism," "regulatory-state capitalism," "restrictivism," "state capitalism," and "state monopoly capitalism."

James Weinstein defines *corporate liberalism*, or the *liberal state*, as including "such names as the New Freedom, the New Deal, the New Frontier, and the Great Society." He called this "the existing political economy."

Herbert Hoover used the term *regulated individualism* to describe his agenda while head of the Department of Commerce (1921–28). His approach was to instruct business groups to form voluntary associations and regulate themselves to address their problems. Government regulation was thus indirect—and less than before, given that such associations were now immune from antitrust prosecution. Hoover adviser Henry Dennison described Hoover's approach as "scientific regulation ... from the inside" in place of "political government" via antitrust agencies or regulatory commissions. The *new associationalism* has been called an "American variant of neo-corporatism." But from a free-market viewpoint, such activity is more a part of capitalism, not political capitalism, particularly given that antitrust law is removed.

The terms "social welfare state" and "public-interest state" connote less business welfare than social welfare, which would include the welfare of employees.

Arthur Schlesinger Jr.'s "affirmative democratic state" connotes a good society crafted by government intervention.

Arthur Bentley spoke of "industrial organization [as a] true government" alongside political government. But he did not develop the theme of political capitalism. John Kenneth Galbraith has posited a strong form of political capitalism in which large corporations and government are intertwined—hence his term *new industrial state*. In his book of the same title, Galbraith finds that "the trend of public policy has been highly favorable to [business] needs." Walter Adams likens Galbraith's concept to "technocracy" and "private socialism."

In his presidential address to the American Economic Association, Galbraith added:

> When the modern corporation acquires power over markets, power in the community, power over the state, power over belief, it is a political instrument, different in form and degree but not in kind from the state itself. To hold otherwise—to deny the political character of the modern corporation—is not merely to avoid the reality. It is to disguise the reality.

This superman view of corporations fails to recognize how even the corporate colossuses can stumble, even crumble (e.g., Samuel Insull's utility empire in 1932 and Enron in 2001). It also ignores the crucial distinction between the government's monopoly on force and the corporation's reliance on voluntary exchange under capitalism proper. Still, the characterization includes important elements of political capitalism.

Government intervention in international affairs to promote export markets is an important area of political capitalism. The foreign policy that has sprung up around this end involves the enormous business sector serving the military. The *military-industrial complex*, a term used by President Eisenhower upon leaving office in 1961, has been called "a state within a state." Economic historian Robert Higgs has expanded the term to "military industrial *Congressional* complex," to explicitly incorporate the crucial role that the government plays in allocating out the sizable defense budget every year. Other terms in this genre are "military State capitalism," "corporate-imperial order," "Hamiltonian-nationalist State," and "empire." "War socialism," "war guildism," and "war corporatism" are other critical terms used to describe this aspect of political capitalism, which all fall within the two most familiar terms, *imperialism* and *militarism*.

Central Planning

A family of terms under the umbrella *corporatism* is popularly used to describe government-owned and directed business activity, where the emphasis is on "community interests over individual interests." Four variants are

"historical or 'natural' corporatism," "ideological corporatism," "manifest corporatism," and "modern neo-corporatism." These uses do not translate to political capitalism as used in this book.

Under national economic planning, also known as "industrial policy,"
"reindustrialization policy," "national foresight capacity," or simply "non-
comprehensive planning" (to differentiate it from comprehensive planning, or
market socialism), private business is directed by government edict and/or
supplemented by government capital allocation. The federal Reconstruction
Finance Corporation (RFC), founded in 1932 by Herbert Hoover and reorga-
nized as the Small Business Administration in 1953, was an instrument of industrial policy. Japan's Ministry of International Trade and Industry (MITI) is a
stronger version. Business leaders in the 1930s strongly supported the RFC, just
as some prominent Wall Street financiers supported the idea of its resurrection
in the 1970s and 1980s. A planned economy, under bureaucratic management,
may be termed *bureaucratism*.

Socialism is defined as state ownership of the means of production (land,
labor, and capital). The entire economy is planned from the center, or under
central planning. The economy is one big firm, as it were, with planner bureaucrats being counterpart to capitalism's industrialists.

Marxism, which evolved into Marxism-Leninism and Stalinism in practice,
is a strident form of socialism where the state invokes mass force—and mass
terror—in an attempt to rid human nature of self-interest and individualism.
Such omnipotent government is also described by such terms as *communism*,
collectivism, and *fascism*. These different forms of *central economic planning* have
been intellectually refuted, although they still exist in practice around the world.
Leading varieties of totalitarianism include *Russian Bolshevism*, *Italian Fascism*,
and *German Nazism*.

Karl Marx and Friedrich Engels never used the term *political capitalism*. But
they recognized in *The Communist Manifesto* the close relationship between the
bourgeoisie ("the class of modern Capitalists") and the political means. "Each
step in the development of the bourgeoisie was accompanied by a corresponding political advance of that class," they wrote in 1848.

Appendix C
Gabriel Kolko's Revisionism Reconsidered

G ABRIEL KOLKO FOUNDED a school of thought with his books *The Triumph of Conservatism* (1963) and *Railroads and Regulation* (1965). Before he burst onto the scene, the public-interest theory of regulation was dominant; after Kolko, the mainstream of thought has acknowledged the primary role of business interests in securing, or at least shaping, important regulations of nineteenth- and twentieth-century America. Yet several decades later, as Thomas McCraw states:

> Kolko's ideas failed to convince many of his colleagues. Some historians pointed out that he ignored contrary evidence and misunderstood basic economics; others argued that he fallaciously assumed a polarity between the public interest and private interests; still others asserted that even the selective evidence he did present, although useful, did not begin to sustain his thesis, in part because he often failed to distinguish what businessmen received from what they originally wanted.

"Still," McCraw concludes, "Kolko's books asked new, challenging questions, and neither the questions nor his evidence could be dismissed easily."

Kolko's interpretation of federal railroad legislation has been subject to numerous, and in places telling, criticism. However, his political-capitalism thesis has been advanced in recent decades by new and more detailed examples, such as those from the energy industries.

Anticipating Kolko

Gabriel Kolko's revisionist interpretation of business/state relations in the so-called Progressive Era had prior development. A book review of *Railroads and Regulation* by Robert Harbeson in the *Journal of Economic History* cited seven prior studies documenting "the fact that the railroads actively sponsored" the Interstate Commerce Act of 1887. A book published in 1955 documented the important role of New York merchants in securing the 1887 law. This example of political capitalism was part of a more general theme documented by Robert Wiebe in a book published a year ahead of Kolko's *Triumph of Conservatism*. In *Businessmen and Reform*, Wiebe found, "The business community was the most important single factor—or set of factors—in the development of economic regulation." He added: "At least one segment of the business community supported each major program of federal control. In this area businessmen exercised their greatest influence on reform and laid their claim as progressives." In his book review of *The Triumph of Conservatism*, Wiebe questioned the originality of Kolko's thesis but concluded that "the whole constitutes a novel, intriguing argument."

Wiebe and others had pieces of the political-capitalism puzzle. Robert Lively documented the "mistake" of believing in nineteenth-century "King Laissez Faire" at the local and state levels. But Kolko put the case together in such a way that transformed the debate. As discussed in chapter 6, Kolko's political-capitalism thesis is amply supported by other case studies to show that he was *generally* correct, although his most detailed example, the railroad industry, was more pluralistic and nuanced than portrayed in *Railroads and Regulation*. Still, shifting causality from carriers to shippers leaves *business lobbying*, or political capitalism, as the heavyweight, and *the people* as the lightweight, in railroad public-policy reform.

Kolko's Caveats

As more than a few of his critics have acknowledged, Kolko considered opposing views, anticipated criticism, and provided caveats in his analysis. From his earliest publications, Kolko noticed that business leaders could disagree on their preferred piece of political capitalism. Some business leaders did not favor government intervention, though for self-interested rather than ideological reasons. It was the historian's job to weigh the different sides of the scale to see who prevailed and why. As Kolko stated:

> One can always find some businessman, of course, who opposed federal regulation at any point, including within his own industry. Historians have relished in detailing such opposition, and, indeed, their larger analysis of the period has encouraged such revelations. But the finding of division in the ranks of business can be significant only if one makes the false assumption of a monolithic common interest among all capitalists, but, worse yet, assumes that there is no power center among capitalists, and that small-town bankers or hardware dealers can be equated with the leaders of the top industrial, financial, and railroad corporations. They can be equated, of course, if all one studies is the bulk of printed words. But in the political as well as in the economic competition between small and big business, the larger interests always managed to prevail in any specific contest.

However, as discussed in chapter 5, *smaller* interests can prevail over *larger* interests if the smaller are better organized and motivated, a point that Arthur Bentley made in *The Process of Government* in 1908.

Regarding the Interstate Commerce Act, Kolko concluded that "the mere fact that [railroads] did not always get their specific legislative demands indicates that not only were the railroads divided among themselves as to precisely what legislative measures they wanted passed, but that they faced opposition on many points from shipping groups who had their own goals and demands."

Railroads and Regulation Revisited

Kolko's "radical reappraisal" of federal railroad regulation in *Railroads and Regulation* consisted of three main points.

- "The railroads, not the farmers and shippers, were the most important single advocates of federal regulation from 1877 to 1916."
- "The ICC [Interstate Commerce Commission] was aligned, for the most part, with the railroads."
- "The federal regulation of railroads from 1887 until 1916 did not disappoint the American railroad industry."

Each point has been challenged in the 40 years since *Railroads and Regulation* was published. Kolko himself has scarcely responded to his critics, and no scholar has rebutted the criticism in toto from Kolko's perspective. Historians have challenged Kolko as follows.

- Major railroads did not support the final draft of what became the Interstate Commerce Act of 1887.
- Shippers were more powerful at both the state and federal levels than railroads in securing regulation.
- Major railroads opposed expanded rate regulation by the ICC.
- Rate-increase denials for railroads by the ICC beginning in 1910 resulted in performance problems and nationalization of the industry in 1917.
- ICC regulation went through periods when some constituencies were favored at the expense of other groups.

Several points can be made in Kolko's defense, beginning with the accepted facts that a distressed railroad industry engaged in price wars and unsuccessfully tried to self-cartelize. Many railroad leaders were hungry for help and longed for the *right* regulation to reverse the situation. Other industries with similar characteristics as railroads (high fixed costs relative to operating costs, and overcapacity) turned to regulation to *limit entry* and accepted rate regulation as a means to this greater end. That these industries did not desire rate regulation by itself and that they worked to moderate rate regulation over time does not invalidate the fact that regulation as part of a practical political package was desired. Some railroad leaders desired rate reform to make fares more uniform and known in the market, as did shippers.

Some of Kolko's critics displayed a naïve view of business and regulation. "It would indeed be remarkable for any industry to cheerfully relinquish control of fundamental economic questions to a politicized agency," James Ely stated. Yet many industries in distress have done this very thing, particularly those with high fixed costs and low variable costs in an oversupplied market. The "idea ghosts" dismissed by Arthur Bentley come to life in such statements by railroad historians as, "By 1886 it was obvious that Americans wanted the federal government to regulate railroads." But Americans wanted many things. Organization and political pressure are what translate wants into accommodative policy reform.

The key role of business in railroad regulation—Kolko's general theme—has been documented in various degrees by Kolko's critics, as the following quotations suggest.

- "When Congress was seriously debating the interstate commerce bill in 1885 and 1886, businessmen throughout the nation supported the idea of regulation in overwhelming numbers."

- "Although independent Pennsylvania oil producers and New York merchants helped originate the interstate commerce bill, when the chips were down, their senators opposed it. . . . [But] the momentum [they initiated] could not be stopped."

- "Transportation charges generally declined during the Gilded Age. The chronic complaint against the carriers, therefore, was not exorbitant charges but unequal treatment of shippers and communities. Every shipper was convinced that someone else was getting a better rate. Resentment of alleged rate discrimination was at the heart of the calls for government controls."

- "The driving force for railroad regulation [in California] came less from an outraged public seeking lower railroad rates than from shippers and merchants who wanted to stabilize their businesses. Public utility [company] officers spearheaded campaigns for the passage, and, later, the enlargement of the [California] Public Utilities Act."

- "Though railroads had favored anti-rebating legislation, they campaigned in 1905 both in and out of Congress against rate regulation."

- "While tension regarding maximum rate restrictions did heighten during [the decades following passage of the 1887 Act], the ICC and the railroads generally seem to have been united in pressing for regulatory controls that would restrict competition."

- "While the railroads in general had been initially opposed to the regulatory provisions of the 1887 statute, the Elkins Act [of 1903] was sponsored by the carriers themselves."

- "That 'big business' had a substantial impact on the implementation of [the Hepburn Act of 1906] is certainly likely."

- "The impetus for change in the Progressive era, at least with regard to federal rate regulation, came from smaller business interests for which rapid industrial growth and market expansion had brought more problems than profits."

What the railroads really wanted but could not get, unlike their counterparts in the gas, electricity, and communications industries, at least on the federal level, was formal *public utility regulation*. "A large majority of the railroads in the United States would be delighted if a railroad commission or any other power could make rates upon their traffic which would insure them six percent dividends," a railroad executive testified before the House Commerce Committee in 1884. "I have no doubt, with such a guarantee, they would be very glad to come under the direct supervision and operation of the National Government."

In any event, the mentality of railroad executives was scarcely antiregulation and pro-laissez-faire. Stated Edward Purcell Jr. in the *Journal of American History*:

> Businessmen were . . . more interested in solving particular problems than they were in adhering to any "business philosophy". . . . The great majority of them rejected laissez-faire economics. . . . Businessmen were much more concerned with the evils of rate discrimination, the effects of pooling, and the value of long-and-short-haul legislation than they were with the laws of nature, the benevolence of competition, or the loss of an abstract liberty.

Thus, it can be hypothesized that federal regulation of the interstate railroad industry would not have occurred if the railroads, for ideological or practical reasons, had not favored such intervention.

Conclusions

The central thesis of political capitalism—business itself as a driving force behind the majority of twentieth-century regulation—remains inviolate even with a partial reinterpretation of Kolko's railroad conclusions. Business includes *shippers*, not only carriers, and "merchants and farmers had their own economic agenda, and were quick to invoke the 'public interest' as a cloak." The rationale for initial regulation as being consumer driven or public-spirited is thus highly questionable. "Historians would do well to look with a critical eye at allegations of rate abuses [against consumers] by the railroads," Ely warned.

Kolko's documentation and focus on business lobbying for *initial regulation* dulled his recognition of regulation as a double-edged sword. Repeated denials of rate increases for the railroad industry by the ICC beginning in 1910 did result in performance problems and nationalization of the industry in 1917.

Antitrust was another two-edged sword, and many business leaders lost faith in using it to hurt the competition. Samuel Insull would have serious second thoughts about public utility regulation of electricity—a regime he fathered (a topic of Book 2). A regulatory agency can have "a life of its own" whether or not a particular business interest favored its creation. As Robert Horwitz has noted: "Because temporality and changes in political dynamics *are* factors in regulatory behavior, there is no *single* pattern to the behavior of agencies."

A regulatory body powerful enough to help a company or an industry is powerful enough to hurt it. There is not only the question of business in a free-market environment proactively seeking intervention but also the question of reactive or defensive business lobbying against the intervention desired by others. Railroads were in this situation in the nineteenth century and after. Business leaders pragmatically come to the table, although they might not have even wanted the issue to be in play.

The "tightest and best established" business organizations "enjoyed the greatest opportunities to affect progressive legislation," stated Robert Weibe, making a point emphasized decades before by Arthur Bentley. But this did not mean that big beat small in all matters political. Standard Oil in Rocke-feller's day lost battles to smaller rivals that had better political connections and/or organization in certain states. Smaller firms can be better organized and focused than bigger, even dominant, competitors, particularly in local set-tings. Indeed, smaller, inefficient competitors had particular reason to exercise the political means against their larger, more efficient rivals. The political victories of shippers over carriers in transportation industries are examples of this as well.

Business conflicts in the political arena—big versus small, integrated versus nonintegrated, diversified versus nondiversified, high-cost versus low-cost, domestic versus international—are all in the orbit of political capitalism. Political capitalism posits that *in the majority of cases at most points in time*, the primary driver of government intervention in markets has been business interests. Gabriel Kolko was the first scholar to forward and substantiate this hypothesis on a grand scale.

Political capitalism has become much more competitive, pluralistic, and transparent since the Progressive Era. Many well-organized and well-funded interests representing age, sex, race, education, religion, environment, family, consumers, taxpayers, and so forth, have made reformers the majority and busi-ness interests the minority in some, if not many, episodes.

Reformers can be strange bedfellows, as previously discussed. Minority business interests allied with reformers can legislatively defeat a business majority. The relative pluralism of modern political capitalism is evidenced by the deregulation of protected U.S. industries in the 1970s and 1980s, which led one scholar to conclude: "The very fact of deregulation tends to invalidate capture and conspiracy theories of regulation, and to restore a measure of autonomy to state action." Still, political capitalism will always be alive and well in the mixed economy if for no other reason than business is such a big player in economic life. This point was made a century ago by William Graham Sumner: "I see no force in modern society which can cope with the power of capital handled by talent, and I cannot doubt that the greatest force will control the other forces."

Appendix D

Resources for the Future: Away from Optimism

ESTABLISHED IN 1952, Resources for the Future (RFF) is the nation's oldest, largest think tank in the field of energy and natural resources. With an annual budget approximating $11 million, RFF fields a research staff of 40, mostly Ph.D. economists. "RFF has pioneered the application of economics as a tool to develop more effective policy about the use and conservation of natural resources," its Web site states. "[Our] scholars continue to analyze critical issues concerning pollution control, energy policy, land and water use, hazardous waste, climate change, biodiversity, and the environmental challenges of developing countries."

RFF's work is applied, not theory for its own sake. "Today's critical concerns involve such areas as climate change, fishery viability, energy efficiency, antibiotic resistance, ecosystem collapse, and forest sustainability," RFF's 2006 annual report states. RFF considers itself "the go-to source of reasoned and dispassionate analysis of complex environmental and natural resources issues." It adds: "RFF is committed to maintaining its status as the single best source of high-quality social science analysis of current environmental and natural resources regulatory policy."

In its first half century, RFF's central message has gone from energy optimism to energy pessimism, complete with an embrace of major government intervention in energy markets. The transformation began in the 1970s with a fixity/depletion view of mineral resources, which spawned conservationism. And when the energy-short 1970s turned into the energy-surplus 1980s, RFF's angst shifted to issues surrounding a human influence on global climate, primarily from carbon dioxide (CO_2) emissions from the burning of coal, oil, and natural gas. RFF embraced climate alarmism even before global warming became a national issue in 1988.

In the 1990s, RFF and Enron found common ground regarding policies related to anthropogenic climate change. RFF proposals to regulate greenhouse gas (GHG) emissions via a cap-and-trade program dovetailed with Enron's interest in becoming one of the world's leading market makers in CO_2 permits. Ken Lay rejoined RFF's board of directors in 2000 (he had been a board member back when he was president of Transco Energy Company), and in spring 2001, Enron's chairman personally donated $2 million to RFF to establish an endowed chair in his name. "As a businessman, I know the difference between public relations and objective research," Lay said in a press release. "And what we need in this nation today to improve policymaking across a range of challenging resource management issues is exactly the kind of fair and measured work that has earned RFF its impeccable reputation as an honest broker." RFF returned the compliment, calling Lay's Enron the archetype of the modern energy company.

RFF is important for the Enron story. Documenting the think tank's public-policy evolution offers a window on the intellectual debates at the center of this book.

From Resource Optimism to Pessimism . . . and Back

A plethora of factual, optimistic studies on natural resources were published from the early 1950s until the early 1970s. Resources for the Future was the locus of much of this activity. Among its studies were:

- Bruce Netschert, *The Future Supply of Oil and Gas* (Baltimore: The Johns Hopkins Press, 1958)

- Sam Schurr and Bruce Netschert, *Energy in the American Economy, 1850–1975* (Baltimore: The Johns Hopkins Press, 1960)

- Neal Potter and Francis Christy, *Trends in Natural Resource Commodities: Statistics of Prices, Output, Consumption, Foreign Trade, and Employment in the United States, 1870–1957* (Baltimore: The Johns Hopkins Press, 1960)

- Hans Landsberg et al., *Resources in America's Future: Patterns of Requirements and Availabilities, 1960–2000* (Baltimore: The Johns Hopkins Press, 1963)

- Harold Barnett and Chandler Morse, *Scarcity and Growth: The Economics of Natural Resource Availability* (Baltimore: The Johns Hopkins Press, 1963)

- Hans Landsberg and Sam Schurr, *Energy in the United States: Sources, Uses, and Policy Issues* (New York: Random House, 1968)

- Joel Darmstadter et al., *Energy in the World Economy: A Statistical Review of Trends in Output, Trade, and Consumption since 1925* (Baltimore: The Johns Hopkins Press, 1971)

Two notable studies not affiliated with RFF were the Twentieth Century Fund's *America's Needs and Resources: A New Survey* (1955) and a 1962 study prepared for the U.S. Senate, *An Assessment of Available Information on Energy in the United States.*

Studies by RFF economist Orris Herfindahl melded theory and data to reach optimistic conclusions. His major works included *Copper Costs and Prices:*

1870–1957 (Baltimore: The Johns Hopkins Press, 1959); *Three Studies in Minerals Economics* (Washington, DC: Resources for the Future, 1961); David Brooks, ed., *Resource Economics: Selected Works of Orris C. Herfindahl* (Baltimore: The Johns Hopkins Press, 1974); and Herfindahl and Allen Kneese, *Economic Theory of Natural Resources* (Columbus, OH: Charles Merrill, 1974).

A 1968 RFF staff report, *U.S. Energy Policies: An Agenda for Research*, reported the "widespread belief that energy requirements for the next twenty years or more can be met without serious upward pressure on real costs." RFF's Joel Darmstadter and Milton Searl testified before Congress in May 1973: "The estimated U.S. resources of shale oil and crude oil are so large that it is unlikely that there will ever be a time at which the nation will not be able to develop substantial additional supplies of oil."

A 1975 book by Mason Willrich, *Energy and World Politics*, on which Darmstadter assisted, took the M. A. Adelman position that "our immediate difficulties are not due to physical scarcity of energy resources or to economic scarcity of low-cost resources; rather, they have arisen because of monopolization by a relatively few governments of the world's known low-cost oil resources."

The New Pessimism

Then the tide turned toward pessimism and alarmism. A 1975 essay by RFF's John Krutilla and Talbot Page, citing helpful input from the Environmental Defense Fund, Natural Resources Defense Council, Sierra Club, and Wilderness Society, was long on conservationism and government intervention and short on the supply side and free market. "Towards a Responsible Energy Policy" was *depletionist* ("we will be forced to rely on new domestic sources and to pay higher prices for energy in the years to come ... [from] our previous policy encouraging [mineral resource] exploitation") and *interventionist* ("we might consider the appropriate taxation of commodities whose prices do not reflect the external or environmental cost of their production, distribution, and consumption"). The authors took a very hard line on allowing greater offshore production, placing the burden of proof on government and drillers to "minimize the social costs" of drilling, extractions, and transportation.

The turmoil in energy markets from federal price and allocation controls got a free ride, and the OPEC-led doubling of oil prices was scarcely considered as intervention enough to remove the case of alleged market failure from underpriced energy. Krutilla and Page ended their essay with a call for greater "public participation" to set energy policy, with "more explicit consideration ... to intertemporal welfare distribution than has been true in the past."

A review of energy developments in 1976, published in RFF's *Resources* magazine, reached a Hotelling-like conclusion: "Nonrenewable and exhaustible fuels supply most of our needs now," the staff article stated, "but they will be increasingly expensive to obtain and use, until, around some distant corner, they will be replaced." A 1977 RFF book, *Conservation & Economic Efficiency*, included a foreword by Walter Spofford Jr., head of RFF's Quality of the Environment Division, referring to "the continual erosion of a finite natural resource base." An RFF book edited by V. Kerry Smith, published in 1979 with papers from a 1976 conference, also cited environmental issues and depletion of mineral resources.

RFF's sea change toward resource pessimism was in full flower with a 1979 book, *Energy in America's Future: The Choices Before Us,* and continued, as discussed in chapter 11, with *Energy Today and Tomorrow: Living with Uncertainty* (1983). It was also evident in the presidential address of Sam Schurr to the International Association of Energy Economists (later renamed the International Association for Energy Economics), when he warned, drawing on *Energy in America's Future,* that the nation was "running out of time . . . for launching the necessary technical and policy initiatives."

Why did RFF turn away from resource optimism? Restated, why did RFF's bevy of Ph.D. economists fail to recognize the institutional (man-made) reasons for the unprecedented energy scarcity, namely, government price and allocation controls? Several things were at work: the nonconfrontational nature of RFF leaders Hans Landsberg and Sam Schurr in the face of contrary thinking, an underlying view of resources as fixed quantities subject to depletion, and the bias of RFF-funding sources toward a government role in addressing resource problems. Perhaps the greatest factor was the death of Orris Herfindahl, head of RFF's mineral-resource program. Herfindahl was no depletionist, and his death in 1972 at age 54 took away a leading thinker in the field. Commented M. A. Adelman, who lost a key intellectual ally: "It was the worst possible moment for him to die, he would be so badly needed."

The proper interpretation, one that RFF was well positioned to champion, was that *government intervention created the resource problem, and reestablished free-market incentives could reintroduce resource abundance.* The American Enterprise Institute, as it turned out, filled the void left by RFF, as discussed in chapter 10.

Energy economist Richard Gordon, a participant in the resource debates in question, offered this view:

> Throughout its history, Resources for the Future has been a major source of penetrating analyses of resource availability and the deficiencies of government intervention. Ironically, during the energy turmoil of the 1970s, RFF's efforts faltered. The main contributions were two externally funded efforts that showed excessive concern over depletion and were too tolerant of government intervention. The main problem was the disappearance of RFF's ability to fund external researchers. Those researchers had produced most of the main contributions to resource optimism and criticism of government. (A critical exception was the work of Orris Herfindahl, who died before the turmoil.) Sam Schurr and Hans Landsberg were astute observers of energy and key in fostering the prior external studies. However, they were not analytic and thus presided over studies that lacked a framework that ensured proper consideration of the underlying resource

situation and the drawbacks of intervention. Later RFF work, undertaken by more analytic people, such as Milton Russell and Douglas Bohi, returned to the prior orientation. Still later, however, funding problems would severely limit RFF activities in energy and increase the long-standing focus on environmental-oriented studies. These were excellent at describing the workings of these policies but weak on skeptical appraisal of the rationales for intervention.

The turn at RFF was also influenced at the very top, beginning with influential members of its board of directors. Board member Maurice Strong, secretary general of the U.N. Conference on the Human Environment, worked with Hans Landsberg in 1972 to organize the first international conference seeking to balance development and environmentalism. The collaborative effort moved RFF toward neo-Malthusianism as RFF tried to move neo-Malthusians toward a more optimistic view of resources.

Changing Thought

In the 1980s, as depletion concerns lessened, RFF's interest in energy turned to a new bread-and-butter issue, anthropogenic (man-made) climate change associated with greenhouse-gas emissions from carbon-based fuel combustion. Still, two RFF books would address natural-resource availability questions. A 1999 book edited by R. David Simpson, *Productivity in Natural Resource Industries*, revisited some classic questions of the 1960s and documented the ability of human ingenuity and technology to overcome the limits of nature. It was depletion itself that inspired solutions: "This book provides many examples of depletion introducing innovation and of the combination and recombination of technologies producing still more innovations." A chapter by Douglas Bohi ("Technology Improvement in Petroleum Exploration and Development") chronicled the breakthroughs in three areas—3D seismic technology, horizontal drilling, and deepwater exploration and production—that increased productivity and controlled cost over time.

A 2003 book by John Tilton, *On Borrowed Time? Assessing the Threat of Mineral Depletion*, returned to some major themes of RFF's 1963 landmark *Scarcity and Growth*. Tilton found that

> new technology has during the past 130 years kept the adverse effects of depletion at bay despite an unprecedented surge in both population and the consumption of mineral commodities. Real production costs of and prices for many mineral commodities have actually fallen, implying that their availability has increased.

He added: "During the next 50 to 100 years . . . mineral depletion is not likely to rank among the most pressing problems confronting society." But he did not hazard a guess about the victor between depletion and technology for the great beyond—hence the title of the book.

These two books, highly influenced by the latest empirical data on cost and prices, effectively refuted the prior depletionist work of RFF—and returned the organization, in a sense, to its 1950s and 1960s tradition. But the damage had been done by a second generation of scholars who embraced Harold Hotelling instead of Erich Zimmermann, Julian Simon, M. A. Adelman, and others in the optimist camp who traced their roots to the Paley Commission report and to Harold Barnett and Chandler Morse's 1963 *Scarcity and Growth*.

Embracing Gapism in the 1970s

Gapism was defined in chapter 10 as the implementation of government measures to reduce demand and increase supply in a quest to engineer a balance of supply and demand in the presence of price controls. In the price-controlled 1970s, RFF embraced gapism for oil and gas, which was related to the organization's aforementioned turn from resource optimism.

A January 1974 RFF *Resources* essay, "Energy in Crisis," although confident about the resource base, was defeatist on the public-policy front. Rather than advocate deregulation of wellhead oil and gas prices to instantly end shortages and set up longer-run gains, the essay stated, "Our ability to cope with [energy] problems in the short run through market adjustments is limited." A constructivist approach was outlined—a "two-pronged approach to the energy problem"—before discussing President Nixon's highly interventionist proposals, outlined in his energy message from the prior November.

Energy conservation as a core government activity was fully embraced by RFF. "For energy users to be able to respond knowledgeably to market conditions," stated Joel Darmstadter in 1975, "government policies designed to guide consumption practices along a more informed path are clearly desirable." He listed a variety of programs, such as information mandates on energy appliances and cars, compulsory insulation standards, a tax on horsepower or vehicle weight, and a higher gasoline tax to fund public transportation.

A fatalistic approach was again in evidence in a 1976 *Resources* essay, "Energy: The Loss of Innocence." "Neither the government nor the public has thus far indicated much capacity for getting on with the transition," leaving the reader guess about what bitter medicine should be taken. Another essay rejected the deregulation of oil prices. "Surely," the staff article read, "the financial return to U.S. producers, and especially producers of [regulated] old oil, should not be dictated by the whim of a foreign monopolistic combine."

RFF's economists did not realize that oil resellers were pocketing much of the money federal regulation was denying domestic producers and that domestic price controls were subsidizing import prices and thus OPEC. The real analysis had to come from elsewhere—prominently including the American Enterprise Institute.

Oil-price decontrol continued to be a nonstarter for RFF scholars. Long-run decontrol was viable and even recommended, but short-run deregulation was left unsupported because of its alleged inflationary and "divisive" wealth-redistribution impacts.

Institutional Advocacy for Energy Alarmism and Interventionism

From the beginning, RFF has described itself as objective and impartial. RFF's nonadvocacy stance means that the institution does not take positions, whereas its staff members do. In 1975, RFF president Charles Hitch added some nuance by stating:

> We're going to address ourselves to policy questions a little more directly, less indirectly. We will achieve this not by advocacy, but by choosing research projects more directly relevant . . . to policy alternatives, and also by improving our communications with the public and the government.

He added, "I think we can do this without prejudicing our one priceless and essential asset—our reputation for objectivity and integrity." RFF's 2006 annual report echoed this theme, stating: "RFF seeks to promote policy innovation without lapsing into advocacy." Further: "RFF's management and research team will rededicate themselves to . . . maintain the reputation of RFF as a nonaligned institution that bears no ideological edges."

But RFF *does* have recognizable institutional positions. RFF takes responsibility for its full-time employees' work product, as well as work done under its imprimatur by outside scholars. RFF's analyses are virtually always consistent; rarely, if ever, are two employees advocating different policies on the same issue. Some combination of employee selection, institutional pressure, and groupthink has ensured that RFF speaks with one voice on major policy issues.

A review of RFF's output identifies an organizational shift from resource optimism to resource pessimism and back again, as well as an organizational embrace of interventionism and gapism instead of thoroughgoing free-market reform. But the American Enterprise Institute embraced what RFF did not in the 1970s public-policy debate, and the energy alarmism embraced today by RFF is countered by the Institute for Energy Research (founded in 1989).

RFF has been careful to speak with one voice on the contentious issue of anthropogenic climate change, embracing the view that there is a clear, significant problem from unregulated emissions of greenhouse gases and a need for government regulation of such emissions. In particular, RFF researchers have endorsed a cap-and-trade program for CO_2, a position that warmed the heart of Ken Lay and Enron in the 1990s.

No employee at RFF has bucked the position of climate alarmism and government CO_2 regulation, and no member of RFF's board of directors has protested this position either. The 2002 appointment of David Hawkins, director of the climate center at the Natural Resources Defense Council, to RFF's board of directors was a clear indication of a prointerventionist ideology. No free-market counterweight exists on RFF's board, indicating that Hawkins was not merely a diversity choice. Foundation funding for RFF includes virtually no free-market donors, leaving such climate-alarmism groups as the Energy Foundation, Environmental Defense Fund, William & Flora Hewlett Foundation, Robert Woods Johnson Foundation, Pew Center on Global Climate Change, and World Wildlife Fund.

A free-market alternative found no champions within RFF. An intellectually viable alternative to government energy planning in the name of climate stabilization or energy security is greater societal wealth through unregulated GHG emissions and an expansion of capitalist institutions worldwide. This view has been stated by this author as follows:

> The major threat to energy sustainability is statism, not [mineral] depletion, pollution, reliability, or anthropogenic climate change. Major government interventions in energy markets, such as price controls, access restrictions, or carbon suppression, create the energy problems that non-politicized, free-market processes work to prevent.

For dozens of RFF's Ph.D. researchers to think in lockstep about today's most contentious energy issue is at odds with the organization's claim to be "a nonaligned institution that bears no ideological edges."

Source Notes

All works cited are as listed in the bibliography.

Introduction
Page 1
a pardon from God (C. Olson, p. 315)

Page 2
WorldCom filing (Romero and Atlas)
"systemic failure" (Will)
"I predict . . . U.S. society" (Krugman 2002)
free-market economics refutation (Kuttner 2002b)

Page 3
"approach . . . citizenship" (Swanson and Frederick, p. 25)
"The wisdom . . . corporation" (Epstein and Hanson, p. xv)
"I believe . . . markets" (quoted in Dolbee)

Page 4
"infrastructure socialism" (Thierer and Crews, p. 6)

Page 5
"the company . . . business" (Leggett, p. 204)
"last-mile" (Coffee, p. 20)
"a problem . . . markets" ("Enron's Sins")

Page 6
Fortune magazine poll (McLean and Elkind, p. 239)
"the crucial. . . Avenue" (F. McDonald 1962, p. viii)
Babe Ruth analogy (ibid., p. 237)
"I think I'm . . . immortal" (quoted in ibid., p. 277)

Page 7
"He took on . . . shoulders" (ibid., p. 284)

Page 10
"prudent man" (A. Smith 1759, p. 213)
"over-weening conceit" (A. Smith 1776, p. 124)

"self-deceit" (A. Smith 1759, p. 156)
"sacred rules" (ibid., p. 163)
"mutual sympathy" (ibid., p. 13)
"How many tricks . . . than others" (S. Smiles 1881, p. 68)

Page 11
"maximizing . . . integrity" (Koch 2007, p. 79)

Page 12
"radical . . . crime" (McCraw 2007, pp. 354–55)

Introduction to Part I: Heroic Capitalism
Page 17
"infectious greed" (testimony before the Banking, Housing, and Urban Affairs Committee, on July 16, 2002, quoted in Goldstein)
"the avenues . . . enormously" (ibid.)
"remarkable . . . capitalism" (Goldstein)
"Whether dealing . . . without referees" (Fox, p. 313)
"a government . . . rules" (Eichenwald, p. 11)
"are now . . . from within" (Partnoy, p. 394)
"Enron . . . twentieth century" (Swartz with Watkins, p. 350)
"was . . . corrupt" (Bryce, p. 12)
"an American . . . wrong" (Seay and Bryan, p. 124)
"Business Ethics and Other Oxymorons" (Norris)
"For decades . . . century" (Kolko 2006, pp. 116–17)

1 The Soul of Commerce: Adam Smith
Figures
1.1 "beau . . . books" (quoted in Skousen, p. 14)

Footnotes
4 *"a predisposition . . . a later date"* (Gintis et al., p. 8)

Page 19
unsightly bundles (Heilbroner 1953, p. 28)
"acute . . . process" (Blaug, p. 57)
founder of economics (Rogge, p. 86; Skousen, p. 13; Viner, pp. 116–17)
"The first . . . Adam Smith" (quoted in Skousen, p. 20 n2)
first treatise (Knight 1933, p. 6)
"great architect" (Schumpeter 1954, p. 185)

Page 20
"The ideal . . . 'invisible hand'" (Kelly)
"The failure . . . regulators" (Millstein, p. 6)
"We must recognize . . . billions of dollars" (quoted in Prashad, p. 53)
"Market failures . . . and investors" (Ehrlich and Ehrlich 2004, p. 291)
"the current . . . capitalism" (Krugman 2005, p. 122)
"deregulation" (ibid., p. 319)
"loving . . . much" (ibid.)
"rigid . . . prejudices" (ibid., p. 295)

"entrust[ed] . . . hand" (ibid., p. 315)
material progress (A. Smith 1776, pp. 23–24)
"universal opulence" (ibid., p. 22)
"the obvious . . . natural liberty" (ibid., p. 687)

Page 21
"as the hand . . . chess-board" (A. Smith 1759, p. 234)
"led by an invisible hand" (A. Smith 1776, p. 456)
"a singular . . . notice" (Stewart 1793, p. 290)
"How selfish . . . seeing it" (A. Smith 1759, p. 9)

Page 22
"mutual sympathy" (ibid., p. 13)
"Whatever . . . spectator" (ibid., p. 10)
concord with the emotions (ibid., p. 16)
emotions identified (ibid, pp. 9–11)
"a disagreeable passion" (ibid., p. 15)
"justice . . . innocence" (ibid., p. 79)
"beat . . . done" (ibid.)
"an unintended . . . order" (Otteson 2002, p. 5)
"self-love" (A. Smith 1759, p. 83)
a desire for approval (ibid., p. 117)
"The love . . . the most" (ibid., p. 114)
"praise-worthy qualities" (ibid., p. 304)
"prudence . . . firmness" (ibid.)
"economy . . . thought" (ibid.)

Page 23
"marketplace of morality" (Otteson 2002, pp. 9, 101)
"experimental . . . behaviour" (Fehr and Fishbacher, p. 790)
positive and negative reciprocity (Otteson, forthcoming; Vernon Smith, p. 31)
cognitive neuroscience and trust (Cook; King-Casas et al.)
"psychological perspective" (Ashraf, Camerer, and Loewenstein, p. 132)
"suggests . . . exploited" (ibid.)
"In short . . . human beings" (ibid., p. 142)
"the care . . . depend" (A. Smith 1759, p. 213)
"success. . . business" (ibid., p. 166)
"perfectly genuine" (ibid., p. 213)
"always sincere" (ibid., p. 214)
"cautious . . . actions" (ibid.)
"reserved . . . speech" (ibid.)
"the steadiness . . . frugality" (ibid., p. 215)

Page 24
"always studies . . . understands it" (ibid., p. 213)
"brilliant" (ibid., p. 214)
"distinguished . . . sensibility" (ibid.)
"imprudent pretender" (ibid., p. 213)
"artful imposter" (ibid.)

"The prudent . . . people" (ibid., p. 215)
"steady . . . fortune" (ibid., pp. 190–91)
"vanity . . . profligacy" (ibid., p. 63)
"imprudence" (ibid., p. 115)
immediate gratification (ibid., p. 189)
"love . . . applause" (ibid., p. 238)
"capitals . . . misconduct" (A. Smith 1776, p. 337)
self-command (A. Smith 1759, pp. 237–62)
"temperance . . . moderation" (ibid., p. 238)
"the great mob . . . greatness" (ibid., p. 62)
"passion . . . ambition" (ibid., p. 173)
"commands . . . admiration" (ibid., p. 216)
"a private . . . injustice" (ibid., p. 173)
"man of enterprise" (ibid.)
"sacred . . . uppermost" (ibid., p. 163)

Page 25
code-of-conduct waiver (Swartz with Watkins, p. 172)
"candidates for fortune" (A. Smith 1759, p. 64)
"too . . . virtue" (ibid.)
"become . . . conduct" (ibid., p. 114)
"self-deceit" (ibid., p. 156)
"there is not . . . own character" (ibid, p. 112n)
"moral looking glass" (ibid.)
"The propriety . . . great distance" (ibid., p. 154)
"Are you . . . fortune" (ibid.)

Page 26
"study . . . virtue" (ibid., p. 62)
"the acquisition . . . greatness" (ibid.)
"proud ambition . . .avidity" (ibid.)
"over-weening conceit" (A. Smith 1776, p. 124)
"every individual . . . principle" (A. Smith 1759, p. 83)
"humble . . . self-love" (ibid.)
"excessive . . . extravagant" (ibid.)
"bring . . . down" (ibid.)
"something . . . with" (ibid.)
"the highest degree. . . wrong" (ibid., p. 234)
"ideal plan of government" (ibid.)
"highest . . . disorder" (ibid.)
"it is . . . luxuries" (A. Smith 1776, p. 346)
"are . . . society" (ibid.)
"trust . . . theirs" (ibid.)
"man of system" (A. Smith 1759, p. 233)
"apt . . . conceit" (ibid.)

Page 27
"The Laws of Justice" (ibid., p. 84)
"Little else . . . things" (quoted in Stewart, p. 322)

"unsocial . . . mean-spirited . . . poor-spirited" (A. Smith 1759, pp. 172–73)
"should have little respect" (ibid., p. 173)
bring down society (ibid., pp. 86–88)
"the first . . . own" (A. Smith 1762–66, p. 5)
"life and person . . . property and possession . . . personal rights . . . others"
(A. Smith 1759, p. 84)
"fraud, falsehood . . . abhorrence" (ibid., pp. 167–68)
"In . . . play" (ibid., p. 83)
"The number . . . a thousand" (A. Smith 1776, p. 342)

Page 28
U.S. bankruptcy rate (American Bankruptcy Institute)
"Bankruptcy . . . gallows" (A. Smith 1776, p. 342)
"presumptuous . . . trades" (ibid., p. 128)
"trade of speculation" (ibid., p. 130)
"a bold . . . ones" (ibid., pp. 130–31)
"the debtor . . . distress" (A. Smith 1762–66, p. 131)
"Trade . . . fault" (Blackstone, vol. 1:388–89)
"allow . . . own" (ibid., p. 388)
"his . . . apparel" (A. Smith 1762–66, p. 131)
"great . . . great" (ibid., p. 132)

Page 29
"The general . . . enterprise" (Story, vol. 2:43–44)
"the negligence . . . affairs" (A. Smith 1762–66, p. 103)
small capitalists (Larson, pp. 94–101)

Page 30
"private copartnery" (A. Smith 1776, p. 740)
"The directors . . . company" (ibid., p. 741)

Page 31
"The greater . . . copartnery" (A. Smith 1776, p. 741)
" 'I don't care . . . done' " (J. Q. Wilson 1989, p. 68)
" 'I can't . . . orders' " (ibid.)
"sacred . . . upon" (A. Smith 1759, p. 121)
"their enterprises . . . exist" (Galbraith 1977, p. 26)
"the most . . . world" (Novak 1997, p. 3)
faith in markets (A. Smith 1776, pp. 342–43, 456)
more capital (ibid., p. 741)
concentrated ownership (ibid., p. 744)
routine business activities (ibid., p. 756)

Page 32
increasing protectionism (Muller, pp. 56, 69)
"a form . . . warfare" (ibid., p. 56)
"the plenty . . . provisions" (A. Smith 1762–66, p. 472)
"exclusive priviledges . . . market" (ibid., pp. 497–98)
"diminishes public opulence . . . one" (ibid., p. 498)
"The mercantilist . . . practice" (Allen, p. 445)

liked commoners and disliked monopolists (Rogge, p. 99; West, p. 143)
"the mean . . . mankind" (A. Smith 1776, p. 493)
"extravagant price . . . monopoly" (Gibbins, p. 137)
"The proposal . . . attention" (A. Smith 1776, p. 267)

Page 33
"people of the same trade" (A. Smith 1776, p. 145)
"conversation . . . raise prices" (ibid.)
"liberty and justice" (ibid.)
"exclusive privilege" (ibid., p. 146)
"I expect . . . Public" (A. Smith 1974, p. 286)
"The legislature . . . already established" (A. Smith 1776, pp. 471–72)
"In the . . . serve" (A. Smith 1759, p. 63)

Page 34
"quiet . . . times" (ibid.)
"the solid . . . legislator" (ibid.)
"perennial . . . destruction" (Schumpeter 1942, p. 83)
"disposition to admire . . . moral sentiments" (A. Smith 1759, p. 61)
"Inattentive observers . . . virtue" (ibid., p. 62)
"It is . . . degrade them" (ibid., p. 64)
"The ambitious man . . . that elevation" (ibid.)
"Every man . . . should be so" (ibid., p. 82)

Page 35
"I have . . . from it" (A. Smith 1776, p. 456)
"restrains . . . negligence" (ibid., p. 146)
"exclusive privilege" (ibid.)
"The uniform . . . administration" (ibid., p. 343)
"private prodigality and misconduct" (ibid.)
"the frugality . . . of others" (ibid., p. 341)
"an unconscious mercenary . . . impulses" (Lerner, p. ix)

Page 36
importance to Smith of *Theory of Moral Sentiments* (Wight, pp. 275–76)
"Surprising . . . ideas" (Wight, "Saving Adam Smith")
"obvious . . . liberty" (A. Smith 1776, p. 687)
laws of justice (A. Smith 1759, p. 84)

2 Character and Success: Samuel Smiles
Footnotes
1 "One is . . . profession" (quoted in Travers, p. 10)
5 "that . . . humility" (F. McDonald, p. 81)
9 "I could not be idle" (quoted in Travers, p. 234)

Page 37
"shocking . . . judgment" (Eichenwald, p. 11)

Page 38
"The greatest . . . attitudes" (quoted in Butler-Bowdon, p. 1)
Victorian England (Briggs 1955, p. 1; Sinnema, pp. 1–4)
"there were . . . Virtue" (A. Smiles, p. 53)

Page 39
"Self-Help . . . lyceums" (Sinnema, p. vii)
U.K. welfarism over Smiles (Harris, pp. vii–viii)
Smiles influence on Insull (F. McDonald 1962, p. 10; Insull 1919, p. 185)
"Corporations . . . age . . . company" (Insull 1917, p. 137)
"be ready . . . knocks" (ibid., p. 136)
"It rests . . . chance" (ibid., p. 135)
"applied . . . work" (F. McDonald 1962, p. 10)

Page 40
translations (S. Smiles 1905, pp. 400–401)
"a bible . . . businessmen" (Butler-Bowdon, p. 275)
"Cholera . . . faster" (Briggs 1955, p. 118)
"the authorized . . . revolution" (ibid., p. 116)
"strong-minded . . . instincts" (quoted in Hughes, p. 8)
"afford . . . established" (S. Smiles 1885, p. 372)
"cheery little soul" (quoted in Travers, p. 45)
"keen . . . benevolence" (quoted in A. Smiles, p. 53)
simplicity ruled (Briggs 1955, p. 137)

Page 41
"retouch . . . picture" (quoted in ibid., p. 120)
"pre-industrial . . . required" (E. J. Hobsbawm, quoted in Travers, p. 5)
Self-Help as guidance for a new age (Jarvis, p. 68)

Page 42
"deterioration . . . principles" (quoted in Briggs 1955, p. 124)
"catalogue . . . practices" (ibid.)
absenteeism, political foibles (Briggs 1958, p. 23)
virtues and their results (S. Smiles 1875, pp. 5, 27, 34, 375, 380)
vices (ibid., pp. 5, 28)
"energetic individualism" (S. Smiles 1866, p. 22)
"Competence . . . them" (S. Smiles 1875, p. 23)
"The will . . . them" (S. Smiles 1866, p. 193)
"Man . . . circumstances" (S. Smiles 1871, p. 22)
"Nothing . . . fault" (quoted in ibid.)
"the ranks" (S. Smiles 1866, p. 21)
"golden age . . . farming" (Briggs 1959, p. 394)
"in an age . . . another" (S. Smiles 1885, p. 3)
"free . . . individuals" (S. Smiles 1866, p. 37)
"the effects . . . our constitution" (ibid.)
"vigorous . . . nation" (ibid.)

Page 43
"makes . . . imaginary woes" (S. Smiles 1875, p. 121)
"among . . . of the people" (ibid., p. 198)
Smiles on labor versus Marx (Travers, p. 229)
"each stage . . . tools" (S. Smiles, quoted in ibid., p. 259)
"drain . . . the ocean" (ibid., pp. 259–60)
resources as means (ibid., p. 258)

"notable" and "remarkable . . . conducted" (S. Smiles 1879, p. xi)
"continuous . . . men" (ibid., p. xii)
"a great . . . happiness" (S. Smiles 1866, p. 249)
"certainly . . . difficult" (ibid.)
"husbanded power" (S. Smiles, quoted in Travers, p. 259)
17:1 ratio (ibid., p. 162)
"character . . . pleases" (S. Smiles 1905, p. 106)
"The philosopher's . . . arrangement" (ibid.)
"The value . . . over-estimated" (S. Smiles 1866, p. 17)
"No laws . . . sober" (ibid.)

Page 44
"We have tried . . . receivers" (S. Smiles 1875, p. 43)
"better habits . . . greater rights" (S. Smiles 1866, p. 17)
reward a person's virtues (Rand 1964a, p. 53)
"The selfish . . . all" (quoted in Travers, p. 227)
"enormous . . . poverty" (S. Smiles 1875, p. 42)
"The function . . . property" (S. Smiles 1866, p. 17)
"Men . . . physical force" (S. Smiles 1881, pp. 282–83)
"uneasy" class (Travers, pp. xiv–xv)

Page 45
"the aristocratic-government complex" (ibid., p. 168)
work over privilege (ibid., p. 16)
feudalism to meritocracy (ibid., p. 258)
"The spirit . . . privileges" (quoted in ibid., p. 137)
Political reform as a moral crusade (Briggs 1959, p. 314)
"detested . . . legislation'" (Sinnema, p. x)
"if a man . . . someone else" (S. Smiles 1866, p. 247)
"morals . . . manifestation" (S. Smiles, quoted in Briggs 1958, p. 15)
"Noble . . . ruled" (S. Smiles 1866, p. 18)
"The solid . . . progress" (ibid.)
"National progress . . . vice" (S. Smiles, quoted in Briggs 1955, p. 125)
"It is . . . empire" (S. Smiles 1866, p. 37)
"A number . . . prosperity" (S. Smiles, quoted in Travers, p. 264)
Adam Smith (S. Smiles 1866, pp. 93–94)
"Where would . . . manufacturers?" (S. Smiles 1875, p. 203)
"Trade . . . life" (S. Smiles 1866, p. 238)

Page 46
"It puts . . . battle" (ibid.)
"high culture . . . judgment" (quoted in S. Smiles 1871, p. 111)
"heartless . . . million" (S. Smiles 1875, p. 196)
"lazy man . . . himself" (ibid., p. 197)
"Put a stop . . . classes" (ibid., p. 196)
nations advance from competition (ibid., p. 197)
"Integrity . . . characteristic" (S. Smiles 1866, p. 317)
"Men whose acts . . . lips" (ibid., p. 318)
"many . . . forms [of] untruthfulness" (S. Smiles 1871, p. 213)

"in reticency . . . a duty" (ibid.)
"'It will do! . . . human good" (S. Smiles 1875, p. 176)
"little things . . . transacted" (ibid., p. 173)
"Where men . . . split" (S. Smiles 1866, p. 226)
"Trifles . . . trifle" (ibid., p. 109)
"As I began . . . small they were" (quoted in Smith and Dalzell, p. 38)

Page 47
"Success . . . shrinks" (quoted in ibid.)
focus, accuracy, thoroughness, promptitude, methodology (S. Smiles 1866, pp. 227–29)
"one thing at a time" (ibid., p. 175)
"quick . . . execution" (ibid., p. 231)
"Philosophers . . . act" (S. Smiles 1881, p. 34)
"must drill . . . impulse" (S. Smiles, quoted in Travers, p. 112)
"immorality . . . society" (S. Smiles 1881, p. 103)
"elasticity . . . success" (S. Smiles 1866, p. 308)
"peace with others" (S. Smiles 1871, p. 181)
"every man . . . feature" (ibid.)
"The wise person . . . suffering" (ibid., p. 370)
"Failure . . . tenderness" (ibid., p. 365)
"Young men . . . o' me" (quoted in Travers, p. 171)
"My object . . . PERSEVERANCE" (S. Smiles 1905, p. 222)

Page 48
"Failure . . . instruction" (S. Smiles 1866, p. 4)
"Crosses . . . heaven" (ibid., p. 282)
"Though . . . where" (ibid., p. 281)
"He who . . . discovery" (quoted in Briggs 1958, p. 10)
"The most . . . endowed" (S. Smiles 1905, p. 222)
"usually . . . common sense" (S. Smiles 1866, p. 223)
"It is not . . . industry" (ibid., p. 292)
"enables . . . dry details" (ibid., p. 190)
"diligent self-education" (ibid., p. 296)
home and biographies (Travers, p. 239)
"school of experience" (S. Smiles 1871, p. 344)
"Precepts . . . women" (ibid.)

Page 49
process of invention (Travers, p. 269)
"Industry . . . distinction" (S. Smiles 1875, p. 19)
"A working . . . skill" (ibid.)
"popular belief" (quoted in Travers, p. 90)
"diligence . . . luck" (ibid.)
"Sheer . . . work" (ibid.)

Page 50
"Luck . . . whistles" (S. Smiles 1875, p. 174)
"*Press On* . . . omnipotent" (quoted in Bowen, pp. 176–77)
"was ignorant . . . multiplication-table" (S. Smiles 1866, p. 225)
"contempt for arithmetic" (ibid.)

"apt . . . misfortunes" (ibid.)
"Important . . . person" (ibid., p. 228)
"If you . . . one else" (quoted in ibid.)
"Those . . . them" (S. Smiles 1871, p. 104)
"The tendency . . . huzzas" (S. Smiles 1881, p. 78)
"Many worship . . . self-help" (ibid., p. 47)

Page 51
"all false . . . them" (quoted in S. Smiles 1875, p. 191)
"Hiding . . . practicing a lie" (quoted in S. Smiles 1875, pp. 191–92)
"Integrity . . . transactions" (S. Smiles 1866, p. 237)
"We may . . . opposite" (quoted in ibid., p. 238)
"great work . . . failures" (S. Smiles 1875, p. 191)
"The spirit . . . gambler" (S. Smiles 1881, p. 68)
"badness of trade" (ibid.)
"In the arithmetic . . . others!" (ibid.)
"young businessmen . . . away" (ibid., p. 69)
"the highest . . . society" (ibid.)
"Young men . . . vintage" (ibid.)

Page 52
"The first . . . creditors" (ibid., pp. 69–70)
"Men . . . lives" (ibid., p. 70)
"Pity us . . . grave!" (ibid.)
" 'To what infamy . . . avail?' " (ibid., p. 72)
"men already rich . . . before" (ibid., p. 71)
"unscrupulous . . . rich" (S. Smiles 1866, p. 239)
"The bubbles . . . blessing" (ibid.)
"keep[ing] . . . honesty" (ibid., p. 250)
"There . . . ruin" (ibid., pp. 250–51)

Page 53
"Though . . . encounter it" (ibid., p. 281)
"Trials . . . not" (ibid., p. 282)
"Man . . . being" (S. Smiles 1875, p. 198)
"He . . . good" (ibid.)
"unfettered individualism" (ibid.)
"the . . . happiness" (ibid.)
"the duty . . . neighbors" (S. Smiles 1866, p. 3)
"Man . . . cause" (S. Smiles 1881, p. 11)
"The middle . . . classes" (S. Smiles 1875, p. 111)
"The object . . . indulgences" (ibid., p. 6)
"A consideration . . . conduct" (S. Smiles 1866, p. 333)

Page 54
"The political economists . . . fill" (S. Smiles 1881, p. 263)
reward for sympathy (S. Smiles 1875, p. 194; 1881, p. 267)
"Mind . . . mischief" (S. Smiles 1866, p. 316)
"It is . . . giant" (quoted in ibid., p. 333)

"Gentleness . . . gentlemanliness" (ibid.)
"values . . . charity" (ibid., p. 326)
"The title . . . neighbors" (ibid., p. 3)
"grand idea" (S. Smiles 1905, p. 133)
"that every . . . accomplish" (ibid.)

Page 55
"Man . . . to enjoy" (S. Smiles 1905, p. 133)
pleasure of labor (S. Smiles 1875, pp. 16–17)
aspects of labor (ibid., p. 198)
"It is not . . . culture" (ibid., p. 370)
"Relax . . . frequently" (ibid., p. 384)
"Be happy!" (ibid., p. 390)
enjoy music, art (ibid.)
"Have a . . . means" (ibid., p. 389)
"Make . . . everything" (ibid., p. 392)
"A benevolent . . . being" (ibid., p. 385)
"Doom . . . vicious" (ibid., p. 393)
"strong . . . amusement" (ibid.)
"wholesome . . ." (ibid.)
"And . . . consummation" (ibid.)
criticism of Smiles and *Self-Help* (Sinnema, p. viii)
"philistinism" (quoted in Muller, p. 208)
"liberalized . . . purged away" (quoted in ibid., p. 226)
"sneer[ed] . . . self-help" (Travers, p. 287)
back-to-nature critics (ibid., p. xix)
leisure utopians (ibid., p. 316)
"Verily . . . realization" (quoted in ibid., p. 252)

Page 56
"teachy-preachy fever" (Henry Mayhew, quoted in ibid., p. 14)
"In many . . . Bible" (Butler-Bowdon, p. 271)
"It is . . . man" (quoted in Travers, p. 252)
"We are . . . now" (quoted in ibid., p. 317)
unionism, socialism, legislation versus Smiles (ibid., pp. 253, 284)
Self-Help sales decline (ibid., pp. 360–62)
Conduct noncommercial (A. Smiles, p. 191)
new self-help genre (Travers, p. 332)
"The success . . . new methods" (quoted in ibid., p. 33)
new psychology, new economics, welfare state (Briggs 1958, pp. 23–25)
"a sort of . . . Alger" (Travers, p. viii)
"we must . . . initiative" (quoted in ibid., p. 1)

Page 57
"Thatcherism . . . equality" (Yergin and Stanislaw, p. 123)
"a mixture . . . populism" (Lawson, p. 64)
"deserves . . . again" (Butler-Bowdon, p. 1)

3 Supply-Side Ethics: Ayn Rand
Footnotes
2 "I can say . . . the world" (Rand 1974, p. 10)
3 "My greatest . . . *counts*" (quoted in Harriman, p. 282)
10 "capitalist . . . adults" (Nozick, p. 163)
15 "The Rand/Branden . . . exist" (Doherty, p. 334)

Page 58
"obvious . . . liberty" (A. Smith 1776, p. 687)
"self-love" (ibid., p. 26)
"led . . . invisible hand" (ibid., p. 456)
"When I . . . moral" (quoted in Tuccille, p. 72)
"superlatively moral system" (Greenspan 1963, p. 121)
"irrational exuberance" (quoted in Goldstein)
"an infectious . . . community" (ibid.)
Greenspan and Enron Prize (Bryce, pp. 323–27)
"I do not . . . ethically" (quoted in ibid., p. 326)

Page 59
post-corporate-scandal publicity (Goldstein; D. Jones)

Page 60
Rand's early life (B. Branden, Part I)
"as they . . . to be" (Aristotle, paraphrased by Rand 1963b, p. 170)

Page 61
three philosophical questions (Peikoff 1999, p. 21)
"while . . . one foot" (Rand 1962, p. 3)
"Metaphysics . . . Capitalism" (ibid.)
"Nature . . . give me death" (ibid.)
existence exists (Peikoff 1993, pp. 4, 6)
law of identify; law of causality (Rand 1974, p. 52)
"Mrs. Logic" (B. Branden 1986, pp. 233, 235)
"good premises . . . luck" (Ayn Rand in 1957, Berliner, p. 498)

Page 62
"If you . . . *think*" (Peikoff 1999, p. 20)
"To run . . . disaster" (Locke and Woiceshyn, pp. 95–96)
"Both . . . talked away" (Schumpeter 1942, p. 74)
"the belief . . . the universe" (Rand 1965b, p. 19)

Page 63
Subjectivism, Kant (Hicks, pp. 42–43)
"primary goal . . . language" (Appleby, p. 201)
"the notion . . . world" (ibid.)
wisdom of science (ibid.)
argument of postmodernism (ibid., pp. 3–4, 7–8)
"Objectivity . . . academy" (ibid., p. 295)
"suspect . . . events" (ibid.)
reject social science (ibid., p. 200)
"the modern . . . life" (ibid., p. 201)
political economy, class-based truth (ibid., p. 203)

Page 64
"deeply disillusioned intellectuals" (ibid., p. 206)
"a playful . . . glitzy" (Blackburn, p. 294)
"workable reality" (Appleby, p. 283)
"the individual as . . . doer" (ibid., p. 202)
"never . . . sorry" ("Jacques Derrida," p. 89)
"in great shape" (Jeff Skilling, quoted in McLean and Elkind, p. xxiv)
"killed a great company" (Jeff Skilling, ibid., p. 414)
"prove . . . great company" (quoted in Romero)
"hubris of power" (Appleby, p. 246)
"smoking . . . dope" (Richard Kinder, quoted in Swartz with Watkins, p. 36)
"drinking . . . whisky" (ibid.)

Page 65
"doped by his own publicity" (Rand 1957, p. 669)
1990s optimism and boom (Shiller, chapter 2)
"in the long run . . . dead" (Keynes 1923, p. 65)
"who couldn't . . . reality" (Jim Alexander, quoted in McLean and Elkind, p. 95)
"opinions . . . about cash" (Partnoy, p. 304)
"facts are facts . . . or fears" (Rand 1962, p. 4)

Page 66
"the refusal . . . are" (Peikoff 1993, p. 267)
"developing . . . contradiction'" (ibid., p. 269)
"more profound . . . soul" (ibid., p. 270)
"fakes . . . others" (ibid., p. 269)
"reality . . . principle" (ibid., p. 271)
"The con man . . . second-hander" (ibid.)
"The liar . . . fooling'" (ibid., pp. 271–72)
"The law . . . reverse it" (Rand 1957, pp. 1037–38)
"The businessman . . . reality" (Locke and Woiceshyn, p. 93)

Page 67
"If you . . . tempted'" (ibid., p. 100)
"the dishonest . . . reality" (ibid., p. 97)
"he has placed . . . evader" (ibid., p. 94)
"man of principle" (A. Smith 1759, p. 163)
"one . . . conduct" (ibid.)
"worthless fellow" (ibid.)
"acts . . . accidentally" (ibid.)
"man of character" (S. Smiles 1871, p. 26)
"guided . . . wisdom" (ibid., p. 23)

Page 68
"Second-handers . . . nothing" (Rand 1943, p. 634)
"The worst . . . power" (ibid., p. 636)
"The code . . . standard" (Rand 1957, p. 100)
"judge . . . judged" (quoted in Greiner and Kinni, p. 103)
"I'm heartless . . . forgiven" (Rand 1957, p. 415)
"Enron was . . . Ayn Rand" (Swartz, pp. 178–79)
"'fierce . . . Rand novel" (McLean and Elkind, p. 253)

Page 69
"pigs *do* fly" (quoted in ibid., p. 257)
"Justice . . . accordingly" (Rand 1957, p. 1019)
"Cronyism . . . subverted" (Greiner and Kinni, p. 110)
"a system . . . *against others*" (Rand 1962, p. 4)
"was not . . . capitalism" (Den Uyl and Rasmussen, p. 173)
morality of capitalism (Rand 1965a, pp. 18–20)
initiation, retaliation of force (Rand 1963d, p. 108)

Page 70
"I am not *primarily* . . . Objectivism" (quoted in Binswanger, p. 344)
"Capitalism . . . explicit" (Rand 1965a, p. 23)
"Capitalism . . . not of vices" (Greenspan 1963, p. 121)
"allows . . . individual rights" (Den Uyl and Rasmussen, p. 173)
"The magnificent . . . historical record" (Rand 1965a, p. 28)
life-expectancy progress (Rand 1971a, pp. 138–39)
"Productive . . . work" (Rand 1961a, p. 25)
"represents . . . values" (Rand 1965a, p. 24)

Page 71
"In my new book . . . regulation" (quoted in Binswanger, pp. 441–42)
"chaotic . . . unearned" (Rand 1963c, p. 29)

Page 72
"Economic . . . *fear*" (Rand 1961b, p. 48)
"He who lives . . . legalized sword" (Rand 1971b, p. 10)
"The bourgeoisie . . . together" (Marx and Engels, p. 85)
"the rapid . . . commodities" (ibid., p. 84)
"gigantic means . . . exchange" (ibid., p. 85)
"exclusive political sway" (ibid., p. 82)
"the modern . . . bourgeoisie" (ibid.)
"We . . . abundance" (quoted in R. Parker, p. 283)
"To furnish . . . quite another" (Galbraith 1958, pp. 355–56)
"all . . . boondoggling" (ibid., p. 198)
"obsolescent . . . goods" (ibid., inside dust jacket)
"Wealth . . . understanding" (ibid., p. 1)
"The rich . . . nations" (ibid.)
revise Puritan ethic (ibid., p. 289)
"the conventional wisdom" (ibid., pp. 152–53, 157)
"consumer . . . imbalances" (ibid., p. 281)

Page 73
"the thralldom . . . efficiency" (ibid., p. 291)
"breath-taking . . . advances" (ibid., p. 352)
reception, popularity of book (R. Parker, pp. 292–93)
Hayek "non sequitur" criticism of Galbraith (Hayek 1961, p. 313)
Stigler criticism (George Stigler, cited in R. Parker, p. 293)

Page 74
"a new concept of egoism" (Rand 1964b, p. iii)
"He raised . . . the dollar" (Rand 1957, p. 1168)

free trade and free minds (Rand 1964b, p. 10)
"a frozen . . . energy" (quoted in Sciabarra 1995, p. 290)
"committed . . . to see" (Rand 1963c, p. 31)
"learns . . . requires" (ibid.)
"We . . . saw wood" (quoted in Tarbell, p. 127)
"diligent . . . was over" (S. Smiles 1879, p. 31)
"money-maker" (Rand 1963c, p. 29)
"money appropriator" (ibid.)
"may become. . . *legalized force*" (ibid.)
"essentially noncreative . . . maneuvering" (ibid.)
"hires . . . 'café society'" (ibid., p. 36)

Page 75
"the system . . . equal" (Rand 1977, p. 129)
"America's abundance . . . fortune" (Rand 1965a, p. 29)
"addiction . . . salvation" (Greenfeld, p. 366)
"worked frightfully hard" (Kolko 1967, p. 353)
"I must . . . them" (ibid.)
"I believe . . . drop" (ibid.)
"stored energy" (quoted in Jonnes, p. 122)
"as many . . . efforts" (ibid.)
"the joy . . . independence" (Schumpeter 1934, p. 93)

Page 76
"grievously misconstrued" (Nevins 1940, p. 711)
"competitive . . . environment" (ibid.)
"Shakespeare . . . applause" (ibid.)
"The real . . . accomplishment" (in a letter to Carol Grant, April 29, 1955, copy in
author's files)
"economic stagnation . . . accordingly" (McCraw 1995, p. 1)
"If [critics] do not choose . . . capitalism" (Ayn Rand in 1960, Berliner, p. 506)

Page 77
"businessmen . . . altruist morality" (Rand in 1960, ibid., p. 583)
"As a group . . . capitalists" (Rand in 1971, quoted in Binswanger, p. 54)
"The two greatest . . . country" (Friedman 1977, p. 21)
"Appeasement . . . 'nonessential'" (Rand 1981, p. 152)
"the real . . . Departments" (Rand 1958, p. 113)

Page 78
"prudent . . . it" (A. Smith 1759, p. 213)
"stop . . . success" (Rand 1958, p. 113)
18-hour work-day (ibid.)
"synthesize . . . possess" (Cole 1946, p. 11)
"Reverse . . . activities" (quoted in B. Branden, p. 222)

Page 79
nationalization in "People's State" (Rand 1957, pp. 22–23, 54–55, 58, 72, 865–66)
work, wealth creation (ibid., pp. 127, 277–78)
frugality (ibid., pp. 219, 233, 354)

detail oriented (ibid., pp. 234, 311)
improvement, perfection (ibid., p. 128)
reality centered, forward, authentic (ibid., pp. 226, 248)
market-oriented (ibid., p. 59)
emotions (ibid., pp. 206, 296)
obligation (ibid., p. 408)
cronyism and nepotism (ibid., pp. 47, 195, 207–08)
extravagance (ibid., pp. 319–20, 666–67)
nonresponsibility (ibid., pp. 596–607, 621)
public relations (ibid., pp. 38–39, 51, 666)
politics (ibid., pp. 52, 55, 197, 342, 878)
government subsides (ibid., p. 181)
appeasement (ibid., pp. 484, 487)
a "gift" and "good press" (ibid., p. 52)
marquee city (ibid., p. 320)
"Washington ability" (ibid., p. 52)
"glossy" (ibid., p. 351)
many speeches (ibid., p. 624)
slogan, symbol, "noble plan" (ibid., pp. 667, 669)
public relations emphasis (ibid., pp. 18–19)
diversity, "fairness" (ibid., pp. 19–20)
"very promising . . . universities" (ibid., p. 320)
legacy, autobiography (ibid.)
overconfident reality shaper (ibid., p. 22)
excuses (ibid., pp. 312–13)

Page 80
"Money will not . . . money" (ibid., pp. 411–12)
"Rational self-interest" as "rational selfishness" (Rand 1964a, p. x)
"analogous emotion" (A. Smith 1759, p. 10)
empathy (ibid., p. 74)
"Men . . . achievement" (Rand 1943, p. 712)

Page 81
"fundamentally . . . doctrine" (Friedman 1962, p. 133)
"There is . . . or fraud" (ibid.)
multiple-masters problem (Sternberg, chapter 2)
"We . . . ethic" (Nixon 1973, p. 150)
"I call . . . part" (ibid., p. 151)
"Whenever . . . now" (ibid., p. 155)
"We have . . . sacrifice" (J. Schlesinger, p. 27)
"sacrifices . . . catastrophe" (J. Carter, pp. 36–37)

Page 82
energy crisis in *Atlas Shrugged* (Rand 1957, pp. 272–73, 339, 343–44, 347, 475, 496–98, 671)
"Pentagon . . . oil crisis" (Sobel 1974, pp. 205, 210, 215, 218, 221, 222, 228–29, 230, 234, 236)
"victory for realism" (Martin 1974, p. 341)
"self-interest . . . regulation"(ibid.)
"find . . . ghosts" (Bentley 1908, p. 172)

Page 83
"Awareness . . . generality" (Chandler 1963, p. 280)
"The good-to-great . . . reality" (Collins, p. 71)
"There . . . away" (quoted in ibid, p. 65)
"'Look . . . great'" (ibid., p. 72)
"We lost . . . war" (ibid, p. 70)
"turned . . . world" (ibid., p. 71)
"creating . . . confronted" (ibid., p. 74)
"have . . . *heard*" (ibid.)
"*Lead . . .mechanisms*" (four rules) (ibid., pp. 74–80)
"allows . . . reality" (ibid., p. 72)
"*Facts* . . . dreams" (quoted in ibid., p. 73)
revolution over incrementalism (Hamel 1994, p. x)

Page 84
"a man . . . ideals" (Arthur Andersen, page 1)
"*think straight—talk straight*" (ibid., p. 13)
"Never . . . storm" (ibid., p. 13)
"a representative . . . no alternative" (ibid., pp. 194–95)
"I am sure . . . established" (ibid., p. 196)
"My motivation . . . life" (Koch 1997, p. 2)

Page 85
three-step process (Koch 1997, p. 7)
"It is . . . *truth*" (Whately, p. 18)
"At Koch . . . economic reality" (Koch Industries)

Page 86
"*Reason* . . . any individual" (Novak 1991, p. 43)
"Faith . . . human affairs" (Maritain, p. 211)
"intellectual . . . trickery" (ibid., p. 212)
"pursuit of truth" (ibid.)
"The pre-eminence . . . objectivity" (Pieper, p. 10)

Page 87
"The prudent . . . concerned'" (ibid.)
Objectivism and the arts (N. Branden 1999, p. 307)
"the Collective" (B. Branden, p. 254; Greenspan 2007, p. 40)

Page 88
"a wholly . . . highest value" (Greenspan 2007, p. 51)
"Forty-five years . . . bureaucrats" (Goldstein)
"she . . . behavior" (D. Kelley 2002)
"Far . . . advantage" (Journo)

Page 89
"the concept . . . absolute" (Rand 1957, "About the Author")

Introduction to Part II: Business Opportunity, Political Opportunism
Footnotes
1 government expenditures and GDP (Caplow, Hicks, and Wattenberg, pp. 192–93)

Page 93
economic versus political means (Oppenheimer, p. 12)

Page 94
"with . . . to conquer" (Friedman 1979, p. 3)
"peculiarly American institution" (Noll and Owen, p. 3)

Page 95
"American . . . reinvention" (Greider 2003, p. 25).

4 Business Opportunity
Footnotes
4 *creative destruction* versus *invisible hand* (McCraw 1991, p. 383); *business strategy* as seminal (ibid., p. 384)
5 "In response . . . on the other" (Swedberg, p. 68)
7 "integrity . . . humility" (Knight, quoted in Coase 1981, p. 15)
13 two sets of financial statements (Koch 2007, p. 176n7)
14 political interference in GAAP setting (Zeff 2005a, 2005b); "On four . . . objections" (Zeff 2005b, p. 24)
15 "When economists . . . 'bilge'" (Coase 1991d, p. 52)

Page 97
hard times, high theory (Elliott, p. xv)
"economics of disorder" (Shackle, p. 134)
"economics of tranquility" (ibid., p. 290)
conceptualists versus mathematicians (ibid., pp. 292, 294)
"What sense . . . foreboding?" (ibid., p. 6)
"When I see . . . my position" (quoted in S. Harris, p. 5)

Page 98
"swashbuckling . . . quasi-heroic" (Machovec, p. 43)
"the function . . . and so on" (Schumpeter 1942, p. 132)
"New Firm" (Schumpeter 1939, p. 93)
"New Plant" (ibid., p. 94)
"New Men" (ibid., p. 96)
"The problem . . . destroys them" (Schumpeter 1942, p. 84)
"Like human beings . . . respectable decay" (Schumpeter 1939, p. 95)

Page 99
"Every piece . . . perennial lull" (Schumpeter 1942, pp. 83–84)
"The Age of Keynes" versus "Age of Schumpeter" (McCraw 1991, p. 382)
book translations and seminal nature (ibid.)
"We need a theory . . . now" (Drucker 1968, p. 165)
"new economics . . . mechanistic" (ibid., p. 166)
theory of organizations (ibid., p. 187)
"scattered" knowledge (ibid., p. 163)
new knowledge (ibid., p. 151)
expectations (ibid., p. 168)
technological change (ibid., pp. 148, 165)
advertising (ibid., pp. 163–64)
growth (ibid., pp. 143, 167)

product differentiation (ibid., p. 164)
"We will . . . is not" (ibid., p. 165)
"who will . . .. fifty years (Drucker 1983, p. 104)
personality traits (McCraw 1991, pp. 372, 378; Skousen 2001, pp. 416–22)
"Given . . . hesitated" (quoted in McCraw 1991, p. 376)

Page 100
"Schumpy" (Swedberg 1991b, p. 114)
"I set out . . . first rate" (anecdote told by M. A. Adelman to author, January 3, 2001)

Page 101
"As much . . . innovation" (Hamel 2000, p. 212)
"Gray-haired revolutionary" (ibid., p. 222)
"helped create . . . revolutionaries" (ibid., p. 212)
"To avoid . . . most" (Popper, p. 186)
"adaptive response"; *"creative response"* (Schumpeter 1947, p. 222)

Page 102
tendency toward equilibrium (McCrea, pp. 520–21)
"law of cost" (Schumpeter 1911/1934, p. 131)
"progressive diminution" (ibid., p. 132)

Page 103
"the more . . . direction" (Langlois, p. 258)
"Good-to-great . . . results" (Collins, p. 165)
"an organic . . . breakthrough" (ibid., p. 183)
"doom loop" (ibid., p. 178)
"big programs . . . new savior" (ibid., p. 183)
discipline (ibid., chapter 6)
"fads . . . hoopla" (ibid., p. 183)

Page 104
"Knight gave . . . intellectual haze" (Buchanan 1995, p. 174)
"a profit theory . . . change" (Schumpeter 1954, p. 894)
"practical . . . system" (Knight, p. 197)
"the first work . . . uncertainty" (Bernstein, p. 219)
true uncertainty (Knight 1921, p. 232)
"Uncertainty . . . separated" (ibid., p. 19)
"It will appear . . . at all" (ibid., p. 20)
"throwing . . . burn" (ibid., p. 215)
"The first . . . experience" (ibid.)
"it is . . . experience" (ibid., p. 215)
"The collection . . . organization" (ibid., p. 261)

Page 105
intuitive judgment (ibid.)
"The best men . . . proportion" (ibid., p. 281)
"The primary . . . cost" (ibid., p. 18)

Page 106
"house advantage" (quoted in Barboza)
equilibrium as foil (Mises 1966, pp. 247–50)

views of mathematics in economics (ibid., pp. 350–57)
"The market is a process" (ibid., p. 257)

Page 107
"Where there is . . . calculation" (Mises 1920, p. 111)
Keynes and the German language (Hayek 1966, p. 284)
"effectively demolished" (Heilbroner 1970, p. 88)
implementation problems (ibid., pp. 91–93)
"Less than . . . has won" (Heilbroner 1989, p. 98)
"socialism . . . easy grasp" (Heilbroner 1990, p. 91)

Page 108
"an Austrian . . . views" (ibid., p. 92)
"It turns . . . was right" (ibid.)
"the most . . . century" (Boettke and Coyne, p. 74)
"We cannot ... economizing" (Mises 1920, p. 120)
"master . . . production" (ibid., 102)
money prices and calculation (ibid., pp. 97–101)
scarcity prices and market preferences (ibid., p. 107)
lack of consumerism (Mises 1922, pp. 448–49)
"full control . . . a good" (Mises 1966, p. 682)

Page 109
dead capital, extralegal sector (De Soto, p. 212)
"Capitalism . . . countries" (ibid., p. 207)

Page 110
"the fundamental . . . profit" (Dewing, p. 509)
"the elaborate . . . statistics" (Mises 1944, p. 32)
"compass" and "conscience" (ibid.)
"The devices . . . details" (ibid.)
"sober" (Mises 1932, p. 374)
"The cool-headed . . . visionary" (Mises 1966, p. 230)
imprecise accounting (ibid., pp. 212–14, 346, 349–50)
overhead (fixed) cost subjectivity (Mises 1944, p. 32; 1966, pp. 346–48)
historical cost versus current value (Mises 1951, p. 127; Mises 1966, pp. 346, 349)
cost accounting versus economic calculation (Mises 1966, p. 349)

Page 111
"Commercial . . . failure" (ibid.)
judgment necessary (Mises 1962, p. 98)
"the incorruptible . . . loss" (Mises 1944, p. 35)
accounting enables economic calculation (Mises 1962, p. 96)
"Financial statements . . . those results" (Koch 2007, pp. 110–11)
political, prescriptive accounting (Zeff 2003, pp. 196–202)

Page 112
"earnings management" (D. Gross)
"the deteriorating . . . reports" (Desai, p. 172)
tax strategies and accounting opportunism (ibid., pp. 176–77)
"gives . . . improvement" (Mises 1944, p. 36)
trust versus economic calculation (Ikeda 2005b)

Page 113
"rhetorical device" (Harold Demsetz, quoted in Williamson, p. 10)
firm depiction (Coase 1988, p. 3)
"commonsense" (Coase 1986, p. 177)
"[Plant] . . . news to me" (Coase 1995, p. 231)
puzzle of firms versus markets (Coase 1991b, p. 230; Coase 1995, pp. 232–33, 246–47)
"that little . . . society" (Coase 1991b, p. 230)
United States trip (Coase 1991a, p. 9; 1991c, pp. 39, 42–44)

Page 114
"absolute bilge" (Coase 1991c, p. 42)
"I was then . . . Nobel Prize" (Coase 1991b, pp. 230–31)
"The main . . . mechanism" (Coase 1937, p. 93)
"The operation . . . are saved" (ibid., p. 94)
"It is true . . . reduced" (ibid., p. 93)

Page 115
nonprice planning (O'Driscoll and Rizzo, p. 123)
"the cumulative . . . firm" (Penrose, p. xiii)

Page 116
"I have . . . high theory" (Coase 1991b, p. 227)
"I started . . . real world" (Coase 1995, p. 235)

Page 117
"You will see . . . pieces" (quoted in Shook, p. 6)
"It is a scandal . . . ownership (Blaug 2000, p. 87)

5 The Business of Politics
Figures
5.4 "greatest political theorist" (Ratner 1969, p. xiii)

Footnotes
3 "allocatively . . . surplus" (Buchanan 1980, pp. 3–4)
6 Beard criticism (Bailyn; F. McDonald 1958)
7 "working amateurs" (Hofstadter 1968, p. 35); "a conservative . . . public" (ibid., p. 7)
11 Schumpeter presidencies (Haberler, p. x)
15 "political economy . . . loose" (Bentley 1953, p. 211)

Page 120
"the utilization . . . long run" (Kolko 1963, p. 3)
"political capitalism . . . every stage" (Kolko to author, March 24, 2004)

Page 121
Rothbard versus Kolko (Rothbard 1965, pp. 38–43)
"There . . . interests" (*State of Louisiana v. FPC*, 503 F. 2d 844 at 869 [1974])

Page 122
"in order . . . regulations" (A. Smith 1776, p. 734)
"To be . . . regulated company" (ibid., p. 735)
"monopolizing spirit" (ibid., p. 738)
"money appropriator" (Rand 1963c, p. 31)
economic versus political power (Rand 1961b, pp. 46–48; 1965a, p. 30)
wealth creation versus distribution (Rand 1965a, pp. 29–30)

"parasitic relationship" (Rand 1943, p. 712)
free market consistency (Fine, pp. 97, 111–12)
"FDR's . . . capitalists" (A. Schlesinger 2002, p. ix)

Page 123
"markets . . . too free" (Rajan and Zingales, p. 311)
"Under . . . too free" (ibid.)
mercantilism: 1500–1800 (Allen, p. 445)
business and laissez-faire (De Santis, p. 5)
"regard . . . society" (Kolko 1963, p. 3)
small and large business (Sklar 1988, p. 33)
"a profound . . . boards" (Heilbroner 1966, p. 38)
"striking . . . commitment" (ibid.)

Page 124
"A passion . . . century" (Beard and Beard 1927, p. 20)
"A frenzy . . . sentiment'" (ibid., p. 21)
"fundamental proposition" (Engels, p. 28)
"the prevailing . . . that epoch" (ibid.)
"modern . . . politics" (Veblen, p. 269)
"has . . . pecuniary color" (ibid.)
"I see no force . . . forces" (Sumner 1905, p. 329)
economic interpretation of history (Hofstadter 1968, pp. 8, 189, 437)

Page 125
"relevant . . . moment" (ibid., p. xii)
"rough . . . neglected" (Hofstadter 1968, p. 184)
"Who . . . want?" (ibid., p. 189)
"new . . . intelligentsia" (ibid., p. xvi)

Page 126
"capitalist reality" (Schumpeter 1942, p. 81)
perfect-competition and the economics profession (Machovec, pp. 269–75)
conditions of perfect-competition (Roberts, vol. 3:838)
imperfect-competition (Kirzner 1973, pp. 112–25)
"imaginary" (Schumpeter 1942, p. 81)
"textbook picture" (ibid., p. 84)
"A perfectly . . . big business" (ibid., p. 106)

Page 127
"perennial . . . destruction" (ibid., p. 84)
"the new . . . organization" (ibid., p. 83)
"keep . . . them" (ibid., p. 84)
"disequilibriating" (ibid., p. 132)

Page 128
"Creative destruction . . . live in" (ibid., p. 83)
"an ever-present . . . attacks" (ibid., p. 85)
potential entry (ibid.)
"the most . . . time" (Galbraith 1981, p. 48)

Schumpeter's career (Swedberg 1991, p. 24)
"invariant conditions" (Schumpeter 1942, p. 84)

Page 129
"Hamlet . . . prince" (ibid., p. 86)
"Schumpeter's . . . problems" (Heertje, p. 266)
Samuelson's textbook (J. Kelley, pp. 14–15)
"An . . . crop" (Samuelson 1948, p. 39)
"One . . . imperfections" (Pegrum, pp. 7–8)
"workhorse statistic" (Shepherd, p. 564)

Page 130
Schumpeter and Austrianism (Ellig and Lin, p. 16)
"wishful thinking" (Schumpeter 1942, p. 81)
"all make-believe" (ibid., p. 85)
"the violence of faction" (Madison, p. 53)
"men of . . . people" (ibid., p. 59)
"well constructed Union" (ibid., p. 53)
"by giving . . . interests" (ibid., p. 55)

Page 131
Madison's legislative experience (Truman, p. 5)
"our . . . protected" (Perry, p. 571)
"No . . . as ours" (ibid.)
"the outstanding . . . epoch" (Schumpeter 1954, p. 866)
"one of . . . economics" (Keynes 1930, p. 233n)
"the burning . . . individual" (Newcomb, p. 445)
"let-alone principle" (ibid., p. 446)
"the custom . . . welfare" (ibid., p. 455)
"could not . . . worth" (ibid., p. 447)

Page 132
business expenditures; "provide . . . Congress" (ibid.)
"individuals . . . injury" (ibid., p. 445)
"other evils equally great" (ibid.)
"the fallacy . . . interference" (Sumner 1913, p. 287)
"clique or faction . . . everybody else" (Sumner 1901, p. 378)
"repel . . . of all" (ibid., p. 380)
"The opinion . . . interests" (Sumner 1877, p. 84)
"control . . . interests" (Sumner 1913, p. 300)
"more crafty . . . action" (ibid.)
"lamentable contest" (ibid.)
"far other . . . intended" (Sumner 1901, p. 380)
"when . . . arena" (Sumner 1913, p. 288)
"Although . . . depends" (Sumner 1888/89, p. 140)

Page 133
"the power . . . talent" (Sumner 1905, p. 329)
"to act . . . America" (ibid., p. 332)

"politicians . . . out of it" (Sumner 1888/89, p. 140)
"every . . . methods" (Sumner 1913, p. 300)
"minimize . . . industry" (ibid.)
"the late . . . to hate" (Bannister, p. ix)
social Darwinist (ibid., p. xxiv; Lee, p. xiv)
leading proponent of laissez-faire (Anderson, p. 14)
"hard work . . . gratification" (Bannister, p. xi)

Page 134
"old school" (R. Ely in 1885, quoted in High and Ellig, p. 8)
"laissez-faire . . . morals" (R. Ely, p. 7)
"combat . . . crowd" (R. Ely in 1885, quoted in High and Ellig, p. 12)
"denunciations . . . oppose" (Macvane, p. 15)
"Well-intending . . . affairs" (ibid., pp. 15–16)

Page 135
"all the politics . . . desk" (Bentley 1953, p. 211)
"two hours . . . my pay" (ibid.)
"hailed . . . genius" (Ratner 1957, p. 32)
"It was . . . groups" (Taylor 1957, p. 5)
"powerful group pressures" (Bentley 1908, p. 447)
felt and *thought* facts (ibid., p. 172)
"soul-stuff" (ibid., pp. 19, 26, 35)
"idea ghosts" (ibid., p. 172)
activity at the margin (ibid., pp. 453–54)

Page 136
"If we try . . . at all" (ibid., p. 213)
"society . . . individuals" (quoted in ibid., p. 157)
more than economic interests (ibid., pp. 209, 212)
inertia, cross currents (ibid., p. 141)
public opinion (ibid., chapter 8)
"'objective utility'" (ibid., p. 213)
"'social whole'" or "established condition" (ibid., p. 220)
"the opinion . . . creed" (ibid., p. 238)
"differentiated activity," examples (ibid., p. 239)
"Freedom . . . interpretation" (ibid., p. 455)
"distorted . . . interests" (ibid., p. 454)
"we see . . . power" (ibid., pp. 454–55)
"the organization . . . pressures" (ibid., p. 453)
"raw material" (ibid., chapter 6)
"the lawbooks . . . 'minds'" (ibid., pp. 179–80)
"very . . . happening" (ibid., p. 447)
"freely . . . lines" (ibid., p. 359)
conflict between interests (ibid., p. 454)
U.S. House of Representatives, Massachusetts (Truman, p. 526)
"body . . . lobbyists" (Odegard, p. xvii)
"dead political science" (Bentley 1908, p. 162)
"your . . . politics" (ibid., p. 163)

Page 137
"the president or governor" (ibid.)
"go behind . . . agency" (ibid.)
"long, crabbed, difficult" (Hofstadter 1968, p. 186)
"unnecessarily rude" (Beard, p. 739)
"thought-provoking . . . belongs" (ibid., p. 741)
"worthy . . . science" (Small, p. 706)
isolation and problems (Lavine, p. xv)
"one of America's . . . inquiry" (Ratner 1957, p. 26)
rediscovery (Gross 1950, pp. 742–43; Gross 1953, p. 4n2; Ratner 1957, p. 33; Taylor 1952, p. 214)
words to *deeds* (Taylor 1952, p. 214)
"the founder . . . political science" (Olson, p. 8)
"the structure . . . associational" (Latham, p. 17)
multidisciplinary contributions (Ratner 1969, p. ix)
"choices . . . people" (Seldon, p. xiii)

Page 138
new political economy (Heckelman et al., p. 1; Ikeda 1997, p. 5)
interest-group theory of government (Tollison, pp. 59, 66)
"politics without romance" (James Buchanan, quoted in Ikeda 1997, p. 6)
"who wins and who loses" (Tollison, p. 66)
"differential advantages" (Buchanan and Tullock, p. 286)
"spiral effect" (ibid.)
"federal . . . legislation" (ibid.)
"political markets . . . groups" (Boettke, p. 8)
"Political equilibrium . . . groups" (Becker, p. 122)
"The economic . . . transactions" (Brickley et al., p. 544)

Page 139
"To develop . . . entrants" (ibid.)
"Benevolent . . . rest of us" (Buchanan 1978, p. 4)
Lincoln quotation recast (Seldon, p. xii)
"It is . . . activists'" (ibid.)

Page 140
"transfer[ing] . . . decision-making" (Royal Swedish Academy, p. 1)
"realistic view" (ibid., p. 3)
"public . . . failures" (ibid., p. 2)
"Individuals . . . life" (ibid.)
"regulation principle . . . service" (G. Smith 1934, p. 705)
"hang . . . business" (ibid., p. 711)
"a type . . . himself" (ibid.)
"is a 'chooser' . . . social drama" (Niskanen, p. 5)
"Analysts . . . interests" (MacLaury, p. vii)

Page 141
"There . . . consumers" (McCormick 1989, p. 28)
"almost . . . profits" (ibid., p. 25)

6 U.S. Political Capitalism
Figures
6.2 "the historian's historian" (Dudden, p. 468)

Footnotes
2 "Laissez faire . . . good" (Bowen, p. 18)
5 industrial revolutions (McCraw 1995, pp. 13–15)
7 "Most histories . . . worldwide" (McCraw 2007, p. 681n10)
11 "new options" and "radical . . . change" (Kolko 1969, p. 138); "While . . . ever"
(Kolko 1994, pp. 480–81)
12 "America's first forester" (Ekirch, p. 147); "a perfect . . . power" (ibid., p. 148)
14 "With . . . economic context" (Kolko 1976, p. 399)

Page 142
"I predict . . . society" (Krugman 2002)
"Enron . . . Harding" (Kuttner 2002a, p. 2)
"The business . . . 1920s" (A. Schlesinger 1957, reprint 2002, p. viii)
"the dynamics . . . greed" (ibid.)
"for one . . . New Deal" (ibid., pp. viii–ix)
"'economic royalists'" (ibid., p. ix)
New Deal programs (ibid.)

Page 143
"Liberalism . . . community" (A. Schlesinger 1946, p. 505)

Page 144
critical intelligentsia (Hofstadter 1968, p. 184)
"the bribe . . . slums" (ibid.)
two thousand articles (Watson, p. 62)
professionalization of economics (High and Ellig, pp. 7–9)
"While . . . morals" (R. Ely, pp. 6–7)
"A vast . . . science" (ibid., p. 7)
"old school . . . solution" (quoted in High and Ellig, p. 8)
"English . . . scholars" (Novick, p. 22)
intellectual influence from Germany (Caine, p. 16)

Page 145
"The German . . . interests" (Schumpeter 1954, p. 802)
graduate social science programs (Sklar 1992, p. 172)
"exhilarated . . . profit" (Leuchtenburg, p. 35)
"had come up . . . hard knocks" (Beard and Beard 1939, p. 864)
"battle of the Ph.D.s" (H. Smith, p. 516)
certification areas (Bradley 1996, p. 558; Wiebe 1967, p. 117)
Uniform System of Accounts (Bradley 1996, p. 558)
"shifting . . . century" (Filene, p. 33)
"steeped in ambiguity" (McCraw 1974, p. 181)

Page 146
"stood clearly for . . . opportunity" (A. Schlesinger 1957, p. 35)
"people's government . . . effective" (ibid.)
"no one . . . *laissez faire*" (quoted in Sklar 1988, p. 58)

"save . . . change it" (A. Schlesinger 1958, p. 5)
"helped . . . unity" (ibid., p. 176)
"permanent depression" (ibid.)
Galbraith and Harris influence (A. Schlesinger 1957, p. xii; 1958, p. ix)
"a major . . . conscience" (Hofstadter 1963, p. 15)
"had been . . . resources" (ibid., p. 2)
"The land . . . plundered" (ibid.)

Page 147
"orderly social change . . . growth" (ibid., p. 3)
"civic alertness . . . the public" (ibid., p. 14)
"heroic efforts" (ibid.)
"high civic ideals" (ibid., p. 7)
"never . . . materialism" (ibid.)
intellectuals and reform (ibid.)
muckrakers, clergy (ibid., pp. 8, 10)
"In their struggles . . . businessmen" (ibid., pp. 9–10)

Page 148
"Government . . . process" (Wilcox, p. 7)
"In their . . . sound" (ibid., p. 876)
"as a . . . culture" (Wheeler, dust jacket quotation)
"Negative . . . Commission" (ibid., p. 58)
industrialists as antiheroes (Josephson 1934, pp. 348, 383)
"fearful . . . society" (Josephson 1934, p. 453)
"idle . . . louts" (ibid.)
"rebels and lawbreakers" (ibid.)
"Frenzied Finance" (Josephson 1934, p. 452)
"mismanagement and stupidity" (ibid., p. 453)
"inherent contradictions" (ibid., pp. 429–30)
anticapitalist influences (Shi, pp. 155–56)
"the whole . . . disaster" (quoted in ibid., p. 157)
book success (ibid., pp. 155–56)
"with . . . novelist" (ibid., p. 158)

Page 149
"I like . . . spirit" (quoted in ibid., 165)
"They are . . . it wants" (quoted in ibid.)
Lloyd background (Bridges, p. 2)
Tarbell bias (Bradley 1996, pp. 1079, 1104–05)
bourgeois bohemian (Shi)
exciting and moralistic writers (McCraw 1974, p. 183)
amateur historians (Novick, pp. 45, 345)
"Without . . . the trusts" (McCraw 1981, p. 20)

Page 150
Rockefeller, Carnegie, Vanderbilt (Folsom, pp. 1–5, 122)
Fulton, Collins (ibid., p. 4)
Villard, Stanford, Gould (ibid., pp. 22–25, 127)
"free competitive economy" (Nevins 1940, p. viii)

"Our . . . work" (ibid., p. vii)
"inextricably mingled . . . strategy" (ibid., p. 707)
"Great Game" (ibid., p. 712)
"Rockefeller . . . society" (ibid., p. 710)
propaganda, not history (Bridges, p. 2)
"journalists . . . in it" (quoted in Kolko 1959, p. 339)
"All historians . . . purpose" (ibid., p. 330)

Page 151
"broader . . . mature" (Nevins 1942, p. 28)
"A thorough . . . future" (ibid.)
"In the past . . . at all" (quoted in "Notes on the Permanent Revolution," p. 83)
"more . . . history" (quoted in ibid.)
praise for Nevins ("Industry and the Historian")
"turning point" ("Notes on the Permanent Revolution," p. 83)
"Not one historian . . . ecology" (Nevins 1954, vol. 1:178)
"superior . . . power" (ibid.)
America gains from industry (ibid., vol. 1:184–85)
McCarthy-like campaign (Josephson 1954, vol. 1:186)
"'Great business . . . enterprises'" (Josephson 1954, 1:189)
changed circumstances for Josephson (Woodruff, p. 245)
"paradise . . . untaxed" (Josephson 1962, p. v)
"of heroic stature" (Josephson 1962, p. vi)

Page 152
"embattled" Kansas farmers (ibid.)

Page 153
Stigler/Boulding over Knight/Schumpeter (Passer, pp. 21–22)
HBS beginnings (www.hbs.edu/about/history.html)
opening curriculum (Harvard University 1908, pp. 13–27)
"the self-centered . . . force" (Gay, quoted in Cole 1946, p. 1)
"rhythm of history" (Gay, quoted in ibid.)
"the cake . . . broken" (Gay, quoted in ibid.)
"social stability" (Gay, quoted in ibid.)
Business History Society; Gras (Cole 1974, pp. 6–7; Larson 1948, pp. 7, 19)
"Gras saw . . . development" (Larson 1948, p. 17)
"the first . . . historian" (Cole 1946, p. 1)
Business History Foundation (Baker; Larson 1954)
Arthur Cole (Miller, p. viii)

Page 154
short-run change versus long-run statics (Cole 1946, p. 3)
"the integrated . . . forces" (ibid., p. 4)
"the central figure" (ibid., p. 8)
"a Schumpeterian" (McCraw 2007, p. 682n10)
"the real purpose . . . strategy" (Cole 1946, p. 5)
"The area of . . . hypothesis" (ibid., p. 15)
Research Center; Schumpeter (Cole 1974, p. 15; McCraw 1988, p. 6; Miller, p. viii)
"Without . . . aborning'" (Cole 1950, p. 56)
"Every economist . . . businessmen" (quoted in Miller, p. 1)

"entrepreneur . . . history" (Sawyer, p. 8)
"new reference group" (Swedberg 1991, p. xxiv)
"Economic . . . will" (Schumpeter 1947, p. 221)
"the . . . change" (ibid.)
"new hypotheses . . . new" (Schumpeter 1949, p. 271)

Page 155
"one of . . . scholarship" (McCraw 1988, p. 2)

Page 156
"My goal . . . environment" (Chandler 1989, p. iii)
strategy, crisis drivers (ibid.)
"resources . . . rationalized" (Chandler 1962, p. 395)
"The market . . . policy" (ibid., p. 384)
"If it does . . . investigation" (ibid., p. 396)
"without . . . hair" (R. J. Wilson, p. 98)
business-history revisionism (Porter, pp. 9, 63, 104–11)
Chandler and economics (McCraw 1988, p. 6n4)
"a collective . . . designed" (ibid., p. 9)
"Dynamic forces" (Chandler 1959, p. 2)
"The historian . . . public?" (ibid., pp. 1–2)

Page 157
"History . . . generality" (Chandler 1963, p. 280)
"Many historians . . . Chandler" (McCraw 1988, p. 12)

Page 158
"'Strategy . . . Japan" (ibid., p. 13)
Chandler and McKinsey (ibid.)
"Jeff may . . . suffer fools" (quoted in Brenner, p. 190)
Rockefeller biography (Swartz with Watkins, p. 42)
"which . . . observations" (McLean and Elkind, p. 32)

Page 159
"Public-spirited undertakings . . . neomercantilism" (Lively, p. 94)
"local aid movement" (ibid., p. 86)
"From . . . regulating" (ibid.)
"Enterprise . . . laid" (ibid., p. 87)
public sentiment (ibid., pp. 91–92)
"King Laissez Faire . . . mistake" (ibid., p. 82)
"The Government . . . corruption" (Godkin, p. 68)
"The error . . . preconception" (Lively, p. 82)

Page 160
"political capitalism" (Kolko 1963, p. 3)
"The dominant fact . . . economy" (Kolko 1963, pp. 57–58)
"combined . . . questions" (Wiener, p. 409)
"a perennial . . . destruction" (Schumpeter 1942, p. 83)
"If economic . . . succeed" (Kolko 1963, p. 58)
competition as unrestricted, "cut-throat," and "ruinous" (ibid., pp. 13–14)
"Laissez faire . . . economy" (ibid., p. 57)

"Ironically . . . lack of it" (ibid., p. 5)
"intense" and "growing" (ibid., p. 26)

Page 161
"Many . . . results" (ibid., p. 286)
"was possible . . . desirable" (ibid.)
"The business . . . The Establishment" (ibid., p. 284)
"It is . . . realities" (ibid., p. 282)
"there . . . manner" (ibid.)
"triumph of conservatism" (ibid., p. 2)

Page 162
"did not . . . society" (ibid., p. 287)
"random . . . regulation" (ibid., p. 6)
nationalized reform (Graebner, p. 174)
"The railroads . . . 1916" (Kolko 1965, p. 3)
dynamics of railroad intervention (Bradley 1996, pp. 976–77, 1788)
"the railroad problem" (Kolko 1965, p. 39)
maximum as minimum rate-setting (ibid., p. 35)
Philadelphia and Reading Railroad authorship (ibid., pp. 21, 44)
"published" and "just and reasonable" (24 *Stat*. 379 at 381; also, Bradley 1996, pp. 622–23)
discounting discouragement (Kolko 1965, p. 57)

Page 163
"We would . . . act" (quoted in ibid.)
"fair return . . . convenience" (*Smyth v. Ames*, 169 U.S. 466 at 547 [1898])
"The committee . . . bring about" (quoted in Kolko 1965, p. 39)
public utility regulation of California railroads (Blackford, pp. 308–13)

Page 164
"It is well . . . public interest" (quoted in ibid., pp. 312–13)
"reached down . . . inside out" (James Harvey Young, quoted in High, p. 1)
"ideological . . . historians" (Kolko 1965, p. 237)
"movement . . . competition" (ibid., p. 238)
"A crusade . . . interests" (Wiebe 1962, p. 207)
"descriptions . . . form" (ibid., p. 206)
"the simplified . . . reformers" (ibid.)
"war cry" (ibid., p. 220)
"'get . . .business'" (ibid.)
"mythology" (Kolko 1963, p. 58)
intense competition (ibid., pp. 7–8)
"The heyday . . . began" (ibid., p. 21)

Page 165
"sufficiently concentrated . . . agencies" (Kolko 1976, p. 8)
"it had . . . .. reality" (G. Kolko to author, May 22, 2003)
real-world competition (Kolko 1963, pp. 24–25)
Kolko and Schumpeter (ibid., pp. 29, 54)
"idealization of the state" (ibid., p. 214)

"Because . . . new problems" (Kolko 1976, p. 20)
"reform . . . problems" (ibid.)
"underconsumptionist . . . demand" (ibid., p. 145)
"intrinsically . . . capitalism" (ibid., p. 149)
"America's . . . mastery" (Kolko 1972, p. 716)
"The main . . . capacities" (Kolko 1976, pp. 1–2)

Page 166
"new politics" (Kolko 1966, p. 220)
"businessmen . . . political economy" (Weinstein, pp. ix–x)
not laissez-faire or Darwinism (ibid., p. x)
"In the . . . interests" (ibid., p. ix)
"businessmen . . . reformers" (ibid.)
"intellectual . . . Kennedys" (ibid., pp. xi–xii)
Schlesinger with Kolko dissertation (G. Kolko to author, May 14, 2003)
Samuel Insull (Weinstein, p. 253)
NAM and NCF (ibid., pp. 5, 92)
"farcical . . . history" (Wiener, p. 400)

Page 167
"The bituminous . . . years" (G. Parker, p. ii)
"Because . . . regulation" (ibid.)
too competitive, "minimum . . . production" (ibid.)
quest for stability (Nordhauser)
"Dollar oil" (quoted in Bradley 1989, p. 41)
domestic oil-industry cartel (A. Kahn 1964, p. 286)
"big business . . . integrated" (Ise, p. 543)
top lobbying organizations (ibid.)
"under pressure . . . economy" (ibid., p. 594)
"One interference . . . competition" (A. Kahn 1971, vol. 2:29)

Page 168
"political . . . benefits" (Stigler, p. 209)
Schlesinger on consumerist legislation (Sobel 1977, pp. 49–50)
Ford Foundation study opinion (Energy Policy Project, pp. 242–49)
"more protective . . . inclusive" (Galambos and Pratt, p. 63)
New York Times and Sherman Act (DiLorenzo, p. 83)
"bogey of monopoly" (Watson, p. 335)
FTC; "unfair" competition (Bradley 1996, pp. 1551–55; Kolko 1963, pp. 262–67; Wiebe 1967, p. 298)
private antitrust suits (Salop and White, pp. 1001–03)

Page 169
"There is . . . activities" (Baumol and Ordover, p. 247)
agricultural subsidies (Wilcox, chapter 15)
shipping subsidies (Bradley 1996, pp. 997–98)
water carrier regulation and ICC (ibid., p. 999)
"nationalistic and protectionist" (quoted in ibid., p. 1003)
"the cumulative . . . competition" (Coppin and High, p. 167)

"were not . . . activity" (ibid.)
"captured . . . bureau" (ibid., p. 15)
Kolko confirmed (ibid., p. 4)
federal child-labor laws (Kolko 1976, p. 14)
"The banking . . . specifically" (Kolko 1963, p. 222)

Page 170
"elastic currency" (Federal Reserve Act of 1913)
gasoline tax and API (Bradley 1996, pp. 1370–77)
"look . . . profit" (quoted in Hofstadter 1963, p. 69)
Roosevelt withdrawals (Bradley 1996, p. 265)
"monopolized . . . men" (quoted in Hofstadter 1963, p. 71)
"the law of Business . . . self-preservation" (Pinchot, p. 127)
"morally imperative" (ibid.)
rid of special interests (ibid., pp. 143, 147)
"In a day . . . whatsoever" (ibid., p. 96)

Page 171
"The object . . . homes" (Hays, pp. 41–42)
people-versus-interests (ibid., p. 277)
"place . . . use" (ibid., p. 266)
timber companies and conservation (ibid., p. 29)
railroad interests and conservation (Shaffer, p. 241)
railroads and conservation-policy gains (Rothbard 1970, pp. 1131–32)
"barbed-wire . . . entry" (Flynn, p. 412)
"was . . . business reform" (Graebner, p. 167)
agenda of Bureau of Mines (ibid., pp. 34–42)
George Huff connections (ibid., pp. 33–34)
"stability, predictability, and security" (ibid., p. 168)
federal mining standard rather than states (ibid., p. 30)
"In short . . . movement" (ibid., p. 167)
"We believe . . . enforced" (quoted in Kolko 1963, p. 180)
"I would . . . competition" (quoted in Kolko 1976, p. 13)
"a truism . . . half-century" (ibid.)

Page 172
milk industry and public utility regulation (H. Gray, p. 293)
"The average . . . regulation" (Flynn, p. 411)
"begging . . . affairs" (ibid.)
"By 1931–32 . . . same" (Larson 1948, p. 942)
planning survey, Donham (ibid., p. 944)
NRA codes (Bradley 1996, p. 1360)
"The business . . . is business" (quoted in Goodman, p. 109)
"Virtually . . . policies" (Wright, p. 4)
"indifferent" (ibid., p. 7)
"negative" (ibid.)
"creative" (ibid.)
"positive" (ibid.)

Page 173
common weal (ibid.)
"urbanization . . . internationalism" (ibid., p. 3)
"new . . . executive" (Canham, p. vii)
"new capitalism" (ibid., p. ix)
"government-business relations . . . development" (Wright, pp. 140–41)
"daily education" (ibid., p. 6)
"legislative . . . techniques" (ibid.)
"that which . . . *Business*" (Flynn, p. 409)
"the legislative . . . commerce" (ibid., p. 410)
"as a huge . . . oar" (ibid., p. 409)
"*Less . . . business*" (ibid., p. 415)
wellhead natural gas price regulation (Bradley 1996, pp. 376–403, 1835–37)
depletion allowance controversy (ibid., p. 338)

Page 174
"Corporate . . . staff" (Holton, p. 57)
"non-economic . . . ones" (Chandler 1969, p. 40)

Page 175
"The corporate . . . agencies" (Holton, pp. 69–70)
"the top . . . Washington" (ibid., p. 72)
"tour of duty" (ibid.)
130 laws; "brought . . . lawyers" (Greider 1992, p. 107)
Walter Heller and "new economics" (Monsen, p. 178)
"I am . . . Keynesian" (quoted in Silk)
"to be . . . CEO" and ARCO mobilization (D. Vogel, p. 178)
"Why . . . adversaries" (Chandler 1980, p. 1)
"The question . . . United States" (ibid., p. 2)
"present . . . government" (Fouraker and Allison, p. x)

Page 176
"Government . . . decades" (Lehne, p. 110)
"analytic . . . responsibility" (ibid.)
"The matrix . . . customary constraints" (Stephens)
"They . . . for Enron" (quoted in ibid.)
"*corporatism* . . . government" (Weaver, p. 182)
"less . . . attitude" (ibid., p. 183)
"whatever . . . they did" (ibid., p. 184)
"Good . . . News" (ibid., p. 186)
"We lied" (ibid.)
"Boundless ambition" (ibid., p. 185)
"good . . . society" (ibid., p. 184)

Page 177
Ford's free-trade legacy (Halberstam, pp. 607, 610)
"A common . . . stealing" (ibid., p. 610)
"In this . . . views" (quoted in ibid.)
"became . . . sessions" (McCraw 1975, p. 165)

Page 178
"intellectual . . . libertarianism" (Heilbroner 1970, p. 11)
"its failure . . . freedom" (ibid., p. 12)
"brilliant" (Rothbard 1965, p. 38)
"monopoly . . . operations" (ibid., p. 39)
"Regulation . . . benefit" (Stigler, p. 3)
Kolko/Stigler thesis (Coppin and High, p. 8)
"liberals mugged by reality" (Irving Kristol, quoted in Yergin and Stanislaw, p. 330)
"law of unintended consequences" (ibid.)
"The neocons . . . decades" (ibid., p. 331)
"as . . . Friedmans" (ibid.)
"While . . . yesteryear" (Derthick and Quirk, p. 29)
"regulatory reform . . . spectrum" (Vietor 1994, p. 15)
"the 'economist's hour'" (McCraw 1984, p. 305)
public-interest theory discredited (Breyer, p. 10)

Page 179
capture to *competition* (Yergin and Stanislaw, pp. 340–42)
dates of regulation and deregulation (Viscusi et al., pp. 302–307)
Natural Gas Policy Act of 1978 (Bradley 1996, pp. 946–47)
Energy Policy Act of 1992 (106 *Stat.* 2276 at 2915)

Page 180
"In most cases . . . reregulation" (S. Vogel, p. 3)
Nader, Kennedy, and consumer groups (Vietor 1994, p. 14)
"to free . . . over-regulation" (quoted in ibid., p. 1)
"an odd . . . Republicans" (Loving, p. 209; McCraw 1984, p. 268)

Page 181
"As . . . mankind" (Beard and Beard 1939, p. 860)
"left-liberal . . . theory" (Horwitz, p. 265)
deregulation and pluralism (ibid., p. 266)
"Our happy . . . capitalism" (Emmott, p. 3)
"governments . . . offered" (ibid., p. 14)
"radical birthday thoughts" (ibid., p. 3)
"pro-market, not pro-business" (ibid., p. 14)
"keep . . . bosses" (ibid.)
"household name" (ibid., p. 7)
"scandal sheet" (ibid.)
"The problem . . . capitalists" (Willi Schlamm, quoted in "Enron's Sins")

Introduction to Part III: Energy and Sustainability
Page 185
"Here is . . . space" (Lane, p. vii)
"The planet . . . earth" (ibid.)
"Since . . . human" (Hudgins)
"the Babe Ruth . . . world" (F. McDonald 1962, p. 237)
"In his role . . . modern energy company" (quoted in *The Nation,* February 11, 2002, p. 7)

Page 186
Insull coal concern (Insull 1911, p. 180)
"The Chief" (F. McDonald 1962, p. 105)
"versatile substitute" (Houston Natural Gas, p. 2)

Page 187
"What . . . dry?" (Ehrlich and Ehrlich 1974, p. 49)
"I'm not . . . a realist" (Simon 1990, p. xi)
"development . . . own needs" (World Commission, p. 43)

Page 188
natural capitalism (Hawken, Lovins, and Lovins)
"Kyoto compliant" (Peggy Mahoney, internal Enron memo to author, May 11, 2000)
three energy visions (Enron, pp. 6–7)

7 Malthusianism
Figures
7.1 "great breakthrough" (Simon 2000, p. 14)
7.3 "powerful face" (Keynes 1933b, 308); "pioneer of modern economics" (Black 1981, p. 1)
7.5 coal-production statistics (B. R. Mitchell 1962, pp. 115–16; Mitchell and Jones, pp. 66–67)
7.6 growing world coal production and reserves (B. R. Mitchell 1962, pp. 115–17; Mitchell and Jones, pp. 66–67)

Footnotes
1 U.S. agriculture boom (Malthus 1798, pp. 40, 68)
2 "It is . . . or vice" (Malthus 1798, p. 41)
10 depletion allowance and controversy (Bradley 1996, pp. 332–49)

Page 189
"wasteland" (quoted in W. T. Jones, vol. 2:296)
"The world . . . dissolution" (quoted in ibid.)

Page 190
"populationist attitude" (Schumpeter 1954, p. 251)
"a numerous . . . to have" (ibid.)
"The ancients . . . idea" (Walter Bagehot [1872], quoted in Nisbet, p. 10)
"the great breakthrough" (Simon 2000, p. 14)
Malthus life (Pullen)
"every day . . . better" (Samuelson 1948, p. 24)
"incontrovertible truths" (Malthus 1798, p. 17)
"the passion . . . sexes" (ibid., p. 8)
geometric versus arithmetic (ibid., pp. 9, 13)
lagging food production (ibid., p. 14)
"mak[ing] . . . a garden" (ibid., p. 12)

Page 191
"misery or vice" (ibid., p. 17)
"The argument . . . leisure" (ibid., p. 10)
"rapidity . . . history" (ibid., p. 40)
"frequent . . . people" (ibid., p. 30)

Page 192
"the foresight . . . family" (ibid., p. 26)
vice out of wedlock (ibid., p. 28)
"preventative check" and "positive check" (Malthus 1798, p. 26)
"Necessity . . . invention" (ibid., p. 129)
"the first . . . body" (ibid., p. 128)
"constant . . . occur" (ibid., p. 142)
"from the . . . population" (ibid.)
"warfare of pamphlets" (Keynes 1933a, p. 99)

Page 193
"impulse" and "from . . . reach" (Malthus 1803, p. 1)
"a new work" (ibid., p. 2)
"moral restraint" (ibid., p. 315)
"preventative check" (Malthus 1798, p. 26; 1803, p. 14)
"promiscuous . . . connections" (Malthus 1803, p. 14);
"superior . . . population" (ibid., p. 19)
moral restraint, misery, or vice (ibid., pp. 13–14)
lack of major change in second edition (Paglin, p. v)
"unexhausted vigor" (Malthus 1872, p. 155)
"Man . . . room" (ibid., p. 154)
"There can be . . . agriculture" (Malthus 1836, p. 288)
"No instance . . . natural resources" (ibid., p. 331)
"the result . . . ingenuity of man" (ibid., p. 351)
"facilitate[d] supply" (ibid., p. 360)
"How very dangerous . . . agents" (ibid., p. 335)
"fertility of soil" (ibid., p. 360)
empirical evidence (Rothbard 1995, pp. 107–08; Weir, p. 292)
inverse relationship (Rothbard 1995, p. 107)
1850 passing (Schumpeter 1954, p. 582)
"dismal science" (Skousen, p. 70)

Page 194
England statistics (W. S. Jevons 1867, pp. 26, 33)
"the coal panic" (Black 1987, p. 1012)
"grave and . . . urgent facts" (Gladstone, p. 265)
"almost exhaustive" (Mill, p. 192)
"all-powerful" (W. S. Jevons 1865, p. vii)
"mainspring . . . civilization" (ibid.)
"With coal . . . earlier times" (ibid., p. viii)

Page 195
"moral . . . retrogression" (ibid., p. ix)
"The progressive state . . . melancholy" (ibid., epigraph)
"the necessary . . . resources" (ibid., p. 344)
"For the present . . . Malthus's doctrine" (ibid., pp. 153–54)
"painful fact" (ibid., p. 154)
"in the increasing . . . progress" (ibid.)
"everything . . . cost" (ibid., p. 39)

Page 196
3.5 percent growth in demand (ibid., p. 213)
"more . . . deepest mine" (ibid., pp. 214–15)
"threatening" (ibid., p. 215)
"perhaps . . . lifetime" (ibid.)
"The exhaustion . . . doomed" (ibid., p. 57)
barriers to coal imports (ibid., chapter 12)
coal in the United States (ibid., pp. 267–70)
"all events . . . coal" (ibid., pp. x–xi)
"Our anxiety . . . *into space*" (ibid., p. 307)
"after a time . . . country" (ibid., p. xvi)
"If we lavishly . . . mediocrity" (ibid., p. 349)
"To allow . . . golden egg" (ibid., p. 345)
"a more . . . heavy" (ibid., p. 328)
"towards . . . cheap coal" (ibid., p. 339)

Page 197
"thorough, scientific" (W. Mitchell 1967, vol. 2:20)
exhaustion terminology (W. S. Jevons 1866, p. xxix; W. S. Jevons 1868, p. 28)
"fixed . . . resources" (W. S. Jevons 1865, p. 344)
"the very . . . use" (ibid., p. 104)
"*It is* . . . parallel instances" (ibid., p. 103)
"the reduction . . . amount" (ibid., p. 114)
"ten-fold . . . industry" (ibid.)
"ten or fifteen-fold" (ibid., p. 108)
"the cheapness . . . affords" (ibid.)
"will only . . . of coal" (ibid., p. 112)

Page 198
"irregular" (Jevons 1865, p. 123)
"supply . . . works" (ibid.)
"open . . . situations" (ibid.)
"upon local circumstances" (ibid., p. 129)
wood and land usage (ibid., p. 140)
limited geothermal (ibid., p. 120)

Page 199
Malthusian influence (ibid., p. 149; Peart, p. 23)
"the voracious . . . woods" (W. S. Jevons 1865, p. 302)
"threatening" (ibid., p. 215)
railway construction peak (Hussey, p. 298)

Page 200
"ingenuity" (W. S. Jevons 1865, p. 55)
"fair fight with difficulties" (ibid., p. 54)
"cheapen[ed] extraction" (ibid., p. 55)

Page 201
"There is no probability . . . forthcoming" (ibid., p. xiii)
"far more limited . . . coal" (ibid., p. 141)
U.K. oil imports (Mitchell and Jones, p. 74)

coal oil (W. S. Jevons 1865, p. 141)
"I naturally . . . exhaustion" (ibid., p. xiii)
"coal famine . . . come" (W. S. Jevons 1875, p. 36)
"a retardation . . . place" (W. S. Jevons 1865, p. 54)
growing U.K. coal production (Hausman, pp. 281–82; W. S. Jevons 1865, p. xiii)
coal price trends (Hausman, p. 282)
increasing coal reserves (W. S. Jevons 1865, pp. 206–09)
U.K. politics and coal problems (Dintenfass, pp. 170–71, 191–96, 204–09, 228; Haynes, pp. 21–34, 48–50; Robinson and Marshall, pp. 11–23; Supple)
no depletion signal (Gordon, pp. 252–53; Krautkraemer and Toman, p. 101)
overproduction and underproduction (Haynes, p. 55)

Page 202
Germany and Belgium versus United Kingdom (Fouquet and Pearson, p. 23)
"British entrepreneurs . . . other countries" (Haynes, p. 49)
overwork from depression (H. Jevons, pp. 201–02, 214–15, 218, 225, 233; Peart, p. 2)
"Almost . . . alive" ("Professor Stanley Jevons," p. 356)
"more . . . basket" (Keynes 1933b, p. 266)
"a psychological . . . resources" (ibid.)
lack of critical comment (Flux, in Jevons 1906)
supply, demand, efficiency (H. S. Jevons 1915, pp. 10, 757, 768)

Page 203
"may . . . shipping" (H.S. Jevons 1915, p. 10)
"the danger . . . us" (ibid.)
"Englishmen . . . heed" (ibid.)
"scare . . . age'" (ibid., p. 694)
"the supply . . . limited" (ibid., p. 706)
Colorado oil production (ibid. 1915, p. 711)
U.S., world oil-production statistics (Zimmermann 1933, pp. 494–95)
predicted world crude production (H. S. Jevons 1915, p. 715)
world crude output, 1970 and 2001 (www.eia.doe.gov/aer/pdf/pages/sec11-321.pdf)
"Practically . . . 100 years" (H. S. Jevons 1915, p. 710)

Page 204
current world crude oil reserves (Bradley and Fulmer, p. 88)
"much deeper . . . seams" (H. S. Jevons 1915, p. 763)
"gradually increase" (ibid.)
250 years (1600–1850) of price stability (Hausman, p. 281)
coal depths in the early 1900s versus today (www.UKcoal.com/commune/story/story06.htm)
"the life . . . more fleeting" (H. S. Jevons 1915, p. 711)

Page 205
"our only . . . power" (H. S. Jevons 1915, p. 717)
"dash for gas" (Fouquet and Pearson, p. 32)
"an imperative call to action" (quoted in National Conservation Commission, vol. 1:1)
natural gas reserves (ibid., vol. 1:101)

Page 206
oil exhaustion (ibid., vol. 1:16, 101)
domestic coal supply (ibid., vol. 1:15)
"exhaustive" (Hammond, p. 17)
"our coal problem" (Hunt et al., p. 25)
"There . . . industry!" (Hammond, p. 17)
"Already . . . wane" (Hunt et al., p. 25)
"Production . . . rate" (ibid.)
"In the . . . attention" (ibid, p. 45)
"Guided . . . business" (ibid., p. 411)
industry-stabilization strategy (Johnson, p. 19)
federal powers over coal; "public interest" (ibid., p. 53)

Page 207
"lightless nights" (ibid., p. 75)
"heatless Mondays" and "non-essential" (Hunt et al., pp. 80–81)
fuel riots, deaths (Johnson, pp. 63–64)
"robber . . . Rhine"; nationalization threat (ibid., p. 57)
"the law . . . property rights" (Harry Garfield, quoted in ibid., p. 63)
federal oil and gas interference (Bradley 1996, pp. 225–33)
"completely . . . system" (Martin 1971, pp. 338–39)
railroad nationalization (ibid., p. 351)

8 A Joined Debate
Footnotes
8 other Ford Foundation grants (Domhoff, p. 96)
9 competing names (RFF 1977b, p. 7)

Page 208
"Resources *are not, they become*" (Zimmermann 1951, p. 15)

Page 209
"the appraising mind . . . decision-maker" (Zimmermann 1933, pp. 3–4)
"the environment . . . man" (ibid., p. 3)
"human wants . . . abilities" (ibid.)
"Creating . . . good" (ibid., p. 9)
variety (ibid., p. 5)
"each invention . . . others" (ibid., p. 73)
"Resources . . . human use" (Zimmermann 1951, pp. 814–15)

Page 210
"Knowledge . . . resources" (ibid., p. 10)
functional, subjective, relative, availability, dynamic (Zimmermann 1933, pp. 3–4, 6, 45)
"mathematical . . . high" (Samuelson 1952, p. 56)

Page 211
"literary economist" (ibid., p. 65)
"To those . . . disconcerting" (Zimmermann 1933, p. 4)
"Nothing . . . become'" (Zimmermann 1951, p. 11)

institutional factors (Zimmermann 1933, pp. 9, 37; Zimmermann 1951, pp. xv, 6, 14–16, 818)

"A functional . . . technological" (Zimmermann 1933, p. 216)

Page 212

"Minerals . . . natural gas" (L. C. Gray, p. 501)

"is the determination . . . resources" (ibid., p. 515)

"plainly . . . decline" (Hotelling, p. 139)

perfect knowledge (ibid., p. 144)

"golden mean" (ibid., p. 139)

"wholesale . . . resources" (ibid., p. 137)

"exploitation . . . good" (ibid., p. 138)

Hotelling influence (Arrow, p. 671)

Page 213

"The Mecca" (Samuelson 1966, p. 1588)

resourceship (S. McDonald)

"ideal state" (Hotelling, p. 146)

Page 214

"a jumble of numbers" (S. McDonald to author, August 2, 2003)

depletion concern (Zimmermann 1933, p. 19)

price and quantity statistics for carbon-based energies (ibid., pp. 461, 463, 494–95, 535, 541)

"obsolete" (ibid., p. 813)

"To the average . . . future" (ibid., p. 18)

"warped appraisal" (ibid., p. 23)

"tempo problem" (ibid., p. 19)

"as the political . . . resources" (ibid.)

"transient" versus permanent civilization (ibid., p. 71)

Page 215

"the necessity . . . of natural resources" (Hayek 1960, p. 370)

"particularly strong . . . reformers" (ibid., pp. 367–68)

"consumption of irreplaceable resources" (ibid., p. 369)

government ignorance (ibid., p. 371)

"Any natural resource . . . future" (ibid., p. 374)

"the conservationist . . . for posterity" (ibid.)

"It is . . . subjectivism" (Hayek 1952, p. 52)

Page 216

depletion fears and conservation movement (Nolan, pp. 49–66)

pessimistic books, 1946–50 (RFF 1977b, p. 4)

"the broader . . . needs" (quoted in President's Material Policy [Paley] Commission, vol. 1:iv)

Paley Commission (Goodwin, pp. 52–61)

increase of U.S. oil and gas production (President's Material Policy [Paley] Commission, vol. 1:5)

materials consumption (ibid., vol. 1:4)

Page 217

"the time will come . . . fossil fuels" (ibid., vol. 1:106)

report upbeat (Goodwin, p. 54)

Mason description (Adelman 1997, p. 14; Adelman to author, June 12, 2002, and April 9, 2003)
"Masonic Lodge" (Papanek, p. 395)
"Where Ed Mason sat . . . table" (quoted in ibid., p. 395)
"popular fallacy" (President's Material Policy [Paley] Commission, vol. 1:21)
"our resource base" (ibid.)
"a fixed . . . survival" (ibid.)
"related . . . waste" (ibid.)
"Hoarding . . . completely" (ibid.)
"using . . . higher" (ibid.)
U.S. oil statistics (ibid., vol. 3:4–5)

Page 218
"the free price system . . . materials" (ibid., vol. 1:17)
"The United States . . . may be found" (ibid., vol. 1:3)
"a courageous . . . industries" (RFF 1987, p. 84)
"prudence . . . uncertainty" (President's Material Policy [Paley] Commission, vol. 1:21)
"comprehensive energy policy" (ibid., vol. 1:129)
"The Nation's . . . field" (ibid.)
historical oil statistics (ibid., vol. 3:4–5)
"If we . . . by 1975" (ibid., vol. 4:213)
atomic energy (ibid., vol. 4:220)
"the United States . . . the present requirement" (ibid., vol. 4:213)
"It is time . . . world" (ibid. vol. 4:220)
coal-based synthetics (ibid., vol. 1:7, 125)
supply-side orientation of study (Goodwin, p. 55)
"We share . . . Growth" (President's Material Policy [Paley] Commission, vol. 1:3)
areas not discussed (RFF 1987, p. 91)

Page 219
"Developing . . . standards" (Belair, p. 1)
"heartening" (quoted in ibid.)
"serious" (ibid.)
"threat" and "many causes for concern" (President's Material Policy [Paley] Commission, vol. 1:1)
media alarmism (Goodwin, p. 59)
Eisenhower refusal (Darmstadter 2003, p. 2)
"substantial groundwork" (Ford Foundation 1952, p. 32)
"a problem . . . resources" (ibid.)

Page 220
1908 and 1952 conferences (Barber, p. 207; RFF 1977b, p. 11)
conference support (RFF 1987, p. 21)
"era of the big books" (RFF 1977b, p. 21)
"We have . . . directions" (quoted in RFF 1954, p. 10)

Page 221
"Every discovery . . . unknown" (Forest Moulton, quoted in RFF, *Resources*, May 1959, p. 1)
U.S. Senate study (National Fuels and Study Group, p. 12)

Page 222
"no society . . . Malthusian diminishing returns" (Barnett and Morse, p. 139)
affluent society (Galbraith 1958, pp. 89–99)
"modern . . . growth" (Barnett and Morse, p. 258)
"gestaltist" and "monumental . . . *Industries*" (ibid., p. 46)
"the basic idea . . . in the mind" (M. A. Adelman to author, April 15, 2003)
"Perhaps . . . the resource" (Adelman 1997, p. 26)
"resources . . . but made" (ibid., p. 41)
Page 223
"resources *are not, they become*" (Zimmermann 1951, p. 15)

9 Neo-Malthusianism
Figures
9.1 "mathematical . . . resource" (Hubbert 1973, p. 119)
9.5 "new agenda" and "solid waste . . . development" (Adler, p. 13)

Footnotes
1 "there is . . . rate" and "the culmination . . . few decades" (Hubbert 1974, p. 68)
6 "The World . . . Man" (quoted in Mesarovic and Pestel, p. 1); "the creation . . . mankind" (quoted in ibid., p. 9); "traumatic . . . catastrophes" (quoted in ibid. , pp. vii–viii)

Page 225
"One . . . population" (Hubbert 1949, p. 104)
"Where . . . up?" (ibid., p. 105)
"overpopulation . . . decline" (ibid., p. 109)
Shell dissent (Deffeyes, p. 2)
"became something . . . conservationists" (ibid., p. 5)
"500 million . . . history" (Hubbert 1956, p. 8)
"progressive exhaustion" (ibid.)
"industrial exploitation" (ibid.)
Ohio curve (ibid., pp. 12–13)
U.S. and world predictions (ibid., pp. 16–18)
"exhaust . . . a century" (Hubbert 1969, p. 205)

Page 226
"about . . . source" (ibid.)
Hubbert's errant predictions (Lynch, pp. 376–79)
"powerful means . . . region" (Hubbert 1973, p. 119)

Page 227
"inspired guess . . . methods" (Deffeyes, p. 6)
warning in 1952 (Wood, p. 279)
"We are . . . economy" (quoted in ibid., p. 241)
"the first . . . visible" (quoted in ibid., p. 280)
"the first twinge" (W. S. Jevons 1875, p. 36)
industry complaints (Bradley 1996, pp. 726–35)
"A Buddhist . . . resources'" (quoted in Wood, p. 248)
"concerned . . . efficiency" (ibid., p. 312)
"Modern . . . man" (Schumacher, p. 275)
"magnanimous . . . enough" (ibid., p. 279)

Page 228
"voice in the wilderness" (Yergin 1991, p. 559)
guru and audiences (Wood, pp. 361, 363–64)
conservation/preservation movement (Adler, chapter 1)

Page 229
founding dates of new environmental groups (ibid., pp. 23, 51)
"The Problem . . . A Dying Planet" (Ehrlich 1968, pp. 17, 36, 46)
"The battle . . . now" (ibid., p. 11)
"death-rate solution" (ibid., p. 69)
"What will . . . dry?" (Ehrlich and Harriman, p. 4)
Johnny Carson shows (Bradley 2000, p. 126)
"hundreds of . . . now" (Ehrlich 1968, p. xi)
I=P·A·T (Ehrlich and Ehrlich 1990, p. 58; Ehrlich and Holdren 1971, pp. 1212–13; Ehrlich, Ehrlich, and Holdren 1973, chapter 7)

Page 231
"firmly . . . camp" (Ehrlich, Ehrlich, and Holdren 1977, p. 954)
"vexing . . . predicament" (ibid., p. 1)
"gloomy prognosis" (ibid., p. 5)
"a growing . . . observers" (ibid.)
"organized . . . government" (ibid.)
Santa Barbara blowout (Bradley 1996, p. 302)
Earth Day (Harrington, p. 9)
"I suspect . . . materials" (quoted in Adler, p. 23)
Simon/Silverman debate (Harrington, p. 8)
Simon conversion (Simon 2002, pp. 237–48)
Simon debate points (ibid., pp. 260, 262)

Page 232
tepid applause; ringing ovation (ibid., p. 260)
"We are . . . intervention" (quoted in ibid., p. 261)
oil concerns (ibid., p. 262)
confrontation (Harrington, p. 8)
Simon's clinical depression (Simon 1993, p. 5)

Page 233
"Ecology . . .thing" (Heilbroner 1970, p. 269)
"There are . . . fad" (ibid.)

Page 234
"Aside . . . urban areas" (Kneese, p. 3)
29 languages, 9 million sold (Suter, p. 2)
"exponential growth" versus "a finite world" (Meadows et al., pp. 51, 87)
"Although . . . *collapse*" (ibid., p. 142)
global equilibrium (ibid., p. 171)
"a totally . . . generations" (ibid., p. 184)
"a realistic . . . society" (ibid.)
"Malthus . . . computer" (C. Freeman, chapter title, pp. 5–13)
"invisible college" of "intellectual technologists" (Simmons, p. 206)

Page 235
"fundamental imperative" to "transform society" (Suter, p. 3)
"astonishingly . . . bright" (Meadows, p. 258)
"to learn . . . coming collapse" (ibid., p. 259)
"We . . . work" (ibid.)
"We dearly . . . action" (quoted in Reinhold, p. 41)
"the soft-spoken . . . project" (ibid.)

Page 236
"known global reserves" (Meadows et al., p. 60)
reserves of 19 minerals (ibid., pp. 55–63)
"'Doomsday . . . policy" (Solow 1973, p. 302)
"Malthus in, Malthus out" (C. Freeman, p. 8)
study problems (Simon 1981, p. 286)
"serious doubts" (Kneese and Ridker)
"housed . . . MIT" (ibid.)
"startling shift" ("Club of Rome Revisited")

Page 237
"evolving strategy" (ibid.)
"a technocratic . . . view" (quoted in Crittenden, p. 58)
"fictitious . . . methodology" (L. Gordon, p. 1)
"didactic . . . utopia" (ibid.)
"almost . . . optimism" (ibid.)
market failure (Pigou 1920, p. 149)
government correction (Pigou 1932, p. 172)
"the clear duty . . . country" (Pigou 1920, p. 28)
"The problems . . . itself" (Galbraith 1958, p. 6)
"the problem . . . together" (ibid., p. 355)

Page 238
"growthmania" as "unimaginative and unworthy" (Mishan, p. 5)
"spillover effects" (ibid., p. xv)
"One may . . . society" (ibid., p. 4)
"post-war . . . destroyed" (ibid., pp. 6–7)
"We do not . . . people'" (ibid., p. 162)
"one of the . . . race" (ibid.)
"broke the spell . . . again" (ibid., p. 165)
"something . . . sex" (Boulding 1970, p. 160)
"with reckless . . . societies" (Boulding 1966, p. 9)
"spaceman economy" (ibid.)

Page 239
"cyclical . . . gain" (ibid., p. 10)
"This idea . . . concepts" (ibid.)
"Economic development . . . spaceship earth" (Boulding 1970, p. 166)
"evil day" (Holdren and Ehrlich, p. 177)
"Resources . . . deluge" (Boulding 1970, p. 164)
"Bigger . . . luxury" (Boulding 1971, p. 33)
"a fundamental . . . traumatic" (Boulding 1970, p. 164)

"collision" (RFF 1970, p. 5)
"At issue . . . in transit" (ibid.)

Page 240
1970 energy problems (ibid.)
"Prophets . . . corner" (Maddox, p. 3)

10 The Dark Decade
Figures
10.3 "conservation . . . increasing supply" (quoted in Nash, p. 22)
10.5 "preacher and engineer" (Yergin 1991, p. 693)

Footnotes
3 "Many . . . War" (Nielsen 1972, p. 10)
10 "The publicly . . . professed goal" (Arrow and Kalt, p. 25)

Page 241
Aramco nationalization (Bradley 1989, p. 4)

Page 242
"neutralizing . . . fuel" (W. S. Jevons 1865, p. 102)
"Britain should be . . . as she is" (ibid., p. 346)
"a classic Malthusian case . . . resource" (quoted in "Opening the Debate," p. 27)
Galbraith congratulations (Rogge, p. 33)
Samuelson support, Friedman criticism (Friedman, Samuelson, and Wallich 1971, pp. 22–23)

Page 243
"One . . . offing" (*Fuel Shortages 2*, p. 525)

Page 244
"the first . . . subject" (*Fuel Shortages 1*, p. 1)
Nixon price-control program (Bradley 1996, pp. 467–78)
Stelzer testimony (*Energy Conservation*)
energy project (Ford Foundation 1974, p. ix)
"liberal domestic reformer" (Nielsen 1985, p. 62)
world's wealthiest foundation (Nielsen 1972, p. 78)
"a man . . . integrity" (Ford Foundation 1974, p. x)
Freeman predisposition (Tavoulareas 1974, p. 400)
three major conclusions; "Conservation . . . supply" (Ford Foundation 1974, p. xi)

Page 245
limited supply-side actions (ibid., pp. 330–33)
conservation and renewables (ibid., p. 331)
federal yardstick enterprise like TVA (ibid., p. 41)
public utility regulation (Bradley 1996, pp. 49–50; Ford Foundation 1974, pp. 41–42)
"if historical growth . . . limits" (Ford Foundation 1974, p. 42)
study's provisions and "high enough" (ibid., p. 333)
"The net effect . . . growth" (ibid., p. 37)
Freeman as prophet of energy conservation (Goodwin 1981, pp. 678, 683)

demand-growth reduction and cessation (Ford Foundation 1974, pp. 325–26)
Energy Policy Council/Citizens' Advisory Board (ibid., p. 329)
"a uniform . . . energy" (ibid., p. 330)
energy stamps (ibid., p. 334)
"unique . . . advantages" (ibid., p. 339)
"selected to reflect . . . outlooks" (ibid., p. 350)

Page 246
"blasted . . . Corporation" (Cochrane, p. 554)
"regrettably . . . demagoguery" (Alchian, p. 1)
"a belief . . . plan" (H. Kahn, pp. 154–55)
"Everything . . . in 1865" (Adelman 1975a, p. 27)
"completely ignores . . . processes" (ibid., p. 28)
"The book's . . . Administration" (ibid., p. 29)
Tavoulareas anger at Freeman (Cochrane, p. 554; Tavoulareas 1974, pp. 25, 29)
introduction by Ford Foundation official (M. Robinson)
"helping . . . policy" (Kaysen, p. 77)
"unhelpful . . . industry" (ibid.)
energy, environment, and social objectives (Ford Foundation 1974, p. 12)

Page 247
"troubled" and "in a very real . . . decade" (*Fiscal Policy*, p. 45)
"Almost . . . rationing" (Hass et al., p. 7)
"although . . . create" (Stiglitz, p. 56)

Page 248
"a scion . . . Brahmins" (Nielsen 1972, p. 93)
"highly . . . program" (Nielsen 1985, p. 83)
"shocking losses," financial losses (ibid., p. 70)
largest loss in history (ibid.)
1,500 staff (ibid., p. 71)
"academics and intellectuals" (ibid., p. 82)
"whisper" to "roar" (Nielsen 1972, p. 94)
"resulted . . . one stroke" (ibid., p. 95)
"quasi-investment, quasi-philanthropic" (ibid.)
"social criteria" (ibid.)
"A policy . . . projects" (ibid.)
"reconfirmed . . . thumb" (Nielsen 1985, p. 67)
"I am not . . . worth preserving" (quoted in Nielsen 1985, p. 83; Dowie, p. 10)

Page 249
"He has . . . course" (quoted in Nielsen 1985, p. 72)
Henry Ford II history (Nielsen 1972, p. 79)
low-price energy era over (S. David Freeman, pp. 78, 89, 333)
"sit-down strike" (ibid., p. 79)
"new ethic . . . theft" (ibid., p. 333)
"the whole structure . . . civilization" (ibid., p. 334)
Freeman and Carter candidacy (Cochrane, pp. 549, 553)
soft energy paths (Lovins 1976a, p. 77)
Ehrlich and Holdren praise (Mayer, p. 108)

Page 250
"selling . . . bill" (J. A. L. Robertson, at www.magma.ca/~jalrober/lovins.htm)
"It is hard . . . unsuspected" (Lovins 1975, p. 113)
"We must . . . grounds" (ibid., pp. 128–29)
"Boundary . . . needed" (ibid., p. 128)
"small is beautiful" (Lovins 1977, p. 12; Schumacher)
oil/gas to coal/nuclear (Lovins 1976a, p. 66)
"transitional technologies . . . 2025" (ibid., p. 84)
"realistic long-term goal" and "modest . . . growth" (ibid., p. 76)

Page 251
technological pessimist toward hard energy (ibid., pp. 70, 88)
"subsidized . . . corporate statism" (ibid., p. 92)
"only cheaper than not doing it" (A. Lovins in Nash, p. 130)
"A final feature . . . conservatives" (quoted in Lanouette, p. 1532)
"we could . . . at all" (Lovins 1979, p. 26)
"we could . . . petrol pigs" (quoted in Jennrich 1982, p. 79)

Page 252
"Strength Through Exhaustion" (Lovins 1976b, p. 16)
"The idea . . . scale" ("Energy: Where Intervention Is Inevitable," p. 80)
2000 prediction and U.S. actual (EIA 2002, p. 5; Lovins 1976b, p. 23)
2025 forecasts (EIA 2007, p. 135; Nash 1979, pp. 37–38)
"urgent" (Lovins 1976b, p. 30)
"the next . . . future" (www.news.harvard.edu/gazette/2000/02.10/holdren.html)
"a soft path . . . groups" (Lovins 1977, p. 220)

Page 253
"temporary" price controls (Nixon, 499)
"the most . . . ever undertaken" (Federal Energy Administration, p. i)
fatalistic about domestic supply (ibid., p. 81)
Ford energy policy (De Marchi, pp. 495, 497, 542–43)
Nelson Rockefeller proposal (ibid., pp. 518–20; Yergin 1991, p. 660)

Page 254
"The diagnosis . . . endangered" (Executive Office of the President, p. vii)
nine groups (Sobel 1977, p. 46)

Page 255
"fundamentally . . . farsighted" (ibid.)
"The . . . ourselves" (ibid.)
"over the next decade . . . could worsen" (Department of Energy, p. 15)
scope of Department of Energy (Sobel 1977, p. 50)
Schumpeter optimism (Schumpeter 1954, p. 263)
"were . . . Friedman" (Cochrane, p. 553)
"Shar[ing] . . . fossil fuels" (ibid., p. 552)
"righteous pragmatism" (ibid.)

Page 256
Galbraith as price controller (Bradley 1996, p. 236)
"The . . . disaster" (Carter 1982, p. 91)
"the moral equivalent of war" (Carter 1977, p. 36)

"widespread belief. . . real costs" (RFF 1968, p. 23)
"While . . . many adjustments" (Schurr et al. 1979, p. 426)
"The increase . . . and use" (ibid., p. 461)

Page 257
"fairness" (ibid., p. 460)
"environmental insults" (ibid., p. 461)
"market failure" (ibid., p. 472)
"social costs" (ibid., p. 440)
"decentralization" (ibid., p. 324)
Amory Lovins (ibid., p. 546)
"private . . . cost" (ibid., p. 440)
"'profit . . . costs" (ibid., p. 441)
"balanced perspective" (Hitch, in ibid., p. xix)
"increasingly . . . availability" (ibid.)
"'satisficing'" rather than "'optimizing'" (quoted in ibid., p. xx)
"personal view . . . needs" (Schurr, p. 9)
"consensus [that] would . . . initiatives" (ibid.)

Page 258
"heavy . . . market forces" (quoted in Landsberg, p. xvii)
"did not . . . forces" (quoted in ibid.)
oil and gas decontrol (ibid., p. 46)
"vigorously . . . source" (ibid., p. 63)
solar energy promotion (ibid., pp. 65–67)
"an increase . . . the future" (Schurr et al. 1979, p. 461)
"explosive revival of interest" (Devarajan and Fisher, p. 65)
"having . . . *Growth*" (Solow 1974, p. 1)

Page 259
"greater reliance on the market" (Stobaugh and Yergin, "The End of Easy Oil," p. 12)
"bleak outlook" (Stobaugh and Yergin, "Conclusion," p. 216)
"transition . . . system" (ibid., p. 229)
"the government . . . conservation and solar" (ibid.)
"within two decades" (Stobaugh and Yergin, "The End of Easy Oil," p. 12)
"modest . . . live" (Yergin 1979, p. 136)
"romantics . . . growth" (Stobaugh and Yergin, "The End of Easy Oil," p. 12)
"even more . . . production" (ibid.)
"Now is the time . . . self-interest" (Stobaugh and Yergin, "Conclusion," p. 233)

Page 260
"the best . . . in print" (quoted in Yergin and Hillenbrand, back cover inside flap)
estimated imported oil price increase (Kalt, pp. 286–87)
oil-reselling boom in the 1970s (Bradley 1996, pp. 681–710, 1806–08)
superfluous entrepreneurship (ibid., pp. 1802–05)

Page 261
hundreds of resellers (ibid., p. 707)
lost million barrels per day (Kalt, p. 287)
"regulatory millionaires" (Bradley 1996, p. 710)

reseller extravagance (ibid., pp. 706–07)
regulation of opportunism (ibid., p. 693)

Page 262
media problems with energy (Reynolds, pp. 5, 8, 13, 20)
"Initial Simplistic Explanation" (ibid., p. 9)
choice of interviews (ibid., p. 12)
Michael Jensen (ibid., p. 6)
Wall Street Journal (ibid., p. 13)
"Why . . . Energy" (Friedman and Friedman, p. 220)

Page 263
avoidance of price controls abroad (E. Mitchell, p. 72)
"market . . . excessive" (OECD, vol. 1:1)
"economic . . . countries" (ibid.)
"a false sense . . . mechanism" (ibid., p. 179)
"reasonable . . . terms" and "long-term . . . development" (quoted in Scott, p. 359)
International Energy Agency (www.iea.org/about/index.htm)
Kissinger price-floor program (De Marchi, pp. 530–31)

Page 264
sentiment for global planning (Wälde, pp. 565–66)
"the only . . . policy" (Carter, p. 91)
"IEA was . . . act" (Stagliano, p. 227)
"Although . . . has ended" (Granville, p. 57)
"brief interlude . . . beyond" (Warner, p. 66)
"committed to remaining an energy company" (ibid., p. 67)
"low-priority" (Lawrence, p. 71)
future of natural gas (ibid., pp. 71–72)
Exxon prediction of falling U.S. oil usage (Darmstadter et al. 1983, pp. 12–13)

Page 265
Royal Dutch Shell and renewables (Hamel 2000, pp. 175–84, 211–33)
"the cornerstone of U.S. energy policy" (quoted in Bradley 1988, p. 310)
thermostat regulation (ibid., p. 308)
Eisenhower veto (Bradley 1996, pp. 381–82)

Page 266
"Economists . . . prevail" (quoted in E. Mitchell, pp. 1–2)

Page 267
shortage policy (ibid., p. 2)
resources not scarcer (ibid., pp. 4–11)
"gap-reducing" and "gapologist" (ibid., p. 19)
gap-filling measures (ibid., pp. 2, 19–26, 71–72)

Page 268
"an altogether . . . one" (Adelman 1975b, p. 89)
Arab OPEC cutback (Adelman 1995, p. 109)
"population controllers" (Simon 2002, p. 264)

Page 269
"If population . . . limit" (Simon 1977, pp. 482–83)
"fell . . . the press" (Simon 2002, p. 265)
"provided . . . evidence" and "a life-time . . . speculation" (reprinted in ibid., p. 268)
"most valuable . . . life" (ibid.)
energy the master resource (Simon 1977, p. 93)
oil not scarcer (ibid., pp. 84–85)
"the human imagination" (ibid., pp. 107, 476)
"the key resource" (ibid., p. 97)
population and economic indicators (ibid., pp. 474–75)
"kind of . . . over time" (C. Robinson 1971, p. 9)
"throws . . . 'famine'" (C. Robinson 1974, p. 27)
"The energy . . . issues" (ibid.)

Page 270
"treating . . . capital items" (Schumacher, p. 12)
"gigantic" (ibid., p. 12)
"foreseeable future" (ibid.)
"income fuels" (ibid.)
"modern man . . . man" (ibid., p. 275)
"the philosophy of materialism" (ibid.)
"magnanimous kind of prudence" (ibid., p. 279)

11 New Light
Figures
11.8 Increasing world proved reserves (American Petroleum Institute, Basic Petroleum
Data Book, Volume XV, Number 1 (January 1995), Section II, Table 1 (oil reserves);
Section XIII, Table 1 (natural gas reserves); Federal Institute for Geosciences and
Natural Resources in Hanover, Germany, and e-mail to author from Dr. Hans Wilhelm
Schiffer, RWE Power AG, July 30, 2007. Oil, gas, and coal production data: Bradley
2000, pp. 28–31, 150.

Footnotes
1 "Morry Adelman . . . market" (Gordon et al., p. xiii)
prediction of $100 oil by 2000 (Hayward, p. 103)
6 "good . . . stock!!"; "The potential . . . for us" (John Palmisano, internal Enron memo,
December 12, 1997)

Page 271
"a flood . . . writers" (Landsberg, p. xxi)
"one of . . . world" (Ziemba et al., p. xviii)
"gapology" (E. Mitchell, p. 17)
"Let . . . Project" (quoted in Yergin 1982, p. 105)
Nixon and Ford energy planning (De Marchi, p. 545)
Carter energy planning (Cochrane, pp. 547–53)
Reagan decontrol (Bradley 1988, p. 306)
$100 oil (Adelman and Watkins, p. 1)

Page 272
"raised . . . points" (Garret Hardin, quoted in Simon 1996, p. 612)
"Why . . . news?" (Simon 1980, p. 1436)

"bad . . . interesting" (ibid.)
"Is . . . improvement?" (ibid.)
"Could . . . count to 20?" (quoted in Simon 1996, p. 612)
"The fact . . . natural gas" (Holdren et al., p. 1297)

Page 273
strategy from Galbraith (Simon 2002, p. 265)
"Hold your hat . . . inexhaustible" (Simon 1981, p. 5)
"The ultimate . . . benefit of us all" (ibid., p. 348)
"Freedom . . . resources" (Zimmermann 1945, p. 159)
"anomaly" (Kuhn, pp. 67, 90)
"paradigm" (ibid., p. 10)
"normal science" (ibid., pp. 10, 24)
"extraordinary science" (ibid., p. 101)
"scientific revolution" (ibid., p. 129)
"gestalt" (ibid., p. 112)
"preformed . . . box" (ibid., p. 24)
"intolerant" (ibid.)
"paradigm shifts" (ibid., p. 120)
"scientists . . . differently" (ibid., p. 24)
"pronounced . . . insecurity" (ibid., pp. 67–68)
"a few . . . remain" (ibid., p. 159)

Page 274
"shift of vision" (ibid., p. 119)
social science paradigm shifts (Rothbard 1997, pp. 197–98)
"mass . . . protoplasm" (Holdren et al., p. 1301)

Page 275
"truth and liberty" (Simon 1996, p. xxxiv)
"gestalt switch" (Kuhn, pp. 111, 122, 204)
"Though . . . policy" (quoted in Simon 1996, p. 615)
Hayek's fame (Yergin and Stanislaw, pp. 141–45, 227)
"parallels" (Kirzner 1983, p. 166)
"spirited . . . thesis" (ibid.)
"'unlimited . . . thoughts'" (ibid.)
"'ultimate resource'" (ibid.)
"My own grounds . . . entrepreneurship" (ibid., p. 167)
"Horizon-expanding discoveries" (ibid.)

Page 276
"ideal" (quoted in Simon 1981, back cover)
"The 1970's . . . perfectly timed" (Bruce-Briggs, p. 10)
"physicists . . . flat Earth" (quoted in Harrington, pp. 18–19)
"pronounced . . . insecurity" (Kuhn, pp. 67–68)
intolerance (ibid., p. 24)
"the economists" (Ehrlich and Ehrlich 1981, p. 245)
"The enemy . . . war" (ibid., p. 242)
energy as the problem (ibid., pp. 174–75)
"If I . . . year 2000" (quoted in Simon, p. 27)

"the doomsdayers . . . are" (ibid., p. 25)
parameters of wager (ibid., p. 27)

Page 277
"accept . . . jump in" (Ehrlich 1981, p. 46)
"the lure . . . irresistible" (Ehrlich 1982, p. 386)
822 million population increase (www.census.gov/ipc/www/worldpop.html)
wager outcome (Simon 1996, p. 35; Tierney)

Page 278
"prices . . . consumption" (Ehrlich and Ehrlich 1996, p. 98)
"more people . . . cleaner environment" (Simon, quoted in Bradley 2000, p. 23)

Page 279
"If present . . . current trends" (Council on Environmental Quality, p. 1)

Page 280
"If present . . . today" (Simon and Kahn, pp. 1–2)
"seems . . . occur" (Brown, p. 385)
Heritage Foundation, Reagan administration, and Simon (Holden)
"the world . . . it" (Darmstadter, Landsberg, and Morton, p. 89)
"As oil . . . decline" (ibid.)
global-warming issue (ibid., p. 156)
"the . . . uninteresting" (E. Mitchell, p. 6)

Page 281
"Low-cost . . . available" (Yergin 1982, p. 95)
"may pose . . . growth" (ibid.)
"glut psychology" (ibid., p. 15)
"by 1982. . . future" (ibid.)
"virtually . . . conservation" (ibid., pp. 15–16)
"an energy . . . Community" (ibid., p. 25)
"Can . . . crisis?" (ibid.)
"research . . . trends" (Cambridge Energy Research Associates, inside cover)

Page 282
"heresy" (Yergin, in ibid., p. 1)
"our outstanding achievement" (S. David Freeman 1988, p. 9)
uneconomic hoarding (Simon 1996, pp. 34–35)

Page 283
"think and do tank" (Stipp, p. 101)
Lovins not a depletionist; against Ehrlich bet (Logan, p. 66)
"The . . . dismal" (quoted in "The 'Soft Path'. . .", p. 96N)
"where . . . it" (ibid.)
"over" (ibid.)
"negawatts" (Fickett, Gellings, and Lovins, p. 72)
1984–2000 electricity growth (EIA 2002, pp. 241–42)
Lovins and California energy policy (Tucker, p. 27)

Page 284
"new era of natural capitalism" (Hawken, Lovins, and Lovins, p. 313)
"Today . . . proposition" (Zimmermann 1933, p. 784)

"The [Hotelling] Principle . . . absent" (Watkins, pp. 1–2, 22)
Hotelling literature (Krautkraemer)
"Hotelling's analysis . . . activities" (Simon, circa 1989, p. 534)

Page 285
"sacrifices . . . life" (quoted in Sobel 1977, p. 37)
"People . . . not America's" (quoted in Hayward, p. 151)
"There . . . now" (Carter, January 14, 1981)
"We're . . . dreams" (Reagan, January 20, 1981)
"In this . . . else?" (ibid.)
"Ending . . . production" (Reagan, January 28, 1981)

Page 286
"The contrast . . . future" (Heclo, p. 51)
"recast . . . knowledge" (Yergin and Stanislaw, pp. 122–23)
"It is possible . . . for reforestation" (Thatcher 1993, pp. 640–41)
Thatcher and Hadley Center, IPCC (Stevens, pp. 162–63)
"green socialism" (Thatcher 1993, p. 639)
"another . . . threat" (ibid., p. 640)

Page 287
"the doomsters' . . . climate change" (Thatcher 2002, p. 449)
"ugly . . . anti-American" (ibid., pp. 452–53)
"Government . . . proven" (ibid., p. 453)
"symbolize[d] . . . with Britain" (Thatcher 1993, p. 340)

Page 288
government/international studies (Simon 2002, pp. 255–57)
"national security" call for oil tariffs (Bradley 1989, pp. 14–22)
"expensive . . . costs" (Holdren 1990, p. 158)
"the trends . . . out" (ibid.)
falling fossil-fuel prices (EIA 2002, 71)
"MacArthur! . . . McDonald's!" (quoted in Regis, p. 195)
Simon and Nobel Prize (M. Friedman to author, September 4, 2003)
Simon's death (Gilpin)
increasing world proved reserves (API, Section II, Table 1; Section XIII, Table 1)

Page 289
emission and energy statistics (U.S. EPA, in Bradley 2003, p. 30)
"our . . . early relief" (Ehrlich and Holdren 1971b, p. 66)
"we have . . . symbols" (Ehrlich 1968, p. 112)
OPEC versus non-OPEC production (EIA 2002, p. 287)
U.S. energy usage, 1970–90 (ibid., p. 13)

Page 290
rearticulated (Kuhn, p. 78)
global-cooling concern (Bryson 1968; Fleming, pp. 132–34)
Carter administration and warming (L. Carter, pp. 376–77)
"very . . . historic" (quoted in ibid., p. 377)

global-warming concern (Fleming, pp. 134–37)
Gore hearings on global warming (Michaels, pp. 14–19)
redefinitions and paradigm strain (Kuhn, p. 78)
"'Cost' . . . components" (Holdren 1992, p. 1)
"the most . . . depleted" (ibid.)

Page 291
"higher . . . fuels" (ibid.)
"that . . . others" (ibid.)
"Shortages . . . response" (Campbell, p. 38)
"Having . . . plausible" (Gordon 1994, p. 12)

Epilogue: Surreal Enron, Real Capitalism
Footnotes
1 "for leading . . . competition" (Stelzer, p. 16); "Enron . . . bottom lines" (White)
2 "many" (Gordon, p. 768); "libertarian antinomian(s). . . regulation" (ibid., p. 769)
3 "Ethical man . . . economic man" (Bowen, p. 235)
4 "create . . . cost" (Epstein, p. 70)
6 "a professor's . . . on it" (Chesher and Machan, p. 136); "intellectual honesty . . .
knowledge" (AAUP, p. 171)
9 "perverse incentives," agency problem (Koch, p. 148)
10 Kuhnian terms (Kuhn, pp. 10, 67, 101, 119)

Page 292
"high culture" (quoted in Smiles 1871, p. 111)
"tries . . . life" (Smiles 1866, p. 238)

Page 293
"Defenders . . . markets" (Kuttner 2001, p. 24)
"Enron . . . standards" (Kuttner 2002, p. 2)
"The problem . . . transactions" (quoted in Niskanen, pp. 7–8)

Page 294
"*Modern* capitalism . . . or die" (McCraw 2007, p. 9)
"Since . . . public interest" (Pinkham, p. 23)
"Many . . . no regulation" (Schnietz, p. 3)
"A serious . . . regulation" (Millstein, p. 6)

Page 295
"Businessmen . . . competition" (Bowen, p. 66)
"the aristocracy of pull" (Rand 1957, p. 404)
"Great Duration" (Higgs, pp. 3–29)
"We definitely . . . are compromised" (quoted in Weisman)
"not much . . . a thousand" (A. Smith 1776, p. 342)

Page 296
"Ultimately . . . first place" (Eichenwald, p. 11)
unintended perverse consequences (Bradley 2006, pp. 75–77; Ikeda, pp. 100–12)
"The proper response . . . age" (R. Epstein, p. 21)
"government . . . traffic" (ibid., p. xiii)
"sacred . . . rules" (A. Smith 1759, p. 163)

"laws of justice" (ibid., p. 84)
"confor[m] . . . custom" (Friedman 1970, p. 406)
"the general rules . . . conduct" (Koch, p. 78)
"The greatest . . . regulation" (Culp and Niskanen, back cover quotation)

Page 297
"One lesson . . . going on" (Reilly)
"A scheme . . . affects" (H. Smith, p. 119)
"Interventionism . . . information" (Ikeda, p. 3)
"stunningly . . . triumph" (McCormick, p. 274)
"open-ended . . . unpredictable" (ibid.)
"Consequences . . . origins" (ibid.)
"It is infeasible . . . economy" (Windsor 2004a, p. 686)
300,000 potential violations (Windsor 2006, p. 47n3)

Page 298
"the more . . . regulations" (Dunlop, p. 368)
"Regulation . . . issues" (ibid., p. 369)
"Designing . . . task" (ibid.)
"Oftentimes . . . deal" (ibid., p. 370)
"The rule-making . . . help" (ibid.)
"The rule-making . . . interests" (ibid., p. 371)
"Regulatory . . . served" (ibid.)
"Legal . . . regulators" (ibid., p. 372)
"no set . . . high" (ibid.)
"encountered . . . compliance" (ibid.)
"Over time . . . positions" (ibid.)

Page 299
"Uniform . . . uniform" (ibid.)
"[There is] . . . responsibilities" (ibid., p. 373)
"The central issue . . . compulsion" (ibid., p. 375)
"new attitudes . . . procedures" (ibid.)
"persuasion . . . problem-solving" (ibid.)
"We live . . . environment" (Hasnas, p. 87)
"vacuous bromide" (ibid.)
"badness of trade" (Smiles 1881, p. 68)
"systemic failure" (Will)
"the study . . . context" (Shaw and Barry, p. 4)
1970s and business ethics (De George, p. 51)
"social responsibility . . . doctrine" (Friedman 1962, p. 133)

Page 300
Friedman's 1970 essay (Friedman 1970)
"If businessmen . . . what it is?" (Friedman 1962, p. 133)
defining purpose of business, ethics therein (Sternberg, pp. x–xi, 32)
"refraining . . . business" (ibid., p. xi)
"central contradiction" (ibid.)
"even when . . . goal" (ibid., p. 25)

distributive justice (ibid., p. 109)
"'ordinary . . . legality" (ibid., p. ix)
"can lead . . . very life" (ibid., p.19)
triple bottom line (Elkington)
"sustainable . . . transition" (ibid., p. 97)
"one . . . negotiate" (ibid.)
"The discussions . . . rigor" (Friedman 1970, p. 406)
"it is . . . regulation" (Windsor, 2004b, p. 737)

Page 301
"thinly veiled business bashing" (Machan, p. 6)
"what we need . . . litigation" (ibid., p. 10)
"Instead . . . denigrated" (ibid., p. 7)
"dangerous . . . knees" (quoted in Swanson, p. 52)
"usually . . . sense" (Smiles 1866, p. 223)
Windsor letter, endorsements (Swanson, pp. 44–45)

Page 302
one-third of business schools (ibid., p. 49)
"crisis . . . interest" (quoted in Swanson, p. 45)
"most MBAs . . . management" (ibid., p. 49)
"an amoral . . . schools" (ibid., p. 53)
complicity of business schools (Swanson and Frederick)
"the Enron . . . markets" (Windsor 2004a, p. 661)
Enron MBAs (Gladwell, p. 28)
$2 million task force (Enron Global Affairs, p. 9)

Page 303
"the difficulty . . . responsibility'" (Friedman1970, p. 407)
"the great . . . purposes" (ibid.)
prophets, profits (Donway, p. 8)
"We cannot . . . maximization" (Bowen, p. 116)
"He recognizes . . . social effects" (ibid.)

Page 304
"If 'business ethics'. . . thing" (Sternberg, pp. 20–21)
course titles (Swanson, p. 46)
enhanced greenhouse effect (Bradley 2003, p. 19)
"green MBAs" (Swanson, p. 57)
"coal panic" (Black 1987, p. 1012)
ultimate resource (Simon 1981, p. 348)

Page 305
Julian Simon debate (Bradley 2000, pp. 19–20, 126–28, 147–49)
global cooling (Bradley and Fulmer, pp. 144, 154–55)
"a planet . . . new one" (Hawken, Lovins, and Lovins, p. 313)
GHG forcing (Bradley 2003, pp. 69–71)
climate inertia (IPCC, pp. 16, 822–31)

Page 306
"In the last . . . 60-fold" (Goklany, p. 19)
"The data . . . population" (ibid., p. 55)
CO_2 benefits (ibid., pp. 158–65)
"master resource" (Simon 1977, p. 93)
fossil-fuel share, GHG emissions (International Energy Agency, pp. 592–93, 608)

Page 307
Kyoto Protocol (Bradley 2003, p. 100)
"If implemented . . . stock!!" (John Palmisano, Enron memorandum, December 12, 1997)
"Enron . . . (monetized)" (ibid.)
Enron talks, Climate Institute award (ibid.)
"energy revolution" (Brown and Mitchell, p. 180)

Page 308
"Enron . . . cells" (ibid.)
"In *Earth* . . . agree" (Lay 2000)
"planetary emergency" (Gore)
"Over time . . . oil and gas" (quoted in Transco, p. 19)

Page 309
"We believe . . . the world" (quoted in Enron Corporate Responsibility Task Force, 2001, p. 5)
"Secured . . . basis" (ibid., p. 8)
"Formally . . . management" (ibid., pp. 9–10)

Page 310
"I have . . . from it" (A. Smith 1776, p. 456)
Friedman on altruism (Friedman 1970, p. 407)
"Mike . . . for money" (Michael Beyer and George McClellan, interview with author, April 10, 2001)
$300 million coal investment (Robert Bradley, internal Enron memorandum to Mark Schroeder, November 3, 1999)
"Our position . . . thin" (Mark Schroeder, internal Enron memorandum to author, November 3, 1999)
"at rates . . . coal" (Myerson)
"Solar Power . . . Affordable" (ibid.)

Page 311
"This establishes . . . industry" (quoted in ibid.)
White support (ibid.)
20 percent cost savings (Tom White, internal Enron memorandum to author, October 6, 1999)
10 percent energy savings (Jones)
"Kyoto compliant" (Peggy Mahoney, Enron memorandum to author, May 11, 2000)
"ESCO's . . . future" (Romm, e-mail to author, July 23, 1999)
"Cool buildings . . . commonplace" (Romm, *Cool Companies*, p. 4)
"*The entire . . . myth*" (ibid., p. 12)

"a company . . . respect" (Romm, e-mail to author, July 1, 1999)
"Something . . . technologies" (quoted in *Business Week* 1984, p. 96L)

Page 312
one-half cut (cited in Stipp, p. 100)
"That's not . . . to eat" (quoted in ibid., pp. 100–101)
"We've bet . . . past" ("Industry Debates," p. 5)
efficiency and usage (Jevons 1865, chapter XI)

Page 313
"The Doomslayer" (Regis, p. 138)
feedback effects, other uncertainties (Bradley 2003, chapter 3; IPCC, p. 805)

Page 314
"Corporate . . . purpose" (Hood, p. 191)
government, charity (ibid., pp. 196–97)
club, family, hobbyist league (Sternberg, pp. 35–40)
goals of firm (Hood, p. 199)
"responsibility . . . operate" (ibid., p. xix)
"guardian activity" (ibid., p. 198)
culture of virtue (Koch, pp. 79–83)
"the sense . . . company" (ibid., p. 132)
"cynicism . . . behavior" (ibid., p. 160)
"emotion . . . feeling" (ibid., p. 117)
"impulsive action" (ibid., p. 151)
"mindless application" (ibid., p. 133)
"gimmicks . . . advertising" (ibid., p. 47)
"entitlement and unaccountability" (ibid., p. 81)
"inaction . . . finger-pointing" (ibid., p. 129)

Page 315
"maximizing . . . integrity" (ibid., p. 79)
"man of enterprise" (Smith 1759, p. 173)
"great work" (Smiles1875, p. 191)
"virtue of *Productiveness*" (Rand 1961a, p. 29)
"a philosophy . . . prosper" (Koch, p. vii)
"miniature societies" (ibid., p. ix)
"property . . . action" (ibid.)
MBM dimensions (ibid., p. 26)
"'From each . . . contribution'" (ibid., p. 152)
"Over-specifying . . . inaction" (ibid., p. 78)
"honesty . . . initiative" (ibid.)
"creating real, long-term value" (ibid., p. 179n13)
"in harmony . . . principles"; economic over political means (ibid., p. 56)

Page 316
setbacks and MBM (ibid., pp. 17, 70)
creative destruction (ibid., pp. 28, 60, 67)
"set of capabilities," not products (ibid., p. 68)
Koch Industries as conglomerate (ibid., pp. 168–69)

"We must . . . make it so" (ibid., p. 30)
"decisions . . . feeling" (ibid., p. 117)
"style . . . substance" (ibid.)

Page 317
"A business . . . results" (ibid., pp. 110–11)
non-GAAP accounts (ibid., p. 176n7)
"A company's . . . animus" (ibid., p. 47)
Public Sector Capability (ibid., pp. 18–19)
"Striving . . . law" (ibid., p. 45)
"because . . . politically" (ibid., p. 46)
"a free . . . association" (ibid., p. 47)
"equality . . . law" (ibid.)

Page 318
"Practicing . . . world" (ibid., p. 44)
"a CEO's . . . thousand-fold" (Welch, p. 381)

Appendix A The Ayn Rand Problem
Page 321
"Mental health . . . at all costs." (Peck, p. 50)
a cult of obedience (Doherty, pp. 261–65)
"Reality . . . the wiper" (Rand 1957, p. 1018)
"goddess of reason" (N. Branden 1999, p. 325)
"a sacred . . . rules" (A. Smith 1759, p. 165)
"must drill . . . impulse" (quoted in Travers, p. 112)

Page 322
split in Objectivist movement (Gladstein, pp. 17–18; Greiner and Kinni, pp. 16–26)
"all people . . . magazines, etc." (B. Branden to author, May 13, 2007)
Rand-Branden break (B. Branden, pp. 299–305)
Rand-Branden affair (ibid., p. 259; N. Branden, 1999, p. 136)
"the nightmare . . . of lives" (B. Branden, p. 258)
affair would last a year (ibid., pp. 259–60; N. Branden 1999, p. 137)
"torture" (Valliant, p. 317)
"Earlier . . . for everything" (N. Branden 1999, p. 143)

Page 323
"Well . . . reality" (ibid.)
Galt's speech (B. Branden, p. 266)
Rand trying to live the novel (ibid., p. 272)
"mountain of words" (Chambers, p. 596)
"remarkably silly" (ibid.)
"preposterous" (ibid.)
"From almost any page . . . 'To a gas chamber—go!'" (ibid.)
"The bitterness . . . questionable" (N. Branden 1999, p. 211)
"a lover . . . to Barbara" (ibid., p. 233)
"the rock of my life" (ibid., p. 278)
"a kind of love . . . plainly" (ibid., p. 299)

Page 324
"an unusual . . . sensitivity" (B. Branden, p. 332)
Barbara's affair (N. Branden 1999, p. 286)
truth would devastate relationship (ibid., pp. 285–86, 287)
relationship with Frank suffered (ibid., p. 329)
"psycho-epistemological" sessions (ibid., p. 326)

Page 325
Rand reached out to Barbara (ibid., p. 330)
Rand became more controlling (B. Branden 1986, p. 331)
"result in . . . the end of everything" (N. Branden 1999, p. 300)
"Now, darling . . . in love again" (quoted in ibid., p. 309)
"the best and closest of friends" (ibid., p. 300)
"I am *dead . . . feel dead*" (quoted in Valliant, p. 245)
"*total* chaos" (quoted in ibid., p. 231)
"horror" (quoted in ibid., p. 280)
"Why don't I . . . now?" (quoted in ibid., p. 213)
"I knew . . . hell" (N. Branden 1999, p. 325)
"Miss X" (Valliant, pp. 247–53, 258–59, 292, 297)
"her rage . . . for her" (N. Branden 1999, p. 332)
Patrecia as Miss X (Valliant, p. 247)

Page 326
"passionately . . . my self-esteem" (N. Branden 1999, p. 335)
12,000-word diary entry (Valliant, p. 310)
"the worst traitor . . . ever met" (ibid., p. 349)
"the total hell . . . 'psycho-epistemological therapy' " (quoted in ibid., p. 332)
"stunned awe . . . authentic greatness" (quoted in ibid., p. 348)
"Well, . . . within him" (quoted in ibid., p. 349)
"There is nothing . . . this earth" (quoted in N. Branden 1999, p. 336)
new demands followed (ibid., p. 339)

Page 327
"If you have . . . moral degradation!" (quoted in ibid., pp. 344–45)
ruin Nathaniel Branden (ibid., pp. 353–64)
"recovery is . . . worth living" (Beattie 1989, Section I: Recovery, epigraph)
resorting to half-truths (Valliant, p. 95)
"very vicious form of lying" (quoted in Mayhew, p. 129)
"paralyzing alienation" (Childs 1982, p. 278)
"a philosophy . . . a dirge" (B. Branden, p. 305)
"a deadly mixture . . . to guilt" (ibid., p. 304)

Page 328
"learned behavior . . . satisfying relationship" (National Mental Health
Association)
"one-sided . . . abusive" (ibid.)
"feeling . . . relationship" (ibid.)
"unable to . . . causes it" (ibid.)

"a disease . . . lost selfhood" (Whitfield, p. 4)
"dysfunction . . . of others" (ibid.)
"the addiction . . . elsewhere" (ibid., p. 3)
"It is not . . . elsewhere" (quoted in Beattie 1987, Part I: Recovery, epigraph)
Rand's drug use (B. Branden, pp. 173–74)
"An exaggerated . . . decisions" (National Mental Health Association)

Page 329
Rand's praise for Branden (N. Branden 1999, pp. 143, 219)
"If anything . . . to have" (quoted in ibid., p. 327)
"The man . . . a wheelchair" (quoted in ibid., p. 328)
"You [want] . . . inferior woman!" (quoted in ibid., pp. 330–31)
"Ayn's blindness . . . Poor Nathan" (quoted in ibid., p. 299)
"near paranoia . . . but her own" (ibid., p. 337)
"The only thing . . . in a nightmare" (ibid., p. 146)
"how disastrous . . . with Ayn" (ibid., p. 375)

Page 330
"a romantic . . .affection" (Valliant, p. 7)
"[Nathaniel] Branden . . . *of a rapist*" (ibid., p. 382)
"monuments of dishonesty . . . historical documents" (ibid., p. 6)
"Certainly . . . intolerable" (ibid., p. 141)
"It's a project . . . can handle" (quoted in ibid., p. 138)
romantic triangle (ibid., pp. 248–49)
Branden's regret (N. Branden 1999, pp. 234–35)
"The luckiest . . . she really was" (N. Branden 1978, p. 61)

Page 331
"If you have . . . it is unrealistic" (ibid., p. 59)
"One must wonder . . . she attained" (B. Branden, pp. 329–30)
"Would a . . . a flaw?" (ibid., p. 330)
"distinguished . . . conversation" (Muller, p. 50)
"They . . . perfections" (ibid.)
"more open . . . orthodoxy" (D. Kelley 2000, p. 96)

Appendix B A Taxonomy of Political Capitalism
Page 332
"unhampered capitalism" (Mises 1966, p. 836)
"Manchesterism" (ibid., pp. 723, 730)
"financial capitalism" (Cole 1946, p. 10)
"a system . . . decision-making" (Kirzner 1989, p. 4)
"consumer economy" (McCraw 1995, p. 1)
"forcible appropriation" (Oppenheimer, p. 12)
"regulatory capitalism" (Micklethwait and Wooldridge, p. 149)
"positive state" (Anderson, p. 8)
"third way" and "third road" (Roepke, p.254)
"third system" (Mises 1966, p. 716)
"third solution" (ibid., p. 859)

"hampered market economy" (ibid., p. 718)
"interest-group pluralism" (Wiarda, p. 22)
"lies behind . . . regulatory origin" (Horwitz, p. 23)
"abounds with . . . economy generally" (ibid., pp. 25–26)
attributes of public-interest regulation (ibid., p. 26)
"capture theory" and "self-interest theory" (High, pp. 8–9; Stigler, *passim*)

Page 333
"any attempt . . . their advantage" (McCormick 1984, pp. 13–14)
"political capitalism" (Kolko 1963, p. 3)
"the merger . . . of capitalism" (Kolko 1976, p. 12)
"the welfare . . . identical" (Kolko 1969, p. 24)
"administrative state" (Galambos and Pratt, p. xi)
"American capitalism" (Greene, p. 64)
"American monopoly statism" (Stromberg 1973, p. 405)
"American oligarchy" (Baran and Sweezy, pp. 186, 207)
"American state corporatism" (Rothbard 1972, p. 145)
"American statism" (Childs 1977, p. 14)
"American syndicalism" (Williams, p. 356)
"aristocratic-government complex" (Travers, p. 168)
"associative state" (Hawley 1974, p. 118)
"broker state" (J. Kelley 1997, p. 5)
"[c]aptive [s]tate" (Monbiot, title)
"corporate-administered stage of capitalism" (Sklar 1992, p. 24)
"corporate capitalism" (Sklar 1988, p. 1)
"corporate capitalist order" (ibid., p. 19; Sklar 1992, p. 35)
"corporate commonwealth" (Galambos and Pratt, p. 41)
"corporate liberal state" (Link and McCormick, p. 43)
"corporate liberalism" (Weinstein, p. xiv)
"corporate state" (Sklar 1988, p. 37)
"corporate statism" (Lovins 1976, p. 92)
"corporate syndicalism" (Stromberg 1977, p. 20)
"corporate welfare state" (Slivinski, p. 1)
"corporation capitalism" (Williams, p. 343)
"corporation political economy" (ibid., p. 372)
"corporative state" (Herring, p. 427)
"corporativism" (Mises 1966, p. 816)
"government capitalism" (Freeman, Martin, and Parmar, pp. 196–97)
"industrial corporate capitalism" (Sklar 1960, p. 91)
"interest group liberalism" (J. Kelley, pp. 5, 28; Rothbard 1965, p. 43)
"liberal corporate capitalism" (Kolko, 1969, p. 85)
"liberal corporatism" (Rothbard 1965, p. 43)
"liberal state" (Weinstein, p. ix)
"lobbying-industrial complex" ("Lobbying-Industrial Complex")
"modern corporate state" (Rothbard 1972, p. 111)
"monopoly capitalism" (Baran and Sweezy, chapter 8)

413

"national capitalism" (Gras, pp. 323–25)
"neo-fascism" (Rothbard 1965, p. 43)
"neomercantilism" (ibid.)
"New Deal capital[ism]" (Feagin, p. 159)
"positive state" (Kolko 1969, p. 5)
"plutocracy" (Sumner 1913, p. 293)
"private government" (Anderson, p. 31)
"progressivism" (Kolko 1976, p. 15)
"regulated capitalism" (ibid., p. 149)
"regulatory-state capitalism" (Ikeda 2005, p. 41)
"restrictivism" (Stromberg 1977, p. 76)
"state capitalism" (Grinder and Hagel, title)
"state monopoly capitalism" (Rothbard 1965, p. 43)
"such names . . . Great Society" (Weinstein, p. x)
"the existing political economy" (ibid.)
Herbert Hoover and *regulated individualism* (Kolko 1976, pp. 109–10)
"scientific . . . from the inside" and "political government" (Hawley 1981, p. 95)
"American variant of neo-corporatism" (ibid., pp. 95–97)
"social welfare state" (J. Kelley, p. 9)
"public-interest state" (Reich, p. 771)
Page 334
"affirmative democratic state" (A. Schlesinger 2000, p. 517)
"industrial organization . . . true government" (Bentley 1920, p. 32)
"the trend . . . to [business] needs" (Galbraith 1967, p. 305)
"technocracy" and "private socialism" (Adams, p. 652)
"When the modern corporation. . . the reality" (Galbraith 1973, p. 6)
"a state within a state" (Grinder and Hagel, p. 71)
"military industrial *Congressional* complex" (Higgs 2006, p. ix)
"military State capitalism" (Rothbard 1965, p. 43)
"corporate-imperial order" (Sklar 1988, p. 440)
"Hamiltonian-nationalist State" (Marshall, p. 271)
"empire" (Stromberg 2001, p. 82)
"War . . . corporatism" (Hawley 1981, p. 99)
"community interests over individual interests" (Wiarda, p. 15)
Page 335
"historical . . . neo-corporatism" (Wiarda, pp. 15–22)
"industrial . . . capacity" (Lavoie 1985, p. 1)
"non-comprehensive planning" (ibid., p. 3)
RFC (Bradley 1996, pp. 545–46; Lavoie 1985, pp. 1–2, 174–86)
MITI (Lavoie 1985, pp. 2, 194–96)
business support for new RFC (Lavoie, chapter 6)
a planned economy as bureaucratism (Mises 1944, p. vii)
leading . . . *Nazism* (Mises 1966, p. 812)
"the class of modern Capitalists" (Marx and Engels, p. 79)
"Each step . . . that class" (ibid., p. 81)

Appendix C Gabriel Kolko's Revisionism Reconsidered
Page 336
"Kolko's ideas . . . originally wanted" (McCraw 1995, p. 165)
"Still . . .easily" (ibid.)
Advance of Kolko's ideas (Bradley 1996; Bradley 2003)
"the fact . . . sponsored" (Harbeson, p. 234)
role of New York merchants (Benson)

Page 337
"The business community . . . regulation" (Wiebe 1962, p. 217)
"At least . . . progressives" (ibid.)
"the whole . . . argument" (Wiebe 1964, p. 121)
"mistake" and "King Laissez Faire" (Lively, p. 82)
"One can . . . specific contest" (Kolko 1963, p. 283)

Page 338
"the mere fact . . . demands" (Kolko 1965, p. 5)
"radical reappraisal" (ibid., p. 231)
"The railroads . . . 1916" (ibid., p. 3)
"The [Interstate Commerce Commission] . . . railroads" (ibid., p. 235)
"The federal . . . industry" (ibid., p. 232)
railroad support for the ICC (J. Ely, pp. 92–93; Purcell, pp. 275–78)
power of shippers (J. Ely, p. 226)
railroad opposition to regulation (J. Ely, 226; Vietor 1977)
Rate-increase denials (Martin 1971)
ICC regulation favored different groups (Hoogenboom, p. 189)
Railroad price wars (Bradley 1996, p. 623; J. Ely, 81–83; Hilton, 89–90)
railroad leaders hungry for regulation (Martin 1974, p. 361)
industries worked to moderate regulation (J. Ely, p. 238)

Page 339
"It would . . . agency" (ibid., pp. 238–39)
"idea ghosts" (Bentley 1908, p. 172)
"By 1886 . . . railroads" (Hoogenboom, p. 8)
"When Congress . . . numbers" (Purcell, p. 575)
"Although . . .stopped" (Hoogenboom, p. 17)
"Transportation . . . controls" (J. Ely, p. 81)
"The driving force . . .Act" (Blackford, p. 307)
"Though railroads . . . regulation" (Hoogenboom, p. 49)
"While tension . . .competition" (Boies, p. 606)
"While the railroads . . . themselves" (ibid., p. 607)
"That 'big business' . . . likely" (Vietor 1977, p. 65)

Page 340
"The impetus . . . profits" (ibid., p. 66)
"A large majority . . . National Government" (quoted in Boies, p. 605)
"Businessmen were . . . liberty" (Purcell, p. 574)
"merchants and farmers . . . as a cloak." (J. Ely, p. 83)
"Historians . . . railroads" (ibid.)
denials of rate increases (Martin 1971)

Page 341
antitrust as a two-edged sword (Wiebe 1962, p. 219)
"a life of its own" (J. Q. Wilson 1971, p. 47)
"Because . . . agencies" (Horwitz, p. 45)
defensive lobbying (J. Ely, p. 92)
"tightest and best . . . legislation" (Wiebe 1962, p. 216)
Standard Oil lost battles (Bradley 1996, pp. 1075–81)
smaller firms as political competitors (Wiebe 1962, p. 45)
"The very fact . . . state action" (Horwitz, p. 266)

Page 342
"I see no force . . . other forces" (Sumner 1905, p. 329)

Appendix D Resources for the Future: Away from Optimism
Page 343
"RFF has pioneered . . . developing countries" (RFF, "RFF Today")
"Today's critical . . . sustainability" (RFF, *2006 Annual Report,* p. 2)
"the go-to . . . resources issues" (ibid., p. 3)
"RFF is . . . regulatory policy" (ibid., p. 2)

Page 344
"As a businessman . . . honest broker" (RFF, quoted in "$4 million")

Page 345
"widespread . . . real costs" (RFF, *U.S. Energy Policies,* p. 23)
"The estimated . . . of oil" (Darmstadter and Searle, p. 7)
"our immediate . . . oil resources" (Willrich, p. 59)
"we will be . . . exploitation" (Krutilla and Page, p. 78)
"we might consider . . . consumption" (ibid., p. 87)
"minimize the social costs" (ibid., p. 92)
"public participation"(ibid., p. 100)
"more explicit . . . in the past" (ibid.)
"Nonrenewable . . . will be replaced" (RFF, January–March 1977, p. 3)

Page 346
"the continual erosion . . . resource base" (Spofford, p. xi)
V. Kerry Smith and depletionism 1979, (Smith, p. xi)
"running out . . . policy initiatives" (Schurr, 1979, p. 9)
"It was . . .badly needed" (M. A. Adelman to author, December 18, 2003)
"Throughout its history . . . for intervention" (Richard Gordon to author, August 3, 2004)

Page 347
International conference (RFF, "50 Years," p. 3)
"This book . . .more innovations" (Simpson, p. 3)
chapter by Bohi (ibid., pp. 73–108)
"new technology . . . has increased" (Tilton, p. 102)
"During the next . . . confronting society" (ibid., p. 119)

Page 348
"Our ability . . . is limited" (RFF, January 1974, p. 6)
"two-pronged . . . problem" (ibid.)

"For energy users . . . clearly desirable" (Darmstadter 1975, p. 4)
"Neither the government . . . the transition" (RFF, Winter 1976, p. 3)
"Surely . . . monopolistic combine" (ibid., p. 5)

Page 349
"divisive" (RFF, January–March 1979, p. 4)
RFF and nonadvocacy (Castle, pp. 6–7)
"We're going . . . the government" (Hitch, p. 3)
"I think . . . integrity" (ibid.)
"RFF seeks . . . advocacy" (RFF, *2006 Annual Report,* p. 3)
"RFF's management . . . ideological edges" (ibid., p. 2)

Page 350
"The major . . . to prevent" (Bradley 2003, p. 15)
"a nonaligned . . . edges" (RFF, *2006 Annual Report,* p. 2)

Bibliography

AAUP (American Association of University Professors). *AAUP Policy Documents and Reports*. Baltimore: Johns Hopkins University Press, 2006. Portions available at www.aaup.org/AAUP/pubsres/policydocs/contents/default.htm.

Adams, Walter. "The Military-Industrial Complex and the New Industrial State." *American Economic Review* 58 (2): 652–65 (May 1968).

Adelman, M. A. "U.S. Energy Policy." In *No Time to Confuse: A Critique of the Final Report of the Energy Policy Project of the Ford Foundation*, edited by M. A. Adelman et al., 27–42. San Francisco: Institute for Contemporary Studies, 1975a.

———. "Population Growth and Oil Resources." 1975b. In M. A. Adelman, *The Economics of Petroleum Supply*, 89–93. Cambridge, MA: MIT Press, 1993.

———. *The Genie Out of the Bottle: World Oil since 1970*. Cambridge, MA: MIT Press, 1995.

———. "My Education in Mineral (Especially Oil) Economics." *Annual Review of Energy and the Environment* 22: 13–46 (1997).

Adelman, M. A., and G. C. Watkins. "Resource Scarcity: Evidence from Values of Oil and Natural Gas Reserves." In *26th International Conference Proceedings*. Prague: International Association for Energy Economics, June 2003 (diskette only).

Adler, Jonathan. *Environmentalism at the Crossroads: Green Activism in America*. Washington, DC: Capital Research Center, 1995.

Alchian, Armen. "An Introduction to Confusion." In *No Time to Confuse: A Critique of the Final Report of the Energy Policy Project of the Ford Foundation*, edited by M. A. Adelman et al., 1–25. San Francisco: Institute for Contemporary Studies, 1975.

Allen, William. "Mercantilism." In *The New Palgrave: A Dictionary of Economics*, edited by John Eatwell et al., vol. 3, 445–49. 1987. Reprint, New York: Palgrave, 1998.

American Bankruptcy Institute, "Quarterly Business Filings by Year (1994–2007), at www.abiworld.org/AM/AMTemplate.cfm?Section=Home&TEMPLATE=/CM/ContentDisplay.cfm&CONTENTID=48425; and "Total Number of U.S. Businesses," at www.bizstats.com/businesses.htm.

Anderson, James. *The Emergence of the Modern Regulatory State*. Washington, DC: Public Affairs Press, 1962.

API (American Petroleum Institute). *Basic Petroleum Data Book*, Volume XV, Number 1 (January 1995).

Appleby, Joyce, et al. *Telling the Truth about History*. New York: W. W. Norton, 1994.

Arrow, Kenneth. "Hotelling, Harold." In *The New Palgrave: A Dictionary of Economics*, edited by John Eatwell et al., vol. 2, 670–72. 1987. Reprint, New York: Palgrave, 1998.

Arrow, Kenneth, and Joseph Kalt. *Petroleum Price Regulation: Should We Decontrol?* Washington, DC: American Enterprise Institute, 1979.

Arthur Andersen & Co. *The First Fifty Years, 1913–1963*. Chicago: Arthur Andersen & Co., 1963.

Ashraf, Nava, Colin F. Camerer, and George Loewenstein. "Adam Smith, Behavioral Economist." *Journal of Economic Perspectives* 19 (3): 131–45 (Summer 2005).

Bailyn, Bernard. *The Ideological Origins of the American Revolution*. Cambridge, MA: Harvard University Press, 1967.

Baker, Ray Palmer. Foreword to *Pioneering in Big Business*, edited by Ralph Hidy and Muriel Hidy, xix–xx. New York: Harper & Brothers, 1955.

Bannister, Robert. Foreword to William Sumner, *On Liberty, Society, and Politics*, ix–xxxviii. Edited by Robert Bannister. Indianapolis: Liberty Fund, 1992.

Baran, Paul, and Paul Sweezy. *Monopoly Capital: An Essay on the American Economic and Social Order*. New York: Monthly Review Press, 1966.

Barber, William. "The Eisenhower Energy Policy: Reluctant Interventionism." In *Energy Policy in Perspective: Today's Problems, Yesterday's Solutions*, edited by Craufurd Goodwin, 205–86. Washington, DC: Brookings Institution, 1981.

Barboza, David. "Despite Denial, Enron Papers Show Big Profit on Price Bets." *New York Times*, December 12, 2002.

Barnett, Harold, and Chandler Morse. *Scarcity and Growth: The Economics of Natural Resource Availability*. Baltimore: Johns Hopkins University Press, 1963.

Baumol, William, and Janusz Ordover. "Use of Antitrust to Subvert Competition." In *Journal of Law & Economics* 28 (2): 247–65 (May 1985).

Beard, Charles. "Book Review: *The Process of Government*." *Political Science Quarterly* 23 (4): 739–41 (December 1908).

Beard, Charles, and Mary Beard. *The Rise of American Civilization*. 1927. Reprint, New York: Macmillan, 1947.

———. *America in Midpassage*. 2 vols. New York: Macmillan, 1939.

Beattie, Melody. *Codependent No More: How to Stop Controlling Others and Start Caring for Yourself*. Center City, MN: Hazelton Foundation, 1987, 1992.

———. *Beyond Codependency: And Getting Better All the Time*. Center City, MN: Hazelton Foundation, 1989.

Becker, Gary. "Pressure Groups and Political Behavior." In *Capitalism and Democracy: Schumpeter Revisited*, edited by Richard Coe and Charles Wilber, 120–46. Notre Dame, IN: Notre Dame Press, 1985.

Belair, Felix. "A Crisis in Raw Materials Found Imperiling Security." *New York Times*, June 24, 1952.

Benson, Lee. *Merchants, Farmers and Railroads: Railroad Regulation and New York Politics 1850–1887*. Cambridge, MA: Harvard University Press, 1955.

Bentley, Arthur. *The Process of Government: A Study of Social Pressures*. 1908. Reprint, Cambridge, MA: Harvard University Press, 1967.

———. *Makers, Users, and Masters.* Unpublished 1920 manuscript. Edited by Sidney Ratner. Syracuse, NY: Syracuse University Press, 1969.

———. Epilogue to *Life, Language, Law: Essays in Honor of Arthur F. Bentley.* 1953. Edited by Richard Taylor, 210–13. Yellow Springs, OH: Antioch Press, 1957.

Berliner, Michael, ed. *Letters of Ayn Rand.* New York: Dutton, 1995.

Bernstein, Peter. *Against the Gods: The Remarkable Story of Risk.* New York: John Wiley & Sons, 1996.

Binswanger, Harry, ed. *The Ayn Rand Lexicon: Objectivism from A to Z.* New York: Meridian, 1982.

Black, R. D. C. "Jevons's Contribution to the Teaching of Political Economy in Manchester and London." 1981. Reprinted in *Economic Theory and Policy in Context,* edited by R. D. C. Black, 162–83. Brookfield, VT: Edward Elgar, 1995.

———. "Jevons, W. S." In *The New Palgrave: A Dictionary of Economics,* edited by John Eatwell et al., vol. 2, 1008–13. 1987. Reprint, New York: Palgrave, 1998.

Blackburn, Simon. *The Oxford Dictionary of Philosophy.* New York: Oxford University Press, 1994.

Blackford, Mansel. "Businessmen and the Regulation of Railroads and Public Utilities in California during the Progressive Era." *Business History Review* 44 (3): 307–19 (Autumn 1970).

Blackstone, William. *Commentaries on the Laws of England.* 1763. Reprint, Philadelphia: J. B. Lippincott, 1870.

Blaug, Mark. *Economic Theory in Retrospect.* Homewood, IL: Richard D. Irwin, 1962.

———. "Entrepreneurship before and after Schumpeter." In *Entrepreneurship: The Social Science View,* edited by Richard Swedberg, 76–88. New Delhi: Oxford University Press, 2000.

Boettke, Peter. "Virginia Political Economy: A View from Vienna." *Market Process* 5 (2): 7–14 (Fall 1987).

Boettke, Peter, and Christopher Coyne. "The Forgotten Contribution: Murray Rothbard on Socialism in Theory and Practice." *Quarterly Journal of Austrian Economics* 7 (2): 71–89 (Summer 2004).

Boies, David. "Experiment in Mercantilism: Minimum Rate Regulation by the Interstate Commerce Commission." *Columbia Law Review* 68 (4): 599–663 (April 1968).

Boulding, Kenneth. "The Economics of the Coming Spaceship Earth." In *Environmental Quality in a Growing Economy,* edited by Henry Jarrett, 3–14. Baltimore: Resources for the Future, 1966.

———. "Fun and Games with the Gross National Product—The Role of Misleading Indicators in Social Policy." In *The Environmental Crisis,* edited by Harold Helfrich Jr., 157–70. New Haven, CT: Yale University Press, 1970.

———. "What Do Economic Indicators Indicate?: Quality and Quantity in the GDP." In *The Economics of Pollution,* edited by Kenneth Boulding and Elvis Stahr, 33–80. New York: New York University Press, 1971.

Bowen, Francis. *American Political Economy.* New York: Charles Scribner, 1870.

Bowen, Howard. *Social Responsibilities of the Businessman.* New York: Harper & Brothers, 1953.

Bowen, Jack, with Eric Fredrickson. *An American Life in the Twentieth Century: The Autobiography of Jack Bowen.* Houston, 2007 (privately printed).

Bradley, Robert. "Market Socialism: A Subjectivist Evaluation." *Journal of Libertarian Studies* 5 (1): 23–39 (Winter 1981).

———. "Energy Policies: A Few Bright Spots." In *Assessing the Reagan Years*, edited by David Boaz, 305–19. Washington, DC: Cato Institute, 1988.

———. *The Mirage of Oil Protection.* Lanham, MD: University Press of America, 1989.

———. *Oil, Gas, and Government: The U.S. Experience.* 2 vols. Lanham, MD: Rowman & Littlefield, 1996.

———. *Julian Simon and the Triumph of Energy Sustainability.* Washington, DC: American Legislative Exchange Council, 2000.

———. *Climate Alarmism Reconsidered.* London: Institute of Economic Affairs, 2003.

———. "The Origins of Political Electricity." In *The End of Natural Monopoly: Deregulation and Competition in the Electric Power Industry,* edited by Peter Grossman, 43–75. Greenwich, CT: JAI Press, 2003.

———. "A Typology of Interventionist Dynamics," in *Humane Economics: Essays in Honor of Don Lavoie*, edited by Jack High, pp. 64–85. Northampton, MA: Edward Elgar, 2006.

Bradley, Robert, and Richard Fulmer. *Energy: The Master Resource.* Dubuque, IA: Kendall/Hunt, 2004.

Branden, Barbara. *The Passion of Ayn Rand.* Garden City, NY: Doubleday, 1986.

Branden, Nathaniel. "Thank You Ayn Rand, and Goodbye," *Reason,* May 1978, 58–61.

———. *My Years with Ayn Rand.* San Francisco: Jossey-Bass, 1999.

Brenner, Marie. "The Enron Wars." *Vanity Fair,* April 2002, 181–209.

Breyer, Stephen. *Regulation and Its Reform.* Cambridge, MA: Harvard University Press, 1982.

Brickley, James, et al. *Managerial Economics and Organizational Architecture.* New York: McGraw-Hill, 2001.

Bridges, Hal. "The Robber Baron Concept in American History." *Business History Review* 32 (1): 1–13 (Spring 1958).

Briggs, Asa. *Victorian People: A Reassessment of Persons & Themes, 1851–1867.* 1955. Reprint, Chicago: University of Chicago Press, 1975.

———. "A Centenary Introduction." In Samuel Smiles, *Self-Help,* 7–31. Reprint, London: John Murray, 1958.

———. *The Making of Modern England, 1784–1867.* Chicago: Harper & Row, 1959.

Brown, Lester, and Jennifer Mitchell. "Building a New Economy." In *State of the World 1998,* edited by Lester Brown, chapter 10. New York: W. W. Norton, 1998.

Brown, William. "The Outlook for Future Petroleum Supplies." In *The Resourceful Earth: A Response to 'Global 2000,'* edited by Julian Simon and Herman Kahn, 361–86. New York: Basil Blackwell, 1984.

Bruce-Briggs, B. "Antineomalthusian." *New York Times Book Review,* September 13, 1981, 9–10.

Bryce, Robert. *Pipe Dreams: Greed, Ego, and the Death of Enron.* New York: PublicAffairs, 2002.

Bryson, Reid. "'All Other Factors Being Constant . . .' A Reconciliation of Several Theories of Climatic Change." 1968. In *Global Ecology,* edited by John Holdren and Paul Ehrlich, 78–84. New York: Harcourt Brace Jovanovich, 1971.

Buchanan, James. "From Private Preferences to Public Philosophy: The Development of Public Choice." In *The Economics of Politics*, 1–20. London: Institute of Economic Affairs, 1978.

———. "Rent Seeking and Profit Seeking." In *Toward a Theory of the Rent-Seeking Society*, edited by James Buchanan et al., 3–15. College Station: Texas A&M University Press, 1980.

———. "Born-Again Economist." In *Lives of the Laureates: Thirteen Nobel Economists*, edited by William Breit and Roger Spencer, 165–82. Cambridge, MA: MIT Press, 1995.

Buchanan, James, and Gordon Tullock. *The Calculus of Consent: Logical Foundations of Constitutional Democracy*. 1962. Reprint, Indianapolis: Liberty Fund, 1999.

Butler-Bowdon, Tom. *50 Self-Help Classics*. London: Nicholas Brealey, 2003.

Caine, Stanley. "The Origins of Progressivism." In *The Progressive Era*, edited by Lewis Gould, 11–34. Syracuse, NY: Syracuse University Press, 1974.

Cambridge Energy Research Associates. *Energy Demand: Decline or Rebound?* CERA Special Report: November 1983.

Campbell, Colin. "Oil Price Leap in the Early Nineties." *Noroil*, December 1989, 35–38.

Canham, Erwin. Foreword to *The Business of Business: Private Enterprise and Public Affairs*, by M. A. Wright, vii–x. New York: McGraw-Hill, 1967.

Caplow, Theodore, Louis Hicks, and Ben Wattenberg. *The First Measured Century: An Illustrated Guide to Trends in America, 1900–2000*. Washington, DC: American Enterprise Institute, 2001.

Carter, Jimmy. "Energy Address to the Nation." April 18, 1977. In *Energy Crisis: 1975–77*, edited by Lester Sobel, vol. 3, 36–37. New York: Facts on File, 1977.

———. "President Jimmy Carter's Farewell Address," January 14, 1981, available at www.jimmycarterlibrary.org/documents/speeches/farewell.phtml.

———. *Keeping Faith: Memoirs of a President*. New York: Bantam Books, 1982.

Carter, Luther. "A Warning on Synfuels, CO_2, and the Weather." *Science*, July 27, 1979, 376–77.

Castle, Emery. "Organizational Characteristics and Performance, 1952–1986." Lectures in Economics, Resources for the Future as a Policy Research Institute, Lecture Series #4, April 1990, Oregon State University.

Chambers, Whittaker. "Big Sister Is Watching You," *National Review*, December 28, 1957, 594–96.

Chandler, Alfred. "The Beginnings of 'Big Business' in American Industry." *Harvard Business Review* 33 (1): 1–31 (Spring 1959).

———. *Strategy and Structure: Chapters in the History of the American Industrial Enterprise*. 1962. Reprint, Cambridge, MA: MIT Press, 1995.

———. "Book Review: *The Age of the Manager: A Treasury of Our Times*." *Business History Review* 37 (3): 279–80 (Autumn 1963).

———. "The Role of Business in the United States: A Historical Survey." *Daedalus* 98 (1): 23–40 (Winter 1969).

———. "Government versus Business: An American Phenomenon." In *Business and Public Policy*, edited by John Dunlop, 1–11. Boston: Harvard University Graduate School of Business Administration, 1980.

———. "Introduction." 1989. *Strategy and Structure: Chapters in the History of the American Industrial Enterprise*, i–vii. 1962. Reprint. Cambridge, MA: MIT Press, 1995.

Chesher, James, and Tibor Machan. *The Business of Commerce: Examining an Honorable Profession*. Stanford, CA: Hoover University Press, 1999.

Childs, Roy. "Big Business and the Rise of American Statism." In Occasional Paper Series #4: *The Political Economy of Liberal Corporativism*, 1–17. Center for Libertarian Studies, November 1977.

———. "Ayn Rand and the Libertarian Movement." 1982. In *Liberty against Power: Essays by Roy A. Childs, Jr.*, edited by Joan Kennedy Taylor, 265–81. San Francisco: Fox and Wilkes, 1994.

"Club of Rome Revisited," *Time*, April 26, 1976.

Coase, Ronald. "The Nature of the Firm." 1937. In *The Economic Nature of the Firm: A Reader*, edited by Louis Putterman and Randall Kroszner, 89–104. Cambridge: Cambridge University Press, 1996.

———. "How Should Economists Choose?" 1981. In *Essays on Economics and Economists*, edited by Ronald Coase, 15–33. Chicago: University of Chicago Press, 1994.

———. "Arnold Plant." 1986. In *Essays on Economics and Economists*, edited by Ronald Coase, 176–84. Chicago: University of Chicago Press, 1994.

———. *The Firm, the Market, and the Law*. Chicago: University of Chicago Press, 1988.

———. "Ronald H. Coase." 1991a. In *Economic Sciences 1991–1995*, edited by Torsten Persson, 7–10. Hackensack, NJ: World Scientific, 1997.

———. "The Institutional Structure of Production." Nobel Lecture, 1991b. In *Economic Sciences 1991–1995*, edited by Torsten Persson, 11–20. Hackensack, NJ: World Scientific, 1997.

———. "The Nature of the Firm: Origin." 1991c. In *The Nature of the Firm: Origins, Evolution, and Development*, edited by Oliver Williamson and Sidney Winter, 34–47. New York: Oxford University Press, 1991.

———. "The Nature of the Firm: Meaning." 1991d. In *The Nature of the Firm: Origins, Evolution, and Development*, edited by Oliver Williamson and Sidney Winter, 48–60. New York: Oxford University Press, 1991.

———. "Ronald H. Coase." In *Lives of the Laureates: Thirteen Nobel Economists*, edited by William Breit and Roger Spencer, 227–49. 3rd ed., rev. and enl. Cambridge, MA: MIT Press, 1995.

Cochrane, James. "Carter Energy Policies and the Ninety-Fifth Congress." In *Energy Policy in Perspective: Today's Problems, Yesterday's Solutions*, edited by Craufurd Goodwin, 547–600. Washington, DC: Brookings Institution, 1981.

Coffee, John, Jr. *Gatekeepers: The Professions and Corporate Governance*. New York: Oxford University Press, 2006.

Cole, Arthur. "An Approach to the Study of Entrepreneurship: A Tribute to Edwin F. Gay." *Journal of Economic History* 6 (Supplement): 1–15 (May 1946).

———. "Joseph A. Schumpeter and the Research Center in Entrepreneurial History." *Explorations in Entrepreneurial History* 2 (2): 56 (1950).

———. *The Birth of a New Social Science Discipline: Achievements of the First Generation of American Economic and Business Historians—1893–1974*. New York: Economic History Association, 1974.

Collins, Jim. *Good to Great: Why Some Companies Make the Leap . . . and Others Don't*. New York: HarperBusiness, 2001.

Cook, Lynn. "Trust Does Come Naturally, Even When It Concerns Money." *Houston Chronicle*, April 15, 2005.

Coppin, Clayton, and Jack High. *The Politics of Purity: Harvey Washington Wiley and the Origins of Federal Food Policy*. 1999. Reprint, Ann Arbor: University of Michigan Press, 2002.

Council on Environmental Quality and Department of State. *The Global 2000 Report to the President: Entering the Twenty-First Century*. Washington, DC: Government Printing Office, 1980.

"The Crisis in Raw Materials." *Fortune*, August 1952, 114–117, 160, 163–64, 166–68, 170. (This is a condensed and slightly reworded version of the opening to Volume 1 of the President's Materials Policy Commission study.)

Crittenden, Ann. "Need for Social Change Is Seen by Club of Rome." *New York Times*, April 15, 1976.

Culp, Christopher, and William Niskanen, eds. *Corporate Aftershock: The Public Policy Lessons from the Collapse of Enron and Other Major Corporations*. Hoboken, NJ: John Wiley & Sons, 2003.

Darmstadter, Joel. "Energy Accounting vs. the Market." *Resources*, October 1975, 4–5.

———. "Hans H. Landsberg and Sam H. Schurr: Reflections and Appreciation." *Energy Journal* 24 (4): 1–16 (October 2003).

Darmstadter, Joel, and Milton Searl. "Prospects for Energy Supply." *Resources*, June 1973, 7–8.

Darmstadter, Joel, Hans Landsberg, and Herbert Norton. *Energy Today and Tomorrow: Living with Uncertainty*. Englewood Cliffs, NJ: Prentice Hall, 1983.

De George, Richard. "The History of Business Ethics." In *The Accountable Corporation*, edited by Marc Epstein and Kirk Hanson, vol. 2, 47–58. Westport, CT: Praeger, 2006.

De Marchi, Neil. "The Ford Administration: Energy as a Political Good." In *Energy Policy in Perspective: Today's Problems, Yesterday's Solutions*, edited by Craufurd Goodwin, 475–545. Washington, DC: Brookings Institution, 1981.

De Santis, Vincent. *The Shaping of Modern America: 1877–1920*. Wheeling, IL: Harlan Davidson, 2000.

De Soto, Hernando. *The Mystery of Capital*. New York: Basic Books, 2000.

Deffeyes, Kenneth. *Hubbert's Peak: The Impending World Oil Shortage*. Princeton, NJ: Princeton University Press, 2001.

Den Uyl, Douglas, and Douglas Rasmussen. "Capitalism." In *The Philosophic Thought of Ayn Rand*, edited by Douglas Den Uyl and Douglas Rasmussen, 165–82. Chicago: University of Illinois Press, 1984.

Department of Energy. *National Energy Plan II*. Washington, DC: U.S. Government Printing Office, 1979.

Derthick, Martha, and Paul Quirk. *The Politics of Deregulation*. Washington, DC: Brookings Institution, 1985.

Desai, Mihir. "The Degradation of Reported Corporate Profits." *Journal of Economic Perspectives* 19 (4): 171–92 (Fall 2005).

Devarajan, Shantayanan, and Anthony Fisher. "Hotelling's 'Economics of Exhaustible Resources': Fifty Years Later." *Journal of Economic Literature* 19 (1): 65–73 (March 1981).

Dewing, Arthur. *The Financial Policy of Corporations*, 2 vols. New York: Ronald Press, 1953.

DiLorenzo, Thomas. "The Origins of Antitrust: An Interest-Group Perspective." *International Review of Law and Economics* 5 (1), 73–90 (Fall 1985).

Dintenfass, Michael. *Managing Industrial Decline: The British Coal Industry between the Wars.* Columbus: Ohio State University, 1992.

Doherty, Brian. *Radicals for Capitalism.* New York: PublicAffairs, 2007.

Dolbee, Sandi. "Prophet or Profit? Energy Chief, Religious Leaders Dispute God's Role in Utility Price Spiral." *San Diego Union-Tribune,* February 2, 2001.

Domhoff, G. William. *Who Rules America Now?* New York: Touchstone, 1983.

Donway, Roger. "The Lengthened Shadow of a Businessman." *The New Individualist,* May 2007, 8–11.

Dowie, Mark. *American Foundations: An Investigative History.* Cambridge, MA: MIT Press, 2001.

Drucker, Peter. *The Age of Discontinuity.* New York: Harper & Row, 1968.

———. "Modern Prophets: Schumpeter or Keynes?" 1983. In *The Frontiers of Management,* edited by Peter Drucker, 104–15. New York: E. P. Dutton, 1986.

Dudden, Arthur. "The Hofstadter Aegis: A Memorial." *American Historical Review* 81 (2): 468–69 (April 1976).

Dunlop, John. "The Limits to Legal Compulsion." 1977. In *A Managerial Odyssey: Problems in Business and Its Environment,* edited by Arthur Elkins and Dennis Callaghan, 368–75. Reading, MA: Addison-Wesley, 1978.

Dunn, Seth, and Christopher Flavin. "Moving the Climate Change Agenda Forward." In *State of the World 2002,* edited by the Worldwatch Institute, 24–50. New York: W. W. Norton, 2002.

Ehrlich, Paul. *The Population Bomb.* New York: Ballantine Books, 1968.

———. "An Economist in Wonderland." *Social Science Quarterly* 62 (1): 44–49 (March 1981).

———. "That's Right—You Should Check It for Yourself," *Social Science Quarterly* 63 (2): 385–87 (June 1982).

Ehrlich, Paul, and Anne Ehrlich. *The End of Affluence.* New York: Ballantine Books, 1974.

———. *Extinction: The Causes and Consequences of the Disappearance of Species.* New York: Random House, 1981.

———. *The Population Explosion.* New York: Simon & Schuster, 1990.

———. *Betrayal of Science and Reason.* Washington, DC: Island Press, 1996.

———. *One with Nineveh: Politics, Consumption, and the Human Future.* Washington, DC: Island Press, 2004.

Ehrlich, Paul, and Richard Harriman. *How to Be a Survivor.* Rivercity, MA: Rivercity Press, 1971, 1975.

Ehrlich, Paul, and John Holdren. "Impact of Population Growth." *Science,* March 26, 1971a, 1212–17.

———. "Overpopulation and the Potential for Ecocide." In *Global Ecology,* edited by John Holdren and Paul Ehrlich, 64–78. New York: Harcourt Brace Jovanovich, 1971b.

Ehrlich, Paul, Anne Ehrlich, and John Holdren. *Human Ecology: Problems and Solutions.* San Francisco: W. H. Freeman, 1973.

———. *Ecoscience: Population, Resources, Environment.* San Francisco: W. H. Freeman, 1977.

EIA (Energy Information Administration). *Annual Energy Review 2001*. Washington, DC: U.S. Department of Energy, 2002.

———. *Annual Energy Outlook 2007*. Washington, DC: U.S. Department of Energy, 2007.

Eichenwald, Kurt. *Conspiracy of Fools: A True Story*. New York: Broadway Books, 2005.

Ekirch, Arthur. *Progressivism in America*. New York: New Viewpoints, 1974.

Elkington, John. "The Triple Bottom Line." In *The Accountable Corporation*, edited by Marc Epstein and Kirk Hanson, vol. 3, 97–129. Westport, CT: Praeger, 2006.

Ellig, Jerry, and Daniel Lin. "A Taxonomy of Dynamic Competition Theories." In *Dynamic Competition and Public Policy*, edited by Jerry Ellig, 16–44. Cambridge: Cambridge University Press, 2001.

Elliott, John. Introduction to *The Theory of Economic Development*. 1983, by Joseph Schumpeter, vii–lix. 1911 (German). 1934 (English translation). Reprint, New Brunswick, NJ: Transaction, 2002.

Ely, James, Jr. *Railroads and American Law*. Lawrence: University of Kansas, 2001.

Ely, Richard. "Report on the Organization of the American Economic Association." *Publications of the American Economic Association* 1 (1): 5–32 (March 1886).

Emmott, Bill. "Capitalism and Democracy: Radical Thoughts on Our 160th Birthday." *The Economist*, June 28–July 4, 2003, 1–18.

Energy Conservation. Hearings before the Senate Committee on Interior and Insular Affairs, 93rd Cong. 1st sess., 1973 ("Prepared Statement of Irwin Stelzer," 23–51).

Energy Policy Act of 1992. (Public Law 102–486; 106 *Stat.* 2276.)

Energy Policy Project of the Ford Foundation. *A Time to Choose: America's Energy Future*. Cambridge, MA: Ballinger, 1974.

"Energy: Where Intervention Is Inevitable." *Business Week*, April 4, 1977, 80–81.

Engels, Frederick. "Preface to the 'Communist Manifesto.'" English Edition, 1888. In *The Essentials of Marx*, edited by Algernon Lee. New York: Vanguard Press, 1926.

Enron Corp. *1995 Annual Report to Shareholders*.

Enron Corporate Responsibility Task Force. "Corporate Responsibility." Presented to the Environmental, Health & Safety Management Conference, October 23, 2001 (copy in author's files).

Enron Global Affairs. "Presentation by Joe Sutton and Enron Global Affairs to Ken Lay and Jeff Skilling." September 21, 1999 (copy in author's files).

"Enron's Sins." Editorial. *Wall Street Journal*, January 12, 2002.

Epstein, Marc, and Kirk Hanson. "Introduction." In *The Accountable Corporation*, edited by Marc Epstein and Kirk Hanson, 4 vols. Westport, CT: Praeger, 2006, vol. 1, vii–xv.

Epstein, Richard. *Simple Rules for a Complex World*. Cambridge, MA: Harvard University Press, 1995.

Executive Office of the President, Energy Policy and Planning. *The National Energy Plan*. Washington, DC: Government Printing Office, 1977.

Feagin, Joe. *Free Enterprise City: Houston in Political and Economic Perspective*. New Brunswick, NJ: Rutgers University Press, 1988.

Federal Energy Administration. *Project Independence Report*. Washington, DC: Government Printing Office, 1974.

Federal Reserve Act of 1913. (Public Law 63–43, 38 *Stat.* 251.)

Fehr, Ernst, and Urs Fishbacher. "The Nature of Human Altruism." *Nature*, October 23, 2003, 785–91.

Fickett, Arnold, Clark Gellings, and Amory Lovins. "Efficient Use of Electricity." *Scientific American*, September 1990, 65–74.

Filene, Peter. "An Obituary for 'The Progressive Movement.'" *American Quarterly* 22 (1): 20–34 (Spring 1970).

Fine, Sidney. *Laissez Faire and the General-Welfare State: A Study of Conflict in American Thought, 1865–1901*. Ann Arbor: University of Michigan Press, 1956.

Fiscal Policy and the Energy Crisis. Hearings before the Subcommittee on Energy of the Committee on Finance, United States Senate, 93rd Cong., 1st Sess., 1973 (S. David Freeman, "Statement of S. David Freeman" and discussion), 38–57.

Fleming, James. *Historical Perspectives on Climate Change*. Oxford: Oxford University Press, 1998.

Flynn, John. "Business and the Government." *Harper's Monthly Magazine*, March 1928, 409–15.

Folsom, Burton, Jr. *The Myth of the Robber Barons*. Herndon, VA: Young America's Foundation, 1991.

Ford Foundation. *Annual Report for 1952*, December 31, 1952.

———. *A Time to Choose: America's Energy Future*. Final report by the Energy Project of the Ford Foundation. Cambridge, MA: Ballinger, 1974.

Fouquet, Roger, and J. G. Pearson. "A Thousand Years of Energy Use in the United Kingdom." *The Energy Journal* 19 (4): 1–41 (October 1998).

Fouraker, Lawrence, and Graham Allison. Foreword to *Business and Public Policy*, edited by John Dunlop, vii–xii. Boston, MA: Harvard University School of Business Administration, 1980.

Fox, Loren. *Enron: The Rise and Fall*. New York: John Wiley & Sons, 2002.

Freeman, Christopher. "Malthus with a Computer." In *Models of Doom: A Critique of the Limits to Growth*, edited by H. S. D. Cole et al., 5–13. New York: Universe Books, 1973.

Freeman, R. Edward, Kirsten Martin, and Bidhan Parmar. "Ethics and Capitalism." In *The Accountable Corporation*, edited by Marc Epstein and Kirk Hanson, vol. 2, 193–208. Westport, CT: Praeger, 2006.

Freeman, S. David. *Energy: The New Era*. New York: Walker, 1974.

———. "Still a Time to Choose . . . Ten Years Later." *Energy Journal* 4 (2): 9–14 (1988).

Friedman, Milton. *Capitalism and Freedom*. Chicago: University of Chicago Press, 1962.

———. "The Social Responsibility of Business Is to Increase Its Profits." 1970. Reprinted in *Morality and the Market: Ethics and Virtue in the Conduct of Business*, edited by Eugene Heath, 405–9. New York: McGraw-Hill, 2002.

———. "Which Way for Capitalism?" *Reason*, May 1977, 18–21, 61.

Friedman, Milton, and Rose Friedman. *Free to Choose*. New York: Harcourt Brace Jovanovich, 1979.

Friedman, Milton, Paul Samuelson, and Henry Wallich. "The Verdict of *Newsweek*'s Three Economists." *Newsweek*, August 30, 1971, 22–23.

Fuel Shortages 1. Hearings before the Senate Committee on Interior and Insular Affairs, 93rd Cong., 1st sess., 1973 ("Opening Statement of the Chairman," by Henry Jackson), 1–4.

Fuel Shortages 2. Hearings before the Senate Committee on Interior and Insular Affairs, 93rd Cong., 1st sess., 1973 ("Opening Statement of the Chairman," by Henry Jackson), 525–27.

Galambos, Louis, and Joseph Pratt. *The Rise of the Corporate Commonwealth.* New York: Basic Books, 1988.

Galbraith, John Kenneth. *The Affluent Society.* Boston: Houghton Mifflin, 1958.

———. "How Much Should a Country Consume." In *Perspectives on Conservation,* edited by Henry Jarrett, 89–99. Baltimore: Johns Hopkins University Press, 1958.

———. *The New Industrial State.* Boston: Houghton Mifflin, 1967.

———. "Power and the Useful Economist." *American Economic Review* 63 (1): 1–11 (March 1973).

———. *The Age of Uncertainty.* London: British Broadcasting Corporation, 1977.

———. *A Life in Our Times.* Boston: Houghton Mifflin, 1981.

Gibbins, H. de B. *The Industrial History of England.* London: Methuen, 1897.

Gilpin, Kenneth. "Julian Simon, 65, Optimistic Economist, Dies," *New York Times,* February 12, 1998.

Gintis, Herbert, Samuel Bowles, Robert Boyd, and Ernst Fehr. "Moral Sentiments and Material Interests: Origins, Evidence, and Consequences." In *Moral Sentiments and Material Interests: The Foundations of Cooperation in Economic Life,* edited by H. Gintis et al., 3–39. Cambridge, MA: MIT Press, 2005.

Gladstein, Mimi. *The New Ayn Rand Companion.* Westport, CT: Greenwood Press, 1999.

Gladstone, W. E. "Ways and Means—The Financial Statement." 1866. Reprinted in *W. S. Jevons: Critical Responses,* edited by Sandra Peart, vol. 1, 233–65. New York: Routledge, 2003.

Gladwell, Malcolm. "The Talent Myth." *New Yorker,* July 22, 2002, 28–33.

Godkin, E. L. "The Moral of the Credit Mobilier Scandal." *Nation,* January 30, 1873, 65–68.

Goklany, Indur. *The Improving State of the World.* Washington, DC: Cato Institute, 2007.

Goldstein, Bill. "'Greenspan Shrugged': When Greed Was a Virtue and Regulation the Enemy." *New York Times,* July 21, 2002.

Goodman, Ted. *The Forbes Book of Business Quotations.* New York: Black Dog & Leventhal, 1997.

Goodwin, Craufurd. "The Lessons of History." In *Energy Policy in Perspective: Today's Problems, Yesterday's Solutions,* edited by Craufurd Goodwin, 665–84. Washington, DC: Brookings Institution, 1981.

———. "The Truman Administration." In *Energy Policy in Perspective: Today's Problems, Yesterday's Solutions,* edited by Craufurd Goodwin, 1–62. Washington, DC: Brookings Institution, 1981.

Gordon, Lincoln. "Limits to the Growth Debate." *Resources,* Summer 1976, 1–6.

Gordon, Richard. *The Evolution of Energy Policy in Western Europe.* New York: Praeger. 1970.

———. "Energy, Exhaustion, Environmentalism, and Etatism." *Energy Journal* 15 (1): 1–16 (January 1994).

Gordon, Richard, et al., eds. *Energy: Markets and Regulation.* Cambridge, MA: MIT Press, 1987.

Gordon, Robert. "A New Role for Lawyers? The Corporate Counselor after Enron." In *Enron: Corporate Fiascos and Legal Implications,* edited by Nancy Rapoport and Bala Dharan, 763–92. New York: Foundation Press, 2004.

Gore, Al. *An Inconvenient Truth: The Planetary Emergency of Global Warming and What We Can Do about It.* Emmaus, PA: Rodale, 2006.

Graebner, William. *Coal-Mining Safety in the Progressive Period.* Lexington: University of Kentucky Press, 1976.

Granville, Maurice. "Petroleum's Role from Now to the End of the Century." In *Petroleum/2000*. Tulsa, OK: *Oil & Gas Journal*, August 1977.

Gras, N. S. B. *Business and Capitalism: An Introduction to Business History*. 1939. Reprint. New York: Augustus M. Kelley, 1971.

Gray, Horace. "The Passing of the Public Utility Concept." In American Economic Association, *Readings in the Social Control of Industry*, 280–303. Philadelphia: Blakiston, 1949.

Gray, L. C. "The Economic Possibilities of Conservation." *Quarterly Journal of Economics* 27 (3): 497–519 (May 1913).

Greene, Murray. "Schumpeter's *Imperialism*: A Critical Note." In *The New Imperialism*, edited by Harrison Wright. Boston: D.C. Heath, 1961.

Greenfeld, Liah. *The Spirit of Capitalism*. Cambridge, MA: Harvard University Press, 2001.

Greenspan, Alan. "The Assault on Integrity." 1963. In Ayn Rand et al., *Capitalism: The Unknown Ideal*, 118–21. New York: Penguin Putnam, 1967.

———. The Age of Turbulence. New York. Penguin Press, 2007.

Greider, William. *Who Will Tell the People: The Betrayal of American Democracy*. New York: Touchstone, 1992.

———. *The Soul of Capitalism*. New York: Simon & Schuster, 2003.

Greiner, Donna, and Theodore Kinni. *Ayn Rand and Business*. New York: Texere, 2001.

Grinder, Walter, and John Hagel. "Toward a Theory of State Capitalism: Ultimate Decision-Making and Class Structure." *Journal of Libertarian Studies* 1 (1): 59–79 (1977).

Gross, Bertram. "Book Review: *The Process of Government*." *American Political Science Review* 44 (3): 742–48 (September 1950).

———. *The Legislative Struggle: A Study in Social Combat*. New York: McGraw-Hill, 1953.

Gross, Daniel. "The Crime: Slow Job Growth. A Suspect: Enron." *New York Times*, September 11, 2005.

Haberler, Gottfried, et al. "Professor Joseph A. Schumpeter." In *Schumpeter: Social Scientist*, edited by Seymour Harris, ix–x. Cambridge, MA: Harvard University Press, 1951.

Halberstam, David. *The Reckoning*. New York: William Morrow, 1986.

Hamel, Gary. *Leading the Revolution*. Boston: Harvard Business School Press, 2000.

Hamel, Gary, and C. K. Prahalad. *Competing for the Future*. Boston: Harvard Business School Press, 1994.

Hammond, John. Foreword to *What the Coal Commission Found*, edited by Edward Hunt et al., 17–18. Baltimore: Williams & Wilkins, 1925.

Harbeson, Robert. "Railroads and Regulation, 1877–1916: Conspiracy or Public Interest?" *Journal of Economic History* 37 (2): 230–42 (June 1967).

Harriman, David, ed. *Journals of Ayn Rand*. New York: Plume, 1999.

Harrington, Walt. "The Heretic Becomes Respectable." *Washington Post Magazine*, August 18, 1985, 8–9, 18–19.

Harris, Ralph. "A New Consensus for a New Millennium." Introduction to Samuel Smiles, *Self-Help*, iv–ix. Reprint, London: Institute of Economic Affairs, 1996.

Harris, Seymour. "Introductory Remarks." In *Schumpeter: Social Scientist*, edited by Seymour Harris, 1–7. Freeport, NY: Books for Libraries, 1951.

Harvard University. *The Graduate School of Business Administration, 1908–09*. Cambridge, MA: Harvard University, 1908.

Hasnas, John. "Unethical Compliance the Non Sequitur of Academic Business Ethics." *Journal of Private Enterprise* 32 (2): 87–105 (Spring 2006).

Hass, Jerome, et al. *Financing the Energy Industry.* Cambridge, MA: Ballinger, 1975.

Hausman, William. "Long-Term Trends in Energy Prices." In *The State of Humanity,* edited by Julian Simon, 280–86. Cambridge, MA: Blackwell, 1995.

Hawken, Paul, Amory Lovins, and L. Hunter Lovins. *Natural Capitalism.* New York: Little, Brown, 1999.

Hawley, Ellis. "Herbert Hoover: The Commerce Secretariat, and the Vision of an 'Associative State,' 1921–1928." *Journal of American History* 61 (1): 116–40 (June 1974).

———. "Three Facets of Hooverian Associationalism: Lumber, Aviation, and Movies, 1921–30." In *Regulation in Perspective,* edited by Thomas McCraw, 95–123. Cambridge, MA: Harvard University Press, 1981.

Hayek, F. A. "The Subjective Character of the Data of the Social Sciences." 1952. In F. A. Hayek, *The Counter-Revolution of Science: Studies on the Abuse of Reason,* 41–60. Indianapolis: LibertyPress, 1979.

———. *The Constitution of Liberty.* Chicago: University of Chicago Press, 1960.

———. "The Non Sequitur of the Dependence Effect." 1961. In *Studies in Philosophy, Politics and Economics,* edited by F. A. Hayek, 313–17. 1967. Reprint, New York: Clarion, 1969.

———. "Personal Recollections of Keynes and the 'Keynesian Revolution.'" 1966. In *New Studies in Philosophy, Politics, Economics and the History of Ideas,* edited by F. A. Hayek, 283–89. Chicago: University of Chicago Press, 1978.

Haynes, William Warren. *Nationalization in Practice: The British Coal Industry.* Boston: Harvard University Graduate School of Business Administration, 1953.

Hays, Samuel. *Conservation and the Gospel of Efficiency.* Cambridge, MA: Harvard University Press, 1959.

Hayward, Steven. *The Real Jimmy Carter.* Washington, DC: Regnery, 2004.

Heckelman, Jac, et al. Introduction to *Public Choice Interpretations of American Economic History,* edited by J. Heckelman et al., 1–9. Boston: Kluwer, 2000.

Heclo, Hugh. "Reaganism and the Search for a Public Philosophy." In *Perspectives on the Reagan Years,* edited by John Palmer, 31–63. Washington, DC: Urban Institute, 1986.

Heertje, Arnold. "Schumpeter, Joseph Alois." In *The New Palgrave: A Dictionary of Economics.* 1987, edited by John Eatwell et al., vol. 4, 263–67. Reprint, New York: Palgrave, 2002.

Heilbroner, Robert. *The Worldly Philosophers.* New York: Simon & Schuster, 1953.

———. *The Limits of American Capitalism.* New York: Harper & Row, 1966.

———. *Between Capitalism and Socialism: Essays in Political Economics.* New York: Vintage Books, 1970.

———. "The Triumph of Capitalism." *The New Yorker,* January 23, 1989, 98–109.

Heilbroner, Robert. "After Communism." *The New Yorker,* September 10, 1990, 91–100.

Herring, Pendleton. *The Politics of Democracy: American Parties in Action.* New York: W. W. Norton, 1940.

Hicks, Stephen. *Explaining Postmodernism: Skepticism and Socialism from Rousseau to Foucault.* Tempe, AZ: Scholargy Publishing, 2004.

Higgs, Robert. *Depression, War, and Cold War: Studies in Political Economy.* New York: Oxford University Press, 2006.

High, Jack. "Introduction: A Tale of Two Disciplines." In *Regulation: Economic Theory and History,* edited by Jack High, 1–17. Ann Arbor: University of Michigan Press, 1991.

High, Jack, and Jerry Ellig. "Economic Theories of Regulation, 1880–1914." George Mason University. Unpublished 1995 manuscript.

Hilton, George. "The Consistency of the Interstate Commerce Act," *Journal of Law and Economics* 9: 87–113 (October 1966).

Hitch, Charles, "RFF: Past and Future." *Resources*, June 1975, 3.

Hofstadter, Richard. "Introduction: The Meaning of the Progressive Movement." In *The Progressive Movement: 1900–1915*, edited by Richard Hofstadter, 1–15. Englewood Cliffs, NJ: Prentice Hall, 1963.

———. *The Progressive Historians: Turner, Beard, Parrington*. New York: Alfred A. Knopf, 1968.

Holden, Constance. "Simon and Kahn versus Global 2000." *Science*, July 22, 1983, 341–43.

Holdren, John. "Energy in Transition." *Scientific American*, September 1990, 157–63.

———. "Prologue: The Transition to Costlier Energy." In *Energy Efficiency and Human Activity: Past Trends, Future Prospects*, edited by Lee Schipper and Stephen Meyers, 1–51. Cambridge: Cambridge University Press, 1992.

Holdren, John, and Paul Ehrlich. "Prospects for a Sane Economics." In John Holdren and Paul Ehrlich, *Global Ecology*, 177–79. New York: Harcourt Brace Jovanovich, 1971.

Holdren, John, et al. "Bad News: Is It True?" Letters to the Editor. *Science*, December 19, 1980, 1296–1301.

Holton, Richard. "Business and Government." In *The American Business Corporation: New Perspectives on Profit and Purpose*, edited by Eli Goldston et al., 57–75. Cambridge, MA: MIT Press, 1972.

Hood, John. *The Heroic Enterprise: Business and the Common Good*. New York: Free Press, 1996.

Hoogenboom, Ari, and Olive Hoogenboom. *A History of the ICC: From Panacea to Palliative*. New York: W. W. Norton, 1976.

Horwitz, Robert. *The Irony of Regulatory Reform: The Deregulation of American Telecommunications*. New York: Oxford University Press, 1989.

Hotelling, Harold. "The Economics of Exhaustible Resources." *Journal of Political Economy* 39 (2): 137–75 (April 1931).

Houston Natural Gas Corporation. *1981 Annual Report to the Stockholders*.

Hubbert, M. King. "Energy from Fossil Fuels." *Science*, February 4, 1949, 103–09.

———. "Nuclear Energy and Fossil Fuels." In *Drilling and Production Practice, 1956*, 7–25. Washington, DC: American Petroleum Institute, 1956.

———. "Energy Resources." In National Research Council, National Academy of Sciences, *Resources and Man*, 157–242. San Francisco: W. H. Freeman, 1969.

———. "Survey of World Energy Resources." 1973. Reprinted in *Perspectives on Energy*, edited by Lon Ruedisili and Morris Firebaugh, 109–39. New York: Oxford University Press, 1978.

———. *U.S. Energy Resources: A Review as of 1972*. Washington, DC: Government Printing Office, 1974.

Hudgins, Edward. "The New Cult of Darkness." At www.solopassion.com/node/2363?PHPSESSID=1cebcff7414d6eff7f6f2ddf71ad5400.

Hughes, Thomas. Introduction to Samuel Smiles, *Selections from Lives of the Engineers,* 1–29. Cambridge, MA: MIT Press, 1966.

Hunt, Edward, et al., eds. *What the Coal Commission Found.* Baltimore: Williams & Wilkins, 1925.

Hussey, Vivian. "Motion for a Royal Commission." 1866. Reprinted in *W. S. Jevons: Critical Responses,* edited by Sandra Peart, vol. 1, 278–321. New York: Routledge, 2003.

Ikeda, Sanford. *Dynamics of the Mixed Economy.* New York: Routledge, 1997.

———. "The Dynamics of Interventionism." In *The Dynamics of Intervention: Regulation and Redistribution in the Mixed Economy,* edited by P. Kurrild-Klitgaard, 21–57. New York: Elsevier, 2005a.

———. "Hubs, Connectors, and Public Characters: Social Capital in Relation to the Market Process." Paper presented to the seventy-fifth annual meeting of the Southern Economics Association, Washington, DC, November 19, 2005b.

"Industry and the Historian." Editorial. *New York Times,* August 7, 1951.

"Industry Debates Kyoto's Benefit for Natural Gas." *Gas Daily,* December 12, 1997, 1, 5–6.

Insull, Samuel. "Satisfy Your Customers." Speech at the banquet of H. M. Nyllesby and Company, January 20, 1911. Reprinted in S. Insull, *Central-Station Electric Service,* 174–181. Chicago: Privately printed, 1915.

———. "A Quarter Century Anniversary." Speech celebrating Insull's 25th anniversary as president of Chicago Edison, Chicago, June 25, 1917. Reprinted in Insull, *Public Utilities in Modern Life,* 133–37. Chicago, 1924.

———. "Looking Backward." Speech, annual dinner of the Public Service Company of Northern Illinois Section of National Electric Light Association (second division), Chicago, October 24, 1919. Reprinted in Insull, *Public Utilities in Modern Life,* 184–98. Chicago, 1924.

International Energy Agency. *World Energy Outlook 2007.* Paris: OECD/IEA, 2007.

IPCC (Intergovernmental Panel on Climate Change). *Climate Change 2007: The Physical Science Basis (Contribution of Working Group I to the Fourth Assessment Report of the Intergovernmental Panel on Climate Change).* Cambridge: Cambridge University Press, 2007.

Ise, John. *Economics.* New York: Harper & Brothers, 1946.

"Jacques Derrida." *The Economist,* October 23, 2004, 89.

Jarvis, Adrian. *Samuel Smiles and the Construction of Victorian Values.* Hartnolls, UK: Sutton, 1997.

Jennrich, John. "Soft Energy Paths." *Oil & Gas Journal,* April 26, 1982, 79.

Jevons, H. Stanley. *The British Coal Trade.* 1915. Reprint, Newton, UK: David & Charles Reprints, 1969.

Jevons, Harriet, ed. *Letters & Journal of W. Stanley Jevons.* London: Macmillan, 1886.

Jevons, W. S. *The Coal Question: An Inquiry Concerning the Progress of the Nation and the Probable Exhaustion of our Coal Mines.* London: Macmillan, 1865; 2nd ed., 1866; 3rd ed., edited by A. W. Flux, 1906. Reprint, New York: Augustus M. Kelley, 1965.

———. "On Coal." 1867. In *Papers and Correspondence of W. S. Jevons,* edited by R. D. C. Black, vol. 7, 18–28. London: Macmillan Press, 1981.

———. "On the Probable Exhaustion of our Coal Mines." 1868. In *Papers and Correspondence of W. S. Jevons*, edited by R. D. C. Black, vol. 7, 28–35. London: Macmillan Press, 1981.

———. "On the Progress of the Coal Question." 1875. In *Papers and Correspondence of W. S. Jevons*, edited by R. D. C. Black, vol. 7, 36–37. London: Macmillan Press, 1981.

Johnson, James. *The Politics of Soft Coal*. Chicago: University of Illinois Press, 1979.

Jones, Del. "Enron Chief: Energy Spending Generates Real Savings." *USA Today*, November 27, 2000.

Jones, Del. "Scandals Lead Execs to 'Atlas Shrugged': 1957 Ayn Rand Novel Sanctions Self-Interest," *USA Today*, September 24, 2002.

Jones, W. T. *A History of Western Philosophy*. Vol. 2, *The Medieval Mind*. New York: Harcourt, Brace, and World, 1952.

Jonnes, Jill. *Empires of Light*. New York: Random House, 2003.

Josephson, Matthew. *The Robber Barons*. 1934. Reprint, New York: Harcourt Brace, 1962.

———. Foreword to *The Robber Barons*, v–vi. 2nd ed. New York: Harcourt Brace, 1962.

———. "Should American History Be Rewritten? NO." 1954. In *The Craft of American History: Selected Essays*, edited by A. S. Eisenstadt, 2 vols. Vol. 1, 185–92. New York: Harper & Row, 1966.

Journo, Elan. "There Isn't Too Much Greed, It's Just the Wrong Kind." *Houston Chronicle*, July 24, 2002.

Kahn, Alfred. "The Depletion Allowance in the Context of Cartelization." *American Economic Review* 54 (4): 286–314 (June 1964).

———. *The Economics of Regulation*. 2 vols. New York: John Wiley & Sons, 1971.

Kahn, Herman. "A General Review." In *No Time to Confuse: A Critique of the Final Report of the Energy Policy Project of the Ford Foundation*, edited by M. A. Adelman et al., 131–44. San Francisco: Institute for Contemporary Studies, 1975.

Kalt, Joseph. *The Economics and Politics of Oil Price Regulation: Federal Policy in the Post-Embargo Era*. Cambridge, MA: MIT Press, 1981.

Kaysen, Carl. "A Time to Choose: A Reply." In *A Debate on A TIME TO CHOOSE*, edited by William Tavoulareas and Carl Kaysen, 71–104. Cambridge, MA: Ballinger, 1977.

Kelley, David. *The Contested Legacy of Ayn Rand*. New Brunswick, NJ: Transaction, 2000.

———. "Ayn Rand and Greed" (letter to the editor). *New York Times*, July 28, 2002.

Kelley, John. *Bringing the Market Back In*. New York: New York University Press, 1997.

Kelly, Marjorie. "Waving Goodbye to the Invisible Hand: How the Enron Mess Grew and Grew. *San Francisco Chronicle*, February 24, 2002.

"Ken Lay's Good Works," *The Nation*, February 11, 2002, 7.

Keynes, John Maynard. *Tract on Monetary Reform*. 1923. Reprint, Amherst, NY: Prometheus Books, 2000.

———. *The Pure Theory of Money*. Vol. 1 of *A Treatise on Money*. New York: Harcourt, Brace, 1930.

———. "Robert Malthus." 1933a. In *Essays in Biography*, by John Maynard Keynes, 81–124. Reprint, New York: W. W. Norton, 1963.

———. "W. S. Jevons." 1933b. In *Essays in Biography*, by John Maynard Keynes, 255–309. Reprint, New York: W. W. Norton, 1963.

King-Casas, Brooks, et al. "Getting to Know You: Reputation and Trust in a Two-Person Economic Exchange." *Science* 308 (5718): 78–83 (April 1, 2005).

Kirzner, Israel. *Competition & Entrepreneurship.* Chicago: University of Chicago Press, 1973.

———. "Entrepreneurship and the Future of Capitalism." 1983. In *Discovery and the Capitalist Process,* edited by Israel Kirzner, 150–80. Chicago: University of Chicago Press, 1985.

———. *Discovery, Capitalism, and Distributive Justice.* New York: Basil Blackwell, 1989.

Kneese, Allen, "Our Polluted Air." *Resources,* September 1962, 3.

Kneese, Allen, and Ronald Ridker. "Predicament of Mankind." *Washington Post,* March 2, 1972.

Knight, Frank. *Risk, Uncertainty and Profit.* New York: Houghton Mifflin, 1921.

———. *The Economic Organization.* 1933. Reprint, New York: Harper & Row, 1951.

Koch, Charles. *Creating a Science of Liberty.* Fairfax, VA: Institute for Humane Studies at George Mason University, 1997.

———. *The Science of Success.* Hoboken, NJ: John Wiley & Sons, 2007.

Koch Industries. "About Koch: Philosophy and Principles." www.kochind.com/about/philosophy.asp.

Kolko, Gabriel. "The Premises of Business Revisionism." *Business History Review* 33 (3): 330–44 (Autumn 1959).

———. *The Triumph of Conservatism.* New York: Free Press, 1963.

———. *Railroads and Regulation, 1877–1916.* New York: W. W. Norton, 1965.

———. "The Decline of American Radicalism in the Twentieth Century." 1966. In *For A New America: Essays in History and Politics from Studies on the Left, 1959–1967,* edited by James Weinstein and David Eakins, 197–220. New York: Random House, 1970.

———. "Brahmins and Business, 1870–1914: A Hypothesis on the Social Basis of Success in American History." In *From the Critical Spirit: Essays in Honor of Herbert Marcuse,* edited by Kurt Wolff and Barrington Moore, 343–54. Boston: Beacon Press, 1967.

———. *The Roots of American Foreign Policy: An Analysis of Power and Purpose.* Boston: Beacon Press, 1969.

———. *The Limits of Power: The World and United States Foreign Policy, 1945–1954.* New York: Harper & Row, 1972.

———. *Main Currents in Modern American History.* New York: Harper & Row, 1976.

———. *Century of War.* New York: New Press, 1994.

———. *After Socialism: Reconstructing Critical Social Thought.* New York: Routledge, 2006.

Krautkraemer, Jeffrey. "Nonrenewable Resource Scarcity." *Journal of Economic Literature* 36 (4): 2065–2107 (December 1998).

Krautkraemer, Jeffrey, and Michael Toman. "Economics of Energy Supply." In *Encyclopedia of Energy,* edited by Cutler Cleveland, vol. 2, 91–101. New York: Elsevier Academic Press, 2004.

Krugman, Paul. "The Great Divide." *New York Times,* January 29, 2002.

———. *The Great Unraveling: Losing Our Way in the New Century.* New York: W. W. Norton, 2005.

Krutilla, John, and Talbot Page. "Towards a Responsible Energy Policy." *Policy Analysis* 1 (1): 77–100 (Winter 1975).

Kuhn, Thomas. *The Structure of Scientific Revolutions.* 1962. Reprint, Chicago: University of Chicago Press, 1970.

Kuttner, Robert. "The Lesson of Enron: Regulation Isn't a Dirty Word." *BusinessWeek*, December 24, 2001, 24.

———. "The Enron Economy." *American Prospect*, January 1–14, 2002a, 2.

———. "Enron: A Powerful Blow to Market Fundamentalists." *BusinessWeek*, February 4, 2002b, 20.

Landsberg, Hans, et al. *Energy: The Next Twenty Years*. Cambridge, MA: Ballinger, 1979.

Lane, Rose Wilder. *The Discovery of Freedom: Man's Struggle against Authority*. New York: John Day, 1943. Reprint, New York: Laissez Faire Books, 1984.

Langlois, Richard. "Do Firms Plan?" *Constitutional Political Economy* 6 (3): 247–61 (Fall 1995).

Lanouette, William. "A Latter-Day David Out to Slay the Goliaths of Energy." *National Journal*, October 1, 1977, 1532–34.

Larson, Henrietta. *Guide to Business History*. 1948. Reprint, Boston: J. S. Canner, 1964.

———. "Editorial Director's Introduction." 1954. In Ralph Hidy and Muriel Hidy, *Pioneering in Big Business, 1882–1911: History of the Standard Oil Company (New Jersey)*, xxi–xxv. New York: Harper & Brothers, 1955.

Latham, Earl. *The Group Basis of Politics: A Study in Basing-Point Pricing*. Ithaca, NY: Cornell University Press, 1952.

Lavine, Thelma. "Introduction to the Transaction Edition." In Arthur Bentley, *The Process of Government*, xi–xxix. New Brunswick, NJ: Transaction, 1995.

Lavoie, Don. *National Economic Planning: What Is Left?* Washington, DC: Cato Institute, 1985.

Lawrence, George. "Gas Industry Outlook Good for 2000." In *Petroleum/2000*, special issue, *Oil & Gas Journal*, August 1977, pp. 71–72.

Lawson, Nigel. *The View from No. 11: Memoirs of a Tory Radical*. New York: Bantam Press, 1992.

Lay, Ken. "Climate Change: Where Do We Go from Here." Presentation to the American Bar Association, Section of the Environment, Energy, and Resources. London, July 20, 2000.

Lee, Alfred. "Introduction to the Transaction Edition." In William Graham Sumner, *Earth-Hunger and Other Essays*, edited by Albert Galloway Keller, v–xxvii. 1913. Reprint, New Brunswick, NJ: Transaction, 1980.

Leggett, Jeremy. *The Carbon War*. London: Penguin Books, 1999.

Lehne, Richard. *Government and Business*. New York: Chatham House, 2001.

Lerner, Max. "Introduction." In Adam Smith, *The Wealth of Nations*, edited by Edwin Cannan, v–x. New York: Random House, 1937.

Leuchtenburg, William. *The Perils of Prosperity, 1914–1932*. 1958. Reprint, Chicago: University of Chicago Press, 1993.

Link, Arthur, and Richard McCormick. *Progressivism*. Wheeling, IL: Harlan Davidson, 1983.

Lively, Robert. "The American System: A Review Article." *Business History Review* 29 (1): 81–95 (Spring 1955).

"The Lobbying-Industrial Complex." *New York Times*, August 26, 2005.

Locke, Edwin, and Jaana Woiceshyn. "Why Businessmen Should Be Honest: The Argument from Rational Egoism." In *Why Businessmen Need Philosophy*, edited by Richard E. Ralston, 81–101. Irvine, CA: Ayn Rand Institute Press, 1999.

Logan, William. "The Futurists." *Worth*, December/January 1993, 63–67.

Loving, Rush, Jr. "The Pros and Cons of Airline Deregulation." *Fortune*, August 1977, 209–17.

Lovins, Amory. *World Energy Strategies: Facts, Issues, and Options*. New York: Friends of the Earth International, 1975.

———. "Energy Strategy: The Road Not Taken?" *Foreign Affairs* 55 (1): 65–96 (October 1976a).

———. "Prepared Testimony of Amory B. Lovins." 1976b. Revised. In *The Energy Controversy*, edited by Hugh Nash, 15–34. San Francisco: Friends of the Earth, 1979.

———. *Soft Energy Paths: Toward a Durable Peace*. 1977. Reprint, New York: Harper Colophon Books, 1979.

Lynch, Michael. "Forecasting Oil Supply: Theory and Practice." *Quarterly Review of Economics and Finance* 42 (2): 373–89 (Summer 2002).

Machan, Tibor. "Business Ethics in a New Key." *Journal of Private Enterprise* 32 (2): 1–33 (Spring 2006).

Machovec, Frank. *Perfect Competition and the Transformation of Economics*. New York: Routledge, 1995.

MacLaury, Bruce. Foreword to Martha Derthick and Paul Quirk, *The Politics of Deregulation*, vii–ix. Washington, DC: Brookings Institution, 1985.

Macvane, S. M. *The Working Principles of Political Economy*. New York: Maynard, Merrill, 1899.

Maddox, John. *The Doomsday Syndrome*. New York: McGraw-Hill, 1972.

Madison, James. "The Federalist No. 10, November 23, 1787: The Union as a Safeguard against Domestic Faction and Insurrection." In *The Federalist*, edited by Robert Scigliano, 53–62. New York: Modern Library, 1937.

Malthus, T. R. "An Essay on the Principle of Population as It Affects the Future Improvement of Society." 1st ed. 1798. Reprinted in T. R. Malthus, *On Population*. New York: Random House, 1960.

———. "An Essay on the Principle of Population or, A View of Its Past and Present Effects on Human Happiness; with an Inquiry into Our Prospects Respecting the Future Removal of the Evils Which It Occasions." 2nd ed. 1803. Reprinted in T. R. Malthus, *An Essay on the Principle of Population*. London: Macmillan, 1926.

———. *Principles of Political Economy Considered with a View to Their Practical Application*. 1820. 2d ed., 1836. Reprint, New York: Augustus M. Kelley, 1968.

———. "An Essay on the Principle of Population: A View of Its Past and Present Effects on Human Happiness; With an Inquiry into Our Prospects Respecting the Future Removal or Mitigation of the Evils Which It Occasions." 7th ed. 1872. Reprinted in T. R. Malthus, *On Population*. New York: Random House, 1960.

Marcoux, Alexi. "The Concept of Business in Business Ethics." *Journal of Private Enterprise* 32 (2): 50–67 (Spring 2006).

Maritain, Jacques. *The Range of Reason*. New York: Charles Scribner's Sons, 1952.

Marshall, Jonathan. "William Sumner: Critic of Progressive Liberalism." *Journal of Libertarian Studies* 3 (3): 261–77 (Fall 1979).

Martin, Albro. *Enterprise Denied: Origins of the Decline of American Railroads, 1897–1917*. New York: Columbia University Press, 1971.

———. "The Troubled Subject of Railroad Regulation in the Gilded Age—A Reappraisal." *Journal of American History* 61 (2): 339–71 (September 1974).

Marx, Karl, and Friedrich Engels. *The Communist Manifesto.* 1848. Reprint, Baltimore: Penguin, 1967.

Mayer, Allan. "Thinking Soft." *Newsweek,* November 14, 1977, 108.

Mayhew, Robert. *Ayn Rand Answers.* New York: New American Library, 2005.

McCloskey, Deirdre. *The Bourgeois Virtues.* Chicago: University of Chicago Press, 2006.

McCormick, Richard. "The Discovery that Business Corrupts Politics: A Reappraisal of the Origins of Progressivism." *American Historical Review* 86 (2): 247–74 (April 1981).

McCormick, Robert. "The Strategic Use of Regulation: A Review of the Literature." In *The Political Economy of Regulation: Private Interests in the Regulatory Process,* edited by Federal Trade Commission, 13–32. Washington, DC: Federal Trade Commission, 1984.

———. "A Review of the Economics of Regulation: The Political Process." In *Regulation and the Reagan Era,* edited by Roger Meiners and Bruce Yandle, 16–37. New York: Holmes & Meier, 1989.

McCraw, Thomas. "The Progressive Legacy." In *The Progressive Era,* edited by Lewis Gould, 181–201. Syracuse, NY: Syracuse University Press, 1974.

———. "Regulation in America: A Review Article." *Business History Review* 49 (2): 159–83 (Summer 1975).

———. "Rethinking the Trust Question." In *Regulation in Perspective,* edited by Thomas McCraw, 1–55. Cambridge, MA: Harvard University Press, 1981.

———. *Prophets of Regulation.* Cambridge, MA: Harvard University Press, 1984.

———. "Introduction: The Intellectual Odyssey of Alfred D. Chandler, Jr." In *The Essential Alfred Chandler: Essays toward a Historical Theory of Big Business,* edited by Thomas McCraw, 1–21. Boston: Harvard Business School Press, 1988.

———. "Schumpeter Ascending." *American Scholar* 60 (3): 371–92 (Summer 1991).

———. Introduction to *Creating Modern Capitalism,* edited by Thomas McCraw, 1–16. 1995. Reprint, Cambridge, MA: Harvard University Press, 1997.

———. *Prophet of Innovation: Joseph Schumpeter and Creative Destruction.* Cambridge, MA: Belknap Press, 2007.

McCrea, R. C. "Schumpeter's Economic System." *Quarterly Journal of Economics* 27 (3): 520–29 (May 1913).

McDonald, Forrest. *We the People: The Economic Origins of the Constitution.* Chicago: University of Chicago, 1958.

———. *Insull.* Chicago: University of Chicago Press, 1962.

McDonald, Stephen. "Erich Zimmermann, the Dynamics of Resourceship." In *Economic Mavericks: The Texas Institutionalists,* edited by Ronnie Phillips, 151–83. Greenwich, CT: JAI Press, 1995.

McLean, Bethany, and Peter Elkind. *The Smartest Guys in the Room: The Amazing Rise and Scandalous Fall of Enron.* New York: Portfolio, 2003.

Meadows, Donella. "The Limits to Growth Revisited." In *The Cassandra Conference: Resources and the Human Predicament,* edited by Paul Ehrlich and John Holdren. College Station: Texas A&M University Press, 1988.

Meadows, Donella, et al. *The Limits to Growth: A Report for THE CLUB OF ROME'S Project on the Predicament of Mankind.* New York: Universe Books, 1972.

Mesarovic, Mihajlo, and Eduard Pestel. *Mankind at the Turning Point: The Second Report to the Club of Rome.* New York: E. P. Dutton, 1974.

Michaels, Patrick. *Sound and Fury: The Science and Politics of Global Warming.* Washington, DC: Cato Institute, 1992.

Micklethwait, John, and Adrian Wooldridge. *The Company: A Short History of a Revolutionary Idea.* New York: Modern Library, 2003.

Mill, John Stuart. "Speech, House of Commons Debates." April 17, 1866. In *W. S. Jevons: Critical Responses*, edited by Sandra Peart, vol. 1, 191–97. New York: Routledge, 2003.

Miller, William. Introduction to *Men in Business: Essays in the Historical Role of the Entrepreneur*, edited by William Miller, 1–6. 1952. Reprint, New York: Harper, 1962.

Millstein, Ira. "A Perspective on Corporate Governance: Rules, Principles, or Both." In *The Accountable Corporation*, edited by Marc Epstein and Kirk Hanson, vol. 1, 3–13. Westport, CT: Praeger, 2006.

Mises, Ludwig von. "Economic Calculation in the Socialist Commonwealth." 1920. In *Collectivist Economic Planning*, edited by F. A. Hayek, 87–130. London: George Routledge & Sons, 1933; Reprint, Clifton, NJ: Augustus M. Kelley 1975.

———. *Socialism: A Sociological and Economic Analysis.* 1922. Reprint, London: Jonathan Cape, 1972.

———. "Economic Calculation under Commercial Management and Bureaucratic Administration." 1932. In *Selected Writings of Ludwig von Mises: Between the Two World Wars*, edited by Richard Ebeling, 372–79. Reprint, Indianapolis: Liberty Fund, 2002.

———. *Bureaucracy.* 1944. Reprint, New Rochelle, NY: Arlington House, 1969.

———. "Profit and Loss." 1951. In *Planning for Freedom*, edited by Ludwig von Mises, 108–50. 1952. Reprint, South Holland, IL: Libertarian Press, 1980.

———. *Liberalism.* 1962. Reprint, Kansas City, MO: Sheed Andrews and McMeel, 1978.

———. *Human Action: A Treatise on Economics.* 3d ed. Chicago: Henry Regnery, 1966.

Mishan, E. J. *Technology & Growth: The Price We Pay.* New York: Praeger, 1970.

Mitchell, B. R. *Abstract of British Historical Statistics.* Cambridge: Cambridge University Press, 1962.

Mitchell, B. R., and H. G. Jones. *Second Abstract of British Historical Statistics.* Cambridge: Cambridge University Press, 1971.

Mitchell, Edward. *U.S. Energy Policy: A Primer.* Washington, DC: American Enterprise Institute, 1974.

Mitchell, Wesley. *Types of Economic Theory.* 2 vols. New York: Augustus M. Kelley, 1967.

Monbiot, George. *The Captive State: The Corporate Takeover of Britain.* London: Macmillan, 2000.

Monsen, R. Joseph. "The American Business View." 1969. In *The American Business Corporation: New Perspectives on Profit and Purpose*, edited by Eli Goldston et al., 175–89. Cambridge, MA: MIT Press, 1972.

Muller, Jerry. *The Mind and the Market: Capitalism in Modern European Thought.* New York: Anchor Books, 2002.

Myerson, Allen. "Solar Power, for Earthly Prices." *New York Times*, November 15, 1994.

Nash, Hugh. "Blackman vs. Lovins." In *The Energy Controversy,* edited by Hugh Nash, 35–43. San Francisco: Friends of the Earth, 1979.

National Conservation Commission. *Report of the National Conservation Commission.* 3 vols. Washington: Government Printing Office, 1909.

National Fuels and Study Group. *An Assessment of Available Information on Energy in the United States,* Committee on Interior and Insular Affairs, United States Senate, 87th Cong., 2nd sess., Senate Document 159, 1962.

National Mental Health Association. "Mental Health Fact Sheets: Co-Dependency." www.mentalhealthamerica.net/go/codependency.

Nevins, Allan. *John D. Rockefeller: The Heroic Age of American Enterprise.* 2 vols. 1940. Reprint, New York: Charles Scribner's Sons, 1969.

———. "American History for Americans." *New York Times Magazine,* May 3, 1942, 6, 28.

———. "Should American History Be Rewritten? YES." 1954. In *The Craft of American History: Selected Essays,* edited by A. S. Eisenstadt, 2 vols. Vol. 1, 176–85. New York: Harper & Row, 1966.

Newcomb, Simon. *Principles of Political Economy.* New York: Harper's, 1885.

Nielsen, Waldemar. *The Big Foundations.* New York: Columbia University Press, 1972.

———. *The Golden Donors.* New York: E. P. Dutton, 1985.

Nisbet, Robert. *History of the Idea of Progress.* New York: Basic Books, 1980.

Niskanen, William. *Bureaucracy & Representative Government.* New York: Aldine Atherton, 1971.

———. "A Crisis of Trust." In *After Enron: Lessons for Public Policy,* edited by William Niskanen, 1–10. Lanham, MD: Rowman & Littlefield, 2005.

Nixon, Richard. "The President's Address on Moves to Deal with Economic Problems" (August 14, 1971). Reprinted in *Contemporary Issues in Economics: Selected Readings,* edited by Robert Crandall and Richard Eckaus, 498–500. Boston: Little, Brown, 1972.

———. "Concerning Energy Resources." April 18, 1973. In *Energy Crisis: Volume 1, 1969–73,* edited by Lester Sobel, 138–55. New York: Facts on File, 1974.

Nolan, Thomas. "The Inexhaustible Resource of Technology." In *Perspectives on Conservation,* edited by Henry Jarrett, 49–66. Baltimore: Johns Hopkins University Press, 1958.

Noll, Roger, and Bruce Owen. "Introduction: The Agenda for Deregulation." In *The Political Economy of Deregulation,* edited by Roger Noll and Bruce Owen, 3–25. Washington, DC: American Enterprise Institute, 1983.

Nordhauser, Norman. *The Quest for Stability: Domestic Oil Regulation, 1917–1935.* New York: Garland, 1979.

Norris, Floyd. "Business Ethics and Other Oxymorons." *New York Times Book Review,* April 20, 2003, 16.

"Notes on the Permanent Revolution." Editorial. *Fortune,* September 1951, 83–84

Novak, Michael. *The Spirit of Democratic Capitalism.* New York: Madison Books, 1991.

———. *On Corporate Governance.* Washington, DC: American Enterprise Institute, 1997.

Novick, Peter. *That Noble Dream.* Cambridge: Cambridge University Press, 1988.

Nozick, Robert. *Anarchy, State, and Utopia.* New York: Basic Books, 1974.

O'Driscoll, Gerald, Jr., and Mario Rizzo. *The Economics of Time and Ignorance.* New York: Routledge, 1996.

Odegard, Peter. "Introduction." In Arthur Bentley, *The Process of Government*. Reprint, Cambridge, MA: Harvard University Press, 1967.

Olson, Cindy. *The Whole Truth . . . So Help Me God: An Enlightened Testimony from an Enron Insider*. Mustang, OK: Tate Publishing, 2008.

Olson, Mancur. *The Logic of Collective Action*. Cambridge, MA: Harvard University Press, 1965.

"Opening the Debate" (a report on Time Inc.'s "Energy Conference '77"). *Time*, April 25, 1977, 27–33.

Oppenheimer, Franz. *The State*. 1914. Reprint, New York: Free Life Editions, 1975.

OECD. *Energy Prospects to 1985*. 2 vols. Paris: Organisation for Economic Co-operation and Development, 1974.

Otteson, James. *Adam Smith's Marketplace of Life*. Cambridge: Cambridge University Press, 2002.

———. *Protagoras Resurrected: The Social and Political Thought of the Scottish Enlightenment*. Forthcoming.

Page, Talbot. *Conservation and Economic Efficiency*. 1977. Reprint, Baltimore: Johns Hopkins University Press, 1981.

Paglin, Morton. "Malthus's *Principles* and the Classical Tradition." 1964. Preface to reprint of T. R. Malthus, *Principles of Political Economy Considered with a View to Their Practical Application*, i–ix. 1836. New York: Augustus M. Kelley, 1968.

Papanek, Gustav. "Edward Sagendorph Mason." In *The New Palgrave: A Dictionary of Economics*, edited by John Eatwell et al., vol. 3, 395–96. New York: Palgrave, 1998.

Parker, Glen. *The Coal Industry: A Study in Social Control*. Washington, DC: American Council on Public Affairs, 1940.

Parker, Richard. *John Kenneth Galbraith: His Life, His Politics, His Economics*. New York: Farrar, Straus and Giroux, 2005.

Partnoy, Frank. *Infectious Greed: How Deceit and Risk Corrupted Financial Markets*. New York: Henry Holt, 2003.

Passer, Harold. "Entrepreneurial History and Economics." *Explorations in Entrepreneurial History*. 1 (5): 21–25 (1949).

Peart, Sandra. *The Economics of W. S. Jevons*. New York: Routledge, 1996.

Peck, M. Scott. *The Road Less Traveled*. 25th anniversary ed. New York: Touchstone, 2003.

Pegrum, Dudley. *Public Regulation of Business*. Homewood, IL: Richard D. Irwin, 1959.

Peikoff, Leonard. *Objectivism: The Philosophy of Ayn Rand*. New York: Penguin, 1993.

———. "Why Businessmen Need Philosophy." In *Why Businessmen Need Philosophy*, edited by Richard E. Ralston, 7–24. Irvine, CA: Ayn Rand Press, 1999.

Penrose, Edith. *The Theory of the Growth of the Firm*. Oxford: Oxford University Press, 1995.

Perry, Arthur. *Elements of Political Economy*. New York: Charles Scribner's Sons, 1878.

Pieper, Josef. *The Four Cardinal Virtues*. 1954. Reprint, New York: Harcourt, Brace & World, 1965.

Pigou, A. C. *The Economics of Welfare*. London: Macmillan, 1920.

———. *The Economics of Welfare*. 1932. 4th edition. London: Macmillan, 1960.

Pinchot, Gifford. *The Fight for Conservation*. 1910. Reprint, Seattle: University of Washington Press, 1967.

Pinkham, Douglas. "Business and Government: Friends and Foes." In *The Accountable Corporation*, edited by Marc Epstein and Kirk Hanson, vol. 4, 23–31. Westport, CT: Praeger, 2006.

Popper, Karl. *Objective Knowledge*. Oxford: Clarendon Press, 1972.

Porter, Glenn. *The Rise of Big Business, 1860–1910*. New York: Thomas Crowell, 1973.

Prashad, Vijay. *Fat Cats and Running Dogs: The Enron Stage of Capitalism*. London: Zed Books, 2002.

President's Materials Policy Commission. *Resources for Freedom*. 5 vols. Washington, DC: U.S. Government Printing Office, 1952.

"Professor Stanley Jevons." *Manchester Examiner and Times*, August 16, 1882. Reprinted in *W. S. Jevons: Critical Responses*, edited by Sandra Peart, vol. 4, 356–59. New York: Routledge, 2003.

Pullen, J. M. "Malthus, T. R." In *The New Palgrave: A Dictionary of Economics*, edited by John Eatwell et al., vol. 3, 280–85. New York: Palgrave, 1998.

Purcell, Edward, Jr. "Ideas and Interests: Businessmen and the Interstate Commerce Act." *Journal of American History* 54 (3): 561–78 (December 1967).

Rajan, Raghuram, and Luigi Zingales. *Saving Capitalism from the Capitalists*. New York: Crown Business, 2003.

Ralston, Richard E., ed. *Why Businessmen Need Philosophy*. Irvine, CA: Ayn Rand Press, 1999.

Rand, Ayn. *The Fountainhead*. 1943. Reprint, New York: Bobbs-Merrill, 1968.

———. *Atlas Shrugged*. New York: Random House, 1957.

———. "Modern Management." 1958. In *The Ayn Rand Column*, edited by Peter Schwartz, 112–13. New Milford, CT: Second Renaissance Books, 1998.

———. "The Objectivist Ethics." 1961a. In Ayn Rand, *The Virtue of Selfishness*, 13–35. New York: Signet, 1964. Reprinted, New York: New American Library, Centennial Edition, 2005.

———. "America's Persecuted Minority: Big Business." 1961b. In Ayn Rand et al., *Capitalism: The Unknown Ideal*, 44–62. New York: Penguin Putnam, 1967.

———. "Introducing Objectivism." 1962. In Ayn Rand et al., *The Voice of Reason: Essays in Objectivist Thought*, 3–5. New York: New American Library, 1989.

———. "The Ethics of Emergencies." 1963a. Reprinted in Ayn Rand et al., *The Virtue of Selfishness*, by 49–56. New York: New American Library, 2005.

———. "The Goal of My Writing." 1963b. In Ayn Rand, *The Romantic Manifesto: A Philosophy of Literature*, 162–72. 1971. Reprint, New York: Signet, 1975.

———. "The Money-Making Personality." 1963c. In *Why Businessmen Need Philosophy*, edited by Richard E. Ralston, 25–38. Irvine, CA: Ayn Rand Institute Press, 1999.

———. "The Nature of Government." 1963d. In Ayn Rand et al., *Capitalism: The Unknown Ideal*, 107–115. New York: Penguin Putnam, 1967.

———. *The Virtue of Selfishness*. 1964a. Reprint, NY: New American Library, 2005.

———. Introduction to Ayn Rand et al., *The Virtue of Selfishness*, vii–xi. New York: Signet, 1964b.

———. "Playboy Interview." 1964c. Conducted by Alvin Toffler. In *Playboy*, March 1964, 35–43, 63. Reprinted as *Ayn Rand: The Playboy Interview*. Poughkeepsie, NY: The Objectivist Center, 1999.

———. "What Is Capitalism?" 1965a. In Ayn Rand et al., *Capitalism: The Unknown Ideal*, 11–34. New York: Penguin Putnam, 1967.

————. "Who Is the Final Authority in Ethics?" 1965b. In Ayn Rand et al., *The Voice of Reason: Essays in Objectivist Thought*, 17–22. New York: New American Library, 1989.

————. "The Anti-Industrial Revolution." 1971a. In Ayn Rand, *The New Left: The Anti-Industrial Revolution*, 127–51. New York, Signet, 1975.

————. "The Moratorium on Brains: Part Two." 1971b. In Ayn Rand, *The Ayn Rand Letter: Volumes I–IV, 1971–1976*, 9–14. Palo Alto, CA: Palo Alto Book Service, 1979.

————. "Philosophy: Who Needs It." 1974. In Ayn Rand, *Philosophy: Who Needs It*, 1–13. New York: Signet, 1984.

————. "Global Balkanization." 1977. In Ayn Rand et al., *The Voice of Reason: Essays in Objectivist Thought*, 115–29. New York: New American Library, 1990.

————. "The Sanction of the Victim." 1981. In Rand et al., *The Voice of Reason: Essays in Objectivist Thought*, 149–57. New York: New American Library, 1990.

Ratner, Sidney. "A. F. Bentley's Inquiries into the Behavioral Sciences and the Theory of Scientific Inquiry." In *Life, Language, Law: Essays in Honor of Arthur F. Bentley*, edited by Richard Taylor, 26–57. Yellow Springs, OH: Antioch Press, 1957.

————. Editor's introduction to Arthur F. Bentley, *Makers, Users, and Masters*. Unpublished 1920 manuscript. Edited by Sidney Ratner, ix–xxv. Syracuse, NY: Syracuse University Press, 1969.

Reagan, Ronald. "First Inaugural Address," January 20, 1981. Available at www.reaganlibrary.com/reagan/speeches/first.asp.

————. "Statement on Signing Executive Order 12287, Providing for the Decontrol of Crude Oil and Refined Petroleum Products," January 28, 1981. Available at www.presidency.ucsb.edu/ws/index.php?pid=43912.

Regis, Ed. "The Environment Is Going to Hell, and Human Life Is Doomed to Only Get Worse, Right? Wrong. Conventional Wisdom, Please Meet Julian Simon, the Doomslayer." *Wired*, February 1997, 137–40, 193–98.

Reich, Charles. "The New Property." *Yale Law Journal* 73 (5): 733–87 (April 1964).

Reilly, David. "Risks Sparking Bailout Were Still in Shadows by Post-Enron Rules." *Wall Street Journal*, October 16, 2007.

Reinhold, Robert. "Warning on Growth Perils Is Examined at Symposium." *New York Times*, March 3, 1972.

Reynolds, Alan. "Energy Economics and Media Misinformation." In *Energy Coverage— Media Panic*, edited by Nelson Smith and Leonard Theberge, 3–21. New York: Longman, 1983.

RFF (Resources for the Future). *The Nation Looks at Its Resources: Report of the Mid-Century Conference on Resources for the Future*. Washington, DC: RFF, 1954.

————. *U.S. Energy Policies: An Agenda for Research*. Baltimore: Johns Hopkins University Press, 1968.

————. "Power—Yes, Power Plant—No." *Resources*, January 1970, 4–6.

RFF. "Behind the Energy Crisis." *Resources*, January 1971, 1–4.

————. "Energy in Crisis." *Resources*, January 1974, 5–11.

————. "Energy: The Loss of Innocence." *Resources*, Winter 1976, 1–3.

————. "Petroleum Prices and the New Energy Act." *Resources*, Winter 1976, 4–5.

————. "Energy: Will 1977 Be Different?" *Resources*, January–March 1977a, 3–4.

————. *Resources for the Future: The First 25 Years*. Washington, DC: RFF, 1977b.

————. "Energy Developments." *Resources*, January–March 1979, 3–4.

————. *Resources for Freedom: 35th Anniversary Edition*. Washington, DC: RFF, 1987.

———. "$4 Million Given to Establish First Endowed Chairs." Press release, May 14, 2001, at www.rff.org/rff/News/Releases/2001/4-Million-Given-to-Establish-First-Endowed-Chairs.cfm.

———. "50 Years of Path-Breaking Research." RFF, 2002. www.rff.org/rff/About/RFFat50/loader.cfm?url=/commonspot/security/getfile.cfm&PageID=4053.

———. 2006 Annual Report. www.rff.org/rff/News/Features/loader.cfm?url=/commonspot/security/getfile.cfm&PageID=26505&CFID=7372655&CFTOKEN=33310187.

———. "RFF Today." www.rff.org/rff/About/RFFat50/Index.cfm.

Roberts, John. "Perfectly and Imperfectly Competitive Markets." In The New Palgrave: A Dictionary of Economics, edited by John Eatwell et al., vol. 3, 837–41. 1987. Reprint, New York: Palgrave, 2002.

Robinson, Colin. Competition for Fuel. London: Institute of Economic Affairs, 1971.

———. The Energy 'Crisis' and British Coal. London: Institute of Economic Affairs, 1974.

Robinson, Colin, and Eileen Marshall. Can Coal Be Saved? London: Institute of Economic Affairs, 1985.

Robinson, Marshall. "Foreword." In William Tavoulareas and Carl Kaysen, A Debate on A TIME TO CHOOSE, xiii–xiv. Cambridge, MA: Ballinger, 1977.

Roepke, Wilhelm. Economics of a Free Society. 1937. Reprint, Chicago: Regnery, 1963.

Rogge, Benjamin. Can Capitalism Survive? Indianapolis: LibertyPress, 1979.

Romero, Simon. "Enron's Chief Offers His Case." New York Times, December 14, 2005.

Romero, Simon, and Riva Atlas. "WorldCom's Files for Bankruptcy; Largest U.S. Case." New York Times, July 22, 2002.

Romm, Joseph. Cool Companies: How the Best Businesses Boost Profits and Productivity by Cutting Greenhouse Gas Emissions. Washington, DC: Island Press, 1999.

Roosevelt, Theodore. "On Conservation." 1907. In The Progressive Movement: 1900–1915, edited by Richard Hofstadter, 69–72. Englewood Cliffs, NJ: Prentice Hall, 1963.

Rothbard, Murray. "Left and Right: The Prospects for Liberty." 1965. In Egalitarianism as a Revolt against Nature and Other Essays, edited by Murray Rothbard, 21–53. 1974. Reprint, Auburn, AL: Ludwig von Mises Institute, 2000.

———. Power and Market. 1970. Reprint, Auburn, AL: Ludwig von Mises Institute, 2004.

———. "Herbert Hoover and the Myth of Laissez-Faire." In A New History of Leviathan: Essays on the Rise of the American Corporate State, edited by Ronald Radosh and Murray Rothbard, 111–45. New York: E. P. Dutton, 1972.

———. Economic Thought before Adam Smith. 2 vols. Brookfield, VT: Edward Elgar, 1995.

———. "Ludwig von Mises and the Paradigm for Our Age." In The Logic of Action One: Method, Money, and the Austrian School, edited by Murray Rothbard, 195–210. Cheltenham, UK: Edward Elgar, 1997.

Royal Swedish Academy of Sciences, Press release of October 16, 1986, available at www.nobel.se/economics/laureates/1986/press.html.

Salop, Steven, and Lawrence White. "Symposium: Economic Analysis of Private Antitrust Litigation." Georgetown Law Journal 74 (4): 1001–64 (April 1986).

Samuelson, Paul. Economics: An Introductory Analysis. New York: McGraw-Hill, 1948.

———. "Economic Theory and Mathematics—An Appraisal." American Economic Review 42 (2): 56–66 (May 1952).

———. "Harold Hotelling as a Mathematical Economist." In *The Collected Papers of Paul A. Samuelson*, edited by Joseph Stiglitz, vol. 2, 1588–92. Cambridge, MA: MIT Press, 1966.

Sawyer, John. "The Entrepreneur and the Social Order." In *Men in Business: Essays in the Historical Role of the Entrepreneur*, edited by William Miller, 7–22. 1952. Reprint, New York: Harper, 1962.

Schlesinger, Arthur, Jr. *The Age of Jackson*. Boston: Little, Brown, 1946.

———. *The Crisis of the Old Order, 1919–33: The Age of Roosevelt*. 1957. Reprint, Boston: Houghton Mifflin, 2002.

———. *The Coming of the New Deal: The Age of Roosevelt*. Boston: Houghton Mifflin, 1958.

———. *A Life in the Twentieth Century: Innocent Beginnings, 1917–1950*. Boston: Houghton Mifflin, 2000.

Schlesinger, James. "Opening the Debate." *Time*, April 25, 1977, 27–28.

Schnietz, Karen. "The Purposes and History of Business Regulation." In *The Accountable Corporation*, edited by Marc Epstein and Kirk Hanson, vol. 4, 3–10. Westport, CT: Praeger, 2006.

Schumacher, E. F. *Small Is Beautiful: A Study of Economics as if People Mattered*. London: Blond & Biggs, 1973.

Schumpeter, Joseph. *The Theory of Economic Development*. 1911. English trans. 1934. Reprint, New Brunswick, NJ: Transaction, 2002.

———. *Business Cycles: A Theoretical, Historical, and Statistical Analysis of the Capitalist Process*. Vol. 1. New York: McGraw-Hill, 1939.

———. "The Creative Response in Economic History." 1947. In Joseph Schumpeter, *Essays on Entrepreneurs, Innovators, Business Cycles, and the Evolution of Capitalism*, edited by R. V. Clemence, 221–31. 1951. Reprint, New York: Transaction, 1989.

———. *Capitalism, Socialism and Democracy*. 1942; 3rd ed., 1950. Reprint, New York: Harper & Row, 1962.

———. "Economic Theory and Entrepreneurial History." 1949. In Joseph Schumpeter, *Essays on Entrepreneurs, Innovators, Business Cycles, and the Evolution of Capitalism*, edited by R. V. Clemence, 253–71. 1951. Reprint. New York: Transaction, 1989.

———. *History of Economic Analysis*. 1954. Reprint, New York: Oxford University Press, 1976.

Schurr, Sam. "America's Energy Choices." *Energy Journal* 1 (1): 1–9 (1980).

Schurr, Sam, et al. *Energy in America's Future: The Choices before Us*. Baltimore: Johns Hopkins University Press, 1979.

Sciabarra, Chris. *Ayn Rand: The Russian Radical*. University Park: Pennsylvania State University Press, 1995.

Scott. Richard. *IEA: The First 20 Years. Vol. 1: Origins and Structure*. Paris: OECD/IEA, 1994.

Seay, Chris, and Chris Bryan. *The Tao of Enron*. Colorado Springs, CO: NavPress, 2002.

Seldon, Arthur. Introduction to *Government: Whose Obedient Servant?* by Gordon Tullock et al., xi–xvi. London: Institute of Economic Affairs, 2000.

Shackle, G. L. S. *The Years of High Theory: Invention and Tradition in Economic Thought, 1926–1939*. Cambridge: Cambridge University Press, 1967.

Shaffer, Butler. *In Restraint of Trade: The Business Campaign against Competition, 1918–1938.* Lewisburg, PA: Bucknell University Press, 1997.

Shaw, William, and Vincent Barry. *Moral Issues in Business.* Belmont, CA: Wadsworth, 2001.

Shepherd, William. "Concentration Ratios." In *The New Palgrave: A Dictionary of Economics,* edited by John Eatwell et al., vol. 1, 563–64. 1987. Reprint, New York: Palgrave, 2002.

Shi, David. *Matthew Josephson, Bourgeois Bohemian.* New Haven, CT: Yale University Press, 1981.

Shiller, Robert. *Irrational Exuberance.* Princeton, NJ: Princeton University Press, 2000.

Shook, Barbara. "Skilling Predicts End of Integrated Companies." *Oil Daily,* November 30, 2000, 5–6.

Silk, Leonard S. "Nixon's Program—'I Am Now a Keynesian,'" *New York Times,* January 10, 1971.

Simmons, Harvey. "System Dynamics and Technology." In *Models of Doom: A Critique of the Limits to Growth,* edited by H. S. D. Cole et al., 192–208. New York: Universe Books, 1973.

Simon, Julian. *The Economics of Population Growth.* Princeton, NJ: Princeton University Press, 1977.

———. "Resources, Population, Environment: An Oversupply of False Bad News." *Science,* June 27, 1980, 1431–37.

———. *The Ultimate Resource.* Princeton, NJ: Princeton University Press, 1981.

———. "The Perverseness of Hotelling's Rule." Circa 1989. In *Economics against the Grain,* edited by Julian Simon, vol. 2, 534–40. Northampton, MA: Edward Elgar, 1998.

———. *Population Matters.* New Brunswick, NJ: Transaction, 1990.

———. *Good Mood: The New Psychology of Overcoming Depression.* La Salle, IL: Open Court, 1993.

———. *The Ultimate Resource 2.* Princeton, NJ: Princeton University Press, 1996.

———. *The Great Breakthrough and Its Cause.* Oxford: Princeton University Press, 2000.

———. *A Life against the Grain.* New Brunswick, NJ: Transaction, 2002.

Simon, Julian, and Herman Kahn. "Introduction." In Julian Simon and Herman Kahn, *The Resourceful Earth: A Response to "Global 2000,"* 1–49. New York: Basil Blackwell, 1984.

Simpson, R. David. *Productivity in Natural Resource Industries.* Washington, DC: Resources for the Future, 1999.

Sinnema, Peter. Introduction to *Self-Help,* by Samuel Smiles, vii–xxviii. Reprint, Oxford: Oxford University Press, 2002.

Sklar, Martin. "Woodrow Wilson and the Political Economy of Modern United States Liberalism." 1960. In *For a New America: Essays in History and Politics,* edited by James Weinstein and David Eakins, 46–100. New York: Random House, 1970.

———. *The Corporate Reconstruction of American Capitalism, 1890–1916.* Cambridge: Cambridge University Press, 1988.

———. *The United States as a Developing Country: Studies in U.S. History in the Progressive Era and the 1920s.* Cambridge: Cambridge University Press, 1992.

Skousen, Mark. *The Making of Modern Economics.* Armonk, NY: M. E. Sharpe, 2001.

Slivinski, Stephen. *The Corporate Welfare State: How the Federal Government Subsidizes U.S. Business.* Policy Analysis, No. 592. Washington, DC: Cato Institute, 2007.

Small, Albion. "Book Review: *The Process of Government.*" In *American Journal of Sociology* 13 (5): 698–706 (March 1908).

Smil, Vaclav. *Energies.* Cambridge, MA: MIT Press, 1999.

Smiles, Aileen. *Samuel Smiles and His Surroundings.* London: Robert Hale, 1956.

Smiles, Samuel. *Self-Help: With Illustrations of Character, Conduct, and Perseverance.* 1859, 2d ed. 1866. Edited by Peter Sinnema. Reprint, Oxford: Oxford University Press, 2002.

———. *Character.* New York: A. L. Burt, 1871.

———. *Thrift.* New York: A. L. Burt, 1875.

———. *Lives of the Engineers: The Locomotive: George and Robert Stephenson.* London: John Murray, 1879.

———. *Duty: With Illustrations of Courage, Patience, and Endurance.* New York: Harper & Brothers, 1881.

———. *Men of Invention and Industry.* New York: Harper & Brothers, 1885.

———. *The Autobiography of Samuel Smiles,* edited by Thomas MacKay. New York: E. P. Dutton, 1905.

Smith, Adam. *The Theory of Moral Sentiments.* 1759. Edited by D. D. Raphael and A. L. Mcfie. Reprint, Indianapolis: LibertyPress, 1984.

———. *Lectures on Jurisprudence.* 1762–66. Edited by R. L. Meek et al. Indianapolis: LibertyPress, 1982.

———. *An Inquiry Into the Nature and Causes of the Wealth of Nations.* 1776. 2 vols. Edited by R. H. Campbell and A. S. Skinner. Reprint, Indianapolis: Liberty Fund, 1981.

———. *Essays on Philosophical Subjects.* 1795. Edited by W. P. D. Wightman and J. C. Bryce. Indianapolis: LibertyPress, 1982.

———. *The Correspondence of Adam Smith.* 1974. 2nd ed., 1985. Edited by E. C. Mossner and I. S. Ross. Indianapolis: LibertyPress, 1987.

Smith, George Otis. "Regulation—More and Better." *Public Utilities Fortnightly,* June 7, 1934, 705–12.

Smith, George, and Frederick Dalzell. *Wisdom from the Robber Barons.* Cambridge, MA: Perseus, 2000.

Smith, Howard. *Government and Business: A Study in Economic Evolution.* New York: Ronald Press, 1958.

Smith, Hubert. *Economic Aspects of State Socialism.* Oxford: B. H. Blackwell, 1887.

Smith, V. Kerry. *Scarcity and Growth Revisited.* Baltimore: Johns Hopkins University Press, 1979.

Smith, Vernon. "The Two Faces of Adam Smith." *Southern Economics Journal* 65 (1): 1–19 (July 1998).

Smyth v. Ames, 169 U.S. 466 (1898).

Sobel, Lester, ed. *Energy Crisis: Volume 1, 1969–73.* New York: Facts on File, 1974.

———. *Energy Crisis: Volume 3, 1975–77.* New York: Facts on File, 1977.

"The 'Soft Path' Solution for Hard-Pressed Utilities." *Business Week,* July 23, 1984, 96L, 96N.

Solow, Robert. "Notes on 'Doomsday Models.'" *Proceedings of the National Academy of Sciences,* December 1972. Reprinted in *Readings in Economics,* edited by Paul Samuelson, 302–305. New York: McGraw-Hill, 1973.

———. "The Economics of Resources and the Resources of Economics" (Richard T. Ely Lecture). *American Economic Review* 64 (2): 1–14 (May 1974).

Spofford, Walter, Jr. Foreword to Talbot Page, *Conservation and Economic Efficiency*, 1977. Reprint, Baltimore: Johns Hopkins University Press, 1981.

Stagliano, Vito. *A Policy of Discontent: The Making of a National Energy Strategy.* Tulsa, OK: PennWell, 2001.

State of Louisiana v. FPC, 503 F. 2d 844 (1974).

Stelzer, Irwin. "The Rise and Fall of Enron: The Good It Did Should Not Be Interred with Its Bones." *Weekly Standard*, November 26, 2001, 16–17.

Stephens, Joe. "Hard Money, Strong Arms and 'Matrix'; How Enron Dealt with Congress, Bureaucracy." *Washington Post*, February 10, 2002.

Sternberg, Elaine. *Just Business: Business Ethics in Action.* Oxford: Oxford University Press, 2000.

Stevens, William. *The Change in the Weather: People, Weather, and the Science of Climate.* New York: Dell, 1999.

Stewart, Dugald. "Account of the Life and Writings of Adam Smith, LL. D." Address to the Royal Society of Edinburgh, January 21 and March 18, 1793, edited by I. S. Ross. Reprinted in Vol. 3, *The Glasgow Edition of the Works and Correspondence of Adam Smith*, ed. D. D. Raphael and A. S. Skinner. W. P. D. Wightman and J. C. Bryce, eds. *Essays on Philosophical Subjects (and Miscellaneous Pieces).* Indianapolis: Liberty Fund, 1982.

Stigler, George. "The Theory of Economic Regulation." *Bell Journal of Economics and Management Science* 2 (1): 3–21 (Spring 1971).

Stiglitz, Joseph. "The Efficiency of Market Prices in Long-Run Allocations in the Oil Industry." In *Studies in Energy Tax Policy*, edited by Gerald Brannon, 55–99. Cambridge, MA: Ballinger, 1975.

Stipp, David. "Can This Man Solve America's Energy Crisis?" *Fortune*, May 13, 2002, 100–108.

Stobaugh, Robert, and Daniel Yergin. "Conclusion: Towards a Balanced Energy Program." In *Energy Future: Report of the Energy Project at the Harvard Business School*, edited by Robert Stobaugh and Daniel Yergin, 216–33. New York: Random House, 1979.

———. "The End of Easy Oil." In *Energy Future: Report of the Energy Project at the Harvard Business School*, edited by Robert Stobaugh and Daniel Yergin, 3–15. New York: Random House, 1979.

Story, Joseph. *Commentaries on the Constitution of the United States.* 1833. 4th ed. 2 vols. Boston: Little, Brown, 1873.

Stromberg, Joseph. "American Monopoly Statism." 1973. In *The Complete Libertarian Forum: Volume 1, 1969–75*, 405–8. Auburn, AL: Ludwig von Mises Institute, 2006.

———. "The Political Economy of Liberal Corporatism." In Occasional Paper Series #4: *The Political Economy of Liberal Corporativism*, 19–35. Center for Libertarian Studies, November 1977.

———. "The Role of State Monopoly Capitalism in the American Empire." *Journal of Libertarian Studies* 15 (3): 57–93 (Summer 2001).

Sumner, William Graham. "Republican Government." 1877. Reprinted in *On Liberty, Society, and Politics*, edited by Robert C. Bannister, 81–92. Indianapolis: Liberty Fund, 1992.

———. "Definitions of Democracy and Plutocracy." 1888. Reprinted in *Earth-Hunger and Other Essays*, edited by Albert Galloway Keller, 290–300. 1913. Reprint, New Brunswick, NJ: Transaction, 1980.

———. "Democracy and Plutocracy." 1888/89. Reprinted in *On Liberty, Society, and Politics*, edited by Robert C. Bannister, 137–48. Indianapolis: Liberty Fund, 1992.

———. "The Bequests of the Nineteenth Century to the Twentieth." 1901. Reprinted in *On Liberty, Society, and Politics*, edited by Robert C. Bannister, 375–92. Indianapolis: Liberty Fund, 1992.

———. "Economics and Politics." 1905. Reprinted in *Earth-Hunger and Other Essays*, edited by Albert Galloway Keller, 318–33. 1913. Reprint, New Brunswick, NJ: Transaction, 1980.

Supple, Barry. *The History of the British Coal Industry, 1913–1946*. Oxford: Clarendon Press, 1987.

Suter, Keith. "The Club of Rome: The Global Conscience." *Contemporary Review*, July 1999, 1–5.

Swanson, Diane. "The Buck Stops Here: Why Universities Must Reclaim Business Ethics Education." *Journal of Academic Ethics* 2 (1): 43–61 (March 2004).

Swanson, Diane, and William Frederick. "Are Business Schools Silent Partners in Corporate Crime?" *Journal of Corporate Citizenship* 9: 24–27 (Spring 2003).

Swartz, Mimi. "Guilty Pleasure." *Texas Monthly*, July 2006, 128–30, 178–82.

Swartz, Mimi, with Sherron Watkins. *Power Failure: The Inside Story of the Collapse of Enron*. New York: Doubleday, 2003.

Swedberg, Richard. Introduction to Joseph Schumpeter, *Essays on Entrepreneurs, Innovators, Business Cycles, and the Evolution of Capitalism*, vii–xxxix. 1951. Reprint, New York: Transaction, 1989.

———. "Introduction: The Man and His Work." In *Joseph A. Schumpeter: The Economics and Sociology of Capitalism*, edited by Richard Swedberg. Princeton, NJ: Princeton University Press, 1991.

———. *Schumpeter: A Biography*. Princeton, NJ: Princeton University Press, 1991.

Tarbell, Ida. *The History of Standard Oil*. 2 vols. New York: McClure, Philips, 1904.

Tavoulareas, William. "William P. Tavoulareas: Advisory Board Comments." In *A Time to Choose: America's Energy Future*, Ford Foundation (final report by the Energy Project of the Ford Foundation), 400–408. Cambridge, MA: Ballinger, 1974.

———. "A Time to Choose: A Critique." In William Tavoulareas and Carl Kaysen, *A Debate on A TIME TO CHOOSE*, 1–68. Cambridge, MA: Ballinger, 1977.

Taylor, Richard. "Arthur F. Bentley's Political Science." *Western Political Quarterly* 5 (2): 214–30 (June 1952).

———. "Life, Language, Law." In *Life, Language, Law: Essays in Honor of Arthur F. Bentley*, edited by Richard Taylor, 3–25. Yellow Springs, OH: Antioch Press, 1957.

Thatcher, Margaret. *The Downing Street Years*. New York: HarperCollins, 1993.

———. *Statecraft: Strategies for a Changing World*. New York: HarperCollins, 2002.

Thierer, Adam, and Wayne Crews. *What's Yours Is Mine: Open Access and the Rise of Infrastructure Socialism*. Washington, DC: Cato Institute, 2003.

Tierney, John. "Betting the Planet." *New York Times Magazine*, December 2, 1990, 52–53, 74, 76, 78, 80–81.

Tilton, John. *On Borrowed Time? Assessing the Threat of Mineral Depletion*. Washington, DC: RFF Press, 2003.

Tollison, Robert. "Regulation and Interest Groups." In *Regulation: Economic Theory and History*, edited by Jack High, 59–76. Ann Arbor: University of Michigan Press, 1991.

Transco Companies. *1st Quarter 1982 Report.*

Travers, Tim. *Samuel Smiles and the Victorian Work Ethic.* New York: Garland, 1987.

Truman, David. *The Governmental Process: Political Interests and Public Opinion.* New York: Alfred A. Knopf, 1953.

Tuccille, Jerome. *Alan Shrugged: The Life and Times of Alan Greenspan, the World's Most Powerful Banker.* Hoboken, NJ: John Wiley & Sons, 2002.

Tucker, William. "The Myth of Alternative Energy." *Weekly Standard*, May 21, 2001, 25–29.

Valliant, James. *The Passion of Ayn Rand's Critics.* Dallas, TX: Durban House, 2005.

Veblen, Thorstein. *The Theory of Business Enterprise.* 1904. Reprint, New York: Charles Scribner's Sons, 1935.

Vietor, Richard. "Businessmen and Political Economy: The Railroad Rate Controversy of 1905." *Journal of American History* 64 (1): 47–66 (June 1977).

———. *Contrived Competition: Regulation and Deregulation in America.* Cambridge, MA: Harvard University Press, 1994.

Viner, Jacob. "Adam Smith and Laissez Faire." In *Adam Smith, 1776–1926: Lectures to Commemorate the Sesquicentennial of the Publication of "The Wealth of Nations,"* edited by John M. Clark et al., 116–55. Chicago: University of Chicago Press, 1928.

Viscusi, W. Kip, et al. *Economics of Regulation and Antitrust.* Cambridge, MA: MIT Press, 2000.

Vogel, David. "The 'New' Social Regulation in Historical and Comparative Perspective." In *Regulation in Perspective: Historical Essays*, edited by Thomas McGraw, 155–85. Cambridge, MA: Harvard University Press, 1981.

Vogel, Steven. *Free Markets, More Rules: Regulatory Reform in Advanced Industrial Countries.* Ithaca, NY: Cornell University Press, 1996.

Wälde, Thomas. "International Energy Law and Policy." In *Encyclopedia of Energy*, edited by Cutler Cleveland, vol. 3, 557–69. New York: Elsevier, 2004.

Warner, Rawleigh. "Petroleum Faces Transition Period." In *Petroleum/2000.* Tulsa, OK: *Oil & Gas Journal*, August, 1977.

Watkins, G. C. "The Hotelling Principle: Autobahn or Cul de Sac?" *Energy Journal* 13 (1): 1–24 (January 1992).

Watson, Richard, Jr. *The Development of National Power: The United States, 1900–1919.* Boston: Houghton Mifflin, 1976.

Weaver, Paul. *The Suicidal Corporation: How Big Business Fails America.* New York: Simon & Schuster, 1988.

Weinstein, James. *The Corporate Ideal in the Liberal State.* Boston: Beacon Press, 1968.

Weir, D. R. "Malthus's Theory of Population." In *The New Palgrave: A Dictionary of Economics*, edited by John Eatwell et al., vol. 3, 290–93. New York: Palgrave, 1998.

Weisman, Robert. "Harvard Raises Its Hand in Ethics: 1st-Year MBA Students Must Take New Course." *Boston Globe*, December 30, 2003.

Welch, Jack. *Jack: Straight from the Gut.* New York: Warner Books, 2001.

West, E. G. *Adam Smith: The Man and His Works.* Indianapolis: Liberty Fund, 1976.

Whately, Richard. *Essays (Second Series) on Some of the Difficulties in the Writings of Apostle Paul, and in Other Parts of the New Testament.* London: John W. Parker & Son, 1854.

Wheeler, Bayard. *Business: An Introductory Analysis.* New York: Harper & Brothers, 1962.

White, Bill. "In These Challenging Times, Enron Deserves Our Thanks." *Houston Chronicle,* October 28, 2001.

Whitfield, Charles. *Co-Dependence: Healing the Human Condition.* Deerfield Beach, FL: Health Communication, 1991.

Wiarda, Howard. *Corporatism and Comparative Politics.* Armonk, NY: M. E. Sharpe, 1997.

Wiebe, Robert. *Businessmen and Reform: A Study of the Progressive Movement.* 1962. Reprint, Chicago: Ivan R. Dee, 1989.

———. "Book Review: *The Triumph of Conservatism,* by Gabriel Kolko." *Journal of American History* 51 (1): 121–22 (June 1964).

———. *The Search for Order: 1877–1920.* London: Macmillan, 1967.

Wiener, Jonathan. "Radical Historians and the Crisis in American History, 1959–1980." *Journal of American History* 76 (2): 399–434 (September 1989).

Wight, Jonathan. *Saving Adam Smith: A Tale of Wealth, Transformation, and Virtue.* Upper Saddle River, NJ: Prentice Hall, 2002. See also "Saving Adam Smith" at www.richmond.edu/~jwight/Adam/Whatsitabout.html.

Wilcox, Clair. *Public Policies Toward Business.* Homewood, IL: Richard D. Irwin, 1955.

Will, George. "Events, Dear Boy, Events." *Newsweek,* January 28, 2002, 64.

Williams, William. *The Contours of American History.* New York: World Publishing, 1961.

Williamson, Oliver. Introduction to *The Nature of the Firm: Origins, Evolution, and Development,"* edited by Oliver Williamson and Sidney Winter, 3–17. New York: Oxford University Press, 1991.

Willrich, Mason. *Energy and World Politics.* New York: Free Press, 1975.

Wilson, James Q. "The Dead Hand of Regulation." *Public Interest* 25: 39–58 (Fall 1971).

———. "Adam Smith on Business Ethics." *California Management Review* 32 (1): 59–72 (Fall 1989).

Wilson, R. J. "United States: The Reassessment of Liberalism." *Journal of Contemporary History* 2 (1): 93–105 (January 1967).

Windsor, Duane. "Business Ethics at 'The Crooked E'," In *Enron: Corporate Fiascos and Legal Implications,* edited by Nancy Rapoport and Bala Dharan, 659–87. New York: Foundation Press, 2004a.

———. "The Development of International Business Norms," *Business Ethics Quarterly* 14 (4): 729–54. (2004b).

———. "Corporate Social Responsibility: Cases For and Against," In *The Accountable Corporation,* edited by Marc Epstein and Kirk Hanson, vol. 3, 31–50. Westport, CT: Praeger, 2006.

Wood, Barbara. *E. F. Schumacher: His Life and Thought.* New York: Harper & Row, 1984.

Woodruff, W. "History and the Businessman." *Business History Review* 30 (3): 241–59 (September 1956).

World Commission on Environment and Development. *Our Common Future.* New York: Oxford University Press, 1987.

Wright, M. A. *The Business of Business: Private Enterprise and Public Affairs.* New York: McGraw-Hill, 1967.

Yergin, Daniel. "Conservation: The Key Energy Source." In *Energy Future: Report of the Energy Project at the Harvard Business School,* edited by Robert Stobaugh and Daniel Yergin, 136–82. New York: Random House, 1979.

———. "America in the Strait of Stringency." In *Global Insecurity: A Strategy for Energy & Economic Renewal,* edited by Daniel Yergin and Martin Hillenbrand, 94–137. Boston: Houghton Mifflin, 1982.

———. "Crisis and Adjustment: An Overview." In *Global Insecurity: A Strategy for Energy & Economic Renewal,* edited by Daniel Yergin and Martin Hillenbrand, 1–28. Boston: Houghton Mifflin, 1982.

———. *The Prize: The Epic Quest for Oil, Money & Power.* New York: Simon & Schuster, 1991.

Yergin, Daniel, and Martin Hillenbrand. *Global Insecurity: A Strategy for Energy & Economic Renewal.* Boston: Houghton Mifflin, 1982.

Yergin, Daniel, and Joseph Stanislaw. *The Commanding Heights: The Battle between Government and the Marketplace That Is Remaking the Modern World.* New York: Simon & Schuster, 1998.

Younkins, Edward. *Capitalism and Commerce: Conceptual Foundations of Free Enterprise.* New York: Lexington Books, 2002.

Zeff, Stephen. "How the U.S. Accounting Profession Got Where It Is Today: Part I." *Accounting Horizons* 17 (3): 189–205 (September 2003).

———. "The Evolution of U.S. GAAP: The Political Forces Behind Professional Standards, Part 1, 1930–73." *CPA Journal* 75 (1): 18–27 (January 2005a).

———. "The Evolution of U.S. GAAP: Controversial Standards Trigger Special-Interest Lobbying, Part 2, 1973–2004." *CPA Journal* 75 (2): 18–29 (February 2005b).

Ziemba, W. T., et al. *Energy Policy Modeling: United States and Canadian Experiences.* 2 vols. Boston: Martinus Nijhoff, 1980.

Zimmermann, Erich. *World Resources and Industries: A Functional Appraisal of the Availability of Agricultural and Industrial Resources.* New York: Harper & Brothers, 1933; 2nd ed., 1951.

———. "Resources: An Evolving Concept." *Proceedings and Transactions of the Texas Academy of Science, 1944,* 28:157–65. Houston: Texas Academy of Science, 1945.

Illustration Credits

Figure 1.1 *Book covers:* Glasgow University; *Adam Smith image:* © The Print Collector/Heritage Images / Imagestate. **Figure 1.2** Edinburgh City Libraries. **Figure 2.1** *Middle:* National Portrait Gallery, London; *right:* Time Life Pictures/Getty Images; *plaque:* East Lothian Council Museums Service. **Figure 2.3** *Left:* Science Museum Pictorial. **Figure 3.1** *Stamp and photograph:* Getty Images. **Figure 3.4** *Photograph:* Harvard News Office. **Figure 3.5** *Arthur Andersen:* Arthur Andersen & Co.; *Charles Koch:* Koch Industries; *Michael Novak:* American Enterprise Institute. **Figure 3.6** *Photograph:* Courtesy of Barbara Branden. **Figure 4.1** *Photographs:* Harvard University Archives: *left:* Call # HUP Schumpeter, J. A. (2); *center:* Call # HUGB S276.90p (2); *right:* Call # HUGB S276.90p (6). **Figure 4.2** *Top:* Enron Corp.; *photograph of Peter Drucker:* Drucker Literary Trust. **Figure 4.3** *Top left:* Horace Knight; *top right and bottom:* University of Chicago Library. **Figure 4.4** *Photograph:* Ludwig von Mises Institute. **Figure 4.5** *Photographs:* Courtesy of University of Chicago. **Figure 4.6** *Logos:* Courtesy of Shell, BP; *EnronOnline:* Enron Corp. **Figure 5.1** *Left:* Front cover of *The Progressive Historians* by Richard Hofstadter. Used by permission of Alfred A. Knopf, a division of Random House. *Right, top:* Culver Pictures, Inc.; *middle:* © Brown Brothers, Sterling, PA; *bottom:* Western History Collections, University of Oklahoma Libraries. **Figure 5.2** Reprinted by permission of Paul Samuelson. **Figure 5.3** *Right:* The Warren Samuels Portrait Collection at Duke University. **Figure 5.4** *Photographs:* Courtesy of Lilly Library, Indiana University. **Figure 5.5** *Title page:* James M. Buchanan and Gordon Tullock, *The Calculus of Consent: Logical Foundations of Constitutional Democracy.* Copyright © by the University of Michigan Press, 1962. *Photographs of James Buchanan and Gordon Tullock:* Reprinted by permission. **Figure 6.2** *Left:* Getty Images; *right, photograph:* Reprinted with permission of the University Archives, Columbia University in the City of New York; Vintage front cover from *The Age of Reform* by Richard Hofstadter. Used by permission of Vintage Books, a division of Random House, Inc. **Figure 6.3** *Left:* Reprinted with permission of the University Archives, Columbia University in the City of New York; *right*: Library of Congress, Prints and Photographs Division, NYWT & S Collection, LC-USZ62-116726. **Figure 6.4** *Photographs of Edwin Gay, Norman Gras, and Arthur Cole:* Harvard Business School Archives Photographs Collection; *photograph of Joseph Schumpeter:* Harvard Business School Portrait Photograph Collection. **Figure 6.5** *Photograph:* Harvard Business School Archives Photographs Collection. **Figure 6.6** *Photograph:* Courtesy of Gabriel Kolko. **Figure 6.7** *Photograph of Ken Lay:* Courtesy of Jack Bowen. **Figure 7.2** *Portrait:* Courtesy of The Warren Samuels Portrait Collection at Duke University; *book cover:* Reprinted courtesy of Penguin Group, UK. **Figure 7.3** *Upper:* Reproduced by courtesy of the University Librarian and Director, The John Rylands University Library, The University of Manchester. **Figure 7.4** *Illustration:* Jean Spitzner. **Figure 7.7** *England map:* Jean Spitzner. **Figure 7.8** *England map:* Jean Spitzner. **Figure 7.9** *Enron logo:* Courtesy of Enron Corp. **Figure 8.1** *Photograph:* Courtesy of Center for American History, University of Texas at Austin. **Figure 8.2** *Photograph and formula:* Reprinted by permission. **Figure 8.3** *Photograph:* © CBS/Landov. **Figure 8.4** *Quotation of principles:* Courtesy of the Ford Foundation. **Figure 8.5** *Book covers:* Courtesy of Resources for the Future. **Figure 8.6** *Photograph of Edward Mason:* Courtesy of Harvard University Archives; *photograph of M. A. Adelman:* Courtesy of the MIT Museum. **Figure 9.1** *Photographs: top:* American Heritage Center, University of Wyoming; *bottom left and right:* The Hubbert Tribute (mkinghubbert.com). **Figure 9.2** *Top:* Courtesy of the E. F. Schumacher Society, www.smallisbeautiful.org; *bottom:* Courtesy of Jimmy Carter Library. **Figure 9.3** *Book cover:* Copyright © 1968, 1971, from *The Population Bomb* by Dr. Paul R. Ehrlich. Used by permission of Ballantine Books, a division of Random House, Inc. *ZPG logo:* Courtesy of Population Connection. **Figure 9.4** *Left:* Courtesy of Chuck Painter / Stanford News Service; *right:* Courtesy of University of California, Berkeley. **Figure 9.5** *Right:* Courtesy of U.S. EPA; *bottom:* Courtesy of Enron Corp. **Figure 9.7** *Photograph of Robert Solow:* Courtesy of Robert Solow. **Figure 10.2** *Top row, book covers:* Courtesy of the Ford Foundation; *photograph of McGeorge Bundy:* Getty Images; *bottom row, left:* Courtesy of S. David Freeman; *center:* Courtesy of Dayna Bealy; *right:* Courtesy of ExxonMobil Corporation. **Figure 10.3** *Photographs:* Courtesy of Amory Lovins. **Figure 10.4** *Upper:* © 1978 Dow Jones & Company, Inc. All Rights Reserved Worldwide; *lower:* Courtesy of Enron Corp. **Figure 10.5** *Upper left:* Courtesy of Richard M. Nixon Library; *lower left:* Courtesy of Gerald R. Ford Library; *right:* Courtesy of Jimmy Carter Library; *inset:* Courtesy of Getty Images. **Figure 10.7** *Left:* Book cover, courtesy of Resources for the Future; *right:* Book cover, copyright © 1979, 1980, 1983, from *Energy Future*, revised edition, edited by Robert Stobaugh and Daniel Yergin. Used by permission of Random House, Inc. **Figure 10.9** *Study covers and photograph:* Courtesy of American Enterprise Institute. **Figure 11.1** *Julian Simon book covers:* Courtesy of Princeton University Press; *photograph:* Courtesy of University of Illinois; *Thomas Kuhn book cover:* University of Chicago Press. **Figure 11.2** *Left, photograph of Paul Ehrlich:* Courtesy of Ed Kashi Studio; *illustration:* Courtesy of Ross MacDonald; *article title image:* Reprinted by permission; *image of check:* Courtesy of Julian Simon family; *right, photograph of Julian Simon:* Dan Borris, courtesy of edge reps, ltd. **Figure 11.7** *Top left, top right, bottom left:* Courtesy of Ronald Reagan Library.

Name Index

Page numbers in italics refer to pages with images of persons.

Cole, Arthur, 153–*155*
Collins, Edward, 150
Collins, Jim, 83–*85*, 103
Constanza, Robert, 239
Cookenboo, Les, 222
Coolidge, Calvin, 172
Coyne, Christopher, 108
Cyprian, Saint, 189

Daly, Herman, 239
Darmstadter, Joel, 280, 344–345, 348
Davis, Gray, 249, 256
Davison, Henry, 171
De Soto, Hernando, 109
Deffeyes, Kenneth, 227
Dennison, Henry, 333
Dewing, Arthur, 110
Donham, W. B., 172
Donway, Roger, 89
Drucker, Peter, 99, 101–103
Dunlop, John, 298–299

Ebbers, Bernard, 1
Edison, Thomas, 75, 185
Ehrlich, Anne, 187, 231, 272, 274, 276, 278
Ehrlich, Paul, 20, 224, 228–231, 234, 239,
        242, 249, 270, 272, 274, 276–278, 283,
        288–289, 305
Eichenwald, Kurt, 17, 37, 296
Eisenhower, Dwight, 219, 265, 334
Elkind, Peter, 68
Elkington, John, 300
Ely, James, 339–340
Ely, Richard, 134, 144
Engels, Frederick, 72, 124, 335
Epstein, Richard, 296

Fastow, Andy, 67
Firestone, Harvey, 47
Flux, A. W., 202
Flynn, John T., 173
Ford, Edsel, *220*
Ford, Gerald, 241, 253–*254*, 265
Ford, Henry, 6, 78, 177, *220*
Ford, Henry, II, 177, *220*, 248
Forrester, Jay, *235–236*
Fox, Loren, 17

Freeman, S. David, 20, 244–249, 260, 282
Freud, Sigmund, 56
Friedman, Milton, 2, 69, 77, 81, 94,
        177–178, 206n10, 242, 255, 262, 266,
        287–288, 295–296, 299–301, 303, 310,
        313, 315, 318
Fulton, Robert, 150

Galbraith, John Kenneth, 31, 72–75, 99,
        146, 217, 222, 227, 229, 237–238, 242,
        256, 270, 273, 283, 288, 334
Garfield, Harry, 207
Garvin, C. C., Jr., 264
Gay, Edwin, 153–*155*
Gladstone, W. E., 56, 194
Goklany, Indur, 306
Gonzalez, Richard, 210
Gordon, Richard, 222, 346
Gore, Al, Jr., 246, 253, 308
Gould, Jay, 150
Graebner, William, 171
Granville, Maurice, 264
Gras, Norman, 153, *155*
Gray, L. C., 212, 214, 217, 223
Greenfeld, Liah, 75
Greenspan, Alan, 17, 58–59, 70, *87–88*
Gullison, Patrecia, 324–327

Hamel, Gary, 83, 101–103, 265
Hansen, James, 286, 290
Harbeson, Robert, 336
Harcourt, Sir William, 56
Harding, Jim, 260
Harding, Warren G., 142, 216
Harris, Seymour, 146
Harte, John, 272, 274, 277
Hasnas, John, 299
Hawken, Paul, 305
Hawkins, David, 349
Hayek, F. A., 69, 73, 107n8, 130n13,
        215–216, 269, 274–275, 287–288, 313
Hayes, Denis, 231
Heath, Edward, 56
Heilbroner, Robert, 107–108, 123–124, 178,
        233
Heller, Walter, 175
Herfindahl, Orris C., 344–346

Subject Index

Accounting, financial, 110
    and economic-calculation debate,
        107–110
    Enron and, 5, 101, 112
    politicization of, 5, 111–112, 119
    trust and, 112–113
Adelman, M. A., 223
    fossil fuels, expansionist view of,
        222–223, 268
    vs. Hotelling, 268, 272
    as methodological realist, 12
    on OPEC as price setter, 268
    and Resources for the Future, 256, 345
    students of, 222, 272n1
Affluent Society, The (Galbraith: 1958)
    as anticapitalist manifesto, 72–73
    criticism of, 73
    neo-Malthusianism in, 237
    Soviet Union praised in, 73
    See also Galbraith, J. K.
Alarmism
    and climate change, 286–287, 312–313
    energy and, 304–305
    vs. human ingenuity, 187, 273, 275, 304
    neo-Malthusianism and, 305
    on population, 288
    on resource depletion, 271, 288–289
    on UK coal, 199–205, 304
    See also Consensus, errant; Neo-
        Malthusianism; Simon, Julian
Altruism in business
    vs. benevolence, 53–54

Friedman opposed to, 81, 299–300, 310
    Objectivism and, 80–82
    vs. rational self-interest, 80
    A. Smith suspicious of, 35, 310
    Sternberg on, 300
Ambition, 24–25. *See also* Hubris
American Economic Association (est.
    1885), anti-laissez-faire origins, 134,
    144
American Enterprise Institute (est. 1943),
    266–268
    vs. Resources for the Future, 268, 346
    See also Mitchell, Edward
American Petroleum Institute, 167, 170,
    210, 225, 263–264, 268
Anti-Enron businesses
    Kinder-Morgan, 65n7, 86
    Koch Industries, 86, 316–317
    in theory (Rand), 79
Arabian-American Oil Company
    (ARAMCO), nationalization of, 241,
    268
Arrogance (hubris)
    in academia, 13, 316
    of Bundy (Ford Foundation), 248–249
    in climate-change debate, 313
    of economic planners, 26
    of P. Ehrlich, 272, 288
    of elites, 26
    at Enron, ix, 1–3, 9
    and failure, 51
    of Freeman, 244–247

Paley and, 216, 219–220
Resourceship, 213. *See also* Expansionism
Revisionist history. *See* Historical
revisionism
Risk vs. uncertainty (Knight), 104–105
and Enron fraud, 106
Rockefeller, John D., 2, 6, 186, 292, 341
as capitalist doer, 46–47, 74, 77, 150, 158
as Mr. Petroleum, 185
Tarbell attack on, 149

Schlesinger, Arthur, Jr., 147
consensus historian of regulatory
reform, 143, 146–147
as Kennedy's historian, 166
Kolko dissertation committee member,
164, 166
Pulitzer Prize winner, 177
and recent corporate scandals, 142
See also Hofstadter, Richard
Schlesinger, James, 254
as central planner, 255
as energy czar (U.S. Department of
Energy), 255
as neo-Malthusian, 81, 242, 249,
254–255, 262
as price controller, 255–266
See also Carter, Jimmy
Schumacher, E. F., 228
and Buddhist economics, 227–228
as conservationist, 227–228
energy alarmism (Malthusianism) of,
227
Small Is Beautiful (1973), 228, 270
as socialist, 227
Schumpeter, Joseph, 97–100, 128, 155
on adaptive vs. creative response, 101
on "business strategy," 99
Capitalism, Socialism, and Democracy
(1942), 99–100
capitalist development, theory of, 98
"capitalist reality," 126–129, 165
"creative destruction," 34, 99, 126–127,
160, 209
criticism of perfect-competition theory,
126–129

on economics/business alliance, 154
on entrepreneurship, 75–76, 97–99
and Harvard Business School, 98–99,
153–155
on law of cost, 102
as methodological realist, 62, 97
as whistleblower, 11–12
Science of Success, The (Koch: 2007), xii,
293, 314, 316, 318
as new business standard, 314
See also Market-Based-Management®;
Principled Entrepreneurship™
Second-hander, 67–68
vs. capitalist doer, 74, 77–78
danger of, 303
Lay/Enron as, 8–11, 13, 68, 302, 321
See also Conformism
Self-deceit
business vice, 303
J. Collins on, 83
and impartial observer need, 10, 25
A. Smith on, 36
Self-Help (Smiles: 1859), 38–41
as handbook for capitalism, 41–42
Insull and, 39
popularity of, 39–40
See also Smiles, Samuel
Self-improvement
pre-Smiles movement for, 38
sympathy and, 22
Victorian era and, 38
See also Smiles, Samuel
Self-interest
vs. altruism, 80–81
and capitalism, 58
consequences of, 20
heroic capitalism and, 319
"invisible hand" and, 21
Nietzsche on, 69
Rand on, 58
Smiles on, 44
A. Smith on, 20, 21, 34–35
Self-interest theory of government.
See Public Choice economics
Simon, Julian, 274, 277
critics of, 187